CRITICAL SURVEY
OF
LONG FICTION

CRITICAL SURVEY
OF
LONG FICTION

Supplement

Edited by
FRANK N. MAGILL

SALEM PRESS
Pasadena, California   Englewood Cliffs, New Jersey

Library of Congress Cataloging-in-Publication Data
Critical survey of long fiction. Supplement.
   Bibliography: p.
   Includes index.
   Summary: Presents critical studies of fifty novel-
ists from all over the world who were not included
in the original multi-volume surveys of long fiction.
   1. Fiction—History and criticism. 2. Fiction—
Bio-bibliography. 3. Novelists—Biography—Dic-
tionaries. 4. English fiction—History and criticism.
5. English fiction—Bio-bibliography. 6. Novelists,
English—Biography—Dictionaries. [1. Fiction—
History and criticism. 2. Authors] I. Magill, Frank
Northen, 1907-   .
PN3451.C75 1984   Suppl. 809.3   87-15559
ISBN 0-89356-368-4

PUBLISHER'S NOTE

The present volume is a supplement to the *Critical Survey of Long Fiction*, English Language Series (1983) and Foreign Language Series (1984). It is being published in conjunction with comparable supplements to the other sets in Magill's Salem Press genre series, which together constitute a forty-five-volume, worldwide study of the major figures in the fields of short fiction, poetry, long fiction, and drama.

The primary purpose of this supplement is to extend coverage to significant novelists who were not included in the earlier volumes—particularly contemporary novelists, who could be covered only very selectively in the original survey. Of the fifty novelists included in the supplement (twelve of whom are women), most are still active; all fifty are from the twentieth century. Roughly half of the novelists included are from the United States; in all, seventeen countries are represented on the list, which includes writers from North and South America, England and Ireland, Eastern and Western Europe, Africa and India, Israel, Japan, Australia, and the Soviet Union.

Among the writers surveyed in this volume are several whose output in long fiction has been sparse (thus their exclusion from the original survey) but whose works in this genre have been judged exceptional by critical consensus. The Nigerian poet, playwright, essayist, and autobiographer Wole Soyinka, winner of the 1986 Nobel Prize for Literature, falls into this category, as do such diverse figures as James Agee, William H. Gass, and Primo Levi.

Increasing critical attention has been devoted to writers of mainstream popular fiction and so-called genre fiction—mysteries, science fiction, Westerns, horror, and the like. This new emphasis, already acknowledged in earlier volumes, is further reflected in the supplement by the inclusion of writers such as Philip K. Dick, P. D. James, Stephen King, Louis L'Amour, Ross Macdonald, and James Michener.

The format of the individual articles in this volume is consistent with that of the earlier volumes. Pertinent top matter is followed by a listing of the writer's principal works of long fiction, with dates of first publication, a brief survey of work in literary forms other than long fiction, a summary of the subject's professional achievements, a biographical sketch, and a critical analysis of the subject's canon, which is the body of the article. Following these critical overviews is a list of major publications other than long fiction and a bibliography of significant criticism.

In addition, the supplement updates information provided in the *Critical Survey of Long Fiction*. For writers who were living when those earlier volumes were published, the supplement provides a record of subsequent publications and awards and, when applicable, a death date. These listings appear in a separate section following the articles on individual novelists.

A comprehensive Index to the volume supplements the original *Critical Sur-*

vey of Long Fiction index, listing all major novelists, titles, and terms discussed. Entries for writers who appear in the volume are in boldface type, followed by an alphabetical listing of those of their works which are analyzed in the text.

CONTRIBUTORS

Patrick Adcock

Linda C. Badley

Peter Baker

Thomas Banks

Dan Barnett

Randi Birn

Frederick Bowers

Harold Branam

Carl Brucker

Rosemary M. Canfield-Reisman

Deborah Core

Bruce L. Edwards, Jr.

Robert P. Ellis

Thomas L. Erskine

June M. Frazer

Robert L. Gale

Terry L. Hansen

Jane Hill

Watson Holloway

D. Barton Johnson

Betty H. Jones

Jane Anderson Jones

Anne Mills King

Paula Kopacz

Penelope A. LeFew

Barbara A. McCaskill

David W. Madden

Anne Laura Mattrella

Jean-Pierre Metereau

Vasa D. Mihailovich

Brian Murray

William Nelles

George O'Brien

Robert C. Petersen

Charles H. Pullen

Victor J. Ramraj

Deborah D. Rogers

June H. Schlessinger

Joan Corey Semonella

Vasant A. Shahane

T. A. Shippey

Charles L. P. Silet

James Sullivan

Charles Trainor

Steven Weisenburger

John P. Welle

Dexter Westrum

LIST OF AUTHORS

CRITICAL SURVEY OF LONG FICTION

CRITICAL SURVEY
OF
LONG FICTION

JAMES AGEE

Born: Knoxville, Tennessee; November 27, 1909
Died: New York, New York; May 16, 1955

Principal long fiction
The Morning Watch, 1951; *A Death in the Family*, 1957.

Other literary forms
James Agee's earliest published book, *Permit Me Voyage* (1934), was a collection of poems, his second a nonfiction account of Alabama sharecroppers in the Depression. He and photographer Walker Evans lived with their subjects for eight weeks in 1936 on a *Fortune* magazine assignment, with a number of critics hailing the resulting book, *Let Us Now Praise Famous Men* (1941), as Agee's masterpiece. From 1941 through 1948, Agee wrote film reviews and feature articles for *Time* and *The Nation*; thereafter, he worked on film scripts in Hollywood, his most notable screenplay being his 1952 adaptation of C. S. Forester's novel *The African Queen* (1935). He also wrote an esteemed television script on Abraham Lincoln for the *Omnibus* series in 1952. *Letters of James Agee to Father Flye* (1962) contains his thirty-year correspondence with an Episcopalian priest who had been his teacher.

Achievements
The prestigious Yale Series of Younger Poets sponsored Agee's first book, Archibald MacLeish contributing its introduction. Agee went on to gain an unusual degree of literary fame for a man who published only three books, two of them slim ones, in his lifetime. Sometimes accused of wasting his talent on magazine and film hack work, Agee lavished the same painstaking attention on film reviews as on his carefully crafted books. His film work was highly prized by director John Huston, and their collaboration on *The African Queen* (1952) resulted in a film classic. His greatest fame developed posthumously, however, when his novel *A Death in the Family* won a 1958 Pulitzer Prize. Three years later, Tad Mosel's dramatization of the novel, *All the Way Home* (1960), earned another Pulitzer. The continued popularity of Agee's work attests his vast human sympathy, his unusual lyrical gift, and his ability to evoke the tension and tenderness of family life in both fiction and nonfiction.

Biography
Born in Knoxville, Tennessee, on November 27, 1909, James Rufus Agee was the son of Hugh James Agee, from a Tennessee mountain family, and Laura Whitman Tyler, the well-educated and highly religious daughter of a businessman. His father sang mountain ballads to him, while his mother

passed on to him her love of drama and music. Hugh Agee's death in an automobile accident in the spring of 1916 profoundly influenced young Rufus, as he was called in the family.

Agee received a first-rate education at St. Andrew's School, near Sewanee, Tennessee, where he developed a lifelong friendship with Father James Harold Flye; at Phillips Exeter Academy, Exeter, New Hampshire; and at Harvard College, where in his senior year he edited the *Harvard Advocate*. Upon his graduation in 1932, he went immediately to work for *Fortune* and later its sister publication, *Time*. Over a sixteen-year period, he did a variety of staff work, reviewing, and feature stories while living in the New York metropolitan area.

From 1950 on, Agee spent considerable time in California working mostly with John Huston, but his health deteriorated. Highly disciplined as a writer, Agee exerted less successful control over his living habits, with chronic insomnia and alcohol contributing to a succession of heart attacks beginning early in 1951. Agee was married three times and had a son by his second wife and three more children by his third, Mia Fritsch, who survived him. He succumbed to a fatal heart attack in a New York taxicab on May 16, 1955, at the age of forty-five.

Analysis

Neither James Agee's novella *The Morning Watch* nor his novel *A Death in the Family* offers much in the way of plot. The former covers a few hours of a boy's Good Friday morning at an Episcopalian boys' school, the latter a few days encompassing the death and funeral of a young husband and father. His fiction develops a remarkable lyric intensity, however, and dramatizes with sensitivity the consciousness of children. He presents the minutiae of life as experienced by his characters at times of maximum awareness and thereby lifts them out of the category of mere realistic detail into the realm of spiritual discovery.

Even a cursory glance at the facts of Agee's life reveals how autobiographically based his fiction is. There is no reason to doubt that St. Andrew's, where he spent the years from ten to sixteen, supplies the framework for *The Morning Watch*, or that Agee's own family, seen at the time of Hugh Agee's fatal accident, furnishes the building blocks of the more ambitious *A Death in the Family*. At the same time, Agee permitted himself artistic freedom in selecting, altering, and arranging the facts of raw experience. It is clear that his literary appropriation of his childhood owes much to reflection and interpretation in the light of maturity.

Agee was a writer who stayed close to home in his work. His fiction displays no trace of the two-thirds of his life spent mainly in New England, New York, and California. As is so often the case with Southern writers, Agee's work is imbued with a sense of his origins, of folk traditions viewed in their own right and in competition with the emerging urban culture. The South, with its insistence on the primacy of personal and familial relationships, was in his bones. In keeping to his earliest and most vividly felt years, Agee created a convincing context in which experiences of universal significance can unfold.

At the beginning of *The Morning Watch*, a preadolescent boy and several of his classmates are awakened in the wee hours of Good Friday morning to spend their assigned time in an overnight vigil in the school chapel as part of the Maundy Thursday–Good Friday devotions. Anyone who has experienced a period of religious scrupulosity in childhood will respond to Agee's presentation of Richard. While his friends fumble and curse in the darkness, Richard prepares for adoration. Once in the chapel before the veiled monstrance, he strives to pray worthily despite the inevitable distractions of potentially sinful thoughts, the dangers of spiritual pride, and the torture of the hard kneeling board. Richard wonders whether he can make a virtue of his discomfort: To what extent is it proper for him to suffer along with the crucified Savior? Agee brings Richard intensely alive and conveys the power and the puzzlement of mighty spiritual claims at this stage of life.

The narrative also develops from the start Richard's sense of his relationships with the other boys, most of whom, he realizes, lack his delicate spiritual antennae. After the stint in the chapel is over, he and two classmates do not return to the dormitory as expected but decide on an early morning swim. Their adventure is presented in a heavily symbolic way. Richard dives into deep water at their swimming hole, stays down so long that his friends begin to worry, and emerges before his lungs give out. The boys torture and kill a snake, with Richard (who, like Agee himself, cannot bear to kill) finishing off the job. He debates in his mind whether the snake is poisonous and whether to wash the slime from his hand, deciding finally in the negative. He carries back to the school a locust shell he has found on the way. The snake, which seemingly cannot be killed, suggests both ineradicable evil and, in its victimization, Christ; the locust shell, which he holds next to his heart, seems to represent suffering in a purer form. Richard's dive into the water and subsequent resurfacing obviously symbolize his own "death" and "resurrection" in this Christian Holy Week.

Some critics have noted the influence of James Joyce on this novella. Certainly Richard resembles in certain ways the young protagonists of some of Joyce's *Dubliners* (1914) stories as well as Stephen Dedalus in *A Portrait of the Artist as a Young Man* (1916). Attracted by religious mysteries and artifacts, Richard wishes to appropriate them for his own purposes. He senses the conflict of religion with the world, evinces distaste for the practices of the latter, and hopes to fashion a life that blends the best of both. While Richard's appropriation of religious rite and doctrine is less consciously the artist's than is that of Stephen Dedalus, the reader senses that his individualistic spirituality will inevitably bring him into a Joycean conflict with conservative religious practice.

Since *The Morning Watch*, despite its provocatively ambiguous conflict between the world and the spirit, is somewhat labored and precious, and since Agee's short stories were few and insignificant, his reputation as an important American novelist rests primarily on one book which he did not quite complete before his early death, *A Death in the Family*. As he left it, the story begins at the supper table of the Follet household in Knoxville, Tennessee, in about 1915, and ends just after Jay Follet's funeral on the third day following. Agee had written a short descriptive essay, "Knoxville: Summer 1915" (which makes an appropriate preface to the novel), and six additional sections, which together make up about one-fifth the length of the narrative.

Although all the six scenes (as they will be termed here) pertain to times prior to that of the main story, it remains unclear where Agee intended to place them, or whether he would have used stream-of-consciousness flashbacks, a story-within-a-story technique, or perhaps another method suggested by his cinematic experience to incorporate them. Surely he intended to use them, for they illuminate and enrich the death story despite the absence of any formal linkage among them or collectively to the narrative. The editorial decision to print three of them after each of the first two parts of the three-part narrative seems as logical as any other way under the circumstances.

The novel has no single protagonist. Jay Follet, strong, tall, and taciturn, is described most specifically, at one point being compared to Abraham Lincoln, though apparently more handsome. Last seen alive a third of the way through the narrative, he appears in five of the six scenes and remains the main object of the other characters' thoughts in the last two parts of the narrative. At various stages, each important family member reflects on him: his wife, Mary, son Rufus, brother Ralph, Mary's parents, Joel and Catherine, Mary's aunt Hannah and her brother Andrew, and even Jay's and Mary's three-year-old daughter, also named Catherine. Agee employs Rufus and Mary as a focus most frequently. No point of view outside the family circle intrudes, and, except on two occasions when the six-year-old Rufus interacts with neighborhood children outside, attention is focused on family members exclusively. Throughout the novel, Agee juxtaposes the tensions and tendernesses of domestic life. The reader is constantly made to feel not only how much the family members love one another but also how abrasive they can be. Recognizing that a family does not succeed automatically, Agee portrays a continual struggle against external divisive pressures and selfishness within.

Jay and Mary's marriage has withstood a number of strains. First of all, their origins differ greatly. Mary's people are the citified, well-educated Lynches; the Follets are Tennessee mountain folk. The couple's ability to harmonize their differences is exemplified in the second of the six scenes.

Rufus notes that when singing together, his father interprets music flexibly, "like a darky," while his mother sings true and clear but according to the book. Rufus particularly admires his father's sense of rhythm. Sometimes, the boy observes, his mother tries to sing Jay's way and he hers, but they soon give up and return to what is natural.

Jay's father, who indirectly causes Jay's death, is one point of difference. Mary's antipathy to him is known to all the Follets, but even Jay realizes that his likable father is weak of character. When Jay's brother calls and informs him that their father is very ill, Jay wastes no time in preparing to go to him, despite his suspicion that the unreliable Ralph has greatly exaggerated the danger. It is on his return trip, after learning that his father is all right, that a mechanical defect in Jay's car causes the crash that kills him instantly.

Jay's drinking problem, a Follet weakness, has also distressed his wife, and Jay has vowed to kill himself if he ever gets drunk again. In one of the scenes, Rufus, aware that whiskey is a sore point between his parents, accompanies his father when he stops at a tavern, and it appears that he has overcome his habit of excess, but his reputation has spread. Both the man who finds Jay's body and the children who later taunt Rufus on the street corner attribute his accident to drunken driving, and Mary has to fight off the temptation to consider the possibility.

Religion is another divisive issue. Jay does not appear to be a denominational Christian, while Mary is, like Agee's own mother, a fervent Episcopalian. The men on both sides of the family are either skeptics or thoroughgoing unbelievers. A devotee of Thomas Hardy's fiction, Mary's father, Joel, has little use for piety or what he calls "churchiness." Although he originally disapproved of Mary's marriage to Jay, he has come to terms with Jay, whom he views as a counterweight to Mary's religiosity. Mary's brother Andrew carries on open warfare with the Christian God. When he first hears of Jay's accident, Mary senses that he is mentally rehearsing a speech about the folly of belief in a benevolent deity. Even young Rufus is a budding skeptic. Told that God has let his father "go to sleep," he ferrets out the details and concludes that the concussion he has heard about, "not God," has put his father to sleep. When he hears that his father will wake up at the Final Judgment, he wonders what good that is. The women accept the inscrutable as God's will, but the men take an agnostic stance and fear the influence of the church. Father Jackson, the most unpleasant person in the novel, ministers to Mary in her bereavement. Rufus quickly decides that the priest's power is malevolent and that, were his real father present, the false father would not be allowed into his home.

Some hours after the confirmation of Jay's death, Mary feels his presence in the room, and though Andrew and Joel will not concede any kind of spiritual visitation, they acknowledge that they too felt "something." Later, Andrew tells Rufus of an event he considers "miraculous": the settling of a butterfly on Jay's coffin in the grave and the creature's subsequent flight, high into the sunlight. The men's unbelief, then, is not positivistic; they recognize the possibility of a realm beyond the natural order, but they bitterly oppose the certified spiritual agent, Father Jackson, as too self-assured and quick to condemn.

To counter the estrangements brought on by cultural and religious conflicts in the family, reconciliations dot the narrative. Rufus senses periodic estrangements from his father and then joyful feelings of unity. Jay frequently feels lonely, even homesick. Crossing the river between Knoxville and his old home, he feels restored. To go home is impracticable, bound up with a vanished childhood. In one of the scenes, the family visits Rufus' great-great-grandmother. It is a long, winding journey into the hills and into the past. It is apparent that none of the younger generations of Follets has gone to see the old woman in a long time. Rufus, who has never been there, comes home in a way impossible to his father. The old woman, more than a hundred years old, barely acknowledges any of her numerous offspring, but she clasps Rufus, the fifth-generation descendant, who is joyful to her. On other occasions, Jay, by imaginative identification with Rufus, can feel as if he is his "own self" again.

Mary also feels alternate waves of friendship with, and estrangement from, her father. He, in turn, has a wife with whom communication is difficult because of her deafness. When Catherine cannot hear her husband, she seldom asks him to repeat himself, as if fearful of exasperating him. In this way, she is insulated from his unbelief. Although they talk little, they communicate by gestures and physical closeness. Agee shows him taking her elbow to help her over a curb and carefully steering her up the street toward their home. Rufus and his father are usually silent on their walks; they communicate by sitting together on a favorite rock and watching passersby.

Much of the talk following Jay's death is irritable and nerve-shattering. Andrew dwells thoughtlessly on the one-chance-in-a-million nature of Jay's accident, for which his father rebukes him. Mary begs Andrew to have mercy and then hysterically begs his forgiveness, upon which her aunt censures her for unwarranted humility. Both Mary and Andrew are enduring crises, however, and are hardly responsible for what they say. She is resisting the temptation to despair of God's mercy; he is trying to come to terms with a possibly meaningless universe. Andrew communicates best with services; throughout the hours of distress, he is unfailingly helpful.

The truest communication exists between Jay and Mary. When he is not silent, he can be sullen or wrathful. As he prepares to set forth on his journey to his father's, Mary dreads the "fury and profanity" she can expect if, for example, the car will not start, but this sometimes harsh husband stops in the bedroom to recompose their bed so it will look comfortable and inviting when she returns to it. She disapproves of his drinking strong coffee, but she makes it very strong on this occasion because she knows he will appreciate it. By dozens of such unobtrusive deeds, Jay and Mary express their love, which prevails over the numerous adverse circumstances and personal weaknesses that threaten it.

Long before he began work on *A Death in the Family*, Agee expressed his intention to base a literary work on his father's death. The eventual novel is thus deeply meditated and very personal. At the same time, it attains universality by means of its painstaking precision. In the Follets can be seen any family that has striven to harmonize potentially divisive differences or has answered courageously a sudden tragedy. As in loving families generally, the tensions do not disappear. At the end, Andrew, for the first time in his life, invites Rufus to walk with him. Sensing the negative feelings in his uncle, Rufus nevertheless is afraid to ask him about them. Walking home with this man who can never replicate his father but who will fill as much of the void as possible, Rufus comes to terms with his father's death in the silence that in Agee's fiction communicates beyond the power of words. In this reconstruction of his own most momentous childhood experience, Agee portrays the most difficult reconciliation of all.

Other major works

SHORT FICTION: "A Mother's Tale," 1952; *Four Early Stories by James Agee*, 1964; *The Collected Short Prose of James Agee*, 1968.

SCREENPLAYS: *The Red Badge of Courage*, 1951 (based on Stephen Crane's novel); *The African Queen*, 1952 (based on the novel by C. S. Forester); *The Bride Comes to Yellow Sky*, 1952 (based on Crane's short story); *Noa Noa*, 1953; *White Mane*, 1953; *Green Magic*, 1955; *The Night of the Hunter*, 1955; *Agee on Film: Five Film Scripts*, 1960.

POETRY: *Permit Me Voyage*, 1934; *The Collected Poems of James Agee*, 1968.

NONFICTION: *Let Us Now Praise Famous Men*, 1941; *Agee on Film: Reviews and Comments*, 1958; *Letters of James Agee to Father Flye*, 1962.

Bibliography

Barson, Alfred. *A Way of Seeing: A Critical Study of James Agee*, 1972.

Kramer, Victor A. *James Agee*, 1975.

Moreau, Geneviève. *The Restless Journey of James Agee*, 1977. Translation by Miriam Kleiger.

Ohlin, Peter H. *Agee*, 1966.

Seib, Kenneth. *James Agee: Promise and Fulfillment*, 1968.

Robert P. Ellis

DEMETRIO AGUILERA MALTA

Born: Guayaquil, Ecuador; May 24, 1909

Principal long fiction

Don Goyo, 1933 (English translation, 1942); *C. Z. (Canal Zone): Los Yanquis en Panamá*, 1935; *¡Madrid! Reportaje novelado de una retaguardia heróica*, 1936; *La isla virgen*, 1942, revised 1954; *Una cruz en la Sierra Maestra*, 1960; *La caballeresa del sol: El gran amor de Bolívar*, 1964 (*Manuela, la Caballeresa del Sol*, 1967); *El Quijote de El Dorado*, 1964; *Un nuevo mar para el rey*, 1965; *Siete lunas y siete serpientes*, 1970 (*Seven Serpents and Seven Moons*, 1979); *El secuestro del general*, 1973 (*Babelandia*, 1985); *Jaguar*, 1977.

Other literary forms

In addition to his novels, Demetrio Aguilera Malta has written, in collaboration with Joaquín Gallegos Lara and Enrique Gil Gilbert, *Los que se van* (1930; those who leave). He has also published several dramas of importance: *España leal* (1938; loyalist Spain), *Lázaro* (1941), *Sangre azul* (1946; *Blue Blood*, 1948), *No bastan los átomos* (1954; atoms are not enough), *Dientes blancos* (1955; *White Teeth*, 1963), *El tigre* (1956; the tiger), *Honorarios* (1957; honorariums), *Fantoche* (1961), *Infierno negro* (1967; black hell), and *Muerte, S.A.* (1968; murder, incorporated). His poetry is collected in *El libro de los mangleros* (1929; the book of the mangleros), and he has published two nonfiction works, *La revolución española a través de los estampas de Antonio Edén* (1938; the Spanish revolution through the engravings of Anthony Eden) and *Los generales de Bolívar* (1965; Bolívar's generals).

Achievements

Aguilera Malta has been hailed as the initiator of Magical Realism in Latin America. This innovative literary tendency constitutes a new way of perceiving the reality of the New World by searching for the collective consciousness of the Latin American countries, probing their history, legends, and psychology. Stylistically, Magical Realism departs from fiction's traditional linear structure, chronological ordering of events, and logic in order to juxtapose past and present, intermix history, legend, and psychology, and integrate multiple elements of time, space, and reality on the same narrative level.

The introduction and development of this new literary tendency reflects Aguilera Malta's dedication to fostering new ideological and aesthetic trends in Latin America. Although he perfected the sophisticated narrative techniques of the vanguard, he looked to the familiar landscapes of his childhood in Ecuador and to the traditions of its people for the expression of his strong sense of social obligation.

Biography

Demetrio Aguilera Malta was born on May 24, 1909, in Guayaquil, Ecuador. One of the most important aspects of his youth which later influenced his literary production was his contact with the countryside and the peasants on the island of San Ignacio, which was owned by his father. He spent much time there and witnessed the massacre of the workers in November, 1922. In this insular environment, he developed an understanding and sympathy for his surroundings and for the island's inhabitants, the *cholos*.

After completing his bachelor's degree at a school in Guayaquil, he enrolled simultaneously in the law school and in the school of fine arts of Guayaquil University in 1928. He abandoned his studies after two years and in 1930 went to Panama, where he worked for four years as a journalist. In 1936, Aguilera Malta went to Spain to study the humanities at the University of Salamanca, but the Civil War thwarted his plans and he was forced to return to Ecuador. In 1937, he became a professor at the institution where he received his secondary education and was also appointed subsecretary of public education. He remained in these positions until 1943 and then served several cultural and consular missions in Chile. In 1958, he moved to Mexico.

Aguilera Malta visited almost all the countries of Europe and the Americas. He offered courses and gave conferences in universities in Chile, Brazil, and Colombia, as well as in universities in Mexico, Central America, and the United States.

Although noted for his friendliness, the most outstanding features of Aguilera Malta's personality are his versatility and dynamism. From his first days as a writer, he was known for his generous and enthusiastic spirit.

He was a member of the Generacíon del Treinta (generation of the thirties), so called because the year 1930 saw the publication of *Los que se van*, the emblematic work of the movement during its first years. Within the Generación del Treinta, he belonged to the division known as the Grupo de Guayaquil, a literary group composed of José de la Cuadra, Alfredo Pareja Diezcanseco, Joaquín Gallegos Lara, and Enrique Gil Gilbert. The works of these authors are marked by denunciation of elite white-power groups and protest against the living and working conditions of the Indians, in the hope of emancipating them from a feudal system that was suffocating them.

Analysis

Demetrio Aguilera Malta's long fiction can be divided into three categories: Magical Realist, historical, and journalistic fiction. The novels which introduce Magical Realism and develop it as a major literary movement in

Latin America are considered to be his best and most important. They are *Don Goyo*, *La isla virgen*, *Seven Serpents and Seven Moons*, and *Babelandia*.

Don Goyo, like most of the works of Aguilera Malta's generation, is a novel of social protest. Unlike the traditional novels of its kind, however, its message was expressed on a narrative level which fused objective reality with magical reality. Magical reality is expressed by the fusion of mythical, legendary, and supernatural elements in the form of animism, totemism, eroticism, and the superhuman powers of some of the characters. The narrative techniques of flashback, stream of consciousness, and metaphor contribute stylistically to convert objective reality into magical reality.

Animism is a primitive vision of nature and the universe which holds that good and evil spirits are responsible for natural phenomena. It also allows man to perceive the cosmic unity of the universe from a simplistic viewpoint. In this environment, man is never alone because nature fully participates in his actions and reflects his emotional states. In *Don Goyo*, the mangle, the native tree of the Guayas Islands, walks, talks, and shares the same emotions and fate of the *cholos* (a group of aborigines believed to be Asiatic immigrants from the Yellow Sea during prehistoric times). For example, until the arrival of the white man on the islands, there existed a special reciprocal relationship of dependency between the mangle and the *cholo*. When the white man arrived, he immediately began to use the mangle for commercial purposes. Not only the *cholos* but also the mangles rebelled.

Totemism is a primitive vision of nature which espouses the belief that man shares a kinship with a totem, be it animal or plant, which is thought to have a human soul and superhuman qualities. In this novel, Don Goyo and the oldest mangle on the island share the same destiny. During the course of their discussions, the relationship between the two becomes evident. The mangle is the only one on the island who addresses him familiarly as Goyo. Their kinship is most evident when the protagonist dies. Don Goyo's wife becomes concerned when her husband leaves home and is gone for a long time. She summons everyone on the island to look for him. During their long and frustrating search, the *cholos* hear a loud, trembling noise reverberating throughout the entire island, caused by the oldest mangle on the island falling to die near the oldest man on the island, Don Goyo. The searchers later find Don Goyo dead next to the mangle, his totem.

Eroticism in *Don Goyo* is of the kind that occurs in the natural habitat and has a positive connotation. In the environment of the Guayas Islands, eroticism forms part of the procreative force of nature. It is not, however, limited to the human species. The relationship between man and nature is also erotic. Man is reduced to his primitive state, governed by instinct, and all the elements of nature participate in the sexual act. There is a fusion and total harmony between all the species and all the objects of nature. For example, after Don Goyo arrived on the islands, they willingly gave themselves to be possessed and conquered by him in a human sexual way.

The two characters who most identify with the magical reality of the novel are Don Encarnación and Don Goyo. Don Encarnación is considered to be part warlock, more mythical than real. He is popular with the *cholos* because of his strong belief in supernatural events and his ability to recount them. For example, he recounts the story of Ño Francia, a black warlock who predicted a great flood. The white man did not believe in witchcraft, made a mockery of him, and in the end was punished for his disbelief by drowning in the flood. He also tells other stories about great natural disasters by magical forces.

Don Goyo is the incarnation of supernatural powers. It is rumored that he is more than 150 years old. He is regarded as the mythical patriarch of the islands and the only one who can control nature. He is also thought to possess magical cures for illnesses which white city doctors have not yet been able to conquer. Don Goyo is phantasmal and human at the same time. In the first two parts of the novel, he rarely appears in human form but seems to be omnipresent. He assumes a human form only when he defends the mangle against the exploitation of the white man. The third part of the novel reinforces the human dimension of Don Goyo by recounting stories of his marriages and children. After his death, Don Goyo becomes a legend. Shortly after Don Goyo and the mangle are found together, uprooted and dead, he appears to his daughter Gertrú and the caretaker of the mangles, Cusumbo. Don Goyo and the mangle are firmly implanted in the consciousness of the *cholo*.

La isla virgen is a continuation of the world of *Don Goyo*: the Guayas Islands, the primitive environment of the *cholos* and a magical vision of reality. It forms part of a novelistic tendency to look to the land to find the identity and roots of the Latin American people. This is done on both a real and a mythical level; many times, nature is perceived through magical rites, legends, and indigenous religious beliefs.

As in his other works, Aguilera Malta's message of social protest is clear. It is more forceful in this novel because nature itself is the chief protagonist, which must always be on the defensive against white civilized man who wishes to exploit it. Unlike the situation in *Don Goyo*, in which nature cooperates willingly with the *cholos*, who learn to understand it and live within its confines in perfect union, nature in *La isla virgen* is hostile and defensive.

La isla virgen recounts the story of Don Nestor, a rich white man who suffers financial failure when his crops are destroyed by a disease called "witches broom." He loses all of his possessions except the island of San Pancracio. He decides to go there to cultivate it and recover his fortune. His plan fails, however, and he dies.

Magical Realism is present in the novel in the savage forces of nature, the story of the tiger, the characters of Don Guayamabe and Don Nestor, the triumph of the *cholo* Don Pablo, and the skillful use of narrative techniques. The savagery of nature manifests itself in a phantasmagoric scene in which all the magical forces on the island unite and awaken all the souls of the dead to protest the presence of the white man. It is further reinforced in the episode of the tiger, which depicts the raw power of nature, controllable only by a brave man such as Don Guayamabe, the only one capable of killing the tiger.

Like Don Goyo, Don Guayamabe is a mythical character who understands the mysteries of the islands. He has supreme wisdom and a superior knowledge of life on the islands. He has conquered nature in a positive way and is therefore tranquil in the face of adversity, while the others manifest panic and desperation. He always knows in advance the fate of Don Nestor's projects but obeys the white owner unfailingly and without question. Don Nestor is the primary victim of the magical forces of the island. Throughout the novel, there is a constant antagonism between his original intention of coming to the island to get rich and his sense of masculinity, which comes alive in the primitive environment. There are moments when his economic goal is totally forgotten, superseded by his emotional state. For example, upon his arrival on the island, nature forces him to lose all capacity to reason. During a later monologue, the erotic aspect is introduced when he expresses his sexual desire to possess the land physically.

The magical forces of the island also surface in the character of Don Pablo Melgor, the son of the *cholo* worker killed by Don Nestor. Don Pablo is Don Guayamabe's godson and has inherited his supernatural wisdom and ability to dominate the brutal forces of nature. Don Pablo declares himself to be the enemy of the white man and avenges his father's death by orchestrating the final downfall of Don Nestor.

The narrative techniques of interior monologue and stream of consciousness allow the reader to become submerged in the mental processes of the characters, in a dream state between reality and fantasy. For example, Don Nestor's monologue occurs while he finds himself in a prerational mental state. Aguilera Malta applies this vanguard technique to a primitive environment, integrating everything in a magical vision.

Like the preceding works, *Seven Serpents and Seven Moons* takes place on the Guayas Islands. Again, Aguilera Malta's strong sense of social obligation is clearly evident. The central theme of this novel is the clash between good and evil, which results in the exposure of a corrupt political system, social exploitation, the prejudice between races, and the corruption of religion. It is in *Seven Serpents and Seven Moons* that Magical Realism realizes its fullest expression. It is the unifying element of this novel and is expressed by the use of classical themes, miracles, psychic phenomena, superstitions, myth, witchcraft, and zoomorphism. The narrative structure further reinforces the magical reality of the novel.

Crisístomo Chalena, with the help of the Devil, to whom he has sold his soul, succeeds in exploiting the poor *santoronteños*, inhabitants of the myth-ical island of Santorontón. This classical theme of selling souls to the Devil adds a mythical dimension to the portrayal of social injustice. Since the main theme deals with the clash of forces between good and evil, the conflict is elevated to a more transcendental level, represented by the clash between Christ and the Devil.

Miracles are supernatural forces capable of altering the natural laws of the universe. In this novel, both Christ and the Devil possess the ability to per-form miracles and do so quite frequently.

Psychic phenomena are manifested in two notable examples: First, the presence of Christ very often seems to be a psychic phenomenon in the minds of the two priests. Second, Clotilde's trauma when the man she saw assassinate her parents also rapes her is manifested in her hatred for men; in a psychic state, she often imagines herself having sexual relations with men and later castrating them. Although this vision exists initially only in Clotilde's mind, it is later converted into an island legend.

This narration is also governed by magical forces resulting from supersti-tions. For example, the origin of the Tin-tines and the episodes with Dominga are effectively explained by resorting to popular beliefs and su-perstitions. The mythical aspect is developed in the episode of the pirate Ogazno. He is created as an archetype of all the pirates who have sacked Guayaquil throughout the ages. He represents all pirates, a fact which places him in a mythical time frame, blurs the borders between history and legend, and transcends reality and temporality. Bulu-Bulu is the incarnation of witchcraft in the novel. His onomatopoeic name, which means "capable of curing people," contributes to the primitive dimension of magical reality in the novel. Like Don Goyo and Don Guayamabe, Bulu-Bulu is privy to all of nature's secrets.

The zoomorphic aspect of Magical Realism is evidenced by the characters' ability to metamorphose into animals: Calendario can become an alligator, Chalena a toad, and Bulu-Bulu a tiger.

The structural elements which contribute to create magical reality in the novel are interior monologue, the chaotic temporal structure (which erases the dividing line between the real and the unreal), and the use of collective mentality (which allows an action or event to be transformed into legend). The language, which is metaphoric and onomatopoeic, infuses the narrative with magical lyricism.

In *Don Goyo*, *La isla virgen*, and *Seven Serpents and Seven Moons*, Aguilera Malta used literature as a vehicle for achieving social reform. In these novels, the language and literary techniques characteristic of Magical Realism created the illusion of a primitive world, all of whose components coexist in perfect harmony. *Babelandia* treats the same themes and utilizes the same literary techniques as the above-mentioned novels, but the result is totally different. It shows a new direction in and a new attitude toward literature.

Like *Seven Serpents and Seven Moons*, *Babelandia* deals with the theme of good and evil. The forces of good are represented by the Amautas and the forces of evil by the dictatorship of Holoformes Verbofilia in the mythical land of Babelandia. Babelandia and the characters who represent these two opposing forces are archetypes. As such, they transcend the physical laws of time and space. Babelandia is illustrative of any underdeveloped country in the Third World. The forces of good are represented by a trinity of characters: Fulgido Estrella, who is a symbol of the eternal revolutionary, similiar to Jesús in *Seven Serpents and Seven Moons*; María, who has been converted into an archetype of the Virgin Mary by the people because she is a young virgin whose husband died on their wedding day before consummating the marriage; and Eneas Roturante, who personifies forgiveness. Their victory represents the beginning of a more humanitarian epoch in Babelandia, where all men are vehemently opposed to any political system that wishes to dehumanize them. The forces of evil are represented by the dictatorial government of Babelandia. The dictator himself, Holoformes Verbofilia, is a parody of death. He is portrayed as a skeleton who speaks through cassettes which are inserted into his throat. He exemplifies the destructive and annihilating force of man's ideals, creativity, and vitality. He is also impotent with his wife. General Jonas Pitecantropo is a caricature of the military man. He symbolizes the military's obsession with power and destructive force of the army. He suppresses freedom of the press and destroys any vestige of humanitarianism in the fight against the Amautas. Like the dictator, he is also impotent with women. The remaining government officials, who also represent the forces of evil, are zoomorphic characters who typify egotism, political and human corruption, and lust.

In this archetypal world, the characters who represent the forces of evil are presented by the stylistic devices of expressionism and distortion. Each character is the physical symbol of a political or social problem. Exterior physical reality is deformed to express an interior reality in order to portray the mechanical, unemotional way of life in Babelandia: The dictator is a skeleton who speaks through cassettes; in order to show the military's obsession with power and authority, the colonel is portrayed as a military uniform. These procedures produce a grotesque and absurd effect which efficiently typifies the corrupt mechanism of the dictatorship, a totally dehumanized world in which the dictator and his subordinates are reduced to robots and puppets.

Zoomorphism also contributes to the grotesque aspect of the novel. Unlike Aguilera Malta's preceding works, it has a negative connotation in this novel. It has a metaphoric function: The characters undergo zoomorphism only when they try to express their suppressed emotions. For example, when Banquero is speaking to the foreigner about business matters, his laughter is compared to that of a defenseless rabbit in an alfalfa field. Esquino Cascabel, one of the dictator's most servile employees, is converted into a horse.

Aguilera Malta's long fiction is a testimony to the depth of his social commitment to the portrayal of the social reality of his day. The themes of war, colonialism, exploitation, and oppression are presented from many perspectives. Their unifying component is Aguilera Malta's desire to promote an awareness of these themes and thereby activate a spirit of reform, not only in Ecuador but also in the entire Spanish-speaking world. Although Aguilera Malta's novels of Magical Realism are perhaps more powerful in the expression of his message, all of his works exude his strong compassion for the underprivileged, his strong sense of nationalism, and his strong commitment to social reform.

Other major works

SHORT FICTION: *Los que se van*, 1930 (with Joaquín Gallegos Lara and Enrique Gil Gilbert).

PLAYS: *España leal*, 1938; *Lázaro*, 1941; *Sangre azul*, 1946 (*Blue Blood*, 1948); *No bastan los átomos*, 1954; *Dientes blancos*, 1955 (*White Teeth*, 1963); *El tigre*, 1956; *Honorarios*, 1957; *Fantoche*, 1961; *Infierno negro*, 1967; *Muerte, S.A.*, 1968.

POETRY: *El libro de los mangleros*, 1929.

NONFICTION: *La revolución española a través de dos estampas de Antonio Edén*, 1938; *Los generales de Bolívar*, 1965.

Bibliography
Barret, Linton Tomás. "The Culture Scene in Ecuador," in *Hispania*. XXXV, no. 3 (1952), pp. 267-273.
Brushwood, John S. "The Year of Don Goyo," in *The Spanish American Novel: A Twentieth Century Survey*, 1975.
Crooks, Esther J. "Contemporary Ecuador in the Novel and Short Story," in *Hispania*. XXIII, no. 1 (1940), pp. 85-88.
Flores, Angel. "Magical Realism in Spanish American Fiction," in *Hispania*. XXXVIII, no. 2 (1955), pp. 187-192.
Irish, James. "Magical Realism: A Search for Caribbean and Latin American Roots," in *Literary Half Yearly*. XI, no. 2 (1970), pp. 127-139.
Rabassa, Clementine Christos. *Demetrio Aguilera Malta and Social Justice: The Tertiary Phase of Epic Tradition in Latin American Literature*, 1980.

Anne Laura Mattrella

VASSILY AKSYONOV

Born: Kazan, U.S.S.R.; August 20, 1932

Principal long fiction

Kollegi, 1960 (*Colleagues*, 1962); *Zvezdnyi bilet*, 1961 (*A Starry Ticket*, 1962; also as *A Ticket to the Stars*, 1963); *Apelsiny iz Marokko*, 1963 (*Oranges from Morocco*, 1979); *Pora, moi drug, pora*, 1965 (*It's Time, My Friend, It's Time*, 1969); *Zatvorennaya bochkotara*, 1968 (*Surplussed Barrelware*, 1985); *Stalnaya ptitsa*, 1977 (novella; *The Steel Bird*, 1979); *Poiski zhanra*, 1978; *Zolotaya nasha zhelezka*, 1979 (*Our Golden Ironburg*, 1986); *Ozhog*, 1980 (*The Burn*, 1984); *Ostrov Krym*, 1981 (*The Island of Crimea*, 1983); *Bumazhnyi peizazh*, 1983; *Skazhi izium*, 1985.

Other literary forms

Vassily Aksyonov is primarily a novelist who has, however, worked in many genres. The young Soviet writer's short stories of the 1960's were enormously popular among Russian readers. He is also the author of numerous Russian film scripts and several plays, of which the best is *Tsaplya* (1980; the heron). Children's books and a fictionalized biography, *Lyubov k elektrichestvu* (1971; love for electricity), are also found in his oeuvre. His travel writings, especially *Kruglye sutki: non-stop* (1976; around the clock nonstop), a collage account of a visit to the United States, are a remarkable blend of fantasy and reportage. A steady stream of diverse journalism has also come from his pen, particularly since his emigration to the United States.

Achievements

Aksyonov holds a unique position in modern Russian literature. From the early 1930's until the death of dictator Joseph Stalin in 1953, Soviet literature stagnated under the official aesthetic doctrine of Socialist Realism. Aksyonov, as a controversial leader of the "young prose" movement in the post-Stalin period, revitalized Russian prose by introducing fresh themes, characters, and living speech into his work. He was an idol of and spokesman for the new generation of young Soviet technocrats, who dreamed of a Western-oriented humanist socialism. As the dream dimmed, Aksyonov was forced to turn to "writing for the drawer," knowing his work could not be published in the U.S.S.R. These new works, increasingly surrealistic, detailed the disillusion of the young intelligentsia. Published in the West only after Aksyonov's emigration, they confirm his reputation as the preeminent chronicler of his generation, as well as its most innovative literary stylist.

Biography

Vassily Pavlovich Aksyonov's parents, both committed Communists, were falsely arrested as "enemies of the people" in 1937. The future writer rejoined his freed mother and stepfather, a Catholic doctor-prisoner, in Siberia at age seventeen. Because "it's easier for doctors in the camps," it was decided that Aksyonov attend medical school in Leningrad, from which he was graduated in 1956, the year in which Premier Nikita Khrushchev denounced the crimes of Stalin. Taking advantage of the cultural "thaw," the young practitioner began writing. After his successful first novel, *Colleagues*, was published, in 1960, Aksyonov turned to full-time writing. The early "optimistic" period of his career came to an end on March 8, 1963, when Khrushchev himself publicly demanded recantation of his work. Publication became increasingly difficult, especially after the Soviet invasion of Czechoslovakia in 1968, but Aksyonov was permitted to accept a one-term Regents' Lectureship at the University of California at Los Angeles in 1975. In the late 1970's, Aksyonov and a number of colleagues boldly undertook to publish an uncensored literary anthology to be called *Metropol*. Those involved were subjected to reprisals, and Aksyonov was, in effect, forced to emigrate in 1980. In the United States, Aksyonov has published several works written earlier and has taught at various universities. He has also been a Fellow at the prestigious Woodrow Wilson International Center. As a resident of Washington, D.C., Aksyonov has continued to write novels, including *Skazhi izium* (say cheese!), a fictionalized version of the *Metropol* affair. An energetic publicist, Aksyonov occupies a leading position in émigré cultural affairs.

Analysis

Vassily Aksyonov's major theme is the nature and fate of the Soviet Union and the role of his generation in trying to reshape the nation after the death of Stalin. His works chronicle these years first from the optimistic perspective of a generation on the rise, confident that a new day has dawned; then, from the perspective of growing doubt; and, finally, in a mood of despair.

A Ticket to the Stars was a landmark book that became the rallying point for the new generation. The young people it portrayed and those whom it inspired took the name "star boys" as their banner. Conservatives of the older generation used the name as a term of condemnation. The story begins in the early summer in Moscow, circa 1960. Three friends who have just finished high school are "hanging out" in the courtyard of their apartment building. The neighbors look askance at their clothes and the music blaring from their tape recorder. From professional families, all three are headed for college and careers in accord with the expectations of society and the wishes of their families. Dimka Denisov, the ringleader, confides to his older brother Victor that they have decided to kick over the traces, defy their parents, and head for the Baltic seacoast for the summer, and perhaps longer.

Victor, who narrates parts of the story, is twenty-eight, a doctoral candidate in space medicine. A model son, a scholarship student, he looks with affection but mild alarm at his aimless younger brother and his friends. Victor's goal in life is represented by the night view from his bedroom window, from which he can see a small rectangle of sky dotted by stars. The sight reminds him of a tram ticket punched with star-shaped holes.

The teenagers pass their summer on the beach. Among their haunts is a restaurant bar with a star-painted ceiling. As their money disappears, they join an Estonian collective fishing enterprise. The young Muscovites first find their companions crude and the work difficult, but at length they begin to take pride in the endeavor. Victor, now on the verge of a brilliant career, comes to visit Dimka, who is still wary of a "programmed" future. Suddenly called back to Moscow, Victor is killed in a plane crash. After the funeral, Dimka lies on Victor's bed and sees for the first time "the starry ticket." It is now his ticket to the stars, but where will it take him?

Soviet readers, unlike their Western counterparts, were not accustomed to sympathetic accounts of youthful alienation. Even though the story has a reassuring ending, readers were shocked by its racy language and its young heroes' flippant attitude toward authority.

The Steel Bird, written in 1965, marks a crucial turning point in Aksyonov's writing both stylistically and thematically. The earlier novels were stylistically within the limits of realism, and their themes were more social than political. The young heroes, whose rebellion is against cant and excessive conformity, ultimately affirm the values of a Socialist society. *The Steel Bird* is a political allegory in a modernist stylistic framework. In the spring of 1948, an odious creature named Popenkov (who subsequently proves to be partly human and partly mechanical bird) presents himself at a large, decaying Moscow apartment building and begs a corner in the entry hall elevator. As the years pass, the creature expands his domain and enlists the residents in an illegal fake antique tapestry business. Eventually the tenants, a diverse cross section of Soviet society, are reduced to entering the building through a cramped backdoor.

The 1960's arrive. Soviet life has changed for the better. The older generation of the residents are retired, and their children are making their mark as leaders of a cultural revolution. The apartment building, weakened by age and Popenkov's constant remodeling, is on the verge of collapse. The Steel Bird nevertheless decides that for the convenience of his nocturnal flights the elevator should be extended through the roof. Seeing their home in danger, the residents finally rise. A coalition of worker-tenants and the young cultural leaders confront the Steel Bird on the roof, but as the residents drive off his minions, the building starts to crack. The building collapses, but all the residents are saved and moved to a splendid new building, while the Steel Bird remains perched atop the old elevator shaft.

Months later, as bulldozers start to clear the rubble, Popenkov slowly flies off. The spirit of Stalinism departs, but it may return at any time.

The story, told by means of third-person narrative, eyewitness accounts, official reports, interludes of poetry, and authorial asides, is punctuated by the Stalinist house manager's cornet improvisations, thus echoing the story's themes. The Steel Bird increasingly lapses into using an autistic bird language.

The Burn, written in the post-Czech invasion years (1969-1975), presents a far bleaker stage in the evolution of Aksyonov's views. The events of *The Burn*—a long, complex, often hallucinatory novel—are perceived through the alcoholic haze that is the intelligentsia's response to the demise of their hopes for a new Russia. There are five more or less interchangeable heroes—or rather antiheroes—all members of Aksyonov's generation, all liberals, all superstars in their professions. Kunitser is a physicist; Sabler, a jazz saxophonist; Khvastishchev, a sculptor; Malkolmov, a physician; and Pantelei, a writer whose past resembles that of author Aksyonov. Although the men have certain almost identical and seemingly concurrent experiences, they lead independent existences. The narrative focus alternates among them, and on occasion they change identities. Most remarkably, they share flashbacks to a single, common childhood when they were Tolya von Steinbock.

The heroes have retreated before a renascent (but much milder) Stalinism, withdrawing into their creative work, sex, and alcohol. On the evening of the first day portrayed in the novel, they individually encounter an old friend, Patrick Thunderjet, a visiting Anglo-American who is obviously their Western counterpart. The day's drinking expands into a binge that takes the collective hero, a friend, and Thunderjet through a set of bizarre experiences ending in the Crimea, where they are ultimately arrested and confined to the drunk tank. The collective hero, too valuable an asset to Soviet society to be abandoned, is sent to a detoxification hospital. Released, the protagonists undertake a sober life, each engaged in a major creative endeavor. Soviet society, however, is too corrupt for their survival. Each has a professional colleague, a close friend from the heady days of the early 1960's. The old friends, who have compromised with the authorities, betray the trust of the heroes, who again succumb to drink. Now merged into a single nameless "I," the protagonist descends into alcoholic hallucinations, ultimately leaping to his death while fantasizing a lunar space flight.

The main story line describes the smashed hopes of a generation. There is also a story behind the story. The five heroes share a childhood very much like Aksyonov's. Tolya von Steinbock joins his mother in Siberia when she is released from a ten-year sentence toward the end of Stalin's reign. He wants nothing more than to be a model Soviet youth and is vaguely embarrassed by his ex-prisoner mother and stepfather, a doctor and Catholic lay priest of German origin. Among a group of new women prisoners, he sees a girl of

Polish-English origin named Alisa and dreams of a daring rescue. As he day-dreams, another young man, an ex-prisoner, offers modest aid to the girl. Tolya becomes friends with the young man, Sanya Gurchenko, who is a friend of his stepfather. Their courage and idealism greatly impress him. Tolya's mother is soon rearrested, as is Sanya. They are interrogated, Sanya brutally, by two political police officers. Sanya eventually escapes to the West, where he becomes a Catholic priest and, years later, briefly encounters the hero.

These events of twenty years before lie deeply buried in the minds of the successful heroes, who do not wish to confront either their impotent past or their compromised present. The past, however, is very much with them. Wherever they go, they encounter two figures, cloakroom attendants, drunk-tank aides, and the like, vaguely reminiscent of the former police officials. They also yearn for a beautiful, promiscuous woman who moves in corrupt, elite Moscow circles and seems to resemble the Polish-English Alisa. The he-roes, however, remain incapable either of vengeance or of rescuing their ideal. Unlike Sanya, who actively resisted evil, they have tacitly compromised with the system.

It is Sanya, the priest, who offers Aksyonov's solution with his philosophy of "the third mode." Its basic postulate is that all men, atheist and believer alike, seek God. There are always two models: an idea and its antithesis. One must seek a third, qualitatively different model through which one may strive to see the face of God. Man comes close to it only in moments of free, irrational creativity, the "burn" of the book's title. The higher emotions, such as compassion for one's neighbor, charity, the urge for justice, are rationally and biologically inexplicable, fantastic. Christianity, precisely because it is concerned with these emotions, is sublime. Christianity is likened to a break-through into space, an image that corresponds to the hero's final, hallucina-tory suicide flight. *The Burn*, Aksyonov's most important novel, is a diagno-sis and indictment of his generation.

The Island of Crimea, written between 1977 and 1979, continues some of the themes of *The Burn*, but with a different emphasis. Although more tradi-tional in style, *The Island of Crimea* is based on two fantastic premises. The Crimea, in reality a peninsula in the Black Sea, is, in the novel, an indepen-dent island-country. Historically, the Red Army defeated the White Armies during the Civil War, and the Whites were driven into overseas exile. Fiction-ally, the Whites have successfully defended the island of Crimea and estab-lished a capitalistic Western political democracy which, in the late 1970's, is a fabulously wealthy, technological supercivilization.

Andrei Luchnikov, a jet-set member of one of the country's most promi-nent White émigré families, is the editor of an influential liberal newspaper. Luchnikov's political program, which reflects his generation's nostalgia for Mother Russia, calls for the voluntary reunification of the Crimea with Russia. Although realizing that the Soviet Union is, by the standards of the Crimea, politically and economically primitive, he believes that the historical motherland is moving forward and that both countries would profit from a symbiotic union. Eventually, the island's voters approve the reunification. The Soviet government, unable to comprehend the idea, responds with a massive military invasion in which most of Luchnikov's family dies, Luchnikov goes mad, and his son flees into exile. The novel, which reads like a James Bond thriller, is, in some sense, a very black comedy.

The Island of Crimea sums up Aksyonov's twenty-year meditation on the nature, history, and fate of his native country. From *A Ticket to the Stars* to *The Island of Crimea*, Aksyonov has charted the evolution of the Russian intelligentsia: from the optimism of the early 1960's, through the cynicism and despair of the late 1960's and early 1970's, to dissidence and emigration. It is the saga of a generation.

Other major works

SHORT FICTION: *Katapulta*, 1964; *Na polputi k lune*, 1965; *Zhal, chto vas ne bylo s nami*, 1969; *The Steel Bird and Other Stories*, 1979.

PLAYS: *Vsegda v prodazhe*, 1967; *Tsaplya*, 1980; *Aristofaniana s lyagushkami*, 1981.

NONFICTION: *Lyubov k elektrichestvu*, 1971; *Kruglye sutki: non-stop*, 1976; *In Search of Melancholy Baby*, 1987.

Bibliography

Meyer, Priscilla. "Aksyonov and Stalinism: Political, Moral, and Literary Power," in *Slavic and East European Journal*. XXX (Winter, 1986), pp. 509-525.

Mozejko, Edward, Boris Briker, and Per Dalgard, eds. *Vasiliy Pavlovich Aksenov: A Writer in Quest of Himself*, 1986.

Proffer, Ellendea. "The Prague Winter: Two Novels by Aksyonov," in *The Third Wave: Russian Literature in Emigration*, 1984. Edited by Olga Matich with Michael Heim.

Slobin, Greta. "Aksyonov Beyond 'Youth Prose': Subversion Through Popular Culture," in *Slavic and East European Journal*. XXX (Spring, 1987), pp. 50-64.

D. Barton Johnson

NELSON ALGREN
Nelson Ahlgren Abraham

Born: Detroit, Michigan; March 28, 1909
Died: Sag Harbor, New York; May 9, 1981

Principal long fiction
Somebody in Boots, 1935; *Never Come Morning*, 1942; *The Man with the Golden Arm*, 1949; *A Walk on the Wild Side*, 1956; *The Devil's Stocking*, 1983.

Other literary forms
Although Nelson Algren is known primarily as a novelist, some critics believe that the short story, because it does not make the structural demands the novel does, is a more appropriate genre for him, and his *The Neon Wilderness* (1947) has been acclaimed one of the best collections of short stories published in the 1940's. *Chicago: City on the Make* (1951) is a prose poem which has been variously described as a social document and a love poem to the city that serves as the center of Algren's fictional world. Similar non-fiction writings include *Who Lost an American?* (1963), a self-described "guide to the seamier sides" of several cities, including Chicago, and *Notes from a Sea Diary: Hemingway All the Way* (1965); both books combine travel writing and personal essays. What little poetry Algren wrote that is not included in his novels (*The Man with the Golden Arm*, for example, concludes with a poem of the same name which Algren terms an "epitaph") is included in *The Last Carousel* (1973), along with some unpublished stories and sketches. He also collaborated with H. E. F. Donohue on the book *Conversations with Nelson Algren* (1964), a series of interviews. *Nelson Algren's Own Book of Lonesome Monsters* (1962), an anthology to which he contributed a preface and the concluding story, sounds Algren's recurring theme: Man is always alone.

Achievements
While Algren's first novel, *Somebody in Boots*, failed commercially, it drew the attention of serious literary critics, who were even more impressed by his second novel, *Never Come Morning*, which won for Algren in 1947 one thousand dollars from the American Academy of Arts and Letters. Also in 1947, he received a grant from the Newberry Library to assist him in the writing of *The Man with the Golden Arm*, which subsequently received the National Book Award in 1950. Since many of the stories in *The Neon Wilderness* had previously appeared in the O. Henry Memorial collections or in *Best American Stories*, Algren's stature as a first-class writer of fiction was assured by 1950. Because his fictional world, for the most part, was Chicago, Algren

is frequently linked with James T. Farrell and Richard Wright, who belong to what some critics have termed the "Chicago School." While he denied any literary indebtedness to Farrell and Wright, Algren admitted that his work was influenced by Carl Sandburg, partly because Algren's prose tends to the poetic, so much so that he has been termed by Malcolm Cowley "the poet of the Chicago slums."

Maxwell Geismar has termed Algren a "neo-naturalist" with roots in the American realistic tradition of Stephen Crane, Theodore Dreiser, and Ernest Hemingway (Algren acknowledged his debt to Hemingway, who in return hailed Algren as, after William Faulkner, among America's first writers). Unfortunately, critics, including Geismar, have also found many of the excesses of naturalism—melodrama, romanticism, oversimplification of characters and motives, and "over-writing"—in Algren's work, which has also been assailed for its formlessness. What Algren lacks in style and form, however, he more than compensates for in rich detail and insightful observations about what George Bluestone has called the "world's derelicts," those unfortunates who had largely been ignored, even by those writers who were ostensibly concerned with the "lumpen proletariat." In fact, so preoccupied is he with the victims of the American Dream, those losers customarily associated with the Depression, that one seldom encounters the other America in his fiction. Consequently, some readers have found his work dated, and while *The Man with the Golden Arm* and *A Walk on the Wild Side* were both filmed (in 1955 and 1962, respectively), thereby testifying to Algren's popularity, his critical standing declined. Yet from 1945 to 1960, he was among America's most acclaimed writers because of his focus and his vision, both of which were compatible with post–World War II America.

Biography

Nelson Ahlgren Abraham was born in Detroit, Michigan, on March 28, 1909, to second-generation Chicagoans, who moved back to Chicago when Algren was three years old. From 1912 until 1928, Algren absorbed the Chicago environment that was to become the center of his fictional world. After receiving his journalism degree from the University of Illinois in 1931, he began traveling across the Southwest, working at odd jobs (door-to-door coffee salesman in New Orleans, migrant worker, co-operator of a gasoline station in Texas, and carnival worker) and gathering the raw material that he later transformed into his fiction, particularly *A Walk on the Wild Side*. After serving time for stealing a typewriter (an oddly appropriate theft for a writer), he returned to Chicago, where he continued his "research" on the Division Street milieu and began to write short stories, poems, and his first novel, *Somebody in Boots*, a Depression tale about the Southwest that became, after extensive revision, *A Walk on the Wild Side*.

After World War II—he served three years in the army—Algren legally shortened his name, returned again to Chicago, and within five years enjoyed a reputation as one of America's finest fiction writers. *The Man with the Golden Arm* received the National Book Award, and several stories were also recognized for their excellence. *A Walk on the Wild Side* and its subsequent filming, as well as the cinematic adaptation of *The Man with the Golden Arm*, brought Algren to the height of his popularity during the 1950's and 1960's, but aside from some travel books and his last novel, his writing career essentially ended in 1956. In his later years, he taught creative writing, before spending his last years on *The Devil's Stocking*, a thinly veiled fictional treatment of the trial and imprisonment of Reuben "Hurricane" Carter, a middleweight boxer. The "novel" did little to restore Algren's literary reputation.

Analysis

Whether the setting is Chicago or New Orleans, Nelson Algren's characters live, dream, and die in an environment alien to most Americans, many of whom have achieved the financial success and spiritual failure endemic to the American Dream. His characters are, at their best, losers in the quest for success; at their worst, they are spectators, not even participants, in that competitive battle. While his protagonists do aspire to escape from their environments, to assume new identities, and to attain that American Dream, they are so stunted by their backgrounds and so crippled with their own guilt that their efforts are doomed from the start and their inevitable fate often involves the punishment that their guilt-ridden souls have unconsciously sought. In *Never Come Morning*, Bruno cannot escape his guilt for allowing Steffi to be raped by his gang and almost welcomes his punishment for the murder of another man; in *The Man with the Golden Arm*, Frankie Machine cannot escape his guilt for the accident that incapacitates his wife and so can end his drug addiction only by hanging himself; in *A Walk on the Wild Side*, Dove cannot escape his guilt for having raped Terasina, to whom he returns after having been blinded in a fight. In all three novels, the guilt that the man experiences from having abused a woman leads to a self-destructive impulse that negates his attempt to escape from his environment and produces the punishment he seeks.

Although it is not his first published novel (*Somebody in Boots*, a commercial failure that Algren revised and reissued as *A Walk on the Wild Side*, was his first published novel), *Never Come Morning* is Algren's first major novel. As the chronicle of a young man's passage from boyhood to manhood, *Never Come Morning* is another, albeit more cynical, American initiation novel, in which Bruno Bicek's initiation leads to his death. Like many young men, Bruno dreams of escaping from the ghetto through professional sports, either boxing or baseball ("Lefty" Bicek is a pitcher), but Algren quickly indicates, through similar chapter headings, that Bruno shares a "problem" with Casey Benkowski, his idol, whose defeat in the ring foreshadows Bruno's eventual defeat in life. Bruno's dreams are illusory, the product of the media: He reads *Kayo* magazine, sees pictures of boxers on matchbook covers, and watches Jimmy Cagney movies. His dream of becoming a "modern Kitchel," a former Polish-American boxing champion, reflects his desire to become someone else, to define his success in terms of other people, not himself. To become a successful man, he seeks status as the president and treasurer of the Warriors, his street gang, but his allegiance to the gang reflects his childish dependence on the group, not his adult leadership of it. His "other-directedness" also affects his relationship with Steffi, whom he seduces partly in order to gain status from the Warriors, who subsequently assert their own sexual rights to her. Rather than defend her and reveal the very "softness" that wins the readers' respect, he yields to the Warriors, thereby forsaking independence and manhood and incurring the guilt that eventually destroys him.

Like most of Algren's women, Steffi has a supporting role and exists primarily in terms of the male protagonist. She is the agent by which he comes of age sexually, acquires his spiritual guilt, eventually becomes an independent man, and finally, since she has alienated the informant Bonifacy, is doomed. Despite being the victim of a gang rape, Steffi retains her capacity for love and forgiveness, limited as that is, and becomes the stereotyped "whore with the heart of gold" whose love enables the "hero," antiheroic as he is, to overcome the odds. Her passivity is reflected symbolically through Algren's description of the fly without wings in Steffi's room: After he "seduces" her, Bruno destroys the fly. Later, when Bruno wins a Kewpie doll and subsequently and unthinkingly destroys it, Algren ties the fate of the doll, an appropriate symbol, to Steffi, who is won and destroyed by Bruno. Steffi's fate seems even crueler than Bruno's, since he will "escape" in death but Steffi will remain trapped with the other prostitutes who endure at "Mama" Tomek's brothel.

Before he is incarcerated, Bruno does mature through a series of tests that prove his manhood. Although he cannot articulate his love and desire for forgiveness, he does come to understand that love is compatible with manhood. When he arranges a fight for himself with Honeyboy Tucker, he acts independently; when he overcomes Fireball Kodadek and Tiger Pultoric, Bonifacy's thugs, he overcomes his fear of physical mutilation (Fireball's knife) and of his idol and father figure (Pultoric is the former champion). Before he can "be his own man," Bruno must overcome his childish dependence and hero worship. Bruno's subsequent victory over Tucker makes his earlier symbolic victory official and gives him the identity he seeks as a promising "contender," but that identity is destroyed when he is arrested only minutes later and sent to jail.

Images of imprisonment pervade the novel, which is concerned with the institutions that house inmates. When Bruno first serves time, Algren digresses to describe prison life, just as he does when he recounts Steffi's life at the brothel, where she is no less a prisoner. While she is there, she dreams of a "great stone penitentiary" and of the "vault" that is the barber's room. The prison and the brothel are appropriate institutions for a city which Algren compares to a madhouse. (Algren also sees the prostitutes as inmates of an insane asylum.) There is no escape for Steffi or Bruno, just as there is no real morning in this somber tale of darkness and night. Algren's Chicago is America in microcosm: As madhouse, prison, and brothel, it is an insane, entrapped world where people "sell out," thereby prostituting themselves.

In *The Man with the Golden Arm*, also set in Polish-American Chicago, Algren reiterates many of the themes, images, and character types that exist in *Never Come Morning*. Although the novel's controversial theme of drug addiction has received much attention, Algren is not concerned with drug addiction per se, but with the forces, external and internal, that lead to the addictive, dependent personalities that render people unable to cope with their environments or escape from them. Once again, Algren's characters are life's losers, "the luckless living soon to become the luckless dead," the "wary and the seeking, the strayed, the frayed, the happy and the hapless, the lost, the luckless, the lucky and the doomed" who become the "disinherited," those who emerge "from the wrong side of its [America's] billboards." The "hunted who also hope" in *Never Come Morning* become the "pursued" in *The Man with the Golden Arm*, which also relies on naturalistic metaphors comparing people and animals.

Since the characters are themselves victims of a system that excludes them, it seems ironic that they should experience guilt, but Algren's protagonist, Frankie Machine, is trapped by the guilt he feels at having been responsible for the car accident that has paralyzed Sophie, his wife. (Since Sophie has induced the paralysis—there is nothing physically wrong with her—his guilt is even more ironic.) Sophie uses Frankie's guilt to "hook" (a word suggesting addiction) him, punish him, and contribute to their self-destructive mutual dependence. Algren describes Frankie's guilt as "slow and cancerous" and even has Louie, the pusher, attribute drug addiction to the desire for self-punishment. Frankie, the "pursued," is not alone in his guilt, for Algren portrays Record Head Bednar, the "pursuer," as also afflicted by a consuming guilt. As the agent of "justice," he feels "of all men most alone, of all men most guilty of all the lusts he had ever condemned in others." Bednar, who is hardly without sin, must nevertheless "cast the first stone."

Sin and guilt permeate this novel, which belabors religious imagery, particularly that concerning the crucifixion. The controlling metaphor in the novel is Sophie's "luminous crucifix," which she uses to enslave Frankie. Sophie states, "My cross is this chair. I'm settin' on *my* cross. . . . I'm *nailed* to mine." When her friend Violet suggests that she is driving in her own "nails,"

Sophie evades the issue because her "crucifixion," while voluntary, is not selfless but selfish. Algren observes the parallels between Sophie and Christ—both have been betrayed and bleed for the sins of others—but Sophie lacks love. In another parody of the crucifixion, Sparrow protests to Bednar, "You're nailin' me to the cross, Captain"; Bednar responds, "What the hell you think they're [the politicians] doin' to me?" Although they have enough religious teaching to mouth biblical allusions, Algren's characters use Christianity only as popular culture, as a source, like advertising and the movies, of reference to their own ego-centered worlds. Although Algren suggests that "God had forgotten His own," at least in Frankie's case, it is at least equally true that, as Sophie confesses, she and Frankie have forgotten God. Sophie's pathetic, self-centered musing about God having gone somewhere and keeping His distance indicate that He has no place in the world of Division Street. Surely Algren's allusion to the gamblers' God, who watches Sparrow's "fall," reflects the post-Christian modern world.

In Algren's naturalistic world, the characters are seen as caged animals waiting to be slaughtered. At the beginning of the novel, Frankie, who waits for justice from Bednar, watches a roach drowning in a bucket and is tempted to help it, but the roach dies before he intercedes, just as Frankie dies without anyone interceding for him. Algren's metaphor for the trapped Sophie is equally flattering. When she hears the mousetrap in the closet snap shut, "she felt it close as if it had shut within herself, hard and fast forever." Even Molly Novotny, who resembles Steffi in being a "fallen woman" and agent of redemption, is depicted as living in a "nest." In fact, Algren uses the animal imagery to suggest Frankie's impending fate. When Frankie is apprehended for stealing irons, Algren uses "over-fed hens" and "bosomy biddies" to describe the saleswomen and then has Frankie glimpse "a butcher holding a broken-necked rooster." Since Frankie finally hangs himself, the glimpse is ironically prophetic. Frankie's addiction is also expressed in animal terms: Frankie has a "monkey on his back," and while he temporarily rids himself of the monkey, permanent escape is impossible. The two caged monkeys at the Kitten Klub shriek insults at the patrons and serve as the metaphor incarnate for Frankie's addiction.

Frankie's addiction is also expressed in terms of an army buddy also addicted to morphine, Private McGantic, whose "presence" is akin to the monkey's. By the end of the novel Frankie has "become" Private McGantic: Frankie calls himself "Private Nowhere," suggesting both the identification and the lack of direction. "Private McGantic" is, however, only one of Frankie's identities; the novel recounts his futile attempt to become someone other than Frankie Machine (the assumed name reflects his lost humanity), the Dealer. He wants Molly to call him the "Drummer," not the "Dealer," but he never becomes a professional musician, and part of his tragedy is that he does not know who he is: "Who am I anyway, Solly?" The answer Solly

(Sparrow) gives, "Be yourself," is a meaningless cliché, an example of circular reasoning because Frankie does not know what his "self" is. The official inquest into the death of Francis Majcinek (Frankie's "real" name) establishes nothing of consequence (his addiction is not even alluded to) except that he is the "deceased," one of the "luckless dead" Algren mentions earlier in the novel. Even his fictional life is not "real": It is a "comic strip" from birth to death.

A Walk on the Wild Side, Algren's fourth novel, is a reworking of *Somebody in Boots*, published some twenty years earlier. As a result, although it resembles the other two in its characters, loose structure, and imagery, it also looks back to an earlier time, the Depression, and its setting is New Orleans rather than Chicago. Once again, Algren focuses on prison inmates, whose "kangaroo court" justice is superior to the justice they receive "outside," and on prostitutes, who also "serve their time" and are compared to caged birds (the brothel is an "aviary"). Despite their situation and their pasts, they are "innocent children" in their naïveté and illusions, and one of them is the means by which the hero is redeemed. Other notable characters include the freaks and the cripples who frequent Dockerty's "Dollhouse" and who are the physical counterparts of the emotional cripples in the novel. Achilles Schmidt, legless former circus strongman, is the exception, for he has found psychological strength through the accident that should have "crippled" him. It is only when Dove Linkhorn, the protagonist, is blinded and therefore "crippled" by Schmidt that he rids himself of the illusions that have weakened him.

A parody of the Horatio Alger myth of the American Dream, *A Walk on the Wild Side* concerns an ambitious young man who "wants to make something of himself" and leaves the farm to find fame and fortune in the city. Dove's journey is "educational," in terms of the reading instruction he receives and the culture he acquires, as well as the "lessons" he learns about capitalism and life in general. At the beginning of the novel, Dove is an "innocent," as his name suggests, but that "innocence" is not sexual—he rapes Terasina, the Earth Mother who is also his first "mentor"—but experiential, in that he believes in the "Ladder of Success" with "unlimited opportunities" for "ambitious young men." Algren offers Dove a naturalistic parable of capitalism, particularly on the tenuous nature of life at the top. The headless terrapin in the fish market struggles to the top by using its superior strength in "wading contentedly over mothers and orphans," but its reign as King of the Turtles is short-lived, and it has literally and symbolically "lost its head." Algren adds that Dove does not know that "there was also room for one more on the bottom." Before he reaches the bottom, Dove becomes a salesman, the epitome of the enterprising capitalist; the coffee scam and the phony beauty-parlor certificate racket, while illegal, are also seen as integral parts of capitalism.

Before he achieves his greatest success as a "salesman" of sex, Dove works, appropriately, in a condom manufacturing plant, which also sells sex. In his role as "Big Stingaree" in Finnerty's brothel, he is paid to perform an art which involves the "deflowering" of "virgins," who are played by prostitutes. In effect, the brothel, the primary setting in the novel, also serves as the symbolic center since Algren presents a society that has sold itself, has "prostituted" itself to survive. Ironically, the real prostitutes in the brothel are morally superior to the "prostitutes" in mainstream American society, the "Do-Right Daddies," the powerful people who crusade against sin but also sin within the laws they create.

Hallie Breedlove, a prostitute, "sins," but she is capable of love and compassion, first with Schmidt and then with Dove, with whom she leaves the brothel. The "escape" is futile, however, for her subsequent pregnancy, in the light of her black "blood," threatens their future, and she believes that she can have her child only if she returns to her past, the mulatto village where she was born. Dove lacks her insight and in his attempt to find her is jailed, released, and then loses his sight in a battle with Schmidt. Metaphorically, however, in searching for her, he finds himself, and in losing his vision, he gains insight. Having learned that the "loser's side of the street" is superior to the "winners'," Dove abandons his quest for success and returns to his Texas hometown to be reconciled to Terasina. Unlike Bruno and Frankie, Dove not only survives but also resolves to deal constructively with the guilt caused by his sin against his woman.

Algren's last novel, *The Devil's Stocking*, is not so much a "novel" as a fictional treatment of Reuben Carter's trial and imprisonment. What began as an *Esquire* assignment, covering a boxer's murder trial, grew to "novel" proportions, probably because of the boxing and the trial, both of which appear in his other novels. The Algren characters—prostitutes, gamblers, police officers, and petty crooks—reappear in the novel about Carter, renamed Ruby Calhoun for fictive purposes. Because of its geographical and chronological distance from his earlier novels, as well as its blending of fact and fiction, it is not among the works for which Algren will be remembered.

Despite the qualified optimism of *A Walk on the Wild Side*, Algren's novels tend to paint a negative image of capitalistic American society with its nightmarish American Dream. Chicago and New Orleans become microcosms of America, a country marked by images of madness, imprisonment, and prostitution. In that world, virtue, such as it is, resides on the "loser's side of the street," in the prisons and the brothels. Constricted by their backgrounds, Algren's male protagonists typically strive to escape and assume a new identity, sin against a woman (thereby incurring guilt that compounds their problems), serve time in prison (presented as a place of refuge), and pursue a self-destructive course that leads inevitably to death or mutilation.

Other major works

SHORT FICTION: *The Neon Wilderness*, 1947; *The Last Carousel*, 1973 (also includes sketches and poems).

NONFICTION: *Chicago: City on the Make*, 1951; *Who Lost an American?* 1963; *Notes from a Sea Diary: Hemingway All the Way*, 1965.

Bibliography

Bluestone, George. "Nelson Algren," in *Western Review*. XXII (Autumn, 1957), pp. 27-44.

Cox, Martha Heasley, and Wayne Chatterton. *Nelson Algren*, 1975.

Donohue, H. E. F. *Conversations with Nelson Algren*, 1964.

Eisinger, Chester E. *Fiction of the Forties*, 1963.

Geismar, Maxwell. "Nelson Algren: The Iron Sanctuary," in *College English*. XIV (March, 1953), pp. 311-315.

Kazin, Alfred. *Contemporaries*, 1962.

Thomas L. Erskine

AHARON APPELFELD

Born: Czernowitz, Romania; 1932

Principal long fiction

Badenheim, 'ir nofesh, 1975 (*Badenheim 1939*, 1980); *Tor-ha-pela'ot*, 1978 (*The Age of Wonders*, 1981); *Kutonet veha-pasim*, 1983 (*Tzili: The Story of a Life*, 1983); *Nesiga mislat*, 1984 (*The Retreat*, 1984); *To the Land of the Cattails*, 1986.

Other literary forms

Aharon Appelfeld's writing career began with poetry published in the 1950's and progressed through short stories to novellas and longer fiction. He has been a prolific writer in Hebrew of countless poems, more than three hundred stories, and more than twenty volumes of fiction and essays. He has also written an autobiography in Hebrew, *Ke'ishon ha-ayin* (1973; like the apple of my eye). Many of his short stories have been published in English-language periodicals, and one collection is available in English, *In the Wilderness* (1965). Like his longer fiction, Appelfeld's short stories revolve principally around the events preceding and following the Holocaust and deal in large part with Jews separated from the mainstream who manage to maintain themselves in a non-Jewish world. Prominently mentioned in significant discussions of his work are "Berta," "The Journey," "The Betrayal," "The Pilgrimage to Kazansk," "Regina," "Kitty," and "1946."

Achievements

Although Appelfeld has been published since the 1950's and emerged in the 1960's as a leading Israeli writer, it was only in the 1980's that his genius was recognized outside Israel, with the publication of several of his novels in English. Prior to that time, however, he had been recognized with several major Israeli awards, including one for his poetry in 1960 and the Bialik Prize in 1978. He was also the recipient of the Israel Prize for Literature in 1983. Most critics writing in English have concentrated on his reputation as one of the great voices of the Holocaust (Alan Mintz says, "Greenberg and Appelfeld are the two great writers of the Holocaust in Hebrew literature") and on his writing techniques of simplicity and understatement and their relationship to the techniques of Franz Kafka. Appelfeld himself has commented on these evaluations of his work, disagreeing in part with both: ". . . I am not writing what is called 'Holocaust literature.' . . . I'm just telling stories about Jews—to Jews—at a certain period in their history. . . . If my work has echoes of both *Kohelet* [Ecclesiastes] and Kafka, that's because I see them both in the tradition of Jewish minimalist literature." Appelfeld's writing achievements are perhaps characterized better by Irving Howe: "No one surpasses Aharon Appelfeld in portraying the crisis of European civilization both before and after the Second World War. . . . He is one of the best novelists alive."

Biography

Aharon Appelfeld was born in Czernowitz, Bukovina, Romania in 1932, into an assimilated Jewish family whose language of choice was German. When Appelfeld was eight, he and his family were removed from their environment. His mother was taken by the Nazis, and he was separated from the rest of his family and shipped to a concentration camp in Transnistria, from which he escaped. After three perilous years of wandering through the forests of Eastern Europe with temporary stays with various refugees along the way, he joined the Russian army in 1944, at age eleven, in the Ukraine as a field cook. At twelve, Appelfeld joined a gang of war orphans who made their way south, living off the land. He was the youngest member and was to remain in touch with others of the gang. Upon their arrival in Italy, the gang members were befriended by a priest and lived for a time at the church, singing in the choir. After this interlude, the gang went on to Naples, where they met a Youth Aliya group and were persuaded to go to Israel. Appelfeld has related that the gang's last night in Naples was spent at a brothel, where he sat up all night in a chair.

After his arrival in Israel in 1947, Appelfeld began writing poetry in his newly acquired language, Hebrew. The Jerusalem editor to whom he sent his poetry corrected it and rejected it for three years, after which time the editor instructed the poet not to send him any more poetry until he learned to write Hebrew. Ten years later, in 1960, Appelfeld has noted, he received an award for his poetry, the award named after the same editor, who had recently died.

In 1962, Appelfeld's first short-story collection was published by an eccentric publisher who had not read the material but liked the author's looks. The book, although not distributed to bookstores initially, enjoyed critical acclaim and started Appelfeld's literary career as a short-story writer and novelist. A graduate of Hebrew University in Jerusalem, Appelfeld taught Hebrew literature at Ben Gurion University in Beersheba, Israel, and eventually made his home in Jerusalem with his three children and his wife, Yehudit, an Argentine and his former student.

Analysis

Careful analysis of Appelfeld's writing suggests that his works consist of detailing different elements of one story, his own story. The seemingly autobiographical aspects of these novels, however, reveal Appelfeld's unusual ability to retell visions and motifs in ever-changing and fascinating literary hues and designs. Appelfeld himself has said,

It's usually pointed out that I draw on my own experience for my stories and novels. I acknowledge that. Yet I have no interest in writing autobiography. . . . Memory can't create a story; the author must. So I objectify my own experience by recreating it in the stories of others.

As noted above, critics have also referred to Appelfeld as one of the great producers of Holocaust literature. Although accurate, that judgment is ironic, for Appelfeld never specifically names or addresses events of the Holocaust in his writing. Nevertheless, in his sparsely written recounting of the pre-Holocaust period, the author evokes the horrors to come by stirring the memories and imagination of those who read with a historical perspective. In like manner, in his stories about those who survived the years of hiding or after being "sucked into" railroad cars, both recurring motifs in Appelfeld's works, he forces the reader's imagination to develop the pictures he never paints but which are responsible for the broken, imperfect souls of the post-Holocaust experience. Appelfeld himself has spoken of this technique: "You can never understand the meaning of the Holocaust. You can just come to the edges of it. If you wrote about it directly, you'd end up trivializing it."

Appelfeld's images and themes are recurrent. The most devastating images recall with chilling understatement and deceptively simple, direct language, the naïve willingness of European Jews to accept resignedly the events, indignities, and humiliations that preceded the Holocaust, and their destructive self-abnegation and anti-Jewish behavior. Appelfeld accents these characteristics by emphasizing stereotypical differences between pre-Holocaust Jews and non-Jews. Jews were timid figures whose long faces were pale from lack of outdoor activity and whose bodies were undeveloped by physical exercise. On the one hand were the intellectual Jews who had assimilated into Western European culture, abandoning their traditions and the Yiddish language; on the other hand were the *Ostjuden* (Jews from the east, Poland in particular), who lacked refinement and who were known for their single-minded pursuit of mercantile occupations and their observance of traditional ways. The two groups disliked each other intensely. Travel, trains, disdaining intellectuals, culpable *Ostjuden*, forests, abandoned children, lost mothers, ugly fathers, unpleasant Jewish characteristics and the coarse, peasantlike behavior of non-Jews: These are the recurring motifs which Appelfeld weaves into an allegorical but realistic fictional world that intensifies the reader's vision of the Holocaust.

Badenheim 1939, the first of Appelfeld's novels to be translated into English, recounts with chillingly understated simplicity the naïve response by a broad spectrum of Jews to unmistakable warning signals just prior to the Holocaust. By not using historical terminology for the victims, the victimizers, or the impending events, Appelfeld increases the horror of his story: The reader is wrenched by historical knowledge of the impending disaster posed against the unawareness of the victims and their almost giddy efforts to ignore what is clear.

The book opens in 1939 as the Austrian resort town of Badenheim slips from sluggish winter into tentative spring, bringing with it a mélange of sybaritic visitors who wait for the entertainment to begin. Dr. Pappenheim, the "impresario," is responsible for providing summer-long entertainment for the guests, many of whom are regulars at Badenheim. To introduce his major theme of willful Holocaust unawareness, Appelfeld introduces the character of Trude, wife of the pharmacist. Like an unwelcome Elijah, Trude is consumed by what the others view as a manic-depressive illness that allows her no peace, as she is obsessed by her vision of a "transparent . . . poisoned and diseased world" in which her absent daughter is "captive and abused" by her non-Jewish husband. She also describes the resort-goers as "patients in a sanitorium."

Additional disharmonies surface when Dr. Pappenheim is disappointed by the musicians' greed and he himself displays melancholic longing for his *Ostjuden* Polish roots. Even more ominous is the increasingly authoritative role taken by the Sanitation Department, which "took measurements, put up fences and planted flags" as "porters unloaded rolls of barbed wire, cement pillars, and all kinds of appliances." Characteristically, the naïve vacationers interpret these preparations as signs of a particularly successful summer festival; otherwise, "why would the Sanitation Department be going to all this trouble?" The palpably clear answer is accentuated by the appearance of the twin performers, "tall, thin and monkish," whose forte is the death poetry of Rainer Maria Rilke and who "rehearsed all the time with morbid melody throbbing in their voices."

The themes of assimilation and levels of Jewishness surface when a "modest announcement" appears on the notice board, saying that all citizens who are Jews must register with the Sanitation Department by the end of the month. Heated discussions among the guests about who must comply, based upon class distinctions that elevate the importance of Austrian Jews and denigrate the *Ostjuden*, increase strife.

All the while, the Sanitation Department has continued its work. It now holds detailed records of each person's heritage and begins to display inviting posters of Poland. Concurrently, the Department prohibits access to or exit from the town, stops all incoming and outgoing mail, and closes the resort pool. As fear and despair begin to envelop the people, "an alien orange shadow gnawed stealthily at the geranium leaves," and the Jews are put into quarantine.

What has been considered up to this time as disease or infection, an unnamed fear in some hearts such as Trude's, becomes real. Delusions disappear and weaker people ignore basic social rules as they loot the pharmacy and consume all the food. The musicians steal the hotel dishes, and even the

dogs become uncontrollable. At the same time, another force begins to operate in the face of chaos. With the common experience of deprivation and
fear of the unknown future, the edges of dissension among the people start
to smooth and closer common bonds draw the captives together.

Badenheim 1939 ends with the recurring Appelfeld image of trains and
journeys signaling a hopeless future. Still uncomprehending, the victims
refuse to recognize the facts, clinging to the illusion that deportation to Poland is only a "transition." Old and young Austrian Jews, *Ostjuden*, and part-
Jews are "all sucked in as easily as grains of wheat poured into a funnel [into]
four filthy freight cars." The last irony is voiced by Dr. Pappenheim, who observes, "If the coaches are so dirty it must mean that we have not far to go."

Badenheim 1939 re-creates Appelfeld's memory of the European pre-
Holocaust world, but the narrator's voice is objective; the characters in this
novel cannot be linked directly with Appelfeld or with those around him. *The
Age of Wonders*, Appelfeld's second book in English translation, on the other
hand appears to be closer to fictionalized biography; in it Appelfeld's own
feelings are more visible. *The Age of Wonders* also affords the reader a view
of both the pre-Holocaust and the post-Holocaust periods, and as a result it
is a more complete and stronger novel than its predecessor.

In the first part of *The Age of Wonders*, the "ugly orange fog" felt in
Badenheim 1939 is an omnipresent, identifiable antagonist. The viscous,
threatening suffocator of the pleasure-seeking vacationers in Badenheim is a
major character in *The Age of Wonders* as it envelops and destroys Austrian-
Jewish lives in pre-Holocaust Vienna. Repeated evocations of Jewish decadence prior to the war enforce the realization that the horror could perhaps
have been averted had the Jews reversed the course of assimilation and self-
hatred.

The three-year prewar history of a doomed intellectual family in Vienna is
reviewed and dispassionately related by the only child, whose name, Bruno,
is not revealed until the second part of the book. The action begins with the
mother and Bruno traveling by train from their last carefree summer vacation
in a forested, "little known retreat." The first clear indication of the impending Holocaust comes when all the passengers who are non-Christian by birth
are commanded to leave the train and register during an unscheduled stop at
an old sawmill. Appelfeld's recurring theme of Jewish alienation from Jews is
introduced when Bruno's relatives come to celebrate his eleventh birthday.
Cousin Charlotte, who has been fired from her position as an actress with the
National Company, represents the reality of Jews being ostracized from the
Austrian culture and also Jewish self-delusion (she acts foreign roles). Uncle
Carl Landman, an attorney, expresses his outrage at Jewish "vulgarity";
some Jews refuse the customs of the prevailing culture. Bruno's Uncle Salo
represents the Jewish merchant who flirts with Gentile women and is
despised by the intellectuals, such as Landman and Bruno's father. The party

ends with bitter debate about what Jewish life should be and displays of hate among the guests; the gathering represents a microcosm of Jewish life before the Holocaust and seems to indicate that Appelfeld sees these divisions as a precursor to the Holocaust.

Bruno's father, a nationally known and acclaimed author/intellectual, despises observant Jews and the *Ostjuden* entrepeneurs, whom he charges with "dark avarice" and whom he believes "should be wiped off the face of the earth, because they ruin everything they touch." Speaking of his own heritage, he says, "My Jewishness mean nothing to me." Ironically, the father's anti-Semitism, which is a theme in his own works, is used against him by another, similarly minded Jew. Michael Taucher destroys the author's reputation and career via repeated attacks in the press. Supported by non-Jewish editors who allow Taucher all the space he can fill, the critic finally writes, about Bruno's father, "the Jewish parasite must be weeded out," and then, having served his purpose, he himself disappears.

Another important thread that unwinds as months go by is the high attrition rate among traditionally observant Jews, as the older generation dies off and the younger traditionalists feel the scorn of their contemporaries. When Bruno's Aunt Gusta dies and is buried according to traditional Jewish rites, Bruno describes the scene as "ugly and shameful."

Kurt Stark, a sculptor and longtime friend of Bruno's father, illustrates the almost militant Jewish opposition to the contemporary traditionalists who wanted to preserve religious observance and practices. In a theme shown in several of Appelfeld's works, notably *To the Land of the Cattails*, Stark, the son of a Jewish mother and Aryan father, seeks refuge from his "tortured [and] cruel perplexities" by conversion to Judaism. In spite of all the difficult hurdles, Stark reaches his goal, but he and his life are horribly altered. After his circumcision, he barely exists in the Paul Gottesman Almshouse for Jews, a dreadful place devoid of spiritual or physical beauty and inhabited by old, dying men. Stark has become a stereotypical Appelfeld Jew—retiring, weak, pale, and unhealthy—whereas before his conversion he had been the stereotypical Aryan—strong, robust, and physically aggressive.

With the family's growing sense of isolation and their increasingly frequent contacts with homeless, dispossessed Jews, Bruno's father seeks escape by appealing to non-Jewish friends. He is representative of the male characters in Appelfeld's works, most of whom are neither strong nor admirable. Bruno's mother, on the other hand, like Tzili in *Tzili*, and Toni and Arna in *To the Land of the Cattails*, gathers strength and courage to do what she can to maintain order, even after her husband abandons the family and escapes to Vienna and a non-Jewish woman.

In one of the most violent scenes in Appelfeld's fiction available in English, all of the town's Jews are herded into and locked in the synagogue, where the frenzied prisoners decide that the rabbi, who represents Judaism, is the source of their misery and beat him almost to death.

Book 1 of *The Age of Wonders* shares the hopelessness of *Badenheim 1939* but appears to place the blame for the coming disaster on the Jewish people themselves, their assimilation, and their self-chosen alienation from Judaism. In Bruno and his family can be seen the autobiographical elements of Appelfeld's own separation from mother and father prior to the Holocaust, and the images of Bruno's summer vacations in the forest as restorative and saving are unmistakably autobiographical.

The darkness of Book 1 is mitigated by Book 2, which introduces hope through survival. Book 2 takes up the same motif with which Book 1 began and ended: Bruno is again on a train, but now he is alone, returning thirty years later to the town of his birth, Knospen, Austria. Bruno comes back with memories of the war years mentioned only in reference to towns—Auschwitz and Thereisenstadt—with the burden of a wife and a failing marriage in Jerusalem, and with an inherited and continuing dislike of Jews as part of his emotional foundation. Although his reason for returning is unclear to both Bruno and the reader, what Bruno experiences is depressingly morbid. Bruno finds only the memories of his town of birth and revisited aspects of the countryside pleasant. In contrast, memories of people and places such as school, perhaps some of them once pleasant, become unwholesome and diseased in revisitation.

The Henrietta Bar, which Bruno frequents and leaves "dull with drink," reveals unpleasant postwar realities. As bizarre as the four swarthy Singapore midgets who entertain bar patrons, not with their talent but with their freakish appearance and wild dancing, are the strange, half-breed waitress and her friends, half-Jewish misfits who have no real identity or past other than their existence. Among these Bruno discovers a half cousin, a bastard daughter of his Uncle Salo. Finally, he confronts old Brum, a prototype of prewar denial and cowardice who echoes Bruno's father.

Demanding that Bruno leave because he is stirring up "evil spirits . . . Jews again . . . the old nightmare," Brum arouses unexpected violence in Bruno by stating, "My hatred for Jews knows no bounds." Bruno hits the Jewish anti-Semite in the face and displays no emotion except vengeance as the old man, a both real and symbolic specter of the past, lies bleeding on the ground.

Never going back to see what happens to Brum, Bruno quietly leaves town early the next morning. The phrase "It's all over" echoes in his mind as epiphany relieves Bruno of a heavy emotional burden. Ironically, even though the Jews Bruno meets on his return initially repel him, he becomes increasingly tolerant of their weaknesses. In a total reversal, Bruno becomes violent against the disease of prewar Jews—the same one he himself had displayed—Jewish anti-Semitism.

Unlike *Badenheim 1939*, *The Age of Wonders* reflects hope and rebirth after death. Bruno, by surviving and returning to his roots, finds truth and reaffirms the faith of his long-dead Aunt Gusta. He becomes a vibrant, unafraid, and robust Jew. The antithesis of prewar stereotypical Jews who hated themselves, their heritage, and would not raise their hands against attack, Bruno undergoes conversion and remains strong and vital.

Appelfeld's third novel to appear in English translation, *Tzili*, continues in the pattern of *The Age of Wonders* with a strong autobiographical element, a pre- and post-Holocaust segment, and the tempering of pessimism by the survival of youth. Appelfeld's use of allegory in *Tzili* sets it apart from his other novels. The minimalist approach places an even greater responsibility upon the reader to interpret meaning while multiple levels of interpretation are added to each word and scene. This approach makes *Tzili* possibly the most rewarding reading of the novels discussed here.

As a young child, Tzili is ignored by her invalid father and shopkeeper mother and is left during summer days to sit alone behind the shop in the dirt and ashes. Feebleminded and unable to learn when she is finally sent to school at age seven, Tzili is scolded by her parents, who are extremely anxious that their children attain high academic goals, and she is ridiculed by her Gentile classmates, who are particularly gleeful at the spectacle of a Jewish child who cannot learn. The parents engage an old Jewish tutor to instruct their youngest child in Jewish customs and laws, but Tzili can only manage to repeat the Judaic formulas drilled into her by rote. Her tutor appreciates the irony, wondering "why it had fallen to the lot of this dull child to keep the spark [of Judaism] alive." Indeed, only the tutor's visits keep the child from total wretchedness. Unintentionally, as a last resort, her parents have unwittingly provided Tzili with the source of her future salvation as well as her present strength—a strong faith.

When troops appear just outside of town, the family deserts Tzili after charging her to "take care of the property"; the rest of them flee to what they mistakenly believe will be safety. Tzili survives an undescribed night of massacre, but her family is never mentioned again.

Indeed, Tzili repeatedly escapes death as if she were divinely protected. In a long, circular journey that never takes her far from her birthplace, Tzili moves from childhood to young adulthood. Her survival is both a celebration of indomitable human courage and an allegorical reference to the undying spirit of Judaism, surviving as if by miracle a series of deadly episodes during the Holocaust years.

When the war ends, Tzili is fifteen, pregnant, and abandoned by her lover-companion, Mark. She falls into the company of liberated but disturbingly petty, quarreling Jews. They ignore Tzili's pain and their own as they travel, but surprisingly, when Tzili's fragile condition prevents her from keeping up with the group, a fat, former cabaret dancer demands that the group stop for the girl, and they do. A stretcher is constructed, upon which Tzili is carried aloft for the rest of the long journey amid "a rousing sound, like pent-up water bursting from a dam." The stretcher bearers are joined by the entire group, who roar, "We are the torch bearers." Tzili, symbol of the Jewish spark noted by her former tutor, unites the group, gives them strong purpose, and helps them survive. Tzili's destiny ultimately leads her aboard a ship bound for Palestine, perhaps with others of the group. While the fate of her assimilated parents and intellectually superior siblings is unknown, the "chosen" child is saved for entrance to the Chosen Land, Palestine.

In *The Retreat*, except for the restorative nature of the forest and other recurring motifs, Appelfeld seems to eliminate the strong autobiographical elements seen in *The Age of Wonders*, *Tzili*, and *To the Land of the Cattails*, as well as their theme of youth and survival. Instead, this book is an echo of *Badenheim 1939*, concentrating, in a very different environment, on the ugliness of the pre-Holocaust Jewish milieu and the assimilation and breakdown of Jews and their community because of self-hatred. There is no hint of a future, no youth present who, like Tzili, can be viewed as a living symbol of the enduring spirit of Judaism. The chilling shadow of the Holocaust comes closer as the narrative continues, and the only hope offered is that the Jews in the Retreat, an isolated mountaintop house which has been established as an "Institute for Advanced Study," will help one another and will not abandon anyone; in a time of extremes, they discover that they need one another for support and comfort.

Lotte Schloss, the novel's protagonist, is the listener among the other cast-offs at the Retreat; she is a prototype of the metamorphosis and becomes an important part of the group's final support system. The "great Balaban," founder of the Institute, envisions his Retreat as a place where Jews can learn to divest themselves of their ugly Jewish characteristics and become more like the Gentiles around them. Thwarted in this goal, Balaban dies unmourned, but ironically he has prepared the group to shift for themselves, help one another, and therefore survive.

At the end of *The Retreat* a faint glimmer of hope for survival through unity appears, but Appelfeld destroys any possibility of salvation: "At night, of course, people were afraid. But they helped one another. If a man fell or was beaten, he was not abandoned." Unity is all the group has.

Appelfeld returns to autobiographical material in his fifth novel published in English, *To the Land of the Cattails*. Its blend of allegory and realism explores what Appelfeld has called a "a love story between a mother and a son," and it ends, as did Appelfeld's own childhood, with the mother lost and leaving her son to find his own way to Jewishness. Although this narrative ends before the Holocaust is at its height, it shares with *The Age of Wonders* and *Tzili* a sense of fulfillment in the characters' acceptance of their Jewishness, and it marks a further development of Appelfeld's almost mystical ability to evoke the Holocaust while never naming it or describing it concretely.

To the Land of the Cattails, interspersing flashbacks and current happenings, recounts a two-year journey during which the two major characters undergo dramatic metamorphoses. In the autumn of 1938, thirty-four-year-old Toni Strauss (née Rosenfeld) and her fifteen-year-old son, Rudi, begin a long journey by horse and carriage from the bustling city of Vienna back to the mother's birthplace of Dratscincz, Bukovina, on the river Prut. Rudi resembles his father, a Gentile "through and through," in appearance and interests. Toni is fearful lest her son also become callous and brutal and abandon her, as his father had fourteen years earlier. She therefore resolves to return to her parents, whom she has not seen since she eloped at seventeen with the Gentile August Strauss. In addition to fulfilling her own yearning to return from exile, Toni also has a "strong wish for [Rudi] to be Jewish."

Although Rudi considers himself a Jew, Toni tells him at the beginning of their journey, "Certainly you are a Jew, but you need a few more things, not many, not difficult . . . you are a Jew in every fibre of your being. And here, in these regions, you will learn the secret easily." Thus the story of Rudi's metamorphosis begins. In the course of their long journey, however, Rudi returns to his Gentile roots rather than becoming more Jewish. Toni watches the transformation with dread. Her own total commitment to Judaism accomplished, she decides to go on alone to her parents' home. Rudi soon follows after her, but his mother is gone, having been "easily sucked in" with other compliant Jews to waiting railway cars and an unknown future.

Rudi wanders off, blaming his mother for leaving him and angry that she did not wait for him, but he suddenly understands what he has guessed, that his mother is in danger. That understanding begins the final stage of Rudi's metamorphosis, achieved through his friendship with Arna, a thin, thirteen-year-old Jewish girl who also has been separated from her family. Arna believes in God and teaches Rudi the ways of observant Jews; she has brought him a "kind of hidden promise." Rudi falls critically ill, and as Arna takes care of him, he wishes for death. During his illness, he hears Arna intone "Hear, O Israel."

Rudi learns the Jewish secrets well, so well that his physical presence changes to match his spiritual change. His gait, which was once swaggering and self-assured, is different after his illness. In fact, Rudi is so different that "he himself did not know how much he had changed."

As the narrative ends and the transformation is complete, Rudi and Arna stand at a railroad station watching a train approach: "It was an old locomotive, drawing two old cars . . . the local apparently. It went from station to station, scrupulously gathering up the remainder." Hope remains that Rudi and Arna, young, vigorous, and secure in their Jewishness, will somehow survive the ensuing Holocaust years and share what they have learned with a future generation.

These Appelfeld novels, all voices from the Holocaust, can be placed into two simple categories: those which describe pre-Holocaust European Jewish society and begin and end with no hope for the future (*Badenheim 1939* and *The Retreat*) and those which seem to indicate that the return to roots, the finding of the true secrets of Jewishness, permits the survival of youth into the post-Holocaust period (*The Age of Wonders*, *Tzili*, *To the Land of the Cattails*).

All these novels share a common base of retold experience, literary techniques, motifs, themes, and symbols, woven into magic by a masterful storyteller. The retold experience is Appelfeld's own life and its connection with the Holocaust. Although, as stated earlier, the Holocaust is never named and its too-familiar scenes of horror are never drawn, the dreamlike superimposition of allegory and realism immerse the reader in visions of impending horror. The reader's historical memory and imagination fill in what Appelfeld's novels do not provide, especially since the understated, simple, sparc and matter-of-fact text demands these additions.

The themes are recurrent—the ugliness of prewar Jewish society, its emphasis on assimilation and self-hate, its rejection of the essence of Judaism, its inability to "raise a hand" against its oppressors. Opposed to this are the themes of inner peace, salvation, and even survival achieved by finding and accepting the secrets of basic Judaism.

Symbols and motifs are other recurrent elements. Forests and nature, havens in Appelfeld's own life, symbolize peace and safety, but trains and other forms of transportation lead to uncertain destinations usually invoking premonitions of the impending Holocaust. Love of books and humanizing education, as opposed to rigidly enforced study in the Austrian *gymnasium*, indicate characters' acceptance of Judaism and humanism, whereas descriptions of people eating usually indicate coarse, peasantlike cruelty to man and beast and are associated with non-Jews.

Although the novels in English translation are based upon retold experience and recurrent themes, symbols, and motifs, each also presents a different view of the same problems, thus affording a multifaceted, in-depth analysis of factors preceding the Holocaust. Although readers can share Appelfeld's stories, they are also left to complete them and draw their own conclusions.

Other major works

SHORT FICTION: *'Ashan*, 1962; *Ba-gai ha-poreh*, 1963; *In the Wilderness*, 1965; *Kefor 'al ha-arets*, 1965; *Be-komat ha-karka'*, 1968; *Adne ha-nahar*, 1971; *Ke-me a edim*, 1975; *Shanim ve-sha ot*, 1976.

NONFICTION: *Ke' ishon ha-ayin*, 1973; *Masot be-guf rishon*, 1979.

Bibliography

Coffin, Edna Amir. "Appelfeld's Exceptional Universe: Harmony out of Chaos," in *Hebrew Studies*. XXIV (1983), pp. 85-98.

Lewis, Stephen. *Art out of Agony*, 1984.

Wisse, Ruth R. "Aharon Appelfeld, Survivor," in *Commentary*. LXXVI (August, 1983), pp. 73-76.

Yudkin, Leon I. *Escape into Seige*, 1974.

June H. Schlessinger

JOHN BANVILLE

Born: Wexford, Ireland; December 8, 1945

Principal long fiction
Nightspawn, 1971; *Birchwood*, 1973; *Doctor Copernicus*, 1976; *Kepler*, 1981; *The Newton Letter*, 1982 (novella); *Mefisto*, 1986.

Other literary forms
John Banville's first published book was a collection of short stories, *Long Lankin* (1970, revised 1984), and he has written a small amount of uncollected short fiction. He has also collaborated in writing television adaptations of *The Newton Letter* and *Birchwood*.

Achievements
Banville is the most original and successful Irish novelist of his generation. His work has received numerous awards, including the prestigious James Tait Black Award and the American-Irish Foundation Award. Reviewers have treated each new work of his with increasing respect for its ambition, verbal felicity, and individuality, and for such a comparatively young writer, Banville has inspired a sizable amount of critical commentary. The development of his career coincides with a period of restlessness and experimentation in Irish fiction. Not the least significant of Banville's achievements is that he has availed himself of the artistic example of such postwar masters of fiction as Jorge Luis Borges, Gabriel García Márquez and Italo Calvino. By admitting such influences, as well as those of the great Irish modernists, James Joyce and Samuel Beckett, John Banville's fiction has embodied a new range of options for the Irish novel and has provided an international dimension to an often provincial literary culture.

Biography
John Banville was born in Wexford, the county seat of Ireland's southeasternmost county, on December 8, 1945. He was educated locally, first at the Christian Brothers School and then at St. Peter's College. After school, he worked for Aer Lingus, the Irish airline. Subsequently, he worked in England for the post office, and briefly, for a London publisher. Returning to Ireland, he worked as a subeditor for *The Irish Press*, a national daily. The recipient of numerous awards, he has also spent a semester in the International Writing Program at the University of Iowa. Banville lives in Howth, outside Dublin, with his wife and two sons.

Analysis
John Banville's short stories, his novella *The Newton Letter*, and his five

novels constitute a remarkably unified and consistent body of work. From the outset of his career, he has shown immense artistic self-possession and an equally assured possession of his themes. Over the years, his style, while not remaining constant, has undergone comparatively little change. It is therefore possible to speak of Banville in terms of a completeness and typicality which most novelists of his age are still in the process of discovering.

The unity and integrity which are the most striking features of Banville's career and oeuvre become more striking still by virtue of being so thematically important in his work. Fascination with the spectacle of the mind in the act of creation is a major concern of this author, and his career may be described in terms of an increasingly deliberate and far-reaching series of attempts to articulate this subject. This preoccupation has given his work a range, ambition, and commitment to large concepts which are extremely rare in modern Irish fiction, and only slightly less rare in contemporary fiction generally.

In addition, the manner in which Banville elaborates his interest in man's creative dimension commands more critical attention than it has received. For example, his fiction is suffused with hints suggesting links between artistic strategies, scientific inquiry, and historical actuality. From these, it is possible to detect a rudimentary, though sustained, critique of traditional epistemological procedures. To complement this critique, the typical Banville protagonist either discovers unsuspected modes of perception or believes that he has no other choice but to set out deliberately to discover them.

Together with the intellectual commitment implicit in such concerns, Banville's work possesses a typically complete and essentially unchanging aesthetic apparatus through which ideas and fiction's critique may be perceived. Since it is central to Banville's artistic vision that fiction's critique of conceptual thinking be considered inevitable and unavoidable, his novels' aesthetic apparatus is largely premised on techniques of doubleness, repetition, echoes, and mirrors. Protagonists often have problematical brothers or missing twins. Personal experience finds it counterpart in historical events. The result is a paradox: The duplicitous character of experience, which renders man's possession of his existence so frail and tentative, impels him, precisely because of that very frailty, to anchor himself in the presumed security of defined abstractions.

Despite the presence of these thematic concerns throughout Banville's output, and despite the fact that his treatment of them has always been marked more by an ironic playfulness than by earnest sermonizing, his first two works of fiction are somewhat callow. In particular, *Nightspawn*, the story of an Irish writer's adventures in Greece on the eve of the Colonel's coup, treats the material with a kind of relentless playfulness which is both tiresome in itself and in questionable taste. Despite the author's admitted—though not uncritical—affection for this novel, and despite its containing in embryonic form the concerns which beset all of his work, *Nightspawn*, as perhaps its title suggests, is an example of a young writer allowing his wonderfully fertile imagination to run to baroque lengths.

It is more appropriate, therefore, to begin a detailed consideration of John Banville's fiction with his second novel, *Birchwood*. Like *Nightspawn*, this novel is written in the first person—arguably Banville's preferred narrative mode. In *Birchwood*, Gabriel Godkin, the protagonist, tells in retrospect the story of his dark heritage and his efforts to escape it. Again, as in *Nightspawn*, much of the material has baroque potential, which the novel's middle section, depicting Gabriel's adventures with the circus of a certain Prospero, accentuates rather than dispels.

The circus escapade shines in the novel like a good deed in an evil world. While Gabriel is within the protected ring of the circus troupe he seems to be essentially immune from the troubles of his past and from the state of famine and unrest which consumes the country through which the circus travels. Thanks to Prospero, he is islanded and becalmed in the surrounding tempest. Yet even under such conditions of childish play, the world is not a safe place. Adult imperfections continually intrude. Crimes are committed in the name of love; futile and obsessive hostilities break out. Innocent Gabriel flees the disintegrating circle—it seems appropriate to think of the circus in etymological terms, since circle and ring possess strong connotations of unity and completeness.

Gabriel forsakes the circus in a state of rather paranoid distress and finds himself, still more distressingly, to have come full circle back to where he started. Now, however, he finds himself compelled to face his origins, which lie in the house of doom which gives this novel its title. The first part of the novel gives the history of the Godkin family. Like the circus sequence, this opening section of *Birchwood* owes more to imagination than it does to actuality. Many readers will be reminded of both Edgar Allan Poe and William Faulkner by Banville's combination of brooding atmosphere and theme of cultural decay upon which this section is premised. Banville's farcical tone, however, without prejudicing young Gabriel's sensitivity, prevents the heavy-handedness and extravagance to which the gothic nature of his material is in danger of giving rise. The seriousness with which the elder Godkins take their insecurities is rendered laughable by the incompetence which ensues from their transparent intensity.

Yet Gabriel, for all of his alienation from his heritage's inadequacies, finds it impossible to do other than to confront them. In a novel which satirically articulates the cultural shibboleth of bad blood, Gabriel feels compelled to carry out an act of blood which will purge his house of the usurper. The usurper in question is Gabriel's twin brother, Michael. The novel ends with Gabriel in sole possession of Birchwood.

This turn of events, however, does not mean that Gabriel is able, or intends, to restore the house to its former glory, a glory in which he never participated. As a writer, his objective seems to be to reclaim the house as it really was, rather than imagine it as something other, something which imaginative treatment would make easier to assimilate. In this objective, students of Irish literature may see a critique of the lofty status often accorded the Big House in the poetry of William Butler Yeats. An appreciation of John Banville's fiction does not require that he be seen as a defacer of the cultural icons of a previous generation. Nevertheless, the status of the Big House in *Birchwood*, coupled with themes of survival, inheritance, and artistic expression, offers a sense of the oblique manner in which this author regards his own cultural heritage, while at the same time situating his regard in the wider, more generic contexts of such concerns as individuality, history, the role of the artist, the nature of the real.

Given the significant, if problematical, status of the Big House in modern Irish literature (Big House being the generic name given to the imposing mansions of the socially dominant, landowning Anglo-Irish class), the degree to which *Birchwood* avoids a specific historical context is noteworthy. There are a sufficient number of clues (the famine and unrest mentioned earlier, the frequent mention of "rebels" in the first part of the novel) to suggest that the locale is Ireland. Yet a larger historical context is obviated by the obsessive, and more psychologically archetypal, quality of Gabriel's sense of his personal history. The result is a novel which is ultimately too reflexive, private, and inward looking to be entirely satisfactory.

It may be that the author himself reached the same conclusion, since in his next two novels, *Doctor Copernicus* and *Kepler*, a specific and detailed sense of history is an important dimension of events. *Doctor Copernicus* inaugurates Banville's most important and ambitious project, and the one on which his international reputation will probably be based. This project consists of four books dealing with the nature of the creative personality, conceived of in terms of the scientific imagination. A subtitle for the series might be, "The Scientist as Artist," meaning that Banville considers that which Copernicus, Kepler, and Isaac Newton (subject of *The Newton Letter*) accomplished in the field of scientific inquiry to be comparable to what an artist might produce. The series concludes with *Mefisto*, which both crystallizes and challenges the assumptions of its predecessors. The most fundamental link between the four books is chronological, *Mefisto* being set in contemporary Ireland. Although there are other more sophisticated connections between each of the four, each may also be read independently.

Doctor Copernicus is a fictionalized biography of the astronomer who revolutionized man's sense of his place in the order of creation. The biography is presented in such a way as to dramatize the crucial tensions between Copernicus and the history of his time. Beginning with the astronomer's unhappy childhood, the novel details the essentially flawed, anticlimactic, unfulfilling (and unfulfillable) nature of human existence as Copernicus experiences it. The protagonist's character is conceived in terms of his inability to give himself fully to the world of men and affairs, whether the affairs are those of state or of the heart.

Sojourning in Italy as a young man, Copernicus has a homosexual affair which temporarily makes him happy. Yet he lacks the self-confidence and will to believe in his happiness and rejects it in an attack of spleen and confusion. Later in his career, he is required to take a political role, negotiating with Lutheran enemies of the Catholic Church, and administering Church properties. Although he discharges his obligations in a responsible manner, it is perfectly clear that, given the choice between being a man of his time or being a student of the stars in their eternal courses, Copernicus prefers the latter isolated, impersonal service. The imperfections of the world—not only in the aggregate, demonstrated by the machinations of history, but also intimately, embodied by the astronomer's syphilitic brother, Andreas—prove emotionally insupportable, philosophically unjustifiable, and morally anesthetizing. Finding no basis for unity and completeness in the sorry state of mortal man, Copernicus takes the not particularly logical, but impressively imaginative, step of considering the heavens.

The astronomer's declared intention in pursuing this line of inquiry is not to bring about the revolution which history commemorates in his name. On the contrary, Copernicus sees his pursuits as conservative, intended to assert a model of order, design, and harmony where it cannot be said for certain one exists. Copernicus' efforts are fueled by his will and spirit, and the intensity of his commitment should not be underestimated because his results are stated in mathematical terms. What his conclusions provide is the fiction of order, a fiction posited on the conceit of mathematics being essentially a rhetoric—a product of mind, not an offspring of matter. Indeed, as Copernicus' career in the world of things and people suggests, his fiction elicits worldlings' assent all the more urgently for being necessarily untrue.

Banville's approach as a biographer in *Doctor Copernicus* is strictly chronological, which gives the novel both scope and a sense of the inevitability of the protagonist's development. Copernicus' integrity, continually challenged, is nourished by the inevitable nature of his spiritual needs and tendencies; in *Kepler*, the approach is fundamentally the same.

Instead of providing a chronology of Kepler's life, however, Banville concentrates on the astronomer's productive years, using flashbacks to illuminate and enlarge aspects of the protagonist's character, as the need arises. This approach shifts the narrative emphasis from the protagonist's temperament, as it was in *Doctor Copernicus*, to the protagonist's working conditions. The effect of this modulation in authorial standpoint is to give historical circumstances greater prominence than previously, and thus provide, from an aesthetic perspective, an image of man in the world which reverses that provided in *Doctor Copernicus*. Kepler is far more life-loving (which Banville communicates as far more capable of love) than his predecessor. He is far more attuned to the eddies and quicksands of the historical forces of his time, consciously aligning himself with one set of forces rather than another, instead of disdainfully and brokenheartedly attempting to rise above them, as Copernicus tries to do.

Kepler's astronomy, therefore, is presented as, in his own eyes, the opposite of Copernicus' model of conservation. Much of Kepler's achievement, in fact, is based on his critique of the predecessor's findings. In addition, Kepler's generally worldly disposition leads him to develop practical applications of astronomical researches. Yet, when most successful in his own eyes, constructing his geometrical model of planetary harmony, he is unwittingly failing. His model is adequate to his own need of it, but is not, by virtue of that adequacy, foolproof. The reader is given a strong sense that Kepler's discoveries, or rather the model which his discoveries serve, introduces as many errors as it corrects in Copernicus' model. In Copernicus' case, the model is the necessary transmutation of sorrow; in Kepler's case, it is the necessary transmutation of joy. Despite fate's cruel blows, Kepler asserts that the world should be considered part of a harmoniously integrated system. Because of fate's cruel blows, Copernicus asserts the same theory.

It would be invidious to conclude that one of these heroic figures suffers more than the others. Banville is at pains, as the dramatic structure of *Kepler* demonstrates, to point out that the astronomer's faith in the world proves to be as destructively alienating as Copernicus' skepticism. The spectacle—which concludes the novel—of this great scientific visionary spending his time and energy attempting to bring his debtors to book is a painfully ludicrous commentary on the all too understandable vanity of human wishes, as well as a cogent expression of Banville's own perspective on his material.

In the novella, *The Newton Letter*, Banville changes his approach, without quite changing his theme. Here the scenario is not biography, but failed biography. The protagonist is not the great scientist, but the apparently less than great modern writer attempting to recapture the scientist's life. This short work, perhaps together with *Doctor Copernicus* the author's most completely successful accomplishment from an artistic standpoint, gives an inverted picture of the procedures which seemed natural in the two earlier works in the series. The presupposition of expository coherence leading to insight and comprehension which was crucial, however unspoken, to the fictionalized biographies has, in *The Newton Letter*, become a subject open to criticism—open, like the procedures of Copernicus and Kepler, to the charge of fiction.

In addition, the fictional biographer (the protagonist of *The Newton Letter*) is failing to complete his work because of Newton's failure to pursue his researches. By this means, the interrelationship between fiction and reality, and the possibility that these terms interchangeably reflect dual perspectives on immutable phenomena, is brought yet more clearly to the forefront of Banville's concerns.

Indeed, as is the case of the earlier novels of the series, life keeps interrupting the Newton biographer. The country house to which he has retreated in order to complete his work, while not possessing the menace and uncertainty of Birchwood, distracts and ultimately ensnares him, so that he is forced to choose between the demands of completeness (his work) and the obligations of incompleteness (his life). The biographer's failed project becomes a synonym for his mortal destiny.

Banville's rejection of the biographical approach to the life of the mind is completed in the final volume of the series, *Mefisto*, in which the protagonist, a mathematician named Gabriel Swan, writes his own story. With this formal development, the procedure of both *Doctor Copernicus* and *Kepler* is completely inverted, and the value of the project both from a biographical and from a scientific point of view is most rigorously challenged. One reason it is possible to make such a claim is that *Mefisto* reaches back beyond its three predecessors to *Birchwood*, to which it bears some strong resemblances.

The most obvious novelty of *Mefisto*, however, is that it does not deal with a historical twentieth century scientist. Most of Banville's readers were not prepared for this development, which is a tribute to Banville's own conception of his project's integrity. It is unlikely, however, that the question of integrity is the only one at issue here. On the one hand, this development is typical of the sly and slapstick humor which pervades Banville's work. On the other hand, the fictitiousness of *Mefisto*'s protagonist is an obvious expression of the status of failure in Banville's oeuvre, the failure from which the artist is obliged to begin, and which his work, by attempting to mask or redeem it, merely makes more obvious. In addition, given that *Mefisto* has a historical context about which it is possible to say much, and that it is a novel which brings to an end a series of works in which historical events were given a prominent and influential place, it must be considered provocative and instructive that *Mefisto* eschews explicit information of a historical nature.

Mefisto is a novel of missing parts. It lacks a sense of specific sense of time and space, though the alert reader will find part 1 of the novel set in a market town in provincial Ireland and part 2 in an Irish city which is presumably Dublin. The hero, Gabriel (a name which, in a novelist as self-conscious as Banville, must be an echo of the protagonist of *Birchwood*, particularly since in part 1 there is a dilapidated, Birchwood-like house) is a mathematician of genius, but it is difficult to deduce what his branch of mathematics is.

It is Gabriel's misfortune to believe that there can be a redemptive function in his symbols and abstractions. He mistakenly believes that, because of the light he finds shining in the purity of math, he can rescue damsels in distress—in genuine distress, like the drug-besotted Adele in part 2. This belief is cultivated by the jauntily cynical and amoral Felix, who fills the role of Mephistopheles, Gabriel's dark angel. There is enough twinning and doubling in the novel to suggest that Felix may also be Gabriel's stillborn twin brother. Events prove both the hopelessness and inevitability of Gabriel's outlook. First, Gabriel is severely burned, the potential fate, no doubt, of all who make Mephistophelian contact. Second, he is brokenhearted by his failure to rescue Adele. Yet the end of the novel finds him rededicating himself to his vision of mathematics, to the rhetoric of perfection and security which it symbolizes.

The combination of failure and rededication on which *Mefisto* ends is an illuminating gloss on one of John Banville's most crucial themes. Echoing a pronouncement of Samuel Beckett's, he believes that the artist necessarily has failure for his theme and that his work articulates that theme's pressing reality. On the other hand, Banville is still romantic enough to conceive of his theme in terms of world-changing, concept-forming figures. Thus, his work is also preoccupied with the meaning of success, which in turn is linked to ideas of progress, clarity, precision, and enlightenment. Failure is relativized by success, and success by failure. The sense of doubleness and unity suggested by such a conclusion is typical of Banville's outlook.

Banville's subject matter and methods of artistic execution are the bases of his reputation for originality. In the context of contemporary fiction, this author is notable for his commitment, for felicity of phrase, and for his relationship to an important fictional genre, the historical novel. He has identified, both by his artistic strategies and his choice of material, with some of the main questions faced by contemporary fiction—identified with them perhaps too conspicuously and with an ease and self-possession uncharacteristic of many contemporary writers. Some readers may find that this author's manner is paradoxically at odds with his central themes. In the context of the modern Irish novel, his voice is precisely the breath of fresh air required to reinvigorate and enlarge an illustrious tradition.

Other major work

SHORT FICTION: *Long Lankin*, 1970, revised 1984.

Sources for Further Study

Barnes, Julian. Review of *Doctor Copernicus* in *New Statesman*. XCII (November 26, 1976), p 766.

Clark, Stephen. Review of *Doctor Copernicus* in *The Times Literary Supplement*. December 10, 1976, p. 1533.

Irish University Review. XI, no. 1. Special Banville issue.

McCormach, Russell. Review of *Kepler* in *The New York Times Book Review*. May 29, 1983, p. 10

Prescott, Peter S. Review of *Kepler* in *Newsweek*. CI (May 2, 1983), p.78.

Soete, G. J. Review of *Doctor Copernicus* in *Library Journal.* CII (February 15, 1977), p. 511.

George O'Brien

PAUL BOWLES

Born: New York, New York; December 30, 1910

Principal long fiction
The Sheltering Sky, 1949; *Let It Come Down*, 1952; *The Spider's House*, 1955; *Up Above the World*, 1966; *Points in Time*, 1982.

Other literary forms
Paul Bowles is probably critically appreciated best for his short fiction, even though he is also known for his novels. Famous as a translator especially of Moroccan fiction, he has translated from Arabic, French, and Spanish, and he is a writer of poetry, travel literature, and even music, to which he devoted himself during the 1930's. His autobiography, *Without Stopping*, was well received when it was published in 1972.

Achievements
Bowles has a unique place in American literature. As an exile, he shares with Gertrude Stein, among others, a distanced perspective on his native culture. Through his translations, he has earned an international reputation as an author with a North African sensibility. His fiction reflects a world more often akin to that written about by Jean-Paul Sartre or Albert Camus, and indeed he has been described as America's foremost existentialist writer, a label more likely to restrict him to a time period than to characterize his fiction accurately. Although his nihilism does strike one as a bit recherché, it also has a modern application, reflecting as it does a dark vision of the world as contemporary as the times demand.

For a while, Bowles became a guru of sorts to the Beat generation, although Bowles's attraction for them was as much for his writings about drugs as for his generally pessimistic philosophy. Never an author of wide appeal, he has nevertheless had a loyal following among those interested in experimental and avant-garde writing, and his work has reflected a steady maturation, his 1982 novel, *Points in Time*, receiving praise from, among others, Tobias Wolfe, who wrote that the novel was a completely original performance. Perhaps in the last analysis, Paul Bowles will be best remembered for his originality, his willingness to challenge definitions and the status quo in his fiction. With every work, he has tried to forge new ground.

Biography
Paul Frederic Bowles has spent most of his adult life living abroad, in permanent exile, mostly in Morocco, although for brief periods he has also lived in France, Mexico, and South America. It obviously suits his life, which

has been unconventional by American standards, and it has provided him with congenial environments within which to work both as a writer and as a composer. Admonished as a young man by his disapproving father that he could not expect merely to sit around and loaf as a writer when at home, Paul Bowles found a place where he could sit and invite his soul.

He was born in the Jamaica section of New York City, the only child of a dentist and a mother who was a former schoolteacher. He was a precocious child and began writing at an early age. By the time he was in grade school, he also began composing music, a passion which occupied him more than did writing until after World War I. Immediately after high school, he attended very briefly the School of Design and Liberal Arts before enrolling in the fall of 1928 as a freshman at the University of Virginia, a choice made primarily because it was the school attended by Edgar Allan Poe. In March, he left the university and ran off to Paris, where he was already known as the writer whose poem "Spire Song" had been published in Eugène Jolas' little magazine *transition*. Bowles returned home the next fall and went to work for Dutton's bookstore while trying to write a novel in his spare time. In the spring, he returned to Virginia to complete his freshman year, at which point he ended forever his college career.

By 1929, Bowles had met and been encouraged by Aaron Copland to pursue a career as a composer by returning to Paris to study with Nadia Boulanger, which he did in the spring of 1931. His second Paris sojourn began his literary life when he met and became friends with Gertrude Stein, who took him under her ample wing and tutored him in writing. It was Alice Toklas who suggested that Bowles and Copland, who had joined him abroad, live someplace warm, and she suggested Morocco, to which the two composers moved in the late summer of 1931. It was the beginning of Bowles's exile, his love affair with North Africa, and his life as a writer: It was from Tangier that Bowles sent Stein his first prose efforts and received back from her the encouragement to continue writing, although, as he admitted later, it was not until the 1930's, while watching his wife, Jane, compose her first novel, that he began to work seriously at the writer's trade.

Since the early 1930's, Bowles has lived and worked in, and translated the literature of, Morocco, becoming one of the country's few voices in the West. For a brief time, his experiments with drugs attracted the attention of the Beat writers who visited him in Tangier, as had Tennessee Williams. Bowles has made forays home to write music for the theater and to further various other literary and musical activities.

Analysis

Because of his small output of novels and because of his problematic relationship with American writing, Paul Bowles's reputation has yet to be firmly established. A writer who has always attracted attention, and serious attention at that, he has not been accorded sufficient critical notice to measure his significance as a writer. To paraphrase Johannes Willem Bertens, one of his most perceptive critics, who has written on the critical response to Bowles's work, Bowles as a novelist can be classified in three categories: romantic, existentialist, and nihilist. As a romantic, Bowles sees modern man in a disjunctive relationship with nature, and that vision has pushed him to depict the march of Western progress in very pessimistic terms, which accounts for one of his most frequently recurring themes, namely, that of a sophisticated Westerner confronting a less civilized and more primitive society in a quest of self-discovery. Such romantic attitudes suggest the reasons for labeling Bowles as an existentialist. The search for an authentic life amid the self-doubts and the fragile, provisional nature of the civilized instincts, as Theodore Solotaroff describes it, places Bowles squarely within the existentialist tradition made more formal and philosophical by such writers as Camus and Sartre. The search for values in a world without God, a world with an ethical vacuum, suggests the third possible interpretation of Bowles's fiction, that of nihilism.

There are those critics, especially Chester E. Eisinger, who understand the novelist's universe as totally without hope, a region devoid of meaning and purpose and thereby representing a nihilistic philosophical position. Again, this position is worked out through the clash between civilizations, or rather through the tension between civilization and the savage. Even Bowles himself has remarked that life is absurd and the whole business of living hopeless, a conviction he shares with most of his central characters, thereby giving credence to any nihilistic interpretation of his fiction. Whichever position one takes, the central details of Bowles's novels remains the same: A Westerner, often an intellectual, searches through an Oriental, less civilized culture for meaning and direction, usually finding neither by the end of the book.

The Sheltering Sky is both Paul Bowles's first novel and his best-known novel. It is a book in which the author set forth those topics or themes which he has pursued throughout the rest of his fiction with almost obsessive tenacity. The story follows an American couple, Port and Kit Moresby, who have traveled to Morocco in search of themselves and to reinvigorate their marriage after years of indifference. The couple appear in Oran shortly after World War II and there experience a series of devastating events which eventually kill Port and destroy the mental stability of his wife, Kit.

Soon after their arrival, Port insists that they travel inland into the desert. Kit is opposed, so Port, accompanied by an Australian photographer and her son, depart, leaving Kit with Tunner, their American friend, who is to escort her on the night train later that day. Bored by the ride, Kit wanders into the fourth-class, or native, section of the train and passes a frightening night among the Arabs, later sleeping with Tunner. Meanwhile, Port has come to the realization that he desires a reconciliation with his wife. The novel follows this hapless pair as they progress farther and farther into the heart of the country, leaving civilization more distantly behind them. Port contracts typhoid and dies, leaving his wife alone to face the rigors of the desert. She is picked up by a passing caravan and made the sexual slave of the leaders of the group. She is both entranced and repulsed by the experience and is soon completely disoriented by her subjugation. Finally, she is rescued by a member of the American embassy only to disappear once again, this time for good, into the Casbah, or native quarter, in Oran.

The Sheltering Sky is considered Bowles's most uncompromisingly existential work and has been read by the critics along this line, with the fragile and provisional nature of civilized instincts being put to the test against the brutality and savagery of the primitive desert. Not only does Port test his febrile psyche against overwhelming powers of the North African terrain, but also he must face the fact that he harbors in himself no reserves, no hope— for it is all too late—of anything better. Unable to commit himself to his wife, or to anything else for that matter, Port is left with a void which, in the end, exacts a heavy price, leaving him utterly alone and unequipped to face the hostile environment. So, too, Kit is stripped of her defenses and forced back on herself, only to discover that she has no inner resolve, either. In the end, these two civilized Americans lack the inner strength to combat the primitive forces, both within and without, which they encounter in their North African adventures.

Although the novel is marred by grave faults, it offers a convincing portrait of the disintegration of a couple of innocents thrust into a cruel environment for which they are totally unprepared. The writing in places is luminescent, the locale wonderfully realized—so much so that the novel's shortcomings pale by comparison, leaving a work, if flawed, at least magnificently so, and convincing in its portrait of nihilism in the modern world.

Bowles's second novel, *Let It Come Down*, continues an existentialist quest by following Nelson Dyer, an American bank clerk, who throws over his job to join an old acquaintance who lives in Tangier and who offers Dyer a position in the travel agency he runs there. When he arrives, Dyer finds that his friend Jack Wilcox does not operate a successful agency and in fact seems to possess a mysterious source of income. As the story advances, Dyer's relationship with Wilcox takes on a Kafkaesque tone, as he is obviously not needed at the agency.

Out of money and in desperate need of a job, Dyer accepts an offer to help in a money scheme by transporting cash between a local bank and a shop. Realizing that he is being used for illegal purposes, Dyer takes the money he has been given and flees Tangier, only to discover that he is utterly helpless in a country where he neither speaks the language nor understands the customs. After he has killed his native guide, the novel concludes with Dyer alone and hunted in a foreign country but curiously pleased with his state of affairs as an isolated individual.

Once again, Bowles has thrust an upper-middle-class American into a North African environment and allowed him to become submerged in the native and alien culture. With his loss of identity, Dyer discovers something far more authentic about himself as he is systematically stripped of his civilized supports and is forced to fall back on what little reserves he possesses as an individual human being. This peeling away of the veneer of civilization reveals underneath an emptiness and void which leaves the protagonist, like Port Moresby, totally unprepared for the unfamiliar culture into which he is thrust. Under such pressure, he collapses and must seek refuge in internal strength, of which he possesses precious little. His plunge into an exotic culture, instead of rejuvenating him, debilitates his vigor, leaving him in a weakened if also enlightened condition.

As with other American writers, such as Edgar Allan Poe and Herman Melville, Bowles writes of the exhaustion exacted by primitive cultures on the more civilized. It is a reversal of the romantic notion that cultured man, tired of his culture, can find rejuvenation through an immersion in a more savage environment. Instead, like Joseph Conrad's heroes, Dyer finds only confusion and despair. At least, it may be argued, he discovers the truth, however unpalatable it might be, and the conclusion of the novel leaves him possessed of a dark actuality, if robbed of a comforting illusion.

Bowles's next novel, *The Spider's House*, was set in 1954 against the political upheaval caused by the deposition of Morocco's hereditary ruler, Sultan Mohammed, by the colonial regime of the French. The fiction traces the tension caused by the collapse of the traditional way of life of the native inhabitants of the city of Fez through a fifteen-year-old boy, Amar, who, halfway through the novel, is befriended by John Stenham, an expatriate American writer, who has fallen in love with an American woman tourist named Lee Burroughs. By the conclusion of the novel, John leaves Fez with Lee, abandoning Amar to deal with the destruction of his way of life any way he can.

Although it is not a political novel, *The Spider's House* uses the tensions of the French colonial rule not only to highlight the theme of the disintegration of Moslem culture under the French but also to provide a backdrop against which to play out the drama of the on-again, off-again love affair between Lee and John. Amar is from a devout family but one which is not caught up in the political conflicts between the Istiqlal, the Nationalist party, with their use of terror, and the colonials. Both the French and the Nationalists are bent on stopping the ritual religious festival of *Aid el Kabir*, and Amar, who has been forbidden to leave the Medina where his family resides, gets caught outside the city's walls and is rescued by Lee and John, who have been observing the unfolding cycle of violence that is developing between the French and the Moroccans. John helps Amar return to his family through the city's walls, and Amar offers to take the couple to see the religious celebration in a village outside Fez. The Americans are fascinated by the exotic quality of the Arab life around them and agree to accompany Amar. The festival turns out badly for them, however, when Lee is shocked and repulsed by the rituals of the feast. After a quarrel, Lee and John decide that they are beginning a love affair.

Meanwhile, Amar has received a large sum of money from Lee so that he can join the Nationalists in their fight against the French. Still apolitical, Amar again gets caught up in the action of the revolution and is manipulated by the Istiqlal, barely avoiding capture by the French. At the end of the novel, he wants to rejoin John and Lee but is rebuffed by the novelist, who is set on going off with his new lover. The fiction concludes when Amar is abandoned by his newly won friend into the political turmoil of a struggle he barely understands.

As the critics have pointed out, *The Spider's House* contains a nostalgia for a past which does not belong to either John Stenham or to Bowles, but it is a longing which is nevertheless keenly felt. It has also been described as a deeply religious book, one in which Bowles mourns for a lost religious belief no longer possible in Western civilization, with its emphasis on the rational and the scientific. Certainly, the book focuses on the consequences of destroying a traditional way of life and on a myopic colonialism which blunders along in an attempt to apply Western methods to a totally unsuitable situation. It is the story of all colonial experiences in which a foreign power tries to forge a new life for a people it only partially understands, which accentuates one of the main achievements of the book, the faithful rendering of the North African landscape with its traditions and cultures.

For his fourth novel, Bowles shifted his location to South America and his plot to that of the detective novel. Yet, although seen by many critics as a genre fiction of the whodunit variety, *Up Above the World* is a far cry from a run-of-the-mill thriller. It is, in fact, a deeply psychological study of the disintegration of another couple, Taylor and Day Slade, who, much in the same vein as the Moresbys, undergo a tragic transformation which ultimately destroys them.

The Slades arrive by ship in an unidentified South American country at the port town of Puerto Farol. A woman whom they had befriended on the ship is found dead in her hotel room—murdered, it is discovered later, at the behest of her son by a thug named Thorny. The son, Grover Soto, afraid that the Slades have been a witness to the killing, hunts down the couple, who have by now taken a train to the interior of the country. The Slades are finally subjected to the use of drugs and a variety of brainwashing techniques in order to erase the memory of Mrs. Rainmantle, the murdered woman, from their minds. While recuperating at the ranch of Grover Soto, Day sees some written instructions which were to have been destroyed, and in a moment of panic, Soto drugs and then kills Taylor. As the novel concludes, he is about to do the same with Day.

The novel is a psychological thriller much in the vein of Graham Greene's "entertainments," a lesser work not demanding the exertion either to read or to write that a more serious novel requires. Yet there are certain themes and characters which immediately label the book as one of Bowles's. The wandering Americans confronting themselves amid the exotic background of a less civilized and unknown world, their eventual disintegration as they experience an alien culture, and the search for meaning in what appears to be meaningless lives echo his earlier novels. Even the appearance of chance events, encounters onto which the critics have latched to tie the volume to the thriller genre, are also present in his earlier work. The big difference in *Up Above the World* is the novel's compactness. It is streamlined, and in that sense it provides a faster, perhaps more accessible read, but it is a novel no less interesting for all that.

The critics, especially Bertens, have been particularly hard on this book, largely because of its thriller status, which is unfair, since the novel goes beyond the requirements of mere genre fiction and into a netherworld of the truly black. In many ways, this book is Bowles's most pessimistic and most nihilistic, and, writing in the thriller vein, Bowles has made a contribution to the American fictional form most foreboding and dark, a form, in short, closest to his own hopeless vision.

Bowles's fiction will remain attractive both to the few who truly admire advanced writing and thinking and to a general reading audience. It is unfortunate that Bowles's reputation as a writer's writer has limited the enjoyment of his work by the public, since he not only deserves a wider readership but also has much to offer the general reader. Too easily dismissed as an expatriate writer and therefore of little interest to students of American literature, Bowles's work is nevertheless central to the American literary experience, dealing as it does with the protagonist facing the frontier on the edge of civilization, a position which recalls that of Melville's Ishmael, James Fenimore Cooper's Natty Bumppo, and even Mark Twain's Huck Finn. Finally, critics and the public alike need to read Bowles's fiction for its relevant encounters between modern humankind and an increasingly mechanistic and depersonalized world, a place truly of nihilism and despair. Paul Bowles has written about it all.

Other major works

SHORT FICTION: *The Delicate Prey and Other Stories*, 1950; *A Little Stone: Stories*, 1950; *The Hours After Noon*, 1959; *A Hundred Camels in the Court-yard*, 1962; *The Time of Friendship*, 1967; *Pages from Cold Point and Other Stories*, 1968; *Three Tales*, 1975; *Things Gone and Things Still Here*, 1977; *Collected Stories, 1939-1976*, 1979; *Midnight Mass*, 1981.

POETRY: *Scenes*, 1968; *The Thicket of Spring: Poems, 1926-1969*, 1972; *Next to Nothing*, 1976; *Next to Nothing: Collected Poems, 1926-1977*, 1981.

NON FICTION: *Yallah*, 1956 (photographs by Peter W. Haeberlin); *Their Heads Are Green and Their Hands Are Blue*, 1963; *Without Stopping*, 1972 (autobiography).

TRANSLATIONS: *No Exit*, 1946 (of Jean-Paul Sartre's play *Huis-clos*); *A Life Full of Holes*, 1964 (of Driss ben Hamed Charhadi's novel); *Love with a Few Hairs*, 1967 (of Mohammed Mrabet's fiction); *The Lemon*, 1969 (of Mrabet's novel); *M'Hashish*, 1969 (of Mrabet's stories); *The Boy Who Set the Fire and Other Stories*, 1974 (of Mrabet's stories); *Hadidan Aharam*, 1975 (of Mrabet's book); *Harmless Poisons, Blameless Sins*, 1976 (of Mrabet's book); *Look and Move On*, 1976 (of Mrabet's book); *The Big Mirror*, 1977 (of Mrabet's book); *Five Eyes*, 1979 (of Abdeslam Boulaich and others' stories); *The Beach Café and The Voice*, 1980 (of Mrabet's stories); *The Chest*, 1983 (of Mrabet's stories); *The Beggar's Knife*, 1985 (of Rodrigo Rey Rosa's stories); *Marriage with Papers*, 1986 (from Mrabet's book).

Bibliography

Bertens, Johannes Willem. *The Fiction of Paul Bowles: The Soul Is the Weariest Part of the Body*, 1979.

Eisinger, Chester E. *Fiction of the Forties*, 1963.

Pounds, Wayne. *Paul Bowles: The Inner Geography*, 1985.

Stewart, Lawrence D. *Paul Bowles: The Illumination of North Africa*, 1974.

Charles L. P. Silet

ANITA BROOKNER

Born: London, England; July 16, 1938

Principal long fiction

A Start in Life, 1981 (U.S. edition, *The Debut*, 1981); *Providence*, 1982; *Look at Me*, 1983; *Hotel du Lac*, 1984; *Family and Friends*, 1985; *The Mis-alliance*, 1986.

Other literary forms

A distinguished historian of eighteenth and nineteenth century French art and culture, Anita Brookner wrote several books of nonfiction before she began to write novels. *Watteau* (1968) is an assessment of the early eighteenth century French artist Antoine Watteau. *The Genius of the Future, Studies in French Art Criticism: Diderot, Stendahl, Baudelaire, Zola, The Brothers Goncourt, Huysmans* (1971) is a collection of six essays on seven French writers; each writer is considered in the context of his time. The greatest space is given to Charles Baudelaire. *Greuze: The Rise and Fall of an Eighteenth-Century Phenomenon* (1972) is a study of the French painter Jean-Baptiste Greuze in a successful attempt to locate the background of a sentimental genre that is distinct from both Rococo and classicism. *Jacques-Louis David* (1980), a biography of the foremost painter of the French revolutionary period, explores the relationship between David's life and work, places that work in the context of contemporary French painting, and details a career that spanned some of the most turbulent years in French history. Brookner's translations include *Utrillo* (1960) and *The Fauves* (1962).

Achievements

Brookner suddenly began to write fiction during her middle years, while still an active teacher and scholar. Although she continued her academic career, she quickly found equal success as a novelist. With the publication of several novels, she gained an international following and widespread critical acclaim. In 1984, Great Britain's prestigious Booker Prize for fiction was awarded to *Hotel du Lac*. Brookner was praised for her elegant and precise prose, her acute sense of irony, and her subtle insights into character and social behavior. Her witty explorations of manners and morals suggest to many a literary kinship to Jane Austen and Barbara Pym. While Brookner's somber, more complex moral vision disallows any sustained comparison to Pym, Austen and Brookner undeniably share a common concern for intelligent, subtle, clever heroines who seek to satisfy both private sensibility and public expectations.

To regard Brookner's novels as simply traditional novels of manners, however, is to misconstrue her art. Brookner's intentions greatly exceed this conventional genre; her achievements, indeed, take her far beyond it. Perhaps it is more useful to note the singularity of her contribution to British letters. Her highly developed pictorial sense; her baroque diction, with its balance of reason and passion; and her allusive, richly textured narratives, haunting in their resonances, reflect at every turn her extensive knowledge of the materials and motifs of eighteenth and nineteenth century paintings and literature.

Her works have been generously admired, but some dissenting voices have been raised. She is occasionally brought to task for fictive worlds too narrow in scope and claustrophobic in their intensity, for overzealous, self-conscious, schematic fiction, and for excessive sentimentality that unfortunately evokes the pulp romance. Brookner's worlds, however, are invariably shaped toward significant moral revelations; technique rarely intrudes to the detriment of story; and her ability to maintain an ironic distance from her characters, one that allows her to reveal sentimentality, to make judgments dispassionately, is one of her greatest strengths as a writer.

Biography

Anita Brookner was born in London, England, on July 16, 1938, to Newson and Maude Brookner. She was educated at James Allen's Girl's School; King's College, University of London; and received a Ph.D. in art history from the Courtauld Institute of Art in London. From 1959 to 1964, she was visiting lecturer at the University of Reading, Berkshire. In 1968, she was Slade Professor at Cambridge University, the first woman to hold this position. Since 1977, she has been reader at the Courtauld Institute of Art, where she lectures on neoclassicism and the Romantic movement. Her fiction career thus far has been crowned by the award of the Booker Prize. Brookner now lives in London.

Analysis

The territory Anita Brookner has claimed for herself is distinctive. In formal, austerely elegant prose, she builds character portraits of scholarly, sensitive, morally earnest young women who lead narrow, attenuated lives. None of these heroines has intended a life so circumscribed. As their stories begin, they seek change, liberation from boredom and loneliness. They seek connection to a wider world. While these women are intelligent, endlessly introspective, and possessed of a saving ironic wit, they do not know how to get the things they most desire: the love of, and marriage to, a man of quality. With compassion, rue, and infinite good humor, Brookner makes it abundantly clear that these worthy women, these good daughters, good writers, and good scholars are unknowing adherents to a romantic ideal. Like the shopgirls and "ultra-feminine" women they gaze upon with such wonder and awe, these intellectually and morally superior women accept without question the cultural assumption that marriage is a woman's greatest good. Consistently undervaluing their own considerable talents and professional achievements, these heroines look to love and marriage as a way of joining the cosmic dance of a rational, well-ordered society. Their intense yearning for a transforming love shapes their individual plots; in each case, the conflict between what the romantic imagination wants and what it indeed does get impels these narratives forward. Brookner's concern is to illuminate the worthiness, the loneliness, the longing of these heroines for love and a more splendid life.

With the exception of *Family and Friends*, in which Brookner widens her scope to focus on the passage of a family through time, each of her novels follows essentially the same path. Determined to become more than watchers at the feast, the heroines establish tentative relationships with remote, elegant, extraordinarily handsome men. Yet these experiences with romantic love inevitably prove corrosive. The much-desired men remain at a tantalizing remove. Brookner's heroines may subtly woo, but they cannot win. Attractive, well dressed, but lacking the authority of truly dazzling beauty, unwilling or unable to employ traditional "feminine" strategies, these luckless heroines are fated to be petitioners before the court of love. Before their stories can end, these women must abandon sentiment and accept their solitary states. Their triumph lies in their ability to confront their fall from romantic innocence and recognize it for what it is. These novels build inexorably toward an ending that is both startling and profoundly moving. While Brookner's heroines must struggle with sentimentality, Brookner herself does not. Her vision is bleak, unsparing. In telling their stories, she raises several other themes: The most notable of these are filial obligation, the "romantic" versus the "realistic" apprehension of life, truth and its relationship to self-knowledge, the determination of proper behavior in society, and the small pleasures that attend the trivia of daily life. Brookner presents her major and minor themes against the background of fictive worlds so powerfully realized that her novels seem to be absorbed as much as read. These are novels of interior reality. Little that is overt happens; dramatic action rests in the consciousness of the heroine, who is always center stage. With the exception of *Family and Friends*, Brookner gives little attention to the interiority of males. Most often, they exist as the distant objects of desire; their physical presence is scant. Her concern lies foremost with her heroines, whose suffering she views with pity and respect.

Brookner's first novel, *The Debut*, lacks the richness and gradation of tone that marks her later fiction, but is nevertheless well crafted. Set against Honoré de Balzac's *Eugénie Grandet* (1833; English translation, 1859), *The Debut* tells the story of Ruth Weiss, a scrupulous, thoughtful scholar, who finds herself at forty with a life "ruined" by literature. A passionate reader from an early age, now a professor of literature specializing in Balzac, Ruth leads a narrow life alternating between teaching students and caring for an aging father. She blames the tradition of filial duty she found in literature for her mostly cheerless state.

Like Frances Hinton of *Look at Me* and Kitty Maule of *Providence*, Ruth began with expectations. In her youth, she once cast aside the burden of an oppressive heritage, one best symbolized by the deep silence and heavy, dark furniture in the mausoleum of a house she shared with her parents, and had fled England for France. Ostensibly, her goal was to write a dissertation on vice and virtue; in actuality, it was as much to seek air and space and light. Although she at first endured a sense of displacement, exile, a condition that at one time or another afflicts many of Brookner's heroines, over time Ruth's transplant into foreign soil proved successful. Away from her charming, eccentric, but infinitely demanding parents, Ruth flourished. She acquired polish, sophistication, lovers. Yet even as she gloried in her new life, Ruth, like many of Brookner's other heroines, engaged in a constant internal debate over the question of how life is best lived. Does vice or virtue bring victory? She concluded that a life of conventional virtue can spell disaster for one's hopes; regretfully, Balzacian opportunism cannot be discounted. It is better to be a bad winner than a poor loser. Even though she observed that conventional morality tales were wrong, however, Ruth lamented the triumph of vice.

Suddenly called back to England because of what proves to be a final deterioration in her mother's fragile health, Ruth is forced to leave the comfortable, satisfying life she built for herself. Her spirited adventure over, Ruth is unable to extricate herself once more. At forty, the long and beautiful red hair indicative of her youthful potential for rebellion now compressed into a tight chignon, Dr. Ruth Weiss is a felon recaptured. She is tender with her father, gentle with her students, and expects little more from life. She is the first of Brookner's heroines who learns to renounce. Ruth's story is told retrospectively, in a way that recalls the French novel of meditation. The bold configurations of her story suggest the quality of a fable. The narrative also gains a necessary solidity and weight by the many allusions to Balzacian characters and texts. These allusions create a substructure of irony that continues to reverberate long after Ruth's story is complete.

If Ruth is disheartened but finally resigned, Kitty Maule in *Providence*, Brookner's second novel, moves toward outright disillusionment. Kitty is also a professor of literature. Her interests lie in the Romantic movement; this novel, then, like the rest of Brookner's fiction, is filled with ideas, good talk, vigorous intellectual exchanges. Here, both Kitty's private musings and her running seminar on Benjamin Constant's *Adolphe* (1816) provide a context for the exploration of Romantic concerns. Brookner's use of Kitty as a teacher of the Romantic tradition is ultimately highly ironic, for Kitty cannot discern her own romanticism. Curiously, she has moments when she is almost able to see her romanticism for what it is. Yet in the end, she suppresses the would-be insights and retreats into her dreams and passionate longings. What Kitty longs for is love, marriage, and, perhaps, God. Her longing for God goes largely unrecognized; like her fellow Romantics, she requires a sign. Yet her longing for love, the love of one man in particular, is at the perceived center of her life.

The handsome, brilliant, but distant lover of the scholarly, sensitive woman in this novel is Maurice Bishop. Maurice, a professor of medieval history, is noted for his love of cathedrals and God. Wellborn, rich, confident in the manner of those accustomed to deference, Maurice is everything that Kitty wants in life: He is the very cultural ideal of England itself. To be his wife is Kitty's hope of heaven; to capture him, she brings to bear all of her weapons at hand: subtle intelligence, grace of manners, enduring patience, and abiding love. That Kitty's love for Maurice has the fervor of a religious acolyte is suggested by his surname. Maurice may be in love with the idea of a religious absolute, but Kitty's religion is romantic love. All of her repressed romanticism is focused in this elegant, remote man.

Kitty's extreme dependence upon Maurice as the repository of her hopes and dreams stems in large part from her sense of cultural displacement. The child of a French mother and a British father, both dead in their youth, Kitty was born in England and brought up there by her immigrant French grandparents. Despite her British birth, however, Kitty never feels at home in England. In the face of concerted and varied efforts to "belong," she retains a sense of exile. Nor is she truly considered English by her colleagues and acquaintances. The product of her doting French grandparents, Kitty is unaware of her true cultural allegiance; ironically, it is the French heritage that dominates in her English setting. Her manners, clothes, and speech belie her English father. In Maurice, Kitty seeks an attachment that anchors, a place to be. Here and elsewhere in Brookner's fiction, the recurrent theme of the search for a home acquires the force and weight of myth. So powerfully realized is Kitty's intense desire for love, acceptance, and liberation from loneliness that it comes as a shock when Kitty, who is expecting Maurice's proposal of marriage, instead learns of his sudden engagement to a woman who shares his aristocratic background. The novel concludes with Kitty's realization that she had indeed lived in a haze of romantic expectation; the truth is, she has been first, last, and always an outsider.

In addition to the major theme of the passive, excellent, but self-deceived young woman in the service of an illusory ideal, Brookner presents in *Providence* themes which are relevant to all of her works. Maurice's betrayal of Kitty, for example, establishes a motif that recurs in later novels, while Brookner's superbly comic depiction of bored and boring academics, a staple in her fiction, reaches perhaps its finest statement here. If Balzacian allusions underlie *The Debut* and give it additional power, allusions to many French writers, but especially to Constant's *Adolphe* are used to provide ironic commentary on and foreshadowings of Kitty's fate. Most important, however, Kitty Maule herself is arguably the quintessential Brooknerian heroine. Like her fictional sisters, Ruth Weiss of *The Debut*, Frances Hinton of *Look at Me*, Edith Hope of *Hotel du Lac*, and Mimi Dorn of *Family and Friends*, Kitty waits patiently for her life to begin. She is blind to her own worth and discounts her singular achievements; longs for order, a place in a rational world; finds joy in the chores, duties, and routines of everyday life; is sensitive, compassionate, morally deserving. Finally, her final inevitable loss of a man morally her inferior leaves her stripped of all romantic illusions, a convert to reality.

By her own admission a relentless observer, Frances Hinton, the heroine of *Look at Me*, Brookner's third novel, tells her own compelling story. To be sure, all of Brookner's heroines are detached observers, though probably none records and stores information so clinically as does Frances. All of Brookner's heroines suffer, yet perhaps none suffers more intensely than Frances. Like other Brooknerian heroines, Frances is virtuous, sensitive, bright, and in need of a more marvelous life. Like other Brooknerian heroines also, she does not know how to get the things she wants. Frozen into inaction, her intense melancholia is mirrored in the images of death and desolation that surround her. A medical librarian who catalogs prints and engravings of Disease Through the Ages, Frances comments ironically on the scenes of madness, nightmare affliction, and death she must sort and mount. She lives in a tomb of a house where her mother has died; Brookner's use of Frances' house recalls her uses of houses elsewhere: They are symbols of oppressive traditions that constrain and weigh heavily upon those who inhabit them. For Frances, the world is somber, dark. The glittering, stylish couple who offer temporary access to a dazzling social world prove cruelly false. In an act of betrayal so profound that Frances cannot but withdraw from the world she has long sought, the beautiful Nick and Alix Fraser hold Frances up to public ridicule. Her brief liberation from solitariness and the eternal prison of self ends abruptly. Always self-analytic, self-deprecatory, Frances blames her failure to find a place in the world as a failure of egotism or will. She observes that others advance through egotism, but she cannot mimic them. She decides to become a writer. Writing will allow her both to comment on life and to retreat from it.

As is usual in Brookner's works, the dramatic action is largely inner. Hers are novels of the interior; the terrain surveyed is that of the soul. Frances presents a commanding narrative voice as she sorts, gathers, and finally reassembles the fragments of her experience into a unified whole. In fullest voice, she provides useful insights into the processes of the creative, transforming imagination. From the detritus of her daily life she, as writer-at-work, will abstract significant form. If Brookner here provides a mirror of herself busy fashioning art from the materials of the ordinary, the details of eating or dressing or chatting that receive so much attention in her novels, she also repeats the characteristic fusion of the comic and the sad that lends such poignancy to her works. Further, the influence of the pictorial is reflected here as well; characters are often framed in an action, presented with a consciousness of scene or setting. Finally, Frances' long commentary on her experience that is the text of *Look at Me* again evokes the French novel of meditation, a literary form that subtly influences and pervades Brookner's fiction. Notably, as Frances begins to write on the last page of the novel, she is free of self-pity. Solitude may be her lot, but art will vindicate her. Art will represent the triumph of the unvanquished self.

Edith Hope, the heroine of *Hotel du Lac*, Brookner's fourth novel and the winner of the 1984 Booker Prize, is also a writer. Edith writes pulp romances for a living. Yet until she learns better, she believes that romance is only her business, not her frame of mind. Brookner's fiction, however, reveals her tendency sometimes to use names to signal character traits or habits of thought. Such is the case here: Edith is indeed a romantic, although an unknowing one. Edith begins her stay at the Hotel du Lac in ignorance of her true nature; she leaves enlightened as to the deeper, more recessed aspects of her moral being.

It was not Edith's choice to leave England and travel to Switzerland, the setting of *Hotel du Lac*. Edith was sent away because of her severe breach of social decorum: She chose not to appear at her own wedding, thus profoundly humiliating a good man and eminently suitable husband. Her action was shocking to all, including Edith herself. Modest, unassuming, and usually anxious to please, Edith is in many ways a typical Brooknerian heroine. She, too, spends too much time alone, condemned to her own introspection. Her marriage would have broken that isolation. Edith's revolt and subsequent removal to Switzerland provide a context for the discussion of numerous moral and psychological questions. While Edith's story is always foremost, the novel itself alternates between first- and third-person narratives, with philosophical positions being argued, accepted, or dismissed. The central fact that emerges about Edith is her passionate love for a married man whom she only seldom sees. Like his fictional predecessors, Edith's David is exceedingly handsome, elegant, intelligent, and remote. For love of him, Edith jilted her dull but safe fiancé. At the Hotel du Lac, Edith's interactions with the other residents move her to a greater understanding of truth, self-knowledge, and the differences between romance and reality. Numerous other themes are present here as well, including that of "ultrafeminine" as opposed to "feminist" women. Edith understands these women as models of feminine response to feminine experience. In relative isolation at this Swiss hotel, she studies these models and rejects both. The will to power, the utility of egotism as a serviceable instrument in the world, a recurrent Brooknerian theme, also receives much discussion here.

What Edith eventually learns as she evaluates her exchanges and relationships with her fellow guests is accorded significant status by the mythological underpinnings of this novel. Inside the hotel, characters are both particular and types, acting out self-assigned roles in a grand comedy of manners. All the inhabitants exhibit a theatrical sense of themselves; they "present" themselves to this community consciously, deliberately. Such attention to the pictorial, personal presentation is a constant of Brookner's fiction. The details of clothes, manners, and mannerisms convey aspects of self and morality in Brookner's works as they do in the works of Henry James, to whom Brookner alludes in this novel. If inside the hotel the characters are on parade, making their statements with dress, or gesture, once outside the hotel, they are subsumed to the mythicized landscape. Gray mist, conveying a sense of menace and oppression, surrounds everything. Characters make journeys that are important only for their mythic impact. Much movement against this drear landscape takes place as characters are directed toward crucial, definitive moral choices. The landscape helps Edith to perceive her dilemmas; she is finally able to reject a diabolical figure, who offers marriage without love. He forces Edith to recognize her romanticism for what it is. At least in the end, however, when she returns to England and her married lover, Edith knows that she has chosen a cold and solitary path. Her self-determination represents a triumph for her and for this book. Edith is finally transformed by her successful journey to knowledge. Although generally considered a good work of wider range than usual, the award of the Booker Prize to *Hotel du Lac* is controversial. It could be argued that *Look at Me* is the more powerful work.

Family and Friends, Brookner's fifth novel, presents a radical departure in form. Written in the historic present with virtually no dialogue, this novel, essentially an extended meditation in the French tradition, does not meet with universal approval. It stems from the ruminations of a narrator who quickly disappears, makes only glancing reappearances, and is curiously never identified. Here, Brookner's concern is not with a particular heroine, but with the Dorn family, rich, most likely German immigrants who fled to England before the start of World War II. The war, when it comes, receives but scant attention; the novel focuses always on the small, interior world of the Dorn family. Little seems to exist outside the family and their immediate interests, sparking again charges of a work too narrow in range.

The lives of the Dorn family and their associates are followed over a period of time. Sofka, the gentle but strong matriarch of the family, is the moral center of the work. Widowed early in life, she rejects the idea of remarriage, directing her loving attentions to her family, instead. Mimi and Betty are her two daughters. While Betty is selfish, willful, theatrical, tricking her family into giving her an independent life quite early, she is nevertheless the child Sofka secretly loves best. Sofka, beautiful and contained, admires her younger daughter's spirit. Mimi is virtuous, dreamy, passive, frozen into inertia in young womanhood when an early feeble attempt to reach out for love was unsuccessful. Mimi languishes for years afterward, until her mother urges her into marriage, and thereby respectability, with a gentle, good man who would normally be her social inferior. A striking and salutary difference in this novel is the extended attention given to men: the sensitive, intelligent responsible Alfred Dorn and his handsome, charming brother Frederick. Interestingly, it is Alfred's plight that mirrors the plight of the usual Brooknerian heroine. It is he who is trapped by filial obligation into a life he had not intended; it is he who suffers forever afterward from an unsatisfying search for love and a desire for a larger, more extended world. It is also he who ultimately becomes inured in long-established habits of insularity.

This, then, is the saga of a family whose interior lives and moral relations are acutely realized. Important themes here include familial relations, especially filial obligation; the search for a transcendent love; the need to venture, to dare, if one is to "win" in life. Structured around four wedding pictures, the novel impresses with its unity and intensity of tone; the pervasive, elegant irony; the discerning moral judgments; and the engrossing character portraits. Especially effective also is the novel's lament for the loss of youthful promise, energy, and innocence. The vibrant Betty, inured in middle-aged stasis, is a case in point. Dominating this entire work is a rich narrative voice, stern, compassionate, and often sad. The Dorn family seems to exist in a twilight, dreamlike world outside time. Yet this world, while admittedly narrow, is nevertheless mesmerizing.

Brookner's novels have brought her remarkable success within a very short time. Her taut, spare narratives share distinctive qualities: grace, precision, and elegance of language; ironic commentaries on character and social behavior that both instruct and delight; a tone compounded of the comic and the melancholy; and a moral vision that is both rigorous and compassionate. What marks Brookner's fictional territory most clearly, though, is her concern for the unclaimed, solitary woman of merit who seeks a place in the cosmic order of a rational, harmonious society. Blind to their own considerable virtues, these intelligent but romantic heroines look to men and marriage for validation. Their intense yearning for liberation from solitariness shapes their respective plots. Perhaps sufficient attention is yet to be paid to the subtle and wide range of Brookner's allied themes. These themes include the question of proper behavior for a woman; the difficulties of making and sustaining friendships; filial obligations; mother and daughter relations; the ethics of the will to power; the search for religious faith; the quest to remain in a state of innocence; the relation between truth and self-knowledge. Further recognition of these sometimes submerged but related themes would no doubt moderate occasional charges that the novels are too narrow in scope: too repetitious of subject matter, too sentimental in intention or execution. Experiments with structure and theme demonstrated in *Hotel du Lac* and *Family and Friends* however, would seem to indicate that Brookner has already begun to broaden her scope. Clearly, despite her early and considerable success, Anita Brookner is a writer still involved in a vigorous exploration of the true nature and range of her talent.

Other major works

NONFICTION: *Watteau*, 1968; *The Genius of the Future, Studies in French Art Criticism: Diderot, Stendahl, Baudelaire, Zola, The Brothers Goncourt, Huysmans*, 1971; *Greuze: The Rise and Fall of an Eighteenth-Century Phenomenon*, 1972; *Jacques-Louis David*, 1980.

TRANSLATIONS: *Utrillo*, 1960 (of Waldemar George's biography); *The Fauves*, 1962 (of Jean Paul Crespelle's book).

Bibliography

Bayles, Martha. "Romance à la Mode," in *The New Republic*. CXCII (March 25, 1985), pp. 37-38.

Jebb, Julian. "Unblinking," in *The Spectator*. CCLIII (September 22, 1984), pp. 26-27.

Lasdun, James. "Pre-Modern, Post Modernist," in *Encounter*. LXIV (February, 1985), p. 42.

McRobbie, Angela. "Fine Disorder," in *New Statesman*. CVIII (September 7, 1984), p. 32.

Betty H. Jones

ANGELA CARTER

Born: Eastbourne, England; May 7, 1940

Principal long fiction
Shadowdance, 1966 (U.S. edition, *Honeybuzzard*, 1967); *The Magic Toyshop*, 1967; *Several Perceptions*, 1968; *Heroes and Villains*, 1969; *Love*, 1971; *The Infernal Desire Machines of Doctor Hoffman*, 1972 (U.S. edition, *The War of Dreams*, 1974); *The Passion of New Eve*, 1977; *Nights at the Circus*, 1984.

Other literary forms
Angela Carter is nearly as well-known for her short fiction as she is for her novels. Her short-story collections include *Fireworks: Nine Profane Pieces* (1974), *Black Venus* (1985; U.S. edition, *Saints and Strangers*, 1986), and the highly praised *The Bloody Chamber and Other Stories* (1979), which contains her transformations of well-known fairy tales into adult tales with erotic overtones. She has also written a number of fantastic stories for children, including *Miss Z, the Dark Young Lady* (1970), *The Donkey Prince* (1970), and a translated adaptation of the works of Charles Perrault, *Sleeping Beauty and Other Favourite Fairy Tales* (1982). In 1979, she published her first book of nonfiction, *The Sadeian Woman: And the Ideology of Pornography*, a feminist study of the Marquis de Sade that remains controversial among both literary and feminist critics. Other nonfiction essays have been published by British journals; *Nothing Sacred: Selected Writings* (1982) is a collection of her journalistic pieces. She also cowrote the screenplay for the British film *The Company of Wolves* (1985), based on her short story of the same title. *Come unto These Yellow Sands* (1985) is a collection of various other scripts adapted from her fiction.

Achievements
With the publication of her first novels in the late 1960's, Carter received wide recognition and acclaim in Great Britain for blending gothic and surreal elements with vivid portrayals of urban sufferers and survivors. She was awarded the John Llewellyn Rhys Memorial Prize for *The Magic Toyshop* and the Somerset Maugham Award for *Several Perceptions*. Critics have praised her wit, inventiveness, eccentric characters, descriptive wealth, and strongly sustained narrative while sometimes questioning her depth of purpose and suggesting a degree of pretentiousness. Such adverse criticism is mostly directed at such novels as *Heroes and Villains* and *The Infernal Desire Machines of Doctor Hoffman*, which are set in postapocalyptic or metaphysical landscapes. Her imaginative transformation of folkloric elements and

examination of their mythic impact on sexual relationships began to be fully appreciated on the appearance of *The Bloody Chamber and Other Stories*, which received the Cheltenham Festival of Literature Award. *Nights at the Circus*, recipient of the James Tait Black Memorial Prize, helped to establish firmly for Carter a growing transatlantic reputation as an extravagant stylist of the Magical Realist school. She is noted for her provocative observations and commentary on contemporary social conditions.

Biography

Angela Carter (neé Stalker) was born in Eastbourne, Sussex, England, on May 7, 1940. After working as a journalist from 1958 to 1961 in Croyden, Surrey, she attended Bristol University, from which she received a B.A. in English literature in 1965. She has traveled widely and lived for several years in Japan. From 1976 to 1978, she served as Arts Council of Great Britain Fellow in Creative Writing at Sheffield University. She has been a visiting professor at Brown University, the University of Texas, Austin, and the University of Iowa, and lives in London, England.

Analysis

The search for self and for autonomy is the underlying theme of most of Angela Carter's fiction. Her protagonists, usually described as bored or in some other way detached from their lives, are thrust into an unknown landscape or enter on a picaresque journey in which they encounter representatives of a vast variety of human experience and suffering. These encountered characters are often grotesques or exaggerated parodies reminiscent of those found in the novels of Charles Dickens or such Southern gothic writers as Flannery O'Connor. They also sometimes exhibit the animalistic or supernatural qualities of fairy-tale characters. The protagonists undergo a voluntary or, more often, forced submission to their own suppressed desires. By internalizing the insights gained through such submission and vicariously from the experiences of their antagonists and comrades or lovers, the protagonists are then able to garner some control over their own destinies. This narrative structure is borrowed from the classic folk- and fairy tales with which Carter has been closely associated. Carter does not merely retell such tales in modern dress; rather, she probes and twists the ancient stories to illuminate the underlying hierarchical structures of power and dominance, weakness and submission.

In addition to the folkloric influence, Carter has drawn from a variety of other writers, most notably Lewis Carroll, Jonathan Swift, the Marquis de Sade, and William Blake. The rather literal-minded innocent abroad in a nightmarish wonderland recalls both Alice and Gulliver, and Carter acknowledges, both directly and obliquely, her borrowings from *Alice's Adventures in Wonderland* (1865) and *Gulliver's Travels* (1726). She has also been influenced by the Swiftian tool of grotesque parody used in the service of satire. It is through Swiftian glasses that she has read Sade. While deploring the depradations on the human condition committed by both the victims and victimizers in Sade's writings, she interprets these as hyperbolic visions of the actual social situation, and she employs in her novels derivatively descriptive situations for their satiric shock value. Finally, the thematic concerns of Blake's visionary poetry—the tension between the contrarieties of innocence and experience, rationality and desire—are integral to Carter's outlook. The energy created by such tension creates the plane on which Carter's protagonists can live most fully. In Blake's words and in Carter's novels, "Energy is Eternal Delight."

Although Carter's landscapes range from London in the 1960's (*The Magic Toyshop, Several Perceptions, Love*) to a postapocalyptic rural England (*Heroes and Villains*) or a sometime-in-the-future South America (*The Infernal Desire Machines of Doctor Hoffman*), a United States whose social fabric is rapidly disintegrating (*The Passion of New Eve*), or London and Russia at the turn of the century (*Nights at the Circus*), certain symbolic motifs appear regularly in her novels. Carter is particularly intrigued by the possibilities of roses, wedding dresses, swans, wolves, tigers, bears, vampires, mirrors, tears, and vanilla ice cream. Menacing father figures, prostitute mothers, and a kaleidoscope of circus, fair, and Gypsy folk people most of her landscapes. It is unfair, however, to reduce Carter's novels to a formulaic mode. She juggles traditional and innovative elements with a sometimes dazzling dexterity and is inevitably a strong storyteller.

At the opening of *The Magic Toyshop*, fifteen-year-old Melanie is entranced with her budding sexuality. She dresses up in her absent mother's wedding gown to dance on the lawn in the moonlight. Overwhelmed by her awakening knowledge and the immensities of possibilities the night offers, she is terrified and climbs back into her room by the childhood route of the apple tree—shredding her mother's gown in the process. Her return to childhood becomes catastrophic when a telegram arrives announcing the death of Melanie's parents in a plane crash. Melanie, with her younger brother and sister, is thrust from a safe and comfortable existence into the constricted and terrifying London household of her Uncle Philip Flower, a toy maker of exquisite skill and sadistically warped sensibility. He is a domestic tyrant whose Irish wife, Margaret, was inexplicably struck dumb on her wedding day. The household is also inhabited by Margaret's two younger brothers, Finn and Francie Jowle; the three siblings form a magic "circle of red people" which is alternately seductive and repulsive to Melanie. Uncle Philip is a creator of the mechanical. He is obsessed by his private puppet theater, his created world to which he enslaves the entire household. In aligning herself with the Jowle siblings, Melanie asserts her affirmation of life but becomes aware of the thwarted and devious avenues of survival open to the oppressed. The growing, but ambivalent, attraction between her and Finn is premature and manipulated by Uncle Philip. Even the love that holds the siblings together is underlined by a current of incest. Finn is driven to inciting his uncle to murder him in order to effect Philip's damnation. The crisis arises when Uncle Philip casts Melanie as Leda in a puppet extravaganza. Her symbolic rape by the immense mechanical swan and Finn's subsequent destruction of the puppet release an orgiastic, yet purifying, energy within the "circle of red people." The ensuing wrath of Uncle Philip results in the conflagration and destruction of the house. Finn and Melanie are driven out, Adam-and-Eve-like, to face a new world "in a wild surmise."

In fairy-tale fashion, Melanie is threatened by an evil father figure, protected by the good mother, and rescued by the young hero. Even in this early novel, however, Carter skews and claws at the traditional fabric. The Jowle brothers, grimy, embittered, and twisted by their victimization at the hands of Philip Flower, are as dangerous as they are endangered. They are unable to effect their own freedom. Melanie's submission to Uncle Philip's swan catalyzes not only her own rescue but also, indeed, the release of the Jowle siblings. Melanie's sacrifice breaks the magic spell that held the Jowles imprisoned.

Several Perceptions, Carter's third novel, depends less on such folkloric structure. In this novel, her evocation of the late 1960's counterculture is so finely detailed that she manages to illuminate the thin line between the idealism and solipsism of that era, without denigrating the former or disguising the latter. The clarity of observation is achieved by viewing the culture through the eyes of Joseph Harker, a classic dropout. He has failed at the university, been dumped by his Jane Austen–reading lover, is disheartened by his job caring for dying old men, despises the contentment of his hippie peers, and, early in the novel, bungles a suicide attempt. Joseph, like his biblical namesake, is a dreamer of dreams: He dreams in the violent images of Vietnam atrocities, the self-immolation of Buddhist monks, and assassinations. His schizophrenic perceptions are colored by shattered images from the books in his room, *Alice's Adventures in Wonderland* and Anne Gilchrist's *Life of William Blake* (1863), by memories of his grandfather, visions of his psychiatrist, the purring of his pregnant cat, Anne Blossom's custard, and the vanilla ice-cream breasts of Mrs. Boulder. The novel narrates Joseph's slow crawl back into the world of the living. Despite a tough-minded acknowledgment of the grubby and quite desolate lives of the characters, the novel is written with a gentle touch and ends on an affirmative note. The Christmas party that takes place at the end of the novel, in which Joseph symbolically reenters society, stands as a classic description of a hippie-generation party, just as F. Scott Fitzgerald's description of Gatsby's party stands as the image for the flapper generation. The connected-disconnected flow, the costumes, the easy sexuality, the simple goodwill, the silliness, and the sometimes inspired personal insights are vividly re-created. Carter wrote the novel as this life-style was being played out, and it is much to her credit that she succumbed neither to sentimentality nor to parody.

Parody and satire are, however, major elements in her three novels that are often classified as science fiction or science fantasy. In *Heroes and Villains*, *The Infernal Desire Machines of Doctor Hoffman*, and *The Passion of New Eve*, Carter's protagonists dwell in societies which are described in metaphysical iconography. Carter seems to be questioning the nature and values of received reality. Marianne's world in *Heroes and Villains* is divided into high-technology enclaves containing Professors, the Soldiers who protect them, and the Workers who serve them. Outside the enclaves, in the semijungle/semicesspool wildernesses, dwell the tribes of nomadic Barbarians and the Out-people, freaks created by nature gone awry. Marianne, the daughter of a Professor, motivated mainly by boredom, escapes from her enclave with Jewel, a young Barbarian chieftain, during a raid. In *The Infernal Desire Machines of Doctor Hoffman*, the aging Desiderio narrates his heroic exploits as a young man when he saved his City during the Reality War. Doctor Hoffman besieges the City with mirages generated from his Desire Machines. Sent by the Minister of Determination to kill Doctor Hoffman, Desiderio is initiated into the wonders of desires made manifest, Nebulous Time, and the juggled samples of cracked and broken reality. His guide is Hoffman's daughter, Albertina, who appears to Desiderio as an androgynous ambassador, a black swan, the young valet of a vampiric count, and finally as his one true love, the emanation of his whole desire. The United States in *The Passion of New Eve* is torn apart by racial, class, and sexual conflicts. Evelyn, a young British teacher, travels through this landscape and is re-created. The unconsciously exploitive and disinterestedly sadistic narrator suffers a wild revenge when captured by an Amazonlike community of women. He is castrated, resexed, raped, forcibly wed and mated, and ultimately torn from his wife's love by a gang of murderous Puritanical boys. Each of these protagonists experiences love but only seems to be able to achieve wholeness through the destruction of the loved one. Symbolically, the protagonists seem to consume the otherness of the loved ones, reincorporating these manifest desires back into their whole beings. Each, however, is left alone at the end of the novel.

Symbolic imagery of a harshly violent though rollicking nature threatens to overwhelm these three novels. The parody is at times wildly exaggerated and at times cuts very close to reality (for example, in *The Passion of New Eve*, the new Eve is incorporated into a polygamous family which closely resembles the Manson cult). Although some critics have decried Carter's heavy reliance on fantasies, visions, and zany exuberance, it is probably these qualities that have appealed to a widening audience. It must also be given to Carter that, within her magical realms, she continues to probe and mock the repressive nature of institutionalized relationships and sexual politics.

With *Nights at the Circus*, Carter wove the diverse threads of her earlier novels into brilliantly realized tapestry. This novel has two protagonists— Fevvers, the Cockney Venus, a winged, six-foot, peroxide blonde aerialist, who was found "hatched out of a bloody great egg" on the steps of a benevolent whorehouse (her real name is Sophia) and Jack Walser, an American journalist compiling a series of interviews entitled "Great Humbugs of the World," who joins Colonel Kearney's circus, the Ludic Game, in order to follow Fevvers, and who is "Not hatched out, yet . . . his own shell don't break, yet." It is 1899, and a New World is about to break forth. The ambivalent, tenuous attraction between Fevvers and Walser is reminiscent of that between Melanie and Finn in *The Magic Toyshop* or Marianne and Jewel in *Heroes and Villains*, but it is now mature and more subtly complex. The picaresque journeyings from London to St. Petersburg and across the steppes of Russia recall the travels in *The Infernal Desire Machines of Doctor Hoffman* and *The Passion of New Eve* but are more firmly grounded in historical landscapes. The magic in this novel comes in the blurring between fact and fiction, the intense unbelievability of actual reality and the seductive possibilities of imaginative and dreamlike visions. Are Fevver's wings real or contrived? Do the clowns hide behind their makeup and wigs or only become actualized when they don their disguises? As in most Magical Realist fiction, Carter is probing the lines between art and artifice, creation and generation, in a raucous and lush style.

Here, after a long hiatus from the rather bleak apocalyptic visions of her 1970's novels, in which autonomous selfhood is only achieved through a kind of self-cannibalization of destroyed love, Angela Carter envisions a route to self-affirmation that allows sexual love to exist. With shifting narrative focuses, Carter unfolds the rebirths of Walser and Fevvers through their own and each other's eyes. Walser's shells of consciousness are cracked as he becomes a "first-of-May" clown, the waltzing partner to a tigress, the Human Chicken, and, in losing consciousness, an apprentice shaman to a primitive Finno-Urgic tribe. As star of Kearney's circus, Fevvers is the toast of European capitals: an impregnable, seductive freak, secure in and exploitive of her own singularity. On the interminable train trek through Siberia, she seems to mislay her magnificence and invulnerability. She becomes less a freak and more a woman, but she remains determined to hatch Walser into her New Man. As he had to forego his socially conditioned consciousness in order to recognize Sophia, however, so she has to allow him to hatch himself. It is as confident seers that Sophia/Fevvers and Jack Walser love at the close of the novel. With *Nights at the Circus*, Angela Carter, too, seems to have entered a confident, strong period in her remarkable literary career.

Other major works

SHORT FICTION: *Fireworks: Nine Profane Pieces*, 1974; *The Bloody Chamber and Other Stories*, 1979; *Black Venus*, 1985 (U.S. edition, *Saints and Strangers*, 1986).

SCREENPLAYS: *Come unto These Yellow Sands*, 1985 (based on her short fiction); *The Company of Wolves*, 1985 (based on her short story).

NONFICTION: *The Sadeian Woman: And the Ideology of Pornography*, 1979; *Nothing Sacred: Selected Writings*, 1982.

CHILDREN'S LITERATURE: *Miss Z, the Dark Young Lady*, 1970; *The Donkey Prince*, 1970; *The Fairy Tales of Charles Perrault*, 1979 (translation); *Sleeping Beauty and Other Favourite Fairy Tales*, 1982 (translation and adaptation of Perrault's tales).

Bibliography

Punter, David. "Angela Carter: Supersession of the Masculine," in *Critique: Studies in Modern Fiction*. XXV (Summer, 1984), pp. 209-222.

Rose, Ellen Cronan. "Through the Looking Glass: When Women Write Fairy Tales," in *The Voyage In: Fictions of Female Development*, 1983. Edited by Elizabeth Abel.

Sage, Lorna. "The Savage Sideshow: A Profile of Angela Carter," in *New Review*. XXXIX/XL (June/July, 1977), pp. 51-57.

Jane Anderson Jones

J. M. COETZEE

Born: Cape Town, South Africa; February 9, 1940

Principal long fiction
Dusklands, 1974; *In the Heart of the Country*, 1977; *Waiting for the Barbarians*, 1980; *Life & Times of Michael K*, 1983; *Foe*, 1986.

Other literary forms
Although J. M. Coetzee has published a number of book reviews and essays, primarily dealing with South African authors and Thomas Hardy, these have not been collected in book form.

Achievements
Coetzee is recognized as one of South Africa's finest writers, one whose allegorical fiction suggests that apartheid is but a particularly virulent expression of man's will to dominate. At the same time, like many contemporary writers, he is acutely aware of problems of language and representation, and his fiction reflects an increasing preoccupation with the complex interplay of language, imagination, and experience. It is Coetzee's distinctive achievement to fuse such philosophical concerns with probing social and psychological insights.

Although Coetzee's career is very much in progress, he has already received many prestigious literary awards. His second book, *In the Heart of the Country*, won South Africa's premier literary award, the Central News Agency (CNA) prize, in 1977. *Waiting for the Barbarians*, chosen as one of the Best Books of 1982 by *The New York Times*, won the CNA prize, the Geoffrey Faber Memorial Prize, and the James Tait Black Memorial Prize; *Life & Times of Michael K* won Great Britain's Booker Prize in 1983. In 1987, Coetzee received the Jerusalem Prize for writing "that contributes to the freedom of the individual in society."

Biography
John Michael Coetzee was born in Cape Town, South Africa, in 1940; he was educated in computer science and in linguistics in South Africa and the United States, and he received his Ph.D. in linguistics from the University of Texas in 1969. He served as an assistant professor of English at the State University of New York at Buffalo, and later as a lecturer in English at the University of Cape Town.

Analysis
Although contemporary South Africa is seldom mentioned or referred to

explicitly in J. M. Coetzee's novels, the land and the concerns of that country permeate his works; one may see this indirect approach as an evasion of the censorship which must be a factor for any writer in that state, but this necessary blurring of temporal and geographic actualities also endows each work with universal overtones. On one level, Coetzee's novels deal with the suffering that human beings inflict on one another, whether as agents of the state or as the victims of their own obsessions. On another level, concurrent with this one, the obsessions and those in their grip form the major thematic centers of the greater part of his fiction.

Coetzee's first major work, *Dusklands*, is composed of two novellas, *The Vietnam Project* and *The Narrative of Jacobus Coetzee*; the common thread that runs through the two seemingly unrelated pieces is the obsession of each protagonist with the personal dimension of colonization. Eugene Dawn, the narrator of *The Vietnam Project*, is a mythographer inquiring into the efficacy of America's propaganda in Vietnam. His discoveries are disturbing and soul-shattering to the point that Dawn is driven to kidnap his child from his estranged wife and use him as a hostage. In the course of his confrontation with the police, Dawn stabs his son, marveling at the ease with which the knife slips into the flesh. He is last seen in an insane asylum, his consciousness peopled with images of power and powerlessness.

The second novella purports to be a narrative of an eighteenth century Boer settler, translated from the Dutch by J. M. Coetzee, with an afterword by Coetzee's father. The account relates a trek undertaken ostensibly to hunt elephants but really to see what lies beyond the narrator's immediate environment. The decorous, antiquarian headings which break up the narrative—"Journey Beyond the Great River," "Sojourn Among the Great Namaqua"—contrast strangely to the horrors endured both by the narrator and by the tribespeople he meets. Stricken with illness, Jacobus remains with the not-yet-colonized Namaqua, whose relations with him are at times contemptuous, at times nurturing, but never the expected ones of respectful native to European explorer. Jacobus' Hottentot servants desert him to stay with the Namaqua, and naked, unarmed, and alone, he returns to civilization after an arduous journey. He goes back to the land of the Namaqua with troops and takes his revenge on the tribespeople, who have shown him less respect than he wanted.

Throughout, the narrator hints, almost unconsciously, at what he is seeking: a sense of limits, and therefore a definition of his self. This motif is introduced in the first novella by Dawn's analysis of the hate felt by Americans toward the Vietnamese: "Our nightmare was that since whatever we reached for slipped like smoke through our fingers, we did not exist. . . . We landed on the shores of Vietnam clutching our arms and pleading for someone to stand up without flinching to these probes of reality. . . but like everything else they withered before us."

This concern with boundaries seems to stem from the physical environment of the vast African plain, into which Jacobus expands endlessly but joylessly. There are no rules, and Jacobus is worried by the possibility of "exploding to the four corners of the universe." There is an unmistakable grandeur in such a concept, one that reflects the position of the powerful in relation to the powerless, but it is a qualified grandeur. It is one that Coetzee's protagonists reject, drawing back from the spurious apotheosis of limitless being, understanding that it is not worth the dreary awareness of the void. Transcendence cannot occur when there is nothing to transcend.

Indeed, transcendence is the object of the quest for all of Coetzee's main characters, and what they seek is the obstinate, obdurate object that will resist them to the point that they know that they exist, and against which they may define themselves. This quest is an important factor in Coetzee's second book, *In the Heart of the Country*, a novel written in the form of a diary kept by a young woman on a sheep farm. The farm is isolated in the featureless landscape, and Magda has recourse to fantasies, terrible and bloody, of revenge on her father, who to her has always remained an "absence." Little by little, Magda peoples her life, writes variations on reasons that she wants to kill her father, imagines situations in which she becomes the servant of her father and his brown mistress, and ultimately kills him, more or less by accident, while he is making love to Anna, the wife of the servant Hendrik. The uncertainty of the act's reality lingers after the occurrence; the father really has been shot, however, and takes several days to die.

At this point, the diary takes on a more straightforward tone, as if the difficulty of disposing of the body has finally focused Magda's life. Hendrik and Anna are moved into the house, and Magda begins sleeping with Hendrik, who now seems to despise her and who treats her as if she were the servant. Eventually, worried that they will be blamed for the murder of Magda's father, Hendrik and Anna disappear in the middle of the night, and Magda is left alone in the great house.

Without money, without any visible means of support, she manages to live into an old age in which she hears voices from airplanes passing overhead. The voices say things which she takes to be comments on her condition: "Lacking all external enemies and resistances, confined within an oppressive narrowness and regularity, man at last has no choice but to turn himself into an adventure." The solipsism which is evidenced in the earlier part of the diary (and which is a function of the diary form) is thus recalled to cast doubt on the truth of what Magda has been writing. Has all the foregoing been the product of a spinster's fevered imagination? Every event surrounding the father's murder and burial may have been so, and Magda herself wonders whether her father will come striding back into her life. Yet the one point in which Magda truly lives is the point where her father has ceased being an absence, when the weight and increasing rigidity of his corpse have lent reality to his dutiful daughter's heretofore thwarted love.

This relationship between the violent act and the affirmation of one's identity, along with the connection between hate and love, between master and slave, between the tortured and the torturer, forms the central theme of *Waiting for the Barbarians* (the title of which alludes to a poem by C. P. Cavafy). An unnamed, aging magistrate of a town on the far borders of "the Empire" narrates the story of an attempt by the Empire to consolidate its northern border against the depredations of "the barbarians," nomads who have heretofore existed peacefully—with the exception of some dubious raids—in the face of increasing expansion by the agrarian settlers. The magistrate is far more interested in comfort, his books, and his antiquarian researches into the ancient sand-buried buildings near the town than he is in the expansion of empire. He is disturbed by the arrival of the sinister Colonel Joll of the "Third Bureau," a police force given special powers for the duration of the "emergency."

At first, the magistrate merely resents the intrusion of such affairs into the somnolent world that keeps him comfortable. He is severely shaken, however, by the torture of two obviously innocuous prisoners (and the killing of one of them) by Joll. As a result, the magistrate is compelled to place himself, quiet servant of the Empire, in opposition to the civilization to which he has been dedicated.

Joll has taken out an expedition to capture barbarians, some of whom he interrogates upon his return. The magistrate cannot simply ignore what is happening, but neither can he act. When Joll leaves, the barbarians are released and they depart; they have left behind a girl who has been tortured: Her eyes have been burned and her ankles broken in order to wring information from her father. The magistrate takes her into his house and enters into a bizarre relationship with her, one which consists of washing her swollen feet and badly healed ankles; the washing progresses to the other parts of her body, but there is no straightforward sexual act. During these ministrations, both the magistrate and the girl fall asleep, a normal sleep for the girl but a heavy drugged torpor for the man.

He cannot fathom his fascination with this girl who has been so cruelly marked, but he begins to understand that perhaps it is her damaged quality which so attracts him. She is unresponsive to him, accepting his tenderness as he imagines she accepted her torture, passive, impenetrable. He decides to take her back to her people after he realizes that to her, he and Colonel Joll are interchangeable, two sides of the same empire.

After an arduous journey, he and his small party come face-to-face with the barbarians in the mountains; he gives the girl back to them, since she expresses her desire to leave him and civilization. Upon his return, he is arrested by the occupying force of the empire on charges of collaborating with the barbarians. A new policeman has installed himself in his office, and the magistrate goes to his cell almost gladly: "I had no duty to her save what it occurred to me to feel from moment to moment: from the oppression of such freedom who would not welcome the liberation of confinement?"

He manages to escape, but returns, knowing that he cannot survive in the open spaces. Eventually he is released: The expedition against the barbarians has been a dismal failure, the town is emptying of soldiers and civilians, and the Empire is crumbling at the edges. He assumes his former responsibilities and tries to prepare the town for approaching winter. The novel ends with the same image that has haunted his dreams: children playing in the snow in the town square. Yet the children are making a snowman, not a model of the empty town, and the faceless girl is not among them.

The Empire could be anywhere: Its geography encompasses Africa as well as Mongolia or Siberia. The townspeople are not described physically, and the barbarians' description is that of Mongols. Colonel Joll and the warrant officer—and their methods—evoke the Gestapo, the KGB, or, for that matter, the South African police. The time appears to be set in a future so distant that sand dunes have engulfed buildings of staggering antiquity. What does endure, Coetzee seems to be saying, are the sad constants of human history: the subjugation of the weak by the strong, the effects of slavery on masters as well as slaves, and the impotence of good intentions. If the magistrate has survived, it is because the Empire has considered his rebellion of no consequence.

It is difficult to present limited expectations as an affirmation of the value of life. This subject, touched on in *Waiting for the Barbarians*, is realized in *Life & Times of Michael K*, a novel set in a South Africa of the future. Coetzee had, until this novel, furnished his readers with introspective, articulate narrators who reveal their complicated thoughts in precise language. With *Life & Times of Michael K*, he departed from this pattern.

Michael K's survival is precarious from the beginning of his life; born with a deformed lip, he must be painstakingly fed with a spoon by a mother repelled by his appearance. Anna K, a domestic worker, takes him with her when she works. When he reaches school age, he is put in an institution for the handicapped, where he learns a bit of reading and writing and the skills of the unskilled: "scrubbing, bedmaking, dishwashing, basket weaving, woodwork, and digging." Eventually, at the age of fifteen, he joins the Parks and Gardens service and becomes a gardener, a job to which he returns after an attempt at night work.

At the age of thirty-one, K receives a message to fetch his mother from the hospital. For a time, they live together in Anna's old "servant's room"—a windowless cubicle under a staircase, originally meant for air-conditioning equipment that was never installed—but a riot in the vicinity of the apartment buildings convinces them to leave. Anna, as her dropsy gets worse, har-

bors a confused dream of returning to the farm where she spent her childhood. She has saved some money, and K attempts to buy a railroad ticket,
but a bureaucratic nightmare of reservations and permits forces them to
walk, the son pushing his mother on a two-wheeled cart which he has built
with persistence and ingenuity.

They travel through a disquieting landscape: At times thronged with
people leaving the city, at times ominously empty, the roads are the domain
of enormous army convoys, whose purpose and destination remain unknown, but which, along with the riots in the cities, indicate an ongoing civil
war in the unnamed country.

Towns still exist, however, and it is in one of these that Anna and K stop;
exhaustion and exposure to the cold rain have aggravated the mother's illness, and K takes her to a hospital where, after a few days, she dies. A nurse
hands K a box of ashes, tells him that these are his mother's remains, and
sends him on his way. He is robbed of his money by a soldier, but he keeps
his mother's ashes, until he reaches an abandoned farm which might be the
one mentioned by his mother. He decides to live there. There is a windmill
pump on the farm, and its leaking has formed an oasis in the barren land. K
plants a garden there and sprinkles his mother's ashes over the soil.

A grandson of the departed owners appears, seeking safety from what is
happening in the cities. Dimly, K realizes that if he stays, it will be as a servant to this boy; he therefore shuts off the pump so that everything will die
and he leaves.

He is interned in a work camp from which he escapes, returns to the farm,
and again plants his garden; the boy is gone, and K builds himself a shelter
with stones and a piece of corrugated iron. One day, he sees men approaching. From concealment, he is somehow aware that these men must be "the
other side," the antagonists to the dispirited government soldiers he has
known. Although their donkeys destroy half his crop, K feels sympathy with
these men. He makes plans to tend his garden so that there will be many
crops and they will have more to eat when they come back. Ironically, the
next soldiers are government soldiers, who appear months later, and they
arrest K under suspicion of being connected to the rebels. They destroy the
garden, explode the pump, and burn the farmhouse. K is again interned.

Up to this point, the third-person account has been from K's point of view:
a registering of random impressions by someone who has no language to
impose a pattern on events, who seldom wonders how he must appear, and
who periodically achieves states approaching the meditative or vegetative.
The second section is a first-person narrative by the medical officer—a pharmacist in civilian life, but it seems that many old men have been called back
to military service, indicating that the civil war has spread everywhere—of
K's new camp. An articulate, compassionate man, reminiscent of the magistrate in *Waiting for the Barbarians*, he is by turns annoyed and inspired by

K's refusal to eat "the food of the camp." When K escapes, the medical officer convinces the aged commandant of the camp to report him dead.

K has returned to the city whence he set out, and there he falls in with others who live by scavenging; he undergoes a sexual initiation among these people, who mean him no harm but by whom he is repelled. At the end of the third section, K has gained self-consciousness. His thoughts are now phrased in the first person and told to the reader: "I am a gardener." This burst of self-awareness does not cut his ties to what he has been before; the final image is an emulation of the slow, patient rhythms of the earth: " . . . he would bend the handle of the teaspoon in a loop and tie the string to it, he would lower it down the shaft deep into the earth, and when he brought it up there would be water in the bowl of the spoon; and in that way, he would say, one can live."

Coetzee has been accused of being too political in his concerns and also of not being political enough; to accuse him of either is to miss the point of his novels. He is concerned with humanity, and what it means to be human. In *Waiting for the Barbarians*, the magistrate says of his torturers, "They came to my cell to show me the meaning of humanity, and in the space of an hour they showed me a great deal." To be human is to suffer, but the one who causes the suffering also suffers, and also is human. His hatred is twisted love, a rage against the victim for not pushing back, not allowing him humanity. This is the root of all evil in the world, and this is what Coetzee shows. Humanity's history is one of suffering, and the only way to escape suffering is to live outside history.

Bibliography

Brink, André. "Writing Against Big Brother: Notes on Apocalyptic Fiction in South Africa," in *World Literature Today*. LVIII (Spring, 1984), pp. 189-194.

Daymond, M. J., et al., eds. *Momentum: On Recent South African Writing*, 1984.

Roberts, Sheila. "South African Post-Revolutionary Fiction," in *Standpunte*. XXXV (June, 1982), pp. 44-51.

Jean-Pierre Metereau

DON DeLILLO

Born: New York, New York; November 20, 1936

Principal long fiction

Americana, 1971; *End Zone*, 1972; *Great Jones Street*, 1973; *Ratner's Star*, 1976; *Players*, 1977; *Running Dog*, 1978; *The Names*, 1982; *White Noise*, 1985.

Other literary forms

Although Don DeLillo's major literary efforts have centered on the novel, he has contributed short stories to periodicals including *The New Yorker*, *Esquire*, *Sports Illustrated*, and *The Atlantic*, and has written several plays.

Achievements

The publication in 1971 of DeLillo's first novel, *Americana*, launched the career of one of America's most innovative and intriguing writers. DeLillo produces satirical novels, novels that drill into and hammer at the chaos of modern society, the lack of coherence and order in institutions, the breakdown of personal relationships, and particularly the failure of language in the world today. He writes a driving, mercurial, upbeat prose that at times smacks of an idiosyncratic pedantry yet abounds in lyricism and musicality. Some readers have labeled his prose "mandarin," after the fashion of Donald Barthelme and Thomas Pynchon. Pynchon definitely influenced him, but DeLillo pushes far beyond the limits of imitation or even derivation and asserts a truly independent voice. The promise of prodigious talent inherent in his first novel has flowered in the later works. In 1984, the American Academy and the National Institute of Arts and Letters presented to DeLillo their Award in Literature. DeLillo's novels, although often criticized as plotless disquisitions that never produce anything but comic-strip characters, nevertheless stimulate and excite readers with their musicality, their rhetorical rigor, and their philosophical depth.

Biography

Don DeLillo was born in New York City in November of 1936. He spent his childhood and adolescence in Pennsylvania and the South Bronx. After studying at Fordham University, he lived for a while in Canada and then returned to New York, where he has lived ever since.

Analysis

What little there is of traditional narrative structure in the Don DeLillo novel appears to serve principally as a vehicle for introspective meanderings, a thin framework for the knotting together of the author's preoccupations about life and the world. Thematically, each novel is a profound reworking of the familiar precepts that make up the core of his literary belief system. This basic set of ideas includes the function (misfunction) of language as it relates to being, the absurdity of death and the meaning of apocalypse, the complications and chaotic workings of societies (particularly governments and institutions), the ontological purity of women and children, the notion of sacred spaces, and the interrelatedness of time, history, and myth. DeLillo's great facility with a language perfectly tuned for irony and satire allows him to range the breadth and depth of these themes.

All these thematic strains are present in *Americana*. The problem of language and meaning finds a penetrating focus in the conversation between the protagonist, David Bell, a dissatisfied minor network executive who seizes upon a documentary assignment to make a cross-country odyssey of self-discovery, and Carol Deming, a distracted yet aggressive young actress who reads a part for David's film: The encounter is set up to be sexual but proves to be nothing more than a bizarre verbal tryst, a duel of wacky hyperbole laced with sarcasm. Beneath the words fired rapidly back and forth between David and Carol, there are the levels of behavior and intensity normally associated with seduction. In this case, words appear to substitute for the great diversity of emotional responses associated with the sex act. The reader, however, knows that verbal intercourse is no substitute for sexual intercourse and commiserates with David on his lack of fulfillment; words are false images that can be made to disguise the multilayered nature of reality. In the end, however, the word is destroyed by the meaning it tries to mask.

This verbal affair takes place in the middle of America, in a town called Fort Curtis, the designated location for the filming of David's documentary. He has been commissioned to film the Navajo Indians but decides that the town will be the backdrop for a film about the central moment of his own childhood, the moment he learned that his mother, for him the bastion of health and security, would soon face disintegration and death. Each stop on his "sacred journey" out West holds a numinous attraction for him: the starting point, the chaotic craziness of the network office with its mad memo writer; the garage of Bobby Brand (a friend who uses his van for the trip); Fort Curtis; and ultimately Rooster, Texas, where David's pilgrimage of self-exploration ends in a boozy orgy in the dust. In Fort Curtis, David hires local people to read absurd lines and then has traveling companion Sullivan, an enigmatic sculptor, play the part of his mother on the day he learned, in the pantry of his parents' home, the tragic truth that women were not what he expected and wanted them to be: They cannot be held as an anodyne against the fear of death. In David's hands, the camera has the power to create from the union of a special place and a particular moment an image that is again an illusion of reality. When he later tries to make a created image real (that is, make Sullivan a real mother figure by having her tell him a precoital bed-time story), he is again instructed in the misalignment between images and the world. DeLillo, by constantly emphasizing the impossibility of the world's true representation in time and place via the word (history), mythologizes his characters and frees them from the bounds of historicity.

One of these mythic characters, Myna Corbett, appears in *End Zone*, the one DeLillo novel that most of the author's critics agree is a brilliant piece. Myna, a student at Logos College in West Texas, is typical of DeLillo's female characters: She is big, carrying 165 pounds, which she refuses to shed because of her desire not to have the "responsibility" of being beautiful; she fills her mind with trivial matter (she reads science-fiction novels); and she has large breasts in which Gary Harkness, the protagonist, hopes to find solace from the world.

Gary is a talented but eccentric footballer at Logos College who, because of his strange behavior, has been cut from the team rosters of larger institutions such as Penn State and Syracuse. He does not change his ways at Logos, walking off the field during the last game, high on marijuana and very hungry. He has a fascination with war and audits the Reserve Officers' Training Corps classes that have to do with mass killing strategy. When Colonel Staley asks him to become a cadet, Gary refuses, saying that he wants only to fantasize about nuclear war. He enjoys playing nuclear destruction games with the colonel, but he will not prepare himself to become an Air Force officer: He will not drop real bombs.

When not engaged in his graphic war daydreams, Gary is either playing football, an abstraction of war, or having picnics with Myna. If war is organized, palpable death, then Myna must be its opposite, an image of life and a defense against the fear of death. The tension between women (as the word or image of antideath) and harsh reality finds expression in the scene in which Gary undresses Myna in the library stacks. He says to himself that it is important to have her completely nude in the midst of the books containing millions of words. He must see her as the word (the image of harmless, uncomplicated femaleness) made flesh. He wants to see Myna, as the embodiment of the illusion of safety that words give, appear to belie the truth behind the image, the truth that women are not immune from the dread of death and therefore cannot offer the security that he seeks. He does not want to confront the mystery and lure of feminine beauty: He is upset when Myna loses weight. When she returns from vacation slender, it is he who does not want the responsibility of Myna's beauty. Women's love can lead to death and words can have deadly connotations.

DeLillo further explores his themes dealing with language, death, women, and time in *Great Jones Street*, the story of a rock star, Bucky, who grows tired of the business, leaves his band in Houston, and returns to a hovel of an apartment in New York City. There his seclusion is destroyed when Skippy, a hippie girl, leaves with him a box full of a special kind of dope that is untested but is thought to be extremely powerful, and therefore of great interest to the drug people. The rest of the novel focuses on the many people who want to get the drugs. One of the agents sent for the drugs is Opel, who eventually dies in Bucky's bed. She is only an image of a living woman as she lies in the bed; the anti-image, death, is the reality of her being there. When she dies, Bucky can contemplate only her dead self; once people leave one extreme of being, they must become the other.

Bucky tries to make his apartment a refuge from the relentless roll of time and the world. He talks into a dead phone, stifling any possibility that words can reach their destination and complete the communication process. He refuses to wind the clock, hoping to arrest time, that hard reality that lies beneath the illusory image of stasis. Opel, although safe in bed in Bucky's timeless, wordless (telephoneless) world of the apartment, dies nevertheless.

The song that has made Bucky famous, "Pee-Pee-Maw-Maw," provides grist for another favorite DeLillo theme, that children, because of their few years, have no thoughts or fears of dying and therefore are immune from death. Bucky sings in the simple, life-giving syllables of children. The Mountain Tapes, traded for the drugs by a boy named Hanes, bring the same release as do the drugs in the box: They reduce language to nonmeaning. Later, when Bucky is injected against his will with the drug, he loses the power of speech; he is silent. Childish babble and wordlessness are equated with a loss of the fear of death and consequently, a loss of humanity. Only humans fear death, says Bucky.

A child is the central character in *Ratner's Star*, a dense and overly long novel about the shortcomings of modern science. Billy, a fourteen-year-old mathematical genius who has just won the first ever Nobel Prize for Mathematics, is called to a futuristic think tank to help decipher a signal presumed to be a communication from Ratner's Star. The boy eventually finds the answer: The pulses of the message are really from the Earth as it existed long ago. The meaning of the mathematical "words," the exact time of day as Billy looks at the clock on the wall (and coincidentally the exact time as an unscheduled eclipse of the sun), is that the secret of all knowledge is what one has at a particular place at the present time. All the supposed power of the modern scientific community can be reduced to the utter simplicity of the time of day in a child's room on our own planet in our own time. When a spontaneous heavenly movement takes place, it is announced first to the child's mind.

The adult scientists with whom Billy is obliged to interact by their utter egregiousness offer DeLillo myriad openings for the insertion of his biting satirical barbs. Endor, for example, the world's greatest mathematician, has given up solving the mystery of the pulses and has gone to live in a mud hole, living off worms and roots which he digs from the ground. Fitzroy-Tapps, the rat-talk scholar, hails from Crutchly-on-Podge, pronounced Croaking-on-Pidgett. Hoy Hing Toy, the obstetrician who once ate a newborn placenta; Grbk, who has to be officially reprimanded for showing his nipples to young children; and Armand Verbene, S.J., a practitioner of red-ant metaphysics, are representative of the resident staff. Of these bizarre characters, one in particular provides DeLillo with an excellent opportunity to hold forth on the meaning of language. Young Billy, a Nobel laureate by virtue of his having conceived the mathematical notion of the zorg (an entity reduced as far as it can be—that is, to nothing), confronts the astronomical mind of Lazarus Ratner. It is necessary to say that Billy confronts the "mind" of Ratner, because that is practically all that is left of the man. He is kept from collapsing in on himself by constant silicone injections, and his bodily functions are kept going mechanically inside a protective bubble. Billy sits astride the biotank, talks to Ratner (who will speak to nobody but the child), and translates what the great scientist says for those who stand near.

DeLillo uses this conversation between the old man and the boy to explore provocative notions about language, knowledge, and God. Ratner tells the boy about the Cabala: The hidden and unknowable name of God is a literal contraction of the superdivinity. The contraction of divine anti- or other-being, *en sof*, makes possible the existence of the world. Being (God) is somewhere on a spectrum between light and darkness, something and nothing, between an integer and a zorg, in Billy's mathematical code. Divinity (pure being) is revealed in the expansion of matter. As the universe expands, human beings, as part of that expansion, come into existence. Existence, then, is like the birth and death of stars, says Ratner: It is manifested with the expansion and perishes with the contraction of its mass. Thus, as elements, or *sephiroth* of the primal being, humans are like tiny sparks of Ratner's Star. Human names, the words that equate with human existence, are merely artificial and abstract images of a constant expansion and contraction. Real being consists of the flux and levels of being behind the image.

Billy puts this theory into simple, incomplete terminology which, complains Ratner, is not fully expressive of the reality of that which is being communicated. Here again is the old problem: Words, as images of reality, cannot possible convey the entire dimension of the meaning of the world. Those who listen to Billy as he interprets Ratner are able to glean only a small portion of the content of Ratner's words.

Of the later novels, *The Names* and *White Noise* offer the most moving and powerful treatment of DeLillo's recurring themes. *The Names* features the decay of the typical American marriage. James and Kathryn are married, have a son named Tap, and live happily for a time on an island in the Eastern United States. They live peacefully until the bright image of marital bliss splinters, broken into a multileveled subset of hard problems, the first of which is separation. Kathryn, yielding to the fascination for digging in the ground in search of lost messages, commits herself to a life of archaeological digging. She joins an excavation site on an island in Greece; James, wanting to be near his fractured family, gets a job in Greece as a so-called risk analyst. Even though this bit of darkness has tarnished the core of the little family, they live on a reasonably even keel until archaeologist Owen Brademas begins an investigation of a cult of hammer killers. These cultists occasionally pound to death a chosen victim who happens to wander into a town, the initials of whose name match the initials of the victim's name: For example, they kill Michaelis Kalliambestos as he enters Mikro Kamini. Brademas, whose profession it is to find and translate ancient script written in stone, really is more interested in the cabalistic power of the alphabet as it is combined and recombined to reveal the hidden names of God. He finds the Names, as the members of the hammer cult refer to themselves, becomes one of them in spirit, witnesses a ritual hammer murder (death comes to him who finds, even if by accident, correspondence in letters and reality), and then retires to read stones and live unmolested in his final sacred place, a hotel room in Bombay. Owen Brademas seems to be merely a mythic extension of an innocent, babbling language spoken by Kathryn and her sister as children, and used by Kathryn and her son: The language inserts the syllable "ob" among the syllables of real words to create a special code. The initials of wordmonger Owen Brademas' name happen to be O.B. OB seeks the meaning of alphabetic combinations even when they lead to death: He is the one who figures out the workings of the Names. In many ways, he is the shadow image of her husband, a writer, who lives by the combinations of words and who follows Brademas in search of the cult. James finds his place of revelation in a Roman ruin just as Brademas finds his in a hotel room. Brademas is also an alter ego of Kathryn, who seeks hidden wisdom by a kind of mindless digging at the site, yet he takes archaeological inquiry to the ultimate degree and ends in a room with nothing but ordered space, a perfect stasis, a state much like death.

In the same way, James's job is nothing but a cover for a CIA operation. His image of a harmless and rather pleasant way of life in Greece is destroyed: He experiences a dark underside of intrigue and deception. It seems that the surface of daily life can never remain innocuously in place; there is always a seepage of antilife. His wife and profession appear to be entities resting on shifting sands; only his son, the child, who writes away at a nonfiction novel, can be counted on for authenticity.

White Noise is a thematic duplicate of *The Names*. The characters are cartoons. Babette is the physically large wife to whom Jack Gladney, her husband, looks for a peaceful domestic life totally removed from danger. Babette, also called Baba, appears to be very capable of fulfilling her husband's needs: She is the perfect image of easygoing housewifery. She volunteers for community service, she shops constantly in the supermarket, and she lovingly cares for the children. The children are precocious and serious-minded. Heinrich, the oldest boy, seems to know much more than his father, a college professor, about the real world. The girls, especially Denise, are concerned about Babette's health, hiding her drugs and looking for hidden habits that might bring her danger or death. Husband and wife, lost in triviality, make inconsequential or erroneous statements, while the children speak with precision and maturity. There is a reversal in the parent-child roles; these children, therefore, are not as innocent as the typical DeLillo child figure. Only Wilder, the baby, embodies the ideal of the deathless child hero: At the end of the novel, he rides his tricycle into the street, across a four-lane street teeming with speeding vehicles, into the grass of the opposite shoulder, miraculously escaping death.

Babette crumbles as the symbolic shield against fear; she is exposed as a woman so terrified of death that she trades sex for a special kind of drug that causes one to forget about the fact that one must die. She takes these pills on the sly and is finally found out by her snooping family. Jack has been happy with Babette because she is open and guileless, unlike his previous wives, who were mysterious, complicated secret agents who worked for the CIA. His illusion is destroyed when he finds out about her pills. Her complicity in this kind of intrigue reinforces his recently discovered vulnerability to death (a physical examination has revealed that his exposure to the toxic chemical spill may leave him only a short time to live). Even Baba, the large, comfortable, unbeautiful, unmysterious, faithful wife, who has consoled Jack as he has lain with his face between her large breasts, proves to be full of duplicity and treachery.

This complication leads Jack to reflect on what Murray Siskind, a fellow faculty member, has told him regarding death; death, says Siskind, can only be purged by killing. Jack has already intuited this precept on his own: His success as a professor of "Hitler studies" (which he established as a full-fledged academic discipline) depends in part on his awareness of the peculiar fascination of the Nazis. Ultimately, Jack shoots Willie Mink, a seedy drug dealer who dispenses death-forgetting pills to women in exchange for sex. He enjoys the bleeding of his wife's seducer for a while but then has pity on the mindless Mink, a victim of his own pills, and drags him by the foot to a hospital. The nuns who attend the wounded man destroy the last great image of security that Jack has left: Jack learns that those whom he had always thought of as sainted women, women firm in their faith that death's dominion has been crushed by the resurrection of Christ, have no more faith in salvation than he, his wife, or anybody else. The white noise of death silences any voice that would offer human beings a verbal sanctuary from its assault.

Not unlike many other writers, Don DeLillo writes the same novel over and over, each time with a bit more force in the dissection and probing of the human spirit. For this reason, the later novels seem more sinister and joyless than the earlier ones. Yet he writes with such brilliance that one never tires of his reiteration of theme. Reading DeLillo continues to be a delightful experience.

Other major works

PLAYS: *The Engineer of Moonlight*, 1979; *The Day Room*, 1986; *A Visit from Dr. Bazelon*, 1986.

Bibliography

Bawer, Bruce. "Don DeLillo's America," in *New Criterion*. III (April, 1985), pp. 34-42.

Bosworth, David. "The Fiction of Don DeLillo," in *Boston Review*. VIII (April, 1983), pp. 29-30.

James, Caryn. "I Never Set Out to Write an Apocalyptic Novel," in *The New York Times Book Review*. XC (January 13, 1985), p. 13.

Watson Holloway

PHILIP K. DICK

Born: Chicago, Illinois; December 16, 1928
Died: Santa Ana, California; March 2, 1982

Principal long fiction
Solar Lottery, 1955; *The World Jones Made*, 1956; *The Man Who Japed*, 1956; *Eye in the Sky*, 1957; *Time Out of Joint*, 1959; *Dr. Futurity*, 1960; *Vulcan's Hammer*, 1960; *The Man in the High Castle*, 1962; *The Game-Players of Titan*, 1963; *Martian Time-Slip*, 1964; *The Three Stigmata of Palmer Eldritch*, 1964; *The Simulacra*, 1964; *The Penultimate Truth*, 1964; *Clans of the Alphane Moon*, 1964; *Dr. Bloodmoney: Or, How We Got Along After the Bomb*, 1965; *The Crack in Space (Cantata 140)*, 1966; *Now Wait for Last Year*, 1966; *The Unteleported Man*, 1966; *Counter-Clock World*, 1967; *The Zap Gun*, 1967; *The Ganymede Takeover*, 1967 (with Ray Nelson); *Do Androids Dream of Electric Sheep?*, 1968; *Ubik*, 1969; *Galactic Pot-Healer*, 1969; *The Philip K. Dick Omnibus*, 1970; *A Maze of Death*, 1970; *Our Friends from Frolix 8*, 1979; *We Can Build You*, 1972; *Flow My Tears, the Policeman Said*, 1974; *Confessions of a Crap Artist*, 1975; *Deus Irae*, 1976 (with Roger Zelazny); *A Scanner Darkly*, 1977; *The Divine Invasion*, 1981; *Valis*, 1981; *The Transmigration of Timothy Archer*, 1982; *Lies, Inc.*, 1984; *Radio Free Albemuth*, 1985; *Humpty Dumpty in Oakland*, 1986.

Other literary forms
Before he began writing long fiction, in 1955, Philip K. Dick went through an extraordinarily prolific period as a short-story writer. His first story, "Beyond Lies the Wub," appeared in 1952. In both 1953 and 1954 Dick published twenty-eight short stories a year. His total output in this genre is more than one hundred stories, most of which he wrote early in his career. Many have been reprinted in his collections *A Handful of Darkness* (1955), *The Variable Man and Other Stories* (1957), *The Preserving Machine and Other Stories* (1969), *I Hope I Shall Arrive Soon* (1985), and elsewhere. He has also collaborated on novels, including *The Ganymede Takeover* (with Ray Nelson) and *Deus Irae* (with Roger Zelazny).

Achievements
In all histories of science fiction, Dick is hailed as one of the greatest and most distinctive exponents of the genre. Literary awards, however, came his way surprisingly rarely. He received the Hugo Award (which is decided by vote of science-fiction fans attending the World Science Fiction Convention) for the best novel of the year 1962, for *The Man in the High Castle*. He received the John W. Campbell Award (decided by a panel of writers and

critics, and also administered by the World Science Fiction Convention) for *Flow My Tears, the Policeman Said*, in 1975. More recognition might have been expected, and would surely have been forthcoming, if it were not for two things. One is that Dick was, for a while, an amazingly prolific author (five novels were published, for example, in 1964), yet one who wrote very few evidently weak or minor novels. His high level of productivity and consistency have accordingly made it difficult for single novels to be chosen as superior to others. Probably few critics would agree even on which are the best ten of his nearly forty novels. A further point is that Dick, while a writer of amazing power and fertility, is also prone to convolution and to the pursuit of personal obsessions.

Biography

Philip Kindred Dick was born in Chicago in 1928, but he lived most of his life in California. He studied for one year at the University of California at Berkeley, but he did not take a degree. Dick held several jobs for short periods, then began writing science fiction with great speed and immediate success, first short stories and then novels. His output slowed markedly at the beginning of the 1970's, as a result of personal problems, involvement with drugs, strong discontent with American society in the Vietnam era, and a sequence of failed relationships. When he resumed writing, his books were significantly more personal and more propagandist. He died on March 2, 1982, following a stroke.

Analysis

Philip K. Dick's novels are, without exception, distinctive in style and theme. Their style may be characterized relatively easily: Dick writes clearly and plainly, and is a master of realistic dialogue. He is, however, also a master of the art of "cutting." Frequently a chapter or a scene will end with a short summary statement, often of doubt, bewilderment, or unease, only to be followed in the next chapter by a longish sentence introducing a new character going about his daily concerns in a manner which seems—but only seems—to have no connection with the foregoing. For all of his plainness, Dick furthermore makes considerable use of words of his own coinage—for example, "flapple," "quibble" (a kind of vehicle), "thungly," "gubbish," or "kipple." The latter has even achieved a certain currency outside its novel, *Do Androids Dream of Electric Sheep?*, to mean the morass of useless objects, such as gum wrappers or junk mail, which seems to reproduce by itself in any modern dwelling. The overall effect of Dick's style is to give an impression of plainness and superficial normality, but to suggest strongly that beneath this surface things are going on which are ominous, disastrous, inexplicable.

This preoccupation is clearly mirrored in Dick's characteristic themes, many of which are shared with the body of science fiction at large. He often writes of androids, simulacra, mechanical men. He bases several plots on consciousness-raising drugs. His later works in particular tend toward the dystopian, presenting visions of a future America as a vast gulag or a slave-labor state. The notions of alternate worlds and of post-Holocaust societies are often exploited. Where Dick differs from other users of these themes is in the strange insecurity which he generates while handling them. Androids are common in science fiction, and so are plots in which androids cannot be told from people. Only Dick produces plots in which the test to distinguish human from android is so deeply infected with the bureaucratic mentality that even people are likely to fail, and be eliminated. Only Dick has a hero giving himself his own test, having come (for good reason) to doubt his own humanity. Similarly, Dick is capable of writing a story which appears to be set in an alternate world, but then begins to suggest that the real world never existed and is merely a drug-induced hallucination—only to switch back again, deny its own hypothesis, and leave the reader quite unsure even of the bases of judgment. Dick is fascinated by forgeries, and by coincidences. In scene after scene, he presents a hero doubting even his own identity, and doing so with total rationality on the basis of all the evidence in the world around him. Most readers soon realize that the common concern that binds Dick's repeated themes and plot elements is the very nature of reality itself, and that Dick doubts common notions of reality more sincerely and more corrosively than almost any writer in any genre. Dick could be described as the poet of paranoia. Yet his cool and sensible style enables him to present horrifying alienations in a way with which even the sanest reader can sympathize.

Dick's overriding concerns are quite apparent in even his earliest novels. *Solar Lottery*, his first novel, presents a future society which is dedicated entirely to chance, as a result of "extrapolation" first of the then-new phenomenon of television quiz shows, and second (as one might have expected) of the "Uncertainty Principle" as a basic rule of the universe. In this world, all authority devolves on "the Quizmaster," but the Quizmaster may be deposed at any moment from his position by a "twitch of the bottle," an event determined by the intrinsically unpredictable forces of submolecular physics. The bottle twitches. Reese Verrick the Quizmaster is deposed. His place goes to an unknown fanatic called Cartwright, whose only interest is the search for a (mythical?) tenth planet. Caught up in all these events is a hero who has had the colossal bad luck to swear irrevocable fealty to Verrick just before he fell from power. Already the sense of an unpredictable world where anything can go wrong is very marked. Even more revealing is *Eye in the Sky*, in which eight characters caught up in a scientific accident find themselves exploring what they slowly realize are the worlds of one anothers' minds: first that of a total believer in an obscure fundamentalist sect, then that of an inhibited housewife, a borderline paranoid, a fanatical Communist, and so on. The worlds themselves are presented with great verve. In the first, for example, a man going for a job asks not about pay but about credits for salvation, and if he presses is told that in his position the God of this world, "(Tetragrammaton)," will probably grant his prayers to the extent of four hundred (dollars?) a week. The job may be constructing a grace reservoir, or improving the wire to Heaven. There is in fact an "eye in the sky," belonging to the unnameable (Tetragrammaton). Underlying the structure of the whole novel, though, is the notion that each person's individual universe is not only private but unreachable; most people are mad. In view of Dick's later development it is also interesting that the novel is strongly anti-McCarthyite, even though one of the characters (ironically a security chief) is indeed a Communist agent.

The novel which best sums up Dick's earliest phase as a novelist, however, is *Time Out of Joint*. This appears for quite some time not to be science fiction at all. It reads instead as a pleasantly pastoral, perhaps rather dull, account of life in a small American town of the 1950's. The only odd feature is that the hero, Ragle Gumm, makes his living by continually winning a newspaper contest "Where Will the Little Green Man be Next?" Slowly, however, this idyllic setting begins to drift by quarter-tones to nightmare. Gumm does not recognize a picture of Marilyn Monroe (something unthinkable if he were really of that time and place). An old phone book found in some ruins has his name in it, with eight phone numbers for all hours of the day and night. A boy's crystal radio picks up voices saying in effect "That's *him* down there, Ragle Gumm." It transpires that the small town with its idealized families is a total deception, all created to shield Ragle Gumm and maintain him in his stress-free delusion while he performs his real job—using extra-sensory powers to predict the fall of enemy rockets on Earth, under the fiction of the newspaper contest.

Gumm is mad at the start. When he thinks he is going mad, he is learning the truth. There is no way to prove that reality is not a perfectly rehearsed plot. This latter is a classic Dick conclusion. In *The Man in the High Castle*— Dick's most famous but not most characteristic work—the reader is plunged into an alternate reality where the Allies lost World War II, California is occupied by the Japanese, and the inhabitants rather like it. The hero here, Robert Childan, is a seller of "ethnic" American curios, such as Mickey Mouse watches, or Civil War handguns, for which the conquerors have an insatiable appetite. His problem is that some of the guns are fakes. The faker's problem is that he is a Jew, and could be deported to German-controlled areas. Still, the predictable theme of resistance, triumph, escape to the real universe where the right side won, hardly materializes. Instead, the reader is presented with a complex argument in favor of Japanese sensitivity, and with strong underlying hints that even the "alternate worlds" of this "alternate world" would not be the same as our world. The novel suggests powerfully that history is chance, merely one possibility among a potential infinity of realities.

By this time Dick was at the height of his power as a writer, and almost any of the sixteen novels published between 1964 and 1969, including *The Simulacra*, *Dr. Bloodmoney*, *Counter-Clock World*, or *Galactic Pot-Healer*, would find admirers. Some especially significant themes emerge, however, from five novels in this group: *The Penultimate Truth*, *Martian Time-Slip*, *The Three Stigmata of Palmer Eldritch*, *Do Androids Dream of Electric Sheep?*, and *Ubik*. The first of these returns to the theme of total, deliberate illusion. In the future imagined in this novel, most of the inhabitants of Earth live underground, in ant-tanks, under the conviction that World War III is still going on and that if they emerge from hiding they will die from the Bag Plague, the Stink of Shrink, Raw-Claw-Paw, or one of a multitude of man-made viruses. In reality, though, the war stopped long ago, and the Earth is a park, divided up into the demesnes of the ruling classes. Like Ragle Gumm, one character digs his way out to discover the truth and to try to lead these latter-day Morlocks up to the light. The particular point which Dick wishes to rub in here, though, is that even outside science fiction people are genuinely at the mercy of their television screens. They cannot tell whether they are watching truth or a construct. They usually have no way of telling true history from the false varieties which Dick makes up. The end of the novel declares that what is essential—and not only in the novel—is a ferocious skepticism. People are too gullible, too easily deceived.

There is no such overt political thesis in *Martian Time-Slip*, of the same year, but in this Dick creates one of his most likable sets of characters, in Jack Bohlen, the Martian repairman, and Arnie Kott, senior member of the Waterworkers' Union—naturally a privileged body on arid Mars, though no one had previously been mundane enough to say so. Dick also brings into the novel what seems to be a personal image of "the Tomb World," a world in which everything is rotten and decaying, with buildings sliding to ruin, and bodies to corruption. This world is perceived only by an autistic child, but that child's perceptions seem stronger than the grandiose claims of governments and land speculators. Still another route into horror is via drugs.

The Three Stigmata of Palmer Eldritch moves rapidly from a protagonist who has the seemingly harmless job of guessing fashion for dolls and dollhouses to the notion of exploitation—for these "Perky Pat Layouts," as they are called, can be experienced only by people who take the drug Can-D to let them into the doll-world; to menace and terror. Can-D is about to be superseded by Chew-Z, a drug allegedly harmless, nonaddictive, government sponsored. This drug, however, puts its users (as in *Eye in the Sky*) in the world of Palmer Eldritch, a demon-figure with steel teeth, artificial hand, and mechanical eyes. Nor can they return from it. Chew-Z takes one into a variant, one might say, of "Tomb World."

Ubik prolongs this theme. Its hero, Joe Chip, finds the "Tomb World" happening around him, as it were. Cigarettes he touches fall into dust; cream turns sour; mold grows on his coffee; even his coins turn out of date. Then he himself starts to age. The only thing that can cure him is a spray of "Ubik," a material which halts the race to corruption and obsolescence. In a memorable scene near the end, Joe Chip reaches a drugstore just before it closes, to demand Ubik, only to find that the store is closing, the stock is out, spray cans too have aged, becoming cardboard packets. What force is doing all this? Are the characters in fact already dead, now existing only in a bizarre afterlife? For whose benefit is the spectacle being played out? Once again, Dick creates a happy ending, but more strongly than usual, one believes that this ending is demanded by the conventions of the field rather than by the logic of the plot.

For depth of paranoia, though, the prize should go to *Do Androids Dream of Electric Sheep?* This novel is best known as the original of the 1982 film *Blade Runner*, both book and film centering on a bounty hunter whose job is to kill androids. What the film could not do is show the depth of devotion which the characters in the book—who live in a world so radioactive that almost all unprotected creatures have died—give to their pets. Deckard the bounty hunter has a counterfeit electric sheep because he is too poor to afford a real one, but like everyone in the book he consistently consults the manual of animal prices. If he kills three more androids, could he buy a goat? If he spares one, will they give him an owl (thought to be extinct)? Would it be an artificial owl? The pitiless slaughter of androids is balanced against the extraordinary cosseting of every nonartificial creature, down to spiders. Yet what is the basis of the division? In a heartrending scene, after Deckard has wiped out his androids, another android comes and kills his goat. Before then, though, Deckard himself has been accused of being an android, been taken to the Hall of Justice, and been quite unable to prove his own identity—because, as soon becomes clear, all the authorities are themselves androids. The notions of undetectable forgery, total illusion, and unanimous conspiracy combine to make the central scenes of this novel as disorienting as any in Dick's work. In the background, a silent struggle goes on in "Tomb World."

Somewhere near this point, Dick's development was cut off. He wrote most movingly on the subject in the "Author's Note" to *A Scanner Darkly*. This novel, he says, is "about some people who were punished entirely too much for what they did." They were real people, the author's friends. They took drugs, like children playing; it was not a disease, it was an error of judgment, called a "life-style." He then lists seven of his friends who have died, three more with permanent brain damage, two with permanent psychosis, one with permanent pancreatic damage . . . the list goes on. How deeply Dick himself was involved in late 1960's California "drug culture," one cannot say. He himself insists this was exaggerated. Yet for whatever cause, Dick wrote less; and his mood became angrier, less playful.

Even so, the great surprise of *Flow My Tears, the Policeman Said* is its ending. In this world—a dystopia based on Nixon-era America—students are persecuted, the "nats" and the "pols" run identification checks in the streets, a quota is taken off daily to slave camps, civil liberties have vanished. Through the world wanders Jason Taverner, in the first chapter a rich and fantastically successful entertainer, who finds himself suddenly (in dream? psychosis? alternate reality?) in a place where everything is familiar, but no one knows him. His hunter is Police General Felix Buckman, as it were the arch-bogey of the liberal conscience, the policy-maker for the police-state. Yet at the end, with his sister dead and Taverner arrested, Buckman, weeping, finds himself at an all-night garage. He climbs out of his "quibble" and goes over to hug a lonely black—one of the very few black people in this world to have got through the sterilization programs. The moral is totally unexpected, as a reaction to incidents such as the Kent State University shootings. It is that even policemen can love. Even men systematically evil can abandon the system. The ending of this novel comes over as an extraordinarily generous gesture from an embittered man. As with the very strongly anti-drug stance of *A Scanner Darkly*, this scene shows that Dick, for all of his liberalism, is not prepared to accept the complete "anti-Establishment" package.

Nevertheless, from this point his works grow weirder, and more connected. Some of his later novels, such as the posthumously issued *Radio Free Albemuth*, were either not submitted or not accepted for publication. This group also includes the best of Dick's non-science-fiction novels, *Humpty Dumpty in Oakland*, a book most easily described as a sequel to John Steinbeck's *The Grapes of Wrath* (1939), recounting what happened after the "Okies" got to California: They settled down, lost their way, ran used-car lots, became "humpty dumpties," passive spectators of the American Dream. The central idea of the last set of Dick's science-fiction novels, however, is a form of Gnosticism, the ancient Christian heresy which insists that the world contains two forces, of good and evil, in eternal conflict, with only a remote or absent God trying occasionally to get through. Dick writes variations on this theme in *Valis, The Divine Invasion, The Transmigration of Timothy Archer*, and *Radio Free Albemuth*, mentioned above.

Valis, at least, makes a direct assault on the reader by including the character "Horselover Fat," a transparent translation of Philip K. Dick. He hears voices, very like the characters from Berkeley in *Radio Free Albemuth*, who believe they are being contacted by a sort of divine transmission satellite. What the voices say are variations on the view that the world is ruled by a Black Iron Empire, by secret fraternities in Rome or the United States; that the President of the United States, Ferris F. Fremont, has "the number of the beast" in his name; that true believers are exiles from another world. Is this mere madness? Horselover Fat remarks himself that the simplest explanation is that the drugs he took in the 1970's have addled his mind in the 1980's. Still, he has to believe his voices. One might say that Dick's corrosive skepticism has finally developed a blind spot; or alternatively, that the novelist has become a sadder and a wiser man. Whatever the decision, Dick's last novels could be characterized not as science fiction, but as theological fiction.

Dick's work as a whole shows clear evidence of his deep social concerns, reacting against Senator McCarthy and President Nixon, first praising and then condemning drugs, testing one notion after another concerning the limits of government. Yet it also remained solidly consistent in its private and personal quest for a definition of reality which will stand any trial. It could be said that Dick's work is obsessive, introspective, even paranoid. It has also to be said that it very rarely loses gentleness, kindness, even a rather wistful humor. Dick has certainly contributed more first-class novels to science fiction than anyone else in the field, and has convinced many also of the genre's ability to cope with serious reflections on the nature of humanity, and of perception.

Other major works

SHORT FICTION: *A Handful of Darkness*, 1955; *The Variable Man and Other Stories*, 1957; *The Preserving Machine and Other Stories*, 1969; *The Book of Philip K. Dick*, 1973; *The Best of Philip K. Dick*, 1977; *I Hope I Shall Arrive Soon*, 1985.

Bibliography

Foundation. XXVI (October, 1982). Special Dick issue.
Gillespie, Bruce, ed. *Philip K. Dick: Electric Shepherd*, 1975.
Greenberg, Martin H., and Joseph D. Olander, eds. *Philip K. Dick*, 1981.
Science Fiction Studies. II, pt. 1 (March, 1975). Special Dick issue.
Taylor, Angus. *Philip K. Dick and the Umbrella of Light*, 1975.

T. A. Shippey

SHUSAKU ENDŌ

Born: Tokyo, Japan; March 27, 1923

Principal long fiction

Shiroi hito, 1954; *Kiiroi hito*, 1955; *Umi to dokuyaku*, 1957 (*The Sea and the Poison*, 1972); *Kazan*, 1959 (*Volcano*, 1978); *Obaka san*, 1959 (*Wonderful Fool*, 1974); *Chimmoku*, 1966 (*Silence*, 1969); *Kuchibue o fuku toki*, 1974 (*When I Whistle*, 1979); *Samuri*, 1980 (*The Samurai*, 1982).

Other literary forms

In Japan, Shusaku Endō is known as a versatile, prolific author of novels, short stories, plays, and essays on history and theology. Only three works in these other genres, however, have been translated into English. *Ogon no kuni* (1966; *The Golden Country*, 1970), a three-act play, dramatizes basically the same historical events as those portrayed in *Silence*, and was first performed in Japan shortly after the publication of the novel. Endō's best-known work in the West besides his novel *Silence* is probably his *Iesu no shōgai* (1973; *A Life of Jesus*, 1973), an interpretive biography that attempts to reintroduce the person of Christ to skeptical Oriental readers; it was joined in 1977 by the companion work *Kirisuto no tanjō* (the genesis of Christ), which won the Yomiuri Literary Prize. *Stained-Glass Elegies* (1984) collects eleven elegantly crafted Endō short stories drawn and translated from two of his earlier Japanese anthologies.

Achievements

Endō's fiction has won for him numerous awards in Japan, including the prestigious Akutagawa Prize, the Mainchici Cultural Prize, the Shincho Prize, and the Noma Prize. In 1981, he was elected to the Japan Arts Academy. He is widely regarded as Japan's most important working novelist and has been hailed by Western writers such as Graham Greene, John Updike, and Irving Howe as perhaps the most significant religious novelist currently writing in any language. That Endō has achieved this recognition writing as a believing Christian in a non-Christian culture generally resistant to Western religious philosophy is all the more remarkable.

Of all postwar Japanese novelists, Endō's work is the most accessible to the West. This is partly because he has explicitly made it his mission to explore and explain the chasm between the two cultures, especially the spiritual abyss that separates them, a theme he has pursued since his first published essay, "The Gods and God," in 1947. Endō's oeuvre is thus unique in the history of modern Japanese literature, illuminating the struggle of Christianity to survive and thrive in the Orient, while providing Western readers with new perspectives for examining their own religious heritage and commitment.

Biography

Shusaku Endō was born on March 27, 1923, in Tokyo, Japan, but spent his early years in Dalian, Manchuria. After divorcing his father, Endō's mother took her two sons back to Tokyo and, with her sister, converted to Catholicism. This religious conversion was the single most important event in Endō's life, since he and his brother soon followed her in accepting the Catholic faith. Though he little understood at the time what a momentous decision he was making, and though he wrestled in his later youth with doubts about his own commitment to Christianity, the adult Endō eventually embraced fully this Western faith. He has become one of Japan's most important and best-known novelists.

After he was graduated from the equivalent of Japanese high school, Endō enrolled at Keio University at the age of sixteen, studying Catholic philosophy. Unable to serve in the war because of his poor health, he continued his education there in French literature, taking his B.A. in 1949. Eventually, Endō became one of the first Japanese to study in Europe after the war, attending the University of Lyons in France from 1950 to 1953, studying French Catholic writers Jacques Maritain, Georges Bernanos, and François Mauriac. His submersion in European culture intensified his appreciation for the impact of Christianity on the West and forced him to recognize the spiritual vacuum in Japan, which made belief in a transcendent deity difficult, if not impossible.

Chronic heart and lung problems prevented Endō from extending his stay in Europe, and he returned home to begin an ambitious career as a novelist and critic. Between 1953 and 1959, he wrote fiction that chronicled the religious indifference of the East and the widening disaffection between Eastern and Western cultures. From 1960 to 1963, Endō underwent a series of major surgical procedures, resulting in the removal of one lung. During his long convalescence in the hospital, Endō renewed his literary craft, developing new themes that explored the possibility of developing a stronger, more indigenous version of Christianity in his native land.

Directly after this period, Endō's reputation and popularity began to grow both within Japan and internationally as he pursued the most important fiction of his career. Translations of his work have appeared in more than ten languages. At home in Japan, Endō is known not only as a writer of serious fiction and nonfiction but also as a television personality, humorist, and uniquely gifted public figure whose opinions and viewpoints are sought and respected by both the cultural elite and the Japanese population at large.

Analysis

Shusaku Endō has been called a "Japanese Graham Greene" by several enthusiastic Western critics. For a writer to be so compared with a successful, highly visible novelist such as Greene is frequently a heavy burden. Whatever the actual merits of a writer so described, a reader too often reminded of his resemblances to another writer will be tempted to dismiss the writer's work as either inferior to his presumed counterpart or merely derivative. In introducing a Japanese writer to a Western audience, however, such comparisons can be useful, even indispensable—and, in this case, entirely apropos. Endō is one of the few Catholic novelists in the East, and his compelling though sinful and often stumbling characters captivate and endear themselves to the reader in the same way that Greene's faltering saints do.

Still, a more pertinent comparison could be drawn between Endō and the American Catholic novelist Walker Percy. Percy's seriocomic exploration of the disintegration of authentic Christianity in the jaded West and his attempts to redeem it novelistically from its secular trappings resemble Endō's own agenda in addressing both his Oriental and his Occidental readers. Like Percy himself, Endō sees his task as taking Jesus out of the realm of commonplaces in his native culture, disarming his Japanese readers and getting past their syncretizing defenses. His key themes are nearly always intertwined with an evocation of Japan as a "mudswamp," that is, a land pervaded by moral apathy and a desperate need to find an ethical center rooted in eternal values—something which, in Endō's view, only Christianity can ultimately provide.

Endō's Christianity emanates from a childhood conversion to Catholicism, a Catholicism tempered by an education in France, where he was exposed to such French Catholic writers as François Mauriac, Paul Claudel, and Georges Bernanos. Endō recognizes that as a Japanese Christian he is a walking oxymoron, an anomaly in his native culture. His own faith, he candidly admits in *Silence*, has been a struggle against tradition and cultural identity:

> For a long time I was attracted to a meaningless nihilism and when I finally came to realize the fearfulness of such a void I was struck once again with the grandeur of the Catholic Faith. This problem of the reconciliation of my Catholicism with my Japanese blood . . . has taught me one thing: that is, that the Japanese must absorb Christianity without the support of a Christian tradition or history or legacy or sensibility.

When Endō looks at his nation through the eyes of a believing Christian, he sees a "swamp" which "sucks up all sorts of ideologies, transforming them into itself and distorting them in the process." As a Christian novelist whose readers have no "objective correlatives" for the concepts he wishes his fiction to incarnate, Endō sees his personal task as a novelist much differently from his contemporaries in Japan. Rather than mirroring the moral and social malaise about him, Endō seeks to foster and exemplify such religious concepts as sin, redemption, and resurrection.

Like most works in translation, Endō's novels have been brought into English not in the order in which they appeared in his native country but in the order of the prestige and interest they have engendered in the West. It is possible, then, to get a somewhat distorted view of Endō's concerns and craft if one considers his work only in terms of what is available in English translation. In fact, Endō's long fiction shows clear signs of development and maturation over time, and can be best and most conveniently discussed and analyzed within two main periods.

The first period covers 1953-1959, the years immediately following his return to Japan from France and during which Endō wrote the short work *Aden made* (1954; till Aden) and five novels. Each dramatizes, in Endō's words, the Japanese "numbness to sin and guilt," by juxtaposing it to the conventional Christianized conscience of postwar Europe. Endō's earliest novels, untranslated into English, bear the marks of a genuinely talented writer who is still seeking the most appropriate voice and characterization to express his thematic vision. The early short piece *Aden made* and the novels *Shiroi hito* (white men), and *Kiiroi hito* (yellow men) deal graphically with the spiritual contrasts between East and West in the postwar period but with thin characterization and heavy sentimentality.

Endō's first two important novels, *The Sea and the Poison* and *Volcano*, emerged as flawed but stirring problem works that scathingly indict the Japanese conscience for its insensitivity to the basic humanitarian impulse Endō saw in Western Christian nations. Set six months before the bombing of Hiroshima and Nagasaki, *The Sea and the Poison* stands out as particularly stirring and harrowing thematically in its exploration of the inhumane operations performed on captured American pilots during World War II and their impact on two young interns. *Volcano* is the first Endō novel that features fully drawn, credible characters, examining the complex relationship between a defrocked French priest and a Japanese volcanologist as they grapple with the natural and supernatural at the foot of a newly active volcano.

At the end of this period, Endō published what may be his most characteristic and ultimately most enduring novel for Western readers, *Wonderful Fool*. Because *Wonderful Fool* is a transitional work that demonstrates Endō's versatility as a novelist with a penchant for combining humor and pathos in his pursuit of a serious theme, and that bridges the gap between Endō's two periods, it warrants special attention. In it, Endō's comic narrative style merges with a mature grasp of characterization to balance his central themes. *Wonderful Fool* features as protagonist the bumbling Gaston "Gas" Bonaparte, a "fool for Christ's sake" whose selflessness and genuine love for his fellowmen reflect the Christlike attributes which Endō wants his reader to recognize. Gaston is a "fool" in a Shakespearean sense, one who may unexpectedly speak as well as live the truth in a most poignant way.

Set twelve years after the end of World War II, *Wonderful Fool* tells the story of Gaston Bonaparte, a bona fide descendant of Napoleon himself, who arrives in Japan on a third-rate steamer, surprising his sometime pen

pal, Takamori, a clerk, and his sister, Tomoe. After their first meeting, neither Takamori nor Tomoe could have suspected that Gas, as they come to
call him, was a failed French seminary student who has launched out on his
own to spread the news of faith and love to the long-neglected Orient. Upon
first acquaintance, Gas seems to be a bumbling, clumsy oaf, well-intentioned
but utterly ineffectual. In an early encounter, the gangly, uncoordinated Frenchman scandalizes his hosts Takamori and Tomoe by brandishing a Japanese
loincloth in the place of table napkin. Later, he mistakes the advances of a
prostitute for the simple congeniality of Japanese people.

Gas is clearly a stranger in a strange land, a wayfarer whose language and
whose thought processes set him apart from everyone. Eventually Gas leaves
behind the warmth and comfort of Takamori's home to set out on his own
pilgrimage, accompanied only by the mongrel dog that has taken up with
him. As Gas moves through the squalor of Tokyo's underworld, he steadily
gropes toward his own destiny, toward his own Gethsemane and later his
own Golgotha.

The key relationship in the novel, however, occurs between Gas and the
gangster Endō. Kidnaped by Endō, Gas repeatedly manifests the innocence
and love that is uncommon in the streets of Tokyo, endearing himself to the
hardened and morally drained underworld figure. Compelled by Endō to
assist him in getting revenge against another criminal, Gas thwarts him twice
and eventually dies in saving both men from killing each other. His climactic
and heroic acts on behalf of two criminals beyond redemption earn for him
the reverence from Takamori and Tomoe which his tenderness and tolerance
so clearly warrant. In a final scene, Gaston, apparently drowned in his mission of mercy, is remembered as a "lone egret, flapping snow-white wings," a
traditional Japanese figure of peace and transfiguration.

Wonderful Fool is thus a parable about faith, the inevitable fate of a trusting soul who determinedly opens his life and his heart to all he encounters.
His naïveté leads him to offend every significant social norm of Japanese
society, and even most patterns of everyday common sense. The final scenes
of the novel powerfully capture Endō's vision of contemporary Japan: a
mudswamp in which a wise fool battles with all of his strength to redeem two
hoodlums who want neither redemption nor life, but whom he redeems all
the same.

The second period in Endō's development as a novelist comprises his work
after 1963 and includes his most celebrated works, exemplified in *Silence*,
When I Whistle, and *The Samurai*. *Silence* and *The Samurai* are historical
novels which focus attention intently on Japan's often ferocious rejection of
Christianity in the seventeenth century and mirror its ambivalence in the
present and should be examined together.

Because few of his lighter, more comic novels and his numerous historical
and theological essays—works no less interesting and provoking than his

other works—have yet to be translated for Western readers, it is possible to form a view of Endō as a rather somber, overly moralistic writer. Certainly, if one knew only Endō's interpretive biography, *A Life of Jesus*, and his historical novels, *Silence* and *The Samurai*, one would gain a distorted picture of both his range of concerns and his innovation as a writer. Nevertheless, *Silence* and *The Samurai* are rightly regarded as two of Endō's major works, and clearly they have drawn the most critical attention and applause in the West. They detail the dismal record of Christianity in Japan, bitterly chronicling both the shallow ambitions of the missionaries who dared to invade the Japanese shores in the seventeenth century and the moral malaise of the Japanese themselves, who first welcomed the visitors and then condemned them to brutal martyrdom.

Silence is a dark, epistolary novel of apostasy and betrayal, a narrative as told from the perspective of a Portuguese missionary priest. It is a tale of faith and faithlessness among both Western and Eastern men, men whose integrity as believers and as human beings is under constant attack. At the beginning of the seventeenth century, the Edo emperors came to the conclusion that Christianity did not "fit" Japan, banishing Christian missionaries and persecuting their flocks of converts. In *Silence*, Endō turns that conclusion on its head, establishing that Christianity and Christ fit *nowhere*, yet everywhere, inasmuch as they dramatize and respond to man's homelessness in the world, his loneliness, his forlorn hope of finding compensation for the pain of life in eternity, if at all.

In *The Samurai*, written nearly fifteen years after *Silence*, Endō again picks up its theme of martyrdom and betrayal. As a novel, it reminds many readers of Grahame Greene's *The Power and the Glory* (1940) and its heroic whiskey priest. *The Samurai* focuses on the enduring faith of a humble, despised servant, Rokuemon Hasekura, a warrior in the service of a powerful feudal lord in seventeenth century Japan, and his cohorts, who escort Father Velasco, an overly ambitious Franciscan missionary, from Japan to Mexico to Rome in his attempt to secure Japanese trading privileges with the West. Velasco's aim is to use his diplomacy to become bishop of Japan. Hasekura is a reluctant envoy who first despises the emaciated man on the cross who serves as the symbol of this baffling faith Velasco represents, and later embraces him as the only light in a civilization growing darker day by day. *The Samurai* takes the reader on the ill-fated diplomatic journey of Velasco and Hasekura, during which both men, stripped of their illusions about self and motive, embrace a common faith. The two men return to Japan as fools for Christ's sake, true believers without pretense or pride, facing an inevitable martyrdom.

Between these two historical novels, Endō wrote *When I Whistle*, a study of contemporary Japan and the relationship between two generations, which focuses on a father and son. Here Endō reveals another aspect of his talent, the ability to write with realism and subtlety, avoiding sentimentality while evoking the antiseptic, forbidding images of hospitals and technology gone mad. Effectively using flashbacks from prewar and postwar Japan, Endō ironically juxtaposes the "new" Japan to the old and finds modern Japan, presumably more open to the West, in its own way even less congenial to Christian values and to simple human kindness. Ozu, the protagonist, is a humble clerk; his ignorance and general nostalgia for the older Japan are in vivid contrast to the preoccupations of his more successful and sophisticated son, Eiichi.

Eiichi is an opportunistic doctor willing to do anything to rise within his profession. His Japan is that of the grim Japanese novelist Yukio Mishima: minimalistic, technological, spiritually barren. Ozu longs for the Japan just after Pearl Harbor in which "at last the time for a confrontation between the spiritual civilization of Japan and the material civilization of a foreign country has come!" Father and son are united at the hospital bed of Ozu's old flame from grammar school days, Aiko, who is dying of cancer. For Eiichi and the other young doctors, Aiko is not a person deserving of care, attention, and love but a convenient depository for experimental cancer treatments. Ozu parts from his old love and his son in muffled despair, confronting a predatory Japan conquering no longer with bayonets or aircraft but with sheer economic and technological prowess, devoid of a spiritual center.

Endō's early works, such as *Volcano* and *The Sea and the Poison*, cleared his vision and provided the foundation for transitional works such as *Wonderful Fool* and later, more mature works such as *Silence* and *When I Whistle*. The backdrop for each of these novels and, indeed, all of Endō's works is the congenital failure of Japanese culture to nurture a transcendent faith and to recognize its eternal relevance for its people. In them Endō attempts to craft an authentically Eastern vision of Christian faith obstinate enough to endure even in soils which have never been fertile for its growth.

The Christian vision of Shusaku Endō thus has at its center a dramatically Eastern Jesus, the humble but single-minded "fool" who abandons all to reach those who are not so much hostile as they are indifferent, not so much faithless as they are cynical. This "foolish" Jesus—distinguished from the often bombastic and authoritarian Jesus imported from the West—drives his readers beyond the shallow, impotent Christianity lurking behind much modern faith. To reach them, Endō is challenged to defamiliarize Christ in his conventionally distant and supernaturally holy character, portraying him instead as a profoundly self-sacrificing, tender, and moral human being—an elder brother, not an omnipotent Lord.

Saint Cyril of Jerusalem, Endō's ancient brother in the Catholic faith, once wrote, "The dragon sits by the side of the road, watching those who pass. Beware lest he devour you. We go to the Father of Souls, but it is necessary to pass by the dragon." In commenting on this passage, the American Catholic writer Flannery O'Connor once remarked, "No matter what form the dragon may take, it is of this mysterious passage past him, or into his jaws, that stories of any depth will be concerned to tell, and this being the case, it requires considerable courage at any time, in any country, not to turn away from the storyteller." Shusaku Endō refuses to turn away from the dragon or the storyteller, and asks of his twentieth century audience—East or West— the same courage.

Other major works

SHORT FICTION: *Aden made*, 1954; *Aika*, 1965; *Stained-Glass Elegies*, 1984.
PLAY: *Ogon no kuni*, 1966 (*The Golden Country*, 1970).
NONFICTION: *Iesu no shōgai*, 1973 (*A Life of Jesus*, 1973); *Tetsu no kubikase*, 1976; *Kirisuto no tanjō*, 1977; *Jū to jūjika*, 1979.

Bibliography

Gallagher, Michael. "Shusaku Endō: Japanese Catholic Intellectual," in *The Critic*. XXXVI (Summer, 1979), pp. 58-63.
Mathy, Francis. "Shusaku Endō: Japanese Catholic Novelist," in *Thought*. XLII (Winter, 1967), pp. 585-614.
Ribeiro, Jorge. "Shusaku Endō: Japanese Catholic Novelist," in *America*. CLII (February 2, 1985), pp. 87-89.
Rimer, J. Thomas. *Modern Japanese Fiction and Its Traditions*, 1978.
Updike, John. "From Fumie to Sony," in *The New Yorker*. LV (January 14, 1980), pp. 94-102.

Bruce L. Edwards, Jr.

J. G. FARRELL

Born: Liverpool, England; January 23, 1935
Died: Bantry Bay, Ireland; August 22, 1979

Principal long fiction
A Man from Elsewhere, 1963; *The Lung*, 1965; *A Girl in the Head*, 1967; *Troubles*, 1970; *The Siege of Krishnapur*, 1973; *The Singapore Grip*, 1978; *The Hill Station: An Unfinished Novel*, 1981.

Other literary forms
J. G. Farrell's perceptive and entertaining account of his 1971 visit to India, posthumously titled "Indian Diary," is appended to *The Hill Station*, an unfinished novel published after Farrell's death. He is known primarily for his novels.

Achievements
In the main, Farrell's early efforts—*A Man From Elsewhere*, *The Lung*, and *A Girl in the Head*—fail to display the power, intricacy, and inventiveness that characterize his fourth book, *Troubles*, and the rest of his completed fiction. Set in rural Ireland between the years 1919 and 1921—a period of bloody civil war—*Troubles* earned for Farrell the Geoffrey Faber Memorial Prize and signaled his interest in producing carefully documented and closely detailed historical fiction. Farrell's fifth novel, *The Siege of Krishnapur*, takes place in India in 1857, when protest of the British presence in that country suddenly grew violent and widespread. *The Siege of Krishnapur* was awarded Britain's prestigious Booker Prize and convinced many critics that Farrell, not yet forty, was fast on his way to a spectacular career. Set during the 1930's in what was then British Malaya, Farrell's sixth book, *The Singapore Grip*, was generally less enthusiastically received than *The Siege of Krishnapur*. Tragically, Farrell's life was cut short when, in 1979, he drowned in waters off Ireland's southern coast. Still, on the basis of his later work, Farrell must be considered a highly original talent and can be ranked among the finest historical novelists of his generation.

Biography
Though born in Liverpool, James Gordon Farrell had strong family ties to Ireland, which he visited regularly as a child and adolescent. After completing his public-school training at Rossall, in Lancashire, Farrell worked briefly as a fire fighter along a NATO defense line in the Canadian Arctic. In 1956, during his first term at Oxford, Farrell contracted polio, which left his chest and shoulder muscles permanently weakened. After taking his degree in 1960, Farrell taught in France and traveled to both Africa and the United

States but spent the bulk of the following decade living in London, where he formed friendships with many fellow writers and developed the highly disciplined work habits that enabled him to produce a series of increasingly lengthy and complex novels.

In the early 1970's, in the wake of the considerable critical and financial success of *The Siege of Krishnapur*, Farrell traveled throughout Asia, where he conducted extensive research for *The Singapore Grip*. In April, 1979, Farrell moved into an old farmhouse on the Sheep's Head Peninsula of Bantry Bay in Ireland's County Cork. Here, while fishing close to his house, Farrell fell from a rock and—according to witnesses—was quickly swept out to sea.

Analysis

J. G. Farrell was essentially a realist, whose most accomplished works draw upon extensive historical research and are both carefully crafted and meticulously detailed. In each of his historical novels, Farrell focuses on various outposts of British colonialism that are under attack and, by implication, in decline. Often, these works bluntly ridicule the cultural codes and biases that made the British empire possible; indeed, they tend to ridicule narrow-mindedness of any kind and suggest, implicitly, that no religion or ideology can convincingly account for the existence of man. Much of Farrell's fiction focuses on the seeming randomness of human life, on the least attractive attributes—particularly on the brutality and the greed—that are part of human nature. Its tone, moreover, is frequently sardonic and aloof—but by no means misanthropic. Instead, as Farrell's friend and fellow novelist Margaret Drabble has observed, "Farrell combined a sense of the pointless absurdity of man with a real and increasing compassion for characters caught up in decay and confusion."

Farrell's first book, *A Man from Elsewhere*, is set in France and focuses largely on a journalist named Sayer, who seeks to expose a former Communist alleged to have dealt too intimately with the Nazis during World War II. In his second novel, *The Lung*, Farrell's principal figure is Martin Sands, a young man confined to an iron lung and in love with Marigold, his stepdaughter and nurse. *A Girl in the Head*, Farrell's third novel, depicts the romantic difficulties of Boris Slattery, a Polish count living in the English resort town of Maidenhair. These novels are certainly not without merit: They contain some fine tragicomic moments, and they feature characters such as Slattery who, in some scenes, come convincingly alive. Farrell's early novels, however, are ponderously paced; they tend to reveal the self-consciousness of a beginning writer who is trying hard to be original and clever but failing to conceal his debt to other authors. In *A Girl in the Head*, for example, it is not difficult to detect the presence of Iris Murdoch, whose celebrated first novel, *Under the Net* (1954), similarly and more successfully combines a disaffected young hero and a supporting cast of eccentrics with serious philosophical themes and, throughout, a charmingly whimsical tone.

The far better *Troubles* is set in the Irish coastal town of Kilnalough and covers the years between 1919 and 1921—a period in which militant Irish nationalists were beginning to employ violence more frequently as a means of freeing their country from British control. The book's central figure, Major Brendan Archer, is a veteran of World War I who comes to Kilnalough's huge Majestic Hotel, where his fiancée, Angela Spenser, resides with her father, Edward, a jingoistic, increasingly unbalanced man who owns the hotel and must work hard to keep it running. The Majestic is—like the British Empire itself—an aging, sprawling structure in a slow but certain state of decay. The Majestic is dusty, gloomy, and filled with odd, elderly guests; in its lobby, one hears the constant ticking of an ancient pendulum clock.

Unlike the protagonists in Farrell's earlier novels, the Major is neither intellectually nor artistically inclined. He is, in fact, a rather bland figure who enjoys reading serialized adventure stories and who has without reflection absorbed most of the prejudices of his nation and his class. Though not a religious man, he regards with particular prejudice and suspicion the tenets and practices of Roman Catholicism. He also takes for granted the notion that Irish Catholics are still simply too irrational and unruly to be trusted with the task of governing themselves. The Irish Republican movement, he unthinkingly assumes, "was merely an excuse for trouble-makers moved more by self-interest than patriotism." Still, Archer is so well-rounded that he cannot be dismissed as a mere bigot and an utterly unsympathetic character. The Major, Farrell makes clear, has been keenly disappointed both in life and in love; as a veteran of trench warfare, he has been on close terms with hunger, fear, and death. Early in *Troubles*, the Major—fresh from war—is shown attending a tea party and causing some discomfort among his fellow guests because of the intensity with which he studies their heads, arms, and legs: "He was thinking: 'How firm and solid they look, but how easily they come away from the body!' And the tea in his cup tasted like bile."

Troubles does contain many comical characterizations and scenes, including a failed sexual interlude which features a pair of fumbling young men and a set of naïvely flirtatious twins and which balances with a stunning deftness the pathetic and the ribald. Most of *Troubles*, however, focuses bluntly on the brevity of life, on the sobering reality of change and decay. The Majestic, for example, literally crumbles bit by bit throughout the novel: It becomes overrun with weeds and rats and—at the novel's close—burns to the ground after being shelled by Irish rebels. Images of skulls and skeletons abound; the silent, mysterious Angela quietly suffers from leukemia and suddenly dies. Meanwhile, not far from the hotel—and, Farrell keeps noting, throughout much of the rest of the world—men continue to slaughter men with brutal gusto. Indeed, by alluding frequently to newspaper accounts of the world's never-ending wars and riots, Farrell not only lends an element of authenticity to his work but also underlines the point that, unfortunately, bloody "troubles" fester wherever men gather; because human beings are territorial and animalistic, they will invariably fail in their attempts to construct a serene and civilized world.

The theme of human brutality is even stronger in *The Siege of Krishnapur*. This work shows the effect of the Sepoy Rebellion of 1857 on some of the English men and women who were then helping rule India in the name of the British-owned East India Company. The novel's principal character, Mr. Hopkins—"the Collector," or chief administrator, at the British outpost at Krishnapur—is a sober, optimistic man who early in the work proclaims his belief that the perfection of mankind will surely be achieved through "Faith, Science, Respectability, Geology, Mechanical Invention, Ventilation, and the Rotation of Crops." Another principal character is George Fleury, a young, melancholic, rather overly sensitive Englishman who is fond of Romantic poetry and no longer certain of the tenets of orthodox Christianity. Fleury—a recognizable Victorian "type," like all the principal characters in *The Siege of Krishnapur*—must then suffer the fulsome proselytism of the Reverend Mr. Hampton, a boorish Anglican clergyman identified throughout the novel as "the Padre."

The early chapters of *The Siege of Krishnapur* portray well-settled British in a world of poetry readings and cricket matches, of elegant meals served by obsequious native servants who, in some cases, must bear with a smile the insulting nicknames that their masters have bestowed upon them. As the remainder of the novel reveals, however, that cozy, very Victorian world is utterly shattered when mutinous Indian soldiers—or "sepoys"—begin an attack on the British compound at Krishnapur that drags on for months and that results not only in countless Indian and English casualties but also—for the English—severe shortages of ammunition and food. Eventually, the survivors find themselves filthy, disease-ridden, rag-clad, and so famished that they willingly devour their horses and prey upon bugs. In the end, they are saved by British reinforcements, but by then, as one of their rescuers observes, they look less like gentlemen and gentlewomen than the pathetic untouchables whom they once automatically scorned.

The Siege of Krishnapur is full of extremely well-paced, graphically described battle scenes. Like *Troubles*, and like Alfred, Lord Tennyson's *In Memoriam* (1850)—perhaps the greatest and most representative poetical work of the Victorian era—*The Siege of Krishnapur* also frequently addresses the most basic of philosophical questions: Does God exist? What is the true nature of man? Is there a divine plan that can account for the ruthlessness of nature and the universality of human pain? In several amusingly constructed scenes, Farrell portrays the Padre arguing at length in favor of the existence of a Supreme Intelligence and offering as proof dozens of such ingeniously practical phenomena as the eel's eyes, the boar's tusks, and the bee's proboscis. Like *Troubles*, however, *The Siege of Krishnapur* focuses principally on a world of nature that is, in Tennyson's famous phrase, "red in tooth and claw"; it conveys strongly the impression that the god or gods who designed the world now seem quite uninterested in its day-to-day operation. It suggests that the margin between civilization and barbarism is frighteningly narrow, and that, moreover, the codes and biases by which men and women order their lives are not only arbitrary but also often bizarre. Indeed, at the conclusion of *The Siege of Krishnapur*, the Collector, older and more cynical and back in England, asserts bluntly that "culture is a sham. It's a cosmetic painted on life by rich people to conceal its ugliness."

The Singapore Grip, Farrell's final completed novel, is a particularly lengthy work that, some critics have suggested, occasionally bogs down under the weight of too many characters and documentary details. Set entirely in Singapore, *The Singapore Grip* focuses principally on the years just prior to December, 1941, when all of British Malaya was rapidly overrun by the Japanese. Its principal characters are related to a large British rubber company run by Walter Blackett, who takes for granted the invincibility of British power in the Pacific and so—like other Britons portrayed in the book—fails to comprehend the seriousness of the Japanese threat. Blackett, who is described as having hairy "bristles" that run up and down his back, is probably too much the stereotypical big-business tycoon: He is aggressive, envious, calculating. Far more appealing is Brendan Archer, who is retired from the military but who, as in *Troubles*, retains the title "the Major." Some of the most poignant scenes in *The Singapore Grip* show Archer "fixed in his habits, apparently suspended in his celibacy like a chicken in aspic" and living out his remaining days in modest quarters in Singapore, surrounded by old, bleary-eyed dogs he no longer likes, but—out of a continuing sense of obligation—continues to board.

The Singapore Grip makes clear that Farrell likes the Major not only for his pluck and respect for duty but also for the many quirks he has accumulated over the years. Indeed, as in *Troubles* and *The Siege of Krishnapur*, Farrell in *The Singapore Grip* reveals a continuing fondness for harmless eccentrics—and underdogs—of all sorts. By focusing extensively on Blackett and his operations, however, Farrell also makes obvious his continuing disdain for cultural chauvinism and the blundering pursuit of profit at any cost. By filling *The Singapore Grip* with vivid, unsettling scenes of war, Farrell also once again indicates his belief that the study of human history is essentially the study of brutality and folly, that only by self-deception can one insist on the universality of human goodness and the inevitability of a saner, more harmonious world.

Bibliography
Bergonzi, Bernard. "Fictions of History," in *The Contemporary English*

Novel, 1980. Edited by Malcolm Bradbury and David Palmer.

Drabble, Margaret. "Things Fall Apart," in *The Hill Station: An Unfinished Novel*, 1981. Edited by John Spurling.

Spurling, John. "As Does the Bishop," in *The Hill Station: An Unfinished Novel*, 1981. Edited by John Spurling.

Stevenson, Randall. *The British Novel Since the Thirties*, 1986.

Brian Murray

GABRIEL FIELDING
Alan Gabriel Barnsley

Born: Hexham, England; March 25, 1916
Died: Bellevue, Washington; November 27, 1986

Principal long fiction
Brotherly Love, 1954; *In the Time of Greenbloom*, 1957; *Eight Days*, 1958; *Through Streets Broad and Narrow*, 1960; *The Birthday King*, 1962; *Gentlemen in Their Season*, 1966; *Pretty Doll Houses*, 1979; *The Women of Guinea Lane*, 1986.

Other literary forms
Gabriel Fielding's literary reputation rests primarily on his prose, but his early work was in poetry, published in two collections, *The Frog Prince and Other Poems* (1952) and *XXVIII Poems* (1955), neither of which matches his prose in quality or critical acclaim. He also published two books of short stories—*Collected Short Stories* (1971) and *New Queens for Old: A Novella and Nine Stories* (1972)—which are substantial enough in literary quality and theme to form a significant part of Fielding's canon.

Achievements
By 1963 Fielding had established the reputation which was maintained, but never enhanced, by his later work. Some critics view Fielding as a Catholic writer, comparable with Graham Greene, Evelyn Waugh, and Muriel Spark, concerned with social and moral issues from a specifically Catholic point of view; this aspect of his work was duly recognized in his being awarded the St. Thomas Moore Association Gold Medal in 1963 and the National Catholic Book Award in 1964. Other critics, however, see him as a writer belonging to the school of European existentialist writers, sharing their philosophic worldview; this second estimate was expressed in the W. H. Smith Literary Award, which Fielding received in 1963.

Biography
Alan Gabriel Barnsley was born in Hexham, Northumberland, Great Britain, on March 25, 1916, the fifth of six children of an Anglican vicar. After going to school at St. Edward's, Oxford, he took a B.A. at Trinity College, Dublin, and from there went to St. George's Hospital, London, from which he was graduated with a medical degree in 1941. He immediately started his war service in the Royal Army Medical Corps, continuing his service until demobilization in 1946. After the war, he was in general medical practice in Maidstone, Kent, until 1966, part of his duties being those of Medical Officer for Maidstone Prison, the experience of which contributed significantly to

several of his novels. He did not start writing seriously until his middle thirties, and in 1966, when he considered his literary career to be established, he left the medical profession to become, first, Author in Residence and then Professor of English at Washington State University, Pullman, a position which he held until retirement. Fielding died in Bellevue, Washington, on November 27, 1986.

Analysis

In the context of British novelists of the twentieth century, Gabriel Fielding presents some characteristics that distinguish his work sharply from that of the mainstream novelist and at the same time place him firmly in a tradition that, in fact, goes back to the realistic social novel of Daniel Defoe. Fielding's distinctiveness lies in a steadiness and explicitness of worldview and ethical philosophy which raise his novels well above mere stories or entertainments; his identification with British literary tradition reveals itself in the spell he casts as a storyteller whose characters, plots, and settings have the dramatic quality of those found in the works of Thomas Hardy and Charles Dickens, striking the reader's mind like reality itself and haunting the memory forever. The result of what is, for a British novelist, an unusual combination of philosophic outlook and intensity of fictional realization is an integrated creativity that expresses the writer's unified sensibility of spirit and mind and that evokes within the reader an intense and often uncomfortable urge to reassess his or her own preoccupations and prejudices, yet whose effect is ultimately cathartic.

Fielding's major novels—*In the Time of Greenbloom*, *The Birthday King*, and *Gentlemen in Their Season*—pursue and explore a theme which is more frequently found in the European novel than the British: that of individual responsibility in an irrational world. Each of the three novels has a different "world" as its setting—a middle-class English county, Nazi Germany, and postwar liberal London—but the dilemmas of decision and action that face the protagonists in each novel are of the same kind. The novels' settings reflect the stages of Fielding's own life: country vicarage and Oxford, wartime military service, and postwar intellectual life in London. In many ways one feels that the novels represent a working-out in fiction of the writer's own perplexities, which were not resolved until his emigration to the United States, to the more primal setting of eastern Washington and the Moscow Mountains, where it is clear that Fielding found a peace and joy of life, and a professional satisfaction, which had eluded him in England.

The autobiographical element of Fielding's work is seen most clearly in the four novels concerning the Blaydon family. The family name itself is a well-known Northumbrian place-name, while the chronicles of John Blaydon— spanning childhood in *Brotherly Love*, adolescence in *In the Time of Greenbloom*, adulthood and medical studies in *Through Streets Broad and Narrow*, and wartime medical service in *The Women of Guinea Lane*—reflect the early progress of Fielding's own life. Of the three Blaydon novels, *In the Time of Greenbloom* is the most striking, in its presentation of a guilt-ridden and domineering adult society bent on finding sin in the young. In the novel, twelve-year-old John Blaydon is wrongly blamed for the death of his friend Victoria Blount, who has been murdered by a hiker in a cave. He is made the scapegoat for an adult crime, and he is ready to acquiesce in the guilt forced on him by the adult world when he is saved by the ministrations of Horab Greenbloom, an eccentric Jewish Oxford undergraduate who applies to John's sense of guilt a bracing dose of Wittgensteinian positivism and Sartrean existentialism. Greenbloom's therapeutic interest is that of one scapegoat for another, and his remedy is to make John see that the empty, abstract categories of the adult moral scheme lead ultimately to personal irresponsibility and inevitable pangs of guilt which must be transferred to the innocent and vulnerable for punishment.

The theme of blame, and the accompanying figure of the scapegoat, had initially been explored in *Brotherly Love*, in which John observes and chronicles the moral demolition of his older brother, David, by his domineering mother, who forces him to become a priest, thereby perverting David's natural creative talents into sordid sexual encounters and alcoholism. In this earlier novel, the adult world is only too successful in transferring its empty notions of duty, faith, sin, and shame to the adolescent, but there is no suggestion of an alternative, redemptive way. *In the Time of Greenbloom* offers hope for redemption in the magus figure of Greenbloom through his resolute opposition to spurious objective abstraction and his insistence that John must make his own moral decisions and not accept those offered by his elders. (In this and in several other respects, Fielding anticipates the concerns and solutions offered in Robertson Davies' *The Deptford Trilogy*.)

The theme of guilt, blame, and the scapegoat principle is one that preoccupies Fielding in all of his major novels, but nowhere does it achieve more compelling realization than in *The Birthday King*, which elevates and generalizes John's suffering in a northern English county to the agony of a whole race in wartime Nazi Germany. The novel chronicles the rise and fall of Nazi Germany through the lives of two Jewish brothers, Alfried and Ruprecht Waitzmann, who are directors of a large industrial group and thus somewhat protected from liquidation by the Nazis. The contrasting responses of the two brothers to the dictatorship of Adolf Hitler represent the twin facts of Jewishness and of humans as a whole in reaction to mindless oppression. Alfried, as a rather self-indulgently pious man, innocent yet provocative, opts for the untidiness of life, represented by the dirty, smelly goat in the Kommandant's garden. His rejection of the hygienic bureaucracy and simple slogans of the Nazis causes him to be imprisoned and tortured in an attempted "cure" of his wayward individuality, and he thus becomes the scapegoat, despised by his friends more than by the Nazis (for whom he actually lightens the burden of guilt). Ruprecht, on the other hand, represents the alternative path: survival at any cost. He is an opportunist and a schemer, preserving the family business by betraying Alfried and running his factories on forced labor for the Nazi regime.

The novel explores the consequences of the brothers' different choices—sacrifice and survival—each of which has been made with existential authenticity, both in their different ways morally "right." Alfried's response, with its mystical innocence and awkward honesty, is that of the child who rejects the adult world of organized belief and consequent absurd moral simplifications. Ruprecht's response is just as true to his own shrewd, aggressive, and lucky nature in a world in which he sees Germany as one gigantic concentration camp in which the only possible choice is for survival. The kind of choice each brother makes is less important than the fact that each actually makes a conscious choice freely, rather than choosing to join the bored sleepwalkers: the camp Kommandant, his puritanical wife, and the aristocratic remnants of old Germany, such as von Hoffbach and von Boehling, who applaud the new Wagnerian romanticism of the Third Reich while sneering at the inferior social status of the Nazi party upstarts. For Fielding, the only corrective to the mind-numbing boredom represented by Nazi Germany is the exercise of free will in subjective decision.

Boredom provides the focus of *Gentlemen in Their Season* as well, but Fielding narrows his scope to marriage in the postwar, liberated world. In many ways, this novel is more complex than the earlier and, arguably, better novels in that issues are less clear-cut and the possibility of authentic decision is consequently much reduced. Moreover, the setting and characters, in their familiarity and ordinariness, are uncomfortably close to the reader, who is unable to distance himself from the action as he is in *In the Time of Greenbloom* and *The Birthday King*. The plot of *Gentlemen in Their Season* concerns two middle-aged, middle-class liberal intellectuals, Randall Coles and Bernard Presage, whose marriages, to an assertive humanist and a rather religiose Catholic, respectively, have stagnated to the point of artificiality, which takes the form of clever parties, esoteric intellectualism, mutual criticism, and automatic churchgoing. Each man drifts into a pointless affair, with tragic consequences for a third party, Hotchkiss, whose simple Christian faith in monogamy has already led to his imprisonment for the manslaughter of his wife's lover, who escapes from prison to confront her current lover, Coles, and to force him to practice the morality that he preaches as director of religious programming for the British Broadcasting Corporation (BBC). In impulsive reaction, and horrified at having to make a simple act of faith in front of Hotchkiss, Coles betrays him to the police, who kill him in their attempted arrest.

This novel, probably the blackest, most ironic and comic of all of Fielding's novels, reduces the sleepwalking quality of a whole nation in *The Birthday King* to the level of ordinary, casual, and unthinking behavior of men whose abstract conceptions of what modern marriage should be make them indecisive, vacillating, and morally irresponsible, while they continue to justify their behavior on intellectualized principles remote from the concerns of real life. Hotchkiss, by breaking out of prison and confronting Coles, makes the only authentic decision in the whole course of events, and by consciously being an agent, rather than a victim to whom things lamely happen, he forces action on the part of others and thus, in his self-sacrifice, atones for the sins of his intellectual and social superiors.

The central concern in all of Fielding's major novels is the moral necessity for human action in the fullest sense of deliberate, self-aware decisiveness in a society that is largely content to go along with the crowd, to rationalize behavior in terms of social, political, religious, and intellectual abstractions. The actions that result from such decisiveness may, in fact, lead to the protagonist's becoming the scapegoat for society's somnambulistic and self-justifying atrocities but ultimately awaken the sleepwalkers for a while, dazzling people into self-awareness by their enormity. Although this theme is existential, it is a Catholic existentialism, reconciling the principles most fundamental to Christian faith with the natural, human, subjective conscience, and promoting will as a necessary accompaniment to belief. Adult institutions of class, politics, and church may, and for most do, substitute slogans for principles and apologetics for action, but the blame lies not in the institutions themselves but in society's slavish and easy acquiescence in the precepts which demand least exercise of will.

The starkness of Fielding's theme associates his work most closely with European preoccupations, constantly reminding the reader of figures such as Jean-Paul Sartre, Albert Camus, Hermann Hesse, and Günter Grass. The only British writer who shares these preoccupations is Graham Greene, whose continentalism makes most British critics, who are more comfortable with what might be called the cardigan-and-post-office kind of novel, suspicious of the underlying philosophic concerns of his fiction. The poor critical response in Great Britain to Fielding's work arises, one imagines, from a similar fear of philosophic depth.

Despite the philosophic significance of Fielding's novels, they are works of literature, not of philosophy. What elevates Fielding beyond the level of mere "messenger," didacticist, or programmatic writer is the other face of his work: the elevation of narrative over precept, of imagery and language over naked theme. His novels are by no means mere illustrative allegories of ready-made themes, but explorations in narrative which lead, perhaps to the surprise of the writer, to inevitable philosophic conclusions. It is the power and richness of plot, character, and language, and the concreteness of setting that put Fielding in the grand tradition of the English novel with Dickens, the

Brontës, and Hardy, making his novels compelling and memorable in themselves, not merely as vehicles of Catholic-existentialist thought. The elemental images of purifying water and oppressive earth, the institutional images of the prison, the school, the hospital, and the bureaucratic machinery, together with the evocative associations of proper names ("Badger," "Toad," "Greenbloom," "Hubertus," and "Presage") interweave with one another and with settings rich in symbolism (the cave where Victoria is murdered, the Anglo-Catholic church with its dead image of Christ, the deserted swimming pool where Ruprecht and Carin make love, the camp of forced workers, Alfried's punishment cell, and Hotchkiss' prison cell), creating a text of such richness as to transcend its constituent parts and to enter the reader's consciousness like reality itself. The texture of Fielding's language is that of the best dramatic poetry: Images, allusions, and references, in the vigorous expression of quite ordinary speech, cluster and weave to engender a depth and breadth of experience which triggers unconscious associations supporting the reader's conscious interpretation of plot and character to produce a wholly new, vital, and often disturbing sensibility.

Other major works

SHORT FICTION: *Collected Short Stories*, 1971; *New Queens for Old: A Novella and Nine Stories*, 1972.

POETRY: *The Frog Prince and Other Poems*, 1952; *XXVIII Poems*, 1955.

Bibliography

Borrello, Alfred. *Gabriel Fielding*, 1972.

Bowers, Frederick. Review of *The Birthday King* in *Queen's Quarterly*. LXXIV (Spring, 1967), pp. 149-158.

——————. "The Unity of Fielding's *Greenbloom*," in *Renascence*. XVIII (Spring, 1966), pp. 147-155.

Grande, Luke M. "Gabriel Fielding: New Master of the Catholic Classic?" in *Catholic World*. CXCVII (June, 1963), pp. 172-179.

Kunkel, Francis L. "Clowns and Saviours: Two Contemporary Novels," in *Renascence*. XVIII (Fall, 1965), pp. 40-44.

Stanford, Derek. "Gabriel Fielding and the Catholic Novel," in *Month*. XXVI (December, 1961), pp. 352-356.

Frederick Bowers

WILLIAM H. GASS

Born: Fargo, North Dakota; July 30, 1924

Principal long fiction
Omensetter's Luck, 1966; *Willie Master's Lonesome Wife*, 1968.

Other literary forms
Chiefly a writer of novels, William H. Gass is also the author of a book of short stories entitled *In the Heart of the Heart of the Country and Other Stories* (1968) and four volumes of essays about literature. In the chief of these, the collections entitled *Fiction and the Figures of Life* (1971) and *The World Within the Word: Essays* (1978), Gass illuminates his own work as a writer of fiction. He prefers novels, as his essay "Imaginary Borges and His Books" suggests, which render fictional worlds which are highly contrived metaphors for the real world. He values the kind of verbal experimentation, and the implications about human consciousness which lie behind it, characteristic of the fiction of Jorge Luis Borges, Gertrude Stein, and Robert Coover. Ultimately, Gass sees the fictional text as less a reflection of objective reality than an artifact created out of the consciousness of the author.

Achievements
While Gass is a highly individual writer, one whose work does not reflect the influence of his contemporaries, his fiction shares with work by authors such as John Barth, Donald Barthelme, and Thomas Pynchon an emphasis on the text as verbal construct. As his *On Being Blue: A Philosophical Inquiry* (1976) indicates, Gass believes that the words used to talk about a thing reveal the essence of the thing being talked about. His prose itself is highly rhythmic and reflexive, filled with images and allusions. The novels Gass has written, *Omensetter's Luck* and *Willie Master's Lonesome Wife*, are as much meditations on the art of writing fiction as narratives about their title characters. His essays, often published in literary journals before their appearance in book form, are cogent statements of Gass's own thematic and technical preoccupations. They influence both other writers and general readers, not only in the way they read Gass's work but also in the way they read the fiction of his contemporaries.

Biography
While born in Fargo, North Dakota, on July 30, 1924, William Howard Gass was reared in Warren, Ohio. He attended Kenyon College and Ohio Wesleyan, served in the United States Navy during World War II, and returned to receive a degree from Kenyon in 1947. Gass came into contact with

John Crowe Ransom there, but his chief interest as a student was philosophy. He went on to do graduate work at Cornell University, and after writing a dissertation entitled "A Philosophical Investigation of Metaphor," he received his Ph.D. in 1954. He has taught at a number of colleges, beginning to publish fiction while teaching philosophy at Purdue University. Since 1969, Gass has been at Washington University in St. Louis, Missouri, where he is Distinguished University Professor in Humanities. He has received grants from the Rockefeller and Guggenheim Foundations.

Analysis

Examination of the stories collected in *In The Heart of the Heart of the Country and Other Stories* reveals the degree to which Gass's fiction reflects his emphasis as a critic on creation of an autonomous verbal construction. In the title story of the volume, for example, he uses recurring images, syntactic patterns, and subject matter to depict a rural community as perceived by a poet who has come to a small Indiana town to recover from a failed love affair. "In the Midwest, around the lower Lakes," the first-person narrator comments, "the sky in the winter is heavy and close, and it is a rare day, a day to remark on, when the sky lifts and allows the heart up. I am keeping count, and as I write this page, it is eleven days since I have seen the sun."

As is typical of all of Gass's work, the first-person narrator of "In the Heart of the Heart of the Country" controls the development of the narrative structure of the story. It is his story, and Gass works through him to reveal its meaning. The narrator's eye for detail is sharp: Nevertheless, he interprets it in terms of his own isolation and despair. "Lost in the corn rows, I remember feeling just another stalk, and thus this country takes me over in the way I occupy myself when I am well . . . completely—to the edge of both my house and body." This metaphor is central to the point of the story, for Gass demonstrates that his protagonist so fuses the data of his sensory experience and his subjective response to it that the two cannot be separated.

In this respect, he is typical of characters in Gass's longer fiction. In the novels, however, the narrative strategy is more complex than in the stories. Gass uses four different narrators in *Omensetter's Luck*, circling about the meaning of the life of Brackett Omensetter without ever entering into his consciousness. According to Henry Pimber, Omensetter's friend and landlord, he

> was a wide and happy man. . . . He knew the earth. He put his hands in water. He smelled the clean fir smell. He listened to the bees. And he laughed his deep, loud, wide and happy laugh whenever he could—which was often, long, and joyfully.

To the citizens of Gilean, a town on the Ohio River to which he comes around 1890, Brackett Omensetter is a mythic figure who is magically in touch with the natural world. That perception precipitates the emotional responses they have to him. It also precipitates a series of human tragedies.

Israbestis Tott, the first narrator Gass uses in *Omensetter's Luck*, functions like the narrator of "In the Heart of the Heart of the Country," in that he chronicles the history of a town. "Imagine growing up in a world," Tott comments at the start of the book, "where only generals and geniuses, empires and companies, had histories, not your own town or grandfather, house . . . none of the things you'd loved." Tott comes at the conflict at the center of Omensetter's story indirectly, not needing to explain to himself as he muses about the past that actually took place. He speaks from the perspective of old age. His Gilean is that of the reader's present, and he refers to Omensetter's life from the perspective of a survivor of the central action of the novel, which took place before the turn of the century.

Gass's use of Tott as his initial focus, and the placement of the action of the first section of *Omensetter's Luck* at an auction of the property of the late Lucy Pimber, enables him to suggest that the lack of vitality in Gilean derives from the community's inability to accept Brackett Omensetter. One of the items at auction is the cradle Omensetter and his wife used for their infant son Amos, and Tott wonders why Mrs. Pimber had it. She never had any children of her own. Her husband, Henry, the character Gass uses to narrate the second section of the novel, is ambivalent about Omensetter's strength and vitality. Both drawn to him and jealous of him, Pimber commits suicide by hanging himself from a tree deep in the woods. This death is the central element in the plot of the novel. Unsure of what has happened to Henry Pimber, the townspeople search for his body and speculate about the role Omensetter has played in his death.

Pimber is convinced that Omensetter is lucky beyond all deserving. On the rainy day on which he brings his family and household goods to Gilean in an open wagon, Omensetter miraculously escapes the rain. The house he rents from Pimber is subject to flooding, but the Ohio River avoids it while Omensetter's family lives there. Even when a fox falls into the well at the house, he is inclined to let nature take its course in confidence that things will work out. Angered by this attitude, Pimber shoots the fox in the well and wounds himself with a refracted shotgun pellet. Neither Dr. Orcutt's drugs nor Reverend Furber's prayers seem to affect the lockjaw Pimber develops, but Omensetter's beet poultice turns the trick. The experience becomes fraught with spiritual significance for Pimber. "It lay somewhere in the chance of being new . . . of living lucky, and of losing Henry Pimber." He sees Omensetter as a sign, as a secret indication of how he himself should live; unable to see that Omensetter is no more than a man like himself, Pimber hangs himself in despair about ever becoming the kind of person he believes Omensetter to be.

While Henry Pimber sees Omensetter as emblematic of positive elements, the Reverend Jethro Furber, the third of Gass's narrators in *Omensetter's*

Luck, sees him as the embodiment of moral evil. Furber is the most difficult to understand of the men Gass uses to narrate the story. His account comes so entirely from within his own consciousness that only the previous evidence of Tott and Pimber serves to put it in perspective. Furber sees Omensetter as a threat to his moral authority. Having coerced him into attending church one Sunday morning, Furber finds himself unable to preach effectively. Speaking to Matthew Watson, the blacksmith in Gilean, he suggests that Omensetter is an agent of Satan. "Listen Matthew, he was in the young corn walking and I said leave us Omensetter, leave us all. Oh I accursed him. I did. Yes, I said, you are of the dark ways, Omensetter, leave us all." When Henry Pimber disappears and foul play is suggested, Furber encourages the townspeople to suspect Omensetter of killing his landlord.

Obsessed by the sight of Omensetter and his pregnant wife Lucy bathing in a stream, Furber makes of the scene an icon of his own lust. He is gored by sexual fantasies, conceding to himself that there is more pleasure in dirty words than real experience, yet the unconstrained relationship of Brackett and Lucy Omensetter excites his jealousy. He titillates himself with words, those drawn from scripture as well as those describing sexual acts, and eventually produces a blasphemous mixture of elements suggesting a parallel between Omensetter, his wife, Lucy, and Furber himself and Adam, Eve, and Satan.

> Now there was in heaven, as you know, an angel, prince among them, Prince of Darkness. And he felt his wife drawn painfully from him, out of his holy body, fully half of himself, and given a place of dazzling splendor. How he hated it, and suffered his loss loudly.

Furber sees himself simultaneously as Adam and Satan; he both displaces Omensetter as the husband of Lucy/Eve and reveals the guilt he feels at this idea. Furber imagines that the sex act reunites the parts that God separated, reintegrating the masculine and feminine halves of His own personality, and he thereby suggests the roots of his own jealousy of Omensetter.

Gass provides the last chapters of *Omensetter's Luck* with an anonymous third-person narrator, one who stays largely outside the consciousness of Furber. The action of the plot develops with absolute clarity at this point. Omensetter comes to the minister with the news that he has located Henry Pimber's body deep in the snowy winter forest. He knows that Furber is trying to persuade others that he murdered Pimber, and he needs to clear his name. "A friend. I've spent my life spreading lies about you," Furber tells Omensetter tauntingly. Yet he does tell the search party the truth when they find Pimber's corpse. By this time, Furber is caught up in his own dark spiritual vision. "God was coming true, coming slowly to light like a message in lemon. And, what was the message? in yet another lingo? Truth is the father of lies; nothing survives; only the wicked can afford to be wise." Since his arrival in Gilean, Furber had tended a shady, walled garden attached to his church. With the graves of his predecessors in its four corners, the garden is an emblem straight from the fiction of Nathaniel Hawthorne or Herman Melville. Furber's dark vision has the same traditional literary source, but the people of Gilean see his words only as the ramblings of a madman. The Reverend Jethro Furber spends his final years in a mental institution.

Omensetter himself does not handle well the roles in which the people of Gilean have cast him. He is essentially a careless, happy man who is not deeply reflective about life. Cast as the embodiment of natural good by Henry Pimber and spiritual evil by Jethro Furber, he himself is unsure of his identity. For Omensetter, his arrival in Gilean was filled with the promise of a new life. "The trees were bare, I remember, and as we came down the hill we could see the tracks of the wagons glistening. You could see what your life would be." He is eager to prove that this promise was not a lie, and so he gambles on the life of his sick son Amos to see if the luck imputed to him by others will hold. "The infant lingered on alive, an outcome altogether outside science, Doctor Orcutt said, and Israbestis swore that Omensetter's luck would be a legend on the river—quite a while, he claimed—perhaps forever." Omensetter and his family leave Gilean, however, suggesting that his self-confidence has been permanently shaken by his experiences. With them, Gass suggests, goes all hope for vitality in the community.

In a fundamental sense, Omensetter, Furber, Pimber, and Tott are aspects of a single personality. They are the voices of human impulses competing for control. The multiple narrators of *Willie Master's Lonesome Wife* are less clearly fragments of a single character, but they are equally strong symbol-making voices. Divided into four sections, each printed on paper of a different color, this novella is more overtly an experiment in narrative construction than *Omensetter's Luck*. It has little coherent plot at all, but there is plenty of action. The central character is Willie Master's wife, a lonesome woman named Barbara who consoles herself with sexual encounters. "Well, I'm busty, passive, hairy, and will serve," she comments in the first, and blue-colored, section of the book. "Departure is my name. I travel, dream. I feel sometimes as if I *were* imagination (that spider goddess and thread-spinning muse)—imagination imagining itself imagine." While engaged in sexual intercourse with a bald man named Gelvin, "Busty Babs"—as her father called her—thinks about differences in the ways men and women think about sexuality. This is a topic to which Gass has returned time and again in his fiction; it fuels the speculations of the narrator of "In the Heart of the Heart of the Country" and the nearly pornographic fantasies of Furber in *Omensetter's Luck*.

Barbara Masters is a former stripper who danced professionally in a blue light. This explains, in part, the blue paper on which her thoughts are printed. She allows her mind to wander while Gelvin works out his fantasies on her body, and she imagines herself the author of a Russian play—printed in Gass's text on yellow paper to suggest its lurid nature—about a Russian named Ivan and his wife. Barbara casts herself in the role of the wife. The subject of the play is Ivan's reaction to evidence of his wife's infidelity, but the play soon gets overwhelmed by the footnotes providing a running commentary at the foot of each yellow page. The notes get longer, they are at times addressed to the reader of *Willie Master's Lonesome Wife*, and eventually they swallow up the play. The text and notes do not match up, so the reader must choose whether to read the pages as printed or to work actively to construct a more coherent text.

Gass refers openly to the proposition that the reader is a collaborator in the section of *Willie Master's Lonesome Wife* which is printed on red paper. The narrator here, perhaps still Barbara Masters, remarks,

> The muddy circle you see just before you and below you represents the ring left on a leaf of the manuscript by my coffee cup. Represents, I say, because, as you must surely realize, this book is many removes from anything I've set pen, hand, or cup to.

Like the play on yellow pages, this section contains simultaneous narratives. There is a dialogue about poetry and sexuality among characters named Leonora, Carlos, Angela, and Philippe; there is a running commentary on the art of writing—containing references to works by Henry David Thoreau, Henry James, and Thomas Hardy; and there is an interior monologue composed of random memories, supposedly events in the life of the narrator. In one sense, this technique re-creates the effect of a single human mind thinking simultaneously about several different subjects. In another, it is simply an elaborate parody of the method Gass uses in *Omensetter's Luck*. In a fictional text such as this one, all interpretations of significance are equally valid (or invalid), and there is ultimately nothing but a subjective reaction to be made out of the materials.

Gass addresses this fact in the final pages of the red section of the book. "You've been had," says the narrator, "haven't you, jocko? you sad sour stew-face sonofabitch. Really, did you read this far?" As Gass has made clear in his essays about literature, the essential nature of a literary text is the fact that it is made up of words. In the fourth section of *Willie Master's Lonesome Wife*, printed on white paper and without the typographical variation to be found in the other sections of the book, the narrator identifies herself as a verbal construct.

> I am that lady language chose to make her playhouse of, and if you do not like me, if you find me dewlapped, scabby, wrinkled, old (and I've admitted as many pages as my age), well sir, I'm not like you, a loud rude noise and fart upon the town.

She is a new incarnation of the most traditional of muses, just as Willie Master is a mask for the author William Gass himself.

Other major works

SHORT FICTION: *In the Heart of the Heart of the Country and Other Stories*, 1968.

NONFICTION: *Fiction and the Figures of Life*, 1971; *On Being Blue: A Philosophical Inquiry*, 1976; *The World Within the Word: Essays*, 1978; *The Habitations of the Word: Essays*, 1985.

Bibliography

Allen, Carolyn J. "Fiction and Figures of Life in *Omensetter's Luck*," in *Pacific Coast Philology*. IX (1974), pp. 5-11.

Carmello, Charles. "Fleshing Out *Willie Master's Lonesome Wife*," in *SubStance*. XXVII (1980), pp. 56-69.

French, Ned. "Against the Grain: Theory and Practice in the Work of William H. Gass," in *Iowa Review*. VII (Winter, 1976), pp. 96-106.

McCaffery, Larry. "The Art of Metafiction: William Gass's *Willie Master's Lonesome Wife*," in *Critique*. XVIII (Summer, 1976), pp. 21-35.

Schneider, Richard J. "The Fortunate Fall in William Gass's *Omensetter's Luck*," in *Critique*. XVIII (Summer, 1976), pp. 5-20.

Robert C. Petersen

NATALIA GINZBURG

Born: Palermo, Italy; July 14, 1916

Principal long fiction

La strada che va in città, 1942 (as Alessandra Tornimparte; *The Road to the City*, 1949); *È stato così*, 1947 (*The Dry Heart*, 1949); *Tutti i nostri ieri*, 1952 (*A Light for Fools*, 1956; also as *Dead Yesterdays*, 1956, and *All Our Yesterdays*, 1985); *Valentino*, 1957 (also includes *Sagittario* and *La madre*); *Le voci della sera*, 1961 (*Voices in the Evening*, 1963); *Lessico famigliare*, 1963 (*Family Sayings*, 1967); *Cinque romanzi brevi*, 1964; *Caro Michele*, 1973 (*No Way*, 1974; also as *Dear Michael*, 1975); *Famiglia*, 1977; *La casa e la città*, 1984 (*The City and the House*, 1987).

Other literary forms

Though Natalia Ginzburg is known primarily as a novelist and short-story writer, she is also a talented dramatist, essayist, and poet. She has published two collections of plays, *Ti ho sposato per allegria e altre commedie* (1967; I married you for the fun of it and other comedies) and *Paese di mare e altre commedie* (1973; sea town and other comedies), some of which have been performed in London and New York. Her three volumes of essays and articles, *Le piccole virtù* (1962; *The Little Virtues*, 1985), *Mai devi domandarmi* (1970; *Never Must You Ask Me*, 1973), and *Vita immaginaria* (1974; imaginary life), range over a wide variety of subjects, including literary and film criticism. Her scholarly biography of the family of Italy's greatest novelist of the nineteenth century, *La famiglia Manzoni* (1983; the Manzoni family), has won critical acclaim. Her poetry has been published in various newspapers and literary reviews.

Achievements

One of the best-known Italian female writers of the second half of the twentieth century, Ginzburg began her career by publishing short stories in *Solaria* and *Letteratura* in the mid-1930's. Her first short novel, *The Road to the City*, was published under the pseudonym Alessandra Tornimparte because of the anti-Jewish laws. Her narrative works of the 1940's and 1950's established her critical reputation and associated her with the brief but significant neorealist movement in Italian literature and film. In 1947, her second short novel, *The Dry Heart*, won the Tempo Prize. Her first long novel, *Dead Yesterdays*, was awarded the Veillon Prize in the year of its publication. In 1957, Ginzburg received the Viareggio Prize for the short novel *Valentino*. Ginzburg's second long novel, *Family Sayings*, which received the prestigious Strega Prize in 1964, is generally considered one of her strongest works, together with the novel that preceded it, *Voices in the Evening*. Ginzburg's uncomplicated narrative style, with which she recounts stories that hover between fiction and nonfiction, has made hers one of the most distinctive voices in postwar Italian letters. One of her several plays, *L'inserzione* (1967; *The Advertisement*, 1968), was honored with the Marzotto International Prize of 1968.

Biography

Although Natalia Levi was born in Palermo on July 14, 1916, she spent her childhood and adolescence in Turin, where her father was a professor of comparative anatomy. The daughter of a Catholic mother and a Jewish father (both nonpracticing), she acquired a sense of social isolation at an early age and was educated at home and in the schools of Turin. (She has told the story of her family in *Family Sayings*.) In 1938, she married Leone Ginzburg, a professor of Russian literature and an active anti-Fascist. From 1940 to 1943, the Ginzburgs, together with their three children, lived in compulsory political confinement in a remote district of the Abruzzi. After moving to Rome, Leone Ginzburg was arrested and imprisoned for the second time in November, 1943, and died in Rome at the Regina Coeli prison on February 5, 1944.

After the war, Natalia Ginzburg returned to Turin and worked there as a consultant for the Einaudi publishing firm. In 1950, she married Gabriele Baldini, a professor of English literature. When Baldini was named head of the Italian Institute of Culture in London, the family took up residence in that city, where they lived from 1959 to 1962, at which time they returned to the Italian capital. In 1968, her second husband died. Thereafter, she took up permanent residence in Rome, working as a consultant for Einaudi in addition to her writing and her occasional contributions to Italian newspapers and magazines.

Analysis

From her first short stories and novellas published in the 1930's and 1940's to her epistolary novels of the 1970's and 1980's, Natalia Ginzburg provides a female perspective on the Italian bourgeoisie during a period of widespread social change. Viewed in its entirety, her career shows a progression from the short story toward the more sustained form of the novel, with a developing interest in the theater. Her dominant themes, which can be related in part to her affinity to Cesare Pavese, revolve around the inevitability of human suffering and isolation, the impossibility of communication, the failure of love, the asymmetries in modern Italy between urban and rural existence, and the influence of the family on the individual human person. Her early novels, *The Road to the City* and *The Dry Heart*, both present first-person female narrators whose interior monologues focus on human emotions rather than external events. Relatively little happens in these early works, which are generally low-key in tone, straightforward in plot structure, and uncomplicated in lexicon and syntax. The elemental character of Ginzburg's prose makes her work accessible to students whose knowledge of Italian may still be rudimentary. In fact, her clear and direct approach to writing has won for her high praise as a stylist. Her later novels depend more on dialogue than on description, and her talent for reproducing realistic speech patterns expresses itself with equal felicity in her writings for the theater.

With *Family Sayings*, which is generally considered to be her best novel, Ginzburg introduced a more openly autobiographical element into her work. A chronicle of the author's family life during Fascism, the Resistance, and the immediate postwar period, *Family Sayings* testifies to the author's statement that memory provides the most important stimulus for her writing. Her interest in the family as a social unit is also manifest in her other works of the 1970's and 1980's and underlies such epistolary novels as *No Way* and *The City and the House*, as well as works as diverse as the novel *Famiglia* (family) and the scholarly biography *La famiglia Manzoni*.

The Road to the City recounts the experience of a sixteen-year-old-girl, Delia, whose boredom with her squalid peasant environment leads her into the trap for which she seems destined. Blinded by the glitter of city life (as personified in her older, more sophisticated sister), she allows herself to be seduced by a young law student named Giulio, for whom she feels only a superficial attraction. She becomes pregnant and marries Giulio while her cousin and true friend, Nino, dies from abuse of alcohol and frustration at being unable to establish a meaningful relationship with her. During the wedding ceremony, Delia realizes that she is marrying a man whom she does not love. Yet she fails to realize the underlying circumstances which have caused her to enter into a loveless marriage. This study in disillusionment contains the typical elements of Ginzburg's early work: Her narrator-protagonists are naïve and simple young women who find themselves attracted to the charms of city life but who are ultimately disappointed by the role that society offers them.

Relying on similarly uncomplicated stylistic devices, *The Dry Heart* recounts a murder story from the perspective of a first-person female narrator, a young schoolteacher from the country whose life in the city is full of disappointments. Like Delia, she enters into a loveless marriage. Unable to draw her husband away from his mistress, the unnamed narrator-protagonist kills him, seemingly against her own will. The murder is related in the novel's opening paragraphs, and the bulk of the novel is made up almost entirely of a monologue in which the protagonist seeks to justify and to understand her own actions. The detached, isolated "I" which appears throughout the narrative mirrors the naïveté, passivity, and resignation of the main character. Brief units of dialogue are embedded in blocks of the narrator's monologue, which is almost completely bereft of commas. This singular punctuation helps create the monotonous, despairing tone of a novel which treats the inability of human beings to establish mutually satisfactory relationships. The failure of a marriage leads to murder and to the protagonist's own drift toward suicide.

With *Dead Yesterdays*, Ginzburg's fiction took a significant step forward. Her first novel of a substantial length, this work seeks to add a historical dimension missing from her previous fiction. Composed while neorealism was enjoying its brief moment in the sun, *Dead Yesterdays* abandons the first-person narrative style of the early short novels in favor of the third person. The novel centers on the sufferings of two Italian families during the reign of Fascism, the war, and the Resistance; the book's plot structure is more developed than the author's previous work, and external events have a greater importance. Indeed, *Dead Yesterdays* seeks to tell the story of an entire generation. For the first time, Ginzburg's strange heroes become involved in the broader fabric of social reality. An unnamed industrial city in the North and a fictional village in the South constitute the settings. The main characters include Anna, the younger sister in the less wealthy of the two families; Concettina, her elder sister; and Cenzo Rena, an intellectual of the Left whose commitment to social problems furnishes Ginzburg's fiction with a successfully drawn portrait of an engagé figure. His decision to take the blame for the death of a German soldier is tantamount to suicide, but it saves the villagers from a brutal Nazi reprisal. His politically motivated self-sacrifice brings the novel to an end on a positive note.

The 1950's and the 1960's witnessed a fruitful development in Ginzburg's maturing narrative production. In 1951, she wrote *Valentino*, a novella published in 1957 together with *Sagittario* (Sagittarius) and *La madre* (the mother) in a single volume. These three novellas were awarded the Viareggio Prize of 1957 and further express Ginzburg's continuing preoccupation with the power of the family as a social unit. In the early 1960's, Ginzburg lived with her husband in London, where in the spring of 1961 she wrote *Voices in the Evening*. Set completely in Italy in an unnamed provincial town, *Voices in the Evening* chronicles the disintegration of an Italian middle-class family. Through a series of flashbacks (each one a portrait of a different member of the family), Ginzburg alternates dialogue with the narrator's monologue. Against a backdrop of Fascism and the war and its aftermath, once again the coming of age of a young woman, Elsa, provides the focal point for Ginzburg's nostalgic narrative. Elsa's unhappy affair with Tommasino, a young man whose family background renders him incapable of giving love, is presented in the flat, unsentimental narrative style which has become Ginzburg's trademark.

Family Sayings was awarded the Strega Prize in 1964 and is regarded by many critics as the author's major work. Having grown up in the anti-Fascist atmosphere of Turin, Ginzburg manages to capture the feeling of an entire epoch in recounting the minimal details of her own family life. In *Family Sayings*, Ginzburg draws a portrait of the people who have mattered the most in her private world, many of whom, it should be noted, such as Leone Ginzburg, Filippo Turati, and Cesare Pavese, have also played a significant role in Italian culture and politics. Paradoxically, the openly autobiographical element of *Family Sayings*, the turning inward to mine her own private stock of memories, seems to have sharpened Ginzburg's abilities as an observer of social reality, abilities which she puts to good use in her three volumes of essays.

In the epistolary novel *No Way*, one finds the themes that Ginzburg elaborates throughout the previous four decades, but here they are brought into the context of the social unrest of Italy in the 1970's: The unhappy marriage of a middle-class Roman couple has disastrous effects on their offspring. The exchange of letters between the novel's various characters revolves around Michele, the young protagonist, who moves to London, where he marries an alcoholic divorcée, and who later dies in Bruges at the hands of a group of neo-Fascists. From a technical standpoint, the epistolary structure of the novel allows Ginzburg to experiment with multiple monologues and multiple points of view.

Famiglia and *Borghesia*, the titles of the two novellas that make up the volume *Famiglia*, indicate the twin themes that Ginzburg has pursued throughout her career. As in the novel that preceded this work, here she brings her focus on the Italian bourgeois family into the highly charged political atmosphere of Italy in the 1970's. With *The City and the House*, Ginzburg returns to the epistolary form used a decade earlier in *No Way*. Her cast of letter-writing characters includes the protagonist Giuseppe, a middle-aged Italian who, in emigrating to New Jersey, cuts himself off from his friends and his roots. The letter as a technical device also fits well with Ginzburg's attempt to fashion a sparse, unadorned style intended to reproduce the rhythms of actual speech. Her focus on the common objects and conflicting emotions of daily life has led critics to compare her work with that of Anton Chekhov. At the same time, as critic Allan Bullock has suggested (an intuition confirmed by the author herself), Ginzburg's use of dialogue beginning in the early 1960's owes a debt to a writer very different from Chekhov: the English novelist Ivy Compton-Burnett. Ginzburg's most accomplished novels, *Voices in the Evening* and *Family Sayings*, combine elements of autobiography, memory, and emotion within the broader context of historical events and social change. Ginzburg's gift for interweaving the private and the social, the personal and the historical in a simple, straightforward prose style may be her most significant contribution to Italian letters.

Other major works

PLAYS: *Ti ho sposato per allegria e altre commedie*, 1967; *L'inserzione*, 1967

(*The Advertisement*, 1968); *Paese di mare e altre commedie*, 1973.

NONFICTION: *Le piccole virtù*, 1962 (*The Little Virtues*, 1985); *Mai devi domandarmi*, 1970 (*Never Must You Ask Me*, 1973); *Vita immaginaria*, 1974; *La famiglia Manzoni*, 1983.

Bibliography

Bowe, Clotilde S. "The Narrative Strategy of Natalia Ginzburg," in *Modern Language Review*. LXVIII (1973), pp. 788-795.

Bullock, Allan. "Natalia Ginzburg and Ivy Compton-Burnett: Creative Composition and Domestic Repression in *Le voci della sera*," in *Rivista di letterature moderne e comparate*. XXX (1977), pp. 203-227.

Heiney, Donald. "Natalia Ginzburg: The Fabric of Voices," in *The Iowa Review*. I (Fall, 1970), pp. 87-93.

Piclardi, Rosetta D. "Forms and Figures in the Novels of Natalia Ginzburg," in *World Literature Today*. LIII (1979), pp. 585-589.

John P. Welle

GAIL GODWIN

Born: Birmingham, Alabama; June 18, 1937

Principal long fiction
The Perfectionists, 1970; *Glass People*, 1972; *The Odd Woman*, 1974; *Violet Clay*, 1978; *A Mother and Two Daughters*, 1982; *The Finishing School*, 1985.

Other literary forms
In addition to her six novels, Gail Godwin has published two collections of short fiction, *Dream Children* (1976) and *Mr. Bedford and the Muses* (1983). In the second collection, "Mr. Bedford" is a novella rather than a short story. Godwin is also a frequent reviewer of contemporary fiction for *The New York Times Book Review* and other publications. In 1985, she served as editor for *The Best American Short Stories*.

Achievements
Godwin has done much to broaden the scope of the contemporary woman's novel. While the struggles of women who seek both an independent life and a productive connection to others are central to her work, she strives in her novels and short fiction to place those efforts within a larger context, especially within the framework of modern theories of art and psychology. In 1971-1972, Godwin was a fellow of the Center for Advanced Studies, University of Illinois at Urbana-Champaign. Her other awards include a grant from the National Endowment for the Arts in 1974 and a Guggenheim Fellowship in 1975. Her story "Amanuensis" was included in the *Prize Stories, 1980: O. Henry Awards* collection.

Biography
Reared by her mother and her widowed grandmother in Asheville, North Carolina, Gail Godwin attended Peace Junior College in Raleigh, North Carolina, and was graduated in 1959 from the University of North Carolina at Chapel Hill (the alma mater of Asheville's other great native writer, Thomas Wolfe). Her B.A. was in journalism. After working as a reporter for the *Miami Herald*, she lived in London and worked with the United States Travel Service at the American Embassy. After returning to the United States, she took an M.A. (1968) and a Ph.D. (1971) in English at the University of Iowa, where she later served on the faculty of the Writers Workshop. She has been married twice, to *Miami Herald* photographer Douglas Kennedy and to British psychotherapist Ian Marshall. Her one-year marriage to Marshall is the basis for her first novel, *The Perfectionists*, as her early years

with her mother and grandmother are for parts of *Glass People* and *The Odd Woman*. Her relationships with her father and her stepfather are also used in her fiction, especially in *Violet Clay* and *The Odd Woman*, respectively.

Analysis

Gail Godwin's novels (and her short fiction as well) all deal with several easily identifiable themes. First, and most often cited perhaps, is the theme of the modern woman, her dilemma in defining self and others in an era when the old frameworks and definitions have broken down, at least for the sort of women about whom Godwin writes. The conflict most often arises between the woman's work, usually an artistic pursuit of some kind, and her desire for security, love, and connection, most often through a relationship with a man. Thus, the theme of the woman struggling for identity divides into two separate thematic strands: her identity as artist and her identity as lover.

Another recurring theme in Godwin's work is, in many ways, the reverse of this quest for self-identity. Often, her characters long to penetrate the identities of the people around them; that is, they consciously seek to violate the human heart's sanctity, to use Nathaniel Hawthorne's description of such activity. Again, however, Godwin's perspective is definitively modern. These characters are all aware of the impossibility of coming to such knowledge in the almost mystical way that Hawthorne describes in "The Custom House" section of *The Scarlet Letter* (1850), and they are also conscious of the questionable morality of such invasions. Therefore, they seek lesser but more concrete knowledge and understanding by prying, by scrutinizing the objects the others possess or the words they write or say, words that the seeker will examine with total (or what he or she assumes to be total) awareness of the ironies and ambiguities involved in both the saying and their interpretation.

These divergent pursuits are most easily forged into a manageable aesthetic form through an artist figure; the role of the artist in relation to self, other, and art itself is, finally, Godwin's most important theme. Her main characters tend to be so self-consciously "artists," even when they are lawyers or psychiatrists or unemployed, that they make life itself into an art, which is to say that they view their own lives as artists view the canvas or the sheet of paper before them.

What makes Godwin an interesting and important figure in the world of contemporary fiction is the narrative technique by which she manages to develop and retell this essentially unchanging story. The noticeable and impressive growth in Godwin herself as an artist can be traced by examining the structural and technical variations in her telling of her stories. In the earlier novels, the distance between narrator and protagonist is less clearly defined. The overblown and romanticized version of the character sometimes seems to be an accurate representation of the narrator's perspective as well.

Beginning with *The Odd Woman*, however, and culminating in *The Finishing School*, Godwin makes that distance itself a matter of chief concern. Her narrators seem acutely aware of the responsibility involved in entering into the lives and souls of "others." The characters seem to move from being primarily concerned with personal happiness and security to doing true and constructive work that recognizes the dignity in whatever lives the artist consumes for the sake of the work and that acknowledges the limitations and fallibilities of the artist himself. These later characters, by having real and constructive work to do, manage to be less obsessed with their personal lives as objects of art; they also manage to find satisfaction in the art and the work itself, whether their personal lives are or are not so satisfying at any given moment.

The protagonists of *The Perfectionists* and *Glass People*, Dane Empson and Francesca Bolt, are both self-absorbed and frustrated in their relationships with their spouses. They are also the last of Godwin's protagonists to be married and unemployed. Not only are they unemployed, but also neither of them shows any desire for doing constructive, creative work. When these novels are read in the context of Godwin's later work, the conclusion that their shared lack of ambition and motivation is crucial to their discontent is inevitable.

Dane Empson has been married to John Empson, a psychologist, for ten months when they go on vacation with John's illegitimate son, Robin, and one of John's female patients, Penelope MacMahon. Although she worked as a journalist prior to her marriage—in fact, she met John when she covered a meeting at which he was the speaker—she no longer pursues her career. Her primary concerns are her relationship with John, in which she has begun to lose interest, and her efforts to become a mother to his son.

Thus, what Godwin does with this character, although it is done in a most unconventional way, is to have her confront the traditional roles and conflicts of the wife and mother. Dane fails in these roles, however, and she is most aware of that failure. She feels nothing, absolutely nothing, of the satisfaction and joy that the mythic versions of those roles provide.

The overt source of conflict in the story is Robin's total refusal to acknowledge Dane. He will not speak in her presence; he will not respond to her displays of affection; he will not compromise in any way in the small, daily struggles between parent and child.

He does, however, make demands on Dane, in both practical and emotional matters. She is expected to feed, clothe, and entertain him. She is also expected to nurture and soothe him while his father is thinking and writing in his journal. Because Godwin sets up the child as a double for the father, a point that John frequently reinforces by comparing himself to the child, the narrator suggests that Dane's real problem is John's refusal to acknowledge her.

Yet, Dane is guilty of expecting her husband to provide her with an identity to be acknowledged. She surreptitiously searches through his journal entries for clues as to what he sees when he looks at her, what he thinks when he thinks of her. When she does rebel, venturing outside the prescribed role that she has accepted with apparent willingness, she takes up with another frustrated wife, Polly Heykoop, who devotes herself to spying on her husband with his lovers, photographing their sexual encounters and compiling a scrapbook of the photos to present to him in their old age.

Dane's act in defiance of this utter decadence of domestic life is to beat the child, almost to kill him, in order to reassert her personal identity. Symbolically, she is also beating John, who, in her imagination, responds to her confession by ruining it. He points out that the action she takes in order to feel a powerful and private emotion is of necessity shared with the child and, by extension, with him. Because she cannot deny the truth of that observation and because she has available to her no other means of self-expression, she remains as self-absorbed and frustrated as she is at the novel's beginning.

Dane's counterpart in *Glass People*, Francesca Bolt, is even less involved in life. Wife to a successful attorney and politician who requires absolutely nothing of her expect that she be beautiful for him, Francesca has retreated from all human activity. She languishes in her bedroom, living for the alternate days when she tweezes the hairs from her legs one by one. At the instigation of Cameron, her husband, she undertakes a quest to discover a life for herself, a quest more dramatic and independent than that of Dane.

After a disappointing visit to her newly remarried and pregnant mother fails to allow Francesca to retreat into a former identity, she embarks upon a series of adventures, each eventually as unsuccessful as her visit home. She has an affair, a one-weekend liaison with a man she meets in the airport, but she romanticizes the encounter into much more than it is. When he does not reappear, she bravely tries to follow the plan the two of them laid to free her from Cameron's worshipful but manipulative grasp.

She rents a room in a cheap New York hotel and briefly takes a job as amanuensis to a bizarre woman named M. She even finds herself buoyed by the successful completion of the tasks she performs for her employer, the basic cleaning, shopping, and cooking chores she could not bring herself to do at home in California. After less than a week of being actively engaged in the world with nothing more than her own identity to define her, she collapses in a complete and devastating illness. She fears that all the fluids within her will leave her body and she will disappear.

Cameron appears, however, a *deus ex machina* in the best romantic tradition—the heroic man come to save the fallen beauty. The problem, as Francesca knows, is that he will save her for his own purposes, and her identity will be defined by those purposes. Still, despite this awareness, she cannot resist the comfort and ease of his salvation. That she is pregnant with the child of her lover seems only to increase Cameron's worshipful desire to hold and control her. As she moves around their beautiful apartment, decorated and maintained by Cameron, and eats plentifully of the food he prepares for her, secure in her knowledge that her husband will never let her get fat, Francesca thinks of the power she holds and of the possibilities for manipulating her husband with that power. She is the last of Godwin's protagonists to accept this traditional sort of power struggle as the best solution for her life.

Narratively, the problem with these novels is a matter of point of view. Because both are dominated by the perspectives of the protagonists, who have so constrained their lives as to have no outside viewpoints against which to test their own (except those of their spouses, whom they can only undermine as valid reference points), Godwin finds herself telling her stories without a reliable observer. Even in *Glass People*, where brief passages are given over to Cameron's point of view, the reader already so distrusts Cameron, from having seen him through his wife's eyes, that the narrator cannot give his view much credence.

The narrative voice, although it is a third-person voice, does not maintain enough distance between itself and the protagonists to convince the reader that the values of that character are not, in fact, the values being espoused by the novel. At the same time, however, the violent impotence of Dane Empson and the luxurious laziness of Francesca Bolt both carry a faintly distasteful flavor for most readers.

The perspective of Jane Clifford, the protagonist of *The Odd Woman*, marks a significant step forward for Godwin as a storyteller. First, her perspective is a much broader one than that of either of her predecessors. Jane works as a teacher of literature, and her work as a graduate student writing her dissertation on George Eliot, in addition to her current work— grading the exams for her just-finished course in visionary literature and preparing to teach a course on women in literature—is an integral part of the narrative.

Furthermore, Jane Clifford has a family, a background, that is richly developed and explored across several generations. Unlike Francesca's fruitless journey back home, Jane's similar trip, to the funeral of her grandmother, produces extended encounters with her memories of the grandmother, her mother, stepfather, sister, and brothers. Kate, mother of Francesca, spends most of her daughter's visit behind the closed door of her bedroom. Jane is involved in talks, reminiscences, and arguments that test her perspective constantly.

Jane also has friends, male and female, to whom she talks, in whom she confides. There is the male colleague with whom she trades confidences about sex and bathroom regularity; there is her old college friend Gerda, the editor of a feminist newspaper in Chicago; and there is Sonia Marx, her colleague at the university where she teaches and the woman who serves as the role model for what Jane wants to be—someone with a career, husband, and family, managing it all with every sign of ease and brilliance. Again, although Jane's point of view is the point of view of the novel, her constant encounters with these others broadens and modifies her view throughout.

Jane also has a lover, a married man, Gabriel Weeks, an art historian. In him, Jane finds an alternative to the cynical and jaded perspective she finds pervasive in the academic world. She gradually comes to realize, however, that the Gabriel she has found is a creature of her own making. She has imagined him and orchestrated their relationship in such a way as to provide herself with a view of the world that must come from within, must be made from oneself, if it is to have true value.

Here, Godwin begins to develop the ironic awareness of self as artist that is crucial to the success of her subject matter. Jane Clifford is painfully aware of her life as an object of art, with herself as the artist. She sees the scenes of her life as just that, scenes, and she manipulates both her own part and the parts of others. The problem is that such a life will never reach the state of natural grace and spontaneity that is Jane's primary goal.

Thus, she is more like Dane and Francesca than she would like to be. She does not find a way to overcome her frustrations with her need to rewrite the role she has been given or has voluntarily taken on. Unlike those predecessors, however, she does not capitulate. She takes actions that give her a chance for progress. She ends her affair; she takes an extension on her temporary appointment at the university, meaning that she will have productive work for another year; she confronts the demons of her past as represented by the family, Greta, and the actor who has been for half a century the arch villain of the family history.

Through these actions and confrontations, she learns that all truths may be artificial and self-imposed, but she also comes to believe in some purer, more absolute version of her own life that will be possible for her, if she acts to pursue it. Thus, despite Jane's own limitations, because Godwin equips her with such an acute sense of irony about herself as well as others, Jane is the first step toward a successful Godwin protagonist.

Interestingly enough, the promise of a truly successful Godwin woman made with Jane is realized in *Violet Clay*, whose story is the first that Godwin told from a first-person point of view. Although it might seem that first-person narration would lead to even greater self-absorption, this does not happen. Using the same principles that make *The Odd Woman* such a step forward, Godwin generated a plot in *Violet Clay* with a death. Jane keeps her job and her lover through most of her story, however, while, in addition to losing her uncle—her only living relative—Violet loses what Jane has been able to keep.

She is forced by these events of plot to confront the essentials of her character, to test the view of herself that she has created. While she probes into her uncle's past to make sense of his suicide, Violet learns much about herself as well and about how the artist manufactures both life and art, each feeding off the other. When she finally paints the painting that will set her on the road she has long aspired to travel, Violet uses some of the same material that her uncle failed to transform into the novel that he had struggled for decades to write.

Violet's success comes because she learns the limits of both life and art, partly through her uncle's example, his legacy to her, and partly through her own increasing ability to forget about "poor little me" and to enter into and learn from the struggles of those around her with compassion and respect. She learns that the artist must not and finally cannot both live and work successfully if she violates the integrity of the other, of the lives out of which her art and her own life are to be constructed.

If *Violet Clay* states an aesthetic credo, *A Mother and Two Daughters* puts that credo into action. In this novel, for the first time, Godwin is able to render a world of multiple viewpoints throughout the story; not coincidentally, it is her longest book to date as well as her most accomplished.

Nell Strickland and her two daughters, Lydia and Cate, are very different women. They, too, find themselves propelled into a plot generated by a death, in this case that of their husband and father. Each also finds herself continuing in the plot of her own life. Nell finds that she relishes the independence and privacy of her widowhood, and she also finds herself in love again before the novel concludes. Lydia, who is recently separated and eventually divorced from her husband and is mother to two teenage sons, returns to school, acquires a lover, and develops a career. Cate struggles with her own love life and the roller coaster of her career as a teacher of drama.

These women are the least self-conscious of all of Godwin's heroines, and their stories are the most straightforward and least manipulated among her works. Even so, the reader is always aware that each of the three women is shaping, in an increasingly conscious way, her life, constructing it so that it gives her the most satisfaction possible within the limitations of a "realistic" environment.

All three of these women also engage in a sustained relationship with a man during the course of the story. For Nell, it is the traditional relationship of marriage, but in her second marriage she is a different woman from the one she was in her first because of the time she spends alone and the things she learns about herself during that time. She is able to bring about a merging of the independent self and the attached self. Lydia and Cate also reach such an integration of these strands of their lives, but for them, traditional marriage is not the form that integration takes. Lydia and her lover, Stanley, live in a hard-won but precarious balance, together but unmarried, separate but irrevocably joined. He thinks at the novel's end, "You can still be independent and mine, at the same time. You are these two things now."

Cate, always more independent and free-spirited than her sister or her mother, has an even more unusual arrangement. She has designed a job to suit her, packaging classes and traveling to the places people want to have them taught, a sort of academic entrepreneur. She has also reached a stability in her relationship with Roger Jernigan after years of tension about how their feelings for each other could be formed into a pattern acceptable to them both. They are good visitors to each other.

The possibilities for marriage are not closed off for either sister, but the necessity of marriage does not exert its terrifying influence over them either. As Godwin goes into and out of the consciousnesses of these women and sometimes briefly into the points of view of the people who make up their worlds, she approaches a compassionate and respectful omniscience that would be unthinkable for the narrators of the earlier work.

In *The Finishing School*, the narrator is again a first-person voice, this time Justin Stokes, a forty-year-old actress remembering the summer she turned fourteen. Justin's preoccupations during that summer are typical of all of Godwin's characters' preoccupations. She has experienced loss: Her father and her beloved grandparents have died, and she, her mother, and her younger brother, Jem, have had to leave their Virginia home and move north to a newly created subdivision in Clove, New York. She develops a special relationship with an older woman, Ursula DeVane, who instructs her in the art of making one's life an artistic creation, lessons that feed into Justin's predisposition for the dramatic and her aspirations to the stage. Most important, however, Justin shares, with the characters from Jane Clifford onward in Godwin's work, a deep desire to come to terms with her own use of others' lives to construct her own, to make it what she needs it to be. In addition, Justin writes to thank Ursula for her contribution to the process of Justin's becoming the adult woman she wanted to be. Despite the fact that their relationship ends badly, Justin cannot overlook the crucial role that the relationship played in helping her through the most difficult summer of her childhood.

Godwin dedicates this sixth novel to "the Ursulas of this world, whoever they were—or weren't"; that dedication seems echoed by Justin's sentiments after remembering and making a story from her summer with Ursula. Justin says:

> I was able to be charmed and possessed by that woman. Such possessions are rare now. I mean by another person. The only thing I can rely on to possess me continually with that degree of ardor is my work. Most of the time I consider this a victory. Sometimes, however, it makes me a little sad. So here I am, in the middle of my own life. . . . And it has taken me this long to understand that I lose nothing by acknowledging her influence on me. . . . I know something of life's betrayals and stupidities myself. . . . I even know the necessity for making constant adjustments to your life story, so you can go on living in it. . . . But I also know something else that I didn't know then. As long as you can go on creating new roles for yourself, you are not vanquished.

The author Gail Godwin has grown in much the same direction as her characters and narrators. The movement has been in the life-affirming direction of compromise, recognition of others, acceptance of responsibility for the self, and productive creativity. The life that gets affirmed is the well-made life, the one shaped out of the complexities and ambiguities of human experience. Godwin's novels speak clearly of the enormous difficulty of being a sensitive and thoughtful woman in today's world. They speak just as eloquently of what such women can make from those difficulties.

Other major works

SHORT FICTION: *Dream Children*, 1976; *Mr. Bedford and the Muses*, 1983.
ANTHOLOGY: *The Best American Short Stories*, 1985.

Bibliography

Frye, Joanne S. "Narrating the Self: The Autonomous Heroine in Gail Goodwin's *Violet Clay*," in *Contemporary Literature*. XXIV (Spring, 1983), pp. 66-85.

Korg, Jacob. "A Gissing Influence," in *Gissing Newsletter*. XII, no. 1 (1976), pp. 13-19.

Lorsche, Susan E. "Gail Godwin's *The Odd Woman*: Literature and the Retreat from Life," in *Critique: Studies in Modern Fiction*. XX (1978), pp. 21-32.

Mickelson, Anne Z. *Reaching Out: Sensitivity and Order in Recent American Fiction by Women*, 1979.

Rhodes, Carolyn. "Gail Godwin and the Ideal of Southern Womanhood," in *Southern Quarterly*. XXI (Summer, 1983), pp. 55-66.

Smith, Marilyn J. "The Role of the South in the Novels of Gail Godwin," in *Critique: Studies in Modern Fiction*. XXI (1979), pp. 103-110.

Welch, Kathleen. "An Interview with Gail Godwin," in *Iowa Journal of Literary Studies*. III, nos. 1/2 (1981), pp. 77-86.

Jane Hill

WILSON HARRIS

Born: New Amsterdam, British Guiana; March 24, 1921

Principal long fiction

Palace of the Peacock, 1960; *The Far Journey of Ouidin*, 1961; *The Whole Armour*, 1962; *The Secret Ladder*, 1963; *Heartland*, 1964; *The Eye of the Scarecrow*, 1965; *The Waiting Room*, 1967; *Tumatumari*, 1968; *Ascent to Omai*, 1970; *Black Marsden*, 1972; *Companions of the Day and Night*, 1975; *Da Silva da Silva's Cultivated Wilderness and Genesis of the Clowns*, 1977; *The Tree of the Sun*, 1978; *The Angel at the Gate*, 1982; *Carnival*, 1985; *The Guiana Quartet*, 1985 (includes *Palace of the Peacock*, *The Far Journey of Ouidin*, *The Whole Armour*, and *The Secret Ladder*).

Other literary forms

Wilson Harris' first published novel appeared in 1960, when he was thirty-nine. Before this, his creative efforts were mainly in poetry, which, given the poetic-prose of his novels, is not surprising. He has published two slim volumes of poems: *Fetish* (1951), issued under the pseudonym Kona Waruk, and *Eternity to Season* (1954). While the first collection is perceived as apprenticeship material, the second is generally praised and seen as complementary to his early novels; it anticipates the novels' symbolic use of the Guyanese landscape to explore the various antinomies that shape the artist and his community. Harris has published two volumes of short stories, *The Sleepers of Roraima* (1970), with three stories, and *The Age of the Rainmakers* (1971), with four. These stories are drawn from the myths and legends of the Aborigines of the Guyanese hinterland. Harris does not simply relate these myths and legends; as in his novels, he imbues them with symbolic and allegorical significance. Harris, conscious of how unconventional and difficult are his novels, has attempted to elucidate his theories of literature in several critical works. His language here, however, is as densely metaphorical as in his novels. Harris' ideas are outlined in *Tradition, the Writer, and Society* (1967), a group of short exploratory essays on the West Indian novel, and *History, Fable, and Myth in the Caribbean and Guianas* (1970), a series of three lectures. These ideas are developed in his two later volumes of essays, *Explorations: A Selection of Tales and Articles* (1981) and *The Womb of Space: The Cross-Cultural Imagination* (1983), in which Harris analyzes the works of a wide range of writers, including Ralph Ellison, William Faulkner, Paule Marshall, Christopher Okigbo, Edgar Allan Poe, Raja Rao, Jean Rhys, Derek Walcott, and Patrick White.

Achievements

From the publication of his very first novel, Harris' work has attracted much attention. Though many readers are puzzled by his innovative techniques and his mystical ideas, his works have received lavish praise. While firmly established as a major Caribbean novelist, Harris is not seen as simply a regional writer. Critics outside the Caribbean perceive him as one of the most original and significant writers of the second half of the twentieth century, and, in trying to come to grips with his ideas and techniques, have compared him with William Blake, Joseph Conrad, William Faulkner, Herman Melville, and W. B. Yeats. As would be expected of one who eschews the conventional realistic novel, Harris is not without his detractors. Some readers have pounced on his work for being idiosyncratic, obscure, and farraginous. Those who defend him indicate that Harris' novels demand more of the reader than the conventional work and that what initially appears to be merely obscure and confused is intended to shock the reader and force him to deconstruct his habitual perceptions and responses. His importance has been acknowledged by the many awards he has received from cultural and academic institutions: He received the English Arts Council Award twice (in 1968 and in 1970) and a Guggenheim Fellowship (in 1972), and has held many visiting professorships and fellowships at such institutions as Aarhus University (Denmark), Mysore University (India), Newcastle University (Australia), the University of Toronto, the University of the West Indies, the University of Texas, and Yale University. In 1984, he received an honorary doctorate from the University of the West Indies.

Biography

Theodore Wilson Harris was born in New Amsterdam, British Guiana (now known as Guyana), on March 24, 1921. He attended Queen's College, a prestigious high school staffed by English expatriates, from 1934 to 1939. He went on to study land surveying and geomorphology, and in 1942 became an assistant government surveyor and made the first of many expeditions into the interior of Guyana. Between 1944 and 1953, he led several expeditions into other interior and coastal areas. The interior, with its dense tropical jungles, vast savannahs, and treacherous rivers, and the coastal region, with its mighty estuaries and extensive irrigation system, had a strong effect on Harris, later reflected in his novels. These expeditions also made Harris aware of the life of the Amerindians and of the various peoples of Guyana of African, Asian, and European ancestry, who have come to populate his novels. While working as a surveyor, he nurtured his artistic talents by writing numerous poems, stories, and short essays for the little magazine *Kyk-over-al*, edited by the poet A. J. Seymour. In 1950, he visited Europe for the first time, touring England and the Continent, and in 1959 he emigrated to Great Britain. That year, he married Margaret Burns, a Scottish writer. (He was married in 1945 to Cecily Carew, but the marriage ended in divorce.) With the publication of his first novel in 1960, Harris became a full-time writer. He resides in

London and constantly travels to take up fellowships and professorships in Europe, Australia, India, the Caribbean, Canada, and the United States.

Analysis

Wilson Harris' novels are variations on one theme. He believes that polarization in any community is destructive in any form it takes, whether it is between the imperial and the colonial, the human and the natural, the physical and the spiritual, the historical and the contemporary, the mythic and the scientific, or even the living and the dead. The healthy community should be in a constant state of evolution or metamorphosis, striving to reconcile these static opposites. The artist himself must aspire to such a unifying perception if he is to be truly creative, and his art must reflect his complementary, reconciling vision. He should reject, for example, the rigid conventional demarcation between past and present, corporeal and incorporeal, literal and allegorical. Time past, present, and future should be interlaced. The dead should exist side by side with the living. The literal should be indistinguishable from the metaphorical. In adhering to such ideas of fictional form, Harris has produced innovative novels that some see as complex and challenging, others as obscure and idiosyncratic.

This perception of society and the artist and of the form his fiction should take informs all of Harris' novels, with gradations in emphasis, scope, and complexity. Some novels, for example, emphasize the polarization rather than the integration of a community. Some accent the allegorical rather than the realistic. Some juxtapose the living with the dead. There are shifts in setting from novel to novel. Harris' artistic psyche is embedded in Guyana, and, though he has lived in Great Britain since 1959, in his fiction he constantly returns to his native land, making use of the varied landscape of coastland, estuaries, jungles, waterfalls, mountains, and savannahs. In his later novels, the range of his settings expands to include the Caribbean, Great Britain, and Latin America.

Palace of the Peacock, Harris' first novel, is the first of *The Guiana Quartet*, four sequential novels which are set in different regions of Guiana. The novel is a perfect introduction to Harris' canon: It establishes the ideas and forms that are found in subsequent works. Of all of his novels, this is the one which has received the most extensive critical scrutiny and explication. Set in the Guyanese interior, the novel recounts the journey upriver of Donne, an efficient and ruthless captain, and his multiracial crew. They are looking for a settlement where they hope to find the Amerindian laborers who earlier fled Donne's harsh treatment. The account of the journey is provided by a shadowy first-person narrator, Donne's brother, who accompanies them. After an arduous journey, Donne and his crew reach the settlement, only to find that the Amerindians have left. They again set out in search of them and, as they travel further upriver, several of the crew meet their deaths—some of them accidentally, some not. Eventually, Donne and two members of the crew reach the source of the river, a waterfall, and, abandoning their boat, begin climbing the cliff, only to fall to their deaths. The narrative is quite thin, and is not given in as linear and realistic a way as this outline suggests. The novel, for example, begins with Donne being shot and killed before undertaking his journey, then proceeds to tell of the entire crew drowning but coming alive just before they reach the Amerindian settlement, and concludes with Donne falling to his death but reaching the mountaintop where stands the Palace of the Peacock.

The novel clearly is allegorical. Critics agree that Harris employs Donne and his strange crew as representations of antithetical yet complementary aspects of human experience. Yet their interpretations of what precisely these characters represent are quite diverse, and the novel accommodates them all. The novel is seen as examining the brotherhood of invader and invaded, the common destiny of the diverse races of Guyana, and the complementary and interdependent relationship between the material and the spiritual, the historical and the contemporary, and the living and the dead. The novel could be interpreted also as an allegorical study of the growth of the artist in an environment inhospitable to art. Drawing from his own experience in the challenging Guyanese hinterland, where he wrote his early pieces while working as a land surveyor, Harris shows that harsh surroundings put the aspiring artist in a quandary, for he is forced to look to his physical well-being by developing a materialistic, aggressive outlook that works against his contemplative, humane, artistic nature. At the end of the novel, Harris' narrator comes to realize that as an artist he must accept that he is the sum total of all the diverse antithetical experiences and impulses that coexist tensely but creatively in his psyche.

A cursory explication of the novel as such an allegorical *Bildungsroman* will provide an insight into Harris' unconventional artistry. Harris examines his narrator-protagonist's progression toward acceptance of the polarities of his artistic psyche in four broad phases which correspond to the four books of the novel. In book 1, the narrator, aspiring toward artistic and humane goals, suppresses his assertive and dictatorial tendencies. From the opening paragraph, it is evident that the narrator and Donne are alter egos: They represent antithetical aspects of one individual, who could be termed the protagonist. Their oneness is emphasized as much as their polarities. The protagonist's rejection of his Donnean qualities is signified by Donne's death in the novel's opening section and by the awakening of the narrator in a maternity ward, suggestive of a birth. After this scene, the journey upriver begins and Donne is found aboard the boat with his crew, but it is the narrator whose voice is prominent. At the end of book 1, Donne is described as being a shadow of his former self.

In book 2, the protagonist discovers that he cannot totally suppress his

Donnean qualities, for to survive as an artist in his harsh environment he must be both the humane, contemplative observer and the assertive, forceful participant. This shift is indicated by the narrator's mellowing attitude toward Donne, who reappears as his former assertive self in book 2. Donne himself, however, mellows toward the narrator, admitting that he is caught up in "material slavery" and that he hates himself for being "a violent taskmaster." Their gradual adjustment to each other is shown in the relationships among the eight members of the crew, who, described by Harris as "agents of personality," represent overlapping but distinct impulses of the divided protagonist. Their personalities tend to run the scale from Donne's to the narrator's. They have their own alter egos. In book 3, as Donne and the narrator adjust to each other—that is, as the protagonist tries to resolve the inner conflict between his contemplative and active natures—various pairs of the crew die.

In book 4, the protagonist attains a new conception of himself as an artist—a conception that accommodates his antithetical feelings and attitudes. He now perceives that though as an artist he must resist the qualities of Donne and members of the crew close to him, he cannot deny them, for the artist incorporates all of their characteristics no matter how unrelated to art they may appear to be. The artist must acquire the all-embracing vision. A host of metaphors suggests this complementary conception. The protagonist reaches the Palace of the Peacock, with its panoramic perspective of the savannah, by falling back into the savannah. The Palace of the Peacock is also El Dorado, which Harris describes as "City of Gold, City of God"; it encompasses both material and spiritual riches. The Palace, moreover, has many windows offering an encompassing view of the world below and stands in contrast to Donne's one-windowed prisonhouse of the opening chapter. Taken together with the peacock's color spectrum, the many eyes of the peacock's tail, and the harmonious singing which pervades the many palatial rooms, the Palace paradoxically suggests both oneness and multiplicity. Such a perception of the artistic vision offered in this interpretation of *The Palace of the Peacock* is not unique; it is found, for example, in the works of Yeats and Blake, whom Harris quotes several times in the novel. The uniqueness of the novel is to be found in the form and setting Harris employs to explore this familiar theme.

The Guyanese hinterland is most evocatively depicted in the novel, though realistic description recedes before the symbolic and allegorical functions of the setting. Though the characters occasionally emerge as living individuals and though their conversations have the authentic ring of Guyanese dialect and speech rhythm, they do not appear primarily as human figures but as allegorical forms. As a result, the protagonist's conflicts are not dramatized in any particularly credible, realistic situation. (*The Secret Ladder*, the last novel of *The Guiana Quartet*, which describes a similar river journey and a similarly ambivalent, tormented protagonist, provides a slightly more realistic, less allegorical study.)

The Far Journey of Ouidin, Harris' second novel, is set in the riverain Abary district of Guyana, which is not too far inland from the Atlantic coast. The setting is as evocatively portrayed as is the Guyanese interior in *Palace of the Peacock*. The inhabitants of this community are East Indian farmers whose forefathers came to Guyana as indentured laborers. A few of these farmers have accumulated material wealth and have established a contemporary version of the master-laborer relationship with the less fortunate. *The Far Journey of Ouidin* emphasizes the community's greed. It tells of Rajah's conspiring with his cousins to murder their illegitimate half brother to whom their father left his property. The murderers suffer for their crime: Ram, a powerful, ruthless moneylender, brings about their ruin, with the help of Ouidin, a drifter, who resembles the murdered half brother. Ram orders Ouidin to abduct Rajah's daughter, Beti. Ouidin, however, elopes with her. Thirteen years later when Ouidin is dying, Ram seeks to make Ouidin and Beti's unborn child his heir.

The narrative is slightly more substantial in this novel than in *Palace of the Peacock*, but it is similarly submerged beneath Harris' allegorical emphasis. The characters, fluctuating between allegorical and literal functions, do not really come alive. The novel begins with Ouidin's death and his vision of the past, which merges with the present and the future. He exists on several levels; he appears, for example, to be the murdered half brother. The novel emphasizes the polarized relationship between Ram, the unscrupulous materialist, and the sensitive, spiritual Ouidin, whose unborn child to whom Ram lays claim symbolizes the possibility in the dichotomized community of reintegration—a factor which is underscored by the novel's circular structure and the recurring images of the union of opposites, such as the reference to the marriage of the sun and moon, to the juxtaposition of fire and water, and to the natural cycle of death and rebirth. Ouidin, who strives to be an integrated individual, refers to "the dreadful nature in every compassionate alliance one has to break gradually in order to emerge into one's ruling constructive self."

The Whole Armour, the third novel of *The Guiana Quartet*, examines the fragmentation and integration of another Guyanese community, that of the riverain-coastal Pomeroon region. While the society of *The Far Journey of Ouidin* is disrupted by greedy materialists, whom Harris perceives as the contemporary equivalents of the exploitative colonizers, that of *The Whole Armour* is disturbed by unbridled passion which erupts into violence and murder. Harris does not want to suppress passion, but he believes that it should be counterbalanced by discipline and control. This complementary Dionysan-Apollonian relationship is suggested by a series of betrothal images and particularly by the image of the tiger (the word used for what in the novel is actually a jaguar), which connotes the antithetical but complementary aspects of Blake's tiger.

The plot is difficult to extract because of the virtual inseparability of the actual and the allegorical, the living and the dead, and because of the elusive metaphors, described by Harris as his "fantastication of imagery." The novel, in bare outline, tells of the protagonist Cristo's fleeing the law, having been accused, apparently without justification, of the murder of Sharon's sweetheart. Cristo is sheltered from the law by his mother, Magda, a prostitute, and Abram, who falsely claims to be his father. Cristo and Sharon become lovers and are fugitives together. Eventually, they are caught but view the future hopefully because of the child Sharon has conceived. Cristo, who is linked with both the tiger and Christ, and the virginal Sharon are set against the passionate older generation. The two constantly yearn for regeneration and perceive themselves as being the founders of a new social order. The explicit discussion of this need for a new order has encouraged some critics to see *The Whole Armour* as Harris' most obviously political novel.

The Secret Ladder could be considered a restatement of and a sequel to *Palace of the Peacock*; it has, however, more plausible characterization and straightforward structuring. Like Donne, the protagonist, Fenwick, is in charge of a crew of men that reflect the racial mixture of Guyana. They are on a government hydrographic expedition that is surveying a stretch of the Canje river as the first step in a planned water conservation scheme. Poseidon, the patriarchal head of a primitive community of descendants of runaway slaves, violently resents their intrusion. Fenwick tries, with the help of Bryant, one of his crew, and Catalena, Bryant's mistress, to win him over. There is much misunderstanding and confrontation. In the end, Poseidon is accidentally killed.

Fenwick, like the protagonist of *Palace of the Peacock*, is torn between "imagination and responsibility," between dominating and accommodating. His boat significantly is named *Palace of the Peacock*. Evidently, he is aware of the importance of integrating his contrary impulses. He is attempting to live in the world of men with the insight his counterpart, Donne, has gained in the Palace of the Peacock. This attempt leads to inner turmoil and disturbing ambivalence, which the novel underscores with numerous images and metaphors. Fenwick frequently mentions the need to unify the head and the heart. His inner contradiction, like Donne's, is externalized in the relationship among his crew: For example, Weng the hunter is compared with Chiung the hunted; Bryant the thoughtful is juxtaposed with Catalena the emotional. Despite the more conventional plot, characterization, and structure, the novel is clearly Harris'. Its theme is polarization and reconciliation, and it is charged with allegorical and symbolic implications.

Harris' next five novels—*Heartland*, *The Eye of the Scarecrow*, *The Waiting Room*, *Tumatumari*, and *Ascent to Omai*—are also set in Guyana and provide further explorations of community and creativity imperiled by various confrontations and polarizations. Yet he places the emphasis now on individuals and on deep probing of their consciousness. The protagonists become progressively more internalized. Subtler dichotomies are examined, such as concrete and abstract realities, scientific and mythic truths, fiction reflecting and being reality, individual and communal aspirations. And in *The Waiting Room* and *Tumatumari*, Harris examines for the first time the psyche of female protagonists. He portrays Prudence of *Tumatumari*, for example, as engaged in an imaginative reconstruction of her brutal past, which she metamorphoses into something meaningful to her present. *Ascent to Omai* similarly affirms the possibility of creativity in catastrophe. In these five novels, Harris' audacious experiments with form continue. In *The Eye of the Scarecrow*, which is perhaps the Harris novel that is structurally furthest removed from conventional form, and *The Waiting Room*, he introduces the disjointed diary form.

In the later novels—*Black Marsden, Companions of the Day and Night, Da Silva da Silva's Cultivated Wilderness and Genesis of the Clowns, The Tree of the Sun, The Angel at the Gate*, and *Carnival*—Harris shifts the emphasis from portraying society's fragmentation, as he did in the early novels, to its possibilities for reintegration. Rebirth and resurrection are common motifs. If the Caribbean's brutal colonial history and its multiracial population provide the ideal context for a heightened consideration of communal disintegration, its "cross-cultural imagination" is similarly suited to an exploration of communal integration. These later novels all feature cross-cultural Caribbean or South American protagonists. In so doing, they are not restrictively regional in scope; they are concerned with the human community at large. This is pointed up by their larger canvases. They are set not simply in the Caribbean and Guyana but in Great Britain, India, and Latin America as well. An increasingly common form of these novels is the employment of narrators as editors and biographers who seek to piece together the protagonists' lives and raise questions about the polarities of art and life and about the literal and representational functions of language itself.

The polarization in the assessment of Wilson Harris' work continues unabated. His advocates lavish praise on him, some perceiving him as a candidate for the Nobel Prize. Many appreciative articles, including two book-length studies, have been written on him. His upbraiders continue to complain that his novels are strange, with, as David Ormerod observes, "no discernible yardstick for meaning—just a simple bland identification, where X is symbolic of something, perhaps Y or Z, because the author has just this minute decided that such will be the case." Shirley Chew, speaking of *The Tree of the Sun*, states: "Harris has failed to rise to some of the more common expectations one brings to the reading of a novel." It is possible that such criticism is indicative of an inability to respond to the demands of Harris' challenging innovations; on the other hand, it is perhaps a reminder to Harris of his own rejection of the static polarization in community and creativity, a warning to him to heed the conventional in his pursuit of the innovative.

Other major works
SHORT FICTION: *The Sleepers of Roraima*, 1970; *The Age of the Rainmakers*, 1971.
POETRY: *Fetish*, 1951 (as Kona Waruk); *Eternity to Season*, 1954.
NONFICTION: *Tradition, the Writer, and Society*, 1967; *History, Fable, and Myth in the Caribbean and Guianas*, 1970; *Fossil and Psyche*, 1974; *Explorations: A Selection of Tales and Articles*, 1981; *The Womb of Space: The Cross-Cultural Imagination*, 1983.

Bibliography

Durix, Jean-Pierre. "Along Jigsaw Trail: An Interpretation of *Heartland*," in *The Commonwealth Novel in English*. II (July, 1982), pp. 127-128.
Gilkes, Michael. *Wilson Harris and the Caribbean Novel*, 1975.
Hearne, John. "The Fugitive in the Forest," in *The Islands in Between*, 1968. Edited by Louis James.
Howard, W. J. "Wilson Harris's *Guiana Quartet*: From Personal Myth to National Identity," in *ARIEL*. January, 1970, pp. 46-60.
James, C. L. R. *Wilson Harris: A Philosophical Approach*, 1965.
James, Louis. "Structure and Vision in the Novels of Wilson Harris," in *World Literature Written in English*. XXII (Spring, 1983), pp. 39-46.
Maes-Jelinek, Hena. *Wilson Harris*, 1982.
Moore, Gerald. *The Chosen Tongue*, 1969.
Ramchand, Ken. Preface to *Palace of the Peacock*, 1968.
Ramraj, Victor J. "*Palace of the Peacock*: A Portrait of the Artist," in *World Literature Written in English*. XXII (Spring, 1983), pp. 47-55.
Sparer-Adler, Joyce. "*Tumatumari* and the Imagination of Wilson Harris," in *Journal of Commonwealth Literature*. July, 1969, pp. 20-31.

Victor J. Ramraj

EDWARD HOAGLAND

Born: New York, New York; December 21, 1932

Principal long fiction
Cat Man, 1956; *The Circle Home*, 1960; *The Peacock's Tail*, 1965; *Seven Rivers West*, 1986.

Other literary forms
Edward Hoagland is known primarily not for his novels but for his essays and travel books. As an essayist and reviewer, he has been published in such periodicals as *Harper's*, *The Village Voice*, *Sports Illustrated*, *Commentary*, and *The Atlantic*; several anthologies of his essays are now in print. His travel narratives include *Notes from the Century Before: A Journal from British Columbia* (1969) and *African Calliope: A Journey to the Sudan* (1979). During the 1960's he also wrote short stories, which appeared in publications such as *Esquire*, *The New Yorker*, *New American Review*, and *The Paris Review*; three of his short stories have been republished in *City Tales* (1986). In addition, he has contributed nature editorials to *The New York Times* since 1979.

Achievements
With the publication of his first novel, *Cat Man*, in 1956, Hoagland received much favorable attention from the critics. The book won for Hoagland a Houghton Mifflin Literary Fellowship, and critics saw in him the makings of a first-rate novelist. They particularly praised his ability to capture a milieu—in this case, the seamy world of circus roustabouts, a world he presents with knowledgeable and detailed frankness. His second novel, *The Circle Home*, confirmed his potential. Once again, he succeeded in vividly re-creating a colorful environment, the sweaty world of a boxing gymnasium. He received several honors during this period as well, including a Longview Foundation Award in 1961, an American Academy of Arts and Letters Traveling Fellowship in 1964, and a Guggenheim Fellowship in 1964.

With the publication of *The Peacock's Tail*, however, Hoagland's career suffered a setback. In both the critics' and his own opinion, this book was a failure, and Hoagland, whose novels had never won for him a wide audience, turned away from long fiction. For the next twenty years, he worked primarily in nonfiction, producing essays and travel narratives to considerable acclaim, but in 1986, he made a triumphal return to the novel. *Seven Rivers West* was well received, combining as it does Hoagland's ability to re-create a sense of place—here, the North American wilderness—with his impressive knowledge of the natural world.

Biography

Edward Hoagland was born on December 21, 1932, in New York City. His father was a financial lawyer whose employers included Standard Oil of New Jersey and the United States Defense and State departments. When he was eight, his family moved to New Canaan, Connecticut, a fashionable community of country estates and exclusive clubs. He was sent off to boarding school at Deerfield Academy, where, because of his bookishness, he was assigned to a special corridor known as the Zoo, which was reserved for those whom the school deemed incorrigible misfits. Hoagland did have great difficulty fitting in as a child. In large part this was because of his stutter. Understandably, he shunned potentially embarrassing social situations, developing a love of solitude and wildlife instead. Indeed, from the age of ten onward, he became very close to nature and kept a variety of pets ranging from dogs to alligators.

He went to Harvard, where he was strongly drawn to writing, a medium in which he could speak unhampered by his stutter. He studied literature under such notables as Alfred Kazin, Archibald MacLeish, and John Berryman; encouraged by his professors, he set to work on his first novel. In his spare time he read Socialist publications and attended meetings of a Trotskyite cell in the theater district of Boston. He was graduated from Harvard cum laude in 1954 with his first novel already accepted by Houghton Mifflin.

Hoagland had to put his literary career on hold, however, when he was drafted. He served in the army from 1955 to 1957, working in the medical laboratory and looking after the morgue at Valley Forge Army Hospital in Pennsylvania. Following his discharge, Hoagland returned to New York City. Financially, times were very difficult. His father, who disapproved of his decision to become a writer, had cut him off. In fact, his father was so opposed to his son's career that he wrote to Houghton Mifflin's lawyer to try to stop publication of his first novel. Hoagland's annual income over the next fifteen years averaged three thousand dollars.

In 1960, his second novel was published and he married Amy Ferrara, from whom he was divorced in 1964. At about this time he also became active politically, marching in civil rights and peace demonstrations and mailing his draft card to President Lyndon Johnson. To supplement his income, he began accepting academic posts as well, teaching at such schools as Rutgers, Sarah Lawrence, the University of Iowa, and Columbia. In 1968, he married Marion Magid, the managing editor of *Commentary*, with whom he has a daughter, Molly. He and his family make their home in West Greenwich Village, but for five months of every year Hoagland lives in an eight-room farmhouse on one hundred acres of woodland near Barton, Vermont.

Analysis

Edward Hoagland's novels are marked by a keen eye for detail and a remarkable sense of place. They masterfully re-create unusual and often male-dominated environments, such as that of the circus or a boxing gymnasium. His protagonists tend to be isolated and lonely men, cut off through their own actions from those they love, men who generally have failed in their relationships with women. They are misfits, drifters, or dreamers, and the novels are often organized around their journeys, which may be merely flight, as in *The Circle Home*, or a clearly focused quest, as in *Seven Rivers West*. Because of this episodic structure, the books have a looseness that can approach the discursive at times, with flashbacks and digressions slowing the pace.

Many of these traits are already apparent in Hoagland's first work, *Cat Man*. Drawn from his own experience working in a circus, *Cat Man* offers a graphic and harrowing portrayal of the life of the low-paid circus roustabouts, most of whom are derelicts or social outcasts. With his usual attraction to the eccentric and offbeat, Hoagland creates a human menagerie, a gallery of grotesques such as Dogwash, who will not touch water and cleans himself by wiping his whole body as hard as he can with paper. The novel presents a brutal world in which violence threatens constantly from both the workers and the animals. In fact, the book begins with an attempted murder and ends with a lion attack. It is also a world of rampant racism, a world in which the insane are to be laughed at and women sexually used and abandoned. As sordid and disturbing as all this is, Hoagland conveys it with remarkable vividness and attention to detail. Indeed, it is the searing portrayal of this world that is the novel's great strength.

Fiddler, the main character, is a classic Hoagland protagonist. A youth who has been with the circus only seven weeks, he has been cut off from his family by his alcoholism and is very much an alienated man. Suffering from low self-esteem, he develops a foolhardy and almost obsessive fascination with the beauty and grace of his charges, the lions and tigers that it is his job, as a cat man, to tend. Hoagland's own interest in and knowledge of animals is quite evident, as he endows the cats with as much individuality as the humans. Yet while Hoagland is clearly as fascinated as Fiddler with the animals, he never sentimentalizes them. The cats may be magnificent but they can also be uncaring and deadly, a lesson that Fiddler finally and fatally learns.

Also typical of Hoagland's novels is the fact that *Cat Man* has a loose structure. Ostensibly, it is the story of one tragic day in Council Bluffs, but interspersed throughout the narrative are the events of other days in other places as Fiddler travels cross-country with the circus. Many of these episodes could stand on their own as quite good short stories, but inserted as they are within the novel's main narrative they interrupt the momentum and slow the book's flow.

Hoagland's second novel, *The Circle Home*, once again features a main character who is a lonely misfit. In this work, the protagonist is an over-the-hill boxer who rightly fears that he is doomed to become a derelict like his father. Again, too, he is a man who, through his own actions, is alienated from his family. Denny Kelly, though, is a less sympathetic figure than Fiddler. He has been so abusive toward his wife, Patsy, that she has repeatedly thrown him out. In fact, Denny seems incapable of committing himself to another person and simply takes advantage of women such as his wife or Margaret, an older woman whom he exploits for whatever material and sexual comforts she can supply.

Essentially, Denny is an immature child (indeed, he is strongly attracted to children), with all the selfishness and irresponsibility that that implies. Moreover, he avoids serious introspection whenever possible and actively fights any inclination toward thought by drowning himself in sensual pleasures. If Hoagland presents animals with considerable understanding in *Cat Man*, in *The Circle Home* he focuses on an individual who exists on little more than an animal level. Denny is a man who is incapable of expressing his feelings or organizing his life, who responds simply to the need for food, shelter, and sex.

If Fiddler clung to the cats in an attempt to give his life meaning, the one element in Denny's life that gives him a sense of achievement is boxing. The novel examines his fate once that is lost to him. Completely demoralized by being brutally beaten in a training bout, Denny abandons the ring and takes to the road, drifting closer and closer to his feared future as a derelict. While the ending of *Cat Man* was utterly bleak, *The Circle Home* offers some hope: In hitting rock bottom, Denny gains some degree of self-awareness. Although his future is far from certain, Denny does at least attempt to overcome his irresponsibility and selfishness as he tries to reconcile with his wife. He has made "the circle home," returning via a long and circuitous route of self-discovery.

Critics were generally enthusiastic about *The Circle Home*, praising in particular its convincing portrayal of the grimy world of the Better Champions' Gym. If *Cat Man* showed Hoagland's detailed knowledge of the circus, this novel shows his thorough familiarity with boxing, as he digresses on such subjects as types of fighters and gym equipment. The book's structure, however, is again quite loose, with repeated shifts in time and place and the use of an episodic journey as an organizing principle.

In Hoagland's third novel, however, the problems are more than simply structural. Regarded by the critics as his weakest piece of long fiction, *The Peacock's Tail* is the rambling story of Ben Pringle, a prejudiced and maladjusted WASP who has taken up residence in a seedy New York City hotel. As usual, Hoagland's main character is a misfit isolated from those he loves. Like Denny, Ben has difficulty maintaining a lasting relationship with a woman and has just been rejected by his lover, an experience that has left him with a badly damaged ego. Indeed, like the earlier protagonists, Ben in his troubled state needs stability and support. While Fiddler clung to his cats and Denny to boxing to retain some sense of pride and avoid a total collapse, Ben turns to children, becoming a storyteller and pied piper to the hordes of youngsters who inhabit his hotel.

If Denny was attracted to children, who mirrored his own arrested development, Ben seems to turn to them out of an inability to deal with adults, using their approval to boost his crumbling sense of self-worth. Powerless and out of control with his peers, he derives a sense of power and control from the adulation of the young. Hoagland apparently intends for the reader to believe that Ben finds happiness and fulfillment leading hundreds of children through the streets of New York to the strains of his newly acquired harmonica. Yet Ben's newfound role as pied piper seems less a solution to his problems than a frenzied attempt to escape them.

Once one doubts the validity of Ben's solution, however, one is also forced to question the reality of the novel's setting. While the faithful depiction of milieu was the great strength of Hoagland's earlier novels, *The Peacock's Tail* takes place in an Upper West Side welfare hotel, which is presented as if it were one large amusement park. The hotel is inhabited by vibrant, lusty blacks and Hispanics who exude an earthiness and enthusiasm that is apparently meant to balance Ben's Waspish reserve and alienation. The earlier novels portrayed their environments with a hard-edged and knowledgeable use of detail. Here the portrait is sentimentalized, a musical-comedy version of a welfare hotel.

This artistic and critical failure represented a setback for Hoagland's promising novelistic career, and he followed it with a twenty-year hiatus from long fiction. With his fourth novel, however, Hoagland fully redeemed himself. *Seven Rivers West* is an entertaining and dazzlingly inventive tale. Set in the North American West of the 1880's, it features the most likable incarnation of the Hoagland protagonist: Cecil Roop. Another man isolated from his loved ones, he, like Denny, has abandoned his family and is now on a journey. Yet while Denny drifted aimlessly, Cecil is on a quest: He wants to capture a grizzly bear. At least, that is his goal until he learns of the existence of Bigfoot, which then becomes his obsession. Like Fiddler's obsession with cats, however, Cecil's fascination with this mysterious creature ultimately proves tragic.

If this sounds like a tall tale, Hoagland grounds it in an utterly convincing reality, presented with documentary exactness. In fact, the novel includes a wealth of information about nature. Yet this information emerges spontaneously as the characters seek to understand their magnificent and overwhelming environment; the pace never slows as the book vigorously follows the characters' picaresque and perilous journey. Moreover, the novel includes Hoagland's most colorful assortment of eccentrics, ranging from Cecil's companion who specializes in jumping forty feet into a tub of water to a trader celebrated for his prowess in bladder-voiding competitions.

Probably the book's greatest achievement, however, as in Hoagland's first two novels, is its stunning and detailed sense of place. The unsentimental portrayal of the unspoiled West is at times rhapsodic as Hoagland presents a world that can chill with its beauty. Hoagland depicts not only the full glory but also the full fury of nature. He offers the reader a world that is as casually violent as that of *Cat Man*, a world where creatures can almost without warning be swept away in torrents or mauled by savage beasts. With its energy, its imaginativeness, and its sheer grandeur, *Seven Rivers West* is Hoagland at his best.

Hoagland's novels, published over a period of thirty years, have a number of traits in common. One is their focus on and sympathy for the downcast and outcast, for the social misfit who finds himself alone as he journeys through a hostile and dangerous world in which his mere survival is tenuous. Isolation is a constant theme, with the protagonists having great difficulty maintaining relationships with women. Yet as harsh and as lonely as these environments are, Hoagland's ability to describe them with honesty and fidelity gives his books a vividness and immediacy that leaves a lasting impact.

Other major works

SHORT FICTION: *City Tales*, 1986.

NONFICTION: *Notes from the Century Before: A Journal from British Columbia*, 1969; *The Courage of Turtles: Fifteen Essays About Compassion, Pain, and Love*, 1970; *Walking the Dead Diamond River*, 1973; *The Moose on the Wall: Field Notes from the Vermont Wilderness*, 1974; *Red Wolves and Black Bears*, 1976; *African Calliope: A Journey to the Sudan*, 1979; *The Edward Hoagland Reader*, 1979; *The Tugman's Passage*, 1982.

Bibliography

Irving, John. "Risking All for Gold and Grizzlies," in *The New York Times Book Review*. XCI (September 21, 1986), p. 1.

Charles Trainor

PAUL HORGAN

Born: Buffalo, New York; August 1, 1903

Principal long fiction

The Fault of Angels, 1933; *No Quarter Given*, 1935; *Main Line West*, 1936; *A Lamp on the Plains*, 1937; *Far from Cibola*, 1938; *The Habit of Empire*, 1939; *The Common Heart*, 1942; *The Devil in the Desert: A Legend of Life and Death in the Rio Grande*, 1952; *The Saintmaker's Christmas Eve*, 1955; *Give Me Possession*, 1957; *A Distant Trumpet*, 1960; *Mountain Standard Time*, 1962 (includes *Main Line West*, *Far from Cibola*, and *The Common Heart*); *Things as They Are*, 1964; *Memories of the Future*, 1966; *Everything to Live For*, 1968; *Whitewater*, 1970; *The Thin Mountain Air*, 1977; *Mexico Bay*, 1982.

Other literary forms

Throughout his long and meritorious career, Paul Horgan has been known as widely for his short fiction and nonfiction as for his novels. Most of his short fiction is found in three collections, but the best of his stories appear in *The Peach Stone: Stories from Four Decades* (1967). Like his fiction, Horgan's histories and biographies revolve around events and people of the American Southwest. His most prestigious history is *Great River: The Rio Grande in North American History* (1954), but *The Centuries of Santa Fe* (1956) and *Conquistadors in North American History* (1963) are also important works. His biographies, most notably *Lamy of Santa Fé: His Life and Times* (1975) and *Josiah Gregg and His Visions of the Early West* (1979), vividly chronicle the struggle of individuals and the clash of Spanish and Indian cultures on the Southwestern frontier. Horgan's work in drama includes the play *Yours, A. Lincoln* (1942) and the libretto to *A Tree on the Plains: A Music Play for Americans* (1943), an American folk opera with music by Ernst Bacon. His *Approaches to Writing* (1973) is composed of three long essays explaining his craft. Horgan's novel *A Distant Trumpet* was filmed in 1964; *Things as They Are* was filmed in 1970.

Achievements

As a novelist as well as a distinguished writer of nonfiction, Horgan has devoted his career to the American Southwest. Although he is regarded as a regionalist, some critics have rightly pointed out that he uses regional figures and settings essentially as vehicles for universal themes, much as William Faulkner used regional materials. Horgan's work should not be identified with the popular, formulaic Western writing of such authors as Zane Grey, Louis L'Amour, and Max Brand; rather, he should be seen as a significant figure in the tradition of literary Western fiction that has attracted the attention of critics and readers since the early 1960's.

Recognition for his writing has come in many forms. He won seventy-five hundred dollars in the Harper Prize Novel Contest for *The Fault of Angels* in 1933. He has been awarded two Guggenheim Fellowships (one in 1945, the other in 1958) to work on his nonfiction. For *Great River*, Horgan won the Pulitzer Prize in History and the Bancroft Prize of Columbia University. In 1957, the Campion Award for eminent service to Catholic letters was presented to him. The Western Literature Association paid tribute to Horgan with its distinguished Achievement Award (1973), and the Western Writers of America cited him with their Silver Spur Award (1976). He has twice been honored by the Texas Institute of Letters (in 1954 and in 1971).

Just as important as these awards, and an indication of the wide range of his interests and abilities, are the ways in which he has served his community and country. Horgan served as president of the board of the Santa Fe Opera (1958-1962) and the Roswell Museum (1946-1952). He became director of the Wesleyan Center for Advanced Studies in 1962 and remained so until 1967. President Lyndon B. Johnson made Horgan one of his first appointees to the Council of the National Endowment for the Humanities. In addition to being visiting scholar and writer-in-residence at a number of colleges and universities, Horgan has served on the board of the Aspen Institute and the Book-of-the-Month Club. Although some of his novels have sold in the millions and despite his fifty-year career, Horgan is not as well-known as many of his contemporaries. Those who are familiar with his work, however, see him as a prescient figure, a writer whose concern with the complex, multicultural history of the Southwest anticipated the challenging revisionism of the 1970's and the 1980's, when scholars and fiction writers alike offered a new, critical look at the West.

Biography

Paul Horgan was born in Buffalo, New York, on August 1, 1903. He moved to Albuquerque, New Mexico, with his parents in 1915, and attended the New Mexico Military Institute in Roswell until 1921, when he left to be at home when his father was dying. After working for a year at the Albuquerque *Morning Journal*, he moved to the East in 1923 to study at the Eastman School of Music in Rochester, New York. He returned to Roswell in 1926 and accepted the job of librarian at the New Mexico Military Institute. He remained in Roswell until 1942 and wrote his first five novels. Horgan spent World War II in Washington as chief of the Army Information Branch of the Information and Education Division of the War Department, where he supervised all the information that was sent to American troops all over the world. Horgan returned to New Mexico after the war and worked on his nonfiction, but after 1960 he became associated with Wesleyan University in different capacities, living and writing on the Wesleyan campus.

Analysis

Paul Horgan's fiction is dominated on one level by a skillful, aesthetic evocation of Southwestern landscape and climate and a sensitive delineation of character. His novels are exceptionally well written, with sharp detail and imagery often matched by a lyrical tone perfectly suited to the basic goodness of his protagonists. Yet to dwell on this strong sense of place is to miss a basic theme in his works and to misjudge the appeal of his writing. The strength of Horgan's fiction lies in the reader's immediate and sympathetic identification with the protagonists. Curiosity is perhaps man's most distinguishing feature. This is true not only in an academic sense but in a personal way as well: To varying degrees, people take an interest in their ancestry and family histories. They want to know who they are and whence they come. It is both a peculiarity and a trademark of Horgan's fiction that this kind of knowing is its constant concern. The dramatic center in Horgan's books revolves around people learning the truth about themselves and their lives.

Horgan employs two main narrative strategies to accomplish his end. In books such as *Far from Cibola* and *A Distant Trumpet*, individuals must deal with an unexpected event upsetting the routine of everyday life and, as a result, are challenged to define their own lives more clearly. On the other hand, in novels such as *Things as They Are* and *Whitewater*, his protagonists conduct a more conscious search for an understanding of who they are and make a deliberate attempt to come to terms with their own pasts.

Often in Horgan's fiction, discovering the truth about oneself occurs after some startling event disrupts the ordinary flow of life. Such is the case in *Far from Cibola*, which many critics regard as Horgan's best novel. This short work, set in and around a small town in New Mexico during the early years of the Great Depression, records what happens to a dozen of the local inhabitants during a day in which they are all briefly brought together as part of a large crowd protesting economic conditions. After the crowd threatens to turn into an unruly mob, the sheriff fires a warning shot above their heads into some trees and accidentally kills a teenager who had climbed up the tree to watch the excitement. The crowd disperses after the gunfire, and the remaining chapters describe what happens to the dozen characters the rest of the day. Although these figures span a broad band of the socioeconomic spectrum of the New Mexican (and American) landscape of the 1930's, *Far from Cibola* is not simply another proletarian novel of that decade. Economic problems and hardships are uppermost in the minds of almost everyone in the story, but the fate of each character hinges on his or her ability to recognize and accept reality as it suddenly appears.

The opening chapter provides a good example of what happens to all the characters in the novel. It begins with serene, pastoral images: Mountains are shimmering in the morning haze, and smoke from breakfast fires rises straight into the clear April sky. In Ellen Rood's kitchen, there is a springlike feeling of peace and well-being. As she lays wood for her own stove, Ellen listens to the sounds of her two small children out in the farmyard. Her son Donald is chopping at some wood with an ax that is too big for his hands, and her daughter Lena is washing her face from a tin dish sitting on the edge of the well. Without warning, however, smoke rolls back into her eyes and sparks sting her arms when Ellen attempts to start the fire. At about the same time, Ellen realizes that her children are strangely quiet. When she investigates, she discovers a huge rattlesnake nearby; she quickly hacks it to death before it can harm her children. There are many scenes such as this one in *Far from Cibola*, in which people suddenly have an idyllic world overturned by a more sober, often harsher reality. How they react is a good measure of their character. Not everyone can prevail as Ellen does.

The incident in the courthouse provides a social context for what happens to the novel's individuals. Until the crowd becomes violent, everything is fairly calm and orderly. There may be hunger and economic desperation in the community, but people have not yet fully faced the fact that there are no hidden food supplies and the government cannot help them. The killing underscores this bleak reality, and society as a whole must deal with this truth, as Ellen had to face the rattlesnake outside her kitchen door.

A Distant Trumpet, written more than two decades later, shows thematic concerns similar to those of *Far from Cibola*, but Horgan achieves this in a slightly different manner. The novel's primary setting is Fort Delivery, a frontier outpost near the Mexican border in the Arizona Territory during the late 1880's. Although there are a number of characters, the story centers on a young army lieutenant named Matthew Hazard and an Apache scout called Joe Dummy. Deftly and incisively, Horgan dramatizes Hazard's and Joe Dummy's roles in helping to make peace with a rebellious band of Indians who had escaped into Mexico, and the novel ends with Hazard, bitter and disillusioned, resigning from the army when Joe Dummy is treated no better than the Indians he helped to defeat.

Rather than using startling and often violent images, as in *Far from Cibola*, Horgan makes extensive use of flashbacks to the Civil War period and earlier as a useful device for pulling down and digging out illusion and sham and seeing the truth clearly. That Matthew Hazard is Horgan's vehicle for showing the necessity not only of recognizing but also of maintaining self-knowledge is brought out in a very short section titled "Scenes from Early Times." Consisting of a series of short questions and answers between Hazard and an unknown person, the conversation reveals the earliest and most important knowledge Matthew can recall: that he was his father's child. Indeed, it is no accident that this book often reads like a biography. To be one's father's child in *A Distant Trumpet* means being able to acknowledge the less well-known aspects of self as well as the more openly accepted parts. Tragedy occurs when individuals cannot or will not see that darker side.

One of the more striking scenes in the novel occurs when Matthew, on his way to Fort Delivery for the first time, meets White Horn. Sargeant Blickner, who has come to take Matthew to the fort, refuses to take an Indian along in his wagon, and Matthew must give him a direct order to do so. Even after this, Blickner baits White Horn on the way back and calls him "Joe Dummy," a nickname picked up later by soldiers at the fort. In previous sections, however, White Horn's courageous and often heroic life has been described at length, so that he has become an individual to the reader. Thus, readers share the narrator's feeling of outrage and indignation that no one at the fort can see Joe Dummy as anything but another "grimy" Indian. Horgan laments bitterly the failure of these people to see clearly and suggests that they will be lost until they somehow discover the truth about themselves and their social structure. In this sense, Fort Delivery becomes an ironic name for an individual's self-imprisonment. Horgan's flashbacks in *A Distant Trumpet* force his readers to look beyond appearance and not accept the false and commonplace, in much the same way the rattlesnake and courthouse incident in *Far from Cibola* made people confront the unpleasant realities in their lives. *A Distant Trumpet* poignantly reveals what happens when individuals (and society) are unable to see worlds other than their own.

In *Things as They Are*, perhaps the most autobiographical of all of his works, Horgan approaches the question of knowing oneself more directly. The novel is narrated by Richard, an adult writer who recounts certain events in his early childhood to help him understand the way he is now. Horgan continues Richard's story in two later novels: *Everything to Live For* and *The Thin Mountain Air*. *Things as They Are*, then, is a *Bildungsroman*, a story of growth and awakening, and through this format, Richard articulates his need to understand himself and others more clearly.

Like most stories about growing up, the boy Richard undergoes a variety of experiences that the adult Richard must now interpret if he is to make some sense of his life. Although he describes a close family life and happy summer trips to the mountains, Richard also discloses certain important conflicts and tensions for the young boy: an uncle who commits suicide, an autocratic grandfather, a well-meaning but overly protective mother, a father who is not quite strong enough. The novel's structure in its simplest terms is a delicate balancing act between Richard honestly depicting these family tensions and then explaining both what they meant to him and how they resulted in his seeing things as they are.

Things as They Are may be regarded as a prelude to *Whitewater*, which is also about a young man, Phillipson Durham, growing up. Set in the West Texas town of Belvedere during the years 1948-1949, the novel describes what happens to Phillipson and two high school classmates (Billy Breedlove and Marilee Underwood) during his senior year. Within this framework, the novel is essentially one long flashback by a much older Phillipson, who has written it, as the last chapter makes clear, for much the same reason Richard told his story in *Things as They Are*. Phillipson is probing for clues in his past that will allow him to understand the events of his senior year and what has happened to him since. Unlike Richard's, Phillipson's search is less successful and his conclusions more tentative.

Phillipson's quest for self-knowledge is marked by three central images in the novel: Lake Whitewater, Victoria Cochran's house, and the town's water tower. Lake Whitewater is a large, man-made lake formed when Whitewater Dam went into operation. What intrigues Phillipson is that deep under the lake's surface lies an abandoned town complete with houses, yards, and streetlamps. Billy informs Phillipson that when the lake is calm, the town can still be seen. The lake and submerged town thus become a metaphor for Phillipson's own lost knowledge about himself. Like the town, his past is still there, waiting to be viewed and understood if only he can see it clearly. Linked with this image is Crystal Wells, the home of Victoria Cochran, an elderly widow who befriends Phillipson and becomes his mentor. At Crystal Wells, Phillipson escapes the dreary provincialism of Belvedere and explores his own ideas and beliefs. It becomes an intellectual oasis where he can begin to define his own life. Opposed to this image is that of Belvedere's water tower, which Horgan unmistakenly identifies with unthinking and impulsive behavior. Caught up in the excitement of springtime and the end of his senior year, Billy Breedlove climbs to the top of the tower to paint the words "Beat Orpha City" on its side. He loses his footing, however, and falls ninety feet to the ground below. Billy's death and Marilee's subsequent suicide are warnings to Phillipson that impulse and feeling by themselves threaten understanding and growth. Phillipson overcomes his grief at Crystal Wells and recognizes that his own education is only beginning. As the last section of *Whitewater* suggests, however, Phillipson years later is still growing, still trying to understand those events and himself, quite aware that there are things that he cannot and perhaps will never know completely. Nevertheless, as Richard does in *Things as They Are*, Phillipson focuses on maintaining moments of wakeful insight.

Horgan's novels are best understood by recognizing that his protagonists are driven by a need to know themselves and their pasts. Given this theme, Horgan uses two main narrative techniques. On the one hand, as in *Far from Cibola* and *A Distant Trumpet*, his characters are confronted with events suddenly disrupting their lives and their normal sense of things. In novels such as *Things as They Are* and *Whitewater*, however, his protagonists deliberately set about exploring their pasts to learn about themselves. Horgan's message is the same with either method: The truth about oneself must be pursued, no matter what the cost. Anything else is escapism, a kind of vicarious participation in life. Horgan's characters do not shrink from this task; they embrace life fully.

Other major works

SHORT FICTION: *The Return of the Weed*, 1936; *Figures in a Landscape*, 1940; *The Peach Stone: Stories from Four Decades*, 1967.

PLAYS: *Yours, A. Lincoln*, 1942; *A Tree on the Plains: A Music Play for Americans*, 1943 (libretto, music by Ernst Bacon).

POETRY: *Lamb of God*, 1927; *Songs After Lincoln*, 1965; *The Clerihews of Paul Horgan*, 1985.

NONFICTION: *New Mexico's Own Chronicle*, 1937 (with Maurice G. Fulton); *Great River: The Rio Grande in North American History*, 1954; *The Centuries of Santa Fe*, 1956; *Rome Eternal*, 1959; *A Citizen of New Salem*, 1961; *Conquistadors in North American History*, 1963; *Peter Hurd: A Portrait Sketch from Life*, 1965; *The Heroic Triad: Essays in the Social Energies of Three Southwestern Cultures*, 1970; *Encounters with Stravinsky: A Personal Record*, 1972; *Approaches to Writing*, 1973; *Lamy of Santa Fé: His Life and Times*, 1975; *Josiah Gregg and His Visions of the Early West*, 1979.

Bibliography

Carter, Alfred. "On the Fiction of Paul Horgan," in *New Mexico Quarterly*. VII (August, 1937), pp. 207-216.

Day, James M. *Paul Horgan*, 1967.

Gish, Robert. *Paul Horgan*, 1983.

Kraft, James. "No Quarter Given: An Essay on Paul Horgan," in *Southwestern Historical Quarterly*. LXXX (July, 1976), pp. 1-32.

Pilkington, William T. "Paul Horgan," in *My Blood's Country: Studies in Southwestern Literature*, 1973.

Terry L. Hansen

P. D. JAMES

Born: Oxford, England; August 3, 1920

Principal long fiction

Cover Her Face, 1962; *A Mind to Murder*, 1963; *Unnatural Causes*, 1967; *Shroud for a Nightingale*, 1971; *An Unsuitable Job for a Woman*, 1972; *The Black Tower*, 1975; *Death of an Expert Witness*, 1977; *Innocent Blood*, 1980; *The Skull Beneath the Skin*, 1982; *A Taste for Death*, 1986.

Other literary forms

Though P. D. James is known principally as a novelist, she is also a short-story writer and a playwright. The great bulk of James's work is in the form of the long narrative, but her short fiction has found a wide audience through its publication in *Ellery Queen's Mystery Magazine* and other popular periodicals. It is generally agreed that James requires the novel form to show her literary strengths to best advantage. Still, short stories such as "The Victim" reveal in microcosm the dominant theme of the long works. James's lone play, *A Private Treason*, was first produced in London on March 12, 1985.

Achievements

James's first novel, *Cover Her Face*, did not appear until 1962, at which time the author was in her early forties. Acceptance of her as a major crime novelist, however, grew very quickly. *A Mind to Murder* appeared in 1963, and with the publication of *Unnatural Causes* in 1967 came that year's prize from the Crime Writers Association. In the novels which have followed, James has shown an increasing mastery of the labyrinthine murder-and-detection plot. This mastery is the feature of her work that most appeals to one large group of her readers, while a second group of readers would single out the subtlety and psychological validity of her characterizations. Critics have often remarked that James, more than almost any other modern mystery writer, has succeeded in overcoming the limitations of the genre. In addition, she has created one of the more memorable descendants of Sherlock Holmes. Like Dorothy Sayers' Lord Peter Wimsey and Agatha Christie's Hercule Poirot, James's Adam Dalgliesh is a sleuth whose personality is more interesting than his skill in detection.

Biography

Phyllis Dorothy James was born in Oxford, England, on August 3, 1920. She was graduated from Cambridge High School for Girls in 1937. She was married to Ernest C. B. White, a medical practitioner, from August 8, 1941, until his death in 1964. She worked as a hospital administrator from 1949 to 1968 and as a civil servant in the Department of Home Affairs, London, from 1968 to 1972. From 1972 until her retirement in 1979, she was a senior civil servant in the crime department.

Analysis

P. D. James's work is solidly in the tradition of the realistic novel. Her novels are intricately plotted, as successful novels of detection must be. Through her use of extremely well delineated characters and a wealth of minute and accurate details, however, James never allows her plot to distort the other aspects of her novel. As a result of her employment, James had extensive contact with physicians, nurses, civil servants, police officials, and magistrates. She uses this experience to devise settings in the active world where men and women busily pursue their vocations. She eschews the country weekend murders of her predecessors, with their leisure-class suspects who have little more to do than chat with the amateur detective and look guilty.

A murder requires a motive, and it is her treatment of motivation that sets James's work apart from most mystery fiction. Her suspects are frequently the emotionally maimed who, nevertheless, manage to function with an apparent normality. Beneath their veneer, dark secrets fester, producing the phobias and compulsions they take such pains to disguise. James's novels seem to suggest that danger is never far away in the most mundane setting, especially the workplace. She avoids all gothic devices, choosing instead to create a growing sense of menace just below the surface of everyday life. James's murderers rarely kill for gain; they kill to avoid exposure of some sort.

The setting for *Shroud for a Nightingale* is a nursing hospital near London. The student nurses and most of the staff are in permanent residence there. In this closed society, attachments—sexual and otherwise—are formed, rivalries develop, and resentments grow. When a student nurse is murdered during a teaching demonstration, Inspector Adam Dalgliesh of Scotland Yard arrives to investigate. In the course of his investigation, Dalgliesh discovers that the murdered girl was a petty blackmailer, that a second student nurse (murdered soon after Dalgliesh's arrival) was pregnant but unmarried and had engaged in an affair with a middle-aged surgeon, that one member of the senior staff is committing adultery with a married man from the neighborhood and another is homosexually attracted to one of her charges. At the root of the murders, however, is the darkest secret of all, a terrible sin which a rather sympathetic character has been attempting both to hide and expiate for more than thirty years. The murder weapon is poison, which serves also as a metaphor for the fear and suspicion that rapidly spread through the insular world of the hospital.

Adam Dalgliesh carries a secret burden of his own. His wife and son died during childbirth. He is a sensitive and cerebral man, a poet of some reputation. These deaths have left him bereft of hope and intensely aware of the fragility of man's control over his own life. Only the rules that humankind has painstakingly fashioned over the centuries can ward off degeneration and annihilation. As a policeman, Dalgliesh enforces society's rules, giving himself a purpose for living and some brief respite from his memories. Those who commit murder contribute to the world's disorder and hasten the ultimate collapse of civilization. Dalgliesh will catch them and see that they are punished.

In *An Unsuitable Job for a Woman*, published within a year of *Shroud for a Nightingale*, James introduces her second recurring protagonist. Cordelia Gray's "unsuitable job" is that of private detective. Gray unexpectedly falls heir to a detective agency and, as a result, discovers her vocation. Again, James avoids the formularized characterization. Gender is the most obvious but least interesting difference between Dalgliesh and Gray. Dalgliesh is brooding and introspective; although the narratives in which he appears are the very antithesis of the gothic novel, there are aspects of the gothic hero in his behavior. Gray, on the other hand, is optimistic, outgoing, and good-natured, despite her unfortunate background (she was brought up in a series of foster homes). She is a truth seeker and, like William Shakespeare's Cordelia, a truth teller. Dalgliesh and Gray are alike in their cleverness and competence. Their paths occasionally cross, and a friendly rivalry exists between them.

In *Death of an Expert Witness*, James's seventh novel, Dalgliesh again probes the secrets of a small group of coworkers and their families. The setting this time is a laboratory that conducts forensic examinations. James used her nineteen years of experience as a hospital administrative assistant to render the setting of *Shroud for a Nightingale* totally convincing, and she uses her seven years of work in the crime department of the Home Office to the same effect in *Death of an Expert Witness*. In her meticulous attention to detail, James writes in the tradition of Gustave Flaubert, Leo Tolstoy, and the nineteenth century realists. Because the setting, characterizations, and incidents of a James novel are so solidly grounded in detail, it tends to be considerably longer than the ordinary murder mystery. This fact accounts for what little adverse criticism her work has received. Some critics have suggested that so profuse is the detail, the general reader may eventually grow impatient—that the pace of the narrative is too leisurely. These objections from some contemporary critics remind the reader once more of James's affinity with the novelists of the nineteenth century.

The laboratory in which the expert witness is killed serves as a focal point for an intriguing cast of characters. Ironically, the physiologist is murdered while he is examining physical evidence from another murder. The dead man leaves behind a rather vacant, superannuated father, who lived in the house with him. The principal suspect is a high-strung laboratory assistant, whom the deceased bullied and gave an unsatisfactory performance rating. The new director of the laboratory has an attractive but cruel and wanton sister, with whom he has a relationship that is at least latently incestuous. In addition, Dalgliesh investigates a lesbian couple, one of whom becomes the novel's second murder victim; a melancholy physician, who performs autopsies for the police and whose unpleasant wife has just left him; the physician's two curious children, the elder girl being very curious indeed; a middle-aged babysitter, who is a closet tippler; and a crooked cop, who is taking advantage of a love-starved young woman of the town. In spinning her complex narrative, James draws upon her intimate knowledge of police procedure, evidential requirements in the law, and criminal behavior.

The publication in 1980 of *Innocent Blood* marked a departure for James. While the novel tells a tale of murder and vengeance, it is not a detective story. Initially, the protagonist is Philippa Rose Palfrey—later, the novel develops a second center of consciousness. Philippa is eighteen, the adopted daughter of an eminent sociologist and a juvenile court magistrate. She is obsessed with her unremembered past. She is sustained by fantasies about her real parents, especially her mother, and the circumstances which forced them to give her up for adoption. Despite these romantic notions, Philippa is intelligent, resourceful, and tenacious, as well as somewhat abrasive. She takes advantage of the Children Act of 1975 to wrest her birth record from a reluctant bureaucracy.

The record shows that she was born Rose Ducton, to a clerk and a housewife in Essex. This revelation sends Philippa rushing to the dreary eastern suburb where she was born, beginning an odyssey which will eventually lead to her mother. She discovers that her fantasies cannot match the lurid realities of her past. Her father was a child molester, who murdered a young girl in an upstairs room of his house. Her mother apparently participated in the murder and was caught trying to take the body away in her car. Her father has died in prison, and her mother is still confined. Though horrified, Philippa is now even more driven to find explanations of some sort and to rehabilitate the image of her mother. She visits Mary Ducton in prison, from which she is soon to be released, and eventually takes a small flat in London, where they will live together.

In chapter 8, James introduces the second protagonist, at which time the novel becomes as much his as it is Philippa's. Norman Scase is fifty-seven and newly retired from his job as a government accounts clerk. Scase is the widowed father of the murdered girl. He retires when he learns of Mary Ducton's impending release, for all of his time will be required to stalk her so that, at the appropriate moment, he may kill her. The murder of young Julia Mavis Scase robbed her father of the same years it stole from Philippa. Philippa is desperately trying to reclaim these lost years by learning to know, forgive, and love her mother. Scase is driven to a far more desperate act.

In form, *Innocent Blood* resembles Tolstoy's *Anna Karenina* (1873-1877). Like Anna and Levin, the dual protagonists proceed through the novel along separate paths. Philippa has no knowledge of Scase's existence, and he knows her only as the constant companion of the victim he is tracking all over London. James makes the city itself a character in the novel, and as Philippa shares her London with her mother, it is fully realized in Dickensian detail. Philippa is the more appealing protagonist, but Scase is a fascinating character study: the least likely of premeditating murderers, a little man who is insignificant in everything except his *idée fixe*. James created a similar character in "The Victim," a short story appearing seven years earlier. There, a dim and diffident assistant librarian stalks and murders the man who took his beautiful young wife away from him. The novel form, however, affords James the opportunity to develop completely this unpromising material into a memorable character. As Scase lodges in cheap hotels, monitors the women's movements with binoculars, and stares up at their window through the night, the reader realizes that the little man has found a purpose which truly animates his life for the first time. He and Philippa will finally meet at the uncharacteristically melodramatic climax (the only blemish on an otherwise flawless novel).

Commander Adam Dalgliesh returns in *A Taste for Death* after an absence of nine years. He is heading a newly formed squad charged with investigating politically sensitive crimes. He is assisted by the aristocratic chief inspector John Massingham and a new recruit, Kate Miskin. Kate is bright, resourceful, and fiercely ambitious. Like Cordelia Gray, she has overcome an unpromising background: She is the illegitimate child of a mother who died shortly after her birth and a father she has never known. The title of the novel is evocative. A taste for death is evident in not only the psychopathic killer but also Dalgliesh and his subordinates, the principal murder victim himself, and, surprisingly, a shabby High Church Anglican priest, reminiscent of one of Graham Greene's failed clerics.

When Sir Paul Berowne, a Tory minister, is found murdered along with a tramp in the vestry of St. Matthew's Church in London, Dalgliesh is put in charge of the investigation. These murders seem linked to the deaths of two young women previously associated with the Berowne household. The long novel (more than 450 pages) contains the usual array of suspects, hampering the investigation with their evasions and outright lies, but in typical James fashion, each is portrayed in three dimensions. The case develops an additional psychological complication when Dalgliesh identifies with a murder victim for the first time in his career and a metaphysical complication when he discovers that Berowne recently underwent a profound religious experience in the church, one reportedly entailing stigmata. Perhaps the best examples of James's method of characterization are the elderly spinster and the ten-year-old boy of the streets who discover the bodies in chapter 1. In the hands of most other crime writers, these characters would have been mere plot devices, but James gives them a reality which reminds the reader how deeply a murder affects everyone associated with it in any way. Having begun the novel with Miss Wharton and Darren, James returns to them in the concluding chapter.

The action of all of James's novels proceeds from that most extreme form of antisocial behavior, murder. The intricacy of her plots and the scrupulosity of her details meet the highest standards of the mystery genre. Her deep probing of personality, however, is more like that of another James, Henry, than like that of her fellow crime writers. Murders are committed by human beings. Dalgliesh muses in *A Taste for Death* that he has learned, like most people, to accept and carry his load of guilt through life. The murderers that he so relentlessly pursues have not.

Other major works

PLAY: *A Private Treason*, 1985.

NONFICTION: *The Maul and the Pear Tree: The Ratcliffe Highway Murders, 1811*, 1971 (with T. A. Critchley).

Bibliography

Bakerman, Jane S. "Cordelia Gray: Apprentice and Archetype," in *Clues*. V (Spring/Summer, 1984), pp. 101-114.

Benstock, Bernard. "The Clinical World of P. D. James," in *Twentieth-Century Women Novelists*, Vol. 16, 1982. Edited by Thomas F. Staley.

Cannon, M. "Mistress of Malice Domestic," in *Macleans*. XCIII (June 30, 1980), p. 50.

Gidez, Richard B. *P. D. James*, 1986.

Siebenheller, Norman. *P. D. James*, 1982.

Winks, Robin W. "P. D. James: Murder and Dying," in *The New Republic*. CLXXV (July 31, 1976), pp. 31-32.

Patrick Adcock

RUTH PRAWER JHABVALA

Born: Cologne, Germany; May 7, 1927

Principal long fiction

To Whom She Will, 1955 (U.S. edition, *Amrita*, 1956); *The Nature of Passion*, 1956; *Esmond in India*, 1958; *The Householder*, 1960; *Get Ready for Battle*, 1962; *A Backward Place*, 1965; *A New Dominion*, 1972 (U.S. edition, *Travelers*, 1973); *Heat and Dust*, 1975; *In Search of Love and Beauty*, 1983.

Other literary forms

Though Ruth Prawer Jhabvala is known mainly as a novelist, she is also an accomplished writer of short stories, film scripts, and essays. Among her collections of short stories are *Like Birds, Like Fishes and Other Stories* (1963), *A Stronger Climate: Nine Stories* (1968), *An Experience of India* (1972), and *How I Became a Holy Mother and Other Stories* (1976); *Out of India* (1986) is a selection of stories from these volumes. *Shakespeare Wallah* (1965; with James Ivory), *Heat and Dust* (1983), and *A Room with a View* (1986; based on E. M. Forster's novel) are her best-known film scripts.

Achievements

Jhabvala has achieved remarkable distinction, both as a novelist and as a short-story writer, among writers on modern India. She has been compared with E. M. Forster, though the historical phases and settings of the India they portray are widely different. The award of the Booker Prize for *Heat and Dust* in 1975 made her internationally famous. Placing Jhabvala in a literary-cultural tradition is difficult: Her European parentage, British education, marriage to an Indian, and—after many years in her adopted country—change of residence from India to the United States perhaps reveal a lack of belonging, a recurring "refugee" consciousness. Consequently, she is not an Indian writing in English, nor a European writing on India, but perhaps a writer of the world of letters deeply conscious of being caught up in a bizarre world. She is sensitive, intense, ironic—a detached observer and recorder of the human world. Her almost clinical accuracy, her sense of the graphic, the comic, and the ironic makes her one of the finest writers on the contemporary scene.

Biography

Ruth Prawer was born in Cologne, Germany, on May 7, 1927, the daughter of Marcus and Eleonora Prawer; her family's heritage was German, Polish, and Jewish. She emigrated to England in 1939, became a British citizen in 1948, and obtained an M.A. in English from Queen Mary College,

London, in 1951. That same year, she married C. H. S. Jhabvala, an Indian architect, and went to live in India. She resided there until 1975, when she moved to New York. She has three daughters, Renana, Ava, and Feroza, who live in India. Jhabvala's friendship and collaboration with filmmakers James Ivory and Ismail Merchant, which began in the 1960's, opened a new phase of her career; her work on film scripts enriched her technique as a writer of fiction and widened her vision.

Analysis

Ruth Prawer Jhabvala's distinctive qualities as a novelist grow from her sense of social comedy. She excels in portraying incongruities of human behavior, comic situations which are rich with familial, social, and cultural implications. Marital harmony or discord, the pursuit of wealth, family to-getherness and feuds, the crisis of identity and homelessness—these are among the situations that she repeatedly explores in her fiction. She writes with sympathy, economy, and wit, with sharp irony and cool detachment.

Jhabvala's fiction has emerged out of her own experience of India. "The central fact of all my work," she once told an interviewer, "is that I am a European living permanently in India. I have lived here for most of my adult life . . . . This makes me not quite an outsider either." Much later, however, in "Myself in India," she revealed a change in her attitude toward India: "However, I must admit I am no longer interested in India. What I am interested in now is myself in India . . . my survival in India."

This shift in attitude has clearly affected Jhabvala's fiction. There is a distinct Indianness in the texture and spirit of her first five novels, which are sunny, bright, social comedies offering an affirmative view of India. The later novels, darkened by dissonance and despair, reveal a change in the novelist's perspective.

Amrita inaugurates Jhabvala's first phase, in which reconciliation between two individuals (symbolic as well of a larger, social integration) is at the center of the action. Amrita, a young, romantic girl, has a love affair with Hari, her colleague in radio. Their affair is portrayed with a gentle comic touch: She tells Hari of her determination to marry him at all costs; he calls her a goddess and moans that he is unworthy of her. Jhabvala skillfully catches the color and rhythm of the Indian phraseology of love.

While this affair proceeds along expected lines, Pandit Ram Bahadur, Hari's grandfather, is planning to get his grandson married to Sushila, a pretty singer, in an arranged match. When Hari confesses to his brother-in-law that he loves Amrita, he is advised that first love is only a "game," and no one should take it seriously. Hari then is led to the bridal fire and married to Sushila. He forgets his earlier vows of love for Amrita, even the fact that he applied for a passport to go with her to England.

The forsaken maiden, Amrita, finds her hopes for a happy union revived when another man, Krishna Sengupta, writes her a letter full of love and tenderness. Enthralled after reading his six-page letter, she decks her hair with a beautiful flower, a sign of her happy reconciliation with life. Amrita shares in the sunshine of love that comes her way.

The original title of the novel, *To Whom She Will* (changed to *Amrita* for the American edition), alludes to a story in a classic collection of Indian fables, the *Pañchatantra* (between 100 B.C. and A.D. 500; *The Morall Philosophie of Doni*, 1570). In the story, which centers on a maiden in love, a Hindu sage observes that marriage should be arranged for a girl at a tender age; otherwise, "she gives herself to whom she will." This ancient injunction is dramatized in the predicaments of Hari, Amrita, Sushila, and Sengupta, the four main characters. The irony lies in the fact that Amrita does not marry "whom she will." Nevertheless, the regaining of happiness is the keynote of Jhabvala's first novel of family relations and individual predicaments.

Alluding to Swami Paramananda's translation of the *Bhagavad Gītā* (c. fifth century B.C.), which Jhabvala quotes, her second novel, *The Nature of Passion*, deals with one of the three kinds of passion which are distinguished in the *Bhagavad Gītā*: that which is worldly, sensuous, pleasure-seeking. This passion, or *rajas*, rules the world of Lalaji and his tribe, who represent the rising middle class and whose debased values become the object of Jhabvala's unsparing irony. She presents a series of vignettes of the life of the affluent—such as Lalaji and the Vermas—who migrated to India after the partition and continued to prosper. Here, Jhabvala's characters are not intended to be fully rounded individuals; rather, they play their parts as embodiments of various passions.

Lalaji's role is to illustrate the contagious effects of greed and corruption. An indiscreet letter written by his older son finds its way into a government file controlled by Chandra, his second son. When Lalaji asks Chandra to remove the incriminating letter, Chandra's self-righteous wife, Kanta, objects. She soon realizes, however, that their comforts and their holidays depend upon Lalaji's tainted money, and she relents, allowing the letter to be removed. Lalaji's daughter Nimmi, too, moves from revolt to submission. Lalaji's tenderness for Nimmi is conveyed beautifully. When she cuts her hair short, Lalaji accepts this sign of modernity. Nevertheless, despite her attraction to another young man, she accepts the marriage partner chosen for her by her family.

Jhabvala's irony is cutting, but her style in this novel has an almost clinical precision, a detachment that discourages reader involvement. By concentrating on social types rather than genuinely individualized characters, she limits the appeal of the novel, which already seems badly dated.

Jhabvala's third novel, *Esmond in India*, as its title suggests, is concerned with the conflict between cultures. Esmond is an Englishman, a shallow man with a handsome face who tutors European women in Hindi language and culture and serves as a guide to visitors. He is an egotistic, aggressive colonial, and Jhabvala is relentless in her irony in sketching him, especially in a scene at the Taj Mahal where he loses his shoes. The pretentious Esmond is cut down to size and becomes a puny figure.

Esmond's relationship with his wife, Gulab, is the novel's central focus. She is a pseudoromantic Indian girl, very fond of good food. Their marriage is in ruins: Esmond feels trapped and speaks with scorn of her dull, alien mind, while she is keenly aware of his failure to care for her. Nevertheless, Gulab, as a true Hindu wife, bears Esmond's abuse, his indulgence in love affairs, until their family servant attempts to molest her. She then packs her bag and leaves Esmond.

Is Gulab a rebel or a complete conformist? In marrying Esmond, an Englishman, she surely seems to have become a rebel. Later, however, she is subservient in response to Esmond's cruelty; the servant assaults her because he knows that Esmond does not love his wife. This sets into motion her second rebellion: separation from Esmond. Gulab is a complex, memorable character.

Esmond, too, though he is drawn with sharp irony, is no mere caricature. At the heart of the novel is his overwhelming sense of a loss of identity, a crisis which grips his soul and makes him unequal to the task of facing India, that strange land.

The Householder is perhaps Jhabvala's most successful, least problematic, most organically conceived novel. A true social comedy, it is a direct, simple "impression of life." It centers on the maturation of its likable central character, Prem, a Hindi instructor in Mr. Khanna's private college. Prem is a shy, unassuming young man, in no way exceptional, yet his growth to selfhood, presented with insight and humor, makes for compelling fiction.

The title *The Householder* is derived from the Hindu concept of the four stages of a man's life; the second stage, that of a family man, is the one which the novel explores. Prem's relations with his wife, Indu, are most delicately portrayed. The scene of Prem loving Indu on the terrace in moonlight is both tender and touching. They both sense the space and the solitude and unite in deep intimacy. Prem realizes that Indu is pregnant and tenderly touches her growing belly—scenes which show Jhabvala at her best and most tender.

Prem's troubles are mainly economic—how to survive on a meager salary—and the comedy and the pathos which arise out of this distress constitute the real stuff of the novel. The indifference, the arrogance, and the insensitivity of the other characters are comically rendered, emphasizing Prem's seeming helplessness, as he struggles to survive and to assert his individuality. (A minor subplot is contributed by Western characters: Hans Loewe, a seeker after spiritual reality, and Kitty, his landlady, provide a contrast to Prem's struggle.) Nevertheless, Prem is finally able to overcome his inexperience and immaturity, attaining a tenderness, a human touch, and a balance which enable him to achieve selfhood and become a true "house-holder."

Get Ready for Battle, Jhabvala's fifth novel, resembles *The Nature of Passion*. Like that earlier novel, it pillories the selfish, acquisitive society of postindependence India. In particular, it shows how growing urbanization affects the poor, dispossessing them of their land. Like *The Nature of Passion*, *Get Ready for Battle* derives its title from the *Bhagavad Gītā*, alluding to the scene in which Lord Krishna instructs Arjuna to "get ready for battle" without fear; similarly, Jhabvala's protagonist, Sarla Devi, urges the poor to get ready for battle to protect their rights. *Get Ready for Battle* is superior to *The Nature of Passion*, however, in its portrayal of interesting and believable characters. While the characters in the later novel still represent various social groups or points of view, they are not mere types.

The central character, Sarla Devi, deeply committed to the cause of the poor, is separated from her husband, Gulzari Lal. They represent two opposite valuations of life: She leads her life according to the tenets of the *Bhagavad Gītā*, while he, acquisitive and heartless, is a worshiper of Mammon. The main action of the novel centers on her attempt to save the poor from being evicted from their squatters' colony and also to save her son from following her father's corrupt life-style. She fails in both these attempts, yet she is heroic in her failure.

Jhabvala brilliantly depicts the wasteland created by India's growing cities, which have swallowed farms and forests, at the same time destroying the value-structure of rural society. Yet *Get Ready for Battle* also includes adroitly designed domestic scenes. Kusum, Gulzari Lal's mistress, is shown with sympathy, while the relationship between two secondary characters, the married couple Vishnu and Mala, is portrayed with tenderness as well as candor. They show their disagreements (even speak of divorce), yet they are deeply in love. For them, "getting ready for battle" is a kind of game, a comic conflict, rather than a serious issue.

Jhabvala's next novel, *A Backward Place*, initiated the second phase of her career, marked by dark, despairing comedies disclosing a world out of joint. In this novel, too, Jhabvala began to focus more attention on encounters between East and West and the resulting tensions and ironies. The novel's title, which refers to a European character's condescending assessment of Delhi, suggests its pervasive irony; neither Indians nor Europeans are spared Jhabvala's scorn. While it features an appealing protagonist, the novel is too schematic, too much simply a vehicle for satire.

A Backward Place was followed by *Travelers*, a novel in the same dark mode, which presents the Western vision of contemporary India with telling irony. European girls seek a spiritual India, but the country that they actually experience is quite the opposite. Despite its satiric bite, the novel must be judged a failure: The great art of fiction seems to degenerate here into mere journalism, incapable of presenting a true vision of contemporary India.

This forgettable novel was followed by Jhabvala's most widely praised work, *Heat and Dust*, the complex plot of which traces parallels between the experiences of two Englishwomen in India: the unnamed narrator and her grandfather Douglas' first wife, Olivia. In the 1930's, Olivia came to India as Douglas' wife. Bored by her prosaic, middle-class existence, Olivia is drawn to a Muslim nawab with whom she enjoys many escapades. Invited to a picnic close to a Muslim shrine, Olivia finds the nawab irresistible. They lie by a spring in a green grove, and the nawab makes her pregnant. She then leaves Douglas, aborts her child, and finally moves to a house in the hills as the nawab's mistress.

After a gap of two generations, the narrator, who has come to India to trace Olivia's life story, passes through a similar cycle of experience. Fascinated by India, she gives herself to a lower-middle-class clerk, Inder Lal, at the same place near the shrine where Olivia lay with the nawab, and with the same result. The young narrator decides to rear the baby, though she gives up her lover; she also has a casual physical relationship with another Indian, Chid, who combines sexuality with a spiritual quest.

Heat and Dust is an extraordinary novel. Unlike many of Jhabvala's novels, it has a strong current of positive feeling beneath its surface negativism. Olivia, though she discards her baby, remains loyal to her heart's desire for the nawab, and the narrator, while not accepting her lover, wishes to rear her baby as a symbol of their love. This note of affirmation heightens the quality of human response in *Heat and Dust*, which is also notable for its fully realized characterizations.

In Search of Love and Beauty, set primarily in the United States but ranging widely elsewhere, centers on the experience of rootlessness which Jhabvala knows so well, and which is so widespread in the twentieth century. The novel is a multigenerational saga, beginning with refugees from Nazi Germany and Austria and concluding in contemporary times. The rootlessness of that first generation to be dislocated from their culture is passed on to their children and their children's children, all of whom go "in search of love and beauty."

The first generation, represented by Louise and Regi, wishes to retain its German heritage, concretely symbolized by their paintings and furniture. The second generation, represented by Marietta, is partly Americanized. The restless Marietta travels to India, falls in love with Ahmad, an Indian musician, and befriends Sujata, a courtesan, sketched with deft accuracy. The image of India is lovable, vital, and glorious, and seems almost a counterpart to Germany's ideal image. The third-generation refugees, represented by Natasha and Leo, are more affluent and still more Americanized, yet they are trapped in drug abuse, depression, and meaninglessness.

In almost all of her novels, Jhabvala assumes the role of an omniscient narrator. She stands slightly aloof from her creations, an approach which has advantages as well as disadvantages. On the one hand, she does not convey the passionate inner life of her characters, many of whom are essentially stereotypes. Even her more fully developed characters are seen largely from the outside. On the other hand, she is a consummate observer. She has a fine eye for naturalistic detail, a gift for believable dialogue, but she is also an observer at a deeper level, registering the malaise that is characteristic of the modern world: the collapse of traditional values, the incongruous blending of diverse cultures: sometimes energizing, sometimes destructive, often bizarre. Thus, her fiction, while steeped in the particular reality of India, speaks to readers throughout the world.

Other major works

SHORT FICTION: *Like Birds, Like Fishes and Other Stories*, 1963; *A Stronger Climate: Nine Stories*, 1968; *An Experience of India*, 1972; *How I Became a Holy Mother and Other Stories*, 1976; *Out of India*, 1986.

SCREENPLAYS: *Shakespeare Wallah*, 1965 (with James Ivory); *Heat and Dust*, 1983 (based on her novel); *A Room with a View*, 1986 (based on E. M. Forster's novel).

Bibliography

Gooneratne, Yasmine. *Silence, Exile and Cunning: The Fiction of Ruth Prawer Jhabvala*, 1983.
Rubin, David. *After the Raj: British Novels of India Since 1947*, 1986.
Shahane, Vasant. *Ruth Prawer Jhabvala*, 1982.

Vasant A. Shahane

ELIZABETH JOLLEY

Born: Birmingham, England; June 4, 1923

Principal long fiction
Palomino, 1980; *The Newspaper of Claremont Street*, 1981; *Mr. Scobie's Riddle*, 1983; *Miss Peabody's Inheritance*, 1983; *Milk and Honey*, 1984; *Foxybaby*, 1985; *The Well*, 1986.

Other literary forms
Elizabeth Jolley's reputation was first established by her short stories, one of which, "Hedge of Rosemary," won an Australian prize as early as 1966. The first works she ever published were her short-story collections *Five Acre Virgin and Other Stories* (1976) and *The Travelling Entertainer and Other Stories* (1979); although her novel *Palomino* won a prize as an unpublished work in 1975, it did not appear in print until 1980. A third volume of short stories, *Woman in a Lampshade*, was published in 1983. Her radio plays have been produced on Australian radio and on the British Broadcasting Corporation (BBC) World Network.

Achievements
Jolley had been writing for twenty years before her first book, a volume of short stories, was published in 1976. In 1975, her novel *Palomino* was given the Con Weickhardt Award for an unfinished novel. *Palomino* was not published, however, until 1980, after a second volume of short stories had already appeared. Not until 1984 was Jolley widely reviewed in the United States.

Sometimes compared to Muriel Spark and Barbara Pym, Jolley is unique in her characterization and tone. Critics variously refer to her novels as fantasy combined with farce, comedy of manners, moral satire, or black comedy. Although most reviewers see a moral dimension beneath the slapstick surface of her work, noting her compassion, her wisdom, and her penetration of complex human relationships, some have insisted that she is merely a comic entertainer. Yet to most thoughtful readers, it is obvious that Jolley's humor often derives from characters who refuse to be defeated by their destinies, who boldly assert their individuality, and who dare to dream and to love, however foolish they may appear to the conformists.

Biography
Elizabeth Monica Jolley was born in Birmingham, England, on June 4, 1923. Her mother, a German aristocrat, the daughter of a general, married a young Englishman who had been disowned by his father because of his pacifist convictions. Privately educated for some years, Elizabeth and her sister

were then sent to a Quaker school. Later, Elizabeth was trained as a nurse at Queen Elizabeth Hospital, Birmingham, and served in that capacity during World War II. In 1959, she moved to Western Australia with her husband and three children. After her move, Jolley began increasingly to divide her time between writing, tending to her farm, and conducting writing workshops.

Analysis

In "Self Portrait: A Child Went Forth," a personal commentary in the one-volume collection *Stories* (1984), Elizabeth Jolley muses on the frequency with which the theme of exile appears in her works. Often her major characters are lonely, physically or emotionally alienated from their surroundings, living imaginatively in a friendlier, more interesting environment. Because of their loneliness, they reach out, often to grasping or selfish partners, who inevitably disappoint them. For Jolley's lonely spinster, widow, or divorcée, the beloved may be another woman. Sometimes, however, the yearning takes a different form, and the beloved is not a person but a place, like the homes of the old men in *Mr. Scobie's Riddle*.

If there is defeat in Jolley's fiction, there is also grace in the midst of despair. Despite betrayal, her characters reach for love, and occasionally an unlikely pair or group will find it. Another redeeming quality is the power of the imagination; it is no accident that almost every work contains a writer, who may, as in *Foxybaby*, appear to be imagining events into reality and characters into existence. Finally, Jolley believes in laughter. Her characters laugh at one another and sometimes at themselves; more detached, she and her readers laugh at the outrageous characters, while at the same time realizing that the characters are only slight exaggerations of those who view them.

The protagonist of Jolley's novel *Palomino* is an exile desperate for love. A physician who has been expelled from the profession and imprisoned, Laura lives on an isolated ranch, her only neighbors the shiftless, dirty tenants, who inspire her pity but provide no companionship for her. Into Laura's lonely life comes Andrea Jackson, a young woman whom the doctor noticed on her recent voyage from England but with whom she formed no relationship. Up until this point, Laura's life has been a series of unsuccessful and unconsummated love affairs with women. At one time, she adored a doctor, to whom she wrote religiously; when the doctor arrived on a visit, she brought a husband. At another period in her life, Laura loved Andrea's selfish, flirtatious mother, who eventually returned to her abusive husband. Perhaps, Laura hopes, Andrea will be different. She is delighted when Andrea agrees to run off with her, ecstatic when she can install her on the ranch, where the women live happily, talking, laughing, and making love. In her new joy, Laura does not realize that, like her other lost lovers, Andrea is obsessed with a man— her own brother, Christopher. It is Christopher's marriage and fatherhood which has driven her into Laura's arms, but Andrea continues to desire Chris, even at moments of high passion. When Andrea admits that she is pregnant with Chris's baby and tries to use Laura's love for her to obtain an abortion, Laura is forced to come to terms with the fact that the love between Andrea and her is imperfect, as it is in all relationships, doomed to change or to dwindle. Obviously, loneliness is the human condition.

Although Jolley's characters must face hard truths such as the inevitability of loneliness, often they move through suffering to new understanding. This is the pattern of *Palomino*. The novel derives its title from the horses on a nearby ranch, whose beauty Laura can appreciate even though she does not possess them. Joy is in perception, not possession; similarly, joy comes from loving, not from being loved. When Andrea and Laura agree that they must part, for fear that their brief love will dwindle into dislike or indifference, they know that they can continue to love each other, even though they will never again be together.

In the graphic dialogue of Laura's tenants can be seen the accuracy and the comic vigor which characterize Jolley's later works. *Mr. Scobie's Riddle*, for example, begins with a series of communications between the matron of the nursing home where the novel takes place and the poorly qualified night nurse, whose partial explanations and inadequate reports, along with her erratic spelling, infuriate her superior. At night, the nursing home comes alive with pillow fights, medicinal whiskey, and serious gambling, at which the matron's brother, a former colonel, always loses. In the daytime, the home is a prison: Old people are processed like objects, ill-fed, ill-tended by two rock-and-rolling girls, and supervised by the greedy matron, whose goal is to part her new guest, Mr. Scobie, from his property. Yet if the patients are prisoners, so are their supervisors. Having lost her husband to an old schoolmate, the matron cannot ignore the fact that the couple cavort regularly in the caravan on the grounds; in turn, the lonely matron saddles her schoolmate with as much work as possible. Meanwhile, the matron is driven constantly closer to bankruptcy by her brother's gambling and closer to a nervous breakdown by her inefficient and careless employees.

Some of the most poignant passages in *Mr. Scobie's Riddle* deal with the yearnings of two old men in Room One, who wish only to return to their homes. Unfortunately, one's has been sold and bulldozed down; the other's has been rented by a voracious niece and nephew. As the patients are driven toward their deaths, no one offers rescue or even understanding. There are, however, some triumphs. The would-be writer, Miss Hailey, never surrenders her imagination or her hope; ironically, her schoolfellow, the matron, who has taken all of her money, must at last turn to Miss Hailey for understanding and companionship. In the battle for his own dignity, Mr. Scobie wins. Even though he is returned to the nursing home whenever he attempts to go home, and even though his uncaring niece and nephew finally acquire his beloved home, he wins, for he never surrenders to the matron, but dies before she can bully him into signing over his property.

The unique combination of farcical humor, lyrical description, pathos, and moral triumph which mark Jolley's later work is also exemplified in *Miss Peabody's Inheritance*, published, like *Mr. Scobie's Riddle*, in 1983. In this novel, a woman writer is one of the two major characters. In response to a fan letter from a middle-aged, mother-ridden London typist, the novelist regularly transmits to her the rough episodes from her new novel, a Rabelaisian story of lesbian schoolmistresses and the troublesome, innocent girl whom they escort through Europe. When at last the typist travels to Australia to meet her writer-heroine, she finds that the writer, a bed-bound invalid, has died. Yet her courage, her imagination, and her manuscript remain for Miss Peabody, an inheritance which will enable her to live as fully and as creatively as the novelist.

In *Milk and Honey*, there is no triumph of love, of laughter, or of the imagination. Alone among Jolley's novels, *Milk and Honey* begins and ends in despair. At the beginning, a door-to-door salesman with a poor, unhappy wife expresses his loneliness, his loss of the woman he loved and of the music he enjoyed. The rest of the novel re-creates his life, from the time when he went to live with his cello teacher and his seemingly delightful family, through the salesman's discovery that he was used and betrayed, to the final tragic climax, when his income vanished—his cellist's hand was charred in a fire—and the woman who made his life worth living was brutally murdered. Although many of the scenes in the novel are grotesque, they are devoid of the humor which is typical of Jolley and which often suggests one way of rising above despair. Nor does the protagonist's art—here, performing music, rather than creating fiction—enable him to transcend his situation. His love for his wife is destroyed with his illusions about her, his mistress is destroyed by his wife, and he and his wife are left to live out their lives together without love.

Foxybaby, published in 1985, is as grotesque as *Milk and Honey* but its characters move through desperation to humor, love, imagination, and hope. The setting is a campus turned into a weight-loss clinic. Typically, the characters are trapped there, in this case by the rascally bus driver, who ensures a healthy wrecker and garage business by parking so that all approaching cars plow into him. The central character of *Foxybaby* is, once again, a woman writer, Alma Porch, who along with a sculptor and a potter has been hired to take the residents' minds off food by submerging them in culture. Miss Porch's mission is to rehearse an assorted group of residents in a film which she is creating as the book progresses. Brilliantly, Jolley alternates the wildly comic events at the campus with the poignant story that Miss Porch is writing, an account of a father's attempt to rescue his young, drug-ruined, infected daughter and her sickly baby from the doom which seems to await them. From his affectionate nickname for her when she was a little girl comes the name of the book.

Like the love story in *Milk and Honey*, the plot in *Foxybaby* illustrates the destructive power of love. Well-meaning though he is, the father cannot establish communication with his daughter. The reason is unclear, even to the writer who is creating the story or, more accurately, is letting the characters she has imagined create their own story. Perhaps the father's love was crushing; perhaps in her own perverseness, the daughter rejected it. At any rate, it is obvious that despite his persistence, he is making little headway in reaching the destructive stranger who is now his "Foxybaby" and who herself has a baby for whom she feels nothing.

Meanwhile, like Jolley's other protagonists, Porch considers escaping from the place which is both her prison and her exile but is prevented from doing so by the very confusion of events. Loquacious Jonquil Castle moves in with her; a Maybelle Harrow, with her lover and his lover, invites her to an orgy; and the indomitable Mrs. Viggars brings forth her private stock of wine and initiates Porch into the joys of the school-like midnight feast. Offstage, the bus driver is always heard shouting to his wife or his mistress to drop her knickers. Love, in all its variety, blooms on the campus, while it is so helpless in the story being shaped in the same place.

Although the campus trap will be easier to escape, bus or no bus, than the nursing home in *Mr. Scobie's Riddle*, Jolley stresses the courage of the residents, a courage which will be necessary in the lives to which they will return, whether those lives involve battling boredom and loneliness, like Miss Porch's, or rejection, like that of Jonquil Castle, the doting mother and grandmother, or age and the loss of love, like the lascivious Maybelle Harrow's. Just as they will survive the clinic, though probably without losing any weight, they will survive their destinies. At the end of the novel, there is a triumph of love, when Mrs. Viggars, admitting her loneliness, chooses to take a young woman and her three children into her home, in order to establish a family once again. There is also a triumph of imagination, when Miss Porch actually sees the characters whom she has created. For her loneliness, they will be companions.

At the end of the novel, the bus stops and Miss Porch wakens, to find herself at the school. Jolley does not explain: Has Porch dreamed the events of the book? Will they now take place? Or is the awakening misplaced in time, and have they already taken place? Ultimately, it does not matter. What docs matter is the power of the imagination which, along with humor and love, make life bearable.

Hester Harper, another spinster protagonist, is somewhat like the doctor in *Palomino* in that she lives on an isolated ranch in Western Australia and yearns for love. In *The Well*, however, the beloved is an orphan girl, whom Hester takes home to be her companion. Refusing to admit her sexual desires, even to herself, Hester persuades herself that her feelings are merely friendly or perhaps maternal; yet she is so jealous of the orphan, Katherine, that she cannot bear to think of the friend who wishes to visit her or of the man who will ultimately take her away. The rival, when he appears, is mysterious, perhaps a thief, perhaps only an animal, whom Katherine hits on a late-night drive and whom Hester immediately buries in the well. Perhaps diabolical, perhaps distraught, Katherine insists that he is calling to her, demanding her love, threatening her and Hester. Although at last his voice is stilled, it is clear that Hester has lost control over Katherine, to whom the outside world of sexuality and adventure is calling with undeniable urgency. Unlike the doctor in *Palomino*, Hester cannot be contented with the memory of love. Imagination, however, once again mitigates the horror of life; at the end of the novel, Hester is making the mysterious nighttime adventure into a story to be told to children.

Because she deals with cruelty, indifference, greed, lust, and, above all, with loneliness, Elizabeth Jolley cannot be considered a superficial writer. The great distances of her Western Australia become a metaphor for the mysterious expanses of time; the small clumps of isolated individuals, trapped together on a ranch, on a weight-loss farm, or in a nursing home, represent society, as did Joseph Conrad's microcosmic ships on an indifferent ocean. Jolley makes it clear that love is infrequent and imperfect, that childhood is endangered by cruelty and that old age leads through indignity to death. Yet most of her works are enlivened by comic characters who defy destiny and death by their very insistence on living. Some of her characters transcend their isolation by learning to love, such as the doctor in *Palomino* or Mrs. Viggars in *Foxybaby*. Others, such as Miss Peabody and Miss Porch, triumph through their imaginations. There is redemption in nature, whether in the beauty of palomino horses or the sunlit shore where Miss Porch sees her characters. There is also triumph in the isolated courage of a human being such as Mr. Scobie, who defies institutionalized and personal greed to save the beloved home to which he can return only in memory. If Elizabeth Jolley's characters are mixtures of the pathetic, the grotesque, and the noble, it is because they are human; if her stories keep the reader off balance between confusion, laughter, and tears, it is because they reflect life.

Other major works

SHORT FICTION: *Five Acre Virgin and Other Stories*, 1976; *The Travelling Entertainer and Other Stories*, 1979; *Woman in a Lampshade*, 1983; *Stories*, 1984.

RADIO PLAYS: *Night Report*, 1975; *The Performance*, 1976; *The Shepherd on the Roof*, 1977; *The Well-Bred Thief*, 1977; *Woman in a Lampshade*, 1979; *Two Men Running*, 1981.

Bibliography

Ackroyd, Peter. "Two Cultures, One Transplanted," in *The New York Times Book Review*. XCI (June 15, 1986), p. 12.

Carter, Angela. "Dreams of Reason . . . and of Foxes," in *The New York Times Book Review*. XC (November 24, 1985), p. 1.

Coover, Robert. "Dotty and Disorderly Conduct," in *The New York Times Book Review*. XCI (November 16, 1986), p. 1.

Disch, Thomas M. "Bound, Gagged, and Left in the Pantry," in *The New York Times Book Review*. LXXXIX (November 18, 1984), p. 14.

Rosemary M. Canfield-Reisman

THOMAS KENEALLY

Born: Sydney, Australia; October 7, 1935

Principal long fiction

The Place at Whitton, 1964; *The Fear*, 1965; *Bring Larks and Heroes*, 1967; *Three Cheers for the Paraclete*, 1968; *The Survivor*, 1969; *A Dutiful Daughter*, 1971; *The Chant of Jimmie Blacksmith*, 1972; *Blood Red, Sister Rose*, 1974; *Gossip from the Forest*, 1975; *Season in Purgatory*, 1976; *A Victim of the Aurora*, 1977; *Passenger*, 1979; *Confederates*, 1979; *Schindler's Ark*, 1982 (U.S. edition, *Schindler's List*, 1983); *Outback*, 1983; *The Cut-Rate Kingdom*, 1984; *A Family Madness*, 1985.

Other literary forms

In addition to his long fiction, Thomas Keneally has written several plays: *Halloran's Little Boat* (1966), *Childermass* (1968), *An Awful Rose* (1972), and *Bullie's House* (1980). He has also written two television plays, *Essington*, produced in the United Kingdom in 1974, and *The World's Wrong End* (1981).

Achievements

Keneally has received international acclaim for his fiction; he has received the Miles Franklin Award (1967, 1968), the Captain Cook Bi-Centenary Prize (1970), the Royal Society of Literature Prize (1982), and the Booker Prize (1982). *The Chant of Jimmie Blacksmith* won for him the Heinemann Award for literature (1973), and *Schindler's Ark* won the *Los Angeles Times* Fiction Prize (1983). Keneally is president of the National Book Council of Australia and a member of the Australia-China Council.

Biography

Thomas Michael Keneally was born in Sydney, Australia, on October 7, 1935. He studied for the Roman Catholic priesthood in his youth but left the seminary two weeks before he was to take Holy Orders. He completed his education at St. Patrick's College, New South Wales. He married Judith Martin in 1965 and had two children. Before becoming a full-time novelist, he taught high school in Sydney, from 1960 to 1964; from 1968 to 1970, he was a lecturer in drama at the University of New England, New South Wales, after which he moved to London.

Analysis

Thomas Keneally has written books on a variety of subjects. His first novel to attain international readership, *Bring Larks and Heroes*, presents the barbarous life of eighteenth century Sydney; *Three Cheers for the Paraclete* concerns a Catholic priest who attacks the Church for its indifference to social evil; *The Survivor* and *A Victim of the Aurora* are stories about Antarctic expeditions, told in flashback by an aged narrator; *A Dutiful Daughter* is a surrealistic tale of a family in which the parents are bovine from the waist down. One may, however, separate Keneally's work into two parts, albeit roughly: the novels which deal with seemingly ordinary, contemporary individuals, and the wide range of what might be called historical novels.

In a large portion of his work, Keneally concerns himself with European history, examining closely the human beings involved, seeing the past not as the present sees it, as a series of neatly wrapped, complete events, but as the participants experience it: as a jumble of occurrences that seem to have little meaning or purpose. Although some reviewers have commented on the portentousness lurking in the background of such works as *Gossip from the Forest*, a fictionalized re-creation of the 1918 peace talks that led to the disastrous Treaty of Versailles, such "damaging knowingness" is only partly Keneally's fault; after all, the present knows what happened in the past, at least in outline.

It must be emphasized that Keneally's historically based fiction is not about ordinary people set against a celebrity-filled background, in the manner of E. L. Doctorow's *Ragtime* (1975). His works deal with the historical figures themselves, presenting them as human beings embroiled in the quotidian matters from which the historical events reveal themselves gradually. The writer's knowledge of history shapes the delineation of the plot. Furthermore, the protagonist's awareness of his or her importance to posterity comes only in flashes. When such awareness occurs, it is as a result of the character's makeup; Joan of Arc, for example, was a visionary, and it is unavoidable that, as a character, she know something of her eventual fate.

It cannot be denied that what Keneally is attempting to do in his historically based novels is difficult; that he succeeds as well as he does is primarily a result of a spare, objective style that is at times brilliant, such as in the description of Yugoslav partisans from *Season in Purgatory*: "Grenades blossomed like some quaint ethnic ornamentation down the front of their coats." The third-person narration, deceptively simple, pretending to mere description, seems detached (at times too detached): *Schindler's List*, based on a German industrialist's widely successful efforts to save "his" Jews, at times suffers from an almost sprightly tone, as if the author were so determined to be objective that he expunged any sense of moral outrage from his account. At its best, however, the stark simplicity of Keneally's prose throws into sharp relief the horrors of which history is made.

The history examined by Keneally is never pretty, no matter how heroic the subject. The final terrible lesson of *Gossip from the Forest* is that well-meaning, intelligent, civilized men have no place in the twentieth century.

Matthias Erzberger, liberal member of the Reichstag, has no success in his negotiations; blind self-interest thwarts his every attempt at justice for his defeated country. He is shot to death several years after the meeting at Compiegne by two young officers, proto-Nazis, as a traitor for his role in the Armistice. Erzberger himself, for all of his excellent qualities and basic decency, seems unequal to the task he has had thrust on him. He is aware of his inadequacy: "Like a cardiac spasm he suffered again the terrible bereft sense that there was nothing in his background that justified this journey. . . . At its most high-flown the true Erzberger's mind wasn't far off steak and red wine and Paula's warm and undemanding bed." His dreamy absentmindedness and his eventual despair seems to remove him from the heroic ranks; it is only toward the end of the novel that the reader realizes the true heroism of the civilian in his struggle against the military mind.

This gradual revelation of heroism is evident also in *Season in Purgatory*, the story of a young British physician, David Pelham, who is sent to the island of Mus to perform emergency surgery on Yugoslav partisans. Pelham arrives on Mus with all the fiery idealism of youth. After being thrust, day after day, into the results of war—both the direct results, such as graphically described wounds, and the indirect, such as Marshal Tito's order that any partisans indulging in sexual relations be summarily executed—he is worn down, no longer convinced of the rightness of any cause: "In his bloodstream were two simple propositions: that the savagery of the Germans did not excuse the savagery of the partisans: that the savagery of the partisans did not excuse the savagery of the Germans."

This final realization that "the masters of the ideologies, even the bland ideology of democracy, were blood-crazed . . . that at the core of their political fervour, there stood a desire to punish with death anyone who hankered for other systems than those approved," does not allow the story to end. It is in this moral vacuum that Pelham becomes a hero, having sacrificed the innocence and illusion of idealism for an embittered realism. Keneally continues to reveal Pelham's personal flaws, as he does with all of his heroic figures: His childishness in love and hate and his typical upper-class British attitudes survive the revelation. Therefore, the apotheosis of the physician at the end of the war comes as much as a surprise to the reader as it must to the character himself.

Pelham's loss of idealism is necessary to Keneally's concept of the heroic figure; idealism bathes reality in a rosy glow that does not fit anything but the usual type of historical novel (or many types of history, for that matter). Generally, Keneally's heroes find themselves chosen to be sacrificial victims, without having wished for it. They are by turn reluctant and filled with fervor, and they are always human, at times perversely flaunting their faults. The positive aspect of their selection is generally far more ephemeral than the certitude of the doom toward which they know they are going. They are often in the situation epitomized by the half-caste protagonist of *The Chant of Jimmie Blacksmith*, the novel on which the 1978 Fred Schepisi film is based: "in tenuous elation and solid desolation between self-knowledge and delirium."

Jimmie Blacksmith has a white father, whom he does not know, and an aboriginal mother. He has been taught Christianity and ambition; he is no longer tribal, but his attempts to show the whites that a black may be as industrious and educated as they are fail to gain for him acceptance in their society. He marries a white girl who has also slept with the station cook (played by Keneally himself in the film); when their baby is born, it is white.

Jimmie has been cheated by the whites, has taken up arms against his tribe in order to be thought white, and has married white to consolidate his ambition, yet he is still rejected by the white society. The birth of the baby makes him explode, and he goes on a methodical rampage, first killing the Newby family, for whom he worked, then taking a sympathetic white schoolteacher as a hostage. He eludes his pursuers for a time, but they catch up with him. Shot in the jaw, delirious, he takes refuge in a convent, where he is eventually captured. His hanging, however, is delayed so that it will not detract from the celebration of the Federation anniversary.

Throughout, Jimmie is seen as a man who might be a bridge between the two cultures, but neither the aborigines nor the whites allow such a resolution; his killing spree seems to represent his only alternative, and while other people die, Jimmie is actually the victim. He wants to become the peaceful link, and when this course proves illusory, he becomes the avenger, knowing that he will not survive. He is doomed, in the way Keneally heroes are usually doomed.

This sense of being the sacrificial victim is most strongly presented in Keneally's retelling of the Joan of Arc story. *Blood Red, Sister Rose* is a fictionalized account of the youth and triumph of Joan of Arc. The novel ends with the few anticlimactic months following the coronation of Charles in Rheims and an epilogue in the form of a letter from her father to the family about his daughter's death. Yet throughout the development of Jehanne's awareness of her destiny, the certitude of her martyrdom is evident, for she is a peasant who knows that Christ's sacrifice was not enough; the king needs one, and she has been chosen. Alternately buoyed and depressed by her fate, she sees herself as a conduit for these forces, the importance of which leaves very little time or passion for Jehanne, daughter of Jacques and Zabillet, to pursue her own humanity.

Described as wide-shouldered and plain, Jehanne goes through adolescence without menstruating, which proves to her that she is not like her sister or her mother, that she is the virgin from Lorraine prophesied by Merlin. She has not chosen her fate, but she must accept it. There are moments when she resents this election: Words of tenderness spoken about another woman, for example, evoke great sadness within her, for she knows that such words will never be spoken about her. The greater part of the time, however, is consumed with her mission, not to France, not to the destruction of the English, not even to stop the slaughter of the farmers who suffered so greatly in the wars of the fifteenth century, but to ensure the consecration of the king, to whom she is mystically bound.

Through ancient ritual, Keneally presents the notion of the human sacrifice. The author's weaving of historical incident with the motivations based in archaic mythologies allows a dimension of verisimilitude to the slippery genre of historical fiction. The inclusion of certain surprising elements of fifteenth century life (for example, the mention that peasants in eastern France plowed their field with a naked woman in the harness so that the earth might be bountiful) reveal a society in which the voices heard by Jehanne cannot be casually dismissed as a frustrated spinster's wishful thinking.

Jehanne is, like her forebears, a mixture of ignorance and hardheaded shrewdness. These qualities, at the service of the obsession that invaded her at the age of nine, ensure her success in reaching the king. Furthermore, the feudal society that she opposes is rapidly approaching dissolution: The battle of Agincourt has demonstrated the impotence of armored knights, Prince Hal has taken to killing noble prisoners instead of ransoming them in the time-honored practice of chivalry, the alliances of dukes and barons have been complicated by the presence of the English, and the ongoing war has caused a near-famine in the countryside. Jehanne's clarity of purpose shines brightly through the morass of confusion and disaster that was fifteenth century France.

Once her objective is reached, however, she becomes an ordinary person again, with no voices telling her the next move. One sees her strength and influence eroding as the king is changed from a timid recluse to a confident monarch. His ingratitude is taken as a matter of course by Jehanne, for she has known all along the fate that awaits the year-king, the sacrificial victim. As if her importance has diminished for the author as well as for Charles, the ending is a mere footnote. One is left with a brilliant picture of a strange and remote past, and a sense of what heroes are—never heroes to themselves, accepting the acclaims of the populace bemusedly, as if the admirers were constantly missing the point. Although there are moments when she is elated by her specialness, more often she sees it as an onus, a word that constantly recurs in Keneally's work.

This realization, in small part exhilarating and in larger part burdensome, is one that recurs in Keneally's work. In the novel *Passenger*, for example, the narrator-fetus views the Gnome as his outside brother and protector; the Gnome is eventually killed in a plane crash, and in dying ensures the birth of the narrator. In *A Victim of the Aurora*, two explorers from a previous expedition have remained in the Antarctic, and one survives by eating the other one; the identities are mixed, so that the one who has survived identifies himself by the name of he who has been eaten. One can see plainly Keneally's Catholic background in the use of the sacrificial victim as theme or motif in many of his works: Christ's sacrifice, rendered bloodless by the sacrament of communion, is constantly reenacted in all its primal violence by either his protagonists or his supporting characters.

This theme links the historical novels with those that deal with supposedly ordinary people. In the latter category, Keneally is more experimental, particularly in the mode of narration employed. The objective third-person narration of the historical novels is replaced by various innovations, such as the second-person, self-addressed narration of *A Dutiful Daughter* or the omniscient first-person narration of *Passenger*. At first glance, there seems to be little similarity between the two types of novels, but the author's concerns form a bridge between them.

Passenger's narrator is a fetus, given consciousness by a laser sonogram. Suddenly, the fetus is no longer happily unaware of anything save the coursing of his blood, an animal faculty that requires a certain kind of innocence; he becomes aware of everything: his mother's thoughts, the historical novel she is writing about her ne'er-do-well husband's ancestor (himself seemingly the prototype of Halloran in *Bring Larks and Heroes*), his father's fear of his birth, the existence of Warwick Jones, the Gnome—"We were Dumas' Corsican twins, the Gnome and I. It was as if we *shared* a placenta and swapped our visions and sensation." Jones feels as though he had never really been born, and that he will be born through the agency of the narrator's own birth. For Jones, however, birth means death, literal death. The narrator also sees his own eventual birth as death, and he resists it, unlike Jones, who actively seeks it.

This notion of the sacrificial double is one aspect that links the two categories of novels. The power of history is another. Keneally's fascination with history and heroes surfaces in *Passenger*: In the narrative is a character who has had the same experiences as David Pelham, the protagonist of *Season in Purgatory*. Maurice Fitzgerald, the eighteen century ancestor of Brian, the narrator's father, was also a reluctant hero in the penal colony of Sydney. The fight against social injustice that characterizes Maurice Fitzgerald forms the thematic center of Keneally's novel *Three Cheers for the Paraclete*.

In this novel, Keneally treats directly the experience that perhaps influenced his life most strongly: the six and a half years of being a seminarian, bound to the doctrine and ideology of the Catholic Church. Again, Father Maitland, the protagonist, is a reluctant hero, unsure of the purity of his motives even as he preaches, afraid of sounding "like a fashionable priest, the glib kind." He tries earnestly to submit to the authority of his bishop, fearing the disappearance of the comforting certainties, but his conscience does not allow him a quiet life.

His working-class cousin has been cheated out of his savings by an unscrupulous housing development corporation; looking into the affair, Maitland
discovers that other people had the same experience with that company, and
furthermore, that his own diocese owns stock in the company. He becomes
the center of controversy, a position he does not want but must take because
of his own convictions. The diocese eventually rids itself of the holdings in
the dishonest company, but on the advice of its legal staff; the question of
morality has been supplanted by one of expediency for the established
Church. Maitland, having indirectly succeeded, submits to the rule of his
church: the censorship of his sermons, a ban on further publications, and
transfer to a rural parish.

The pervasiveness of social injustice and its force makes its appearance in
all of Keneally's novels, in one degree or another. Jehanne of *Blood Red, Sister Rose*, a peasant and a woman, is herself a statement against the class and
gender inequities of the fifteenth century, at times bringing a modern flavor
to a time when such inequities were seldom questioned. Her liberationist tendencies are diluted by the importance of her vision, but it is impossible for
her to witness late medieval war without realizing who suffers the most: The
farmers, the peasants who form the major part of the armies, are never held
for ransom. They are killed outright when captured. The noncombatants,
women and children, are raped and killed by the rampaging armies. The
sexism inherent in the way she is treated makes her rage impotently.

Jehanne's story appears in *A Dutiful Daughter*; Barbara Glover, the sister
of the narrator, possesses what might be a fifteenth century transcript of
Jehanne's first examination by priests, which might have saved her from the
stake had it not been lost. Barbara sees in Jehanne's story elements which
might explain her own life to her.

The Glover family has settled on a swampy bit of land, Campbell's Reach,
and has tried to make a living on it with only minimal success. The son,
Damian, who is the narrator, has been sent to college, while Barbara has
stayed behind to take care of the parents. In a flashback that is evocative of
Jehanne's own awakening to the voices, Barbara runs off into the swamp,
pursued by her parents; when they finally come back, the parents have
undergone a bizarre metamorphosis: They have been turned into cattle from
the waist down, "like centaurs, except that the horse half was a cow half."
They seem to have not noticed, but Barbara tells them what has happened;
they never forgive her, but from that day forward, she has complete control
over them. As Damian writes, "It is the duty of a good child to let his parents
know the second they turn into animals."

Barbara's control has its responsibilities, and she finds them onerous. She
cannot evade them, however, no more than Jehanne can escape her destiny.
She therefore perserveres, although life on Campbell's Reach is dismal at
best, and in conjunction with the caring for her parents, absolutely deaden-

ing. For the parents are indeed cattle from the waist down; the transformation is literal, and Keneally leaves no doubt about that fact. The mother suffers from mastitis, a bovine disease of the udder that is fatal in cows. Most farmers, it is said, kill the cows that contract it. Obviously, Barbara cannot put her mother out of her misery, so she treats her with massive doses of antibiotics, and her mother querulously suffers nearly all the time.

The father really is a bull from the waist down, and goes out in search of heifers, stricken by suicidal shame every time he succeeds, but driven to repeat his quest by his animal self. It is obvious that Barbara is sacrificing herself: The only love she experiences is the incestuous passion that Damian has for her, and that is consummated only once before she puts a stop to it—for his sake. Eventually, she takes the parents with her so that they may all drown in the flood that is sweeping over Campbell's Reach, and so that her brother may finally be free of his unwholesome family ties.

Family, history, the tormented personalities of those who are present at great events, the sacrificial victim: These are the themes that are interwoven in all of Keneally's works. Perhaps the fact that Australia has very little history of its own has contributed to Keneally's fascination with the topic. His novel *A Family Madness* juxtaposes two families: Terry Delaney's working-class family and that of Radislaw Kabbelski. The Delaneys seem not to be touched by history, but the Kabbelskis, Belorussian refugees, have bathed in it for a long time. The third-person narrative, set in contemporary Australia, is interspersed with the journals of the Kabbelski family. The relative degrees of innocence or experience of the two groups are thus seen as contingent on how deeply one is embedded in history.

There is a wholeness about Keneally's work that belies one's initial impression of diversity. Not that diversity does not exist: Geographically and temporally, his work ranges from the Antarctic to Europe and America, from the dim past to the present. Yet certain themes are always prevalent. In the introduction to an interview with Keneally, Janette Turner Hospital writes, "The protagonists of the novels of Thomas Keneally are Jeremiahs of a sort, reluctant prophets or messiahs . . . prophets by random circumstance only." It is Keneally's fascination with circumstance and its effects that stands out as the major lesson that history has taught him: Those who do great deeds, either public or private, are no better or worse than anyone else. If they are holy, they are so in the ancient sense of the word: "different from, other than." It is in revealing the humanity in their holiness that Keneally makes his greatest contribution.

Other major works

PLAYS: *Halloran's Little Boat*, 1966; *Childermass*, 1968; *An Awful Rose*, 1972; *Bullie's House*, 1980.

TELEPLAYS: *Essington*, 1974; *The World's Wrong End*, 1981.

Bibliography

Ackroyd, Peter. "Burning Down," in *The Spectator*. CCXXXIX (September 3, 1977), pp. 19-20.

Carter, Angela. Review of *A Dutiful Daughter* in *The New York Times Book Review*. September 12, 1971, p. 53.

Cook, Bruce. "Suspicions of Sainthood," in *The Washington Post Book World*. January 26, 1975, p. 3.

Fussell, Paul. Review of *Gossip from the Forest* in *The New York Times Book Review*. April 11, 1976, p. 7.

Haynes, Muriel. Review of *A Dutiful Daughter* in *The Saturday Review*. LIV (July 24, 1971), p. 53.

Hospital, Janette Turner. "Keneally's Reluctant Prophets," in *Commonweal*. CIII (May 7, 1976), pp. 295-300.

Maddocks, Melvin. "Joans of Arc," in *Time*. CV (February 10, 1975), p. 76.

Steiner, George. "Petrified Forest," in *The New Yorker*. LII (August 23, 1976), pp. 80-82.

Jean-Pierre Metereau

WILLIAM KENNEDY

Born: Albany, New York; January 16, 1928

Principal long fiction

The Ink Truck, 1969; *Legs*, 1975; *Billy Phelan's Greatest Game*, 1978; *Ironweed*, 1983; *The Albany Cycle*, 1985 (includes *Legs*, *Billy Phelan's Greatest Game*, and *Ironweed*).

Other literary forms

In addition to the four novels cited above, William Kennedy's nonfiction *O Albany! An Urban Tapestry* (1983), pamphlets for the New York State Library, Empire State College, and the *Albany Tricentennial Guidebook* (1985) largely center on his native Albany, New York. In addition, he wrote the screenplay for the film *The Cotton Club* (1984) with Francis Coppola and Mario Puzo, and with his son, Brendan, a children's book, *Charlie Malarkey and the Belly Button Machine* (1986).

Achievements

Kennedy is a former newspaperman from Albany, New York, a city in which politics plays an important role. He was born there of Irish Catholic heritage, struggled at writing for years while teaching as an adjunct at the State University of New York (SUNY) at Albany. He brings all these traditions to his writing: the bite of the newsman, the literary allusions of the professor, and the mysticism of the American Irishman. His first books—*The Ink Truck*, *Legs*, and *Billy Phelan's Greatest Game*—drew some notice but sold sluggishly, so *Ironweed* was rejected by thirteen publishers until Saul Bellow, Kennedy's teacher and mentor, persuaded Viking to reconsider. Viking reissued the previous two novels along with *Ironweed* as *The Albany Cycle*, and *Ironweed* won the National Book Critics Circle Award in 1983 and the Pulitzer Prize in fiction in 1984. Kennedy received a MacArthur Foundation Fellowship in 1983. This unsolicited "genius" award freed him for creative work; he used part of the proceeds to start a writers' institute in Albany, later funded by New York State with him as director. His novels' characters are drawn from the world of bums and gangsters and have been compared in brilliance to those of James Joyce and William Faulkner. *The Albany Cycle*, with its interlocking characters and spirit of place, has been compared to Faulkner's Yoknapatawpha stories and Joyce's *Dubliners* (1914) and *Ulysses* (1922). Kennedy's style has won praise as a combination of naturalism and surrealism, yet critics have faulted what they call his overwriting and pandering to the public's demand for violence, explicit sex, and scatological detail. Critics generally agree that *Ironweed*, the culmination of *The

Albany Cycle, is also Kennedy's best, fusing the style, characterization, attention to detail, and mysticism of the other two and focusing them with mastery.

Biography

William Kennedy was born in Albany, New York, on January 16, 1928. He was graduated from Siena College in 1949 and went to work for the Glens Falls, New York, *Post Star*, as sports editor and columnist, followed by a stint as reporter on the Albany *Times Union* until 1956. He went to Puerto Rico to work for the *Puerto Rico World Journal*, then for the *Miami Herald* (1957), returning to Puerto Rico as founding managing editor of the San Juan *Star* from 1959 to 1961. Deciding to make fiction writing his career and Albany his literary source and center, he returned to the Albany *Times Union* as special writer and film critic from 1963 to 1970, while he gathered material and wrote columns on Albany's rich history and its often scabrous past. Upon the success of *Ironweed*, he was promoted to Professor of English at SUNY/Albany in 1983. The university and the city sponsored a "William Kennedy's Albany" celebration in September, 1984.

Analysis

William Kennedy's fiction is preoccupied with spirit of place, language, and style, and a mystic fusing of characters and dialogue. The place is Albany, New York, the capital city, nest of corrupt politics, heritor of Dutch, English, and Irish immigrants, home to canallers, crooks, bums and bag ladies, aristocrats, and numbers-writers. Albany, like Boston, attracted a large Irish Catholic population, which brought its churches, schools, family ties, political machine, and underworld connections.

Kennedy's style has been compared to that of François Rabelais for its opulent catalogs and its ribald scatology. Kennedy is not, however, a derivative writer. As his books unfold, one from another, he makes novel connections, adeptly developing the hallucinations of Bailey, the protagonist of *The Ink Truck*, the extrasensory perception of Martin Daugherty, one of the central consciousnesses of *Billy Phelan's Greatest Game*, and the ghosts of his victims visiting Francis Phelan on his quest for redemption in *Ironweed*.

Kennedy's first published novel, *The Ink Truck*, connects less strongly to these themes and styles than do later works. The novel focuses on the headquarters of a Newspaper Guild strike committee on the one-year anniversary of its strike against the daily newspaper of a town resembling Albany. Only four Guild members remain: Bailey, Rosenthal, Irma, and Jarvis, their leader. Bailey, the proverbial blundering Irish reporter, mixes his libido and marital problems with his earnest belief in the strike, now bogged down in trivialities.

Bailey's relationship with his wife is strained and crazed: She is madly jealous, as she has reason to be. Bailey mixes idealism about the strike with several sexual romps and psychic encounters, punctuated by savage beatings from the scabs and company agents determined to break the strike.

Bailey's fantasy is to open the valve on the ink truck coming to the newspaper plant, bleeding the newspaper's black blood into the snow of the mean streets. In the Guild room near the paper plant, Bailey attempts to revive his affair with Irma, another of the few remaining strikers. Joined by Deek, a collegiate type and an executive's son who wants to join the strike, the four members try to harass the paper's owners, whose representative, Stanley, refuses to grant their demands, which, by this time, have become niggling. As they attempt to block the ink truck in the snow and release the ink, everything goes wrong. When Bailey sets fire to the vacant store where the gypsies congregate, Putzina, the queen, is fatally burned, and she dies in the hospital amid a wild gypsy rite. Antic writing celebrates Bailey's subsequent kidnaping by the gypsies so that they seem comic despite the violence. Bailey escapes after cooperating with the company secretary in her sexual fantasy but is disillusioned when he finds that he must sign an apology to the newspaper company for the action of some members.

More setbacks emerge: Bailey takes back the apology, then finds that the motor has been taken out of his car. Rosenthal's house has been trashed viciously. Bailey, expelled from the Newspaper Guild, goes home to find that his wife, Grace, has put all of his belongings on the curb to be pilfered. His uncle Melvin refuses to help but invites him to an elaborate pet funeral for his cat. Just after this event, the cat's body disappears, a ludicrous culmination of all Bailey has lost: Guild, Guild benefits, apartment, and wife. Going literally underground, Bailey takes a job shelving books in the State Library, where Irma visits him to tell him that despite all setbacks, he, Rosenthal, and Deek are being hailed as the Ink Truck Heroes. In this aspect, Bailey prefigures the gangster hero, Legs Diamond, and the hero as transfigured bum, Francis Phelan, of the later books.

Becoming a media hero, Bailey makes one more futile try at the ink truck. In a grand finale, the orgiastic end-of-strike party hosted by Stanley becomes another humiliation for Bailey. Kennedy's low-key and inconclusive ending leaves the characters where they began: looking at the place on the wall of the Guild Room where a sign hung over the mimeograph machine saying DON'T SIT HERE. Bailey tries to make sense of his experiences, but even the reader cannot understand. Some of the richest of these experiences—a religious pilgrimage by trolley car and a trip backward in time to a cholera epidemic in 1832—seem almost gratuitous, loose ends without much relationship to the rest of the story. Bailey realizes that "all the absurd things they'd all gone through, separately or together... were fixed in time and space and stood only for whatever meaning he, or anyone else, cared to give them."

Kennedy's next novel, *Legs*, develops clearer patterns and meanings, though with the same mixture of realism and surrealism as in *The Ink Truck*. Kennedy demonstrates the truth of his 1975 novel's epigraph, "People like killers," a quote from Eugène Ionesco, through his portrayal of John "Jack" Diamond, also known as "Legs," an idolized, flamboyant underworld figure, a liquor smuggler during Prohibition, a careless killer, and a tough womanizer. Finally brought to justice by New York governor Franklin D. Roosevelt, Jack was mysteriously executed gangland style in Albany in December, 1931.

The story begins in a seedy Albany bar, where four of the book's characters meet in 1974 to reminisce about the assassination of their gangster-hero, Jack "Legs" Diamond. The novel is a fictionalization of Jack's life, superimposing fictional characters, fictional names for real people, and Kennedy's imagination on real events. Three of the four in the frame story are minor, therefore surviving, members of Jack's entourage. The fourth member of the group is Marcus Gorman, Jack's attorney, mouthpiece, and friend, who gave up a political career to lend respectability and a capacity for legal chicanery to Jack. Marcus is the narrator of the novel, providing a less-than-intimate portrait, yet one filtered through a legal mind accustomed to the trickery of the profession as it was practiced then in Albany.

The book is tightly crafted, with parallel scenes, apt literary allusions, well-constructed flashbacks, foreshadowing throughout, and, always, the map of Albany and its neighboring Catskills in mind. The sordid historical account is elevated with signs and coincidences: Marcus, employed by Jack after he successfully represented another gangster, visits Jack in the Catskills after speaking at a police communion breakfast in Albany; a copy of Rabelais is in the Knights of Columbus Library frequented by Marcus in Albany; one is in Jack's bookcase at his Catskills hideaway. Literary allusions combined with Bonnie-and-Clyde violence produce Kennedy's most transcendental effects. Marcus seems a divided consciousness: He regrets the straight-and-narrow life of Irish Catholic Albany and a secure role in politics, yet he has a way of suborning witnesses, getting them to pretend insanity, and ignoring obvious hints about Jack's grislier killings (such as the garage murder of an erstwhile ally).

Jack Diamond became a mythical imaginative popular hero, a "luminous" personality who appealed to the crowds, and remained their darling even in his final trials. He survived assassination attempts, though his murder is foretold from the beginning. The story is interwoven with parallels and coincidences. Kiki, Jack's gorgeous mistress, engages in a monologue reminiscent of Milly Bloom's in Joyce's *Ulysses* when she learns (from a newspaper she has hidden in her closet) that Jack really kills people. Then, when Jack is shot in a hotel (he recovers), Kiki leaves for a friend's apartment and hides in her closet from both the police and the rival gangsters.

Finally, Jack comes to trial over his torture of a farmer in the matter of a still. The farmer complains, and a grand jury is called by Roosevelt. Though

acquitted of the assault on the farmer, a federal case against him nearly succeeds because of the testimony of an aide Jack betrayed. Following this, Jack
is shot and killed in a rooming house in Albany.

Part of the novel's theme relates to the legal profession. Marcus insists that
he defends those who pay his fee. In Jack's second trial, he uses an old nun, a
courthouse regular, telling the court in a rambling summation that this old
nun came to tell him how compassionate Jack Diamond was. Though a complete fabrication, these emotional touches win juries.

Kennedy's manic touch is evident in his portrayal of scenes on an ocean
liner as Jack and Marcus try to conclude a drug deal, scenes in the Kenmore
bar in Albany in its art deco heyday, and of the singing of "My Mother's Ro-
sary" at the Elk's Club bar in Albany. The final coda is a lyrically written, but
puzzling, apotheosis: Jack, dead, gradually emerges from his body, in a transfiguration worthy of a Seigfried or a Njall of Nordic sagas.

Kennedy's next novel, *Billy Phelan's Greatest Game*, tells the story of
another of Albany's historical crimes—the real kidnaping of the political
boss Dan O'Connell's nephew—through the framework of a series of games
of chance played by a young hanger-on of the city's underside. He is Billy
Phelan, son of an absent father, Francis, who will be the protagonist of *Ironweed*. The other consciousness of the book is Martin Daugherty, old neighbor of the Phelans and a newspaperman. The time frame covers several days
in late October, 1938, the time of the greatest game—the kidnaping.

Family interrelationships loom importantly in this novel. Billy Phelan has
lost his father, Francis, by desertion twenty-two years before; Martin's father,
a writer with an insane wife and a lovely mistress, now lies senile in a nursing
home. The politically powerful McCall family almost loses their only heir, the
pudgy, ineffectual Charlie. Martin lusts after his father's mistress, who plays
sexual games with him. Similarly, Billy's lady friend, Angie, cleverly outwits
him by pretending to be pregnant, to see what Billy will do. They have never,
she says, really talked about anything seriously. Billy reminisces about rowing
down Broadway in a boat, during a flood in 1913, with his father and uncle.
Soon, he finds his father in a seedy bar, along with his companion Helen, and
gives Helen his last money for his father.

This novel frames and mirrors an unsavory crime in the lives of ordinary,
yet complicated, human beings. Kennedy's wealth of language, his handiness
with an anecdote, sometimes leads him to leave loose ends in his otherwise
tightly constructed narratives. For example, Martin Daugherty has extrasensory perception; moreover, he lusts after his father's former mistress Melissa,
who also has a taste for women. These details are interesting, yet, unlike the
appearance of the vagrant Francis Phelan, these anecdotes do not further the
plot or embellish the theme.

Still, Kennedy's novels unfold in a profusion of ideas, one from the other,
both in language and in plot. The same time frame and some of the same

characters appear in *Ironweed*, the final book of the cycle and the Pulitzer Prize winner.

Ironweed takes place immediately after the events in *Billy Phelan's Greatest Game*, on Halloween and All Saint's Day, 1938, just after the radio broadcast of Orson Welles's adaptation of H. G. Wells's *The War of the Worlds* (1898). The dates are not randomly chosen: The story, though on the surface the saga of a failed, homeless man, is actually a religious pilgrimage toward redemption from sin. Ironweed is described in an epigraph as a tough-stemmed member of the sunflower family, and Francis, like the weed, is a survivor. These analogies, like the Welles broadcast, hinge on a question of belief important to this novel.

Unlike Kennedy's previous books, *Ironweed* has no narrator or central consciousness. The main character, Francis Phelan, first left home after he killed a man during a transit strike by throwing a stone during a demonstration against the hiring of scab trolley drivers. Subsequently he returned, but left for long periods when he played professional baseball. Later, he disappeared for twenty-two years after he dropped his infant son while diapering him; the child died, yet Francis' wife, Annie, never told anyone who dropped Gerald. Francis and another bum, Rudy, dying of cancer, get jobs digging in St. Agnes' Cemetery, where Gerald and other relatives are buried.

Reason and fact are supremely important in the book, yet within one page Francis' mother, a disagreeable hypocrite, twitches in her grave and eats crosses made from weeds, and the infant Gerald converses with his father and wills him to perform acts of expiation, as yet unknown, that will cease his self-destructiveness and bring forgiveness. Francis has killed several people besides the scab driver, yet it is not for these crimes that he needs forgiveness but for deserting his family. The rest of the book chronicles his redemption. Throughout, shifts to fantasy occur, triggered by passages of straight memory and detailed history. Ghosts of the men Francis killed ride the bus back to Albany, yet they do not seem as horrible to Francis as a woman he finds near the mission, freezing in the cold. He drapes a blanket around her, yet later he finds her dead, mangled and eaten by dogs.

During the night, Francis meets with his hobo "wife," Helen, a gently educated musician (she once went to Vassar) with enough energy, though dying of a tumor, to sing proudly in a pub on their rounds. In the mission, Francis gets a pair of warm socks; on the street, Helen is robbed of the money given to her by Francis' son Billy. Then follows a nightmare search through the cold streets for shelter for the delicate Helen. In desperation, Francis goes to a friend's apartment, where he washes his genital region in the toilet and begs a clean pair of shorts. The friend refuses them shelter, so Francis leaves Helen in an abandoned car with several men, though he knows she will be molested sexually.

The next day, Francis gets a job with a junkman. While making his rounds, he reads in a paper about his son Billy getting mixed up in the McCall kidnaping. Making the rounds of old neighborhoods, buying junk from housewives, releases a flood of memories for Francis: He sees his parents, his neighbors the Daughertys in their house, now burned, where one day the mad Katrina Daugherty walked out of her house naked to be rescued by the seventeen-year-old Francis. Because of this memory, he buys a shirt from the ragman to replace his filthy one. While he is buying the shirt, Helen goes to Mass, then listens to records in a record store (stealing one). Retrieving money she has hidden in her bra, Helen redeems the suitcase at the hotel. In her room, she recalls her life, her beloved father's suicide, her mother's cheating her of her inheritance, her exploiting lover/employer in the music store. Washing herself and putting on her Japanese kimono, she prepares to die.

Francis, meanwhile, revisits his family, bringing a turkey bought with his earnings from the day's job. He bathes, dresses in his old clothing his wife has saved, looks over souvenirs, meets his grandson, gets his daughter's forgiveness as well as his wife's, and is even invited to return. He leaves, however, finds Rudy, and together they look for Helen. Finding Helen registered at Palumbo's Hotel, Francis leaves money with the clerk for her. The final violent scene occurs in a hobo jungle, as it is being raided by Legionnaires. Francis kills Rudy's attacker with his own baseball bat and carries the fatally injured Rudy to the hospital. Returning to the hotel, Francis discovers Helen dead and leaves swiftly in a freight car.

The ending, typical of Kennedy's novels, is inconclusive. The reader can assume either that Francis leaves on a southbound freight or that he returns to his wife Annie's house and lives hidden in the attic. The use of the conditional in narration of this final section lends the necessary vagueness. Nevertheless, in *Ironweed*, the intricacy of poetry combines with factual detail and hallucinatory fugues to create a tight structure, the most nearly perfect of *The Albany Cycle* and its appropriate conclusion. The parallelism, for example, of a discussion of the temptations of Saint Anthony with the name of the Italian Church of St. Anthony, where Helen hears Mass on her last day of life, shows the craftsmanship of the author. The interconnections of theme, plot, and character in the three Albany novels, their hallucinatory fantasies, their ghostly visitations, ennoble the lowest of the low into modern epic heroes.

Other major works

SHORT FICTION: "The Secrets of Creative Love," 1983; "An Exchange of Gifts," 1985; "A Cataclysm of Love," 1986.

SCREENPLAY: *The Cotton Club*, 1984 (with Francis Coppola and Mario Puzo).

NONFICTION: *Getting It All, Saving It All: Some Notes by an Extremist,*

1978; *O Albany! An Urban Tapestry*, 1983; *Albany and the Capitol*, 1986.

CHILDREN'S LITERATURE: *Charlie Malarkey and the Belly Button Machine*, 1986 (with Brendan Kennedy).

Bibliography

Bonetti, Kay. "An Interview with William Kennedy," in *Missouri Review*. VIII, no. 2 (1985), pp. 71-86.

Croyden, Margaret. "The Sudden Fame of William Kennedy," in *The New York Times Magazine*. CXXXIII (August 26, 1984), p. 33.

Hunt, George W. "William Kennedy's Albany Trilogy," in *America*. CL (May 19, 1984), pp. 373-375.

Kennedy, William. "Be Reasonable—Unless You're a Writer," in *The New York Times Book Review*. XCII (January 25, 1987), p. 3.

Mitgang, Herbert M. "Inexhaustible Albany," in *The New York Times Book Review*. LXXXVIII (November 13, 1983), p. 84.

Nichols, Loxley F. "William Kennedy Comes of Age," in *National Review*. XXXVII (August 9, 1985), pp. 46-48.

Prescott, Peter S. "Having the Time of His Life," in *Newsweek*. CIII (February 6, 1984), pp. 78-79.

Pritchard, William H. "The Spirits of Albany," in *The New Republic*. CLXXXVIII (February 14, 1983), pp. 37-38.

Whittaker, Stephen. "The Lawyer as Narrator in William Kennedy's *Legs*," in *Legal Studies Forum*. IX, no. 2 (1985), pp. 157-164.

Anne Mills King

STEPHEN KING

Born: Portland, Maine; September 21, 1947

Principal long fiction

Carrie, 1974; *'Salem's Lot*, 1975; *The Shining*, 1977; *Rage*, 1977 (as Richard Bachman); *The Stand*, 1978; *The Dead Zone*, 1979; *The Long Walk*, 1979 (as Bachman); *Firestarter*, 1980; *Roadwork*, 1981 (as Bachman); *Cujo*, 1981; *The Dark Tower: The Gunslinger*, 1982 (illustrated by Michael Whelan); *The Running Man*, 1982 (as Bachman); *Christine*, 1983; *Pet Sematary*, 1983; *Cycle of the Werewolf*, 1983 (novelette, illustrated by Berni Wrightson); *The Talisman*, 1984 (with Peter Straub); *Thinner*, 1984 (as Bachman); *The Eyes of the Dragon*, 1984, 1987; *The Bachman Books: Four Early Novels by Stephen King*, 1985 (includes *Rage*, *The Long Walk*, *Roadwork*, and *The Running Man*); *It*, 1986; *Misery*, 1987; *The Tommyknockers*, 1987.

Other literary forms

Stephen King has published more than ninety short stories (including two collections, *Night Shift*, 1978, and *Skeleton Crew*, 1985) and the four novellas contained in *Different Seasons* (1982). Two of these novellas are central to his work. In *The Body*, a boy's confrontation with mortality shapes his developing identity as a writer. In *The Mist*, King in his satirical and apocalyptic mode brings Armageddon to the Federal Foods Supermarket as an assortment of Grade B movie monsters that inhabit a dense fog.

The relations of King's fiction with the electronic media are many and complex. Much of his fiction has been adapted to film, although it usually plays best in the mind's eye. He has written several mediocre screenplays, four of which have been produced, including *Maximum Overdrive* (1986), which he directed. A relatively successful mixed-media venture was his collaboration with George Romero on *Creepshow* (1982), a film anthology inspired by the E. C. Comics' blend of camp and gore and based on King's own book version. *Creepshow II*, written by Romero and based on King's stories, appeared in 1987. King has published numerous articles and one critical book, *Danse Macabre* (1981).

Achievements

King is perhaps the most widely known American writer of his generation, yet his distinctions include publishing as two authors at once: From 1977 to 1984, he wrote five novels under the pseudonym Richard Bachman. Special World Fantasy and British World Fantasy awards for his contributions to the field in 1980 and 1981 suggest a fraction of his achievement. The most appropriate distinction was the October 9, 1986, cover of *Time* magazine, which depicted a reader, hair on end, transfixed by "A Novel by Stephen King." The cover story on the "King of Horror" correctly suggested that his achievement and the "horror boom" of the 1970's and 1980's are inseparable. Yet, like Edgar Allan Poe, King turned a degenerated genre—a matter of comic-book monsters and drive-in movies—into a medium embodying the primary anxieties of his age.

King's detractors attribute his success to the sensational appeal of his genre, whose main purpose, as he readily confesses, is to scare people. He is graphic, sentimental, and predictable. His humor is usually crude and campy. His novels are long and loosely structured, and increasingly so: *It* comprises 1,138 pages. In an environment of "exhaustion" and minimalism, King's page-turners are the summit of the garbage heap of a mass, throwaway culture. Worst of all, he is "Master of Postliterate Prose"—as Paul Gray put the issue in 1982—of writing that takes readers mentally to the movies rather than making them imagine or think.

On the other hand, King has provided the most genuine example of the storyteller's art since Charles Dickens. He has returned to the novel some of the popular appeal it had in the nineteenth century and turned out a generation of readers who vastly prefer some books to their film adaptations. As Dickens drew on the popular culture of his time, King reflects the mass-mediated culture of his own. His dark fantasies, like all good popular fiction, allow readers to express within conventional frames of reference feelings and concepts they might not otherwise consider. In imagination, King is not merely prolific; his vision articulates universal fears and desires in terms peculiar to contemporary culture.

Biography

The second son of Donald and Nellie King, Stephen William King has lived most of his life in Maine, the setting for most of his fiction. Two childhood traumas, neither of which he remembers, may have been formative. In 1949, when he was two years old, his parents separated and his father disappeared. In 1951, he apparently saw a train dismember a neighborhood friend.

King's conservative Methodist upbringing was supplemented early with a diet of comic books and *Weird Tales*. When twelve, he began submitting stories for sale. In 1970, he was graduated from the University of Maine at Orono with a B.S. in English and a minor in dramatics. He encountered two lasting influences, the naturalist writers and contemporary American mythology. He also met Tabitha Jane Spruce, whom he married in 1971.

After graduation, he worked in an industrial laundry until 1971, when he became an English instructor at a preparatory school in Hampden, Maine. He wrote at night in the trailer he shared with his wife and two children. In the early 1970's, he sold stories to men's magazines. Then, in 1974, he published *Carrie*, which was followed by several best-sellers and motion-picture rights. In 1987, he was living in Maine with his wife, Tabitha King, novelist of *Small World* (1981) and *Caretakers* (1983), and their three children.

Analysis

Stephen King may be known as a horror writer, but he calls himself a "brand name," describing his style as "the literary equivalent of a Big Mac and a large fries from McDonald's." His fast-food version of the "plain style" may smell of commercialism, but that fact perhaps makes him the contemporary American storyteller without peer. From the beginning, his dark parables spoke to the anxieties of the late twentieth century. As a surrogate author in *The Mist* explains King's mission, "when the technologies fail, when . . . religious systems fail, people have got to have something. Even a zombie lurching through the night" is a "cheerful" thought in the context of a "dissolving ozone layer."

King's fictions are naturalized fantasies. They begin with premises accepted by middle Americans of the television generation, opening in suburban or small-town America—Derry, Maine, or Libertyville, Pennsylvania—and have the familiarity of the house next door and the Seven Eleven store. The characters have the trusted two-dimensional reality of kitsch: They originate in clichés such as the high school "nerd" or the wise child. From such premises, they move cinematically through an atmosphere resonant with a popular mythology taken from brand names, the electronic media, and comic strips as well as traditional sources. King applies naturalistic methods to an environment created by popular culture. This reality, already mediated, is translated easily into preternatural terms, taking on what A.D. Hutter calls the quality of a "shared nightmare."

King's imagination is above all archetypal: His "pop" familiarity and his campy humor draw on the collective unconscious. In *Danse Macabre*, a study of the contemporary horror genre which emphasizes the cross-pollination of fiction and film, he divides his subject according to four "monster archetypes": the ghost, the "thing" (or man-made monster), the vampire, and the werewolf. As in his fiction, his sources are the classic horror films of the 1930's, inherited by the 1950's pulp and film industries. He hints at their derivations from the gothic novel, classical myth, Brothers Grimm folktales, and the oral tradition in general. In an anxious era both skeptical of and hungry for myth, horror is fundamentally reassuring and cathartic; the tale-teller combines roles of physician and priest into the witch doctor as "sin eater," who assumes the guilt and fear of his culture. In the neoprimitivism of the 1970's and 1980's, this ancient role and the old monsters have taken on a new mystique.

In this light, *The Eyes of the Dragon*, advertised as "a fairy tale for adults," is not exceptional. In *The Uses of Enchantment* (1976), Bruno Bettelheim argues that the magic and terrors of fairy tales present existential problems in forms children can understand. King's paranormal horrors have similar cathartic and educative functions for adults; they externalize the traumas of later life, especially adolescence.

Stephen King's first published novel, *Carrie*, is such a parable of adolescence. Sixteen-year-old Carrie White is a lonely ugly duckling, an outcast at home and at school. Her mother, a religious fanatic, associates Carrie with her own "sin"; Carrie's peers hate her in a mindless way and make her the butt of every joke. *Carrie* concerns the horrors of high school, a place of "bottomless conservatism and bigotry," as King explains, where students "are no more allowed to rise 'above their station' than a Hindu" above caste. The novel is also about the terrors of passage to womanhood. In the opening scene, in the school shower room, Carrie experiences her first menstrual period; her peers react with abhorrence and ridicule, "stoning" her with sanitary napkins, shouting "Plug it up!" Carrie becomes the scapegoat for a fear of female sexuality as epitomized in the smell and sight of blood. (The blood bath and symbolism of sacrifice will recur at the climax of the novel.) As atonement for her participation in Carrie's persecution in the shower, Susan Snell persuades her popular boyfriend Tommy Ross to invite Carrie to the Spring Ball. Carrie's conflict with her mother, who regards her emerging womanhood with loathing, is paralleled by a new plot by the girls against her, led by the rich and spoiled Chris Hargenson. They arrange to have Tommy and Carrie voted King and Queen of the Ball, only to crown them with a bucket of pig's blood. Carrie avenges her mock baptism telekinetically, destroying the school and the town, leaving Susan Snell as the only survivor.

As in fairy tales, there is a consolation: The bad die and the good survive. As in most folk cultures, initiation is signified by the acquisition of special wisdom or powers. King equates Carrie's sexual flowering with the maturing of her telekinetic ability. Both cursed and empowered with righteous fury, she becomes at once victim and monster, witch and White Angel of Destruction. As King has explained, Carrie is "Woman, feeling her powers for the first time and, like Samson, pulling down the temple on everyone in sight at the end of the book."

Carrie catapulted King into the mass market; it immediately went into paperback and was adapted into a critically acclaimed film directed by Brian De Palma. The novel touched the right nerves. Feminism was one. William Blatty's *The Exorcist* (1971), which was adapted to a powerful and controversial film, had touched on similar social fears in the 1960's and 1970's with its subtext of the "generation gap" and the "death of God." Although Carrie's destructive power, like that of Regan in *The Exorcist*, is linked with monstrous adolescent sexuality, the similarity between the two novels ends there. Carrie's "possession" is the complex effect of her mother's fanaticism, her peers' bigotry, and her newly realized, unchecked female power; it is the combined failure of nature and civilization. Like Anne Sexton's *Transformations* (1971), a collection of fractured fairy tales in sardonic verse, King's novel explores the social and cultural roots of its evil.

King's *Carrie* is a dark modernization of "Cinderella," with a bad mother, cruel siblings (peers), a prince (Tommy Ross), a godmother (Sue Snell), and a ball. King's reversal of the happy ending is actually in keeping with the Brothers Grimm; it recalls the tale's folk originals, which enact revenge in bloody images: The stepsisters' heels, hands, and noses are sliced off, and a white dove pecks out their eyes. As King knows, blood flows freely in the oral tradition.

King represents that oral tradition in a pseudodocumentary form which depicts the points of view of various witnessess and commentaries: newspaper accounts, case studies, court reports, and journals. Pretending to textual authenticity, he alludes to the gothic classics, especially Bram Stoker's *Dracula* (1897). *'Salem's Lot*, King's next novel, is a bloody fairy tale in which Dracula comes to Our Town.

By the agnostic and sexually liberated 1970's, the vampire had been demythologized into what King called a "comic book menace." In his most significant departure from tradition, he diminishes the sexual aspects of the vampire. He reinvests the archetype with meaning by basing its attraction on the human desire to surrender identity in the mass. His major innovation, however, was envisioning the mythic small town in *American Gothic* terms and then making it the monster; the vampire's traditional victim, the populace, becomes the menace as mindless mass, plague, or primal horde. Drawing on Richard Matheson's grimly naturalistic novel *I Am Legend* (1954) and Jack Finney's novel *The Body Snatchers* (1955), King focused on the issues of fragmentation, reinvesting the vampire with contemporary meaning.

The sociopolitical subtext of *'Salem's Lot* was the ubiquitous disillusionment of the Watergate era, King has explained. Like rumor and disease, vampirism spreads secretly at night, from neighbor to neighbor, infecting men and women, the mad and the senile, the responsible citizen and the infant alike, absorbing into its zombielike horde the human population. King is especially skillful at suggesting how small-town conservatism can become inverted on itself, the harbored suspicions and open secrets gradually dividing and isolating. This picture is reinforced by the town's name, 'Salem's Lot, a degenerated form of Jerusalem's Lot, which suggests the city of the chosen reverted to a culture of dark rites in images of spreading menace.

King's other innovation was, paradoxically, a reiteration. He made his "king vampire," Barlow, an obvious reincarnation of Stoker's Dracula that functions somewhere between cliché and archetype. King uses the mythology of vampires to ask how civilization is to exist without faith in traditional authority symbols. His answer is pessimistic, turning on the abdication of Father Callahan, whose strength is undermined by secret alcoholism and a superficial adherence to form. Representing external authority without inner resources, he leaves on a Greyhound bus. The two survivors, Ben Mears and Mark Petrie, must partly seek, partly create their talismans and rituals, drawing on the compendium of vampire lore—the alternative, in a culture-wide crisis of faith, to conventional systems. (At one point, Mears holds off a vampire with a crucifix made with two tongue depressors.) The traditional paraphernalia, they find, will work only if the handler has faith.

It is significant that the two survivors are, respectively, a "wise child" (Mark Petrie) and a novelist (Ben Mears, King's self-portrait); only they have the necessary resources. Even Susan Norton, Mears's lover and the gothic heroine, succumbs. As in *The Shining*, *The Dead Zone*, and *Firestarter*, the child (or childlike adult) has powers which may be used for good or for evil. Mears is the imaginative, nostalgic adult, haunted by the past. The child and the man share a naïveté, a gothic iconography, and a belief in evil. Twelve-year-old Mark worships at a shrinelike tableau of Aurora monsters that glow "green in the dark, just like the plastic Jesus" he was given in Sunday School for learning Psalm 119. Mears has returned to the town of his childhood to revive an image of the Marsten House lurking in his mythical mind's eye. Spiritual father and son, they create a community of two out of the "pop" remnants of American culture.

As in fairy tales and Dickens' novels, King's protagonists are orphans searching for their true parents, for community. His fiction may reenact his search for the father who disappeared and left behind a box of *Weird Tales*. The yearned-for bond of parent and child, a relationship signifying a unity of being, appears throughout his fiction. The weakness or treachery of a trusted parent is correspondingly the ultimate fear. Hence, the vampire Barlow is the devouring father who consumes an entire town. In *The Shining*, King domesticated his approach to the issue, focusing on the threat to the family that comes from a trusted figure within it. Jack Torrance is the abused child who, assuming his father's aggression, in turn becomes the abusing father. The much beloved "bad" father is the novel's monster: The environment of the Overlook Hotel traps him, as he in turn calls its power forth. King brilliantly expands the haunted-house archetype into a symbol of the accumulated sin of all fathers who were one-night stands. In the epic fantasy *The Stand*, King explores the issue in the terms of an apocalyptic Western, as survivors of a superflu struggle across the continent, rebuilding civilization out of the new wilderness, the open future. The haunting and haunted father is the "Walkin' Dude" named Flagg who draws loners and outlaws to Las Vegas, thwarting community and growth; he is opposed by the idealized tribal Mother Abigail, who is also the childlike seer. Then, in *Cujo*, King naturalizes the issue, making the monster the family dog after it contracts rabies—the objective correlative for a spectrum of domestic and social ills: marital problems, wife beating, business failure, food additives.

In *Christine*, King examines the same threat by way of American popular culture. The setting is Libertyville, Pennsylvania, in the late 1970's. The monster is the American Dream as embodied in the automobile. The epigraph to chapter 14, a song ("Less than Zero") by punk rock artist Elvis Costello, makes the point: "about a couple/ living in the U.S.A." who "traded in their baby/ for a Chevrolet:/ Let's talk about the future now,/ We've put the past away."

King gives *Christine* all the attributes of a fairy tale for "postliterate" adolescents. *Christine* is another fractured "Cinderella" story—*Carrie* for boys. Arnie Cunningham, a nearsighted, acne-scarred loser, falls "in love with" a car, a passionate (red and white) Christine, "one of the long ones with the big fins." An automotive godmother, she brings Arnie, in fairy-tale succession, freedom, success, power, and love: a home away from over-protective parents, a cure for acne, hit-and-run revenge on bullies, and a beautiful girl, Leigh Cabot. Soon, however, the familiar triangle emerges, of boy, girl, and car, and Christine is revealed as a femme fatale—driven by the spirit of her former owner, a malcontent named Roland LeBay. Christine is the vehicle for its death wish on the world, for its all-devouring, "everlasting Fury." LeBay's aggression possesses Arnie, who reverts into an older, tougher self, then into the "mythic teenaged hood" that King has called the prototype of 1950's werewolf movies, and finally into "some ancient carrion eater," or primal self.

As automotive monster Christine comes from a variety of sources, including the folk tradition of the "death car" and a venerable techno-horror premise. King's main focus, however, is the mobile youth culture that has come down from the 1950's by way of advertising, popular songs, film, and national pastimes. Christine is the car as a projection of the cultural self, Anima for the modern American Adam. To Arnie's late 1970's–style imagination, the Plymouth Fury, in 1958 a mid-priced family car, is an American Dream. Her sweeping, befinned chassis and engine re-create a fantasy of the golden age of the automobile: the horizonless future imagined as an expanding network of superhighways and unlimited fuel. Christine recovers for Arnie a pre-lapsarian vitality and manifest destiny.

Christine's odometer runs backward and she regenerates parts. The immortality she offers, however—and by implication, the American Dream—is really arrested development in the form of a *Happy Days* rerun and by way of her radio, which sticks on the golden oldies station. Indeed, *Christine* is a recapitulatory rock musical framed fatalistically in sections titled "Teenage Car-Songs," "Teenage Love-Songs," and "Teenage Death-Songs." Fragments of rock-and-roll songs introduce each chapter. Christine's burden, an undead 1950's youth culture, means that most of Arnie's travels are in and out of time, a deadly nostalgia trip. As Douglas Winter explains, *Christine* reenacts "the death," in the 1970's "of the American romance with the automobile."

The novel's uncanny narrative perspective is best described as déjà vu. Early New Year's Day, 1979, Arnie takes the narrator, Dennis, on a last ride. "We went back in time," he says, "but did we?" The present-day streets look "like a thin [film] overlay" superimposed on a time "somehow more real" whose "dead hands" reach out to draw them in forever. The epilogue from four years later presents the fairy-tale consolation in a burned-out monotone. Arnie and his parents are buried, Christine is scrap metal, and the true Americans, Leigh and Dennis, are survivors, but Dennis, the "knight of Darnell's Garage," does not woo "the lady fair"; he is a limping, lackluster junior high teacher and they have drifted apart, grown old in their prime. Dennis narrates the story in order to file it away, all the while perceiving himself and his peers in terms of icons from the late 1950's. In his nightmares, Christine appears wearing a black vanity plate inscribed with a skull and the words, "ROCK AND ROLL WILL NEVER DIE." From Dennis' haunted perspective, *Christine* simultaneously examines and is a symptom of a cultural phenomenon: a new American gothic species of anachronism or déjà vu, which continued after *Christine*'s publication in films such as *Back to the Future* (1985), *Peggy-Sue Got Married* (1986) and *Blue Velvet* (1986). The 1980's and the 1950's blur into a seamless illusion, the nightmare side of which is the prospect of living an infinite replay.

The subtext of King's adolescent fairy tale is another coming of age, from the opposite end and the broader perspective of American culture. Written by a fortyish King in the final years of the twentieth century, *Christine* diagnoses a cultural midlife crisis and marks a turning point in King's career, a critical examination of mass culture. The dual time frame reflects his awareness of a dual audience, of writing for adolescents who look back to a mythical 1950's and also for his own generation as it relives its undead youth culture in its children. The baby boomers, King explains, "were obsessive" about childhood. "We went on playing for a long time, almost feverishly. I write for that buried child in us, but I'm writing for the grown-up too. I want grown-ups to look at the child long enough to be able to give him up. The child should be buried."

In *Pet Sematary*, King unearthed that child, which is the novel's monster. *Pet Sematary* is about the "*real* cemetery," he told Winter. The focus is on the "one great fear" all fears "add up to," "the body under the sheet. It's our body." The fairy-tale subtext is the magic kingdom of our protracted American childhood, the Disney empire as mass culture—and, by implication, the comparable multimedia phenomenon represented by King himself. The grimmer, truer text-within-the-text is Mary Shelley's *Frankenstein: Or, The Modern Prometheus* (1818).

The novel, which King once considered "too horrible to be published," is also his own dark night of the soul. Louis Creed, a university doctor, his wife Rachel, and their two children (five-year-old Ellie and two-year-old Gage) move to Maine to work at King's alma mater; a neighbor takes the family on an outing to a pet cemetery created by the neighborhood children, their confrontation with mortality. Additionally the "sematary," whose "Druidic" rings allude to Stonehenge, is the outer circle of an Indian burial ground that sends back the dead in a state of soulless half life, resurrecting with primitive simplicity. Louis succumbs to temptation when the family cat Church is killed on the highway; he buries him on the sacred old Indian burial grounds. "Frankencat" comes back with his "purr-box broken." A succession of accidents, heart attacks, strokes, and deaths—of neighbor Norma Crandall, son Gage, Norma's husband, Jud, and wife Rachel—and resurrections follow.

The turning point is the death of Gage, which his father cannot accept and which leads to the novel's analysis of modern medical miracles performed in the name of human decency and love. Louis is the heavy father as baby boomer who cannot relinquish his childhood. The larger philosophical issue is Louis' rational, bioethical *creed*; he believes in saving the only life he knows, the material. Transferred into an immoderate love for his son, it is exposed as the narcissistic embodiment of a patriarchal lust for immortality through descendants, expressed first in an agony of sorrow and rage, then ghoulishly, as he disinters his son's corpse and makes the estranging discovery that it is like "looking at a badly made doll." Later, reanimated, Gage appears to have been "terribly hurt and then put back together again by crude, uncaring hands." Performing his task, Louis feels dehumanized, like "a subhuman character in some cheap comic-book."

The failure of Louis' creed is shown in his habit, when under stress, of taking mental trips to Orlando, Florida, where he, Church, and Gage drive a white van as Disney World's "resurrection crew." In these waking dreams, which echo the male bond of "wise child" and haunted father from as far back as *'Salem's Lot*, Louis' real creed is revealed: Its focus is on Oz the Gweat and Tewwible (a personification of death to Rachel) and Walt Disney, that "gentle faker from Nebraska"—like Louis, two wizards of science fantasy. Louis' wizardry is reflected in the narrative perspective and structure, which flashes back in part 2 from the funeral to Louis' fantasy of a heroically "long, flying tackle" that snatches Gage from death's wheels.

In this modernization of *Frankenstein*, King demythologizes death and attacks the aspirations toward immortality that typify the 1980's. King's soulless Lazaruses are graphic projections of anxieties about life-support systems, artificial hearts, organ transplants, Baby Faye—what King has called "mechanistic miracles" that can postpone the physical signs of life almost indefinitely. The novel also indicts the "waste land" of mass culture, alluding in the same trope to George Romero's "stupid, lurching movie-zombies, . . . T. S. Eliot's poem about the hollow men,L and *The Wizard of Oz*: "headpiece full of straw." Louis worries that Ellie knows more about Ronald McDonald and "the Burger King" than the "*spiritus mundi*."

If the novel suggests one source of community and culture, it is the form and ritual of the children's pet "sematary." Its concentric circles form a pattern from their "own collective unconsciousness," one that mimes "the most ancient religious symbol of all," the spiral. In *It*, a group of children similarly create a community and a mythology as a way of confronting their fears, as represented in It, the monster as a serial-murdering, shape-shifting boogey that haunts the sewers of Derry, Maine. In 1958, the seven protagonists, a cross-section of losers, experience the monster differently, for as in George Orwell's *Nineteen Eighty-Four* (1949), It derives its power through its victim's isolation and guilt and thus assumes the shape of his or her worst fear. (To Beverly Rogan It appears, in a sequence reminiscent of "Red Riding Hood," as her abusive father in the guise of the child-eating witch from "Hansel and Gretel.")

In a scary passage in *Pet Sematary*, Louis dreams of Disney World, where "by the 1890s train station, Mickey Mouse was shaking hands with the children clustered around him, his big white cartoon gloves swallowing their small, trusting hands." To all of *It*'s protagonists, the monster appears in a similar archetypal or communal form, one that suggests a composite of devouring parent and mass-culture demigod, of television commercial and fairy tale, of 1958 and 1985: as Pennywise, the Clown, a cross between Bozo and Ronald McDonald. As in *Christine*, *Pet Sematary*, and *Thinner*, the monster is mass culture itself, the collective devouring parent nurturing its children on "imitations of immortality." Like Christine, or Louis' patched-up son, Pennywise is the dead past feeding on the future. Twenty-seven years after its original reign of terror, It resumes its siege, whereupon the protagonists, now professionally successful and, significantly, childless yuppies, must return to Derry, like the ex-hippies of *The Big Chill* (1983), to confront as adults their childhood fears. Led by surrogate horror writer Bill Denborough, who now stutters only in his dreams, they defeat It once more, individually as a sort of allegory of psychoanalysis and collectively as a rite of passage into adulthood and community.

It was attacked in reviews as pop psychology and by King himself as a "badly constructed novel," but the puerility was partly intended. As John Barth's magnum opus, *Letters* (1979), was self-referentially abstruse, Stephen King's is self-consciously naïve. (The last chapter begins with an epigraph from Dickens' novel of 1849-1850, *David Copperfield*, and ends with an allusion to William Wordsworth's "Intimations of Immortality.") In the 1970's, his fiction was devoted to constructing a mythology out of shabby celluloid monsters to fill a cultural void; in the 1980's, looking back with postmodern self-consciousness, he demythologized the culture he had in part created. *It* is multiple exorcism, a calling forth and unmasking of motley Reagan-age monsters. It, the monster *in* motley, is King himself, the "gentle faker" from Bangor posing as Oz the Gweat and Tewwible.

Putting It to rest, King seems in 1987's *The Eyes of the Dragon* (published in a limited edition in 1984) to return to the springs of his fantasy, the fairy tale. There, he tells much the same story but assumes the mantle of adulthood. Says reviewer Barbara Tritel, this "pellucid" and "elegant" fairy tale has "intimate goofiness of an extemporaneous story" narrated "by a parent to a child."

Other major works

SHORT FICTION: *Night Shift*, 1978; *Different Seasons*, 1982; *Skeleton Crew*, 1985.

SCREENPLAYS: *Creepshow*, 1982 (with George Romero; adaptation of his book); *Cat's Eye*, 1984; *Silver Bullet*, 1985 (adaptation of *Cycle of the Werewolf*); *Maximum Overdrive*, 1986 (adaptation of his short story "Truck").

NONFICTION: *Danse Macabre*, 1981.

MISCELLANEOUS: *Creepshow*, 1982 (adaptation of the E.C. Comics).

Bibliography

Gray, Paul. "Master of Postliterate Prose," in *Time*. CXX (August 30, 1982), p. 87.

Kanfer, Stefan. "King of Horror," in *Time*. CXXVIII (October 9, 1986), pp. 74-78, 80, 83.

Norden, Eric. "Playboy Interview: Stephen King," in *Playboy*. June, 1983, pp. 65-82, 230-239.

Underwood, Tim, and Church Miller, eds. *Fear Itself: The Horror Fiction of Stephen King*, 1982.

Winter, Douglas. *Stephen King: The Art of Darkness*, 1986.

Linda C. Badley

DANILO KIŠ

Born: Subotica, Yugoslavia; February 22, 1935

Principal long fiction
Mansarda, 1962; *Psalam 44*, 1962; *Bašta, pepeo*, 1965 (*Garden, Ashes*, 1975); *Peščanik*, 1972; *Grobnica za Borisa Davidoviča*, 1976 (*A Tomb for Boris Davidovich*, 1978).

Other literary forms
In addition to novels, Danilo Kiš has written two books of short stories that are sometimes mistakenly labeled as novels: *Rani jadi* (1969; early sorrows) and *Enciklopedija mrtvih* (1983; the encyclopedia of the dead). His short stories lose some of their significance in that Kiš often writes his novels as a collection of related stories, thus blurring the line between the two genres. His attempts at television drama, *Noć i magla* (1968; night and fog), *Papagaj* (1969; parrot), *Drveni sanduk Tomasa Wulfa* (1974; the wooden trunk of Thomas Wolfe), have been less successful than his other works. Kiš is also an essayist and polemicist, advocating new approaches to literature and expounding his own views on literary art. His *Po-etika* (1972; poetics), *Po-etika, knjiga druga* (1974; poetics, book two), and especially *Čas anatomije* (1978; a lesson in anatomy) are examples of a spirited and passionate defense of his own works against detractors. In addition, they trace for younger writers the path to a more modern approach to writing. Kiš has also skillfully translated some major writers from the original French, Hungarian, and Russian.

Achievements
Kiš belongs to the generation of Serbian writers who burst upon the literary scene in the mid-1960's with a fresh outlook on literature and with surprisingly mature works. As one of the most articulate and cosmopolitan among them, he has been able to bring down the barriers of traditionalism and provincialism prevalent in Serbian prose up to that time. To be sure, that process had begun before Kiš's generation, but it reached its full potential with that generation, finally bringing Serbian prose into the mainstream of contemporary world literature. His second important contribution can be seen in his highly accomplished style. His seemingly simple yet rather sophisticated realism, broad erudition, and uncanny dexterity with words have made him the undisputed leader among the Serbian writers in the second half of the twentieth century. With these qualities, Kiš has appealed to readers beyond his homeland, resulting in translations of his works into many languages. Among other awards, he has received the French Legion of Honor medal as a Knight of the Arts and Literature.

Biography

Danilo Kiš was born in Subotica, a northern city of Yugoslavia that is near the Hungarian border, on February 22, 1935, of a Jewish father and a Montenegrin mother. As a consequence, his family was subjected to terror during World War II, which his father and other relatives did not survive. He spent his childhood in Novi Sad until the infamous massacre of Serbs and Jews in 1942, after which he fled to his father's home village in Hungary. After the war, working on farms and reading voraciously adventure, mystery, and crime books, he nurtured his imagination and the love for books that eventually brought him to Belgrade University, from which he was graduated with a degree in world literature. As a young lecturer, he spent two years in Bordeaux, France, an experience that led to a long-standing love affair with that country.

Analysis

In most of his works, Danilo Kiš has been preoccupied with the suffering of people during wartime, especially those the hardest hit—the Jews and other minorities. He does not dwell on suffering per se but rather on what war forces the victims to do under such unusual circumstances. The mistreatment of the innocent and their outward dehumanization offer them a chance to observe their past and to arrive at some rudimentary understanding of the meaning of existence. This process pertains even to those who suffered in peacetime at the hands of oppressors, since their suffering, too, was often the result of war. By transforming the tragic fate of specific individuals into general experience, Kiš has imbued his works with universality and pathos. His sophisticated approach to both form and subject matter raises the artistic value of his works.

Kiš's first work, the short novel *Mansarda* (the attic), did not foreshadow his primary concerns discussed above. The work of a novice, *Mansarda* reveals the ebullience of a writer flexing his muscles. One impressionistic chapter follows another in no discernible order; the characters find it difficult to separate reality from hallucinations; there is hardly any plot; and the themes crystallize only after a tortuous course of events. What the novel does show, however, is the age-old problem of young people in search of identity amid growing pains, and the seductive and often tragic combination of love and suicide. The central feature of this fledgling yet remarkably mature work is the metaphor of an attic, where the protagonist lives, to which he constantly returns yet from which he is pulled down to earth, where he must face the reality of everyday existence. Although *Mansarda* did not solve this perennial dilemma, it promised even more mature accomplishments by the young author.

In *Psalam 44* (Psalm 44), there appears for the first time the theme that would recur in most of Kiš's subsequent works. Written in a more controlled style than *Mansarda*, *Psalam 44* depicts, in an almost entirely realistic fashion, a few hours in a Nazi concentration camp during the last days of World War II. Again, Kiš does not so much describe what happens to the main characters—a captive Jewish doctor forced to ply his trade in the camp and a young Jewish girl who has just given birth to their child—as he does reveal their thinking and feelings. Tortured by their tense inner world and the bizarre real world crumbling around them, they are nurtured by the concern and help they receive from other inmates and, most important, by their own love, which conquers all obstacles. The author does not succumb to this potentially trite subject matter, nor does he moralize. Resisting these temptations, Kiš creates a deeply felt artistic document of man's inhumanity toward man.

In his third novel, *Garden, Ashes*, Kiš's main theme gains full force. Through the reminiscences of his dolorous childhood, he builds a monument to the memory of his remarkable father—to his memory because, a victim of a pogrom, he left the child's world before there could be a closer, more prosaic relationship. The father was an eccentric and an incorrigible dreamer, a frustrated genius, a poet, a philosopher, a grotesque Don Quixote, a drunkard, a proud squanderer of his many gifts, a giant among Lilliputians, a misplaced wanderer from some exotic land. He was the focal point of the child's imagination and preoccupations for a long time. His most important function, as far as the boy is concerned, was to impress on the child's feverish imagination a firm belief that life is not what it seems to be—a sequence of cruel, frightful, seemingly meaningless events—or that at least it does not have to be so. The fact that the father was always an alien among the people around him only enhances the boy's awe and love for him. The tragic circumstances of his disappearance and the passage of time have added an aura of pathos and unreality to the already unreal experiences of a growing boy—learning to accept and cope with his father and his memory. The reader is left with the feeling that the bonds between the precocious child and his wayward father are indestructible and that the father's shadow will accompany the child's every step into manhood.

These events are related by Kiš in a poetic tone and with an accomplished style. He incorporates many modern techniques, skillfully blending reality and dream and following the rampant imagination of a gifted, painfully sensitive child. The result is more than another confessional, cathartic farewell to childhood by a young man who has outgrown it: It is, rather, an artistic creation with a life of its own. The exceptional beauty and richness of the language come through even in translation.

Kiš returns to this, by now more or less constant, theme in his next novel, *Peščanik* (hourglass). There are, however, significant differences, seen primarily in the noticeable maturation in the author's style and in his approach to the theme. While in *Garden, Ashes* and in the short-story collection *Rani jadi* the reminiscences of Eduard Sam are those of a son, in *Peščanik*, the father, or E. S. as he is called, appears in his own right, telling his own story. The telling of the story also marks an advance for Kiš: While in earlier works the narrative mode was personal, sentimental, and often poetic, this novel features a dazzling variety of narrative devices.

The novel is composed of several sections, "Pictures from a Journey," "Notes of a Lunatic," "Investigation," and "The Investigation of Witnesses," which represent various approaches to reality and which recur in the novel when a particular approach is being used. The novel ends with a letter written by the protagonist that can be seen as his last will. Each chapter has a specific function that corresponds to the author's varying points of view. In the first of these chapters, impressions of various objects that meet the observer's eye are given in minute detail, underlining one possible method of observation—the purely realistic one. In "Notes of a Lunatic," reality is seen through the mind and emotions of a victim of persecution and suffering. Here the author penetrates the realistic surface created by the previous method. In the chapters on investigation, Kiš employs a purely dramatic technique of direct questions and answers used in a criminal investigation, thus underscoring the unspeakable tension under which every moment of the protagonist's life is spent. Yet these different approaches are intrinsically related through the author's constant return to the same object in a different guise, as if to say that there is only one reality but there are different perceptions of it. While it is true that this technique makes the novel somewhat complex and at times difficult to follow, it is also true that Kiš is willing to experiment and that the experimentation has added a new dimension to his craft.

In the last analysis, however, the significance of *Peščanik* lies not so much in its artistic virtuosity as in the treatment of the theme that has preoccupied Kiš ever since he began to write: The tragedy of men involved in conflict with one another, whether because of race, religion, politics, or greed. Kiš sees the atrocities and the ensuing suffering in World War II as inevitable as long as man continues to ignore the need for understanding, compassion, and respect for each human being, no matter what the circumstances. The universality of these concerns, combined with its artistic virtues and complexity, make *Peščanik* not only one of the most important achievements in modern Serbian writing but also one of the outstanding works on a central theme of postwar European literature.

That Kiš is not interested exclusively in the atrocities committed during World War II in his homeland is confirmed by his next novel, *A Tomb for Boris Davidovich*. The focus here shifts to the few years before the outbreak of the war in the Soviet Union—a period during which that country experienced one of the worst cases of man's inhumanity to man, the infamous purges of the so-called dissidents. That the main victims are again Jews is both coincidental and purposeful; while many of the purge victims were Jewish, many others were not. In Kiš's vision, Boris Davidovich is again a universal symbol, as was Eduard Sam in the previous works.

The novel is composed of seven seemingly loosely related stories which, on a closer look, reveal an organic unity. The author follows the crisscrossing paths and intertwined destinies of several people, most of whom again fall victim to persecution through no fault of their own. Yet it is peacetime, and the persecutors are not Nazis. Thus, Kiš returns to one of the basic lessons of *Peščanik*: Man will commit the same crime, regardless of motives, if he loses respect for the dignity of his fellowman. People do not have to be officially at war to exterminate one another; they can do it whenever they take it upon themselves to be the final judges of their fellowman or, what is yet more deadly, gods on earth.

Five of the stories in *A Tomb for Boris Davidovich* deal with the victimization of the Jewish revolutionaries in the Soviet Union. The sixth goes back six centuries, to medieval France, where another Jew, not coincidentally bearing the initials of Boris Davidovich, succumbs to persecution. The only way to combat this perennial evil is through courage and constant resistance, which is exactly what the protagonist of the last story, a Soviet writer, lacks in his refusal to face reality.

Kiš employs here a mixture of facts and fiction, a method new to the literatures of Yugoslavia. His reliance on historical facts provoked widely publicized accusations of plagiarism, which he was able to refute easily by pointing out that, though relying on facts, he gave them artistic garb, weaving them into the intricate web of his imagination.

The combination of significant subject matter and artistic prowess in almost all of his works has established Kiš's reputation as one of the best among the contemporary Eastern European writers. What makes him even more important is his ability to transcend narrow regional boundaries and to appeal to readers of all persuasions. Danilo Kiš is indeed the most accomplished and modernistic of all contemporary Yugoslav writers.

Other major works

SHORT FICTION: *Rani jadi*, 1969; *Enciklopedija mrtvih*, 1983.

TELEPLAYS: *Noć i magla*, 1968; *Papagaj*, 1969; *Drveni sanduk Tomasa Wulfa*, 1974.

NONFICTION: *Po-etika*, 1972; *Po-etika, knjiga druga*, 1974; *Čas anatomije*, 1978.

Bibliography
Bynum, David E. "Philosophical Fun and Merriment in the First Fiction of Danilo Kiš," in *Serbian Studies*. II, no. 4 (1984), pp. 3-20.

Czarny, Norbert. "Imaginary—Real Lives: On Danilo Kiš," in *Cross Currents 3*, 1984.

Vitanović, Slobodan. "Thematic Unity in Danilo Kiš's Literary Works," in *Relations*. Nos. 9/10 (1979), pp. 66-69.

White, Edmund. "Danilo Kiš: The Obligations of Form," in *Southwest Review*. LXXI (Summer, 1986), pp. 363-377.

Vasa D. Mihailovich

LOUIS L'AMOUR

Born: Jamestown, North Dakota; March 22, 1908

Principal long fiction

Westward the Tide, 1950; *Hondo*, 1953; *Sitka*, 1957; *Last Stand at Papago Wells*, 1957; *The First Fast Draw*, 1959; *The Daybreakers*, 1960; *Sackett*, 1961; *Shalako*, 1962; *Lando*, 1962; *Mojave Crossing*, 1964; *The Sackett Brand*, 1965; *The Broken Gun*, 1966; *Mustang Man*, 1966; *The Sky-Liners*, 1967; *Down the Long Hills*, 1968; *The Lonely Men*, 1969; *The Man Called Noon*, 1970; *Galloway*, 1970; *North to the Rails*, 1971; *Ride the Dark Trail*, 1972; *Treasure Mountain*, 1972; *The Ferguson Rifle*, 1973; *The Man from Skibbereen*, 1973; *Sackett's Land*, 1974; *Rivers West*, 1975; *The Man from the Broken Hills*, 1975; *Over on the Dry Side*, 1975; *To the Far Blue Mountains*, 1976; *Borden Chantry*, 1977; *Fair Blows the Wind*, 1978; *Bendigo Shafter*, 1979; *The Iron Marshal*, 1979; *The Warrior's Path*, 1980; *Lonely on the Mountain*, 1980; *Comstock Lode*, 1981; *Milo Talon*, 1981; *The Cherokee Trail*, 1982; *The Lonesome Gods*, 1983; *Ride the River*, 1983; *Son of a Wanted Man*, 1984; *The Walking Drum*, 1984; *Jubal Sackett*, 1985; *Last of the Breed*, 1986; *The Haunted Mesa*, 1987.

Other literary forms

Although Louis L'Amour has achieved his greatest success as a Western novelist, he began his career as a writer of short pulp fiction, now partly assembled in thirteen collections. He also wrote some hard-boiled detective stories. In addition, he issued a book of undistinguished poetry early in his career.

Achievements

L'Amour is the most phenomenal Western writer America has ever produced. Each of his eighty-five novels, mostly traditional Westerns, has sold at least a million copies; ten of his novels have doubled that figure. His books have been translated into more than a dozen foreign languages. More than thirty of his plots have been made into motion-picture and television dramas. In 1981, with *Comstock Lode*, L'Amour became a formidable presence in the hardbound-book market; he immediately made the best-seller list; all of his subsequent hardbound novels have matched this performance. By 1977, L'Amour had sold fifty million copies of his books. In 1987, the figure was 175 million.

L'Amour has also received important awards and honors. He won the Western Writers of America (WWA) Golden Spur Award in 1969 for *Down the Long Hills* and the Western Writers of America Golden Saddleman

Award in 1981 for overall achievement and contributions to an understanding of the American West. When, in 1985, the WWA published a list of the twenty-six best Western novels of all time, L'Amour's *Hondo* made the list. In 1982, the United States Congress awarded him a National Gold Medal, and one year later, President Ronald Reagan awarded him the United States Medal of Freedom.

L'Amour has not been averse to peddling his own wares. In June of 1980, he cruised the Midwest and the Mid-South in a leased luxury bus, meeting fans and selling autographed copies of his seventy-five books then available. He has appeared on television to promote his Louis L'Amour Collection of novels. His publisher (Bantam Books, Inc.) now offers L'Amour calendars, audiotape dramas (multivoiced, with sound effects) of certain L'Amour stories, and an audiocassette of their star author's personal reminiscences.

Biography

Louis L'Amour was born Louis Dearborn LaMoore in Jamestown, North Dakota, on March 22, 1908, into a rugged, French-Irish pioneering family. His father, Louis Charles LaMoore, reared by his paternal grandparents in Ontario, was a veterinarian, a Jamestown police chief, and a civic leader. The novelist's mother, Emily, whose father was a Civil War veteran and an Indian fighter, attended the normal school at St. Cloud, Minnesota, and married L. C. LaMoore in 1892. Louis was the youngest of the couple's seven children, four of whom survived to distinguished maturity.

After a healthy early boyhood of outdoor activity and voracious reading, L'Amour moved in 1923 with his family to Oklahoma but soon struck out on his own. An incredible sequence of knockabout jobs followed: sailor, longshoreman, lumberjack, boxer, circus worker, cattle skinner, fruit picker, hay shocker, miner, friend of bandits in China, book reviewer in Oklahoma, lecturer there and in Texas, neophyte writer, and a United States Army tank-destroyer and transportation officer in World War II in France and Germany.

In 1946, L'Amour decided to live in Los Angeles, where he still maintains a residence (another being in Durango, Colorado), and became a professional writer. Some of his short-story pulps and slicks into the mid-1950's were under the pen names Tex Burns and Jim Mayo. A turning point for L'Amour came with the publication of "The Gift of Cochise" in *Collier's*, the story which formed the basis for *Hondo* a year later. This was not, however, L'Amour's first Western novel, which was the competent *Westward the Tide*, published in London in 1950.

The biography of Louis L'Amour from 1953 onward is largely an account of one popular success after another, adaptations of his plots to the screen, fine efforts at versatility in a career which too many regard as merely capitalizing on the formulaic Western, and steady personal happiness.

With the publication of *Night over the Solomons* (a collection of old prewar stories) in 1986, L'Amour saw his one-hundredth book into print. Of the many films made from his fiction, the most notable are *Hondo* (1953), *The Burning Hills* (1956), *Apache Territory* (1958), *Heller in Pink Tights* (1960), *Shalako* (1968), and *Catlow* (1971). The best television adaptation from L'Amour fiction was called *The Sacketts* (based on *The Daybreakers* and *Sackett*), which first aired in 1979. Beginning in 1960, L'Amour started the first of three family sagas, novels in multiple numbers featuring generations of families. *The Daybreakers* opened the ongoing Sackett saga, which by 1986 had grown to eighteen volumes. The 1971 publication of *North to the Rails* began another ongoing series, the Chantry family series. In 1975, *Rivers West* began the Talon family sequence.

Abetting L'Amour is the former Kathy Adams, who relinquished her career as an actress to marry him in a gala 1956 ceremony at the Los Angeles Beverly Hilton. In the 1960's, she bore him a daughter, Angelique, and then a son, Beau, and has served as his business manager, informal editor, and chauffeur. The durable L'Amour (who stands six feet, one inch, and weighs 215 pounds) writes early in the morning, six hours a day, seven days a week, combining this spartan routine with tough afternoon workouts using a punching bag and weights. He has a library in excess of ten thousand volumes, plus maps and memorabilia, mostly concerned with history. He lectures and travels widely and personally scouts locales to make his work more authentic.

Analysis

Louis L'Amour will be remembered for his action-filled Western novels, especially his family sagas. He is appreciated by readers from all walks of life who want to follow the exploits and suffering of heroic men, attractive and dutiful women, and manifestly evil villains, in exciting, well-knit plots, against a backdrop of accurately painted scenery. L'Amour extols the old American virtues of patriotism, respect for the land, go-it-alone courage, stoicism, and family loyalty. He offers his updated vision of the Old West as the locus of increasingly endangered mankind's last, best hope.

Critics should not look to L'Amour for aesthetic subtleties. His unvaried boast is that he is an old-fashioned storyteller, of the sort that sits by a campfire after a hard day's work and spins his tales in a straightforward manner. He does not worry, then, about critics who categorize Western fiction into formulaic narratives, romantic-historical reconstructions, or historical reconstructions. Such critics would probably define his *Hondo* as formulaic, his *Sitka* as romantic-historical, and nothing he wrote as genuinely historical (though he meticulously researched *The Walking Drum*, for example). In addition, critics complain to no avail when they claim that L'Amour's slapdash, unrevised writing betrays compositional errors by the gross.

L'Amour is pleased to be put in the same company as James Fenimore Cooper, Honoré de Balzac, Émile Zola, Jules Romains, and William Faulkner. L'Amour's Tell Sackett bears comparison with Cooper's Natty Bumppo. L'Amour follows Balzac's habit of creating reappearing characters, who help produce both unified, multivolumed fiction and loyal readers. The hero of L'Amour's *Shalako*, between wars in Paris, meets Zola, whose Rougon-Macquart cycle may have inspired L'Amour to build his Sackett/Chantry/Talon series. Romains employed historical figures, real events, and even specific dates to augment the verisimilitude of his monumental *Les Hommes de bonne volonté* (1932-1946; *Men of Good Will*, 1933-1946); L'Amour, to be sure, deals with three centuries of American frontier Sacketts rather than France in a mere quarter-century, but he uses Romains-like details in doing so. Moreover, Faulkner's love of his native soil, his combination of different races together in weal and woe, his praise of the old virtues of enduring and prevailing, and his construction of interlocked families are echoed in L'Amour's novels.

Since it is impossible to discuss all or even most of L'Amour's fiction, long and short, in a few pages, it seems best to concentrate on several salient titles, which illustrate his peaks of accomplishment, and also to consider his monumental three-family saga. In "Ride, You Tonto Raiders!" (*New Western Magazine*, August 6, 1949; reprinted in *Law of the Desert Born*, 1983), L'Amour prophetically introduces many of his books' most typical features. The broad-shouldered hero is a hard-bitten adventurer with a military, cosmopolitan, cattleman background, and he is now a gunslinger. He kills a bad man in Texas, then delivers the victim's money to his sweet widow and small son. She owns some Arizona land and is aided but also jeopardized by an assortment of L'Amouresque types: rich man, gunslinger, bumbling lawman, codger, literary drunk, Europe-trained pianist, loyal ranch hand, half-breed, and Hispanic. Other ingredients include surrogate fatherhood, dawning love for a red-haired heroine, the taking of the law into one's own hands, berserker fighting lust, hidden documents, place-names aplenty, the dating of the action by reference to historical events, cinematic alternation of close-up and wide-angle lens scenes, the use of key words (especially "alone," "eye," "home," "land," "patience," "shoulder," "silence," and "trouble"), and compositional infelicities. In short, this story is a fine introduction to L'Amour and, in addition, incidentally prefigures *Hondo*.

Hondo remains L'Amour's best Western. It features a typical loner hero, torn between moving on and settling down. It is datable and placeable: Hondo Lane scouts for General George Crook in the Arizona of 1874. Hondo cannot quickly woo and win the fetchingly home-loving heroine, not only because he killed her husband but also because Vittorio's Apaches grab and torture him. Hondo is half in favor of the white man's progress and half in love with violence in Apacheria; similarly, L'Amour mediates between the twentieth century and starker, earlier American epochs.

Last Stand at Papago Wells has an unusually complex set of narrative lines, neatly converging at a desert well and featuring a gallery of characters in varied movement: hero heading west, couple eloping, outraged father of bride-to-be in hot pursuit, survivor of party butchered by Apaches, near-rape victim, frustrated Apaches and two of their chronic enemies, posse remnants, fat woman with heavy saddlebags (is she hiding gold?), and rogue Apache-Yaquis circling and then attacking the forted-up well occupants.

Sitka is L'Amour's first big romantic-historical novel and has a refreshingly different setting. It concerns the Alaska Purchase, features real-life figures such as Secretary of the Treasury Robert Walker and Russian Ambassador Édouard de Stoeckl, and moves scenically from Pennsylvania to the Far West to Pacific Ocean waters (even to Russia)—Jean LaBarge, the hero, is L'Amour's first important fictional sailor—and up by Jean's wheat-laden schooner to Sitka, Alaska. L'Amour charmingly delays an indispensable love affair by having stalwart Jean smitten by a beautiful Russian princess who is demurely wed to a nice old Russian count, whose greasy enemy, another Russian, is Jean's enemy as well. Toward the end of *Sitka*, the plot takes on comic-book coloration, with interludes in Czar Alexander II's court, Washington, D.C., Siberia, and a Sitka prison.

The First Fast Draw never deserved its best-selling celebrity. It is supposedly based on the well-documented life of Cullen Montgomery Baker, the infamous Texas gunman whose bloody career got its impetus from Texas Governor Edmund Davis' vicious Reconstruction laws. L'Amour includes so many other real-life characters and events that naïve readers may think they are reading a historical reconstruction—but this is not so. L'Amour ignores the real Baker's first two marriages, his Quantrill-like antiblack and anti–Union army conduct, and even his death in 1869. L'Amour was enamored enough of thug Baker to shove him tangentially into five later books.

The Daybreakers is the first volume of L'Amour's tremendous, million-word Sackett sequence. It introduces the most famous Sacketts. They are five Tennessee-born brothers: William Tell, Orrin, Tyrel, Bob, and Joe Sackett. An 1866 feud with the evil Higgins family, during which a Higgins kills Orrin's fiancée and is hastily gunned down by narrator Tyrel, obliges both brothers to head out. They go west to gather wild cattle, in spite of dramatic adversities, along the Santa Fe Trail. Once in New Mexico, Orrin marries disastrously: His vicious wife is the daughter of a dishonest and anti-Hispanic politician and land grabber from New England. Tyrel, on the other hand, while on the trail is taught to read by an ex-army officer who later turns alcoholic, jealous, and lethal; Tyrel becomes the gun-handy marshal of Mora and marries a lovely heiress of an old Spanish land grant there. Orrin and Tyrel send for their widowed Ma and younger brothers Bob and Joe. The plot is energized by much violence, though not involving offstage Tell Sackett; having fought in the Civil War, he is now campaigning against the Sioux in the Northwest and is soon to leave Montana for Mora. (Incidentally, Tell was first presented in the story "Booty for a Bad Man," *Saturday Evening Post*, July 30, 1960; reprinted in *War Party*, 1975.) Even while writing much else, L'Amour continued his narrative of these Sackett brothers in six more novels, which, not in order of publication (1961 to 1980) but in chronological order of events (1867 through 1878 or so), are *Lonely on the Mountain*, *Sackett*, *Mojave Crossing*, *The Sackett Brand*, *The Lonely Men*, and *Treasure Mountain*.

During this time, L'Amour was turning his Sackett clock back more than two centuries. In 1974, he published *Sackett's Land*, which introduces Barnabas Sackett of the Welsh fenlands, in 1599. The first of the Sackett dynasty, he and his wife Abigail, daughter of an Elizabethan sea captain, generate a wild brood in the Carolinas: sons Kin Ring, Brian, Yance, and Jubal Sackett, and daughter Noelle Sackett. In the later novels, the three brothers, Kin, Yance, and Jubal (in *To the Far Blue Mountains*, *The Warrior's Path*, and *Jubal Sackett*, respectively), are shown to be different, and their stories shift from the Eastern seaboard, New England, and the Caribbean to the Far West, and advance to the year 1630 or so. In 1983 came *Ride the River*, which tells how a feisty Tennessee girl named Echo Sackett (destined to become the aunt of Tell and his brothers) ventures to Philadelphia to claim an inheritance as Kin Sackett's youngest descendant and gets it home again.

L'Amour has written six other Sackett novels (*Lando*, *Mustang Man*, *The Sky-Liners*, *Galloway*, *Ride the Dark Trail*, and *The Man from the Broken Hills*), which star a dusty array of cousins of Tell and his brothers and bring in still more Sacketts. These cousins, from different parts of Tennessee, Arizona, and New Mexico, include Lando, twins Logan and Nolan, brothers Flagan and Galloway, and Parmalee. The action, ranging through the Southwest and into Mexico, may be dated 1867-1878.

There are about sixty Sacketts in the ambitious Sackett sequence, amid a gallery of more than 750 characters in all. The Chantry/Talon novels, less expansive than the Sackett saga, are usually independent of it but occasionally connect with it. They may be most sensibly read in the chronological order of events narrated. *Fair Blows the Wind* concerns a swashbuckling Rafael Sabatini–like hero-narrator called Tatton Chantry (not his real name, L'Amour oddly insists), in the very late sixteenth century, in Ireland, England, Spain, France, the southern colonies in America, and back to Ireland. *The Ferguson Rifle* tells about a Chantry named Ronan, in the newly acquired lands of the Louisiana Purchase. L'Amour has thus left the 1600's and 1700's open for more Chantry narratives to fill. The picaresque *Rivers West* introduces an early Talon (in the year 1821). He is Jean, hinted to be a descendant of legendary Talon the Claw, a rich old pirate of the glorious Gaspé Peninsula. Western rivers take ambitious builder, lover-manqué Jean Talon to the Louisiana Purchase regions roamed by Ronan Chantry. Enter scholarly, verbose, often violent Owen Chantry in *Over on the Dry Side*, searching in Utah (1866) for his lost brother Owen (dead) and a reputed treasure (really a historical manuscript). The next Talon segment stars Milo Talon, one of Tell Sackett's countless cousins, in *Milo Talon*, a detective story fashioned largely from earlier Western mystery novels by L'Amour, specifically *The Man Called Noon*, *The Man from Skibbereen*, and *The Iron Marshal*, but rendered weird by ridiculous plot improbabilities. Milo does nothing for L'Amour's Talon saga. Then, in 1977, came *Borden Chantry*, perhaps his best Western mystery, because it is direct and gripping. Cleverly, L'Amour makes the victim in the puzzle Joe Sackett, who is the long-unmentioned younger brother of Tell and Tyrel and whose mysterious murder in Colorado (c. 1882), Borden Chantry, storm-ruined cattleman turned town marshal, must solve—or else Tyrel Sackett, who gallops in, will take the law into his own rough hands. The unexceptional *North to the Rails* already featured Borden Chantry's East-softened son Tom and reported that the father had been murdered about 1890, before the action starts, after which young Tom elects to drive cattle from Cimarron, near Santa Fe, north to a railhead for transport east. Obstacles to the hero in his *rites de passage* are varied and absorbing, but the novel is marred by much silliness and an improbable villainess.

As early as 1974, in his preface to *Sackett's Land*, L'Amour informed his public of plans to tell the epic of the American frontier through the westward movement of generations of three families, in forty or so novels. In 1981, he added that he had traced his Sacketts back to the fifteenth century and planned ten more Sackett, five more Chantry, and five more Talon books; further, that his Talons are builders, his Chantrys, educated statesmen, and his Sacketts, frontiersmen. (It has already been seen that L'Amour's practice has often blurred his theoretical distinctions.) Finally, in 1983, the author explained that he sees his three families as periodically linking and splitting. For two tiny examples, in addition to what has already been noticed: In *Ride the River* may be found strong but spoiled Dorian Chantry, whom his splendid old uncle, Philadelphia-lawyer Finian Chantry, orders to help heroine Echo Sackett; in the popular but flawed *Son of a Wanted Man*, Borden Chantry is revived and joins forces with Tyrel Sackett in gunning for law and order.

Brief mention may be made of seven of L'Amour's best works, simply to suggest his versatility and undiminished professional ambition. They are *The Broken Gun*, *Down the Long Hills*, *Bendigo Shafter*, *The Cherokee Trail*, *The Lonesome Gods*, *The Walking Drum*, and *Last of the Breed*.

The Broken Gun offers a brilliant translation of nineteenth century Western ingredients—rugged hero, mysterious murder, Hispanic friend, admirable lawman, land-hungry villains, sweet heroine, and villainess—all into twentieth century terms. In addition, the protagonist, a combat veteran and a writer, is partly autobiographical. *Down the Long Hills* is unique in

L'Amour's canon: It has strict Aristotelian unities and features a seven-year-old hero saving a three-year-old girl from an assortment of dangers, in a diagrammable plot of villains avoided and rescuers frustrated. *Bendigo Shafter* is L'Amour's classic Western blockbuster—in balanced, numbered thirds, nicely structured, and huge. The admirable hero-narrator describes the establishment in Wyoming's South Pass region (starting about 1862) of a Western community whose inhabitants represent everything from saintly to depraved, young and old, married and single, gauche and nubile. Nearby are Indians good and evil, and assorted white renegades. Nature here can be cruel but rewards those who surrender to its potent beauty. Notable are the hero's return to the East and meeting Horace Greeley there; his rejuvenating visit to the sacred Indian Medicine Wheel in the Big Horns; and L'Amour's skillful depiction of nineteen varied females. *The Cherokee Trail* also dramatizes assorted women's activities: A young widow takes over the management of a Colorado stagecoach station, protects a daughter and an Irish maid there, and has a rich rancher's spoiled daughters for neighbors nearby. *The Lonesome Gods* is epic in its sweep, with a varied plot and such bizarre effects as a disowning, the attempted murder of a little boy, gigantism, an uncannily svelte heroine with an unnecessary Russian background, a wild stallion, ghostly visitations, and—best of all—the loneliness of sad, patient gods in need of human adoration.

The Walking Drum, L'Amour's most ambitious novel, is a sprawling, episodic romp from Brittany through Europe to the Black Sea and beyond, in the years 1176-1180, starring an impossibly talented hero. He is Mathurin Kerbouchard, sailor, horseman, fighter, scientist, magician, caravan merchant, linguist, scholar, and lover. It must be added at once that L'Amour, in these days of depraved adult Westerns, is restraint itself: He limns no torrid love scenes on either side of any ocean. In addition, his violence is never offered in splashes of current cinematic gore.

Finally, *Last of the Breed*, another innovative effort, is nothing less than an eastern Siberian Western, cast in contemporary times (Mikhail S. Gorbachev is mentioned). Pitted are a Sioux-Cheyenne United States Air Force super-pilot and squabbling Soviet secret police. It has the most elaborately detailed escape since *The Count of Monte Cristo* (1844-1845) by Alexandre Dumas, *père*: here, from a prison camp east of Lake Baikal. Though crafted with care, this novel smacks of the film character Rambo, most of its more than forty characters have hard-to-remember names, the pages are dotted with twice that number of place names, and the hero's success depends on protracted good luck. Sympathetic readers will accept his exploits, however, because they accept the true hero of the novel—hauntingly rendered Siberia.

Louis L'Amour's two most admirable traits are his troubadour wizardry as a narrator and his profound love of Mother Nature and American derring-do. His late-career ambition to broaden his fictive scope, while admirable, can never diminish the significance of what will probably remain his most lasting contribution—namely, his best Westerns, among which the Sackett saga retains a high place. It is certainly to those works that he can attribute his immense popularity.

Other major works

SHORT FICTION: *War Party*, 1975; *Bowdrie*, 1983; *The Hills of Homicide*, 1983; *Law of the Desert Born*, 1983; *Riding for the Brand*, 1986; *The Rider of the Ruby Hills*, 1986; *Night over the Solomons*, 1986.

POETRY: *Smoke from This Altar*, 1939.

NONFICTION: *Frontier*, 1984 (with photographs by David Muench).

Bibliography

Gale, Robert L. *Louis L'Amour*, 1985.

Gonzalez, Arturo F. "Louis L'Amour: Writing High in the Bestseller Saddle," in *Writer's Digest*. LX (December, 1980), pp. 22-26.

Hinds, Harold E., Jr. "Mexicans and Mexican-American Images in the Western Novels of Louis L'Amour," in *Latin American Literary Review*. V (Spring/Summer, 1977), pp. 129-141.

Hubbell, John G. "Louis L'Amour: Storyseller of the Old West," in *Reader's Digest*. CXVII (July, 1980), pp. 93-98.

Marsden, Michael T. "Louis L'Amour (1908-)," in *Fifty Western Writers: A Bio-Bibliographical Sourcebook*. Edited by Fred Erisman and Richard W. Etulain.

Nesbitt, John D. "Change of Purpose in the Novels of Louis L'Amour," in *Western American Literature*. XIII (Spring, 1978), pp. 65-81.

Robert L. Gale

ROSAMOND LEHMANN

Born: Bourne End, England; February 3, 1901

Principal long fiction
Dusty Answer, 1927; *A Note in Music*, 1930; *Invitation to the Waltz*, 1932; *The Weather in the Streets*, 1936; *The Ballad and the Source*, 1944; *The Echoing Grove*, 1953; *The Sea-Grape Tree*, 1976.

Other literary forms
Rosamond Lehmann's preferred art form has been the novel, but in addition, she has published a volume of short stories, *The Gipsy's Baby and Other Short Stories* (1946), and a play, *No More Music* (1939). Her autobiography, *The Swan in the Evening: Fragments of an Inner Life*, appeared in 1967.

Achievements
Lehmann's first novel, *Dusty Answer*, appeared in 1927, when the author was twenty-six years old. The novel struck a responsive chord with the post–World War I generation, and Lehmann soon found herself famous. Her subsequent novels and other works have found a considerable audience, especially in England, where her writing has been highly regarded by the reading public as well as critics. In 1982, Lehmann was honored as a recipient of the Order of the British Empire. Those of her novels which had been out of print were republished by Virago Press.

Biography
Rosamond Nina Lehmann was born near London on February 3, 1901. On the same day, Queen Victoria was buried, a fact that would later strike Lehmann as having symbolic significance. She received her early education at home, partly through the use of the enormous library of her father, Rudolph Lehmann, an editor of *Punch* magazine. Her later education was at Girton College of Cambridge University.

An early marriage ended in divorce, attributable, Lehmann believed, to the upheaval arising from her sudden fame. A second marriage, to the Honorable Wogan Philipps, also ended in divorce; a long relationship with the poet C. Day-Lewis also ended unhappily. Lehmann's primary bonds were with family: her brother, poet-critic John Lehmann; her sister, actress Beatrix Lehmann; and her two children, Hugo and Sally. Sally's sudden death from polio in 1958 ended Lehmann's writing for some time; when she began to write again, her works reflected her new interest in what may imprecisely be called spiritualism. In her eighties, she served as vice president of the British College of Psychic Studies, and she counseled other parents who had lost children.

Analysis

The great theme of Rosamond Lehmann's fiction is the evanescent quality of love in a world where love is the only thing worth having. This emphasis on love and on female characters has sometimes caused her to be considered a "woman's novelist," an evaluation which would have surprised her audience early in her career. To many of her contemporaries in the 1920's, Lehmann was part of the vanguard, a peer of Virginia Woolf, Dorothy Richardson, and May Sinclair, writers who chose female characters as the voices of a new fictional style which these women, along with James Joyce and others, were creating. This style is generally called "stream of consciousness," although the term is somewhat imprecise: Lehmann's style requires neither the intense, allusive language of Joyce nor the changing viewpoints of Woolf. Lehmann learned from her contemporaries to stay within the mind of one character and to show the sensibilities and sensitivities of that character.

Lehmann's first novel, *Dusty Answer*, is a fine achievement as a novel of consciousness, especially of the special consciousness of adolescence. The novelist stays within the mind of the young Judith Earle as she grows into early adulthood. Like other popular novels of the 1920's (Michael Arlen's *The Green Hat*, 1924, is a good example), the novel traces the character's development by her relationship with a person or group of people whom the central character views as somehow enchanted. That the enchanted ones are also destructive comprises the fascination and also the growth experience for the central character.

Judith grows up in a wealthy home, in an isolation which creates her bookishness and romantic turn of mind. Her loneliness is broken occasionally by a family of five cousins who visit next door; Judith sees them as a closed unit, incredibly mysterious and desirable. Her fascination with them continues even when she goes off to Cambridge (Lehmann herself was at Girton College, Cambridge) and meets a fellow undergraduate, Jennifer Baird, to whom she is also drawn. The novel traces Judith's intense friendship with Jennifer and with each of the cousins. As the book ends, she has been separated from all of them by the differing courses of their maturity. She believes that enchantment is gone from the world and that she must now live in the cold light of reality.

Dusty Answer had an immediate and intense popularity. For some readers, it powerfully evoked their university days, and in this regard the book bears comparison with Evelyn Waugh's *Brideshead Revisited: The Sacred and Profane Memories of Captain Charles Ryder* (1945, 1960), which is set at Oxford in the same time period, the early 1920's. A reader desiring a portrait of those days could do no better than to read these two novels. A second reason for the novel's popularity is its relative frankness with regard to sexual attitudes; Lehmann shows her heroine eager to "give herself" to the man she loves. Homoerotic relationships also abound. Although there are no explicit sexual scenes, the novel was considered shocking by many critics. Some of her contemporaries thought that *Dusty Answer* was a flash in the pan which would both begin and end Lehmann's career. On the contrary, as she continued to write, maturity deepened her powers of observation.

Lehmann's third novel, *Invitation to the Waltz*, shows her mastery of atmosphere in a novel. The main character is Olivia Curtis, an adolescent on the verge of adulthood, and it is primarily through her that Lehmann conveys a wonderful atmosphere of expectation, anticipation. The story opens on the morning of Olivia's seventeenth birthday. Her upper-middle-class home in the snug village of Little Compton is carefully described. A gentle air of mystery, however, is developed: "Something is going on. The kettle's boiling, the cloth is spread, the windows are flung open. Come in, come in! Here dwells the familiar mystery. Come and find it! Each room is active, fecund, brimming over with it." The invitation to the reader is explicit: Enter this novel, this home, to watch the dance of life. What one finds is both common and marvelous—common in the easy familiarity and give-and-take of family life and marvelous in the recurring mystery of girl growing to young woman. That Lehmann can have it both ways, in both its common and its marvelous aspects, testifies to her growth as a novelist.

An invitation necessarily inculcates expectation. At the opening of the novel, the invitation to the Spencers' dance, one week hence, has already been extended. Even as she lies in bed, reveling in its delicious warmth and in the slow, pleasant moments before the hectic day must begin in earnest, Olivia anticipates the dance. Indeed, thoughts about the dance subsume Olivia's anticipation of a more immediate event, breakfast with the family— the presents to be opened and the good wishes to be received. That the prized gift of the day turns out to be some flame-colored fabric for a new dress to wear to the Spencers' dance indicates something of Lehmann's skill in developing a sense of expectation in ever-expanding circles of anticipation. Mundane events of plot resonate with increasingly meaningful, open-ended implications, all circumferences being blurred in the subjective consciousness, the magical visionary world, of an innocent, naïve, alert, and sensitive seventeen-year-old.

After the early-morning anticipation of the birthday breakfast, the plot points to the big dance, a week away. The dress is to be readied. An escort is to be speculated on. On the night itself, Olivia and her sister Kate are to prepare themselves carefully—with long baths and manicures and attentive dressing of hair. Kate, the older sister who is at once rival and best friend, does much better in the business of appearance than Olivia, but having turned Olivia's dress around and suggested how to fashion her hair, she and Olivia are finally ready for the dance. Part 2 of the novel explains the day's preparation for the dance, while part 3 focuses on the dance itself. Thus, the structure of the novel supports the atmosphere of anticipation.

If this were all there were to it, however, part 3 of the novel would be something of a disappointment to the reader, as it surely seems to be at times for Olivia. Reggie Kershaw, the man Olivia and Kate have invited to escort them, first asks Marigold Spencer for a dance. Olivia's dance program gradually fills, but her predominant emotion is gratitude that she will not be humiliated by being a wallflower rather than excitement over the young men with whom she will be dancing. She feels clumsy and awkward when she finally dances with Reggie; she feels intellectually inferior and unstylish with Peter Jenkin; she feels very much out of her social class with George; she feels crude and unsophisticated with Podge; and so the evening goes. She feels surprise, shock, pity, sorrow, resentment, and even repulsion at her various partners through the evening. Yet there are minor triumphs, too. When dashing Rollo Spencer returns from walking the dogs, he invites her into his father's library, where Olivia meets Sir John Spencer himself. As Olivia leaves the library, she is overwhelmed with good feeling and a sense of accomplishment: Far "from being outcast, flung beyond the furthest rim, she had penetrated suddenly to the innermost core of the house, to be in their home." At the end of the evening, sitting in the armchair, waiting for the last dancers to finish and for Kate and Reggie to appear, she reflects on the evening: "Nothing for myself really," yet "to have come to the place of not caring was very soothing, very peaceful." She anticipates "with longing . . . her dark bedroom, her bed waiting for her at home."

The power of the novel lies in the wider implications of Olivia's anticipations, for the events of the story are only the pretext for the grand anticipation of Olivia's life, the fulfillment of which the reader is left to imagine. Early in the novel, Olivia had looked at herself in the mirror, wondering if this would be one of those days when the mirror reflected back not what was familiar, but a new Olivia, a new self, a different person, a beginning life. Throughout the novel, the people whom Olivia meets and the episodes she experiences resonate as options for Olivia in her adult life. Will she become bitter and poor, like the spinster dressmaker Miss Robinson? Will scandal rob her of simple companionship and neighborly friendship, as it did Major Skinner? Will she be a victim of calculated pathos, as she is with the lace maker, who takes advantage of her pity so that she wastes the ten shillings given to her by Uncle Oswald for her birthday? Will her life be reduced to a tragedy of isolation, restriction, and emptiness, as is the life of blind Timmy Douglas, married to a former nurse in an arrangement of convenience rather than of passion?

As one anticipates Olivia's adult life, one realizes that not all options are equally available to her. The Spencers represent an aristocratic life-style that is clearly beyond the Curtises. Marigold and Rollo live in a world made brilliant and dashing by their parents' social status; theirs is a self-confidence that comes from solid and long-standing foundation in the bedrock of social place. Kate, too, may represent an option that proves not to be viable for Olivia, for Kate, during the course of the evening, becomes separated from Olivia, each sister following her individual pathway to the future. Kate falls in love with Tony Heriot and secretly makes plans to meet him in Paris; they share a vision to which Olivia is not party.

At the end of the novel, though, Olivia, too, has a vision. Running out beyond the garden, recognizing that every woman makes the trip to adulthood by herself, Olivia feels a sense of new beginning. Her future, in the image of a winged gigantic runner, hastens toward her from a great distance: "On it came, over ploughed field and fallow. The rooks flashed sharply, the hare and his shadow swerved in sudden sunlight. In a moment it would be everywhere. Here it was. She ran into it." The future is now. The girl is a young woman with a full life ahead. The dance of life is now beginning.

With good reason, Lehmann's fifth novel, *The Ballad and the Source*, is widely considered her best. It has an evocative power and strength of characterization that linger long after the book has been read. Furthermore, the narrative technique is at once complex and suggestive: Rebecca Landon tells the tale of a period during her childhood, between the ages of ten and fifteen, the years 1912 to 1917, when she first came to know a neighbor, Mrs. Jardine, and Mrs. Jardine's grandchildren. As she recalls the long afternoons at tea with Mrs. Jardine and the conversations with Maisie, the grandchild with whom she developed the closest of friendships, she seems at times to be reliving the experience, to return again to those childhood days of innocence threatened only sporadically by glimpses into the adult world of evil. Occasionally, the adult consciousness reflects on the limitations of the child's awareness and the reader is reminded of the retrospective perspective, but the child's consciousness prevails, and the movement between today's adult and yesterday's child is blurred and inconsistent.

This is not to say that the shifting consciousness is a flaw in the novel. Indeed, it is one of the novel's triumphs, for like other of Lehmann's novels, *The Ballad and the Source* creates a highly subjective consciousness that colors what it encounters. Rebecca is a sensitive, romantic child, strongly attracted to the unusual situation and the magnetic personality of the suspect Mrs. Jardine. The novel presents Rebecca's attempt to solve the puzzle that is Mrs. Jardine. In rehearsing those preadolescent years, Rebecca is even now trying to reach some resolution, some recognition that ever eludes her. The novel gains in immediacy because one is not presented with the adult's conclusions but learns the pieces of information as the child did many years ago, and one can follow her engaged understanding through the maze of hints and innuendos, biased accounts and tortured confessions, shadings and concealments to which she is subject.

The amazing thing about this novel is that Rebecca is not ultimately the main character, even though her consciousness and experience govern the reader's access to information. She is an observer of the developments in the Jardine/Thomson family and a receiver of information about their past, not an involved participant in the ongoing drama of their lives. What Rebecca says or does or thinks relative to the Jardines and Thomsons is ultimately of little importance. Sibyl Anstey Herbert Jardine is really the main character, the source, and the subject of all the ballads. It is her strong personality that so attracts the love of Rebecca and the hatred of her granddaughter Maisie.

The novel is a detective story of sorts, including all the material of high drama—adultery, abandoned children, runaway wives, insanity, lifelong hatred, empty and wasted lives, early death, kidnaping, jealousy, secrecy, plots, shifting conspiracies, and passion, as well as loyalty, dedication to truth, independence, and love. Young Rebecca has led far too sheltered a life to be able to take in what she hears, but the reader is not hindered by Rebecca's limitations. That the reader has greater understanding than does the narrator of the story is possible through Lehmann's strategy of allowing several different people to reveal what they know. Rebecca learns something about Mrs. Jardine first from Mrs. Jardine herself. In fact, Mrs. Jardine at times actually confides in Rebecca, using her as the "listener" she always needs. It is largely because Rebecca is so fascinated by Mrs. Jardine that she has difficulty accepting some of the other accounts she subsequently hears. Rebecca recognizes good qualities in Mrs. Jardine—a strong maternal instinct, a fondness for children, courage, loyalty, and strength. These are not the traits about Mrs. Jardine that most impress other people.

Tilly, for example, the poor, elderly seamstress who makes a yearly visit to the Landon family to do necessary work and who formerly was employed by Rebecca's grandmother, certainly does not share Rebecca's fondness for the woman. When Rebecca discovers that Tilly knew Mrs. Jardine years ago, she pumps her to tell her story of Mrs. Jardine's life. Part 2 of the novel is a long narration by Tilly, interrupted by prompts and questions from Rebecca. To Tilly, Mrs. Jardine is an evil woman who violated her friendship with Rebecca's grandmother by asking her to assist her in deceiving her former husband, Charles Herbert, in order to gain access to their daughter, Ianthe. Despite her loyalties toward her grandmother, Rebecca still sides with the cause of the mother deprived of her only child. When Sibyl Anstey Herbert (later Mrs. Jardine) left her husband, she had never intended to leave the child Ianthe behind as well, but Charles Herbert insisted on total estrangement between Ianthe and her mother, an estrangement Sibyl was never able to overcome, despite a life dedicated to winning Ianthe back.

Part 3 is a long conversation between Mrs. Jardine and Rebecca, during which Rebecca learns much about the life of Ianthe. In veiled suggestions of incest that Rebecca cannot quite grasp, Mrs. Jardine tells of the "sick" relationship between Charles Herbert and his daughter, when they are everything to each other. After his death, Ianthe moves in with a Mr. and Mrs.

Connor. Again, there are suggestions in the narrative of illicit sex and corruption that young Rebecca does not understand; an adult world is being opened up to a child. Mrs. Jardine, aware that her daughter is involved in a scandalous situation but still unable to approach her directly, sends a male relative to Ianthe, and they run away together. Later, Mrs. Jardine admits that sending this young man was a mistake. Ianthe conceives a child and goes to Bohemia with Tilly to bear it. The long-standing enmity between Tilly and Mrs. Jardine stems from Tilly's refusal even at this point to allow Mrs. Jardine access to her daughter.

The story covers three generations, and the sins of the one are visited upon the next. As Sibyl left her child, so Ianthe, having married Thomson, leaves him and ultimately must abandon her children, Maisie, Malcolm, and Cherry, Mrs. Jardine's three grandchildren who became friends with Rebecca and Rebecca's sister Jess. Their father, Mr. Thomson, developed an intense hatred of both Ianthe and her mother, Mrs. Jardine—Ianthe for leaving him and Mrs. Jardine for having ruined Ianthe. As another husband with custody of children, he refused to allow any contact between his children and either their mother or grandmother. Maisie tells Rebecca that her mother Ianthe is beautiful and that she loves the children very much, although she cannot be with them. It is Mrs. Jardine who tells Rebecca that Ianthe never cared for the children. As with every aspect of this complicated web of right and wrong, love and hate, Rebecca receives different and sometimes flatly contradictory information. Despite Mr. Thomson's hatred for Mrs. Jardine, he allows the children to live with her when he becomes too ill to care for them himself. Finally, upon his death, Mrs. Jardine recovers what had always eluded her with Ianthe; she gains custody of her grandchildren.

The influence of Henry James is sometimes noted in connection with this novel, and surely no more so than in the almost demoniac passion with which Mrs. Jardine seeks to gain possession of the soul first of her own child, Ianthe, and then, when that fails, of her grandchildren. Jamesian, too, is the immature consciousness accosted with hints and suggestions, indirectness and obscurity, contradiction and variety. The quest for truth is not an easy one. The success of this novel depends in large measure on the reader's willingness to bear the burden of judgment and opinion, to make his or her own distillation of the facts and arrive at truth, and then to make a moral judgment if such is deemed necessary, for Lehmann does not make the moral judgment for the reader. Indeed, the need for the rights of women and their freedom from the bondage of marriage comes across strongly, especially from the mouth of Mrs. Jardine. Yet the novel unremittingly insists, too, that the consequences of such freedom are devastating and evil. Rebecca is drawn to this saga because she, too, is one of those intelligent, sensitive, strong women who may find social restrictions too binding to tolerate. An awareness of the plight of such women and a recognition of the confused and incremental way in which one learns truth are the main accomplishments of Lehmann's fifth novel.

Creating and interweaving the experiences and attitudes of both Rebecca and Mrs. Jardine, *The Ballad and the Source* attains a power that is unique in Lehmann's fiction. Her other novels are likelier to be regarded as "period pieces." Such a label does not discount the value of her work: Lehmann has the gift, shared by many other minor writers, of being able to populate a time and place—her own closely observed day, whether the 1920's or 1950's. Reading her novels, one senses instinctively that she has "gotten it right," shown the university, the seaside villa, the run-down flat, all as they must have been. The inhabitants of those locales have life in her fiction. To create such portraits is no small feat. Lehmann's work may lack the resonance and depth of some of her more famous contemporaries, but she has contributed to the British novel: All of her novels represent some experiments with the representation of consciousness, they add to the tradition of realism, and several give powerful portrayals of the anxieties of youth and love.

Other major works

SHORT FICTION: *The Gipsy's Baby and Other Short Stories*, 1946.

PLAY: *No More Music*, 1939.

NONFICTION: *The Swan in the Evening: Fragments of an Inner Life*, 1967 (autobiography).

Bibliography

Beach, Joseph Warren. *The Twentieth Century Novel*, 1932.

Dangerfield, George. "Rosamond Lehmann and the Perilous Enchantment of Things Past," in *The Bookman*. LXXVI (1933), pp. 172-176.

Dorosz, Wiktoria. *Subjective Vision and Human Relationships in the Novels of Rosamond Lehmann*, 1975.

Gustafson, Margaret T. "Rosamond Lehmann: A Bibliography," in *Twentieth Century Literature*. IV, no. 4 (1959), pp. 143-147.

Humphrey, Robert. *Stream of Consciousness in the Modern Novel*, 1954.

Kaplan, Sydney Janet. *Feminine Consciousness in the Modern British Novel*, 1975.

Lehmann, John. *The Whispering Gallery*, 1955.

LeStourgeon, Diana E. *Rosamond Lehmann*, 1965.

Mooney, Bel. "Lost Loves of a Soul Survivor," in *The Times* (London). February 9, 1984, p. 8.

Thornton, Lawrence. "Rosamond Lehmann, Henry James and the Temporal Matrix of Fiction," in *Virginia Woolf Quarterly*. I, no. 3 (1973), pp. 66-75.

Tindall, Gillian. *Rosamond Lehmann: An Appreciation!*, 1985.

Deborah Core
Paula Kopacz

PRIMO LEVI

Born: Turin, Italy; July 31, 1919
Died: Turin, Italy; April 11, 1987

Principal long fiction

La chiave a stella, 1978 (*The Monkey's Wrench*, 1986); *Se non ora, quando?*, 1982 (*If Not Now, When?*, 1985).

Other literary forms

Associated with Holocaust literature, Primo Levi was a novelist, short-story writer, essayist, and poet, although he is known primarily for his memoirs. These include *Se questo è un uomo* (1947; *If This Is a Man*, 1959; revised as *Survival in Auschwitz: The Nazi Assault on Humanity*, 1961) and *La tregua* (1963; *The Reawakening*, 1965). Levi himself, in a preface, characterized his collection of stories *These Moments of Reprieve* (1986) as a record of experiences left out of *If This Is a Man* and *The Reawakening*. (Most of these autobiographical short stories were previously published in 1981 in *Lilìt e altri racconti*.) *Il sistema periodico* (1975; *The Periodic Table*, 1984), a collection of autobiographical pieces unified by its organization according to the chemical elements, mixes traditional genres. Levi's poems about his experiences during the Holocaust are collected in *Shema: Collected Poems* (1976). Additional poems are collected in *L'osteria di Brema* (1975). His early pseudonymous short-story collections *Storie naturali* (1966) and *Vizio di forma* (1971) combine autobiography, science fiction, and fantasy to describe his experiences after the war. Levi's essays are collected in *La ricera della radici* (1981).

Achievements

An Italian Jew who survived Auschwitz, Levi is widely acclaimed as a fictional, historical, and autobiographical chronicler of the Holocaust and its aftermath. Highly praised by such important writers as Umberto Eco, Italo Calvino, Studs Terkel, Claude Lévi-Strauss, Irving Howe, Alfred Kazin, Philip Roth, and Saul Bellow, Levi's work is distinguished by an attempt to understand his wartime experiences and by a compassionate, sensitive, and astonishingly optimistic view of humanity. Levi's epigraph for *The Periodic Table* is a Yiddish saying: "Troubles overcome are good to tell." Levi's works are ample proof of the proverb, his life a testament of the resiliency of the human spirit. In recognition of his many achievements, Levi won Italy's prestigious Premio Bagutta, Viareggio, Strega, and Campiello literary prizes.

Biography

Primo Levi was born on July 31, 1919, in Turin, Italy, to a cultured middle-class couple, Ester and Cesare Levi. Levi attended the University of Turin and in 1941 received his Ph.D. in chemistry. A Jew in occupied Italy during World War II, he joined the Italian Resistance and was soon arrested for anti-Fascist activities. Upon discovering that Levi was a Jew, the German SS deported him to their death facility in Auschwitz. There, where he was tattooed number 174517 on his left arm, he remained until the concentration camp was liberated. For his survival, he credits luck, which manifested itself in terms of his health, which was good most of the time he was in Auschwitz and poor at precisely the right moment (when the Germans fled the concentration camp, taking with them all "healthy" prisoners). In addition, he worked as a chemist part of the time that he was in Auschwitz, and his friend, an Italian bricklayer, smuggled extra food to him.

After the war, Levi found employment as technical director of a paint factory. In 1947, Levi married Lucia Morpurgo, a teacher, who helped him adjust to his new life. Still deeply depressed, he turned to writing in an attempt to understand his concentration camp experience. The Holocaust turned the chemist into the writer. Levi describes his time in Auschwitz as "the fundamental experience of my life." He goes on to say, "I knew that if I survived, I would have to tell the story." In 1947, he chronicled his imprisonment at Auschwitz in *If This Is a Man*, and later, in *The Reawakening*, he described his bizarre, circuitous journey home from Poland. Many of his other works, including *Shema*, *These Moments of Reprieve*, and *If Not Now, When?* were also inspired by the Holocaust. In 1977, Levi devoted himself to writing full-time. Levi died in his hometown of Turin on April 11, 1987, survived by a son, Renzo, a physicist, and a daughter, Lisa, a biologist.

Analysis

Most of Primo Levi's work (with the exception of *The Monkey's Wrench*) can be placed within the genre of Holocaust literature. As a survivor of Auschwitz, Levi blended personal reminiscence and reflection to depict his major preoccupation, the unfathomable horror that was the Holocaust.

Almost totally devoid of self-pity, Levi reserved his concern for others. Levi never indulged in luridness or melodrama. Rather, his tone is clear, straightforward, and moderate; his passion, muted. Although his writing deals with the deepest of human emotions and feelings, it remains restrained in a manner that makes for a quiet intensity, which is only emphasized by his subtle (if somewhat startling) humor. Through his unflinching and careful use of detail, he presents a picture of human degradation. Yet, despite the bleakness inherent in Levi's usual subjects, his portrayal leads not to bitterness, but, astoundingly, to a compelling affirmation of life, to a sense of faith in humanity, to a compassionate understanding of both victims and victimizers, and, finally, to a powerful and moving vision of the dignity of man.

Although Levi's first piece of long fiction, *The Monkey's Wrench*, represents a divergence from his usual concerns (and therefore is lighter and even more amusing in tone), it still reflects Levi's life experiences, and Levi himself is one of the main characters. This work has been widely classified as a novel. In actuality, however, *The Monkey's Wrench* defies classification, being a combination of autobiography and long and short fiction. Indeed, in an interview with Philip Roth, Levi implied that he does not consider *The Monkey's Wrench* to be a novel. The work is, perhaps, best regarded as a collection of short stories linked by a narrative situation: The unnamed narrator/ writer, who represents Levi, for the most part listens to and records stories related by Faussone, the protagonist and Levi's self-styled alter ego. This frame automatically emphasizes the complex relationship between storyteller and listener, between writer and reader.

In the street-smart, cocky, energetic Faussone, Levi created one of his most fully realized characters. An itinerant steelworker, Faussone (like Levi and the narrator) comes from Turin. In seemingly artless monologues, Faussone articulates his devotion to work, a passion he shares with the narrator, who finds, "If we except those miraculous and isolated moments fate can bestow on a man, loving your work (unfortunately, the privilege of a few) represents the best, most concrete approximation of happiness on earth." In fact, the central metaphor of the novel has to do with the relationship between life and work, whether the comparison is to rigging, to chemistry, or to writing.

Like Levi, the narrator is a chemist (a paint specialist) and author from Turin. Just as Levi became a full-time writer in 1977, the narrator (who, in describing his writing generally alternates between the language of rigging and of chemistry) relates his last adventure as a chemist and marks his impending transition:

> With nostalgia, but without misgivings, I would choose another road . . . the road of the teller of stories. My own stories . . . then other people's stories . . . his [Faussone's], for example. . . . [I]t was possible that, having spent more than thirty years sewing together long molecules . . . I might have learned something about sewing together words and ideas.

If in his previous works Levi depended primarily on his own individual experience, *If Not Now, When?* is based on the true story of Jewish partisans who banded together to fight the Nazis. Levi described this deliberate new direction in his writing in his interview with Roth: "I had made a sort of bet with myself: after so much plain or disguised autobiography, are you, or are you not, a full-fledged writer, capable of constructing a novel, shaping characters, describing landscapes you have never seen? Try it!" In *If Not Now, When?*, for the first time Levi imagines rather than recalls events surrounding the Holocaust. He reconstructs a people (Yiddish-speaking Eastern European Jews whom Levi had not known before his concentration camp experience), a period (World War II), a setting (the countryside of Eastern

Europe), and even a language (Yiddish) to celebrate the active resistance of the Jews, arguing against the commonly held notion that all Jews passively submitted to their fate at the hands of their Nazi murderers. Levi outlined his intentions thus:

> I wished to assault a commonplace still prevailing in Italy: a Jew is a mild person, a scholar (religious or profane), unwarlike, humiliated, who tolerated centuries of persecution without ever fighting back. It seemed to me a duty to pay homage to those Jews who, in desperate conditions, had found the courage and the skills to resist. . . . I cherished the ambition to be the first (perhaps only) Italian writer to describe the Yiddish world.

The story begins in 1943 as two Russian Jews—Mendel, one of the main characters, a resourceful and philosophic watchmaker whose wife has been slaughtered by the Nazis, and Leonid, an uncommunicative young concentration camp escapee—try to elude the Nazis. Living hand-to-mouth as they travel over marshes, forests, and countryside, they join with various ragged groups of refugees, stragglers, and partisans attempting both to survive and to fight the Germans. Eventually, the two meet a group of Jewish partisans, the Gedalists, named for their leader, Gedaleh. This courageous band— comprising a wide variety of Polish and Russian men and women, from former Soviet soldiers to fugitives of Nazi roundups and concentration camps— aims to survive, to harm the Germans, and eventually, to reach Palestine. Traveling over much of the same territory Levi himself crossed on his protracted journey home from Auschwitz (chronicled in his memoir, *The Reawakening*), the partisans get as far as Italy before the novel ends, as does the war in Europe, in August, 1945.

The novel oscillates in atmosphere from romantic to epic. The tone is not indignant, but rather reflective, understated, and at times quietly humorous. What distinguishes this work from most Holocaust literature is that Levi rarely details the German atrocities that form the backdrop of this story. Explicitly, "this story is not being told in order to describe massacres." Nevertheless, images of the grotesqueness of the Holocaust are a silent presence, almost more notable in their absence. As one character explains to another, "It's the first rule. . . . If we kept on telling one another what we've seen, we'd go crazy and instead we all have to be sane, children included."

Action-packed, tense, and suspenseful, the plot of this stirring war story is (like the plot of *The Reawakening*) picaresque. Levi is a master of the episodic, a painter of poignant vignettes. As they travel westward from Russia to Italy, their springboard to Palestine, the Gedalists risk considerable danger to sabotage the Germans, engaging in a series of rearguard acts of harassment and guerrilla warfare—from ambushing trains to liberating concentration camps—that are variously amusing, frightening, exciting, and moving.

Yet *If Not Now, When?* is also a novel of character. In fact, as Levi confessed, "For the first and only time in my life as a writer, I had the impression (almost a hallucination) that my characters were alive, around me, behind my back, suggesting spontaneously their feats and their dialogues." Irrepressible and courageous, individual members of the Gedalists are sharply and insightfully drawn. The characters are made all the more vivid and striking through a series of elegant and wonderful metaphors.

Mendel's character is the most fully developed, as the third-person narrator continually presents his innermost thoughts. This is in direct contrast to the presentation of the elusive Gedaleh, whose interior consciousness, and consequently his character, remain remote. Introduced as "the legendary leader" of the partisan group, Gedaleh, with his violin as talisman, is appropriately mysterious and heroic.

As for the group itself, the narrator presents the inner thoughts of the band as a whole, expressive of a developing Jewish collective consciousness. It is here that Levi strikes a chord of universality: The possibility for community, camaraderie, mutual responsibility, and unity emerges as the final lesson to be learned from the Holocaust and from all of Levi's works. Perhaps this lesson is best expressed in the words of Rabbi Hillel: "If I am not for myself, who will be for me? If I am for myself alone, what am I? If not now, when?"

Other major works

SHORT FICTION: *Storie naturali*, 1966; *Vizio di forma*, 1971; *Il sistema periodico*, 1975 (*The Periodic Table*, 1984); *Lilít e altri racconti*, 1981; *These Moments of Reprieve*, 1986.

POETRY: *L'osteria di Brema*, 1975; *Shema: Collected Poems*, 1976.

NONFICTION: *Se questo è un uomo*, 1947 (*If This Is a Man*, 1959; revised as *Survival in Auschwitz: The Nazi Assault on Humanity*, 1961); *La tregua*, 1963 (*The Reawakening*, 1965); *La ricera della radici*, 1981.

Bibliography

Denby, David. "The Humanist and the Holocaust," in *The New Republic*. CXCIII (July 28, 1986), pp. 27-33.

Eberstadt, Fernanda. "Reading Primo Levi," in *Commentary*. October, 1985, pp. 41-47.

Howe, Irving. "How to Write About the Holocaust," in *The New York Review of Books*. XXXII (March 28, 1985), pp. 14-15.

Hughes, H. Stuart. *Prisoners of Hope: The Silver Age of the Italian Jews, 1924-1974*, 1983.

Kazin, Alfred. "Life and Steel: A Rigger's Tale," in *The New York Times Book Review*. XCI (October 12, 1986), p. 1.

Levi, Primo. "Beyond Survival," in *Prooftexts*. IV (1984), pp. 9-21.

Mitgang, Herbert. "Tales of 1944 Troubles Overcome," in *The New York Times*. XC (May 27, 1985), p. 14.

Roth, Philip. "A Man Saved by His Skills," in *The New York Times Book Review*. XCI (October 12, 1986), p. 1.
Vincenti, Fiora. *Invito alla lettura di Primo Levi*, 1973.

Deborah D. Rogers

CLARICE LISPECTOR

Born: Chechelnik, USSR; December 10, 1925
Died: Rio de Janeiro, Brazil; December 9, 1977

Principal long fiction

Perto do coração selvagem, 1944; *O lustre*, 1946; *A cidade sitiada*, 1949; *A maçã no escuro*, 1961 (*The Apple in the Dark*, 1967); *A paixão segundo G. H.*, 1964; *Uma aprendizagem: Ou, O livro dos prazeres*, 1969 (*An Apprenticeship: Or, The Book of Delights*, 1986); *Água viva*, 1973; *A hora da estrela*, 1977 (*The Hour of the Star*, 1986); *Um sopro de vida: Pulsações*, 1978.

Other literary forms

Clarice Lispector was a prominent short-story writer as well as a novelist; among her collections of stories are *Alguns contos* (1952; some stories) and *Laços de família* (1960; *Family Ties*, 1972). *A legião estrangeira* (1964; *The Foreign Legion*, 1986) is a collection of stories and brief miscellaneous prose pieces.

Achievements

Lispector is regarded as one of the most influential and important Brazilian fiction writers. A member of the revisionist school of writers that emerged in the period following World War II, she was a force in the move, in Brazilian fiction, from the regionalism and sociological orientation of the 1930's to an intense interest in subjective experience.

She first achieved general acclaim with *Family Ties*, a collection of inward-looking short stories. *The Apple in the Dark* marked Lispector's major artistic breakthrough. Lengthy and complex, symbolic and mythic, its intense, lyrical style recalls the works of Djuna Barnes, Virginia Woolf, and Katherine Mansfield.

Lispector was the recipient of many literary prizes. In 1943, the publication of *Perto do coração selvagem* (close to the savage heart) won for her the Graça Aranha Prize. She received the Cármen Dolores Barbosa Prize for *The Apple in the Dark* in 1961, a prize from the Campanha Nacional da Criança for a children's story, "O mistério do coelho pensante" (the mystery of the thinking rabbit) in 1967, the Golfinho de Ouro Prize for *An Apprenticeship* in 1969, and was awarded first prize in the tenth Concurso Literário Nacional for her overall contribution to Brazilian literature in 1976, one year before her death.

Biography

Clarice Lispector was born in Chechelnik, in the Ukraine, in 1925, of Jewish parents. The family moved to Brazil when the child was two months old. Lispector attended school first in Recife, then in Rio de Janeiro. In 1943, she was graduated from the Faculty of Law in Rio. She married a diplomat and lived in Italy, Switzerland, Great Britain, and the United States for many years. After her divorce, she settled permanently in Rio de Janeiro in 1959. She died from cancer in 1977.

Analysis

Most, but not all, of Clarice Lispector's protagonists are female, and the author is keenly aware of women's problems and of the female side of the psyche. Her major works deal with internal guests. An occurrence in the protagonists' lives causes them to move out of their daily routines and enter into new types of relationship with themselves and with the physical world. They live each moment intensely, as if every breath of existence is a major experience, tightly connected to the pulsating rhythm of life itself. The protagonist's quest has no specific goal except to move forward:

> Still in his favor was the fact that he knew he should walk in a straight line because it would not be very practical to lose the thread of the maze. In his disfavor there was a danger he was on the lookout for: the fact that there were pleasure and beauty in a person's losing himself.

(The Apple in the Dark). Lispector's major protagonists are all making their way through the maze of life, lost at times, but always eventually able to resume their journey toward enlightenment.

Perto de coração selvagem, Lispector's first novel, published when she was still a teenager, is considered a breakthrough in Brazilian literature because of its modernistic style. It is the story of Joana, a young orphan who, after an introspective adolescence, lives through a marriage and a subsequent divorce. In part 1, descriptions of Joana's childhood alternate with descriptions of her life as Octavio's wife. Part 2 tells the story of her marriage, her husband's infidelity, her divorce, and her ultimate encounter with herself as a free entity in the world. The epigraph for the novel, "He was alone. He was abandoned, happy, close to the savage heart of life," is taken from James Joyce's *A Portrait of the Artist as a Young Man* (1916).

As a child, Joana is keenly aware of the cycle of life and death. Eating a chicken makes her think of the worm in the earth on which the chicken once nourished itself. Behind all life there is death, and the only thing that distinguishes human beings from other organisms is consciousness. A feeling of being connected with the physical world through a common destiny provides moments of profound pain and profound joy to Joana as well as to most of Lispector's later protagonists. "Oh, pity, that is what I sense then. Pity is my form of love. Of love and of communication."

Marriage proves to be a very disturbing experience for Joana, who as a child quizzed her teacher about the goal of happiness: "Be happy in order to obtain what?" she had wondered. While her need to touch another human being through love nevertheless remained strong, her marriage resulted in a sense of imprisonment. How does one tie oneself to another human being without becoming imprisoned by that person's construction of walls around one's body and soul? How is it possible to possess things without having things possess one? These are questions that will haunt all of Lispector's major protagonists. In her marriage, Joana's quest for self-fulfillment constantly comes into conflict with the bland happiness she finds with Octavio: "Lightly surprised she dilated her eyes, perceived her body plunged into a comfortable happiness. She did not suffer, but where was she?"

Part 2 describes Joana's long struggle to free herself from Octavio: "His presence, and more than his presence: knowing that he existed left her without liberty." Her time is no longer her own: "Now all her time was handed over to him and the minutes that were hers, she felt them allotted, distributed in small cubes of ice that she must swallow rapidly, before they melted." Marriage, she believes, is betrayal of herself and of the vision of life that she developed during adolescence. For Octavio, on the other hand, Joana's restlessness, which originally attracted him to her, proves too disturbing, and he seeks refuge in his former fiancée, Lidia, a woman whose dream is to create a conventional family. Victimized by irrational jealousy, Joana, too, takes a lover, at the same time attempting to retain Octavio. The drive toward self-fulfillment, however, proves stronger than the forces that link her to either her husband or her lover, and in the novel's last chapter Joana is alone. Her only goal now is to walk humbly down the road of life, without fear, receptive to the world and to death. Finally in harmony with the fluidity of life itself, Joana experiences within herself a burst of creative energy.

The Apple in the Dark is considered to be Lispector's most important novel. Martim, the protagonist, is fleeing a crime. At the beginning of the novel, he is in bed in a womblike hotel room. The balcony outside his room overlooks a garden bathed in darkness. Still half asleep, Martim walks out onto the balcony, observes that a car which has been parked in front of the hotel has disappeared, and suspects that a German who lives in the hotel has gone to turn him in to the police. Totally awake now, Martim jumps from the balcony into the garden and begins a long, slow walk into the dark.

The Apple in the Dark is a dreamlike narrative of Martim's quest for a side of the self with which he has lost contact while living as a married man in a conventional social setting. Unsure of where he is going, his only goal is to move in a straight line so as to avoid a circular return to the walls of the hotel. Martim's quest ends on an ambiguous note, since at the end of the novel he appears to have given up and is ready to be captured and returned to the world he left behind.

Nevertheless, Martim's journey has provided him with experiences and in sights which he did not possess at the beginning of the book. "We don't know where we came from and we don't know where we're going; but we just experience things, we experience! And that's what we have, Ermelinda." Surrounded by stones and plants, Martim experiences exquisite moments of connection with the mystery of the natural world, as all of his senses open and his mind abdicates its power and accepts being merely a part of life "with the nakedness of his lack of understanding." He makes the surprising discovery that "the more stupid he was the more face to face with things he was." In his new state of consciousness, Martim replaces understanding with awareness. He senses the air he breathes with the delicate tension of a plant and attempts to adopt the patient rhythm of grazing cows.

The Apple in the Dark is a novel about love, both for the world itself and for other human beings. A significant part of the book describes Martim's stay at a farm and his encounter with two women, Ermelinda and Vitória. Ermelinda seeks, in her love for Martim, protection against her obsessive fear of death, only to discover that physical love, on the contrary, brings her closer to an experience of dying than does any other emotion. This newly won insight finally enables Ermelinda to accept her own mortality. Martim's encounter with Vitória is different, a communion of souls rather than bodies. In a moving description, Lispector shows how Martim's resistance to intimate contact with another person is gradually broken down, as Vitória for the first time in her life gives expression to her innermost thoughts and emotions. While communication does not last, the experience proves crucial to Martim, who is finally able to look upon himself with love and respect: "The man was loving himself for the first time, which meant that he was ready to love others. . . ." Martim no longer needs to flee, and he willingly consents to cut short his quest and return to society.

The title of the novel is important. *The Apple in the Dark* can be read as a commentary on the biblical myth on the tree of knowledge. The understanding of the world that Martim achieves is intuitive rather than rational. He never actually eats the apple, he merely reaches out for it in the dark, hoping that he will be able to hold onto the fruit: "And I have that clumsy way of reaching for an apple in the dark—and trying not to drop it."

The quest for identity continues in *A paixão segundo G. H.* (the passion according to G. H.). While Martim's quest took the form of a voyage through external space, G. H.'s quest is wholly internal. The killing of a cockroach triggers in the protagonist an extensive and painful meditation on life, death, and writing, and on her own place within the order of things. Toward the end of the novel, G. H., like Martim, will emerge from her introspection with an increased awareness which will enable her to live her daily life in a more productive way than before.

An Apprenticeship, written five years later, is Lispector's most optimistic novel. The novel has two protagonists, a woman and a man, engaged in an extensive dialogue. Lori, a physically attractive young teacher, lives an empty, nonreflective life until she falls in love with Ulysses, a professor of philosophy. Although Lori has had several affairs, Ulysses refuses to consummate their love until she has completed her "apprenticeship" and learned the secret meaning of life. Only then, he believes, is a permanent union of two people possible. Lori, feeling frustrated and rejected, reluctantly starts her slow, painful route toward self-discovery under his guidance.

Until the meeting with Ulysses, Lori had eliminated pain from her life, but she had also cut off any potential for meaningful contact either with herself, with other people, or with life itself: "Without pain, she had been left without anything, lost in her own world and that of others without any means of contact." Love, reduced to sex, failed to connect her to anything outside herself. Ulysses realizes this and decides that Lori must reestablish contact with her own body and soul before she will be able to love him or anybody else: "I could have possessed you already with my body and my soul, but I will wait even though it takes years, for you, too, to have a body and a soul to love with," he tells her.

During her apprenticeship, Lori experiences an increased sense of awareness of the world around her, and of the silence of death which perpetually lurks behind the bustling noises of life. Lori discovers that pain and pleasure, life and death, are inextricably linked. By attempting to escape from pain she has excluded pleasure from her life as well. Consequently, her new receptivity to pain will restore her ability to experience pleasure. It is only after having accepted the pain of death that she can start to feel a genuine joy of living.

The pleasure results from her growing ability to strip away façades and protective mechanisms and dare finally to be herself. Lori soon experiences flashes of communication and insights accompanied by a keen sense of genuinely existing. During this period of profound introspection, Lori needs to distance herself from society and from Ulysses as well, in order to be more fully with herself. Her ultimate goal, however, is connection, not isolation. First, she must be reattached to the earth itself. Then, she hopes to reestablish the link between herself and other people.

In an episode typical of Lispector's fiction, Lori is walking slowly and wearily down the street. She notices a girl waiting for the bus, and her heart begins to throb—she has decided to try to make contact with another person. After the brief encounter, Lori realizes that what she is looking for is more profound. She returns home and calls Ulysses. She bites into an apple and discovers that the eating of the fruit leads her to a state of grace rather than exile: "Unlike Eve, when she bit into the apple she entered paradise. . . . It was the beginning . . . of a state of grace." The state of grace is the state of someone who does not have to guess any longer, according to the narrator, someone who simply knows. The world around her acquires a kind of halo that radiates almost perfectly from things and people, a kind of energy consisting of very fine particles of light. Lori, at the same time, realizes that she does not want to experience grace often, she does not want to become addicted to it, because it would distance her from the struggle, from the perplexity and joy of an ordinary human destiny: "It was important not to forget that the state of grace was merely a small opening to the world which was like paradise—it was neither an entrance into it nor did it give one the right to eat from the fruits of its orchards."

Lori, then, does not stay in paradise but emerges from her experience of grace as a better human being. Ulysses, in the following chapter, tells her that she is now ready for love. Before leaving her apartment to join him, Lori stands by her window, watching the rain. She feels neither pain nor pleasure, only a keen sense of connection and release: "She and the rain were busy with their violent outpouring." She intuitively knows that she will be able to transfer her newly won intimacy with the world to her relationship with Ulysses, leaves her apartment without putting on her customary makeup, and takes a taxi to his place. Somehow, living and loving have finally become simple, as Lori has discovered that it is possible for her to give herself without losing herself. After a period of passionate lovemaking, she sees in a vision the fruit of the world, "And it was in midair that she placed her mouth on the fruit and managed to bite into it, yet leaving it intact gleaming in space." Ulysses is no longer a teacher to Lori. The two of them are equal, united through mutual love.

An Apprenticeship, with its vision of a mature, passionate, conscious relationship between a man and a woman, is an exception within Lispector's total work, a pleasant detour along the road. In *Água viva* (sparkling water), written four years later, the author returns once again to a solitary, questing protagonist. The novel is an intense, fluid monologue addressed to an absent *you*, a person with whom the narrator was once intimately involved. In the novel's first paragraph, the narrator bursts out in a cry of joy upon realizing that she is once again free. It is a joy mixed with the sadness of separation and the fear of an unknown future. Nevertheless, she wants to capture the present moment, to connect with the spirit of life, and to sing out the joy she experiences from being in the world: "And I sing hallelujah in the air like the bird does."

Água viva is a glorification of the self alone in the world, detached from material possessions and from other people. The prevailing emotion in the book is one of being intensely alive, bought at the price of separation from the person she loves. Her new lover is nature, a feminine principle both soothing and ferocious. This love affair with life itself is for the narrator a way of approaching God. Such a radical break is necessary for Lispector's narrator in order to escape from a society which flattens out emotional lives and turns people into automatons, unable ever to grasp the present moment.

Separation, thus, becomes a gift of life that she, through her writing, wants to bestow upon her former lover as well. Separation is seen as a birth trauma, painful but necessary for the lover to experience the exquisite joy of liberty: "I give you liberty. First I break the waterbag. Then I cut the umbilical cord. And you are alive in your own right." On the book's final page, she addresses the lover for the last time: "Look at me and love me. No: you look at yourself and love you. And that is what is just."

Água viva is a long meditation on love, separation, life, death, and God, seemingly inspired by Oriental mysticism: "Profound prayer is a meditation on nothingness," according to the narrator. Faced with the pain of separation, analogous to the pain of dying, the narrator chooses to respond with joy: "... because it is too cruel, so I respond by the purity of indomitable joy. I refuse to be sad. Let us be joyous." The style of *Água viva* is fluid and poetic, each sentence giving birth to the next with no preconceived structure, as Lispector attempts to capture the rhythm of her own respiration.

The Hour of the Star is also a detour. It is different from Lispector's other novels in that it focuses on a social rather than a metaphysical problem. Macabéa, the protagonist, is a young woman who moves from the poor northeast part of Brazil to the city. The novel deals with the problems of the rural North versus the urban South, of poverty and the dream of a better life, and, finally, of an uneducated woman's struggle to survive in a sexist society.

In her final novel, *Um sopro de vida* (a breath of life), Lispector returns for the last time to an intensely personal inquiry into the problems of life, death, and writing. Completed shortly before the author's own death, the novel is the ultimate statement of an artist whose own road has come to an end, for whom reality has caught up with her life's vision, and for whom each breath now literally encapsulates the essence of life itself. The novel was published posthumously.

Other major works

SHORT FICTION: *Alguns contos*, 1952; *Laços de família*, 1960 (*Family Ties*, 1972); *A legião estrangeira*, 1964 (*The Foreign Legion*, 1986); *Felicidade clandestina: Contos*, 1971; *A imitaçã da rosa*, 1973; *Onde estivestes de noite*, 1974; *A via crucis do corpo*, 1974; *A bela e fera*, 1979.

NONFICTION: *Para não esquecer*, 1978.

CHILDREN'S LITERATURE: *O mistério do coelho pensante*, 1967; *A mulher que matou os peixes*, 1969.

MISCELLANEOUS: *Selecto de Clarice Lispector*, 1975.

Bibliography

Borelli, Olga. *Clarice Lispector: Um esboço para um possível retrato*, 1981.
Brasil, Assis. *Clarice Lispector*, 1969.
Campedelli, S. Y., and B. Abdala, Jr. *Clarice Lispector*, 1981.

Fitz, Earl E. *Clarice Lispector*, 1985.
Nunes, Benedito. *Leitura de Clarice Lispector*, 1973.
_____. *O mundo de Clarice Lispector*, 1966.
Pereira, Teresinha Alves. *Estudo sôbre Clarice Lispector*, 1975.
Sá, Olga de. *A escritura de Clarice Lispector*, 1979.

Randi Birn

ALISON LURIE

Born: Chicago, Illinois; September 3, 1926

Principal long fiction
Love and Friendship, 1962; *The Nowhere City*, 1965; *Imaginary Friends*, 1967; *Real People*, 1969; *The War Between the Tates*, 1974; *Only Children*, 1979; *Foreign Affairs*, 1984.

Other literary forms
Besides writing fiction, Alison Lurie has distinguished herself in two other areas, children's literature and the semiotics of dress, and her novels reflect both concerns as well. Her interest in children's literature is reflected in *Only Children*, in which two little girls pose their fantasies against the shocking reality exposed to them by their parents, and in *Foreign Affairs*, in which one of the two central characters, Vinnie Miner, spends her sabbatical in England collecting playground rhymes. (Real children's rhymes, Lurie has observed, are surprisingly subversive, not like the "safe" literature written for children by adults.) Lurie's fascination with the semiotics of clothing is reflected frequently in the novels, where she pursues the relationship between clothing and personal identity. An especially provocative example can be found in *Imaginary Friends*, where Roger Zimmern, forced by a strange religious group to abandon his normal academic dress in favor of cheap suits, loses his sense of identity.

Achievements
Lurie's fiction has received much praise from critics, and her work has been very popular with the broader reading public. Her first novel, *Love and Friendship*, appeared in 1962 and was followed by several prestigious grants and fellowships: Yaddo Foundation fellowships in 1963, 1964, and 1966; a Guggenheim grant in 1965-1966; a Rockefeller Foundation grant in 1967-1968; a New York State Cultural Council Foundation Grant in 1972-1973. *The War Between the Tates* in 1974 brought Lurie a popular audience and more critical acclaim. An American Academy of Arts and Letters award followed in 1978. All of Lurie's fiction displays a remarkable control of language, a style which surprises and amuses. Both for her wit and for her sharp-edged, satiric depiction of human follies, she has often been compared to Jane Austen.

Biography
Alison Lurie was born September 3, 1926, in Chicago, Illinois, but grew up in White Plains, New York. An avid reader as a child, she began at about

the age of thirteen or fourteen to read such authors as Charles Dickens, George Bernard Shaw, and Jane Austen. In 1947, she was graduated from Radcliffe, where she had met many people who later became important literary figures—Barbara Epstein, for example, later an editor of *The New York Review of Books*, and Jonathon Peale Bishop, a teacher, critic, and essayist whom she married in 1948. Lurie is a professor of children's literature at Cornell University in Ithaca, New York, where she has taught since 1969. She and her husband have three grown sons, John, Jeremy, and Joshua.

Analysis

Alison Lurie's novels are known for their comedy and satire, and her acute observation is most often trained on the complications of love, marriage, and friendship as they affect the lives of the upper classes, the educated, the academic. Many of her novels take place at the fictional Convers College in New England or at Corinth University in upstate New York (based on Cornell University, where Lurie has taught for many years) or concern characters who teach at or have been associated with Corinth. These novels are not, however, all academic satire; the academics often travel to other places or become involved in issues beyond the campus.

Lurie's style is most often detached and ironic, a treatment that has won for her both blame and praise. Her novels, except for *Only Children*, explore the time in which they are written and reflect the events and culture of Lurie's own adult years. The novels typically cover a short space of time, a crisis point in the lives of the characters, but several of the characters are seen at different points in their lives because of Lurie's use of the same characters in different novels, sometimes as major, sometimes as minor characters. Lurie works successfully with a variety of narrative points of view: omniscient narration in *The War Between the Tates*, first-person narration in *Real People*, third-person focus narration in *Imaginary Friends* (expanded to include two focus characters in *Foreign Affairs*). She shows no penchant for either the happy or the unhappy ending, realistically leaving her characters to continue to work out their lives as best they can.

At the heart of Lurie's first two novels are couples trying to work out their relationship. Her first novel, *Love and Friendship* (a title taken from Jane Austen), draws out the main lines of the issue. What is love and what is friendship? Are they different in what is best and most enduring? In this novel, the main character, Emmy Turner, "loves" her lover more than she does her husband. In the end, however, she chooses her husband over her lover because he needs her and to him she can be a friend. Indeed, what first led her to enter into a love affair was a frustration with her husband's failure to make a friend of her, to discuss with her his work and his concerns. Ultimately, Lurie suggests, friendship is more satisfying and lasting than love; indeed, love at its best is friendship at its best. In her second novel, *The Nowhere City*, the ending is the opposite, but the implication seems the same. Paul Cattleman rediscovers his wife at the end after much neglect and many adulteries. It is too late, however: Friendship is lost, and with it love; she tells him that she is not angry with him, but she just does not know him anymore.

While the love and friendship theme becomes a secondary issue in *Imaginary Friends*, she made it once again the central focus of *Real People*. In this novel, Janet Belle Spencer, a writer, has taken up residence at Illyria, a haven for writers and artists. She has gone there primarily to work, since she cannot seem to write at home, but she is also drawn there by her love for an artist, Ken, with whom she believes she has much more in common than with her insurance-executive husband. The artists' colony of Illyria is an unreal world, however, and Janet discovers that she and Ken are not really friends; she learns much about her writing that she resolves to change. It is at home with her husband, Clark, not at Illyria, she finally realizes, that she will be able to put to work her new understandings.

Love and friendship in marriage are explored most intensively in Lurie's next and most celebrated novel, *The War Between the Tates*. Erica and Brian Tate, a young academic couple, are in their own eyes and the eyes of their friends the perfect couple, but as middle age looms, Brian becomes increasingly frustrated at not being famous, while the children become rebellious teenagers. True love and friendship appear to be lacking. Finally, Brian has an affair with a student whom he makes pregnant, Erica befriends the student, and both Brian and Erica, but especially Erica, wander through a bewildering maze of events that leave their earlier sense of themselves and their marriage damaged. As the novel ends, they drift back together, confused, "out of love," but basically seeking a peace they can find only with each other.

Love and friendship in marriage is the topic once again of *Only Children*, but this time the actions of the adults are seen through the eyes of two little girls, Lolly and Mary Ann, who respond to what they see in the behavior of their elders, especially their parents. In each set of parents there is one serious, deeply dedicated person (Lolly's mother, Mary Ann's father) and one shallow, egotistic, flamboyant hunter of the other sex. The two sets of parents ultimately stay together, but, lacking a love based on friendship, they are merely maintaining a façade, and their example will cripple their children's ability to love.

The love and friendship theme appears again in *Foreign Affairs*, which juxtaposes two main characters, one married and one not. Vinnie Miner, a middle-aged professor, finds love surprisingly where she had least expected it, in a friendship with a man totally unlike her, a retired sanitary engineer. The other main character, a handsome young man in Vinnie's academic department, begins the novel estranged from his wife, is temporarily dazzled and infatuated by a far more glamorous Englishwoman, but returns to his wife at the end, finding her superior in trust, honesty, and common decency.

Lurie's novels concern themselves with relationships between people, and these relationships are at the center of all of her work. Yet the lives of Lurie's characters are affected by more than personal forces alone. Context, temporal and physical alike, is also central to these novels, and the direction of the lives of Lurie's characters is profoundly affected by the times and the places in which they live. The most persistent context, moreover, is academic, since many of these characters, like Lurie herself, are university professors or members of their families. In this case again, *Love and Friendship* sets a pattern which other novels will follow. Emmy Turner's husband, Holman Turner, is a young instructor at Convers, a small, exclusive liberal arts college in New England. Emmy wants to share her husband's academic interests but he shuts her out, treasuring her as an ideal wife and mother but bored by her attempts to enter into his intellectual concerns. Ironically, Emmy should be more at home at Convers (her wealthy father is a trustee, and two brothers are alumni), while Holman has come from a very different background, yet it is he, not Emmy, who seems the "Convers type." Emmy's love affair flaunts the Convers traditions, while Holman seems the perfect instructor. In the end, however, he falls afoul of those same Convers traditions, and it is Emmy who must stay to save him.

The academic world is also a factor in *The Nowhere City*, although the story takes place in a Los Angeles setting which dominates the novel. Paul, in the end, will retreat to the Eastern academic world that he knows (remaking his relationships with his old Harvard friends and taking a teaching post at Convers College), while Katherine, who had initially seemed the more Eastern academic of the two, refuses to return with him there and seems to find a new self in Los Angeles.

The War Between the Tates again makes the academy not only strong backdrop but also actor in the events. Brian Tate is a highly successful sociology professor at Corinth University in upstate New York; his wife, Erica, a faculty wife. Their two closest friends, who divorce in the novel, are Leonard Zimmern, an English professor, and Danielle Zimmern, Erica's closest female friend, a part-time faculty member in the French department. The convulsions of American academe in the late 1960's interfere directly in Brian's and Erica's lives. Brian, though very successful academically, has always dreamed of fame as an adviser to governments and presidents, and his middle-aged frustration makes him susceptible to trying to recover his lost youth by mixing socially with his graduate students, increasingly adapting his clothing and other styles to theirs, finally indulging in his affair with Wendy. Erica, like Katherine Cattleman in *The Nowhere City*, attempts to preserve her traditional moral values in the face of all this upheaval and tries not only to adapt herself to these values but also to give direction to Brian and Wendy, even to the point of insisting that Brian divorce her and marry Wendy. She becomes peripherally involved, through her friend Danielle, in the Hens, a local feminist group, and finding the local Hare Krishna guru of the students to be an old school friend, under his guidance has her own adventure with LSD. Brian and Erica, then, experience their marital troubles amid the student rebellions of the 1960's. Though the novel does not probe as deeply as *Imaginary Friends* into the political and intellectual doubts and troubles of academe, these influences are present, shaping their reaction.

In *Foreign Affairs*, the two main characters are again college professors, both from the English department at Corinth University: the middle-aged, internationally famous expert in children's literature, Vinnie Miner, and the young specialist in the eighteenth century, Fred Turner, both on leave to do scholarly work in London. The novel for the most part tells their stories separately, their paths crossing significantly only twice. While their common background does make their lives cross in significant ways, and while both their lives are shaped by their academic backgrounds, the primary focus of the novel is on other aspects of their lives, which will be discussed below.

The university campus, then, demonstrates the importance of time and place in Lurie's novels. This is also true in a larger sense, since American culture itself, with its regional and sociological tensions, plays just as important a role as the characters do. If *Love and Friendship*, the first novel, works off a Jane Austen theme, it also echoes a peculiarly American, Fitzgeraldian theme in which the different regions and classes of America become important players in the conflicts of the novel. Emmy is New Jersey rich, her lover Will Thomas Southern shabby genteel, and her husband Holman Chicago shabby but respectable poor. As the marital couple work out their conflicts with traditions of Convers College playing an important role, these different regional and class conflicts do much to shape their actions and reactions. In *The Nowhere City*, 1960's America, with its new and strange customs and dress, almost overpowers its characters' ability to work out their human problems. Here, Los Angeles is the city in which "nowhere" comes to mean "present but lacking history and future." Strange and mixed new forms of architecture in both house and public building design, styles of hair and dress, sexual life-styles, artistic forms, even subjects being studied in the universities are all strange, macabre, and new, dividing Katherine and Paul Cattleman as they respond to them so differently. Setting plays just as important a role in *Imaginary Friends*, which brings two very traditional strongholds, the enclosed small town and the principles of academic inquiry, together with the strains of the world without.

Real People, again, though it removes its main characters to an isolated, protected, ideal world of the artists' colony, nevertheless shows that the best work cannot be done in an artificial atmosphere but only when the artists are living and writing truthfully about the world in which they are "real people."

Again, too, despite all the 1960's campus shenanigans of *The War Between the Tates* (drugs; strange new life-styles, clothes, and hairstyles) the novel presents a strong sense that the campus is only reflecting all the major movements, confusions, and displacements of the society at large. In *Only Children*, which is set during the Great Depression, the characters reflect the concerns of that time, including its powerful economic and political conflicts. Bill Hubbard, for example, is an example of the FDR-type liberal democrat, dedicated to social reforms which will lift the poor, while Dan Zimmern represents the nascent Madison Avenue type, flamboyant and driven to succeed. *Foreign Affairs*, in the experiences of both Vinnie Miner and Fred Turner, discloses the tensions of many cultural mores, especially different class and sexual expectations, complicated further by differences between Great Britain and the United States.

The lives of the individual characters are additionally set against the backdrop of the world of literature itself. In *Real People*, Janet Belle Spencer images Ken as the ideal reader of her fiction, largely because he recognizes every literary reference—which in turn is reminiscent of Lurie's own rich texture of literary reference. In this regard, as already observed, she uses the "love and friendship" theme from Jane Austen. Another novelist to whom Lurie is greatly indebted is Henry James, especially in *Imaginary Friends* and *Foreign Affairs*. Indeed, *Imaginary Friends* in many ways duplicates the plot of James's *The Bostonians* (1886), in which a young woman named Verena leads a band of truth-seekers, by an extraordinary gift of public speaking, which seems to proceed from a trancelike ability to contact higher powers. Lurie's Verena, like James's heroine is torn between her group and her believers there, and a young man in love with her who wishes to carry her away. This role, taken by Basil Ransome in James's novel, is split in *Imaginary Friends* between the narrator, Roger, and the young man Ted, who does finally marry Verena and carry her off to the University of Arizona, where they are last seen as student agitators.

Foreign Affairs enlarges on the Jamesian theme not only by explicitly introducing James's work by name but also by exploring one of his most insistent themes: what happens when basically good, decent Americans encounter a far more culturally sophisticated European society. In James's novels of this type, the balance is struck in favor finally of the basic, honest decency of Americans against the more sophisticated but possibly corrupt world of the Europeans, and Lurie's novel arrives at the same resolution. This exploration is complicated by the fact that, of the two Americans, Vinnie Miner is very sophisticated in the ways of the English, knowing their ways and customs so well that she really feels more culturally at home there than in the United States. Fred Turner, on the other hand, despite his great physical charms and handsomeness and his knowledge of eighteenth century literature, is basically a raw recruit to European culture. Both, however, have "foreign affairs":

Vinnie, with an almost illiterate Oklahoman whom she meets on the plane on the way over, so embarrassingly crude that she dreads presenting him to her friends; Fred, with an English aristocrat and actress so elegant and sophisticated that his American life appears crude by comparison. Despite this structural converse, in which Vinnie loves an American far less presentable than her European friends, and in which Fred loves an Englishwoman far more sophisticated than his American wife and friends, both find, despite all of their differences, their American loves superior after all, and their European friends, for all of their sophistication, less satisfying morally as friends and lovers than their American friends. Thus, the pattern of James's international novels in which superior American decency confronts and ultimately wins out over superior European elegance and sophistication, is repeated here in Lurie's fiction.

If Lurie's readers often spot resonances from other fiction, they also have the pleasure of recognizing characters they have met in other Lurie novels, for Lurie frequently works with recurring characters. Emmy Turner's four-year-old boy Freddy from *Love and Friendship* is one of the grown-up main characters in *Foreign Affairs*, while Fred's wife Roo in that same novel appeared as a child in the earlier *The War Between the Tates*. Sometimes Lurie will in a later novel go back to an earlier period in a character's life: Miranda, the grown-up, married mother of three children in *Love and Friendship*, is seen as a child in the later novel *Only Children*. Of all the characters that recur, the most persistent one is Leonard Zimmern, first seen in *Real People* as a middle-aged, distinguished critic of American literature living in New York; later, in *The War Between the Tates*, as a friend of Brian and Erica. He is also the father of Roo, a child here but an adult in *Foreign Affairs*. In *Only Children*, the Depression-era story, Zimmern is a teenager, and in *Foreign Affairs* he is the father of a grown-up Roo, the famous critic whose harsh article on Vinnie Miner's work in children's literature haunts Vinnie as she goes to England. Roger Zimmern of *Imaginary Friends* is mentioned briefly in *The War Between the Tates* as Leonard Zimmern's cousin. This remarkable amount of recurrence suggests Lurie's strong interest in understanding how her characters came to be who they are, despite her novels' time frames. Her novels, as noted before, cover only short periods of time—one, *Only Children*, takes place in a single weekend. In order to continue her characters' development, then, Lurie often spreads out their lives over several novels, the recurrence of her characters in different novels doing much to tie their lives together.

As in the other novels, all the themes discussed so far are treated as well in *Imaginary Friends*. Their treatment in that novel, however, represents perhaps Lurie's broadest and deepest effort, for the academic backdrop she uses so often elsewhere is broadened here to embrace the most fundamental of human questions, questions of knowledge, of identity, of sanity, and finally of

madness. The main character in this novel, sociologist Roger Zimmern—
a young, brand-new Ph.D. at a large, upstate New York university—goes to
Sophis, a nearby small town, as the research assistant of Thomas McCann, a
famous senior professor in his department whom Roger admires despite ru-
mors he has heard about him from other young faculty members and despite
the realization that McCann's form of empirical sociology (the case-study
method) is passé. To investigate McCann's hypothesis that small groups can
build so powerful a belief system that it can withstand, rationalize, and incorporate doubting attacks from within and without, Roger infiltrates, under
the cover of a public opinion seeker, a group of religious fundamentalists
called the Truth-seekers, whose young leader, Verena, leads and directs
through automatic writing from superior beings on another planet, named
Varna. McCann is introduced as a businessman friend, also interested in
their theories. Roger's secure identity is overset by his mentor's unscientific
attempt to control the experiment in the direction of this hypothesis rather
than merely observe and record, by the degree to which he sees this tendency
in his mentor, driven by academic rivalry and jealousy. Also tormented by his
sexual attraction for Verena, he reaches a point where he no longer knows
what he believes in, no longer knows who he is, no longer knows whether
there is in his discipline any objective basis for scientific inquiry. He believes
that he is going mad but decides that it is, rather, his mentor who is insane
and becomes unwillingly the primary witness whose testimony results in
McCann's being committed to an asylum. The novel ends with Roger maintaining tenuous but commonsensical hold on his own sanity. Here, Lurie has
touched upon questions central not only to academic life but to the lives of
everyone else as well: How can one truly observe and know? How real is our
own sense of self?

Taken as a whole, Lurie's novels reveal a remarkable uniformity. Her own
background in academe provides the most common setting for her novels,
and frequently this setting is broadened to reflect the central questions with
which Lurie is concerned. Her interest in clothing and identity, in the lives of
children, indeed in the lives of all of her characters, is unusual. Her work is
best considered not as a series of separate novels but as a continuity in which
her characters' lives continue, not ceasing with the end of a particular novel
but continuing as do all our lives: growing and changing through time.

Other major works

NONFICTION: *The Language of Clothes*, 1981.

CHILDREN'S LITERATURE: *The Heavenly Zoo: Legends and Tales of the Stars*,
1979; *Clever Gretchen and Other Forgotten Folktales*, 1980; *Fabulous Beasts*,
1981.

Bibliography

Lehman, David. "A Kind of Witchery," in *Newsweek*. CIV (September 29, 1984), p. 80.

"Lurie, Alison," in *Current Biography*. XLVII (February, 1986), p. 26.

Parini, Jay. "The Novelist at Sixty," in *Horizon*. XXIX (March, 1986), p. 21.

Shapiro, Harriet. "*Foreign Affairs* Earns Novelist Alison Lurie Domestic Acclaim and a Place Beside Henry James," in *People Weekly*. XXII (December 3, 1984), p. 73.

June M. Frazer

ROSE MACAULAY

Born: Rugby, England; August 1, 1881
Died: London, England; October 30, 1958

Principal long fiction

Abbots Verney, 1906; *The Furnace*, 1907; *The Secret River*, 1909; *The Valley Captives*, 1911; *The Lee Shore*, 1912; *Views and Vagabonds*, 1912; *The Making of a Bigot*, 1914; *Non-Combatants and Others*, 1916; *What Not: A Prophetic Comedy*, 1918; *Potterism: A Tragi-farcical Tract*, 1920; *Dangerous Ages*, 1921; *Mystery at Geneva*, 1922; *Told by an Idiot*, 1923; *Orphan Island*, 1924; *Crewe Train*, 1926; *Keeping Up Appearances*, 1928 (U.S. edition, *Daisy and Daphne*, 1928); *Staying with Relations*, 1930; *They Were Defeated*, 1932 (U.S. edition, *The Shadow Flies*, 1932); *Going Abroad*, 1934; *I Would Be Private*, 1937; *And No Man's Wit*, 1940; *The World My Wilderness*, 1950; *The Towers of Trebizond*, 1956.

Other literary forms

Though principally a novelist, Rose Macaulay wrote prolifically in several genres. Early in her career, she published two slim volumes of verse, *The Two Blind Countries* (1914) and *Three Days* (1919), both of which earned favorable reviews in the British press. For many years, Macaulay contributed reviews and essays to such publications as *The Spectator*, *The Guardian*, and the *New Statesman*; she produced two generally well-received book-length critical studies, *Milton* (1934, revised 1957) and *The Writings of E. M. Forster* (1938). Some of Macaulay's best prose can be found in two of her widely acclaimed travel books, *Fabled Shore: From the Pyrenees to Portugal* (1949) and *Pleasure of Ruins* (1953).

Achievements

Throughout much of her lifetime, Macaulay was one of Great Britain's best-known authors. Many of her lighter sketches and essays appeared in the *Daily Mail*, the *Evening Standard*, and other newspapers and periodicals aimed at large, general audiences; some of her fiction appeared in serialized form in *Eve*, a popular English magazine aimed at women and filled mainly with froth. Yet Macaulay's more serious works consistently earned high praise in Great Britain's most respected literary publications; her twenty-third and final novel, *The Towers of Trebizond*, won the prestigious James Black Tait Memorial Prize. In 1951, Macaulay was awarded an honorary doctorate of letters from Cambridge University; in 1958, she was named a dame commander of the British Empire. Her death from heart seizure in 1958 brought forth warm and respectful tributes from many leading literary figures, including Harold Nicolson, Rosamond Lehmann, and Anthony Powell.

Biography

Emilie Rose Macaulay was born in Rugby, England, on August 1, 1881. Her father, George Macaulay, was a schoolmaster and Latin scholar; her mother, the former Grace Conybeare, was a bright, energetic, but rather severe woman who sought to impart to her children a High Church interpretation of Anglican Christianity. Rose Macaulay was related to a long line of ministers, teachers, and authors (the celebrated historian Thomas Babington Macaulay was her paternal grandfather's first cousin); not surprisingly, she was so well schooled by her parents that, by early adolescence, she was already on very familiar terms with, among other classics, Dante's *Inferno* (c.1320) and Shakespeare's plays. Because doctors prescribed warmth and sunshine as a means of treating her mother's tuberculosis, Macaulay spent the better part of her childhood in Varazzo, Italy—a place she would later recall with considerable fondness. In 1900, she entered Oxford's Somerville College, where she studied modern history and became—as her biographer Constance Babington Smith records—"a chatterbox who gabbled away so fast that at times she was hardly intelligible, a ready speaker who made lively contributions to undergraduate debates." Soon after completing her studies at Oxford, Macaulay—while living with her parents in Wales—began work on her first novel, *Abbots Verney*, which critics praised for its artistic promise. In 1915, Macaulay acquired a flat of her own in London, where she quickly developed friendships with such influential literary figures as Hugh Walpole, J. C. Squire, and Walter de la Mare, and where, in 1917, she entered into what became a twenty-five-year love affair with Gerald O'Donovan, a married man and a former Catholic priest who was himself well-known in London's literary circles as the author of the highly autobiographical and anticlerical novel *Father Ralph* (1913). Though she traveled frequently, widely, and often intrepidly to locations that saw little tourist activity, Macaulay continued to make her home in London, where even in old age she was seen—as one friend recalled—"at every party, every private view, protest meeting, cruise, literary luncheon, or ecclesiastical gathering." Macaulay began openly to identify herself as an agnostic during her university days; much of her fiction pokes generally gentle fun at organized religion. After O'Donovan's death in 1942, however, she experienced a renewed interest in orthodox Christianity, an interest much in evidence in her later novels.

Analysis

Over a writing career that spanned fifty years, Rose Macaulay produced twenty-three novels. She understandably came to regard the earliest of these—including *The Furnace*, *The Secret River*, and *The Valley Captives*—as immature and rather badly made, and she did nothing to encourage their republication. In her novels, Macaulay utilizes a wide variety of carefully rendered settings (some of which are quite exotic); her prose is beautifully cadenced and richly detailed. Occasionally, however, the exuberance and ornateness of Macaulay's prose can be distracting, and, occasionally, her plots bog down beneath the weight of the descriptive digressions and authorial intrusions that pepper her texts. Many of Macaulay's characters are both convincing and memorable. Some, however, are both stereotypical and stiff and appear to be exchanging speeches rather than engaging in spontaneous conversation. Macaulay recognized that, as a novelist, she was least skilled at characterization; indeed, she was sometimes urged by friends and critics to concentrate on the essay form. Yet Macaulay also recognized that her fiction had a large and rather devoted readership and that, moreover, fiction could provide her with an entertaining vehicle for disseminating, and dissecting, a wide range of stimulating ideas.

As a novelist, Macaulay returned again and again to the same provocative themes. It is plain that, on the whole, she very much liked human beings. Still, she was severely critical of the intellectual laziness that she found epidemic in the human race. Repeatedly, her novels mock and sometimes savage characters who unthinkingly digest easy answers to the questions of life and who are prone, then, to sentimentality and cant. Though she is not generally ranked among her generation's more overtly feminist authors, Macaulay frequently reveals in her work a deep disdain for a social system that continued to deny women equal access to education and adventure. She regularly features as central figures young women who are witty, well-read, and intellectually ambitious.

Many of Macaulay's recurring concerns are overtly stated in *Potterism*, one of her most enduring novels—and the first to sell impressively in the United States. *Potterism* is, in fact, dedicated to "the unsentimental precisians in thought, who have, on this confused, inaccurate, and emotional planet, no fit habitation." It features among its five epigraphs Dr. Johnson's injunction to "clear your mind of cant. . . . Don't *think* foolishly." At the core of *Potterism* is the abrupt death of a young newspaper editor recently wed to Jane Potter, whose father is the publisher of a string of superficial, cant-spewing newspapers, and whose mother, under the pseudonym of Leila Yorke, churns out foolish and schmaltzy novels that enjoy huge sales. In order to discuss and analyze this somewhat suspicious demise from varying perspectives, Macaulay presents "extracts" from the "private journals" of several characters who knew the young editor, including his novel-writing mother-in-law. Employing clichéd and rather empurpled prose, Mrs. Potter shows herself to be quite capable of the sort of overemotionalism and muddled thinking that Macaulay, throughout her career, so thoroughly disdained. The three authors of the other journal entries are the friends of the Potter twins, Johnny and Jane, who have sought to distance themselves from what they disparagingly refer to as the "Potterism" of their parents. Macaulay demonstrates that Johnny and

Jane and their university-trained friends are not without their own pretensions and illusions, but she makes it clear that their crusade against vulgarity and stupidity—though quite probably quixotic—is well worth the taking.

Macaulay's thirteenth novel, the highly praised *Told by an Idiot*, is set in England between 1879 and 1927 and takes its title, and its epigraph, from Macbeth's well-known observation that life is a "tale told by an idiot, full of sound and fury,/ Signifying nothing. . . ." In this work, Macaulay focuses on the family of Maurice Garden, whose continuing struggles with faith and doubt have made him at various times a Catholic, a Baptist, a Positivist, an Anglican, "a plain agnostic," and, when the novel opens, an enthusiastic member of the Ethical Society. Garden's theological gyrations are well tolerated by his calm wife and his bright children, whose ranks include lively daughters named Imogen, Stanley, and Rome. Through her portrait of Maurice, Macaulay not only conveys something of her sense of the futility of most conflicting "isms" but also provides an acute portrait of the mental landscape of Victorian England. Through her depiction of the Gardens' daughters, she is able to portray young women who, though by no means perfect, possess energy, perspicacity, and a desire for independence.

In *Orphan Island*, perhaps Macaulay's most satisfactorily plotted novel, she harshly satirizes the sort of narrow-minded smugness that was not uncommon among influential people in the Victorian age. In the novel's early chapters, Macaulay describes how in 1855 a ship carrying dozens of young English orphans is blown off its California-bound course during a violent storm and winds up wrecked along the coast of a small, uncharted island in the South Pacific. In succeeding chapters, she shows how the prim and proper Miss Charlotte Smith—the orphans' supervisor—gradually turns the island into a model of Victorian England and establishes herself as its stern and platitudinous queen. In the 1920's, Miss Smith's island is rediscovered by a team headed by Mr. Thinkwell, a Cambridge lecturer in sociology. Thinkwell is astonished to discover that, in the remotest part of the South Pacific, Victorian England—complete with pronounced social inequities and an obsession with propriety—is, in effect, frozen in time. Still, Thinkwell enjoys the island's remarkable beauty, which Macaulay effectively renders through frequent and detailed descriptions of its sunny skies, lush plant life, and exotic vegetation. He also becomes attached to his growing status as a man of great intelligence and learning. In fact, near the novel's close and soon after the ancient Miss Smith's long-expected death, he becomes the island's prime minister, bent on reforming the corrupt monarchy into a republic where freedom and social justice can thrive. Macaulay does not reveal whether Thinkwell succeeds, though she does point out that, in the end, human folly has a way of winning out, and that the island is "likely" to become "as tyrannous, as unfair, as oligarchic in constitution and economic condition" as it was during Miss Smith's curious reign.

Macaulay's sole historical novel is *They Were Defeated*, called *The Shadow Flies* in its American edition, which takes place in England and covers an eight-month period beginning in the fall of 1640. Essentially, the novel centers on the often bloody and self-defeating religious conflicts that were then taking place between Puritans, Anglicans, and Roman Catholics. Among its characters are several well-known historical and literary figures, including the poets Robert Herrick, John Cleveland, and John Suckling. The scholarly and highly analytical Dr. Conybeare, himself based on one of Macaulay's distant relations, is one of the many central characters in her fiction who finds himself struggling with religious doubts. Similarly, his daughter Julian is a recognizable Macaulay "type": She bears what is commonly regarded as a male name and desires for herself the male prerogative to ask questions and obtain knowledge. In a prefatory "Note" to this long, intricately plotted and largely convincing book, Macaulay explains,

> I have done my best to make no person in this novel use in conversation any words, phrases, or idioms that were not demonstrably used at the time in which they lived; though I am aware, for all the constant and stalwart aid of the Oxford Dictionary, and the wealth of literature, letters and journals of the period that we possess for our guidance, that any such attempt must be extremely inadequate; or, at least, that mine is so.

In fact, after the publication of *The Shadow Flies*, Macaulay received assurances from several students of the language that her errors in word usage were both minor and few.

Going Abroad, Macaulay's next novel, represents a decided change of pace. Dedicated to two friends "who desired a book of unredeemed levity," *Going Abroad* is set largely in Zarauz, a coastal resort town in the Basque country of Spain. It features a large cast of British eccentrics, including a Dante scholar, a young aesthete, a rigid colonel, and a woman schooled in the classics who seeks to relocate and re-create the Garden of Eden. Also featured in *Going Abroad* is a pair of vulgarians who run a string of beauty parlors and a group of hearty Oxford students who seek to spread goodness and religion through the Moral Re-armament Movement, and who are successfully portrayed by Macaulay as both foolish and, in their own sort of way, admirable. By focusing on the often strained interaction of these diverse types, Macaulay created a highly successful comic novel set in an appealingly sunny climate—one that deserves to be ranked among the most amusing of its time.

During the 1950's, Rose Macaulay produced two novels that are generally placed among her most accomplished. The first of these, *The World My Wilderness*, draws heavily upon the recent events of World War II. Its central figure, a seventeen-year-old girl named Barbary, spent the war years in France, where she witnessed or was touched by a host of brutalities, including her stepfather's murder by Resistance fighters who believed, wrongly, that he collaborated regularly with the Nazis. After the war, Barbary moves to London to live with her father, a wealthy barrister. She studies art and tries to start a more ordered life. As Macaulay repeatedly emphasizes, however, the ruins of war still dominate London: Blocks and blocks of buildings have been shattered, and so have innumerable lives. Thus, Barbary and her brother Raoul eventually fall in with a group of young Londoners who have been similarly affected by the recent violence and chaos and who spend their days wandering around in the city's many ruins, their energies focused on petty crime. During the war, Macaulay's small flat was itself destroyed by German bombs; she lost all of her letters, manuscripts, and books. Certainly, much of her sense of loss and despair informs *The World My Wilderness*.

The Towers of Trebizond, Macaulay's final novel, begins with the delightful and arresting words, "Take my camel, dear." This work—which is set principally in Turkey, along the Mediterranean coast—seems at first glance to be an outrageous and funny farce in the manner of *Going Abroad*. For example, one of its main characters, the camel-riding Aunt Dot, is immediately recognizable as yet another of Macaulay's eccentric—and harmless—fanatics. Her goal is to spread single-handedly the doctrine of female emancipation throughout Islamic Turkey, while along the way bringing wayward Moslems into the Anglican fold. She is accompanied on her trip by a priggish, relic-scavenging and very High Church priest, and by a niece, Laurie, who relates the novel's action.

Like many of Macaulay's earlier novels, *The Towers of Trebizond* pokes gentle, rather affectionate fun at zealous churchgoers. Like many of her novels, it displays a subtle, complex, and rhythmical prose style that sometimes dazes and more frequently dazzles. Laurie, its narrator, is certainly very much in keeping with Macaulay's earlier central figures. She is witty, intelligent, and widely read. In the final analysis, Laurie's observations on many serious matters give *The Towers of Trebizond* a far less farcical tone than *Going Abroad*. Indeed, Laurie—Macaulay's last heroine—is, perhaps appropriately, her most autobiographical. She not only freely expresses a mixture of guilt and joy at having maintained a long and intimate relationship with a married man, but—like Macaulay after Gerald O'Donovan's death—she repeatedly reveals a deep desire to return to the Church which she denied for so many years. Even more revealing, however, is her zest for life. Like Macaulay, Laurie has read and traveled and carefully observed because, as she points out,

> life, for all its agonies of despair and loss and guilt, is exciting and beautiful, amusing and artful and endearing, full of liking and of love, at times a poem and a high adventure, at times very gay; and whatever (if anything) is to come after it, we shall not have this life again.

Other major works

POETRY: *The Two Blind Countries*, 1914; *Three Days*, 1919.

NONFICTION: *Some Religious Elements in English Literature*, 1931; *Milton*, 1934, revised 1957; *The Writings of E. M. Forster*, 1938; *They Went to Portugal*, 1946; *Fabled Shore: From the Pyrenees to Portugal*, 1949; *Pleasure of Ruins*, 1953; *Letters to a Friend, 1950-1952*, 1961; *Letters to a Friend, 1952-1958*, 1962.

Bibliography

Bensen, Alice R. *Rose Macaulay*, 1969.

Fromm, Gloria G. "The Worldly and Unworldly Fortunes of Rose Macaulay," in *The New Criterion*. V (October, 1986), pp. 38-44.

Smith, Constance Babington. *Rose Macaulay: A Biography*, 1972.

Brian Murray

CORMAC McCARTHY

Born: Providence, Rhode Island; July 20, 1933

Principal long fiction

The Orchard Keeper, 1965; *Outer Dark*, 1968; *Child of God*, 1974; *Suttree*, 1979; *Blood Meridian: Or, The Evening Redness in the West*, 1985.

Other literary forms

Cormac McCarthy is almost exclusively a writer of novels. Short excerpts from his novels in progress have sometimes appeared in such literary magazines as *Yale Review*, *Sewanee Review*, and *TriQuarterly*. He also wrote the script for *The Gardener's Son*, a teleplay in the "Visions" series shown on national public television. First broadcast in January, 1977, the drama is based on an actual murder in 1876 in Graniteville, South Carolina. In a story full of dark implications, crippled Rob McEvoy, son of a poor working family, kills the son of the local textiles mill owner. The teleplay's director, Richard Pearce, recruited McCarthy to write the script.

Achievements

Few writers have received such critical acclaim as McCarthy without also gaining wide popularity. He has consistently been praised for his carefully crafted work, his unflinching, dark vision, his immense range of vocabulary, and his powers of observation and description. These qualities have also won for him rich recognition in the form of prizes and grants. *The Orchard Keeper* won the 1965 William Faulkner Foundation Award as the best first novel by an American writer and helped win for McCarthy an American Academy of Arts and Letters traveling fellowship to Europe in 1965-1966. The following years, as more of McCarthy's work appeared, brought him grants from the Rockefeller, Guggenheim, Lyndhurst, and MacArthur foundations. McCarthy has been compared to Faulkner, Edgar Allan Poe, and Mark Twain.

The same qualities in McCarthy that have been praised have also been the cause of criticism and help to explain why he has not been more popular. He writes slowly, having taken at least twenty years to produce his first five books; thus, McCarthy seems to fade from the public eye between books. His subjects—killings, incest, necrophilia, Knoxville lowlife, and scalp-hunting Western marauders—may repel some readers, and others may find his dark vision too unrelenting and morbid. Finally, his tendencies to ransack the dictionary for unusual words and to describe his dripping horrors in overwritten prose make him sound occasionally like gothic writer H. P. Lovecraft.

McCarthy has, however, continued to develop as a novelist. Despite the recognized high quality of his first three works, as exemplified by the praises and prizes given his very first novel, there is evidence that these works are derivative, that McCarthy was assimilating various influences as he wrote them. Although McCarthy continued to assimilate influences as he wrote *Suttree* and *Blood Meridian*, he also seemed to find his own voice in these novels, which are undoubtedly his best. McCarthy's control of his description has improved as his settings have widened, and his thematic perspective has widened with his settings. At first, pigeonholing critics thought McCarthy an East Tennessee regionalist, and then a Southern gothic, but *Blood Meridian* is a dark Western with hints about Western civilization itself. These terms illustrate the dangers of labeling a developing writer, but they also suggest the continuity, progression, and extent of McCarthy's development. His original gifts and his ability to grow make McCarthy a formidable writer who has yet to be fully recognized.

Biography

Cormac McCarthy is the product of a middle-class Catholic family—about as far as one can get from the background of most of his characters (with the notable exception of Suttree). He was born in Providence, Rhode Island, in 1933. When McCarthy was four, his family moved to the Knoxville, Tennessee, area, where his father was chief legal counsel to the Tennessee Valley Authority (TVA). There, McCarthy grew up, attending parochial school, Catholic High School, and the University of Tennessee. He dropped out of the university after one year, traveled for a year, and then joined the United States Air Force, in which he served for four years. Afterward, he attended the University of Tennessee for three more years but finally left in 1959 without getting a degree.

McCarthy did discover his writing vocation at the University of Tennessee, where he began work on a novel. After the publication of *The Orchard Keeper*, he traveled in Europe for three years, living in London, Paris, and on the Spanish island of Ibiza. While in Europe, he married Anne de Lisle of Hamble, England. Later, they lived on a small farm in Rockford, Tennessee, just outside Knoxville. McCarthy moved to El Paso, Texas, during the time he was writing *Blood Meridian*.

As *Blood Meridian* and his East Tennessee novels show, McCarthy is influenced by the landscape around him and is good at absorbing local talk, color, and tradition. Whether he was more directly influenced by his father's work with the TVA is an interesting question. For many families who had been living in the mountain valleys for generations, the TVA was their first contact with big government—a traumatic one that has still not been forgiven. The permanent flooding of their land by TVA projects, despite "compensation," resulted in massive dislocations within the traditional mountain culture. One of the more gruesome aspects was transferring the contents of cemeteries to higher ground—a scene of the restless dead that seems to be echoed repeatedly in McCarthy's work, as is the theme of the government's bringing of change.

Analysis

Like British Catholic writer Graham Greene, Cormac McCarthy is reluctant to develop any optimistic themes. He is also reluctant about stating his themes, although some of his titles offer strong hints. For the most part, he merely tells his stories and leaves it up to the reader to interpret their meanings. As a result, one critic has judged McCarthy to be nihilistic, but surely this judgment is incorrect. McCarthy's reluctance to preach about the good news masks a profoundly moral sensibility that is forced to face the worst in human nature and to recognize the power of evil. In this way, his novels are comparable to the medieval morality play or to such films by Ingmar Bergman as *Det sjunde inseglet* (1956; *The Seventh Seal*, 1958).

There is also a softer, more modern side to McCarthy's morality. Few writers identify so thoroughly with people beyond the pale—the poor, the homeless and dispossessed, the criminal and degenerate, the outcasts. He manages to find some humanity even in the worst of these and to ascribe their conditions partly to contingency, bad luck, or the operations of respectable society. Their nemesis (besides themselves) is often the law and its officers, who, for them, become additional embodiments of the death and destruction that pursue everyone. McCarthy's refusal to avert his sympathies from the outcasts thus raises some complex social and theological issues.

McCarthy's first novel, *The Orchard Keeper*, introduces the outcasts as members of the disappearing mountain culture of East Tennessee. Young Marion Sylder lives by bootlegging, and in self-defense he kills a man and disposes of the body in an abandoned peach orchard that symbolizes the dying culture. Old Arthur Ownby, who fondly watches over the orchard, finds the body, but he does not report it. He lets it rest in peace for seven years. The old man also believes in his own peace and privacy, and when these are disturbed by a government holding tank erected on a nearby hill, he shoots his *X* on the tank's side. Both the men live by old mountain codes which, by definition, are outside the law of the intruding modern world. Yet the enforcers of the law, who finally arrest and beat Sylder and send the old man to a mental institution, seem degenerate in comparison to them. The novel's theme is also represented in John Wesley Rattner (ironically, the son of the dead man), a boy who hunts and traps, is befriended by the two men, and comes of age in the novel. He decides to cast his loyalties with the old ways even if they have become anachronistic.

The episodic converging stories and italicized flashbacks of *The Orchard Keeper* recall Faulkner's narrative techniques, and McCarthy's second novel,

Outer Dark; also owes a debt to Faulkner. The novel takes place in some vaguely Deep South setting early in the twentieth century and deals with the horrible consequences of incest between Culla and Rinthy Holme, brother and sister. Rinthy delivers a baby boy, and Culla abandons it in the woods, where a passing tinker finds and takes it. Culla tells Rinthy that the baby died, but Rinthy digs up the shallow grave, discovers his lie, and intuitively goes in search of the tinker. Culla goes after Rinthy to bring her back. Their wanderings on the roads recall those of Lena Grove and Joe Christmas in Faulkner's *Light in August* (1932). Everyone she encounters befriends Rinthy, who moves along dripping mother's milk for over six months, but Culla meets nothing except suspicion and trouble. These episodes also recall the journey down the river in Mark Twain's *The Adventures of Huckleberry Finn* (1884), particularly a wild incident in which a loose ferry is swept down a raging river.

McCarthy's most original and unforgettable creation in *Outer Dark* is a set of three avenging angels, or devils, who rove about the landscape murdering people. On a realistic level, they are lawless, asocial drifters who have gone totally beyond the pale into the "outer dark." They have lost all caring. Appropriately, Culla meets this unholy trio of blood brothers near the novel's end. The three hang the tinker and dispose of the baby (now symbolically scarred as in a Nathaniel Hawthorne story) before Culla's eyes: One slits the baby's throat and another sucks its blood.

If *Outer Dark* does not contain horror enough, McCarthy followed it with *Child of God*, which returns to a rural East Tennessee setting. Here, mountain man Lester Ballard loses his farm for failure to pay taxes; embittered and alone, he sinks gradually into necrophilia and then murder. His degeneration is marked by movement from the farm to an abandoned shack that burns to a cave where he stores his supply of dead women. He is finally captured, dies in a state mental hospital, and is dissected in a medical laboratory. His neighbors, whose choruslike, folksy comments are interspersed throughout the story, always thought him a bit strange, with bad blood. McCarthy suggests that all Lester ever needed, however, was a home and love. Lester was only "a child of God much like yourself perhaps."

A short, tightly unified work, *Child of God* contrasts with McCarthy's next novel, *Suttree*, usually considered his masterpiece. *Suttree* displays the variety and range of McCarthy's talent. Set in Knoxville during the 1950's, the novel is a long, rambling work rich in incident, character, language, and mood, including some surprisingly amusing, bawdy humor. Yet *Suttree* has certain features in common with *Child of God*. Misery and unhappiness also predominate here, and instead of one child of God, *Suttree* has hundreds— drunks, prostitutes, perverts, petty criminals, and the poor generally, black and white—all dumped together in a slum known as McAnally Flats. The characters have such names as Gatemouth, Worm, Hoghead, and Trippin

Through The Dew, and their dialogue is spiced with slang and expletives.

The central character is Cornelius "Buddy" Suttree, scion of a prominent local family. He has deliberately chosen to live in this slum on a houseboat moored in the Tennessee River, from whose filthy waters he catches a few carp and catfish to sell. Why he has made this strange choice gradually becomes clear. On the one hand, he has made a mess of his life. He and his parents are no longer on speaking terms, and his wife left him long ago, taking their child (who dies in the novel). Suttree sank to drink and served a term in the prison workhouse. Now he lives in McAnally Flats because, on the other hand, he feels at home there. There, he can find the company of like-minded, fun-loving pals who can help him pass the time and avoid involvement in the pain of life. There he sits, the fisher king in his wasteland, and with dread and longing he awaits the oblivion of death.

A happy flaw in Suttree's character, however, prevents his nihilistic scheme from taking effect: compassion. He cannot avoid feeling compassion for the people around him, such as the ignorant but irrepressible Gene Harrogate, a country boy who serves a term in the workhouse for having sex with a farmer's watermelons and who dynamites the city's sewer system down on himself trying to rob a bank (the "country mouse," as he is first called, soon becomes the "city rat"). Further involvement with people leads to further pain for Suttree—a girl he falls in love with is killed, his long affair with a rich prostitute breaks up, and most of his pals are killed or imprisoned. Deeper emotional commitment on Suttree's part, however, might have saved both the girl and the affair with the prostitute. After a solitary retreat to the Great Smoky Mountains and a near-fatal illness, Suttree decides to embrace life—pain and all—and to leave Knoxville. He leaves just as the McAnally Flats are being torn down to make room for an expressway. His parting words of advice concern the hounds of death: "Fly them."

McCarthy's fifth book, *Blood Meridian*, is a historical novel set in the American Southwest and northern Mexico around the middle of the nineteenth century. The novel's protagonist is a nameless character known only as "the kid" (with suggested parallels perhaps to Billy the Kid), who runs away from his Tennessee home when he is fourteen and heads west. His story might be that of Huck Finn after Huck "lit out for the territory" and left civilization behind. After repeated scrapes, always moving west, the kid joins a band of scalping bounty hunters who hunt the Apaches when the Apaches are not hunting them. The massacres go on endlessly, all duly noted in the running summaries that head each chapter.

In some ways, *Blood Meridian* provides a useful retrospective view of McCarthy's work. It returns to the horrors of his earlier novels but seems to relate these to the social themes of *Suttree*. The scalp hunters are, after all, the advance guard of Western civilization. They suggest a terrible moral ambiguity at the heart of civilization, as in the hearts of individuals, that enables it to stamp out Apaches and backward mountaineers and to create such slums as McAnally Flats. Judge Holden, the repulsive and evil philosopher of *Blood Meridian*, argues that God made man thus, that morality is irrelevant, and that superior violence shall triumph. The naked judge finally embraces the kid with an apparent death hug inside a jakes behind a whorehouse in Fort Griffin, Texas. Readers can probably find a warning in this to flee such philosophers.

Other major work
TELEPLAY: *The Gardener's Son*, 1977.

Bibliography
Cox, Dianne L. "Cormac McCarthy," in *Dictionary of Literary Biography*. 2d series, vol. 6, *American Novelists since World War II*, 1980. Edited by James E. Kibler, Jr.
Longley, John Lewis, Jr. "Suttree and the Metaphysics of Death," in *The Southern Literary Journal*. XVII (Spring, 1985), pp. 79-90.
Schafer, William J. "Cormac McCarthy: The Hard Wages of Original Sin," in *Appalachian Journal*. IV (Winter, 1977), pp. 105-119.

Harold Branam

ROSS MACDONALD
Kenneth Millar

Born: Los Gatos, California; December 13, 1915
Died: Santa Barbara, California; July 11, 1983

Principal long fiction
The Dark Tunnel, 1944 (as Kenneth Millar; British edition, *I Die Slowly*, 1955); *Trouble Follows Me*, 1946 (as Millar; British edition, *Night Train*, 1955); *Blue City*, 1947 (as Millar); *The Three Roads*, 1948 (as Millar); *The Moving Target*, 1949 (as John Ross Macdonald; reissued as *Harper*, 1966); *The Drowning Pool*, 1950 (as John Ross Macdonald); *The Way Some People Die*, 1951 (as John Ross Macdonald); *The Ivory Grin*, 1952 (as John Ross Macdonald; reissued as *Marked for Murder*, 1953); *Meet Me at the Morgue*, 1953 (as John Ross Macdonald; British edition, *Experience with Evil*, 1954); *Find a Victim*, 1954 (as John Ross Macdonald); *The Barbarous Coast*, 1956; *The Doomsters*, 1958; *The Galton Case*, 1959; *The Ferguson Affair*, 1960; *The Wycherly Woman*, 1961; *The Zebra-Striped Hearse*, 1962; *The Chill*, 1964; *The Far Side of the Dollar*, 1965; *Black Money*, 1966; *The Instant Enemy*, 1968; *The Goodbye Look*, 1969; *The Underground Man*, 1971; *Sleeping Beauty*, 1973; *The Blue Hammer*, 1976.

Other literary forms
Ross Macdonald's reputation is based primarily on his twenty-four published novels, particularly on the eighteen which feature private detective Lew Archer. He also published a collection of short stories, *Lew Archer, Private Investigator* (1977), which includes all the stories from an earlier collection, *The Name Is Archer* (1955). *Self-Portrait: Ceaselessly into the Past* (1981) gathers a selection of his essays, interviews, and lectures about his own work and about other writers, including two essays first published in his *On Crime Writing* (1973). Macdonald edited a collection of short stories, *Great Stories of Suspense* (1974). He also wrote dozens of book reviews and several articles on conservation and politics.

Achievements
Macdonald was recognized early in his career to be the successor to Dashiell Hammett and Raymond Chandler in the field of realistic crime fiction, and his detective, Lew Archer, was recognized to be the successor to Sam Spade and Philip Marlowe. Macdonald's advance over his predecessors was in the greater emphasis he placed on psychology and character, creating a more humane and complex detective and more intricate plotting. He is generally credited with raising the detective novel to the level of serious literature. The Mystery Writers of America awarded him Edgar Allan Poe

scrolls in 1962 and 1963. In 1964, *The Chill* was awarded the Silver Dagger by the Crime Writers' Association of Great Britain. The same organization gave his next novel, *The Far Side of the Dollar*, the Golden Dagger as the best crime novel of the year. Macdonald served as president of the Mystery Writers of America in 1965 and was made a Grand Master of that organization in 1974. In a review of *The Goodbye Look* in *The New York Times Book Review*, William Goldman called the Lew Archer books "the finest series of detective novels ever written by an American." His work has gained popular as well as critical acclaim: *The Goodbye Look*, *The Underground Man*, *Sleeping Beauty*, and *The Blue Hammer* were all national best-sellers. Three of his books have been made into successful motion pictures, two starring Paul Newman as Lew Archer: *The Moving Target* was made into the film *Harper* (1966) and *The Drowning Pool* was filmed in 1975. *The Three Roads* was filmed as *Double Negative* in 1979.

Biography

Ross Macdonald, whose real name is Kenneth Millar, was born in Los Gatos, California, on December 13, 1915. He published his early novels as Kenneth Millar or as John (or John Ross) Macdonald, but settled on the pseudonym Ross Macdonald by the time he wrote *The Barbarous Coast*, in order to avoid being confused with two other famous mystery writers: his wife, Margaret Millar, whom he had married in 1938, and John D. Macdonald. His family moved to Vancouver, British Columbia, soon after he was born, and he was reared and educated in Canada. After he was graduated with honors from the University of Western Ontario in 1938, he taught English and history at a high school in Toronto and began graduate work at the University of Michigan in Ann Arbor during the summers. He returned to the United States permanently in 1941, when he began full-time graduate studies at Ann Arbor, receiving his M.A. in English in 1943. During World War II, he served as communications officer aboard an escort carrier in the Pacific and participated in the battle for Okinawa. In 1951, he was awarded a Ph.D. in English from the University of Michigan, writing his dissertation on the psychological criticism of Samuel Taylor Coleridge. Macdonald belonged to the American Civil Liberties Union and, a dedicated conservationist, was a member of the Sierra Club and helped found the Santa Barbara chapter of the National Audubon Society. He lived in Santa Barbara, California, from 1946 until his death there of Alzheimer's disease on July 11, 1983.

Analysis

Ross Macdonald's twenty-four novels fall fairly neatly into three groups: Those in which Lew Archer does not appear form a distinct group, and the Archer series itself may be separated into two periods. His first four books, *The Dark Tunnel*, *Trouble Follows Me*, *Blue City*, and *The Three Roads*, together with two later works, *Meet Me at the Morgue* and *The Ferguson Affair*, do not feature Lew Archer. These six novels, especially the first three, are rather typical treatments of wartime espionage or political corruption and are primarily of interest to the extent that they prefigure the concerns of later works: *The Three Roads*, for example, is Macdonald's first explicit use of the Oedipus myth as a plot structure and of California as a setting.

The first six Archer books, *The Moving Target, The Drowning Pool, The Way Some People Die, The Ivory Grin, Find a Victim,* and *The Barbarous Coast,* introduce and refine the character of Archer, build the society and geography of California into important thematic elements, and feature increasingly complex plots, with multiple murders and plot lines. Archer still shows traces of the influence of the hard-boiled detectives of Hammett and Chandler (he is named after Miles Archer, Sam Spade's partner in Hammett's *The Maltese Falcon,* 1930, but closely patterned after Philip Marlowe), but he also shows marks of the sensitivity and patience, the reliance on understanding and analysis, that separate him from his models. Even in these early books, Archer is more often a questioner than a doer.

The next twelve Archer novels constitute Macdonald's major achievement. Crimes in these books are not usually committed by professional criminals but rather by middle-class people going through emotional crises. They followed a period of personal crisis in Macdonald's own life, during which he underwent psychotherapy; all these novels deal more or less explicitly with psychological issues. *The Doomsters,* although begun before his psychoanalysis, presents his first extended treatment of the plot of intrafamilial relations that dominates all the later books. Carl Hallman, a psychologically disturbed young man, appears at Archer's door after escaping from the state mental hospital. He has been confined there as a murder suspect in the mysterious death of his father. Although he knows himself to be legally innocent, he feels guilty for having quarreled violently with his father on the night of his death. This Oedipal tension between father and son, following the pattern of Sigmund Freud's famous interpretation, often serves as the mainspring of the plot in Macdonald's later novels. After hiring Archer to investigate the death, Carl panics and escapes again as Archer is returning him to the hospital. Carl's brother, Jerry, and sister-in-law, Zinnie, are subsequently murdered under circumstances which appear to incriminate Carl.

As it turns out, the case really began three years earlier, with the death by drowning, apparently accidental, of Carl's mother, Alicia. She had forced Carl's wife, Mildred, to undergo an abortion at gunpoint at the hands of Dr. Grantland. Mildred hit Alicia over the head with a bottle when she came out of anesthesia and assumed that she had killed her. Dr. Grantland actually killed Alicia and made it look like drowning, but he conceals this fact and uses his power over Mildred, who is becoming psychologically unstable, to persuade her to kill Carl's father. He has designs on the family's money and

Mildred is greedy herself. She is also influenced, however, by her hatred of her own father, who deserted her mother, and by her desire to possess Carl entirely, to gain his love for herself by eliminating conflicting familial claims to it. She murders his brother and sister-in-law, his only remaining family, as she increasingly loses touch with sanity. Women are frequently the murderers in Macdonald's books, and he analyzed the reasons behind this in an interview. He considered that people who have been victims tend to victimize others in turn, and he regarded American society as one which systematically victimizes women. Mildred's difficult childhood and gunpoint abortion provide a clear illustration of this theme.

While the focus on family psychology constituted a clean break with the Hammett and Chandler school as well as with most of his own early work, the next Archer novel, *The Galton Case*, was of even greater importance for Macdonald's career. In *The Doomsters*, the case is rooted in a crime committed three years earlier; in *The Galton Case*, as in most of the novels to follow, the present crime is rooted deeper in the past, in the preceding generation. This gives Macdonald the means to show the long-term effects of the influence of the family upon each of its members. The elderly Maria Galton hires Archer to trace her son Anthony, who had stolen money from his father after a quarrel (reminiscent of that between Carl Hallman and his father) and run off to the San Francisco area with his pregnant wife, Teddy, twenty-three years before. Archer discovers that Anthony, calling himself John Brown, was murdered not long after his disappearance. He also finds a young man calling himself John Brown, Jr., who claims to be searching for his long-lost father. Events lead Archer to Canada, where he learns that the young man is Theo Fredericks, the son of Nelson Fredericks and his wife. Mrs. Galton's lawyer, Gordon Sable, has planned Theo's masquerade as her grandson to acquire her money when she dies. Yet a further plot twist reveals that Theo really is Anthony Galton's son. Fred Nelson had murdered Anthony twenty-three years before for the money he had stolen from his father and had taken Anthony's wife and son as his own under the name Fredericks.

This summary does not reflect the true complexity of the novel, which ties together a number of other elements, but does bring out the major theme of the son searching for his father, a theme which will recur in later works such as *The Far Side of the Dollar*, *The Instant Enemy*, *The Goodbye Look*, *The Underground Man*, and *The Blue Hammer*. As Macdonald explains in his essay "Writing *The Galton Case*" (1973), this plot is roughly shaped on his own life. His own father left him and his mother when he was three years old. Like Macdonald, John Brown, Jr., was born in California, grew up in Canada, and attended the University of Michigan before returning to California. It is interesting that each man assumed his lost father's name: Macdonald was Kenneth Millar's father's middle name. This transformation of personal family history into fiction seems to have facilitated the break-

through that led him to write the rest of his novels about varying permuta-
tions of the relations between parents and children.

The exploration of the relations between three generations of fathers and
sons in *The Galton Case* was followed by examinations of father and daughter relationships in *The Wycherly Woman* and *The Zebra-Striped Hearse*.
Macdonald always counted the latter among his favorites for its intensity and
range. In *The Zebra-Striped Hearse*, Archer is hired by Mark Blackwell to
investigate his daughter Harriet's fiancé, Burke Damis, with a view to
preventing their marriage. The implication is made that Mark sees Damis as
a rival for his daughter's love. Archer discovers that Damis is really Bruce
Campion and is suspected of having murdered his wife, Dolly, and another
man, Quincy Ralph Simpson. Suspicion shifts to Mark when it is revealed
that he is the father of Dolly's baby and then to Mark's wife, Isobel, who
knew Dolly as a child. Harriet disappears and Mark confesses to murdering
her, Dolly, and Simpson before committing suicide. Yet Archer believes that
Harriet is still alive and tracks her down in Mexico. She had killed Dolly to
clear the way for her marriage to Bruce and had also killed Simpson when he
discovered her crime. Underlying her motive for Dolly's murder, however, is
another Freudian pattern. The child of Mark and Dolly is Harriet's half
brother, making Dolly a sort of mother figure and, by extension, making her
husband, Bruce, a sort of father figure. Harriet thus symbolically kills her
mother and marries her father.

The Chill features one of Macdonald's most complex plots, but at its center
is another basic family relationship, this time between a mother and son. Archer is brought into the case by Alex Kincaid, who hires him to find his wife,
Dolly, who has disappeared the day after their wedding after a visit from an
unknown man. The visitor turns out to have been her father, Thomas
McGee, who has just been released from prison after serving a ten-year sentence for the murder of his wife and Dolly's mother, Constance. Later it is
revealed that he had convinced her of his innocence and told her that Constance was having an affair with Roy Bradshaw. To learn more about Roy,
Dolly has left Alex to go to work for Roy's mother, Mrs. Bradshaw, as a
driver and companion. Shortly thereafter, she is found, hysterical, at the
Bradshaws', talking about the murder of her college counselor, Helen
Haggerty. Helen is soon discovered murdered and the weapon used is found
under Dolly's mattress, though under circumstances that suggest that it may
have been planted there. Archer learns from Helen's mother that she had
been deeply affected by a death that occurred twenty years before. Luke
Deloney had been killed in a shooting that was ruled accidental on the basis
of an investigation that was conducted by Helen's father, but Helen was convinced that the facts had been covered up. Luke's widow admits to Archer
that there had been a cover-up, that her husband committed suicide. Archer
later discovers another connection between the recent death and those of ten

and twenty years ago: Roy Bradshaw was the elevator boy at the building in which Deloney died.

Investigation of Roy reveals that he has been secretly married to Laura Sutherland, having recently obtained a divorce from a woman named Letitia Macready. Archer confronts Mrs. Bradshaw with the latter fact (though not the former), and after an initial denial she confirms that twenty years ago Roy had briefly been married to a much older woman. Letitia turns out to have been the sister of Luke's wife, and it was rumored that she was having an affair with her sister's husband. Letitia apparently died in Europe during World War II, shortly after Luke's death. Archer eventually draws a fuller story out of Roy: Deloney, who was indeed Letitia's lover, found her in bed with Roy. There had been a violent struggle, during which Letitia accidentally shot and killed Luke. Roy married her and took her to Europe, later returning with her to America. He had been leading a secret double life ever since, concealing Letitia, now quite old and sick, from all of his friends as well as from the police and, especially, from his possessive mother. During this confession, Archer answers a telephone call and hears Laura, who believes that she is speaking to Roy, tell him that "she" has discovered their secret marriage. Roy attacks Archer at this news and escapes in his car to attempt to intercept the other woman, who had vowed to kill Laura. Roy is killed when Mrs. Bradshaw's car crashes into his. Archer knows by now that Mrs. Bradshaw is not Roy's mother, but his first wife: She is Letitia Macready. Roy has acted out the Oedipal drama of the death of a father figure, Letitia's lover Luke, and the marriage to a mother figure, the older woman who posed as his real mother. (Macdonald develops the obverse of this plot in *Black Money*, which pairs a young woman with a much older man.) Letitia murdered Constance McGee because Roy had been having an affair with her and murdered Helen Haggerty in the belief that it was she rather than Laura Sutherland whom Roy was currently seeing.

This unraveling of the plot has come a long way from Alex Kincaid's request that Archer find his wife, but one of the characteristics of Macdonald's later novels is the way in which seemingly unrelated events and characters come together. The deeper Archer goes into a set of circumstances involving people who know one another, the more connectedness he finds. These novels all have large casts of characters and a series of crimes, often occurring decades apart. Once the proper connections are made, however, there is usually only one murderer and one fundamental relationship at the center of the plot. All the disparate elements, past and present, hang together in one piece.

While Freudian themes continued to dominate Macdonald's work, he often combined them with elements adapted from other stories from classical mythology or the Bible. *The Far Side of the Dollar* has been seen as a modern, inverted version of the story of Ulysses and Penelope. Jasper Blevins, the fratricidal murderer of *The Instant Enemy*, explicitly draws the analogy between his story and that of Cain and Abel. He has also murdered one of his stepfathers, adding the Oedipal masterplot to the biblical plot, and murdered his own wife in one of the series' most violent books, perhaps reflecting the violence of the wartime period during which the book was written. The complex events of *The Goodbye Look* are catalyzed by the search for a gold box which is specifically compared to Pandora's box. Again the myth is combined with the primal story of the parricide, this time committed by a child. All three of these books also repeat the quintessential Macdonald plot of a young man's search for his missing father.

The search for the absent father also sets in motion the events of *The Underground Man*, probably the most admired of Macdonald's works. This novel, together with his next, *Sleeping Beauty*, also reflects its author's abiding concern with conservation. Each novel examines an ecological crime as well as a series of crimes committed against individuals. In *Sleeping Beauty*, Macdonald uses an offshore oil spill, inspired by the 1967 spill near his home in Santa Barbara, as a symbol of the moral life of the society responsible for it, in particular that of the Lennox family, which runs the oil corporation and is also the locus of the series of murders in the book. In *The Underground Man*, the disaster of a man-made forest fire serves similar ends. The story begins unexceptionally: Archer is taking a day off at home, feeding the birds in his yard. He strikes up an acquaintance with young Ronny Broadhurst and Ronny's mother, Jean, who are staying at the home of Archer's neighbors. The boy's father, Stanley, disrupts the meeting when he drives up with a young girl, later identified as Sue Crandall, and takes his son to visit Stanley's mother, Elizabeth Broadhurst. They never pay the planned visit, and when Jean hears that a fire has broken out in that area, she enlists Archer to help her look for them. On the way there, Jean explains that her husband has gradually become obsessed by his search for his father, Leo, who apparently ran away with Ellen Kilpatrick, the wife of a neighbor, Brian, some fifteen years ago. It turns out that Stanley, accompanied by Ronny and Sue, obtained a key from Elizabeth's gardener, Fritz Snow, and had gone up to her cabin on a mountain nearby. There, Archer finds Stanley, murdered and half-buried. The fire originated from a cigarillo Stanley dropped when he was killed, creating a causal as well as symbolic link between the personal and ecological disasters.

After an investigation that is complex even by Macdonald's standards, Archer is able to reconstruct the past events that explain those of the present. The seeds of the present crimes are found in the previous generation. Eighteen years ago, Leo Broadhurst got Martha Nickerson, an underage girl, pregnant. She ran away with Fritz Snow and Al Sweetner in a car they stole from Lester Crandall. The incident was planned by Leo and Martha to provide a scapegoat to assume the paternity of her coming child. When they were tracked down, Al went to jail for three years, Fritz was sentenced to work in a forestry camp for six months, and Martha married Lester Crandall. Three years later, Leo was having an affair with Ellen Kilpatrick. She went to Reno to obtain a divorce from her husband, Brian, and waited there for Leo to join her. While she was gone, however, Leo went up to the cabin with Martha and their child, Sue. Brian, who knew about his wife's affair with Leo and wanted revenge, discovered the renewal of this earlier affair and informed Leo's wife, Elizabeth. She went up to the mountain cabin and shot her husband, believing that she killed him. Stanley, who had followed his mother that night, was an aural witness to the shooting of his father, as was Susan, also Leo's child. Yet Leo had not been killed by the bullet. He was stabbed to death, as he lay unconscious, by Edna Snow, Fritz's mother, in revenge for the trouble that Leo and Martha's affair had caused her son and also as a self-appointed agent of judgment on Leo's adulteries. She forced Fritz and Al to bury Leo near the cabin. Fifteen years later, on almost the same spot, she murders Stanley, who is on the verge of discovering his father's body and Edna's crime. Life moves in a circle as Ronny witnesses Stanley's death in the same place that Stanley witnessed Leo's shooting. The connection is reinforced by Sue's presence at both events.

The last novel Macdonald wrote is *The Blue Hammer*, and whether he consciously intended it to be the last, it provides in certain ways an appropriate conclusion to the series. It is the first time, apart from a brief interlude in *The Goodbye Look*, that Archer has a romantic interest. The effects of a lack of love preoccupy all the Archer novels, and Archer recognizes in this book that the same lack has had its effects on him. He has been single since his divorce from his wife, Sue, which took place before the first book begins. In the last book, he meets and soon falls in love with Betty Jo Siddon, a young newspaper reporter. Yet Macdonald knew that Raymond Chandler was unable to continue the Philip Marlowe novels after marrying off his detective, and perhaps he intended to end his own series similarly. It seems that the genre requires a detective who is himself without personal ties, who is able to and perhaps driven to move freely into and then out of the lives of others. Indeed, the involvement of Betty in the case does create a tension between Archer's personal and professional interests. Another suggestion that *The Blue Hammer* may have been intended to be the last of the Archer novels lies in its symmetry with the first, *The Moving Target*. In the earlier book, Archer kills a man in a struggle in the ocean, the only such occurrence in the eighteen books and an indication of the extent to which the compassionate Archer differs from his more violent predecessors. In the last book, he finds himself in a similar struggle, but this time manages to save his adversary. Archer specifically parallels the two events and feels that he has balanced out his earlier sin, somehow completing a pattern.

The plot of *The Blue Hammer* is built around the Dostoevskian theme of the double, a theme that Macdonald treated before in *The Wycherly Woman*, in which Phoebe Wycherly assumes the identity of her murdered mother, and in *The Instant Enemy*, in which Jasper Blevins takes on the role of his murdered half brother. The motif is developed here in its most elaborate form and combined with the familiar themes of the crimes of the past shaping those of the present and of the son's search for his true father, forming an appropriate summation of the major themes of MacDonald's entire Archer series.

Thirty-two years ago, Richard Chantry stole the paintings of his supposed half brother, William Mead, then serving in the army, and married William's girlfriend Francine. William murdered Richard when he returned and assumed his identity as Francine's husband, though he had already married a woman named Sarah and had a son, Fred, by her. Seven years later, Gerard Johnson, a friend of William from the army, appears at William's door with Sarah and Fred, threatening to blackmail him. William kills Gerard and then takes his name, in a doubling of the theme of doubleness. He returns to live with Sarah and Fred and remains a recluse for twenty-five years to hide his crimes.

The case begins for Archer when he is called in to locate a painting which has been stolen from Jack Biemeyer. He learns that it was taken by Fred Johnson, who wanted to study it to determine whether it was a recent work by the famous artist Richard Chantry, who had mysteriously vanished twenty-five years before. If genuine, it would establish that the painter was still alive. Fred had seen similar pictures in the Johnson home and had formed the idea that Chantry might be his real father. William steals the painting, which is one of his own works, in a doubling of his earlier theft of his own paintings from Richard. The painting had been sold by Sarah to an art dealer, and William is forced to kill again to prevent the discovery of his true identity and his earlier murders. By the book's guardedly positive resolution, three generations of men—Fred Johnson; his father, William Mead; and Jack Biemeyer, who turns out to be William's father—have all come to the admission or recognition of their previously concealed identities and have come to a kind of redemption through their suffering.

Macdonald's work, in terms of quantity as well as quality, constitutes an unparalleled achievement in the detective genre. The twenty-four novels, particularly the eighteen which feature Lew Archer, form a remarkably coherent body of work both stylistically and thematically. The last twelve Archer books have received especially high critical as well as popular acclaim and have secured Macdonald's standing as the author of the finest series of detective novels ever written, perhaps the only such series to have bridged the gap between popular and serious literature.

Other major works

SHORT FICTION: *The Name Is Archer*, 1955; *Lew Archer, Private Investigator*, 1977.

NONFICTION: *On Crime Writing*, 1973; *Self-Portrait: Ceaselessly into the Past*, 1981.

Bibliography

Bruccoli, Matthew J. *Kenneth Millar/Ross Macdonald: A Checklist*, 1971.

_____. *Ross Macdonald/Kenneth Millar: A Descriptive Bibliography*, 1983.

Sipper, Ralph B., ed. *Inward Journey*, 1984.

Sokolov, Raymond A. "The Art of Murder," in *Newsweek*. LXXVII (March 22, 1971), pp. 101-104.

Speir, Jerry. *Ross Macdonald*, 1978.

Wolfe, Peter. *Dreamers Who Live Their Dreams: The World of Ross Macdonald's Novels*, 1976.

William Nelles

JOSEPH McELROY

Born: Brooklyn, New York; August 21, 1930

Principal long fiction

A Smuggler's Bible, 1966; *Hind's Kidnap: A Pastoral on Familiar Airs*, 1969; *Ancient History*, 1971; *Lookout Cartridge*, 1974; *Plus*, 1977; *Ship Rock, a Place: From Women and Men, a Novel in Progress*, 1980; *Women and Men*, 1987.

Other literary forms

Joseph McElroy's reputation stands on his achievements as a novelist. A number of excerpts from his massive novel *Women and Men* first appeared in short-story form; the excellence of three of these pieces ("The Future," "The Message for What It Was Worth," and "Daughter of the Revolution") was acknowledged by their selection for the *O. Henry Prize Stories* and *Best American Short Stories*. In addition, McElroy has published a number of uncollected essays on topics as various as the Apollo 17 launch, the influence on his generation of Vladimir Nabokov's fiction, and autobiographical aspects of his own work. Between 1971 and 1976 he was also a regular reviewer for *The New York Times Book Review*.

Achievements

From the start, McElroy was received as one of the generation of American novelists that includes William Gaddis, Robert Coover, and Thomas Pynchon—writers of long and technically demanding fictions. Among them, McElroy remains the dark star, outshone by their well-publicized brilliance while being acknowledged among his peers as the writer's writer, one who is committed to giving fictional order to a complex "information society" by optimistically recognizing its possibilities for narrative art and human growth. In 1977, McElroy's writing was acclaimed by an Award in Literature from the American Academy of Arts and Letters. Still, the regard of critics has been slow in coming, and reviewers have argued that the complexity of internal reference and detail in McElroy's work is too demanding of the reader. In a 1979 interview, McElroy countered that he continues to "hope . . . for readers who would be willing to commit themselves to a strenuous, adventurous fiction." The reissue of several of McElroy's novels, in addition to blooming scholarly acclaim, suggests that this hope is well placed.

Biography

Joseph Prince McElroy was born in Brooklyn, New York, on August 21, 1930, and has lived near there for most of his life. He received a baccalaureate from Williams College in 1951 and a master of arts degree from Columbia University in 1952. After two years with the United States Coast Guard (1952-1954), he returned to graduate studies at Columbia, completing the Ph.D. in 1962 with a dissertation on seventeenth century poet Henry King. From 1956 to 1961, he held positions as instructor and assistant professor of English at the University of New Hampshire. Since 1964, he has been a full professor of English at Queens College, City University of New York. McElroy has been a visiting professor or a writer-in-residence at a number of major universities, has received a wide range of fellowships and awards, and has served editorial terms on several literary magazines. He continues to make his home in New York City.

Analysis

Joseph McElroy's novels unfold in the topographies of mind. He has called them "neural neighborhoods." Within those imaginary spaces, McElroy's fictions grow from a profound desire for order, for a meaningful landscape of human intentions and actions. Also, they grow from a profound recognition that such orders may be unobtainable amid the fragmenting stresses of advanced machine culture. The point, as his books illustrate, is not to kick against this crux but to set the mind in motion within it, thus to create form and meaning. This precept is the source of both difficulty and great achievement in McElroy's writing.

Not that McElroy's neural landscapes stand apart from ordinary surroundings. Quite the opposite: His novels are saturated with the stuff of contemporary society, with references to and metaphors from urban culture, and from such wide-ranging pursuits as cinematography, information processing, linguistics, and the space program. Richly detailed and technically specific, these familiar endeavors illustrate the fragmentary nature of human knowledge. At the same time they point out unsuspected possibilities for human growth. McElroy's narrator-protagonists are imbued with an almost claustrophobic variety of concise memories and everyday desires. Yet within these mental topographies they are driven to discover order, or "plot," for novels are also "plotted," and it is of the essence of McElroy's novels that the action, the narrators' attempted discoveries, be seen as contemporary variations on the detective plot. They solve no significant enigmas. Not "representations" of events that have been rarefied by memory, McElroy's fictions are instead "demonstrations" of the complexities involved in reconstructing any past event. Inevitably the character's memory involves his own categories of feeling and linguistic mapping, which themselves become objects of scrutiny. The best one can do, suggests McElroy, is to "smuggle" or "kidnap" a perception or idea over the received boundary of some other. By thus learning to manipulate them, one surmounts the inadequacies and paradoxes of human knowledge.

This brief sketch of McElroy's principal concerns will suggest the interests he shares with many modern and contemporary writers. With modernists such as Marcel Proust and André Gide, he is concerned to show both the complexity and the potential illicitness of narratively reconstructed events, which are "counterfeit" creations precisely to the degree that they recognize themselves as ordered rememberings of life's dismembered orderings. With contemporaries such as Michel Butor, William Gaddis, Nicholas Moseley, and Thomas Pynchon, he reflects on the linguistic nature of this narrative activity. Like them, he sees the ability to manipulate hypothetical, alternative structures—for example, the worlds of "stories"—as a condition of social existence, and he reflects on how we too hastily suppose that continuity and causality are absolute requirements of that structuring work.

A Smuggler's Bible was a brilliant first articulation of these themes. By McElroy's own account, this novel was not his first, but developed after several aborted attempts at a rather conventionally sequential, causal type of long narrative. Its title describes the book's main emblem: a "smuggler's Bible" is a hollowed-out volume designed for carrying contraband over borders. Similarly, McElroy's narrative develops by making illicit leaps. Even though its eight parts are essentially disconnected, the reader still "smuggles" bits of information across their boundaries to reconstruct a "story" about its narrator-protagonist, David Brooke. In fact, readers are encouraged in this by another, omniscient narrative voice, which appears in short interchapters. This voice advertises itself as David's "creator" and comments on his task, itself also the reader's, which is to "analyze, synthesize, [and] assimilate" details gleaned by "projecting" oneself into others' experience. This is the task framed by a conventional, "realistic" novel. Yet a smuggler's Bible is also a clever deception: an illegal, profane business tucked inside an authorized, holy cover. In similar ways, David's eightfold story, a kind of experimental writing, can be read as trying, and failing, to disguise itself as an artistically conventional novel replete with causal plot.

The essentials of that inner narrative are as follows. David and his wife, Ellen, are passengers aboard a ship, the *Arkadia*, bound for London. There he must deliver to a mysterious "Old Man" the manuscript of a book he has written, each of its eight parts the story of an event or of characters with special significance in his own life. The ship's passage takes eight days. During that time, at the rate of a story per day, David struggles to give the manuscript continuity. He provides narrative transitions and "smuggles" characters from one narrative into another. He even attempts to structure each story according to some mythic subtext, such as those of Oedipus, Midas, or the Golden Ass. This technique of highly self-conscious parody—what T. S. Eliot called the "mythic method" in reference to James Joyce's *Ulysses*— is revealed as yet another mode of smuggling, which has lost that sacred magic it once promised to modernist writers. Thus, while David may think of himself as "an epistemological reuniac" attempting an integral, totalizing reconstruction of the past, *A Smuggler's Bible*, especially in its interchapters, tends contrariwise toward disjunction and incompleteness. McElroy has said that it "was designed to fracture."

Throughout this long, stylistically brilliant performance, the image one gets (not a "picture" but an immanence or field theory) is of women and men existing in a grand relational network. Yet only David's acts of memory hold that web in balance. This field of charged particles did exist, and had "reality," but only when a single mind was composing it, and that mind is, in the best sense of the term, *trivial*: It finds pattern and meaning in the accidental minutiae of ordinary lives.

A few examples: In the fourth of his "principal parts," David recounts the story of his acquaintance, at the University of New Hampshire, with an intellectual con artist named Duke Amerchrome. An immensely popular historian and theorist of American culture, Duke engineered his fame on forged sources and blustering rhetoric. He is an exemplar of the literati who smuggle themselves into positions of "authority." Tony Tanner thinks that the character is patterned on Norman Mailer, yet almost any other (such as Marshall McLuhan) would do, and one could also point to the autobiographical aspects and note that McElroy may have been exorcising personal as well as professional demons. In any event, much of Duke's story is transmitted to David through his son Michael, who discloses the man's use of counterfeited trivia about the Battle of Ticonderoga. Michael, however, has selfish motives for these disclosures, such as coveting his father's nubile young wife (Duke's third). This Oedipal motif broadens; the idea of "shadowing" a (supposed) father, tracking him and absorbing the minutiae of his days until one knows enough to expose and supplant him, recurs in other chapters. The first memory concerns a bored rare-book dealer named Peter St. John who is being followed by a boy who thinks that the man resembles his father. In the second, David's association with a group of eccentric fellow boarders eventually centers on a rare-coin dealer named Pennitt, who may be a counterfeiter; whether he is is never certain, because the old man brushes David off before disclosing any conclusive evidence. In the final part, David's father spins through his last, trivial thoughts while dying of angina and rectal cancer. David *inhabits* these memories, seeking safe harbor between antinomies: the imploding heart of man, symbolizing powers of empathy and connection, versus the exploding rectum, David's symbol of dispersal and "apartness." The book ends there, with the mind shuttling in between, never resolving that antinomy but finding art in the act of composing.

Hind's Kidnap, McElroy's next novel, takes these ideas a step further. Once again the concern is with detection, with the mind moving inside a labyrinthine network of information that points equally to integral order and to zeros of disorder. Yet this novel falls short of its ambition. Critics have aptly noted that the book succeeds better in its idea than in its stylistic performance, which often becomes tiresome.

The reasons are several. One is that the narrator's attention to matters of trivial but feasibly significant detail achieves a still closer focus than in *A Smuggler's Bible*, but this attention must be borne by units of narrative (sentences on up to chapters) that strain from sheer length, and hence from the span of attention demanded of readers. Another reason, and doubtless an attempt to explain (that is, to naturalize) the first, is that in *Hind's Kidnap* the narrator-protagonist is virtually obsessed with the dialectic of detection.

The story is related by Jack Hind, a six-foot, seven-inch, lookout tower of a man who, for years, has been intermittently tracking his way back and forth through the same case. A four-year-old boy, Hershey Laurel, was kidnapped from his rural home, and for seven years there has been no trace of the boy. Desperate to solve the enigma, Hind tells and retells the known facts to everyone he knows; in time, his auditors become so knowledgeable as to seem implicated in the original crime. Hind's recollections thus become a labyrinth without boundaries, as if all were "suspicioned" into the plot, often on the slightest of linguistic associations, such as a name. Midway through the narrative, with the book's reader now equally knowledgeable of the main "facts," it becomes necessary for Hind to "de-kidnap" everyone, to extricate them from the paranoid plottings of his own mind. Thus, Hind, too, becomes implicated. In the novel's second part, he turns his detective skills onto his own past: the early deaths of both parents, his childhood with a guardian (a linguist, as it happens), and the question of his own paternity (the guardian appears to have been his actual father). These matters explain his obsession. Jack's quest for the boy is a means of asserting his own guardianship, and so of questing into the self, of separating illusion from reality and discovering how he was misled by language. As the novel's subtitle implies, Jack thereby seeks to become a truer shepherd of both memories and the discourses used to shape them.

Yet the discourse of *Hind's Kidnap* is often so meditative, so far removed from the pitch and flow of narrative as to read like a poetic anatomy. This tendency continues in *Ancient History*, McElroy's third (and least satisfying) novel, in which the narrator, Cy, searches to explain the evident suicide of his friend, Dom. Like Hind, he discovers that every force expended in the effort of detection tends to reverberate throughout the web of his friend's associations, and eventually through his own memories. Yet the stylistic and technical demands of this novel also bring diminishing returns to the reader. The book becomes, at the last, a poetic demonstration of the spatial possibilities in linguistically organized memory. It has little in it of narrative action.

Lookout Cartridge, arguably McElroy's best work, resolves these problems. The plot crackles with action and the style surges ahead in a more declarative mode, while never weakening the complex power of its main idea.

A further "demonstration" of the dynamics and the essential incompleteness of memory in an information society, *Lookout Cartridge* asks to be read as a mystery-thriller.

The narrator-protagonist, Cartwright, a filmmaker who has been collaborating with a director named Dagger DiGorro on a politically radical documentary project, is literally pushed into his detective research. The narrative opens with the momentary fall (as a result of mechanical failure) of a helicopter hovering over a terrorist explosion in New York, itself partly explained at the novel's end. This recollection spins Cartwright into another beginning: an unseen hand that pushed him violently down an escalator, a fall he transforms by half-coordinated steps into a self-preserving forward stagger. In the narrative order, Cartwright's second "fall" thus redeems the mindless near-accident of his first. It also eventually emblematizes the detective activity, as a type of half-random, half-volitional motion. For a novel preoccupied with kinds of drive (physical and cinematic, social and narrational, epistemological and historical), this paradox is crucial.

Persons unknown, for reasons never fully explained, want Cartwright and Dagger's film destroyed, along with Cartwright's shooting diary, Cartwright himself, and perhaps even members of Cartwright's family who have knowledge of the film at second hand. All of this is apparently necessary because the film may have inadvertently recorded minute details of "an international power struggle." It may have, but without replaying or at least mentally reconstructing the footage, Cartwright can never know for certain. Therefore he sets to work. Like McElroy's previous detectives, he takes up the fragmentary evidence: the remaining chunks of the diary, recollections (often prompted) of friends and associates, material objects, whatever comes to hand during his headlong plunge through England, where much of the footage was shot, and New York City.

This urgency of self-survival gives *Lookout Cartridge* a sense of immediate purpose missing from the more abstract plots of *Hind's Kidnap* and *Ancient History*, and is something McElroy would capitalize on again, in *Plus*. As Cartwright shuttles back and forth between London and New York, and between pieces of contrary evidence, his in-betweenness becomes the basis for an uncannily creative power. Though he imagines himself as a "lookout cartridge" of film inserted "in someone else's system," still Cartwright discovers how, "between blind coghood" (the camera as simple recording instrument) and "that sinister hint of godhead" (in the conspiracies of unknown others), he himself has the power—even by using purest accident—of pushing events toward disclosure. Indeed, Cartwright finally nails both his assailants and their banal secrets. This resolution is the result, equally, of his power to manipulate details of story and his power simply to act by lunging forward, by reacting. Through it all, readers "have" only this Cartwright-Cartridge: the mind as recording machine, the machine as uncanny intercessor for the mind. What the lens records will depend entirely on where one is, what one wants to see, how long one rolls the film, and, later, how it is spliced. The camera thus becomes, like the remembering human subject, part of a relational system or associational grid whose power is greater than its parts.

This idea underwrites the lexicons of cinematography and information processing evident on the novel's every page. There is much, much more. Cartwright's narrative also includes speculations on Mayan calendars, on Mercator maps, and on Stonehenge or the standing stones of Callanish as ancient data-processing systems; details about the topographies of Corsica, London, or New York; and countless oblique references to the conspiracy-racked politics of the 1960's and 1970's. Involving readers in this labyrinth of events, representation techniques, and forms of knowledge, *Lookout Cartridge* surpasses the excesses and the feigned completion of other contemporary encyclopedic novels, such as Pynchon's *Gravity's Rainbow* (1973) or Coover's *The Public Burning* (1977).

By comparison to these, *Lookout Cartridge* makes far more demands on the reader. As the title suggests, the reader is also inserted into this survival-experience and discovers that what matters is not a final why, but how one might manipulate the journey. Yet many of the novel's critics were so taken by its profusion of reference and detail that they missed commenting on one of its completed enigmas, a palpable bit of political absurdity worthy of Joseph Conrad's *The Secret Agent* (1907). That explosion in chapter 1 was set off by a faction of Cartwright's assailants, who were terrorizing the city for towing their illegally parked car. This detail points to a wry, detached satire of a contemporary society in which politics is managed as sequences of media events.

At first glance, that potential for satire would also seem to be the motive force of McElroy's fifth novel, *Plus*, easily his most accessible work of fiction. Given the novel's premise, the chances for targeting the absurdities of contemporary "information society" were numerous. Its story concerns a disembodied brain inserted, cartridgelike, in an orbiting space platform called Imp, whose computer he—or it—was programmed to be. The engineers dubbed the combination "Imp Plus." Relaying technical data, controlling Imp's self-sustaining internal environment, with its glucose-producing algae—these are its simple programmed functions. Yet as a relational network, an ecosystem, Imp Plus is more than a mere machine. It has the power of self-induced growth. In sum, once more the narration unfolds in the topography, now absolute, of mind, and the primary action again involves the composition of a self from fragments of memory.

In a reconstruction of its past and present states (made difficult by its linguistic limitations), Imp Plus forms a new identity. Looking backward from this perspective, its story is simple. Exposed to lethal doses of radiation, a space scientist donates his brain, and Imp Plus is launched as an experiment in photosynthesis and symbiosis—the algae providing necessary glucose for the brain, the brain respiring carbon dioxide necessary for the algae, the brain and its mechanical platform interpreting and relaying data. Then, however, the brain begins re-forming itself. Imp Plus expands inwardly by recovering discrete sensual memories and thereby reconstructing language. (In an elegantly structured argument, Brooke-Rose shows how this develops from a hypothetically "nonsensical" sentence by linguist Noam Chomsky: "Colorless green ideas sleep furiously.") Imp Plus also expands outwardly by linking the neural sites of previous sensory activity, such as vision, to the platform's circuitry. It thereby realizes the practical and virtual reciprocity of mind and matter, a discovery tantamount to the age-old philosopher's stone. It also begins disregarding and disobeying signals from Earth, and when Ground Control threatens fiery destruction, Imp Plus carries out a ploy which will carom the platform off Earth's atmosphere and into deep space. There Imp Plus envisions further growth—leaving matter behind to become pure light, the wholly disembodied "Plus" of McElroy's title.

Plus can be read as a recapitulation of the principal themes of McElroy's previous books—a work of summary and consolidation. With *Plus*, he had published five challenging novels in just over a decade; his sixth novel, *Women and Men*, was itself ten years in the writing.

Everything about *Women and Men* proclaims its enormous ambition. Its title has the immodest sweep of Fyodor Dostoevski's *Crime and Punishment* (1866) or Leo Tolstoy's *War and Peace* (1865-1869). In sheer bulk, nearly twelve hundred pages, it easily outweighs any of McElroy's earlier books. In the complexity of its structure, the density of information it conveys, it is even more daunting than *Lookout Cartridge*. Reviewing the novel in *The Washington Post Book World*, Tom LeClair suggested that "*Women and Men* is the single book—fiction or nonfiction—that best manifests what human beings can know and be and imagine now and, just as importantly, in the future."

Whether such claims will stand up is a matter for time to tell. A first reading of *Women and Men* is essentially a reconnaissance mission. The action of the novel is set primarily in the mid-1970's. The two central characters—James Mayn, a journalist specializing in science and technology and economic issues, and Grace Kimball, a radical feminist guru—live in the same apartment building in New York. They do not know each other, but they have mutual acquaintances, and they are connected in more subtle ways as well. This pattern of coincidence is a model for the novel as a whole, which traces a multitude of unexpected connections both in the private lives and family histories of the characters and in the life of the planet.

While the intertwining stories of Mayn and Kimball constitute a loose narrative line, many chapters are self-contained vignettes that illuminate, from diverse perspectives, the relation between women and men at a time of significant change: change in assumptions concerning sexual roles, but also more broadly change in the assumptions by which we organize our experience. "The ways in which we embrace the world and embrace other people," McElroy has said, "can be more precise and clear than we sometimes think." Weather patterns, body chemistry, economic cycles: These are not merely esoteric academic subjects but rather the stuff of everyday life. All that is required is attentiveness to available knowledge.

Much of the knowledge that informs *Women and Men* is scientific, but this is complemented by a strong emphasis on what has been called New Age spirituality. Native American lore plays an important role in the book; Grace Kimball frequently invokes the Goddess (the primeval Earth Mother who, many feminists contend, was universally worshipped by humankind before the onset of patriarchy); and there are hints of reincarnation throughout the novel.

Indeed, several long sections, set in the future, are given to a chorus of disembodied spirits who comment on the action and the characters of the main narrative. Here McElroy seems to suggest a collective consciousness in which individual identity is subsumed. It is not clear how literally this vision is to be taken; even readers who find it unpersuasive will be left with a vivid sense of intricate order within the dizzying multiplicity of things.

Bibliography

Brooke-Rose, Christine. "Joseph McElroy: *Plus*," in *A Rhetoric of the Unreal: Studies in Narrative and Structure, Especially the Fantastic*, 1983.

Karl, Frederick. "Joseph McElroy," in *American Fictions, 1940-1980: A Comprehensive History and Critical Evaluation*, 1983.

LeClair, Tom. "Interview with Joseph McElroy," in *Anything Can Happen*, 1983. Edited by Tom LeClair and Larry McCaffery.

_____. "Joseph McElroy and the Art of Excess," in *Contemporary Literature*. XXI (1980), pp. 15-37.

Tanner, Tony. "Toward an Ultimate Topography: The Work of Joseph McElroy," in *TriQuarterly*. XXXVI (Spring, 1976), pp. 214-52.

Steven Weisenburger

THOMAS McGUANE

Born: Wyandotte, Michigan; December 11, 1939

Principal long fiction

The Sporting Club, 1969; *The Bushwhacked Piano*, 1971; *Ninety-Two in the Shade*, 1973; *Panama*, 1978; *Nobody's Angel*, 1982; *Something to Be Desired*, 1984.

Other literary forms

In addition to writing novels, Thomas McGuane has produced work for motion pictures and for popular magazines. He wrote the screenplay and directed the film version of *Ninety-Two in the Shade* (1975), wrote the scripts for *Rancho DeLuxe* (1973) and *The Missouri Breaks* (1975), and shared credit with Bud Shrake for *Tom Horn* (1980). *An Outside Chance: Essays on Sport* (1980) contains many of his magazine pieces, and *To Skin a Cat* (1986) is a collection of short fiction.

Achievements

Early in his career, McGuane was heralded as one of the most promising writers of his generation, one with a good chance to become a major American writer. He appeared on the cover of *The New York Times Book Review* and was compared favorably with Ernest Hemingway, William Faulkner, and Saul Bellow. *The Bushwhacked Piano* won the Rosenthal Award, and *Ninety-Two in the Shade* was nominated for a National Book Award. In the mid-1970's, however, when he began to devote the majority of his energies to writing for films, McGuane was dismissed as a sellout. In the late 1970's, his film career seemingly over, McGuane returned to publishing novels. Because he centers most of his work on the fictional town of Deadrock, Montana, some critics fear that he is becoming too much of a regionalist. McGuane does not take this label seriously, however, and maintains his personal goal of becoming "a true man of literature, . . . a professional." Many in the critical community believe that with *Something to Be Desired* he has begun to fulfill his earlier promise.

Biography

Thomas McGuane was born in Wyandotte, Michigan, on December 11, 1939. He was graduated with honors from Michigan State University in 1962, took an M.F.A. from the Yale Drama School in 1965, and spent 1966-1967 at Stanford on a Wallace Stegner Fellowship. His parents were New England Irish who migrated to the Midwest, where his father became an auto-parts tycoon. He believes that he inherited his storytelling impulse from his mother's family, who loved verbal sparring and yarn-spinning. McGuane is a highly visible writer, articles about him appearing regularly in newspapers and slick magazines. These articles usually center on the manic behavior, heavy drinking, and drug use that marked his film years, and his eventual return to sobriety, family life, and hard work. McGuane has preferred to pursue a career as a writer apart from life in the academic world, believing that his chances of writing interesting novels would be diminished were he to confine himself to life in English departments.

Besides writing, McGuane supports himself by raising cutting horses. He is a champion steer roper who competes regularly in rodeos, and an accomplished sailor and fisherman who spends a part of every year at fishing haunts in Florida and Georgia.

Analysis

Thomas McGuane's fictional universe is a "man's world." His protagonists appear to do whatever they do for sport and to escape ordinary reality. They seek a world where they can, without restraint, be whoever they choose to be. This goal puts them at odds with prevailing social customs and middle-class ideas of morality and achievement. Unfortunately, most of these quests end in frustration. Finding themselves quite apart from the normal flow of society, McGuane's protagonists must try all the harder to fulfill themselves. As a result, they easily become self-absorbed and further jeopardize whatever ties they might once have had to conventional life. Usually this tie is to a woman, who, for her own self-fulfillment, must forsake the protagonist in the end.

McGuane's first novel, *The Sporting Club*, concerns the adventures of well-to-do Michiganders who maintain the exclusive and grand Centennial Club, to which they repair to fish and hunt. The story is limited to the point of view of James Quinn, who has emerged from a protracted adolescence to take over the family's auto-parts factory. Quinn's friend Vernor Stanton, however, refuses to take up the ordinary life and spends his time in the pursuit of games. Stanton is bored by the elitist pretensions of the club members and the pride they take in its noble heritage, and he is frustrated with Quinn for outgrowing the need for freedom and frolic. Stanton engineers a series of adventures which ultimately result in the collapse of the club. The noble pretensions of the membership are exploded when Stanton unearths a photograph which shows their ancestors engaged in an outlandish "sexual circus at full progress." Once the current members see the photograph, the pretense upon which they build their lives collapses and they run rampant with, as Quinn puts it, "moral dubiousness" emulating the sexual circus of the forefathers. In this way, McGuane manages to show that the established social order is rotten at its foundation, and the only sensible thing to do is to quest for a life in which one determines one's own values. Exposing this truth does nothing, however, for the survival of the McGuane protagonists. By the end of the aftermath occasioned by the photograph, Stanton is living under the surveillance of mental health workers at what is left of the club, and Quinn returns to the family business. They are no longer freewheeling protagonists able to make "the world tense."

In *The Bushwhacked Piano*, Nicholas Payne is more fortunate. Even though his father has the finest law practice in Detroit, Payne has no intention of doing anything respectable. He wants no part of his father's "declining snivelization" and "the pismire futilities of moguls." Payne does, however, want Ann Fitzgerald, an aspiring poet and photographer, whom he sees as almost a goddess.

Ann's parents do not approve of Payne; appearances, hard work, and achievement mean everything to them. They take Ann from Michigan to their ranch in Montana, but Payne follows because movement appeals to him, as well as the romantic idea of an almost unworldly mate. Ann is also sleeping with an establishment boyfriend whom she will not give up completely because she knows that someday she will have to behave like a conventional adult. For now, however, camera in hand, she joins Payne on an expedition to Florida to sell fraudulent bat towers. She goes more for the experience than simply to be with Payne, and ultimately she leaves him.

Payne not only loses Ann but also is arrested for selling a useless bat tower. Still, breaking the law is not as serious as breaking conventions. Payne goes free when he agrees to reenact his trial for a television program. Life, McGuane seems to say, is indeed a bewildering proposition, and the only way to emerge victorious is to determine one's own goals and always keep them uppermost in mind. Indeed, neither the loss of Ann nor the scrape with the law has a lasting effect on Payne. Those who live the conventional life will never understand Payne, but he will not relent. The novel ends with Payne proclaiming: "I am at large," which is the same language used to describe an outlaw on the loose. Payne's movement outside conventional spheres will not stop. He is, for better or for worse, in charge of his own life, the artist of his own destiny.

In *Ninety-Two in the Shade*, Thomas Skelton attempts to engineer his own fate when he tries to become a fishing guide with his own skiff off Key West. Nicole Dance, an established guide and murderer, forbids him to do so. When Dance plays a joke on Skelton, the young man burns Dance's skiff in retaliation. Dance vows to kill Skelton if he guides, but Skelton guides anyway, his fulfillment depending on it. The situation here is much the same as in earlier McGuane fiction. The protagonist must assert himself against the normal flow of life. With his life in danger, Skelton ought not to guide, but he knows that "when what you ought to do [has] become less than a kind of absentee ballot you [are] always in danger of lending yourself to the deadly farce that surrounds us." Couched in McGuane's wisecracking language is the idea that the deadly farce occurs when one absents oneself from vital energies and capitulates to the flow of ordinary life. Skelton must stand up for the self he desires to be and attempt the life he wants.

Ninety-Two in the Shade could be considered McGuane's most optimistic book if it were not for the fact that when Skelton becomes a fishing guide, Dance kills him. Until the very end, Tom seems to have everything going his way. He has determined his own values and his own fulfillment. He has the support of family and a fulfilling love relationship with Miranda, a local schoolteacher. Yet he also has his feud with Nicole Dance, who shoots him "through the heart." In spite of the protagonist's courage to pursue goals and the conviction to stand up to adversity, life does not come equipped with happy endings.

McGuane's fourth novel, *Panama*, more clearly points up the frustrations of the unconventional life. Protagonist Chester Hunnicutt (Chet) Pomeroy has become an overnight sensation, performing all the loathsome acts of the imagination for audiences. He has, for example, crawled out of the anus of a frozen elephant and fought a duel in his underwear with a baseball batting practice machine. He also vomited on the mayor of New York, which ended his career. As the novel opens, Chet has returned to Key West, Florida, in the hope of putting his life back together by reconciling with his wife, Catherine, who stuck by him until he became a national disgrace.

Even though she still loves him, Catherine wants nothing to do with him because his behavior is still bizarre. At one point, he nails his hand to her door; at another, he snorts cocaine off the sidewalk. He has lost his memory and given up all hope. Catherine accepts the fact that she cannot change him and leaves him for good to the emptiness he calls home.

Chet combats this emptiness by evoking a transcendent presence of Jesse James, who has the power to inhabit his loved ones. He prefers that James inhabit his father, a snack-foods tycoon. A typical McGuane protagonist, Chet is bothered by the security and ordinariness of his background. He insists that his father is dead and claims James as an ancestor, suggesting that Chester Hunnicutt Pomeroy really wishes he were someone else. Since the glories of the Old West are not available to him, he creates the myth of himself through bizarre behavior.

Chet's outlaw myth leads him nowhere. At the novel's conclusion, his father forces a reconciliation. Chet knows that all his father wants is for Chet to say hello, to acknowledge him as his father. To admit that his father lives will be to agree that Jesse James is dead. Chet will have to accept himself for who he is: the son of an unillustrious packager of snack foods, the perfect symbol of conventional modern life.

Nobody's Angel is McGuane's first novel to be set entirely in the West, a West which McGuane characterizes as "wrecked." In Deadrock, Montana, farmers abuse the land, cowboys are lazy, and Indians are nowhere to be found. Returning to this damaged world is thirty-six-year-old Patrick Fitz-patrick. Patrick is as unconventional as earlier McGuane protagonists. As a whiskey addict and a professional soldier, he has been a tank captain in the army for all of his adult life, most recently in Europe, and the only place he feels secure is inside his womblike tank. Suffering from "sadness for no reason," he has returned to the family ranch, which he will someday own. He feels stranded on the ranch because becoming a property owner is not a meaningful achievement for him. Patrick appears to be in the worst shape of any McGuane protagonist. He is not only without goals but also without any sense of himself, conventional or unconventional.

The effect of the wrecked West is seen in the character of Patrick's grand-father. The old man has been a cowboy all of his life, has known real gunfighters, and has run the ranch like an old-time outfit. The West has changed, however, and everything from sonic booms to valleys cluttered with yard lights has got the old man down. The only things he feels good about are Australia, which he has heard is open country like Montana once was, and Western films. His one fit of excitement comes when he signs on to be an extra in a Western about to be filmed locally. Even that, however, is accompanied by overtones of sadness and ends in disappointment. The film is *Hondo's Last Move*, evocative of a legendary but nonexistent West popular-ized by John Wayne and Louis L'Amour. Even then, the "last move" refers to the dying of the West and perhaps Hondo himself. To make matters worse, the project folds when the distributor forsakes Westerns for science fiction. In the end, the old man moves into town and takes an apartment from which he can see the local film theater, which plays old Westerns, and a little bar in which hangs the head of the best elk he ever shot. The open West has been reduced to one-bedroom apartments, yesterday's movies, and mounted animals, which serve only to remind him of a glorious past.

In *Nobody's Angel*, McGuane continued to work the theme of unfulfilled love. Patrick hopes to bring purpose into his life by means of a love affair with Claire Burnett. Claire and her husband, Tio, are second-generation nouveau-riche Oklahomans summering in Montana. Not a genuine stockman like Patrick's grandfather, Tio is mainly interested in oil, cattle futures, row crops, and running horses. Since Tio's main hobby is pretending to be a good old boy, Patrick sees him as a personification of the substanceless modern West.

Patrick believes that "Claire could change it all" and wishes theirs could be a sentimental love story, the kind found in romantic books. Claire, however, will not become a part of Patrick's dream. Her commitment to Tio goes beyond Patrick's understanding. Her family provided the money to support their life-style. Tio's people are poor Okies, and this discrepancy in their backgrounds has driven him to incurable delusions of grandeur, to the point that Claire has promised that she will not abandon him. Even though she tells Patrick that she loves him, she never stops loving Tio, and Patrick's dream of a storybook romance crumbles. Even when Tio dies, Claire will not marry Patrick. She makes love to him one last time, explaining that love is "nothing you can do anything with." Patrick is not able to cope with Claire's pragmatic attitude about love and their relationship. She gives him a picture of herself, but he does not keep it with him, because it reminds him of the frustrations of his romantic hopes.

In the end, Patrick survives, but not in the West. When he was a teenager, Patrick invented an imaginary girlfriend named Marion Easterly. Even though he was eventually discovered, the fantasy has remained a part of his consciousness. He had hoped that Claire would replace Marion, but a living woman will never become the woman of a man's imagination, and when Claire dismisses him, Patrick rejoins the army and finds fulfillment in his fantasy. Word filters back that he is now a blackout drinker in Madrid and that he is living with a woman named Marion Easterly. Patrick Fitzpatrick remains "at large"—in the sense that his heavy drinking and fantasy lover keep him outside the normal boundaries of life—but without the hope and energy of Nicholas Payne. The McGuane protagonist seemingly must find a way to accommodate himself, at least partially, to the concerns of conventional life.

In *Something to Be Desired*, the McGuane protagonist combines both unconventional and conventional goals. Lucien Taylor grows tired of normality and destroys his perfectly fine marriage with self-absorbed erratic behavior. Once his single life becomes empty, he, like Chet, tries to put it back together again by reuniting with his former wife, Suzanne, and their son, James. Lucien's plight is not entirely the result of his disenchantment with conformity; he is victimized by his capricious lust.

Lucien's sense of sexual discipline was broken in college by Emily, who slept with him on their first meeting. Emily was engaged to a medical student and continued to sleep with both young men at the same time. Ultimately, she is abused by her surgeon husband and becomes totally self-absorbed and manipulating. Emily is a woman as selfish as Claire, and she continues her self-absorbed actions throughout the novel, exploiting everyone, including Lucien. Lucien, however, married Suzanne, who "took the position that this was a decent world for an honest player." This basic decency is what Lucien eventually comes to value, but when he hears that Emily is free of her marriage, he thinks nothing of destroying his own and returning to Montana in quest of her. Lucien is troubled by the lack of romance in his life, an element that Suzanne and James cannot provide. Suzanne sums up Emily by calling her the queen of the whores, an assertion which is borne out when, on her penultimate appearance in the novel, she is seen sleeping naked next to her purse.

Such a portrayal of women who do not measure up to male ideals or fantasies is not rare in McGuane's fiction: Ann (*The Bushwhacked Piano*) and Claire (*Nobody's Angel*) are two other disappointing women. Lucien has dreamed of Emily since their first encounter. Not until he finally decides that he wants nothing more to do with her does she tell him that she regards his concern for her an infantile gesture, a thing she holds in contempt. Indeed, she does not even think enough of him to shoot him, which she has done to her husband and, by this time, another lover. Lucien, however, like Nicholas Payne in *The Bushwhacked Piano*, does not lose momentum. He pulls off a crackpot piece of venture capitalism. Through a series of exchanges, he comes to own Emily's ranch and develops its sulfur spring into a thriving health spa. In short, he becomes rich. In this way Lucien remains unconventional, at the same time—new for a McGuane protagonist—gaining that which is admired by conventional society. Even though McGuane still maneuvers his protagonist through some outlandish paces because of his peripatetic penis, McGuane at the same time imbues Lucien with a sense of purpose higher than sport or making the world tense. Lucien, once his new wealth requires him to bring a semblance of order into his life, begins to want to think of himself as a working man with a family to support.

When Suzanne and James come for a visit, Lucien first attempts to reach James from the security of his own masculine interests. He takes him out to band some hawks. He baits the trap with a live pigeon. When the hawk strikes the pigeon, James screams and crawls off. As Lucien bands the hawk, James shakes. While Lucien admires the hawk, James's natural inclination is to cradle the dead pigeon; he manifests a sense of compassion that his father lacks. The violent world of nature is awful to him. Lucien actually finds himself liking the fact that his son is timid and made of more delicate and sensitive stuff than his father. Still, McGuane is not becoming sentimental. Later, when he understands how nature works, James explains that killing pigeons is how hawks have to live, but the fact remains that James was terrified by the killing. His explanation is not so much an emulation of his father's more hard-boiled ways as it is an acceptance of them as his father's ways. James is actually reaching toward a relationship with his father.

What is important here is that Lucien is attempting to reestablish his family because such a reestablishment would be better for all of them, not only for him alone. Lucien's is one of the few nonselfish acts committed by a McGuane protagonist. He would like not to see the child become a "hostage to oblivion." He wonders how he could leave him unguarded. His reward is that James begins not to fear his father.

Winning back Suzanne, however, is not as easy. She is too skeptical to welcome the sadder-but-wiser protagonist back into her arms. She tells him the truth about himself: He is self-absorbed, insensitive to those who love him, and not worth the effort of reconciliation. Lucien is going to have to recognize her as an independent and worthy person. Before the novel's end, she works through her sense of him as a totally selfish person, but even though she admits to loving Lucien, she is not sure if she is ready to trust him. As she and James drive away from the ranch, she does not look back. She is charting her own course, which may or may not include Lucien.

What is important here is that the McGuane protagonist has progressed through the state of self-absorption with adventure and sport. He has begun to understand that what matters about life is not being "at large" to commit glorious exploits, but being a part of a larger whole that includes the other people in the world. The full life is not lived in furious battle with the forces of conventionality, but in achieving deep and lasting relationships with human beings.

Other major works

SHORT FICTION: *To Skin a Cat*, 1986.

SCREENPLAYS: *Rancho DeLuxe*, 1973; *Ninety-Two in the Shade*, 1975; *The Missouri Breaks*, 1975; *Tom Horn*, 1980 (with Bud Shrake).

NONFICTION: *An Outside Chance: Essays on Sport*, 1980.

Bibliography

Carter, Albert Howard, III. "McGuane's First Three Novels: Games, Fun, Nemesis," in *Critique*. XVII (August, 1975), pp. 91-104.

Grant, Kerry. "On and Off the Main Line: The Failure of Compromise in the Fiction of Thomas McGuane," in *Mid-American Review*. III (Spring, 1983), pp. 167-184.

McCaffery, Larry. "On Turning Nothing into Something," in *Fiction International*. IV/V (Fall/Winter, 1975), pp. 123-129.

Masinton, Charles G. *"Nobody's Angel*: Thomas McGuane's Vision of the Contemporary West," in *New Mexico Humanities Review*. VI (Fall, 1983), pp. 49-55.

Welch, Dennis M. "Death and Fun in the Novels of Thomas McGuane," in *Windsor Review*. XIV (Fall/Winter, 1978), pp. 14-20.

Dexter Westrum

JAMES A. MICHENER

Born: New York, New York?; February 3, 1907?

Principal long fiction

Tales of the South Pacific, 1947; *The Fires of Spring*, 1949; *The Bridges at Toko-Ri*, 1953; *Sayonara*, 1954; *The Bridge at Andau*, 1954; *Hawaii*, 1959; *Caravans*, 1963; *The Source*, 1965; *The Drifters*, 1971; *Centennial*, 1974; *Chesapeake*, 1978; *The Covenant*, 1980; *Space*, 1982; *Poland*, 1983; *Texas*, 1985.

Other literary forms

Although James A. Michener considers himself primarily a novelist, he is also an accomplished short-story writer, essayist, art historian, and editor. Major themes in his nonfiction are travel and American politics. *The Voice of Asia* (1951) is in the same tradition, although it includes no fiction at all. *The Floating World* (1954) is a philosophical essay on Japanese art, a theme he treats in four other works, most notably in *Japanese Prints from the Early Masters to the Modern* (1959).

Achievements

In the early 1950's, Michener was heralded as the new voice in American fiction. Still basking in the considerable praise that followed his first book, *Tales of the South Pacific*, and the Pulitzer Prize that accompanied it, he shared the reflected glow of Richard Rodgers and Oscar Hammerstein's musical adaptation, *South Pacific* (1949). Although critics objected to the romantic cast of his early novels, they also found much to praise. Critical reaction to his later novels has also been mixed: While some consider them brilliant for their sweeping panoramic scope, others have condemned the novels for their mass of information, undeveloped characters, and lack of depth. Despite the doubts of literary critics as to the merits of Michener's novels, an eager public has responded to them enthusiastically.

In addition to the Pulitzer Prize, Michener's writing has earned for him a number of honorary degrees and awards, including the appointment to several government committees. His work on two of these committees—the Centennial Commission and the National Aeronautics and Space Administration (NASA) Advisory Council—contributed to research for his fiction.

Biography

Although standard references state that James Albert Michener was born on February 3, 1907, in New York City to Edwin and Mabel Michener, the facts of his birth are unknown; he was a foundling whom Mabel Michener reared from birth, moving at times to the county poorhouse to help the family through poverty and illness. On a scholarship, he attended Swarthmore College, from which he was graduated summa cum laude in 1929. For ten years, he taught at a variety of schools and universities, including the School of Education at Harvard, and in the early 1940's he became an editor at Macmillan Company. Although as a practicing member of the Society of Friends (Quakers) he might have been exempted from combat, in 1942 he volunteered for active duty in the United States Navy and was sent to the Pacific. Royalties and a small percentage of ownership in the musical *South Pacific*, which opened in April, 1949, assured him financial freedom to travel and write. Michener thus became an independent writer and scholar, publishing more than thirty major works, and an even greater number of articles, from his home base in Bucks County, Pennsylvania.

Analysis

In almost all of James A. Michener's novels, the story line is a loosely woven thread, a framework, a context in which to tell tales and provide geographic and historic detail. Although in his notes on *Centennial* Michener explains four different narrative devices he developed in the course of his writing career, each is still a framing device for a series of related events or information. Throughout all of his work Michener is the social science editor and teacher, using quantities of well-researched data and imaginative incidents to explain issues from his particular point of view. While each of his novels has a historical basis that covers hundreds or thousands of years, each is rooted in its own time as well.

Much of Michener's writing, both fiction and nonfiction, is journalistic in style, but his staccato rhythms are interrupted from time to time by florid descriptions and precise diversions, such as recipes and statistical contrasts. All of his writing is permeated by an unmistakable creed that affirms human values and a deep concern for America. The harsh facts of his early life shaped Michener's career, and his writing is that of a grateful man driven to repay society for the chances he was given in life. There is more to his writing, however, than a need to express gratitude: His broad panoramas are peopled with Dickensian characters from every part of society, although his sympathies remain with the sad and the unfortunate—even rogues such as Oliver Wendell in *Centennial* and Jake Turlock in *Chesapeake*—who can get by on their wits. Underscoring all of Michener's work is a strong statement of human courage and human tolerance, coupled with a driving concern for man's relationship with his environment. All of his novels (except perhaps *The Bridges at Toko-Ri*, *The Drifters*, and *Poland* focus on racial discrimination of some kind, and each teaches the value of hard work and the necessity for change. As in his nonfiction, Michener does not hesitate to portray society's weaknesses. While critics have frequently panned both his style and the values it embodies, particularly in his later work, these same late novels have consistently been best-sellers.

Ironically, *Tales of the South Pacific* was not a best-seller, even though of all Michener's works it is perhaps the most familiar. Although it continues to sell as many copies today as when it was originally published and has won the Pulitzer Prize, the book was first printed on the cheapest paper with the poorest binding available—so little did the publisher think of its chances—and new chapters did not even begin at the tops of new pages. Even after its award, the novel would have continued to die a slow death were it not for the musical comedy based on it. Few successful writers have had a less auspicious beginning.

Tales of the South Pacific is a framing story that sets up many of Michener's themes; with it the author began a literary romance with the Pacific islands that would last for more than fifteen years and characterize much of his work. In this work, nineteen related episodes tell the story of America's commitment to the Pacific theater during World War II. The treatment of character as well as setting is significant to the body of Michener's work. No one character can be called the protagonist, although Tony Fry (a navy lieutenant) and the narrator are most central to the plot. By not having a protagonist, Michener implies that this is not the story of one man but rather the shared experience of all those who were in the Pacific during the war years. The narrator makes no moral judgments: Men and women are presented at their finest and their weakest moments; some die in war, but life somehow goes on.

With the exception of *The Fires of Spring*, a semiautobiographical novel that develops much of Michener's personal life through 1929, both the fiction and nonfiction which followed *Tales of the South Pacific* are steeped in Pacific history and his own war experience. All are connected as part of a cumulative statement; *Return to Paradise* (1951), for example, with its alternating essays and stories, begins with the description of islands emerging from the sea, the same technique Michener employs in the first of his "blockbuster" novels, *Hawaii*. Of these early works, *The Bridges at Toko-Ri* is particularly significant. The novel exemplifies Michener's typical blend of fact and fiction, as he exposes his reader to the Asian world and the Korean War experience. With the publication of the novel, the author observed that it was the "purest writing" he had done so far.

Although *The Bridges at Toko-Ri* is a short novel and neatly divided into sections—"Sea," "Land," and "Sky"—in it, Michener provides his strongest development of character. The protagonist is Harry Brubaker, a twenty-nine-year-old veteran of World War II and promising Denver lawyer, who resents fighting in Korea. In the first section, Brubaker is rescued from the frozen sea by another three-dimensional character, Mike Forney, a cocky Irishman from Chicago. Michener included an expanded version of both these characters in his later novel *Space*. The "Land" interlude takes place in Japan, a liberty stop, where Brubaker must rescue Forney and his friend from jail before he can visit with his family, who has come to see him there. In a human brotherhood scene typical of Michener, the Brubakers meet a Japanese family in a private pool at their hotel; paddling naked, the families intermingle and converse, resolving any conflict left over from the days before. At this point, the major conflict of the novel begins, however, as the carrier crew starts to plan its assault on four bridges across the canyon of the enemy center at Toko-Ri. Connected to the questions about the attack are more rhetorical ones, addressed to the reader: Will the flyers knock out the bridges? Will this make the Communists stop the war? Have Americans lost the strength to make this sacrifice? Where will America's last stand against the Communists come—in California, or Colorado, on the banks of the Mississippi?

The climax of the novel comes in "Sky," when the heroic Brubaker and Forney destroy the bridges but are killed in the aftermath of the attack. The action reaffirms that America has produced men who will always fly against bridges. The energy of this short section is powerful, deeply rooted in Michener's own naval air experience and the passion of his convictions.

Caravans is a transitional novel for Michener; while the setting is still Asia, it marks a western movement in both action and thought. Precursor to *The Drifters*, *The Source*, and to a lesser extent *Poland*, *Caravans* begins in 1946, in the aftermath of World War II. Here, the journalistic style that marks much of Michener's fiction is handled through a first-person narrator, Mark Miller, a junior-grade State Department officer stationed in Afghanistan. During the opening pages of the novel, Miller is sent on a mission to locate Ellen Jaspar, a high-spirited college girl from Dorset, Pennsylvania, who left Bryn Mawr College to marry an Afghan exchange student named Nazrullah. The plot is a series of adventures laced with romance, even after Ellen is found with a nomad caravan in the desert. The connecting link for the related incidents is the ancient route of the Kochis, whom Miller joins in the hope of convincing Ellen Jaspar to return to her parents. Again, in usual Michener fashion, the plot provides a context within which to describe geographic and historic detail and argue thematic questions.

In his excellent discussion of Michener's major works, George J. Becker points out that for more than twenty years the author was concerned with the "stresses and false values that beset American youth"; Becker applies his insight to *The Drifters*, but it is equally true of *Caravans*. Although the time of the story is 1946, Ellen Jaspar is almost a stereotype of college youth in the early 1960's, when the novel was written, in her dress, ideas, and life-style. For the last third of the book, she and Miller articulate the fiery rhetoric of campuses across America.

The thematic substance of *Caravans* goes further than any of Michener's previous work in its discussion of racial and religious prejudice. The dark-skinned Nazrullah explains his educational experience in Germany and America, infuriating Miller by comparing the American treatment of blacks to the German treatment of Jews. Although the reader's sympathy is with Miller, Nazrullah's point is well made. It is underscored in the climactic moment of the novel, when Miller—a Yale man, perhaps the most civilized member of the cast—announces that he is Jewish and nearly kills Dr. Stiglitz for his wartime Nazi efforts.

The majority of characters in the novel are Muslim, and a few are Christian. Repeatedly, however, the novel turns on a Jewish element, directly anticipating Michener's next major novel, *The Source*. Even Kabul, the Afghan capital, is used to show "what Palestine was like at the time of Jesus."

Chesapeake was the first of Michener's highly popular novels to deal with an indigenously American subject (one might take exception here with *Hawaii*, but that work seems clearly to belong to his earlier preoccupation with the Pacific). As in *Centennial* and later in *Texas*, Michener hoped to chronicle the making of America and to celebrate the courage of those who took part in that achievement. Spanning nearly four hundred years, the novel moves from the first Indians who settled the land to the funeral, in 1978, of one of the Quaker descendants of the earliest white men. In part, it is an instructive, political book, dealing with governments in Great Britain and France as well as the United States, culminating with Pusey Paxmore's suicide over his involvement in the Watergate scandal. For the most part, the focus is narrow—the Eastern Shore of Chesapeake Bay—despite the long roster of historical characters, from John Smith and George Washington to Daniel Webster and Henry Clay.

Here the episodes are organized in a fairly straightforward pattern—allowing for slight digression with a chapter devoted to a family of geese and another to a batch of crabs—and the third-person omniscient point of view does not shift. Four fictional families provide the substance of the book: the Catholic family of Edmund Steed who flees religious persecution in England and joins John Smith in exploring the land in 1607; the family of London thief and indentured servant Timothy Turlock, who arrives a generation later; the Quaker family of Edward Paxmore, who comes in search of religious freedom by way of Barbados and ironically receives the first slaves in the area; and the Caters, a family of former slaves, who build their contribution to the novel from the time just before the Civil War. Although there is great discussion of loyalties, each of the first three families fares well in the Revolution: Steed is an interpreter for the French, Turlock a sharpshooter, Paxmore a builder of fine ships. The War of 1812 continues the tension that creates the climax of the novel, with the Emancipation Proclamation and the War Between the States. Certain characters are given focus—Rosalind Steed, for example—but Michener does not slow down to develop any of them fully; many are types used to maintain the human element while the narrative sweeps over succeeding generations. This large movement does not, however, mitigate the value of the novel.

From the outset, Michener's emphasis is on human courage and tolerance and man's relationship with his environment. Ample descriptions build a love for the land and for the watermen who work it; later chapters deal with ecological concerns—erosion, litter, and landfill. Early chapters ennoble the Indian and lament his passing. Perhaps the greatest weight throughout is given to the issues of racial and religious freedom. The suffering of both the Steeds and the Paxmores offers compelling insight into the theocracy of Puritan New England and those who came to America seeking religious freedom. In ironic contrast, both the Steeds and the Paxmores own slaves. The final struggle for black freedom comes at the start of the twentieth century, with an amendment to the Maryland constitution intended to disenfranchise blacks. Although the Steed and Turlock clans support it, Emily Paxmore champions the defeat of the bill by arguing that it can be applied equally to all European immigrants after 1869, and the campaign becomes her own personal Armageddon.

Chesapeake is a big novel, and it includes even a recipe for oyster stew; the fragments that fill the end are the unresolved conflicts of modern time—except for an account of the passing of Devon Island. As the scene of much of the action slips into the sea, Michener affirms that it will come again and again until at last the "great world-ocean" reclaims it.

Although his other novels touch on the twentieth century, *Space* is Michener's one piece of fiction that concentrates solely on life in twentieth century America. In it, he chronicles the space program from its inception in 1944 to an ebb in 1982 through a series of incidents that connect neatly to his work before and after it.

The novel begins on October 24, 1944, with scenes that introduce four major characters. The first is Stanley Mott, an American engineer, in London at the request of the American president, whose job it is to see that the German installation at Peenemunde is not bombed before three of the chief scientists can be captured alive. The second is Norman Grant, drawn much like Harry Brubaker, in the climactic naval battle of Leyte Gulf. The third is John Pope, a seventeen-year-old football hero from Grant's hometown of Clay. Finally, there is Dieter Kolff, one of the scientists whom Mott must rescue, who survives the bombing because he is with his girlfriend. The next part of the novel introduces the women who are loved by these men and advances the story through them. Because of the ingenuity of a Nazi officer who later becomes a leader of the American aerospace industry, Dieter Kolff and Leisl come to the United States, shepherded by Mott and his wife, Rachel. Pope gets appointed to Annapolis, on the recommendation of Grant, who has become senator from the state of Fremont; Pope's wife, Penny, earns a law degree and goes to work for Grant when he is appointed to the space committee; Grant's wife, Elinor, preoccupied with little green men, becomes the principal supporter of Leopold Strabismus and the Universal Space Associates.

These characters, and those who flesh out their stories, create the substance of the novel. While Michener's focus is on the space program, these people are among the most fully developed in all of his work. Systematically moving through the various stages of America's efforts in outer space, he keeps the weight of his research in careful balance with the stories of human lives. This is particularly true in the second half of the novel, which centers on six fictional astronauts (Pope among them). While the reader is drawn into the explorations (particularly the Gemini flight, which Pope shares with his likable opposite, Randy Claggett, and their adventures on the dark side of the moon), one's interest is held by the characters at least as much as by the technology. This is particularly true of the capable con man Strabismus.

At first Strabismus seems an unnecessary diversion—similar to the recipes Michener offers for Polish sausage or oyster stew—but as the story builds, he becomes an integral part of the work. Playing off the initials U.S.A., Strabismus moves through a series of lucrative rackets until he sets himself up as a preacher with the United Salvation Alliance. As he panders to the fears of the uneducated, he crusades against "atheistic humanism" and advocates a return to fundamentalism that will prohibit the teaching of evolution and forbid national park rangers from describing the geological history of their areas. He launches impassioned attacks on homosexuals and fosters a virulent anti-Semitism. Michener clarifies his point of view in the final confrontation between Strabismus and the "heroes" of his novel. Finally, Michener suggests, the conflict is part of the long march of history and will continue thousands of years hence.

In the fall of 1981, Michener said that he had two big novels left in him, one on Poland and the other on Texas; both of these have subsequently been written. The first is a well-researched chronicle of Polish history that moves backward and forward, connecting the Communist country of modern time to the thirteenth century raids of Genghis Khan through the development of three fictional families. In the acknowledgments, in which the author explains his reasons for choosing this particular subject, he sounds very much as he did three decades before, when clarifying his interest in Asia. In both instances, the geographical and ideological positions of the areas indicate that they will become political focal points. Again, Michener is using his fictional format to educate readers of his time, moving through history to explain the present.

Texas is perhaps Michener's largest novel: More than two hundred characters are involved in its story, a number of whom are historical figures, and dialogue is the primary vehicle through which their story is told. With its narrative framework and blending of fact and fiction, the novel compares neatly with many of its predecessors. Despite its scope, however, one would be hard-pressed to claim that *Texas* is among the finest of Michener's works.

Whatever the critical verdict on Michener the novelist, it is clear that Michener the educator-through-fiction has been a great success. To a popular audience numbering in the millions, he has communicated the uniquely modern sense of the long view of history, and that is a considerable achievement.

Other major works

SHORT FICTION: *Return to Paradise*, 1951.

NONFICTION: *Proposals for an Experimental Future of the Social Sciences: Proposals for an Experimental Social Studies Curriculum*, 1939 (with Harold Long); *The Unit in the Social Studies*, 1940; *The Voice of Asia*, 1951; *The Floating World*, 1954; *Rascals in Paradise*, 1957 (with A. Grove Day); *Japanese Prints from the Early Masters to the Modern*, 1959; *Report of the County Chairman*, 1961; *The Modern Japanese Print: An Appreciation*, 1962; *Iberia: Spanish Travels and Reflections*, 1968; *Presidential Lottery: The Reckless Gamble in Our Electoral System*, 1969; *The Quality of Life*, 1970; *Facing East: The Art of Jack Levine*, 1970; *Kent State: What Happened and Why*, 1971; *A Michener Miscellany, 1950-1970*, 1973; *Sports in America*, 1976; *In Search of Centennial: A Journey*, 1978; *Testimony*, 1983; *Collectors, Forgers, and a Writer: A Memoir*, 1983.

ANTHOLOGY: *The Hokusai Sketchbooks: Selections from the Manga*, 1958.

Bibliography
Becker, George J. *James A. Michener*, 1983.
Day, A. Grove. *James A. Michener*, 1964.
Hayes, John P. "James A. Michener," in *Conversations with Writers II*, 1978.
_____. *James A. Michener: A Biography*, 1984.
Kings, John. *In Search of Centennial: Journey with James A. Michener*, 1978.
Michener, James A. *About Centennial: Some Notes on the Novel*, 1974.

Joan Corey Semonella

DAVID PLANTE

Born: Providence, Rhode Island; March 4, 1940

Principal long fiction

The Ghost of Henry James, 1970; *Slides*, 1971; *Relatives*, 1972; *The Darkness of the Body*, 1974; *Figures in Bright Air*, 1976; *The Family*, 1978; *The Country*, 1981; *The Woods*, 1982; *The Francoeur Novels*, 1983 (includes the preceding three novels); *The Foreigner*, 1984; *The Catholic*, 1985.

Other literary forms

David Plante is a frequent contributor of short fiction to *The New Yorker* magazine, including stories such as "Mr. Bonito" (July 7, 1980), "Work" (September 21, 1981), "The Accident" (August 9, 1982), and "A House of Women" (April 28, 1986). Plante has also published one book of nonfiction, *Difficult Women: A Memoir of Three* (1983), an account of his relationships with Sonia Orwell, George Orwell's widow, and writers Jean Rhys and Germaine Greer.

Achievements

While Plante has never enjoyed a large readership, he has achieved considerable recognition among his peers, winning the acclaim of Philip Roth and other prominent contemporaries. Plante began his career with several self-consciously artistic novels, but in his later works he has fashioned a spare, radically simplified style with a deceptive look of artlessness. In contrast to the minimalist writers to whose works his fiction bears a superficial resemblance, Plante uses this pared-down style as a vehicle to explore the consciousness of his protagonists, which he presents in a manner that differs sharply from the involuted style of most novels of consciousness. This is Plante's distinctive achievement in contemporary American fiction.

Plante's sixth novel, *The Family*, was nominated for the National Book Award in 1979. In 1983, while teaching writing at the University of Tulsa, in Tulsa, Oklahoma, Plante received a Guggenheim grant, and in the same year he won the Prize for Artistic Merit from the American Academy and Institute of Arts and Letters.

Biography

David Plante was born in Providence, Rhode Island, on March 4, 1940, the son of Anaclet Joseph Adolph and Albina (Bison) Plante. From 1959 to 1960, he attended the University of Louvain in Belgium, and in 1961 he was graduated with a B.A. from Boston College. After graduation, Plante taught at the English School in Rome, Italy, at the Boston School of Modern Languages, and at St. John's Preparatory School. He also worked for two years (1962-1964) as a researcher for *Hart's Guide to New York* in New York City. Plante has been a writer-in-residence at the University of Tulsa (1979-1983) and at King's College, Cambridge (1984-1985). He has lived in England since 1966.

Analysis

The dominant themes in the novels of David Plante concern the nature of relationships and the efforts of the individual to break out of his own self-consciousness in order to participate in these relationships. He explores the forces which unite people, whether family members, friends, or lovers, and the ability of these forces to bind as well as alienate, create as well as destroy. His method of narration in his early works reveals unconventional techniques which he would later incorporate into his more traditional novels. In his earliest works, such as *The Ghost of Henry James*, *Slides*, *Relatives*, *The Darkness of the Body*, and *Figures in Bright Air*, Plante experiments with an almost plotless structure with an emphasis on language and the expression of consciousness, echoing Henry James, Nathaniel Hawthorne, James Joyce, and Gertrude Stein. Instead of a narrative of progression and movement within a defined space and time, these novels present random associations from constantly changing perspectives. Plante often creates snapshots of consciousness in the form of numerous brief narrative sections which flash in front of the reader, revealing not concrete images but glimpses of various characters' impressions, perceptions, and emotions. Through this technique, Plante attempts to use a character's consciousness to define and describe meaning, leading many critics to observe that these early novels are not novels at all but rather collections of psychological fragments which, though often powerful, ultimately confuse and disappoint the reader.

With the publication of his largely autobiographical trilogy, *The Francoeur Novels*, in 1983 (which includes *The Family*, *The Country*, and *The Woods*), Plante continued to develop his theme of relationships between family members through the perspective of subjective consciousness and fragmented images, but he integrated these experimental techniques into a more traditionally defined narrative. The first book of the trilogy, *The Family*, introduces Daniel Francoeur, Plante's autobiographical counterpart in the trilogy, and his six brothers born to a Catholic, working-class, French-Canadian couple, Jim and Reena Francoeur. The novel is set primarily in Providence, Rhode Island, at the Francoeur's newly acquired lake home. Plante traces the emotional struggle of the nine family members to remain unified, communicative, and productive in the face of internal tension and external threat. Because of their ethnic background and unsophisticated social orientation, the family members feel alienated from the Providence community, and when the father loses his job through union pressure, the internal problems within the family are magnified at the same time that the bonds of love and dependency between individual members are tested. Though most of the narrative is seen and evaluated through Daniel's consciousness, the focus of the novel is not on him or any one character but rather on the Francoeur family as a single living organism trying to support and nurture all of its parts for the survival of the whole. The dependency of each family member on the others' well-being is exemplified by the hysterical disintegration of the family unit when the mother experiences a recurrence of an emotional illness.

Plante develops Reena's character more fully than he does the others in *The Family*, and he examines her closely through Daniel's eyes, making her the touchstone for the novel's major theme: the fragility of the seemingly indestructible. Reena possesses the objectivity to see quite clearly the flaws in each son's character while simultaneously loving each totally; she is unable, however, to acknowledge her husband's inability to cope with his unemployment. Her failure to deal with her husband as a fallible human being forces her sons to take sides against their father and ultimately to question their familial duties. Despite her strength and authority as the Francoeur matriarch, Reena remains a child-wife, puzzled and victimized by an uncommunicative, brooding husband. She confides frequently in Daniel, who comes to see his mother's position in the family as isolated and vulnerable. The only woman in a world full of men, an interloper in a fraternity house environment, Reena has tried to remain as unobtrusive as possible in her husband's and sons' world, from avoiding flowers and lacy decorations which might intrude upon their male starkness to suppressing her fears and anger. She has created, literally, seven times over, a world which she can never enter. When her emotional breakdown occurs and Jim resists medical help for her, afraid she would come back from the sanatorium as something other than his submissive wife, the family organism suffers a shock and responds with violence: sons against father, mother against sons, brothers against brothers. The novel concludes with a semblance of unity, but the organism has been damaged.

The damage is subtly revealed in the second (though last written) book of the trilogy, *The Woods*. Peace has returned to the Francoeur home, but only because Jim and Reena have surrendered to a self-imposed isolation and stagnant existence. They appear only peripherally in the novel, and the focus remains on Daniel, who visits his parents' home during a vacation from college. An extremely self-conscious adolescent, Daniel finds himself facing terrifying indecision and overwhelming freedom. Though little action takes place in the novel's three brief chapters, Plante conveys in simple yet intense language Daniel's need to belong, to anchor himself somewhere, to overcome his apathy and lack of ambition. Daniel's first sexual experience brings him no closer to what he wants as he becomes increasingly obsessed with the maleness of his own body. His decision to file with the draft board as a conscientious objector, despite the influence of his older brother Albert, a life-long military man, role model, and major source of financial support for the Francoeurs, does give Daniel a sense of definition, though mixed with shame. In *The Woods*, Plante creates in Daniel a representation of the time in adolescence when passivity is the safest action, when any other action seems too great a risk, and when even one's own body appears strange and threatening.

This period in Daniel's life has long passed when *The Country* opens. Once again Daniel, now a writer living in London, returns to his parents' home in Providence, where he joins his six brothers, not for any holiday or family celebration but as a response to the final assault on the family unit: the slow, degrading physical and mental deterioration of Reena and Jim Francoeur. Now in their eighties, they are weakened to the point of partial immobility and senility. The sons, some with wives and children, gather to take care of their parents' basic needs as well as attempt, in quiet desperation, to restore the bonds of familial understanding and love. Reena's mental problems have intensified with age, and Daniel listens, as always, to her frightened and often bitter ramblings about her sacrifices to her husband and family. In more tender moments, however, Reena shows her devotion to her dying husband, frequently enveloping his withered body in her arms, grasping his hands in silence, and kissing his cheek. Reena is also still able to express love toward her sons, sharing their secrets and laughing at the jokes whispered to her in French.

The Country does not, however, use Reena as a symbol for the state of the Francoeur family as the first novel did. Except for a brief flashback to twenty years earlier at a tense family gathering at the lake house, the last book of the Francoeur trilogy explores the character of Jim, who, in the earlier works, received uneven and ambiguous treatment. Through a first-person narrative, Daniel attempts to understand the complexities of a man who once seemed so simple. In moments of lucidity, Jim expresses to Daniel his doubts about having been a good father, husband, and worker, and Daniel realizes that, despite his father's domination over his mother and the unrelenting sense of social and familial duties imposed on his sons, Jim loved his family in every way that his old-world cultural background permitted, limited greatly by an inability to express his emotions. As Daniel witnesses the pathetic deterioration of his once hearty and active father, he frantically tries to re-establish communication and a sense of tradition. In response, his father awkwardly attempts to understand his son's life as a writer in a foreign country. Ultimately, the father, drifting in and out of the present in a cloudy mind, leaves his son the only wisdom he knows: "Work hard. . . . And be a good boy." When his father dies, Daniel is able to grieve honestly for a man who, he now realizes, "could not think of himself, but had to think of his duty to the outside world." Reena, after an initial feeling of emancipation from her husband's authority, reacts to his death by retreating into incessant speech and fearful imaginings, once again alone among the men she created.

In *The Country*, the strongest work in the trilogy, Plante achieved what he had been working toward since his first novels: the subordination of plot with an emphasis on emotion and perception. The only significant action in *The Country* is the observation of time and death, but the helplessness of every member of the Francoeur family is a haunting and consistent echo throughout the novel. This echo gives *The Country* a power never realized in the earlier works.

In the two novels succeeding the Francoeur trilogy, Plante's protagonist continues to narrate in the first person, though he is never mentioned by name in the earlier work, *The Foreigner*; only through allusions to the hero's family background does the author identify him as a member of the Francoeur family, probably Daniel once again. Adam Mars-Jones suggests in his review of *The Foreigner* in the *The Times Literary Supplement* that the narrator may be Daniel's older brother Andre, noting that at the end of *The Family* the Francoeurs receive a postcard from Andre, who is in Europe, the same postcard which is mentioned in *The Foreigner*. This connection does exist, but the narrator of *The Foreigner* undeniably possesses the same history, voice, and sensibility as the protagonist of *The Francoeur Novels*, whatever name the reader gives him.

The Foreigner does not relate to the trilogy in any other way, nor does it follow the previous work chronologically. In this novel, the hero is twenty and leaving his Rhode Island home in 1959 to travel to Europe, hoping to shed his "Americanisms" and experience the expatriate life-style in the fashion of Ernest Hemingway, whose epigraph, "In Spain you could not tell anything," introduces the book. Instead of the romance and rebirth he expected, the narrator discovers loneliness and alienation from the environment and the people, even his American college friends who meet him in France. Wanting to get as far away as possible from what these friends represent, he is grateful to find in Spain a mysterious black woman he met previously on his crossing from America. From the moment he links himself with Angela Johnson and her emotionally disturbed lover Vincent, the strangeness and danger he craved are never far from him, though never fully defined. Angela and Vincent demand all of their new friend's money, leaving him totally dependent upon them by the time he realizes that they are possibly involved in illegal activities. The narrator's odd relationship with Angela and Vincent is revealed in the Hemingway style of terse dialogue and matter-of-fact description blended with Plante's characteristically fragmented narrative and vivid images of consciousness. *The Foreigner* is a unique work for Plante, however, in that it does make some attempt, though sporadic and uneven, toward a climactic scene, the street-dance suicide of Vincent. No other Plante novel uses this traditional narrative element. Yet the circumstances which lead up to the story's climax remain subordinate to Plante's interest in the objective correlatives of his protagonist's consciousness, the means of representing his thoughts and emotions as concrete objects or communicable expressions. Many of these thoughts reflect the narrator's voyeuristic, homosexual obsession with Vincent and the total sense of alienation brought about by this attraction.

Daniel's homosexuality, only obscurely implied in *The Francoeur Novels*, is made explicit in *The Foreigner* and becomes the major focus of *The Catholic*. Early in the Francoeur trilogy, Daniel became obsessed with the figure of the nude, crucified Christ, a ubiquitous presence in his Catholic home. As he grew older, Daniel developed strange correlations between the body of Christ and the power of male sexuality. In *The Catholic*, Daniel decides that the only way for him to overcome his intense self-consciousness and escape from his body's prison is to surrender himself physically and spiritually to another man. Women, in Daniel's perception, have no spirituality: They are fixed, concrete, earthbound objects and therefore can only give him back to himself as a mirror does, thus increasing his awareness of himself. Although Daniel turns to women as confidantes and advisers, sexually they cannot provide the transcendental experience he seeks. When Daniel falls in love with Henry, he mistakes sexual obsession with heightened consciousness. They spend only one night together, and Daniel immediately realizes that Henry wants to maintain his autonomy and selfhood as desperately as Daniel wants to lose his. The novel becomes little more than an explication of Daniel's frightening sexual compulsions and the aftermath of grief and guilt. *The Catholic* does not develop the narrative structures attempted in *The Francoeur Novels* and *The Foreigner* and resembles more closely the earlier novels in its extremely obscure language and disturbing images.

Plante's work is significant mostly for its contribution to the genre of the modernist novel of consciousness. His early experimental novels, though static and highly derivative, adumbrate the techniques Plante would later refine in novels which artfully explore the self-consciousness of the individual as he strives to understand his relationship with the external world. Especially in *The Francoeur Novels*, Plante succeeds in creating, through an often masterful command of language, a powerful synesthesia, blending paintings of the mind with the art of storytelling.

Other major work
NONFICTION: *Difficult Women: A Memoir of Three*, 1983.

Bibliography
Baker, John F. "David Plante," in *Publishers Weekly*. CCXXII (December, 1982), pp. 12-13.
Byatt, A. S. "Standing and Falling with the Body," in *The Times Literary*

Supplement. December 20, 1985, p. 1463.

Hunt, George W. "A Catholic Family Trilogy," in *America.* CL (1984), pp. 262-263.

Mars-Jones, Adam. "Performing a European Act," in *The Times Literary Supplement.* November 16, 1984, p. 1301.

Plante, David. "Conversations with Philip [Roth]," in *The New York Times Book Review.* LXXXIX (January, 1984), p. 3.

Penelope A. LeFew

CHAIM POTOK

Born: New York, New York; February 17, 1929

Principal long fiction

The Chosen, 1967; *The Promise*, 1969; *My Name Is Asher Lev*, 1972; *In the Beginning*, 1975; *The Book of Lights*, 1981; *Davita's Harp*, 1985.

Other literary forms

Wanderings: Chaim Potok's History of the Jews (1978) is a personal reconstruction of four thousand years of Jewish history. Potok has also written essays and book reviews for Jewish and popular periodicals and newspapers.

Achievements

Critical acceptance and public acclaim have greeted Potok's novelistic explorations of the conflict between Orthodox Judaism and secular American culture. Potok received the Edward Lewis Wallant Award and a National Book Award nomination for *The Chosen*, his first novel. He received the Athenaem Award for its sequel, *The Promise*. His sympathetic (critics would say sentimental) portrayal of Jewish fundamentalism and those who choose to leave it highlights the poignancy of an individual's break with tradition. Indeed, Potok's novels test the ability of traditional communities to contribute to the modern world without themselves being assimilated. His evocation of Jewish life in New York in the middle third of the twentieth century has universal appeal and disturbing implications.

Biography

Born of Orthodox Jewish parents in the Bronx in 1929, Chaim Potok was reared in a fundamentalist culture. Potok's father, Benjamin Potok, was a Polish émigré and no stranger to the pogroms of Eastern Europe. The young Potok was taught that the profound suffering of the Jews would one day transform the world. Yet, as Potok suggests in *Wanderings*, his service as a Jewish chaplain with the United States Army in Korea (1956-1957) confronted him with a world of good and evil that had never heard of Judaism. His attempt to come to terms with this larger world led Potok to a critical investigation of his own Jewish heritage and the limitations of the fundamentalist perspective. Though he had been ordained a Conservative rabbi in 1954, attracted by doctrines more liberal than those of strict Jewish Orthodoxy, Potok has continued his struggle to reconcile fundamental Judaism with the findings of science (as historiography and textual criticism shed new light on ancient traditions). *The Chosen* inaugurated his public search for a voice with which to speak to his heritage as well as to the larger world.

In the early 1960's, Potok taught at the Jewish Theological Seminary in New York, edited *Conservative Judaism*, and in 1965 became an editor with the Jewish Publication Society of Philadelphia. He was married to Adena Mosevitzky in 1958, with whom he resides in Merion, Pennsylvania. The Potoks have three children: Rena, Naama, and Akiva.

Analysis

In his novels, Chaim Potok returns again and again to the story of a young protagonist coming of age in a culture (usually Jewish) at once mysterious, beautiful, sad, and somehow inadequate. Usually told in the first person, Potok's stories surround the reader with forebodings of the larger, evil world (news of pogroms in Europe, the Holocaust, the first atom bomb) into which his characters are plunged. Potok creates a microcosm of feeling and reaction to events that shake the world. His sentences are simple and reportorial, at times almost a parody of the staccato style of Ernest Hemingway. The stories develop chronologically, though they are frequently invaded by dreams, visions, or voices from the "Other Side."

In each of his stories, Potok sets for himself a question to be answered and reworks his own experiences until he is satisfied with at least a provisional resolution. Controlling metaphors help shape the questions. In *The Chosen*, the baseball game symbolizes the competition between two Jewish cultures, the very strict Hasidic and the more openly assimilationist. What happens to those caught in between those two traditions? The vision of pups being born in *The Book of Lights* represents the entrance of fertile Cabala mysticism into a world of strict Jewish law. How can Jewish mysticism enrich Orthodoxy? Asher Lev's dreams of his mythical ancestor foreshadow the young artist's confrontation with his own culture. What happens when art brings great hurt? The sound of a little door harp symbolizes the transforming power of the imagination for Ilana Davita Chandal of *Davita's Harp*. What is the place of the imagination in Jewish Orthodoxy? What is the place of women? (Davita is Potok's first female protagonist.)

The Chosen recounts the story of Danny Saunders, brilliant son of a Hasidic rabbi, chosen by tradition to one day succeed his father as leader of the fundamentalist community in Brooklyn, New York. Yet Danny is less interested in studying the Talmud (Jewish law) than in probing the works of Sigmund Freud and other secular psychologists. The story closes with the inevitable confrontation between Danny and his father, which is mediated by Danny's friend Reuvan Malter. In the climactic scene in Reb Saunders' office, the old rabbi turns to his son and addresses him as a father for the first time. (For years, Danny had been reared in silence, except for times of Talmud study.) With fatherly tears, Reb Saunders explains that the years of silence created a soul of compassion within his brilliant son. Though he may well leave the Hasidic community for secular studies, Danny will always carry with him the legacy of Jewish suffering. That legacy will provide the moral force to change the world.

Reuvan, son of a Talmud scholar of the new school of textual criticism, chooses to become a rabbi. The choices, for Reuvan and for Danny, do not, however, come easily. Reuvan faces ostracism by the Hasidic community for suggesting that some Talmudic texts were of inferior quality and subject to misinterpretation. Danny must seemingly turn against his father if he is to pursue secular studies and abandon his leadership obligations.

The novel is structured almost as a diary, with pages of detailed descriptions of schoolwork in the Jewish high school, visits to the local synagogue, and the ebb and flow of Reuvan's life. Though at times tedious, the very innocence of the language contributes to a certain dramatic intensity. The conflict in the novel is mirrored in the frequent news reports of World War II and in the ensuing controversy over the creation of a Jewish state, Israel, in 1949. The Hasidic community is content to wait for the Messiah to create such a state; Reuvan's father calls for an immediate political settlement. Political questions are present in each of Potok's novels and are of central interest in *Davita's Harp*.

Silence is again present in Potok's second novel, *The Promise*, which continues the story of Danny Saunders and Reuvan Malter as they enter their professional lives. The novel begins with shouts of rage from young Michael Gordon, the son of Professor Abraham Gordon, a controversial Jewish philosopher. Michael has been cheated at a carnival booth by an old Jewish man, and both Reuvan and his date, Rachel Gordon, Michael's cousin, stare in horror as Michael angrily denounces Orthodoxy. Michael's father had questioned the supernatural accounts in the Hebrew Bible and, as a result, was excommunicated from the Orthodox community; now Michael is releasing his hate on those who persecuted Professor Gordon. Subsequently, Michael is taken to Danny Saunders, now a psychologist at a residential treatment center. When the boy refuses to speak, Danny isolates him. The agonizing silence breaks Michael's will and he reveals the hate he feels for his father and his writings, writings that have brought condemnation to them both. Eventually, Michael is finally able to accept his own feelings and reconcile with his parents, and Danny and Rachel are married, the powerful coupling of the brilliant Hasid with the cosmopolitan daughter of a secularist philosopher.

The Promise continues the exploration of Reuvan's choice to receive his rabbinate from an Orthodox seminary and his refusal to become a secular Jew, as Professor Gordon has done. Yet Reuvan is uneasy with the traditional method of Talmud study advanced by Rav Kalman, one of his teachers. If the Talmud is the sacred oral tradition of the Jews in written form, contradictory commentaries from rabbis down through the centuries must always be reconciled by newer interpretations, so as not to call God's Word into question. For Reuvan, there is another possibility; a corrupt text could be the source of confusion. Any correction, however, would mean violence to sacred scripture. Reuvan will become a rabbi so that he might debate Rav Kalman and the others from within a common tradition.

Reuvan's father, David Malter, is the voice of quiet wisdom throughout both books. Though a proponent of the new Talmud studies, he is sympathetic toward those whose tightly knit culture is being threatened. As he tells Reuvan in *The Promise*, "We cannot ignore the truth. At the same time, we cannot quite sing and dance as they do. . . . That is the dilemma of our time, Reuvan. I do not know what the answer is." Earlier, Reuvan's father had challenged his son to make his own meaning in the world. Those who had committed themselves to the Hasidic traditions had kept the faith alive through incomprehensible persecution. Now Reuvan must also choose with the greatest seriousness and fervency, for he, too, must make a mark on the world and endure hardship of his own.

Potok picks up this theme in his third novel, *My Name Is Asher Lev*. Covering the period of the late 1940's through the late 1960's, the book is an apologia for the artist. The Orthodox Jewish surroundings are familiar, but this time the controversy is not over textual criticism but rather representational art. Painting is not strictly forbidden to the Orthodox Jew, but it is regarded as useless, as foolishness, as a waste of time better devoted to the study of the Torah, the five books of Moses. Moreover, certain pictures could come close to violating the Commandment forbidding graven images. Asher Lev is a born painter, however, and throughout the novel, as he develops his talent, he is increasingly isolated from his family and culture. Asher is born in Crown Heights in Brooklyn in 1943. His father travels extensively for the local Rebbe in an effort to establish Ladover Hasid communities throughout Europe and to aid families emigrating to the United States. Asher's mother must stay with her son in New York because Asher refuses to leave his familiar streets to join his father in Europe. There are long nights of loneliness, waiting for Asher's father to return from some mission or other. Asher's mother suffers a breakdown when her brother, also on a mission for the Rebbe, is killed. She begins to find herself again by plunging into her Russian studies, picking up the work her brother left unfinished. Metaphors of things unfinished and things completed permeate the novel. Asher's father is continually on the move because of the great unfinished work of the Ladover. Asher himself finds that he must bring some kind of completeness to the world by painting not only what he sees with his eyes but also what his inner vision reveals to him. Those visions are not always beautiful; his paintings can be like knives, plunging the reality of evil into the soul of the onlooker. The wise Rebbe, sensing Asher's vast talent, entrusts him to Jacob Kahn, himself an artistic genius and a nonobservant Jew. Kahn forces Asher to absorb the work of Pablo Picasso, especially *Guernica* (1937), a painting inspired by the German bombing of the Basque capital during the Spanish Civil War. In time, Asher begins to surpass his teacher.

Asher becomes virtually a stranger to his father. At the end of the novel, Asher's parents stare with mixed rage and amazement at the two crucifixions he has painted. Both are of his mother, looking in abstract fashion at Asher the stranger on one side and the always-traveling husband on the other. The image of the cross for Asher has become the supreme symbol of suffering, devoid of any Christian preoccupation. The image is too much, however, for his parents, Orthodox Jews. As the Rebbe tells him, "You have crossed a boundary. I cannot help you. You are alone now. I give you my blessings."

There is a marked contrast between Asher's sensitive paintings (an effort to say what must be said about the evil in the world) and his selfish behavior toward his parents. He is one of the least sympathetic of Potok's protagonists because he struggles less with his own anguish than with his need to express his artistic gift at whatever cost. Jacob Kahn's advice, "Be a great painter, Asher Lev. . . . That will be the only justification for all the pain your art will cause," seems too facile. Asher is determined to remain an observant Jew, but he will do so on his own terms. The Commandment about honoring one's parents must be radically reinterpreted. The book suffers from the technical difficulty that Asher Lev must be identified as a genius early in the story in order for Potok to create the kind of tension he needs to interest a reader. A mediocre artist who causes pain is merely self-indulgent.

Yet the book reveals something of Potok's larger purpose. Art must be true to itself even if that means surprise or hurt. The artist, painter, or writer must speak from the heart; anything else is mere propaganda. Potok is seeking to provide a rationale for his novelistic critiques of fundamentalist communities.

Potok introduces something else into Asher's story: Asher often dreams of his "mythic ancestor," a Jew who served a nobleman only to have the nobleman unleash evil upon the world. Just as Asher envisioned that ancient Jew traveling the world, seeking to redress the wrong he had a part in, so must the artist reshape evil into art and so bring a kind of balance to the world. Asher's visions are forerunners of Potok's use of mysticism or imaginative visions themselves as ways of coming to terms with a world gone crazy.

In the Beginning is the story of young David Lurie and his childhood in an Orthodox family in the Bronx in the 1920's. The novel is patterned after the Book of Genesis: David falls from his mother's arms, develops a keen interest in the accounts of the Flood, and learns through the study of the Torah the power of words to shape a world. Potok's fourth novel was his most complex to date, departing from the forthright exposition found in *The Chosen* in favor of a more subtle panoply of impressions of growing up. Like all Potok's protagonists, David is precocious, constantly questioning the world around him, trying to have it make sense. He is sickly, bullied by other boys, and

plagued with recurring nightmares. David functions in the novel as an ideal-
ized figure to focus the reader's attention on how Orthodoxy confronts anti-
Semitism and growing secularization. David imagines the Golem of Prague
crushing those who would harm the Jews like some powerful living robot; as
David grows, though, he learns that words can be more powerful than the
Golem. Eventually, helped by those who practice textual critique of the Torah, David heads for graduate study at the University of Chicago. Yet, as in
Potok's other works, there must also be some kind of reconciliation of the
demands of Jewish Orthodoxy with those of secular learning. It is achieved
through a vision David has years later as he tours the site of the Bergen-
Belsen death camp. David's vision of his dead father, and of his father's
brother, David's namesake, is a moving conclusion to the book. David's father despairs that he has lost his son to the evil world, to the very world that
took the lives of millions of Jews. He is reassured by David's uncle, however,
that the son must journey into that world in order to bring something back to
enrich Orthodoxy, which has become moribund. The son must venture out
but must never forget his own roots. No anger of man can strike evil from the
world. Only the patient use of words, with faith in their power to transform
creation, can accomplish the task. That will be a new beginning for the
world, and for Orthodoxy.

Potok's earlier novels tell the story of those in conflict with their Orthodox
heritage. For the first time, *In the Beginning* pictures a reconciliation as a vision or story within the context of the novel. It is a kind of blessing from the
beyond; here is the artist at work, crafting the resolution to the story.

The Book of Lights, narrated in the third person, uses the technique of
mystical reconciliation for a more universal purpose. If the Master of the
Universe truly exists, how is a believer to accept the death light of the twentieth century, the atomic bomb? Potok's answer is that through the imaginative
use of Jewish mysticism, the spark of God can be found in an evil world.

The story departs from Potok's previous novels, which traced the childhood of the protagonist. Only a few pages are devoted to Gershon Loran's
early life before his seminary days and subsequent chaplaincy in Korea.
Those first pages, however, are significant. Gershon witnesses the birth of
some pups on a rooftop in the midst of his rundown neighborhood; he is
awed by the presence of life even amid wreckage.

In seminary, Gershon is introduced to the study of the Cabala and its *Zohar*, a Jewish mystical work from the thirteenth century. The *Zohar* is the
book of lights of the novel's title, describing the creation of the world through
the emanations of God. There are places where God has withdrawn his light;
that has enabled humankind to come on the scene but it has also ushered in
great evil. Now the mystic is called to ascend through those emanations to
find God.

Such mystical tradition is complex and even contradictory. For Gershon, however, it is the pounding heart of a living faith. Gershon's quiet moments of reverie serve him well during his chaplaincy. Though Potok paints a detailed picture of Gershon's activities in Korea, the crucial story is elsewhere. Gershon's seminary friend, Arthur Leiden, travels with him to Kyoto and Hiroshima. At the Hiroshima monument, Arthur reads from the Psalms and pleads to God in vain for some kind of atonement. Arthur's father had worked with other scientists in developing the atom bomb, and Arthur is haunted by the memory. Later, Arthur is killed in a plane crash; Gershon, visiting Arthur's parents, hears a portion of one of Arthur's letters: "All the world, it seems, is a grayish sea of ambiguity, and we must learn to navigate in it or be drowned." That is Potok's message in the novel; "Loran" is itself a navigational acronym. If Judaism were merely the law, the faith would break on the shoals of the gritty world. Its mystical tradition infuses the faith with the ambiguity of real life. It does not explain but rather affirms the nature of God's creation. The *Zohar* is an imaginative understanding of the nature of God; in it, God enfolds both good and evil. It is a light by which to view a decaying civilization, a light that will survive the death light. In his final mystical vision of his old cabala teacher, Gershon learns that the mystical light will help mend the world so that it can be broken again in yet new acts of creation.

It is the "mending power" of imagination that is at the heart of *Davita's Harp*. The harp referred to is a small instrument that fits on a door, with little balls that strike piano wires when the door is opened or closed. Here Potok returns to the first-person narrative, tracing the childhood of Ilana Davita Chandal, his first female lead character. She is the daughter of a nonbelieving Jewish mother and a nonbelieving Christian father. Spanning the years from the mid-1930's to 1942, the novel speaks with a new voice yet recapitulates some familiar themes. Davita grows up in the New York area; she remembers frequent moves, strange people coming and going, and the constant singing of the door harp. Her parents are involved in the Communist Party, attempting to fight Fascism in Spain and in the United States. Davita is precocious and inquisitive and her mother intelligent and cool, forever supplying Davita with the meaning of new words: proletariat, strike, idea, magic, war. Davita is spurred in her imaginative development by Aunt Sarah, a devout Episcopalian nurse, who tells her Bible stories, and by Jakob Daw, an Austrian writer, now suffering from having been gassed in World War I, who had loved Davita's mother when they were both in Vienna. Daw is sheltered for a time by Davita's parents and spins odd stories for her. There is the story of the little bird, flying to find the source of a beautiful music that soothes the world of the horrors of war. Only if the bird could stop the deceitful music would the world wake to its pain.

Davita's father, Michael Chandal, a journalist with *New Masses*, is killed during the bombing of Guernica during the Spanish Civil War. Soon after, both Jakob Daw and Davita's mother, Channah, become disillusioned with the Stalinists because the Communists, too, have committed atrocities. Davita has taken to attending a Jewish high school and becomes an outstanding student. Jakob Daw returns to Europe, where he dies, though his stories live in Davita's heart. Not long afterward, Ezra Dinn, an Orthodox Jew who had loved Davita's mother years ago, marries Channah. Slowly, Davita's mother regains her sense of place.

Davita's time of innocence is over. Before Jakob Daw left for Europe, he finished his strange story of the bird. The bird, he said, gave up searching for the music of the world and became very small to fit inside the door harp. There, said Daw, the music was not deceitful but full of innocence. Now, however, Davita encounters something sinister in her adopted tradition. She is the most brilliant student at her yeshiva but she is passed over for the Akiva Award because, she is told, she is a woman. It is 1942. Another student is selected for the award but learns the truth and refuses it. He is Reuvan Malter, first introduced in *The Chosen*.

Ilana Davita had wanted the prize because it would have given her the opportunity to tell her Jewish community a few words of farewell. "I had made this community my home, and now I felt betrayed by it. . . . I felt suddenly alone. And for the first time I began to understand how a single event could change a person's life." Later, in a vision, Jakob Daw and Davita's father appear, as well as Aunt Sarah. They want to hear her words, and so Davita speaks. She does not understand a world that kills its very best. She had wanted to speak public words of goodbye to her father and Jakob Daw the storyteller. The harp appears in her vision as well, singing in memorial to all the Davitas who would never have an opportunity to "speak their few words to this century."

In the end, Davita will go on to public school, angry with "sacred discontent." In an interview, Potok explained that Davita's experience was based on that of his wife, who was passed over as valedictory speaker because of her sex. *Davita's Harp* is a new exploration for Potok, that of Orthodoxy and feminism. Yet the novel also draws from Gershon Loran, David Lurie, and Asher Lev in recognizing the power of the artist's imagination to transform pain and ambiguity into some kind of meaning. A writer is a kind of harp, playing new music that mends the world.

These six novels of Chaim Potok are offered as a gift of imagination to the Orthodox world and to all who are children of a restrictive past. The gift is risky, but it may well infuse new life into old ways or serve as a beacon for those who must plunge into the world in their search for meaning.

Other major work

NONFICTION: *Wanderings: Chaim Potok's History of the Jews*, 1978.

Bibliography

Kauvar, Elaine M. "An Interview with Chaim Potok," in *Contemporary Literature*. XXVII (Fall, 1986), pp. 290-317.
Potok, Chaim. Essay in *The Condition of Jewish Belief*, 1966.

Dan Barnett

RAYMOND QUENEAU

Born: Le Havre, France; February 21, 1903
Died: Paris, France; October 25, 1976

Principal long fiction

Le Chiendent, 1933 (*The Bark Tree*, 1968); *Gueule de Pierre*, 1934; *Les Derniers Jours*, 1936; *Odile*, 1937; *Les Enfants du Limon*, 1938; *Un Rude Hiver*, 1939 (*A Hard Winter*, 1948); *Les Temps mêlés: Gueule de Pierre II*, 1941; *Pierrot mon ami*, 1942 (*Pierrot*, 1950); *Loin de Rueil*, 1944 (*The Skin of Dreams*, 1948); *On est toujours trop bon avec les femmes*, 1947 (as Sally Mara; *We Always Treat Women Too Well*, 1981); *Saint-Glinglin*, 1948; *Journal intime*, 1950 (as Sally Mara); *Le Dimanche de la vie*, 1952 (*The Sunday of Life*, 1976); *Zazie dans le métro*, 1959 (*Zazie in the Metro*, 1960); *Les Œuvres completes de Sally Mara*, 1962; *Les Fleurs bleues*, 1965 (*The Blue Flowers*, 1967); *Le Vol d'Icare*, 1968 (*The Flight of Icarus*, 1973).

Other literary forms

Raymond Queneau was a prolific writer in many forms in addition to long fiction. He published a dozen major collections of poetry, in addition to many opuscules published in private or limited additions. His poetry spoofs the seriousness of twentieth century poetry through the use of odd end-rhymes, slang, and invented forms; at the same time, he also manages to deal with serious subjects. One of Queneau's best-known works is the unclassifiable *Exercises de style* (1947; *Exercises in Style*, 1958). In this work, he takes the kernel of a narrative and in a dazzling series of ninety-nine variations investigates the limits of the possibilities of language. Queneau also wrote essays, criticism, and the dialogue for several of the film adaptations of his novels.

Achievements

Raymond Queneau is an unclassifiable author, which is just what he would have wished. His novels of the 1930's, when he was associated with the Surrealists, abound in wordplay and experiments with colloquial language, but they are generally set against a sombre backdrop of war and working-class life. The characters seem to be controlled by the language which they speak, with the consequence that they are viewed from an ironic distance. In the 1940's, with his literary reputation firmly established, Queneau took some daring chances. He published *Exercises in Style*, which, if judged by its narrative content, is of no substance whatsoever; he also published a semi-serious parody of the then-popular scandal novel under an assumed name. Yet these were precisely the sorts of risks that Queneau enjoyed taking and that, in turn, make him both so hard to pin down and such a source of invention for subsequent writers. Queneau's novels of the 1950's brought him a wide popular audience for the first time, with their bright and zany depiction of ordinary people having the time of their lives. In 1960, along with François Le Lionnais, he founded OuLiPo, l'Ouvoir de Littérature Potentielle (the Workshop of Potential Literature), a group of writers who meet regularly to discuss the infinite potential of language for recombination and creative invention. His association with this group, along with the experimental quality of his work, is often mentioned as leading to Queneau's strong influence over the practitioners of the *nouveau roman*, or New Novel, of the 1960's. Overall, Queneau enjoyed a productive, highly varied, yet playful career as a writer, introducing slang and colloquial language into "serious" literature. In some ways, he is the most significant literary figure to provide a link between the Surrealists of the 1920's and 1930's and the more language-oriented writers of the 1960's and 1970's.

Biography

Raymond Queneau was born on February 21, 1903, in Le Havre, France. His family background was modest; his parents ran a haberdashery. Queneau took his *lycée* degree in Le Havre in 1920 and then went to Paris to study philosophy. During the following decade he associated with the Surrealists and helped to edit the journal *La Révolution surréaliste*. For two years, Queneau fulfilled his military service obligation as a Zouave in North Africa; he eventually wrote of the experience in *Odile*. After his discharge, in 1928, he gained employment at a bank and married Janine Kahn.

Queneau's career as a novelist received some initial impetus from a voyage to Greece in 1932. There he wrote most of his first novel, *The Bark Tree*. Once started in his career as a writer, Queneau began to publish frequently in several genres. His first collection of poetry, *Chêne et chien* (1937), plays off the ambiguous Norman etymology of the Queneau family name, Quêne/Chêne, "oak tree," and Quenot/Chien, "dog." In like manner, throughout his career as a man of letters, Queneau would continually seek to blend humor with noble literary aspirations.

The literary contacts Queneau cultivated in his early years led in part to a position with the prestigious French publishing house Gallimard. In 1945, he assumed the role of editor for the *Encyclopédie de la Pléiade*, a multivolume encyclopedia of history, natural sciences, and social sciences. Queneau's was never purely a literary mind to begin with, and his association with the encyclopedia allowed him to continue to develop his wide-ranging interests in mathematics and science. In 1947, Queneau's poem "Si tu t'imagines" ("If You Would Think") was set to music and became the most popular song of the year. In the same year, Queneau published a parody of the scandal-novel, under the pseudonym Sally Mara. Only several years later, when he published *Journal intime* under the same name, did he admit to being the author of both works.

The decade of the 1950's saw Queneau reach his greatest popularity as a novelist with two cheerful, funny, "popular" novels, *The Sunday of Life* and *Zazie in the Metro*. Both novels were turned into critically acclaimed, popular films—the former by Claude Chabrol, the latter by Louis Malle—with Queneau's assistance in both projects. The popularity Queneau enjoyed at first hampered the acceptance of his work as literature. With the rise of the New Novel in the 1960's, however, and the new emphasis given by criticism to the significance of language itself in literary works, Queneau eventually came to be seen as a forerunner of contemporary novelistic practice.

Toward the end of his life, a writer both popular and honored, Queneau continued to publish collections of poetry, as well as two of his most profound novels, *The Blue Flowers* and *The Flight of Icarus*. Queneau died in Paris, on October 25, 1976, at the age of seventy-three.

Analysis

Raymond Queneau's long fiction can be characterized by its wordplay, humor, and attentive concern with the lives of people living in ordinary circumstances. Queneau's pursuit of radical linguistic measures—like that of James Joyce, who among other English-language authors served as his literary model—is almost always tied to a depiction of working-class and lower-middle-class conditions. In fact, the language experiments that most identify Queneau's originality are his various ways of representing colloquial and slang expressions, or how real people actually talk. Interwoven with the depiction of the lives of ordinary people are an extraordinary number of learned allusions, buried quotations, and philosophical statements. Paradoxical as it may seem, Queneau's work points to the level of what might be called "metaphysical" thinking even by characters who would not know the meaning of the word. For Queneau, philosophy is interesting and useful primarily as it reflects the insights of simple people, which are often of a startling profundity.

Queneau's novels of the 1930's deal with a range of subjects, from the lives of ordinary people in Le Havre, his birthplace, to his war experience in North Africa, to some of the crazy artists he knew in part through his associations with the Surrealists. *A Hard Winter* may be taken as representative of Queneau's work from this decade. Set during World War I, the winter of 1916 specifically, the novel examines with cool and detached humor some of the contradictions in popular sentiment and the reality of wartime existence. Through a slowly developing romance seen through the perspective of the main character, Lehameau, the novel also investigates the repressed emotional lives of the people from this world.

The novel takes place in Le Havre and clearly incorporates elements of Queneau's background and family experience. Lehameau, the protagonist, enlisted, was wounded in action, and is now working as a liaison with the English armed forces stationed in Le Havre. At the opening of the book a group of Chinese soldiers are marching through the streets to the general amusement of the population. Lehameau expresses his feelings to a young woman (Miss Weeds) in the uniform of the British WAAC:

—Zey làffe, bicose zey dou notte undèrrstande.
Il dit encore:
—Aïe laïe-ke zatt: you dou nott làffe.

Here Queneau's humor and wordplay are at the foreground of the passage, representing a Frenchman speaking accented English through the use of French orthography. Throughout Queneau's work the way people speak reveals more about them than they know about themselves. The passage has a deeper meaning as well, concerning the necessary understanding of people from other cultures. The dialogue also serves to set up a relationship between Lehameau and Miss Weeds, which the rest of the novel explores.

Lehameau's sentiments of universal understanding are placed in an ironic light. He is in fact a racist and a proto-Fascist who, behind a pacifist ideology, harbors the belief in the necessity of a German victory to restore France to her true greatness. Queneau's underlying motive for portraying such a character in a book published in 1939 can only be guessed. It is clear from the work itself that the intended effect is one of ironic distancing. Lehameau's stunted emotional life becomes the amusing subject of the book, in spite of the antipathy his political views almost necessarily provokes in the reader.

The low level of Lehameau's emotional development is further explored in the book through the relationship he cultivates with an adolescent girl and her younger brother, following a random encounter on a bus. Lehameau courts the two of them through an appeal to English regimental badges and an obviously phony patriotism. He also takes the two to the cinema, after receiving the benevolent blessing of the head of the household, Madeleine, their older sister, who runs a brothel. Annette, the young girl, is one of Queneau's typically precocious nymphets, and in this way she anticipates two of Queneau's most famous characters, Sally Mara and Zazie. The way in which Lehameau's relationship with Annette develops in parallel fashion with his relationship to Miss Weeds is the true core of the novel.

Lehameau and Miss Weeds gradually fall in love, but they are prevented from fulfilling their relationship by a mixture of ignorance and institutional prudery. Miss Weeds, in the service of the British armed forces, at first resists Lehameau's overtures. When she later gives in to her feelings and they are on the verge of consummating their relationship, Miss Weeds is abruptly transferred back to England, effectively ending their relationship. The double standard of British morality is clearly Queneau's target here: Miss Weeds is protected by the military bureaucracy from the morally dangerous Frenchman; at the same time, Madeleine's primary customers in her bordello are the English soldiers stationed in Le Havre. Lehameau temporarily overcomes his sorrow at losing Miss Weeds through a brief tryst with Madeleine, at which time he also loses his virginity. In a surprise ending, on the last page of the book Lehameau marries—Annette. The various levels of irony at work in the novel prevent the reader finally from making any rigorous moral judgments on the actions of the characters.

Queneau's career as a novelist took a strange turn in 1947, when he published two very different works. *Exercises in Style* is not a novel at all, but there are many who regard it as Queneau's greatest achievement. In a dazzling series of ninety-nine variations, the writer tests language to the limits of its possibilities. The narrative kernel remains constant throughout the various treatments: the speaker sees a strangely dressed man on a bus; the man angrily accuses a fellow passenger of stepping on his toes, then quickly grabs a vacant seat; two hours later, the speaker sees the man again talking with a man near the Gare Saint-Lazare. From formal logical analysis to haiku, from street slang to Anglicisms to Italianisms, Queneau shows that the work of the literary imagination has as its primary material language itself.

Queneau's other work published in 1947 is his parody of the scandal-novel, *We Always Treat Women Too Well*, which he published under the pseudonym Sally Mara. Ostensibly, the work is the translation into French by one Michel Presle of a work originally written in Gaelic by one Sally Mara, and presents an account of the events in a post office taken over by Irish nationalist insurgents during the Easter Rising of 1916. The insurgents are inconvenienced when they find, after securing the post office and releasing the postal workers, that one Gertie Girdle has been left behind, locked in a ladies room. Poking fun at the macho posturings of men during wartime (as the title suggests), Queneau shows how the insurgents' freedom of speech and behavior are seriously constrained by this woman's presence. Gertie also turns out to be more than they bargained for when her long-repressed sexuality reaches full flower and she becomes an active seductress. Queneau has great fun with the conventions of both the action novel and the pornographic novel and characteristically enjoys manipulating language and literary reference: The insurgents' password, for example, is "Finnegans wake!"

The reader is instantly alerted to the tongue-in-cheek nature of the book through its style. The doorman who guards the post office opens the novel with "God save the King!" but is quickly dispatched, as follows:

> He did no more than murmur, this time, for he had already manifested his loyalty to such an extent that Corny Kelleher had wasted no time in injecting a bullet into his noggin. The dead doorman vomited his brains through an eighth orifice in his head, and fell flat on the floor.

As the insurgents' names suggest, Queneau's Ireland owes more to a reading of the work of James Joyce than to the accounts of Irish history. By the conclusion of the first chapter, the insurgents have expelled the remaining postal employees—they think—and have secured the post office. From the perspective of one of the insurgents, Dillon, the chapter concludes, "No more virgins offended his view."

While spoofing the action-and-sex novel, Queneau also incorporates his more serious literary models, using the unreliable narrator associated with the work of Joseph Conrad and the interior monologue style of Joyce. When Gertie Girdle takes over the narrative in chapter 4, it is as though she had stepped straight from the pages of Joyce right into (where else?) the ladies' room. Her simple mind reviews its limited contents: the state of modern plumbing, her intended, whether she should fix her hair again. When she sees an armed insurgent, her mind follows its own logic: He is armed and dangerous, he must be a Republican, only the British can save me, I will wait in the ladies room, they cannot touch me in here, it is only proper. As in *A Hard Winter*, the French perspective on Anglo-Saxon prudishness gives the writer plenty of material for his humorous purposes.

The humor turns dark as the novel progresses. Gertie is initiated into sex in the prurient style that the novel parodies, then begins to take an active role. At the same time the military position of the insurgents deteriorates, and they come under direct attack from British gunboats. The two situations intertwine in the narrative. As the shelling begins, one shot takes off Caffrey's head as he makes love to Gertie: "The body continued its rhythmic movement for a few more seconds, just like the male of the praying mantis whose upper part has been half-devoured by the female but who perseveres in his copulation." After Gertie frees herself, she considers the situation and concludes: "That's one less." Though shaken by the violence and initiated into not only sex but also, strangely enough, tenderness, Gertie's deepest feelings remain those of patriotism. She even evinces her satisfaction when the post office finally falls and the remaining insurgents are summarily executed before her eyes. Throughout the book, humor and wordplay predominate, rendering the outrageous situations of the narrative pathetic and human in Queneau's unique way.

Queneau returned to Sally Mara and eventually admitted to his authorship of "her" works with the publication of her *Journal intime* (intimate diary) in 1950. Once again, Queneau plays off the supposed prudishness and simple-mindedness of his characters in the Irish setting, but as always through the lens of language. *Journal intime* is set in 1934-1935, at which time Sally is studying Gaelic in order to write a novel and is still an almost incredibly naïve late adolescent. *Journal intime* is the story of her initiation into sexual matters in spite of rampant simplicity and a total lack of knowledge at the outset. In the manner of the five blindmen and the elephant, Sally slowly progresses in her knowledge of the male sexual organs through a long process of trial-and-error experimentation.

The journal opens with Sally on the pier lamenting the return to France of her French teacher, Michel Presle. Through his inspiration, she resolves to write her journal in French (with the accompanying humoristic possibilities this opens up for the author). As she makes her way back down the gangplank, someone identified only as "un gentleman" advises her to "Tenez bon la rampe, mademoiselle," or "Hang on tight, Miss." At the same time: "At the same time was placed effectually in my free hand an object which had both the rigidity of a steel bar and the softness of velvet." Sally retains from this experience an everlasting respect for the kind qualities of the "gentleman" and the beginnings of her inquiry into that object she had held.

Sally's Gaelic lessons with one Padraic Baoghal plunge her at once into the ambience of Irish nationalism as well as into a fertile arena for contact and further knowledge of men. One of these is her fellow student, Barnabé Pudge, who admires Sally from a repressed distance, but with the tenacity required to succeed eventually. During a sequence of darkened séances conducted by Baoghal's wife, who is a spiritual medium, Sally conducts her researches, which she began that night on the pier and continued in the darkness of a motion-picture theater one afternoon with Barnabé. Meanwhile, Sally's home life reveals how she could be so ignorant in the first place.

Sally's mother is a simpleminded woman who awaits the return of her husband by knitting socks for him. Sally's father left the family one night, saying he needed to buy a box of matches, and has yet to return though many years have passed. This suits Sally, whose memories of her father are dominated by his practice of administering prolonged bare-bottomed spankings to her on a daily basis. Her brother is another simpleton, who sees life through an alcoholic stupor but who nevertheless manages to father a child by the family cook, Mrs. Killarney. As the birth of the child approaches, Sally wonders how the conception could have taken place in the absence of a marriage ceremony, and Mrs. Mara denies that her son could have played any role at all. In short, Sally's family, like some primitive culture from the dawn of time, remains at least partially in ignorance of the connection between sex and reproduction. Almost like someone who must reinvent the alphabet, Sally is left to discover the connection on her own.

And discover the connection she does. Her curiosity is satisfied to some extent when her uncle takes her that summer to see the coupling of two goats (a neologism made from the word for "billy-goat" remains her verb for intercourse throughout the book). She is also aided by the discovery of the mythological miniatures painted by Mrs. Baoghal, which show the heroes' full equipment. At this time she also has her first experience of sexual pleasure, with the Baoghal's lesbian housemaid Mève. While Sally's researches continue, her brother makes an honest woman of Mrs. Killarney, her father returns for a time, and she loses her virginity to a tough named Tim. At the end of the book, she does indeed marry Barnabé Pudge. This time, however, as they are boarding the boat for their honeymoon and Barnabé urges her to hold on tight, she is disappointed: "I moved my hand in the darkness, but all I found was a damp, cold rope. I understood then that my conjugal life had begun." The verve and humor that Queneau brings to Sally's exploits gently mock conventional morality while constructing a sense of the contradictory nature of sexual wisdom and ignorance.

Queneau took the title for his next novel, *The Sunday of Life*, from a celebrated passage by Georg Wilhelm Friedrich Hegel in which the philosopher is discussing the depiction of peasant life in Dutch painting. Queneau's understanding runs parallel to the philosopher's belief that there is something so bright, so cheery in the lives of simple people that it seems that they must by their very nature be closer to the Ideal. This understanding by Queneau informs all of his work, and, whether the setting is Le Havre, Ireland, or the working-class sections of Paris, it is what keeps the humor in the work from simply demeaning the characters. Queneau would rather investigate the naïve wisdom of the simpleton than the pompous idiocies of the wise man.

Valentin Brû, the protagonist of *The Sunday of Life*, is one of Queneau's most fascinating characters. From his speech and his reactions to other people, one would have to judge him a simpleton, yet his clear-sighted view of the large scale of world events enables him to prosper in even the most difficult circumstances. The reader first sees Valentin through the eyes of two sisters, Chantal and Julia, who watch him from the window of their mother's haberdashery. Chantal teases her sister that she should marry this attractive soldier. Valentin has just returned from a campaign in Madagascar and is being housed in one of the local barracks. Through the machinations of Chantal and her husband Paul, Valentin is indeed discharged and marries Julia, though she is some fifteen years his senior.

As in all of Queneau's work, the main action of the novel is in the language itself. In this case the simplicity of the characters' thought processes actually regulates their subsequent actions. Here, Valentin and Julia discuss their honeymoon and whether they can afford to let it interrupt their shopkeeping:

> No, of course, not, said Valentin. You see, then, said Julia. And yet, said Valentin, and yet, it's obligatory, a honeymoon . . . . Maybe we could put the honeymoon off until our next vacation, suggested Valentin. And when will we take the vacation, then? Julia objected. And he had no answer to that.
>
> They ended up by adopting the only possible solution, the one and only, to wit that Valentin alone would go on the honeymoon alone.

So Valentin sets off on an uproarious trip that involves humorous encounters with taxi drivers, prostitutes, and hoteliers. His simplicity both gets him into trouble and keeps him from being affected by it. The next thing he knows, he is at graveside of a funeral and reunited with his spouse, by accident.

The very next chapter contains another funeral, that of the mother Nanette, who leaves her shop and money to Valentin. Besides the recriminations he faces from his wife's family, he must face one of his worst fears at the dinner that follows the funeral: oysters. The language gains in exuberance from the protagonist's fears. The oysters are referred to as *animaux ostréicultivés*, *glaviusque molleux*, *lamellibranches*, and *mollusques crus*. These coinages test the ingenuity of the translator, who rises to the occasion with "ostreicultivated animals," "goblike mollusk," "lamellibranchia," and "raw mollusks." Valentin defends his distaste with the claim that they are living animals:

> "They're only just alive," said Paul.
> "They're just as alive as you and me," said Valentin.
> "Funny comparisons you make," said Julia.
> "It's true, though," said Valentin. "An oyster, it's a living creature. Just as much as I am. Zno difference. Zonly one difference: between the living and the dead."
> "You aren't very tactful," said Chantal.

All this wordplay and ludicrous conversation does come in the context of a commemoration of a departed relative. Yet this is simply Queneau's way of dealing with the eternal mysteries of human existence. Behind the apparently subhuman intelligence of a character such as Valentin, there is a deeper understanding of human existence than that found in many other more portentous works of literature.

The Sunday of Life takes a final series of narrative turns when Julia becomes a fortune-teller under the name Madame Saphir. Valentin's failing business allows him plenty of time to gossip, which gossip he, in turn, feeds to Julia. When Julia suffers a stroke, Valentin must take her place, and with his simpleminded wisdom he enjoys a greater success than she ever did. As the outbreak of World War II approaches, the prophecies grow darker. Even war, however, cannot fundamentally affect Valentin's destiny. He is remobilized, made a prisoner of war, and released. When Julia finds him at last, he is helping three female refugees climb into a crowded train through the window: "Julia choked with laughter: it was so as to get his hand on their behinds." *The Sunday of Life* is buoyant with such good cheer.

Zazie in the Metro is probably Queneau's best-known work. From its celebrated opening word, *Doukipudonktan* (or, in English, "Howcanaystinksotho")—in other words, "Who is it thus emitting such a stench?"—through its full sequence of zany adventures and outrageous word creations, *Zazie in the Metro* is a tour de force of comic wit and invention. A spiritual sister of Annette and Sally Mara, Zazie is all street-smarts and foul language. In the novel, the title of which bears her name, the joke is on her: What she most looks forward to doing in Paris, riding the Metro, is the one thing she does not do in the book, since the Metro workers are on strike during her visit.

Zazie arrives in Paris for a visit with her uncle Gabriel so that her mother can spend some time with her lover. Uncle Gabriel fits the pattern of Queneau's male characters and is a bit of a simpleton. For the first part of the book, he hides the true nature of his nocturnal employment from Zazie; in fact, he is a male stripper in a gay bar. Gabriel and his even more simpleminded friend Charles, who drives a taxi, meet Zazie at the train station and bring her back to the apartment that Gabriel shares with his wife, Marceline. Much of the action in the first half of the book takes place in the apartment or in the bar in the basement of the same building. The bar's owner is named Turandot, and his only waitress is Mado (short for Madeleine), but he also has a parakeet to keep him company. The parakeet's name is Laverdure, and he has one comment that he makes throughout the book: "Tu causes, tu causes, c'est tout ce que tu sais faire" ("Talk, talk, that's all you can do"). Interestingly, his comment almost always rings true in context.

Zazie has trouble staying put, so on the morning of her second day, while Gabriel is still asleep after his night's work, she leaves the apartment. Charles tries to catch up to her and protect her from harm, but she accuses him of molesting her and, after an indignant crowd gathers, makes her escape. She then picks up the novel's other main character, at first only referred to as the *type* (guy). At first it appears that he is a child molester; later in the book he reappears as Trouscaillon, an undercover policeman; still later he appears as Bertin Poirée and Aroun Arachide. It is to the *type* that Zazie recounts the story of her life, particularly that her mother murdered her father. Her father, it seems, was a drunk who had sexual designs on the nubile Zazie. The mother is aware of this and borrows an ax from her lover, George (a fact which is revealed during Zazie's testimony at the trial). One day, the mother says that she is going to the store for some spaghetti, but she actually lies in wait for the father to make his move. As Zazie recounts the events:

> "Just then, she opens the door, quiet as can be, and comes in calmly, my papa he had his mind on other things the poor slob, he wasn't paying attention you might say, and that's how he got his skull split open. You have to hand it to her, she made a good job of it, my mamma. It wasn't a pretty sight. Even sickening. Enough to give me a complex."

Yet Zazie, in fact, seems to be one of the least "complexed" characters in the book. Her cheerful, worldly-wise naïveté carries her through the book's events and situations with a casual aplomb.

An ill-starred trip to see the Eiffel Tower, their encounter there with a busload of tourists, a subsequent chase through the streets of Paris, Gabriel's treating everyone to an evening at his nightclub, a subsequent celebration, fracas, and shooting—all this and more finds Zazie cheerful and wisecracking as usual. She is a very tired girl, however, when her uncle Gabriel returns her to her mother the next day. Zazie's madcap adventures seem cinematic in their conception, and it is probably no accident that Louis Malle's film adaptation is one of the small gems of the French cinema.

Queneau's last novels, *The Blue Flowers* and *The Flight of Icarus*, are moving works that continue and extend Queneau's concern with the materiality of language. Throughout his career as a novelist, Queneau brought a wise and compassionate concern to the lives of ordinary people. That he used sometimes brilliant humor and an always engaging sense of play with language are two reasons that his work is now seen as a forerunner to the successive generation of French New Novelists. No matter what tradition literary historians place him in, Queneau will always remain a unique literary figure.

Other major works

POETRY: *Chêne et chien*, 1937; *Les Ziaux*, 1943; *Foutaises*, 1944; *L'Instant fatal*, 1946; *Petite cosmogonie portative*, 1950; *Si tu t'imagines*, 1951; *Le Chien à la mandoline*, 1958; *Cent mille milliards de poèmes*, 1961 (*One Hundred Million Million Poems*, 1983); *Texticules*, 1961; *Courir les rues*, 1967; *Battre la campagne*, 1968; *Fendre les flots*, 1969; *Morale élémentaire*, 1975; *Pataphysical Poems*, 1985.

NONFICTION: *Bâtons, chiffres, et lettres*, 1950.

MISCELLANEOUS: *Exercises de style*, 1947 (*Exercises in Style*, 1958).

Bibliography

Guicharnaud, Jacques. *Raymond Queneau*, 1965.
Shorley, Christopher. *Queneau's Fiction*, 1985.
Thiher, Allen. *Raymond Queneau*, 1985.

Peter Baker

ISHMAEL REED

Born: Chattanooga, Tennessee; February 22, 1938

Principal long fiction

The Free-Lance Pallbearers, 1967; *Yellow Back Radio Broke-Down*, 1969; *Mumbo Jumbo*, 1972; *The Last Days of Louisiana Red*, 1974; *Flight to Canada*, 1976; *The Terrible Twos*, 1982; *Reckless Eyeballing*, 1986.

Other literary forms

Ishmael Reed may be best known as a satirical novelist, but he is also a respected poet, essayist, and editor. His four poetry collections—*Catechism of D Neoamerican Hoodoo Church* (1970), *Conjure: Selected Poems, 1963-1970* (1972), *Chattanooga* (1973), and *A Secretary to the Spirits* (1977)—have established him as a major Afro-American poet, and his poetry has been included in several important anthologies. In two well-received collections of essays, *Shrovetide in Old New Orleans* (1978) and *God Made Alaska for the Indians* (1982), Reed has forcefully presented his aesthetic and political theories. He has also proved to be an important editor and publisher. *19 Necromancers from Now* (1970) was a breakthrough anthology for several unknown black writers. *Yardbird Lives!* (1978), which Reed edited with Al Young, includes essays, fiction, and graphics from the pages of the *Yardbird Reader*, an innovative periodical that published the work of minority writers and artists. Reed's most ambitious editing project resulted in *Calafia: The California Poetry* (1979), an effort to gather together the forgotten minority poetry of California's past.

Achievements

Reed has earned a place in the first rank of contemporary Afro-American authors, but such recognition did not come immediately. Most established reviewers ignored Reed's first novel, *The Free-Lance Pallbearers*, and many of the reviews that were written dismissed the novel as offensive, childish, or self-absorbed. Although *Yellow Back Radio Broke-Down* was even more untraditional than its predecessor, it received much more critical attention and became the center of considerable critical debate. Some reviewers attacked the novel as overly clever, bitter, or obscure, but many praised its imaginative satire and technical innovation. Moreover, the controversy over *Yellow Back Radio Broke-Down* stirred new interest in *The Free-Lance Pallbearers*. Reed's increasing acceptance as a major Afro-American author was demonstrated when his third novel, *Mumbo Jumbo*, was reviewed on the front page of *The New York Review of Books*. Both *Mumbo Jumbo* and *Conjure*, a poetry collection published in the same year, were nominated for the National Book Award.

Subsequent novels have maintained Reed's position in American letters. In 1975, Reed's *The Last Days of Louisiana Red* received the Rosenthal Foundation Award, and some reviewers viewed *Flight to Canada* as Reed's best novel. Yet his work has consistently been controversial. His novels have, for example, been called sexist, a critical accusation that is fueled by comparison of Reed's novels with the recent, powerful fiction written by Afro-American women such as Alice Walker and Toni Morrison. The charge of sexism is further encouraged by Reed's satirical attack on feminists in *Reckless Eyeballing*. Reed has also been called a reactionary by some critics because of his uncomplimentary portrayals of black revolutionaries. His fiction has been translated into three languages, and his poetry has been included in *Poetry of the Negro*, *New Black Poetry*, *The Norton Anthology of Poetry*, and other anthologies.

Biography

The jacket notes to *Chattanooga* glibly recount Ishmael Scott Reed's life: "born in Chattanooga, Tennessee, grew up in Buffalo, New York, learned to write in New York City and wised up in Berkeley, California." Each residence played a crucial role in Reed's development.

Reed was born the son of Henry Lenoir and Thelma Coleman, but before he was two years old, his mother remarried autoworker Bennie Reed. When he was four years old, his mother moved the family to Buffalo, New York, where she found factory work. Reed was graduated from Buffalo's East High School in 1956 and began to attend Millard Fillmore College, the night division of the University of Buffalo, supporting himself by working in the Buffalo public library. A satirical short story, "Something Pure," which portrayed Christ's return as an advertising man, brought Reed the praise of an English professor and encouraged him to enroll in day classes. Reed attended the University of Buffalo until 1960, when he withdrew because of money problems and the social pressures that his financial situation created. He moved into the notorious Talbert Mall Projects, and the two years he spent there provided him with a painful but valuable experience of urban poverty and dependency. During these last years in Buffalo, Reed wrote for the *Empire Star Weekly*, moderated a controversial radio program for station WVFO, and acted in several local stage productions.

From 1962 to 1967, Reed lived in New York City. As well as being involved with the Civil Rights movement and the black power movement, Reed served as editor of *Advance*, a weekly published in Newark, New Jersey. His work on the *Advance* was admired by Walter Bowart, and together they founded the *East Village Other*, one of the first and most successful "underground" newspapers. An early indication of Reed's commitment to encouraging the work of minority artists was his organization in 1965 of the American Festival of Negro Art.

In 1967, Reed moved to Berkeley, California, and began teaching at the University of California at Berkeley. Although he was turned down for tenure in 1977, he continued to teach there and at other universities: the University of Washington, the State University of New York at Buffalo, Yale University, and Dartmouth College. In 1971, with Al Young, Reed founded the Yardbird Publishing Company, which from 1971 to 1976 produced the *Yardbird Reader*, an innovative journal of ethnic writing and graphics. The Reed, Cannon, and Johnson Communications Company, which later became Ishmael Reed Books, was founded in 1973 and has published the work of William Demby, Bill Gunn, Mei Mei Bressenburge, and other ethnic writers. In 1976, Reed and Victor Cruz began the Before Columbus Foundation. In all of his publishing ventures, Reed has tried to expose readers to the work of Asian Americans, Afro-Americans, Chicanos, and Native Americans in an effort to help build a truly representative and pluralistic national literature.

Analysis

Ishmael Reed is consciously a part of the Afro-American literary tradition that extends back to the first-person slave narratives, and the central purpose of his novels is to define a means of expressing the complexity of the Afro-American experience in a manner distinct from the dominant literary tradition. Until the middle of the twentieth century, Afro-American fiction, although enriched by the lyricism of Jean Toomer and Zora Neale Hurston, concentrated on realistic portrayals of black life and employed familiar narrative structures. This tendency toward social realism peaked with Richard Wright's *Native Son* (1940) and *Black Boy* (1945), but it is continued today by authors such as James Baldwin. Reed belongs to a divergent tradition, inspired by Ralph Ellison's *Invisible Man* (1952), a countertradition that includes the work of Leon Forrest, Ernest Gaines, James Alan McPherson, Toni Morrison, and Alice Walker.

Because he believes that the means of expression is as important as the matter, Reed argues that the special qualities of the Afro-American experience cannot be adequately communicated through traditional literary forms. Like Amiri Baraka, Reed believes that Afro-American authors must "be estranged from the dominant culture," but Reed also wants to avoid being stifled by a similarly restrictive countertradition. In *Shrovetide in Old New Orleans*, Reed says that his art and criticism try to combat "the consciousness barrier erected by an alliance of Eastern-backed black pseudo-nationalists and white mundanists." Thus, Reed works against the stylistic limitations of the Afro-American literary tradition as much as he works with them. Henry Louis Gates, Jr., has compared Reed's fictional modifications of Afro-American literary traditions to the Afro-American folk custom of "signifying," maintaining that Reed's novels present an ongoing process of "rhetorical self-definition."

Although Reed's novels are primarily efforts to define an appropriate Afro-American aesthetic, his fiction vividly portrays the particular social condition of black Americans. In his foreword to Elizabeth and Thomas Settle's *Ishmael Reed: A Primary and Secondary Bibliography* (1982), Reed expresses his bitterness over persistent racism and argues that the personal experience of racism that informs his art makes his work inaccessible and threatening to many readers: "I am a member of a class which has been cast to the bottom of the American caste system, and from those depths I write a vision which is still strange, often frightening, 'peculiar' and 'odd' to some, 'ill-considered' and unwelcome to many." Indeed, Ishmael seems to be an ironically appropriate name for this author of violent and darkly humorous attacks on American institutions and attitudes, for the sharpness and breadth of his satire sometimes make him appear to be a man whose hand is turned against all other men. His novels portray corrupt power brokers and their black and white sycophants operating in a dehumanized and materialistic society characterized by its prefabricated and ethnocentric culture. Yet Reed's novels are not hopeless explications of injustice, for against the forces of repression and conformity he sets gifted individuals who escape the limitations of their sterile culture by courageously penetrating the illusions that bind them. Moreover, in contrast to many white authors who are engaged in parallel metafictive experiments, Reed voices a confident belief that "print and words are not dead at all."

Reed's narrative technique combines the improvisational qualities of jazz with a documentary impulse to accumulate references and allusions. In his composite narratives, historical and fictional characters coexist in a fluid, anachronistic time. In an effort to translate the vitality and spontaneity of the oral, folk tradition into a literature that can form the basis for an alternative culture, Reed mixes colloquialisms and erudition in novels which are syncretized from a series of subtexts. The literary equivalent of scat singing, his stories-within-stories parody literary formulas and challenge the traditional limits of fiction.

Reed claims that his novels constitute "an art form with its own laws," but he does not mean to imply that his work is private, for these "laws" are founded on a careful but imaginative reinterpretation of the historical and mythological past. The lengthy bibliography appended to *Mumbo Jumbo* satirizes the documentary impulse of social realist authors, but it also underscores Reed's belief that his mature work demands scholarly research in order to be decoded. This artistic process of reinterpretation often requires the services of an interlocutor, a character who explicitly explains the events of the narrative in terms of the mythological past. Reed's novels describe a vision of an Osirian/Dionysian consciousness, a sensuous humanism that he presents as an appropriate cultural alternative for nonwhite Americans. His imaginative reconstructions of the American West, the Harlem Renaissance, the American Civil War, and contemporary American politics, interwoven with ancient myths, non-European folk customs, and the formulas of popular culture, are liberating heresies meant to free readers from the intellectual domination of the Judeo-Christian tradition.

Reed's first novel, *The Free-Lance Pallbearers*, takes place in a futuristic America called HARRY SAM: "A big not-to-be-believed out-of-sight, sometimes referred to as O-BOP-SHE-BANG or KLANG-A-LANG-A-DING-DONG." This crumbling and corrupt world is tyrannized by Sam himself, a vulgar fat man who lives in Sam's Motel on Sam's Island in the middle of the lethally polluted Black Bay that borders HARRY SAM. Sam, doomed by some terrifying gastrointestinal disorder, spends all of his time on the toilet, his filth pouring into the bay from several large statues of Rutherford B. Hayes.

The bulk of the novel, although framed and periodically informed by a jiving narrative voice, is narrated by Bukka Doopeyduk in a restrained, proper English that identifies his passive faith in the establishment. Doopeyduk is a dedicated adherent to the Nazarene Code, an orderly in a psychiatric hospital, a student at Harry Sam College, and a hapless victim. His comically futile efforts to play by the rules are defeated by the cynics, who manipulate the unjust system to their own advantage. In the end, Doopeyduk is disillusioned: He leads a successful attack on Sam's Island, uncovers the conspiracy that protects Sam's cannibalism, briefly dreams of becoming the black Sam, and is finally crucified.

The Free-Lance Pallbearers is a parody of the Afro-American tradition of first-person, confessional narratives, a book the narrator describes as "growing up in soulsville first of three installments—or what it means to be a backstage darky." Reed's novel challenges the viability of this Afro-American version of the *Bildungsroman*, in which a young protagonist undergoes a painful initiation into the darkness of the white world, a formula exemplified by Wright's *Black Boy* and James Baldwin's *Go Tell It on the Mountain* (1953). In fact, the novel suggests that Afro-American authors' use of this European form is as disabling as Doopeyduk's adherence to the dictates of the Nazarene Code.

The novel is an unrestrained attack on American politics. HARRY SAM, alternately referred to as "Nowhere" or "Now Here," is a dualistic vision of an America that celebrates vacuous contemporaneity. The novel, an inversion of the Horatio Alger myth in the manner of Nathanael West, mercilessly displays American racism, but its focus is the corruptive potential of power. Sam is a grotesque version of Lyndon B. Johnson, famous for his bathroom interviews, and Sam's cannibalistic taste for children is an attack on Johnson's Vietnam policy. With *The Free-Lance Pallbearers*, Reed destroys the presumptions of his society, but it is not until his later novels that he attempts to construct an alternative.

Yellow Back Radio Broke-Down is set in a fantastic version of the Wild West of popular literature. Reed's protagonist, the Loop Garoo Kid, is a proponent of artistic freedom and an accomplished voodoo *houngan* who is in marked contrast to the continually victimized Doopeyduk. Armed with supernatural "connaissance" and aided by a white python and the hip, helicopter-flying Chief Showcase, the Kid battles the forces of realistic mimesis and political corruption. His villainous opponent is Drag Gibson, a degenerate cattle baron given to murdering his wives, who is called upon by the citizens of Yellow Back Radio to crush their rebellious children's effort "to create [their] own fictions."

Although *Yellow Back Radio Broke-Down* satirizes Americans' eagerness to suspend civil rights in response to student protests against the Vietnam War, its focus is literature, specifically the dialogue between realism and modernism. The Loop Garoo Kid matches Reed's description of the Afro-American artist in *19 Necromancers from Now*: "a conjurer who works JuJu upon his oppressors; a witch doctor who frees his fellow victims from the psychic attack launched by demons." Through the Loop Garoo Kid, Reed takes a stand for imagination, intelligence, and fantasy against rhetoric, violence, and sentimentality. This theme is made explicit in a debate with Bo Shmo, a "neo-social realist" who maintains that "all art must be for the end of liberating the masses," for the Kid says that a novel "can be anything it wants to be, a vaudeville show, the six o'clock news, the mumblings of wild men saddled by demons."

Reed exhibits his antirealist theory of fiction in *Yellow Back Radio Broke-Down* through his free use of time, characters, and language. The novel ranges from the eighteenth century to the present, combining historical events and cowboy myths with modern technology and cultural detritus. His primary characters are comically exaggerated racial types: Drag Gibson represents the white's depraved materialism, Chief Showcase represents the Indian's spirituality, and the Loop Garoo Kid represents the Afro-American's artistic soul. Reed explains the novel's title by suggesting that his book is the "dismantling of a genre done in an oral way like radio." "Yellow back" refers to the popular dime novels; "radio" refers to the novel's oral, discontinuous form; and a "broke-down" is a dismantling. Thus, Reed's first two novels assault America in an attempt to "dismantle" its cultural structure.

In *Mumbo Jumbo*, Reed expands on the neo-hoodooism of the Loop Garoo Kid in order to create and define an Afro-American aesthetic based on voodoo, Egyptian mythology, and improvisational musical forms, an aesthetic to challenge the Judeo-Christian tradition, rationalism, and technology. Set in Harlem during the 1920's, *Mumbo Jumbo* is a tragicomical analysis of the Harlem Renaissance's failure to sustain its artistic promise. Reed's protagonist is PaPa LaBas, an aging hoodoo detective and cultural diagnostician, and LaBas' name, meaning "over there" in French, reveals that his purpose is to reconnect Afro-Americans with their cultural heritage by reunifying the Text of Jes Grew, literally the Egyptian Book of Thoth. Reed takes the phrase Jes Grew from Harriet Beecher Stowe's Topsy and James Weldon Johnson's description of Afro-American music's unascribed development, but in the novel, Jes Grew is a contagion, connected with the improvisational spirit of ragtime and jazz, that begins to spread across America in the 1920's. Jes Grew is an irrational force that threatens to overwhelm the dominant, repressive traditions of established culture. LaBas' efforts to unify and direct this unpredictable force are opposed by the Wallflower Order of the Knights Templar, an organization dedicated to neutralizing the power of Jes Grew in order to protect their privileged status. LaBas fails to reunify the text, a parallel to the dissipation of the Harlem Renaissance's artistic potential, but the failure is seen as temporary; the novel's indeterminate conclusion looks forward hopefully to a time when these artistic energies can be reignited.

The novel's title is double-edged. "Mumbo jumbo" is a racist, colonialist phrase used to describe the misunderstood customs and language of dark-skinned people, an approximation of some critics' description of Reed's unorthodox fictional method. Yet "mumbo jumbo" also refers to the power of imagination, the cultural alternative that can free Afro-Americans. A text of and about texts, *Mumbo Jumbo* combines the formulas of detective fiction with the documentary paraphernalia of scholarship: footnotes, illustrations, and a bibliography. Thus, in the disclosure scene required of any good detective story, LaBas, acting the part of interlocutor, provides a lengthy and erudite explication of the development of Jes Grew that begins with a reinterpretation of the myth of Osiris. The parodic scholarship of *Mumbo Jumbo* undercuts the assumed primacy of the European tradition and implicitly argues that Afro-American artists should attempt to discover their distinct cultural heritage.

In *The Last Days of Louisiana Red*, LaBas returns as Reed's protagonist, but the novel abandons the parodic scholarship and high stylization of *Mumbo Jumbo*. Although LaBas again functions as a connection with a non-European tradition of history and myth, *The Last Days of Louisiana Red* is more traditionally structured than its predecessor. In the novel, LaBas solves the murder of Ed Yellings, the founder of the Solid Gumbo Works. Yellings' business is dedicated to combating the effects of Louisiana Red, literally a popular hot sauce but figuratively an evil state of mind that divides Afro-Americans. Yelling's gumbo, like Reed's fiction, is a mixture of disparate elements, and it has a powerful curative effect. In fact, LaBas discovers that Yellings is murdered when he gets close to developing a gumbo that will cure heroin addiction.

In *The Last Days of Louisiana Red*, Reed is examining the self-destructive forces that divide the Afro-American community so that its members fight one another "while above their heads . . . billionaires flew in custom-made jet planes." Reed shows how individuals' avarice leads them to conspire with the establishment, and he suggests that some of the most vocal and militant leaders are motivated by their egotistical need for power rather than by true concern for oppressed people. Set in Berkeley, California, *The Last Days of Louisiana Red* attacks the credibility of the black revolutionary movements that sprang up in the late 1960's and early 1970's.

Flight to Canada, Reed's fifth novel, is set in an imaginatively redrawn Civil War South, and it describes the relationship between Arthur Swille, a tremendously wealthy Virginia planter who practices necrophilia, and an assortment of sociologically stereotyped slaves. The novel is presented as the slave narrative of Uncle Robin, the most loyal of Swille's possessions. Uncle Robin repeatedly tells Swille that the plantation is his idea of heaven, and he assures his master that he does not believe that Canada exists. Raven Quickskill, "the first one of Swille's slaves to read, the first to write, and the first to run away," is the author of Uncle Robin's story.

Like much of Reed's work, *Flight to Canada* is about the liberating power of art, but in *Flight to Canada*, Reed concentrates on the question of authorial control. All the characters struggle to maintain control of their stories. After escaping from the plantation, Quickskill writes a poem, "Flight to Canada," and his comical verse denunciation of Swille completes his liberation. In complaining of Quickskill's betrayal to Abraham Lincoln, Swille complains that his former bookkeeper uses literacy "like that old Voodoo." In a final assertion of authorial control and the power of the pen, Uncle Robin refuses to sell his story to Harriet Beecher Stowe, gives the rights to Quickskill, rewrites Swille's will, and inherits the plantation.

In *The Terrible Twos*, Reed uses a contemporary setting to attack Ronald Reagan's administration and the exploitative nature of the American economic system. In the novel, President Dean Clift, a former model, is a mindless figurehead manipulated by an oil cartel that has supplanted the real Santa Claus. Nance Saturday, another of Reed's Afro-American detectives, sets out to discover Saint Nicholas' place of exile. The novel's title suggests that, in its second century, the United States is acting as selfishly and irrationally as the proverbial two-year-old. The central theme is the manner in which a few avaricious people seek vast wealth at the expense of the majority of Americans.

Reckless Eyeballing takes place in the 1980's, and Reed employs a string of comically distorted characters to present the idea that the American literary environment is dominated by New York women and Jews. Although *Reckless Eyeballing* has been called sexist and anti-Semitic by some, Reed's target is a cultural establishment that creates and strengthens racial stereotypes, in particular the view of Afro-American men as savage rapists. To make his point, however, he lampoons feminists, using the character Tremonisha Smarts, a female Afro-American author who has written a novel of violence against women. Reed's satire is probably intended to remind readers of Alice Walker's *The Color Purple* (1982).

Because the novel's central subject is art and the limitations that society places on an artist, it is appropriate that Reed once again employs the technique of a story-within-a-story. Ian Ball, an unsuccessful Afro-American playwright, is the novel's protagonist. In the novel, Ball tries to succeed by shamelessly placating the feminists in power. He writes "Reckless Eyeballing," a play in which a lynched man is posthumously tried for "raping" a woman with lecherous stares, but Ball, who often seems to speak for Reed, maintains his private, chauvinistic views throughout.

Ishmael Reed's substantial body of fiction has established him as an important satirist. His innovative narrative techniques have stretched the limits of the American novel and dramatically broadened the scope of Afro-American literature.

Other major works

POETRY: *Catechism of D Neoamerican Hoodoo Church*, 1970; *Conjure: Selected Poems, 1963-1970*, 1972; *Chattanooga*, 1973; *A Secretary to the Spirits*, 1977.

NONFICTION: *Shrovetide in Old New Orleans*, 1978; *God Made Alaska for the Indians*, 1982.

ANTHOLOGIES: *19 Necromancers from Now*, 1970; *Yardbird Lives!*, 1978 (with Al Young); *Calafia: The California Poetry*, 1979.

Bibliography

Fabre, Michel. "Postmodern Rhetoric in Ishmael Reed's *Yellow Back Radio Broke-Down*," in *The Afro-American Novel Since 1960*, 1982. Edited by Peter Bruck and Wolfgang Karrer.

Gates, Henry Louis, Jr. "The 'Blackness of Blackness': A Critique of the Sign and the Signifying Monkey," in *Critical Inquiry*. IX (June, 1983), pp. 685-723.

Lindroth, James R. "From Krazy Kat to Hoodoo: Aesthetic Discourse in the Fiction of Ishmael Reed," in *Review of Contemporary Fiction*. IV (Summer, 1984), pp. 227-233.

O'Brien, John. "Ishmael Reed," in *Interviews with Black Writers*, 1973.

_____. "Ishmael Reed," in *The New Fiction*, 1974. Edited by Joe David Bellamy.

Schmitz, Neil. "Neo-HooDoo: The Experimental Fiction of Ishmael Reed," in *Twentieth Century Literature*. XX (April, 1974), pp. 126-140.

Settle, Elizabeth A., and Thomas A. Settle, eds. *Ishmael Reed: A Primary and Secondary Bibliography*, 1982.

Carl Brucker

MARY LEE SETTLE

Born: Charleston, West Virginia; July 29, 1918

Principal long fiction

The Love Eaters, 1954; *The Kiss of Kin*, 1955; *O Beulah Land*, 1956; *Know Nothing*, 1960; *Fight Night on a Sweet Saturday*, 1964; *The Clam Shell*, 1971; *Prisons*, 1973; *Blood Tie*, 1977; *The Scapegoat*, 1980; *The Killing Ground*, 1982 (revision of *Fight Night on a Sweet Saturday*); *Celebration*, 1986.

Other literary forms

In addition to her novels, Mary Lee Settle has written several nonfiction books. Her juvenile works, *The Story of Flight* (1967) and *Water World* (1984), the latter being a parallel history of man's exploration of the sea, are not as significant as her autobiographical *All the Brave Promises: Memories of Aircraft Woman Second Class 2146391* (1966) or her historical study *The Scopes Trial: The State of Tennessee vs. John Thomas Scopes* (1972). *All the Brave Promises* describes her experiences as an American volunteer in the Women's Auxiliary Air Force of the Royal Air Force (RAF) in 1942 and 1943. *The Scopes Trial*, like *All the Brave Promises*, deals with human responses to a historical confrontation.

Achievements

As late as 1978, when she won the National Book Award in Fiction for *Blood Tie*, critics were calling Settle an "unknown" writer. With the earlier publication of four of her historical novels, some of them had praised her for research-based realism, resulting in works more respectable than the typically lurid products of that genre. Critics, however, found her complexity sometimes confusing, pointing out the changes in point of view, the flash-forwards and flashbacks, and sometimes the assumption that the reader knew the history of her characters as well as the writer did. There was a lack of agreement as to whether her characters were well developed. After the completion of the Beulah Quintet in 1982 (*O Beulah Land*, *Know Nothing*, *Prisons*, *The Scapegoat*, *The Killing Ground*), however, critics recognized the depth and scope of her vision, arguing that Settle's structural complexity was justified by her aim: to present the truth about human relationships in their historical context. To her early champions, among them Malcolm Cowley and George Garrett, were added numerous other reviewers, who saw evidence of her considerable talent in her contemporary works as well as in the historical novels. To them, the award for *Blood Tie* was a belated recognition, rather than an unexpected one. When *Celebration* was published, Settle received praise, rather than blame, for her stylistic and technical feats, and she was no longer faulted for her characterization. With such articles as that by Peggy Bach in the October, 1984, *The Southern Review*, Settle's reputation was established as a skillful, serious writer, whose approach to her material is necessitated if she is to document her own search and that of her characters for, in Bach's words, "their own personal past and the taproot that was cut."

Biography

Mary Lee Settle was born in Charleston, West Virginia, on July 29, 1918. She attended Sweet Briar College from 1936 to 1938. After serving in the RAF Women's Auxiliary Air Force during World War II, she became a freelance writer and journalist, working briefly as an editor for *Harper's Bazaar* and later as English correspondent for *Flair*. After writing several plays, still unpublished, she turned to fiction, publishing her first novel in 1954. She was awarded Guggenheim Fellowships in 1957-1958 and in 1959-1960. She lives with her husband, writer and historian William Tazewell, in Charlottesville, Virginia.

Analysis

Whether her works are set in the present or in the past, in Europe or in West Virginia, Mary Lee Settle's preoccupations are always the same: the quest for freedom and the pursuit of love in a threatening, changing social environment. Like a Greek dramatist, she employs a background of ordinary people, who ignore the issues and the dangers of their time and place, who accept their intellectual and social prisons, blindly assuming that all is for the best, no matter what persons or what ideals they betray. In contrast to this chorus are a few exceptional people who are incapable of that blind and easy acceptance. Whatever the social cost, they insist on honesty. Whatever the political and economic cost, they seek freedom. Their ideals are ultimately democratic, for they will not judge others by narrow social standards or limit their associations by social formulas. Because they are uncompromising, they are destined to be misunderstood, ridiculed, deserted, even betrayed, but they may also be followed, admired, and loved.

Settle's novels fall into three categories: the Southern novels, such as her first two published works, *The Love Eaters* and *The Kiss of Kin*, and *The Clam Shell*; the Beulah Quintet, five historical novels published between 1956 and 1982, out of chronological order; and the European novels, the award-winning *Blood Tie*, set in contemporary Turkey, and *Celebration*, set in London but tracing the past lives of its characters to Kurdistan, Hong Kong, and Africa. Before *Celebration*, Settle had finally concluded the Beulah Quintet with *The Killing Ground*, which brought her several families into the present. In *Celebration*, although her characters deal with their past, they find redemption. More than any of her other works, *Celebration* moves joyfully into the future, symbolized by the central section, in which the characters of the work gather to watch the moon walk.

The Love Eaters is set in Canona, West Virginia, among the Country Club people who will appear again in the final novel of the quintet, *The Killing Ground*, Anne Randolph Potter, for example, the drawling Virginian, and her "real American" husband George Potter. The men work, talk, and drink; the women decorate their homes, plan community projects, talk, and drink. With her fine ear for dialogue, Settle captures their sterile lives by carefully recording that talk, the beauty-shop gossip blaring under the hair dryers, the brief exchanges between husbands and wives, mothers and daughters, men in the Country Club locker-room. The marriages in Canona have become the routine relationships of people who live politely in the same house, like the Potters and like their friends the Dodds, Jim and Martha. Because she was tired of the meaningless talk, Martha married Jim, and when she feels alone in their silent home, she reminds herself that she got exactly what she wanted. What Jim himself wanted was a quiet routine; knowing this, Martha has not even permitted herself to bear him a child.

The bored women of the Canona Country Club have brightened their lives by organizing an acting company, and it is through this venture that one of the two disrupting forces in *The Love Eaters* comes to Canona. As the novel opens, the itinerant director Hamilton Sacks descends from the train, accompanied by his devoted mother. Sacks is a physical and emotional cripple, who delights in "playing" the people he meets as if he were playing to an audience, as indeed he is, and who has no sense of moral responsibility for the effect that his wicked hints may have on their lives.

The second disrupting force comes, ironically, through the placid Jim Dodd. Through a letter, he has learned the whereabouts of the son whom he had by a previous marriage, about whom he had never told his childless present wife. With the arrival of charming, slender, handsome, and above all, lovable Selby Dodd in Canona, the lives of Jim and Martha are changed forever.

In Settle's modern version of *Phaedra* (c. A.D. 45-55), the passion of a menopausal woman, trapped in the aimless days and nights of a society which thinks in stereotypes and in a marriage whose value has been its placid silence, is no more surprising than the fact that George Potter keeps the local beautician as his mistress. Martha's upcountry old mother is familiar with the yearnings of middle-aged women, familiar enough to warn that infatuations with young men, while not surprising, are generally unwise. Martha is not the only one who is taken with Selby Dodd, who, as Hamilton comments, lives on love and, without exerting himself, attracts women of all ages, as well as men such as Hamilton; Martha's contemporary Anne Randolph Potter and her seventeen-year-old daughter Sally Bee Potter vie for Selby from the first time they meet him. There is, then, very little shock in speculations about Martha's feelings. It is Martha herself who inflicts the punishment upon herself, and her emphasis is not on the immorality of incestuous feelings or fear of a heroic husband—for neither moral rectitude nor heroism are common in Canona society—but on her own need for Selby's physical and emotional love. As Hippolytus, Selby is neither morally outraged nor committed to a young princess. He trifles with Sally Bee Potter under the same rules which she observes in teasing him, but no love is involved, for Selby, like Hamilton, is too narcissistic to love anyone but himself and too opportunistic to be troubled by morality. Because his long-range plans include acquiring as much of Jim's property as possible, however, Selby cannot afford to risk angering Jim, and his pose must remain that of loving son and considerate stepson.

The differences between the traditional tragic characters in this account of a stepmother's passion for her stepson and Settle's characters, who lack the tragic stature and the rigid moral sense of those in the earlier versions of the story, indicate the diminished standards of modern society, which imprisons its members within patterns which have no moral dimension, but merely the force of mindless custom. At the end of the novel, Martha at least briefly takes responsibility for Selby's death, but instead of dying, she loses her mind. Jim, too, escapes from reality; having made his dead son into a hero, he waits for Martha to become her old self.

In *The Kiss of Kin*, the imprisoning society is a Southern family, brought together for a funeral. Into this society comes Abraham Passmore, summoned to claim his inheritance and determined also to discover the wrong which his father's people once did to his mother. By the end of the novel, Abraham has forced the members of the family to admit the truth, but it is obvious that they will not therefore become honest. Only the cousin who leaves with him has been forced by the day's events to reject the family, as well as her similarly dishonest Yankee lover, in order to find her own freedom.

While entertaining, *The Kiss of Kin* is too clearly an adaptation of the light comedy which Settle had first written. Like *The Love Eaters*, it was skillfully constructed, hilariously satirical, accurate in dialogue; avoiding authorial comment, it depends upon dramatic scenes and upon the meditations of the few sensitive characters to comment upon the society which is its target. At this point, Settle made an important turn in her literary career. She produced the first of the Beulah Quintet novels, which plunged into the historical past to find the roots of that Southern society realized in her first two novels.

Settle's first two historical novels were written in chronological order. *O Beulah Land* is set in what was later to be West Virginia at the time of the French and Indian War, *Know Nothing*, in the 1840's and 1850's. It is significant that both of these novels take place just before a momentous historic event, in the first case, the American Revolution, in the second, the Civil

War. In both of them, exceptional people understand the issues of their time and respond heroically. Others either insist on living in a changeless world, clinging to a familiar pattern, or blindly refuse to admit that change is inevitable.

In *O Beulah Land*, a massacre results from the insistence of two English men, at opposite ends of the social scale, that the New World pattern is no different from the old. "Squire" Josiah Devotion Raglan steals, as he did in England; the arrogant British commander is rude, as he could afford to be in England. Unfortunately, the Indians, whose tomahawk is stolen and whose pride is offended, are not governed by Old World rules, and the massacre is the outcome. Significantly, Hannah Bridewell, a transported prostitute and thief, survives captivity by the Indians and reaches safety in the arms of a frontiersman, Jeremiah Catlett. Adapting to the New World, they create a marriage outside the church, which has not yet come to the wilderness, and later defend their home by the justifiable murder of the blackmailing Squire, who once again has miscalculated in the New World.

In the Lacey family, Settle again contrasts the selfish and the blind with those perceptive, freedom-loving individuals who refuse to enslave them-selves to an old pattern. Sally Lacey, the pretentious, spoiled wife of Jona-than Lacey, refuses to adapt to frontier life. Failing in her lifelong crusade to make over her homely neighbors, Sally at last goes mad. In contrast, the printer Jarcey Pentacost has lost his shop rather than tailor his efforts to the values of a community already stagnating; for him, the frontier means freedom.

In *Know Nothing*, although the historical background is very different, the descendants of the characters in *O Beulah Land* must choose between enslavement to older patterns, which no longer suit the changing country, and emerging new patterns. Another Sally Lacey and her husband, Brandon, must move west because the plantation economic system has failed them. Unable to adapt, Brandon kills himself and Sally retreats permanently into the contemplation of her heredity. Other casualties of inherited patterns are Johnny Catlett, who cannot escape from his role as slaveowner and finally as Confederate officer; Lewis Catlett, the prisoner of his religious obsession, whose abolitionism, the result of his mother's influence, has in it no grain of compassion; Melinda Lacey and Sara Lacey, both trapped in miserable mar-riages from which, in a society which does not permit divorce, only death can release them. Already in *Know Nothing*, the same kind of social prisons from which American immigrants escaped have been established in the New World, and the quest for freedom has become more and more difficult.

In 1964, Viking Press published *Fight Night on a Sweet Saturday*, which was to have been the concluding work in a "Beulah Trilogy." In that book, Hannah McKarkle, who is named for the heroic Hannah of *O Beulah Land*, comes to Canona, West Virginia, originally to see her brother and then to investigate his death. During her visit, she begins to explore the past of her family and of her region, thus, in a sense, becoming Mary Lee Settle herself. Unfortunately, the publishers so cut *Fight Night on a Sweet Saturday* that Settle found the relationships obscured. Eventually, she was to add two volumes to the Beulah works, *Prisons* and *The Scapegoat*, and to rewrite *Fight Night on a Sweet Saturday*, which was published as *The Killing Ground*.

Still pursuing the democratic ideal, Settle returned to Great Britain, where she tracked down a chance reference to John Lilburne, the leader of a group of radicals, a number of whom were executed by the forces of Cromwell, who were averse to the "Leveling" principles of true egalitarians. It is the story of one of these executed radicals which Settle tells in her seventeenth century novel *Prisons*, which becomes the first novel in the Beulah Quintet, viewed chronologically. Its hero, the brave, idealistic Johnny Church, enmeshed in amoral public policy, refuses to save his own life by becoming Oliver Cromwell's agent among the men who see Johnny as a natural leader. It is the descendants of Johnny Church, both literal and spiritual, who continue to fight for freedom in Settle's historical and contemporary novels.

Meanwhile, Settle had published another novel set in the contemporary South, *The Clam Shell*, which is set among the same Country Club set as *The Love Eaters*. In Canona in 1966, Anne Randolph Potter, "Plain" George Potter, and their friends are involved in their usual rituals. This time, however, the disrupting influence is one of their own friends, the woman protagonist, who watches them watching football, drinking, and reminiscing. Unlike Martha Dodd, she learned young that she was unable to fit the mold of her friends in Canona, just as she could not fit the mold of the Virginia finishing school to which she was sent. Musing on her youth, remembering her unjust treatment at the finishing school, she realizes that she has long ago ceased wishing to be accepted by mindless, restrictive upper-class Virginia or West Virginia society. Like Abraham Passmore, she is content to be an honest exile.

In literary quality, *The Clam Shell* is one of Settle's less effective novels. Satirical and often angry, it divides its characters into two groups: those who understand life and those who, from dullness or from choice, choose not to understand but, instead, to persecute those who do.

After this simplistic novel came one of Settle's best, *Blood Tie*, a contemporary work set on a Turkish island. The protagonist, idealistic, innocent Ariadne, has come to Ceramos to recover from a mid-life divorce. There she becomes acquainted with a group of expatriates, the sensationalist Basil, a German archaeologist, a Jewish bar owner, a wealthy American girl, and the CIA agent Frank Proctor. None of the expatriates understands the language well enough to realize the disapproval, the contempt, and the ridicule with which they are viewed by the natives. Nor have the expatriates any idea of the intrigue with which they are surrounded. The archaeologist, for example, does not guess that a hunted university student is hiding in the sacred caverns which he cannot find. As the Turks manipulate the expatriates for gain, the expatriates utilize one another and the Turks for the sensations they seek. Through the corruption walks Ariadne, mothering the spoiled American girl and the mute Turkish child, struggling with her sense of rejection and with her own troublesome sexuality, unintentionally shocking the Turks, who misinterpret her actions. When she and the other expatriates at last leave the island, the Chief of Police praises her because of all the visitors only Ariadne tried to see the Turks as individuals, rather than as background figures in an exotic environment. Although Ariadne does not know it, she has made a difference to the troubled, mute child, for at last he is able to speak.

In *The Scapegoat*, published only three years after *Blood Tie*, Settle again created complex characters who have a moral sense. Foolish, innocent, and idealistic though they may be, such individuals do provide some hope for the future. Like its predecessors in the series, *The Scapegoat* takes place at a time of confrontation, on a single day, June 7, 1912, when the hostility between British mine owners and their hired thugs, on one hand, and the mines with their union leaders, on the other, results in armed conflict. In the middle of the conflict are the mine owners, Beverley and Ann Eldridge Lacey, who hope to keep their mine, their home, and their friendships apart from the approaching violence. Ironically, the idealism of their daughter Lily Ellen Lacey, home from college, leads directly to the violence. Her friendship with a young striker is exploited to inflame both the strikebreakers and the strikers. As the day develops, basically good people do evil. To save her son, Lily's friend sacrifices a new immigrant, the "scapegoat" of the title; to help the friend escape, Lily and Beverley take advantage of the death of the scapegoat, thus in a sense participating in the guilt.

In her later books, however, Settle is dealing more realistically with guilt, seemingly recognizing that in this world every act is tainted. Rather than expecting her exceptional characters to be flawless and fully cognizant of the situation in which they are placed, Settle is more compassionate toward the well meaning, even if, like Lily, they unintentionally play into the hands of clearly evil forces. Granted, ignorance cannot exempt one from guilt. Lily's service as a nurse in World War I, which results in her death, is a course deliberately chosen because she must take the responsibility for her tragic blindness. Yet in her later works, Settle castigates fewer characters for their blindness and permits more of them the possibility of redemption.

In her final volume of the Beulah Quintet, *The Killing Ground*, Settle's writer Hannah McKarkle sums up what she has learned of history. In clash after clash, people struggle for freedom. Often, as Johnny Church learned in the English Civil War, as the Laceys saw in the American mine wars, both sides in a confrontation seek power, and it is a third group which must struggle for real freedom. Whatever its pretensions, every society is made up of many who are blind, often for their own comfort, and of many who, though perceptive, are unprincipled. Because of that convenient or deliberate blindness, the rebels, the seekers for freedom, must always struggle, first to see the truth, then, and only then, to act upon it.

Because critics are now becoming aware of Settle's themes, they can justify the shifts in point of view and the movements back and forth in time which make her work difficult. In *The Scapegoat*, for example, Settle tells her story through the eyes of several different characters, whose testimony, weighed and judged by the reader, can add up to objective truth. Similarly, in *Blood Tie*, the mutual misunderstandings between the Turkish and the expatriate populations are dramatized by frequent changes in point of view, often revealing opposite interpretations of events and statements. Thus, the thematic emphasis on the pursuit of truth is exemplified by Settle's own method of revealing the truth.

Moreover, because as William Faulkner believed, the truth of any one moment involves the past of an individual, a community, a people, and because the human mind never lives purely in present consciousness, Settle's frequent shifts in time are also a technical expression of a thematic emphasis. In a comic novel such as *The Kiss of Kin*, the thrust of the work is toward the revelation of a single element in the past, and therefore the dramatic technique is effective. In a complicated novel such as *The Killing Ground* or *Blood Tie*, however, in which characters attempt to understand the present while always being conscious of the past, the shifts in time are both effective and thematically necessary.

Settle's increasing technical mastery and her developing theme of redemption are both evident in *Celebration*. The six chapters of the novel alternate between London and three distant areas where various characters once lived, Kurdistan, Hong Kong, and Africa. The process through which the main characters must go is that of the mass: an honest facing of the past, the acceptance of guilt, repentance, redemption, and joy. Each of the characters has crossed what Settle terms "the Styx," directly confronting death and despair. For Teresa Cerrutti, it was the death of her husband in Malakastan, followed by her own surgery for cancer. For Noel, Lord Atherton, it was a disastrous encounter with a Chinese lover in Hong Kong. For Ewen Stuart McLeod, it was the betrayal by his uncle, who trapped him in an unsavory African expedition and involved him in the murder of innocent people.

The movement toward a joyful future is suggested in the fourth of Settle's chapters, when her major characters and their friends together watch the moon landing, which is an affirmation of mankind's possibilities. That chapter, however, is followed by the darkest account in the novel, Ewen's African adventure, revealing man at his treacherous, murderous worst. Ewen's life was saved by the black Roman Catholic priest, Pius Deng, who is also now in London, one of the friends.

In the final chapter, there is a celebration of death and of life. The priest is killed by London muggers, but as the guilt-stricken youngest of them comments, he died in a state of grace. Furthermore, the commitment for which he had hoped, the marriage of Ewen and Teresa, concludes the novel. Under the influence of the saintly Pius and through their ever-increasing love for one another, the London friends have made the Styx not a river of death, but one of life.

Thus, in her works, Mary Lee Settle has always stressed the need for personal honesty, for emotional and political freedom, and for a democratic acceptance of others on an individual basis. In the three Southern novels, she emphasized the stagnant, snobbish, superficial society which broke the weak and drove the strong into exile. In the Beulah Quintet and in the European novels, however, while still castigating the cruel, the selfish, and the blind, Settle has increasingly emphasized the possibility of expiation or of redemption. As her imagination has moved backward in time and outward in space, her sense of human possibilities has intensified. With *Celebration*, she seems to have expressed an honest hope for those who are willing to face life with honesty and courage; with that novel, she has also almost faultlessly synthesized her matter and her manner.

Other major works

NONFICTION: *All the Brave Promises: Memories of Aircraft Woman Second Class 2146391*, 1966; *The Scopes Trial: The State of Tennessee vs. John Thomas Scopes*, 1972.

CHILDREN'S LITERATURE: *The Story of Flight*, 1967; *Water World*, 1984.

Bibliography

Bach, Peggy. "The Searching Voice and Vision of Mary Lee Settle," in *The Southern Review*. XX (Autumn, 1984), pp. 842-850.

Sanoff, Alvin P. "Life Is Really a Dance," in *U.S. News and World Report*. CI (December 22, 1986), p. 64.

Shattuck, Roger. "A Talk with Mary Lee Settle," in *The New York Times Book Review*. LXXXV (October 26, 1980), pp. 43-46.

Smith, Wendy. "Mary Lee Settle," in *Publishers Weekly*. CCXXX (October 10, 1986), p. 73.

Rosemary M. Canfield-Reisman

WOLE SOYINKA

Born: Abeokuta, Nigeria; July 13, 1934

Principal long fiction
The Interpreters, 1965; *Season of Anomy*, 1973.

Other literary forms
Wole Soyinka is best known as a dramatist. He has written more than twenty plays in various modes, including *The Swamp Dwellers* (1958), *The Lion and the Jewel* (1959), *A Dance of the Forests* (1960), *Madmen and Specialists* (1970, revised 1971), and *Death and the King's Horseman* (1975). He is also a director and filmmaker. He has published several collections of poetry, including *Idanre and Other Poems* (1967) and *A Shuttle in the Crypt* (1972), and the long poem *Ogun Abibiman* (1976). His nonfiction prose includes the impressive book of criticism *Myth, Literature, and the African World* (1976) and two autobiographical works: *The Man Died* (1972), a memoir of his prison experiences, and *Aké: The Years of Childhood* (1981), a recreation of his early life in Nigeria. In addition, he has translated the Yoruba novel *Ogboju Ode Ninu Igbo Irunmale*, by D. O. Fagunwa, as *Forest of a Thousand Daemons: A Hunter's Saga* (1968).

Achievements
Soyinka is a writer of international stature and is perhaps the most talented and versatile to have emerged during the literary flowering in Africa beginning in the 1950's. He is, without doubt, the finest dramatist; he is also an accomplished poet and has written two novels so experimental that critics are not yet sure what to make of them. While tapping numerous twentieth century fictional devices, the novels are based on his own cultural heritage, combining ritual, myth, comedy, and hard realism in a new configuration. He draws from the Yoruba mythology of his native region but makes contact with a larger public by frequent references and parallels to myths and literatures of other cultures. Not only his literary achievements but also his championing of individual freedoms have gained for him recognition both in his native Nigeria and abroad. He has received numerous awards, including first prize at the Dakar Negro Arts Festival in 1960, the John Whiting Drama Prize in 1966, the Jock Campbell Award for Fiction in 1968, and the Nobel Prize for Literature in 1986.

Biography
Akinwande Oluwole Soyinka was born July 13, 1934, at Abeokuta, in western Nigeria. A Yoruba by birth, he has studied Yoruba mythology and

theology and has made it the basis of his literary themes. His formal educa- tion, however, was British. He attended primary and secondary schools in Abeokuta and Ibadan, began his undergraduate work at University College, Ibadan, and received his bachelor of arts degree with honors in English (1957) at the University of Leeds. He has continued to be associated with various universities throughout his academic and literary career and has held lectureships, delivered papers at academic meetings, and published critical reviews and articles. His career as a dramatist began at Leeds and continued with his establishment of acting companies in Lagos and Ibadan. Aside from the theater and his own literary endeavors, he has been a political activist; the Nigerian authorities detained him in prison during the Biafran War, from August, 1967, to October, 1969. Individual freedom and social responsibility are themes in his earliest work, but his commitment to social justice became even more intense after his prison experiences and the Nigerian atrocities during the war.

Analysis

Like other novelists in Africa during the years just before and after inde- pendence, Wole Soyinka faced the question of ethnic and cultural identity. The now notorious negritude movement, begun in the 1930's, had attempted to promote a pan-African identity by distinguishing between two mentalities: the rational, methodical, categorical tendency of the industrialized Westerner and the emotional spontaneity of the African still in tune with the rhythms of nature. Many, including Soyinka, came to see this definition as a sign of cul- tural dependency—the African described by contrast to the dominant Eu- ropean culture. In his most famous remark on the subject, Soyinka declared that "the tiger does not proclaim his tigretude!" Soyinka presumably meant that the African need not be defensive about his identity; at any rate, Soyinka has proclaimed unabashedly, in all of his works, including his two novels, the indigenous source of his themes and inspiration.

As Soyinka makes clear in his book of criticism, *Myth, Literature, and the African World*, his own cultural heritage is Yoruba. Drawing from its fas- cinating and complex mythology, Soyinka concentrates on two central events. One is the disintegration of primal oneness, which he calls Orisa-nla. In the beginning, only Orisa-nla existed, with his servant Akunda; in a moment of revolution or treachery, depending upon the point of view, Akunda rolled a boulder down the back of Orisa-nla, shattering him into the fragments that became the human race and the gods of the Yoruba pantheon; god and man were thenceforth separated from each other. Among these individuated gods, two stand out, Obatala and Ogun, as aspects of the original oneness. Soyinka uses human representations of them both in his novels. Obatala ap- pears as the titular leader of a traditional community. While not actively pursuing the rejuvenation of society, he tries to hold things together: "He is the embodiment of the suffering spirit of man, uncomplaining, agonised, full of the redemptive qualities of endurance and martyrdom." Soyinka also includes a third human figure in the novels, a woman, who appears as the fertility principle inherent in Orisa-nla and promises continuity.

The most important god for Soyinka, however, is Ogun, whose story is central to the plots in the two novels and whose complex character makes him the most complete symbol of the original oneness. Most simply, he is the god of creation and destruction, and man is his incarnation. After the original disintegration, Ogun took upon himself the task of entering the abyss that separated men from the gods and of building a bridge across the primeval gulf to reunite them. To accomplish this task, he had to "die," to risk total disintegration of the personality (thus repeating the original fragmentation) and to reintegrate himself through an act of the will. Ogun's success was his grand triumph that man must strive to emulate. Ogun's cautionary tale does not, however, end here. At the call of human beings, he reluctantly descended to aid them, but his gift of "Promethean" fire—Ogun is the god of the forge—gave man the power of destruction as well as creation. During his sojourn among men, Ogun, as god of wine and of war, then experienced his most shameful moment, the massacre in battle, while in a drunken rage, of both friends and enemies. This destructive power of the will repeated the drunken act of Akunda and symbolizes the ever-present threat of man's own destructiveness. It is especially Ogun's personality and social roles that provide for Soyinka a rationale for contemporary events. Ogun's story proclaims the will as the crucial ethical faculty, individual heroism as the dynamic factor in social change, and the communal function of the heroic act as its sanction.

Soyinka's first novel, *The Interpreters*, is a dark comedy. The settings are the capital city of Lagos, the university city of Ibadan, and the surrounding lagoons, at a time soon after Nigeria's independence, in the early 1960's. Soyinka presents a directionless society seen mainly through the eyes of a few university-educated observers who have just returned from abroad to take up their roles, which they have yet truly to discover, in the new state. What they see is an assortment of professional people holding on to or seeking status and power; their attractive public image is but a disguised sleaziness, a combination of Old World corruption and Victorian hypocrisy. Moving through this structured society are various lost people seeking stability: an American black homosexual, an evangelical preacher, a thief, and occasional transients from outside Africa. The novel traces the lives of the five interpreters—Egbo, Sagoe, Kola, Sekoni, and Bandele—as they get in touch with themselves and their society. What sets them apart, in particular, is their refusal to accept wholesale imported Western values and mores, and a vague sense that an indigenous worldview should mold the new state. The problem is to get in touch with it and revive it. Soyinka does not offer any hope of immediate success.

Of all the interpreters, Egbo and Sekoni are most closely associated with the Ogun experience. Sagoe, Kola, and Bandele do not share the risky heroism of Ogun's nature but seem closer to the passive, suffering attitude of the god Obatala, though it is difficult and undesirable to make such identifications with any allegorical rigidity. Sagoe, the newspaper reporter whose experiences give insight into the corrupt practices of business and politics and into the religious void of modern Nigeria, suffers in the first part of the novel from inebriation and a morning hangover. He has developed an absurd philosophy of Voidancy, a solipsistic return to original oneness, a passive loss of identity. A recurring childhood memory perpetuates a Western, Manichaean split between divine and human nature. He finally agrees to abandon his philosophy and commit himself to his fiancée, Dehinwa, but Sagoe never displays any deep internal struggle. Kola is a painter who is intellectually aware of Yoruba tradition; he spends several months finishing his huge canvas, a symbolic representation of the Yoruba pantheon using contemporary models. Kola gradually recognizes his own inadequacy as an artist—Ogun is Soyinka's divine symbol of the true artist—and is almost ready to accept his role as simply a teacher of art. The painting itself would suggest, at least in the eyes of Egbo, an inadequate conception of human struggle and redemption. Kola presents Ogun (Egbo) not in his creative role as architect of order but as a drunken murderer. Bandele is the clearest image of the god Obatala. Throughout the novel, he tries to mediate among the various interpreters and to judge and encourage ethical behavior. He also tries to live a life of compromise, to prevent a complete split between the intellectuals and the rest of society. In the end, he continues his role of judge—as the traditional Oba—but strikes out at the society itself, ensuring a split, as he sarcastically accuses the hypocritical professional class of burying its own children.

Soyinka measures human character against divine behavior after the original fragmentation. Only Ogun, among all the gods, risked the loss of individuation in the abyss of transition. Egbo, the grandson and heir of a village chief, is on the edge of the abyss. The novel places two choices before him: between the power and privileges of the Osa chiefdom and a life in a modern state, and between a sensuous life with Simi, a nationally famous and beautiful courtesan, and a New World university student, a feminist rebel pregnant with his child. While he has not made either choice definitively at the end of the novel, he leans toward contemporary demands. Such a commitment would be a denial of African heritage as superficially perceived but an assertion of it in essential terms. The university student is herself a heroine, defying artificial conventions of the day and committed to her child and to her education in spite of bitter rejection by the professional elite. She is also the only person with whom Egbo has shared his religious commitment to the Yoruba gods; their night of love takes place in his sacred retreat under the bridge crossing the Ogun River. Egbo has at least three initiation experiences, all sexual, described as symbolic leaps into the abyss of death and rebirth: twice during his first night with Simi and once during his more mature "venturing" with the unnamed student girl. By the end of the novel, he knows, though he has not yet made the decision, that "he could not hold her merely as an idyllic fantasy, for the day rose large enough and he was again overwhelmed by her power of will."

While Egbo's Ogun experience is still on the level of "idyllic fantasy," Sekoni's has a degree of fulfillment and a tragic finality. Like Egbo, at the beginning of the novel he perceives the sacred through physical reality. Egbo calls the fleshy black dancer at the Club Cabana "the exaltation of the Black Immanent." For Sekoni, she is a symbol of the original oneness: It would be profane, he says in his stuttering excitement, "t-t-to bring her in c-c-conflict." In moments of inspiration, as he comes into contact with spiritual reality, his language breaks down and his stuttering increases. Sekoni's first profession is engineering. His dream is to harness the powers of nature. A flashback has him returning home aboard ship, imagining the ocean as "a deafening waterfall defying human will," and his creative fingers as shapers of bridges, hospitals, derricks, and railroads. The sea, however, proves to be too strong; the bureaucracy at home gives him a desk job and then allows him to build a rural power plant only to have it condemned by an expatriate expert. The failure drives him insane. When he is released from the mental hospital, he goes on a pilgrimage to Jerusalem (not to Mecca, as his devout Muslim father would have wished), and by putting his fingers through the broken walls of the city, he has a mystical experience. Soyinka's description of it suggests an identification between the Jewish and the African diaspora, the disintegration of traditional community, and, by implication, a repetition of the original fragmentation of Orisa-nla. Sekoni returns to Nigeria as an inspired artist. His one great work, a sculpture which he calls "The Wrestler," seems a race against time. Using Bandele as a model and a rough incident with a bouncer at the Club Canana as the inspiration, Sekoni depicts what appears to be Ogun just beginning to relax after subduing the forces of chaos in the abyss. Kila admires and envies Sekoni's genius, his ability to create "that something which hits you foully in the stomach."

When Ogun grants such powers, however, he demands a sacrifice in return. In a symbolic scene, with obvious mythological references and a typical Soyinka setting, Sekoni dies in an automobile accident during a raging storm, near a bridge that spans a precipice. As god of the forge, Ogun is associated with automobiles and bridges and with the metal that draws down lightning from the heavens. On that chaotic night, the "dome" of heaven "cracked," and, like Ogun in the abyss, Sekoni loses his identity, literally, except as he survives in his sculpture. His death leaves the other interpreters drained of energy, searching desperately for a myth that will convince them of rebirth. That Sekoni is not reborn seems to provoke estrangement. At the end, the four remaining interpreters are no longer a close-knit group: They experience "a night of severance, every man . . . going his way." The Ogun paradigm would suggest that, since everyone is an incarnation of Ogun, the interpreters are facing the transition experience.

Like *The Interpreters*, *Season of Anomy* has as its major theme the reestablishment of cultural and spiritual continuity. Bandele's searing rebuke of his peers, that they are burying their own children, applies even literally to the generation in power in Soyinka's second novel. The ruling Cartel (a conglomerate of business, political, and military leaders) use their positions to exploit the country (a fictionalized Nigeria) and to intimidate, suppress, and massacre in order to maintain control. The novel's main antagonist is the innocuous-appearing community of Aiyéró, headed by the wise Pa Ahime, which perpetuates the traditional African values of community and harmony with nature. Ahime resembles the Obatala personality in his passive, suffering role as priest. Beneath his surface calm dwell "doubts upon doubts, thicker than the night" about African ideals ever overcoming the forces of exploitation. He himself, however, does not struggle actively against the forces outside the community. The conflict in the novel begins when Ofeyi, the novel's protagonist and the Ogun personality in its artistic, creative aspect, goes out into the larger world to combat the Cartel. Ofeyi is at first a propagandist jingle writer for the Cocoa Corporation, an ally of the Cartel; under the influence of Ahime and his own vision of a new Africa, however, he uses his position to undermine the corporation, until he has to resign under fire. The novel, then, presents a conflict between these two forces, creation and destruction, but the plot is a tracing of Ofeyi's growing commitment to his cause, his debate in particular over using either peaceful or military means, his eventual acceptance of violence, and his personal and communal quest for Iriyise, his mistress, whom Soyinka develops as a goddess of fertility, an aspect of Orisa-nla, who gave birth to the Yoruba pantheon. Ofeyi travels into the center of the Cartel's massacres in order to rescue Iriyise from the enemy prison and carry her, though comatose, safely back to the refuge of Aiyéró.

While the novel often operates on a realistic level—with its vivid pictures of war, for example—its language is infused with ritual and myth. Ofeyi's actions take on a ritualistic meaning and, as in ritual and myth, detailed, causal explanations are not always forthcoming. The novel does not follow a clear chronological line; it oscillates between the communal life in Aiyéró and the outside world and between the inner life of Ofeyi, his memories and reflections, and public action. The novel tries to make sense of the chaotic events through which Ofeyi moves. It judges the Cartel according to traditional values and myths. In particular, it condemns an exploitation that forgets the obligation of one generation to another. Ofeyi's subversive jingles accuse the Cocoa Corporation of milking the country dry: "They drained the nectar, peeled the gold/ The trees were bled prematurely old/ Nor green nor gold remained for the next generation." The proverb that defines the Cartel, one of its own choosing, damns it: "The child who swears his mother will not sleep, he must also pass a sleepless night." The mother (the Cartel) accusing the child of the crime, fails to acknowledge that the child is restless and screams for attention because the mother has not been nurturing him. The Cartel fails in its function of ensuring continuity from one generation to the next. Aiyéró, on the other hand, through its rituals and myths, maintains the three necessary connections, between generations, between the living and the dead, and between gods and men. Aiyéró is not a pastoral paradise; it has a reputation for its boatbuilding, uses hydroelectric power, and manufactures guns. Soyinka's notion of the idyllic community is not backward. Still, its communal ideal suggests strongly its allegorical representation of the divine world attempting to reestablish ties with the fragmented human race to achieve wholeness.

Ogun's transitional journey is the paradigm for the novel's plot and theme. Individual scenes and incidents reinforce the idea. Ofeyi's main concern is whether his actions will make any impact on history: whether the attempt to create order out of chaos is hopeless and whether his own personal contribution will soon be covered in obscurity. When he is still debating his role, sitting in a canoe on the pond that the people of Aiyéró use as a retreat for reflection, Ofeyi watches the wake quickly disappear as the waters resume their calm cover. Even "this simple rite of passage," he says, seems a meaningless challenge. Beneath the pond are centuries of history—"Slaves, gold, oil. The old wars"—and his efforts seem doomed to join them. The oil could be a promise for the future; like Ogun, Ofeyi regards resources as the raw materials of creativity. As he contemplates the Cartel's exploitation of them, he determines, through an act of the will, that victory requires "only the rightful challenger."

The novel's central symbol of the new Nigeria, as conceived by Ahime and Uteyi, is the dam at Shage, which will, when completed, span the river into Cross-river, the region most antagonistic to Aiyéró's ideas and known for its xenophobia. Mainly Aiyéró men, living outside their native community, are engaged on the project, and Ofeyi, as idealogue, has been its inspiration. It, like Iriyise's dance performed for the workers on the construction site, celebrates the harmonious creation of power—hydroelectric power—out of natural forces. Later, however, after the Cartel has begun to react to the initiatives of the Aiyéró men and has begun to repress them, Ofeyi passes by Shage Dam on the way to Cross-river. The site is abandoned, the dam only partially finished, and dead bodies—perhaps the men of Aiyéró—lie floating in the artificial lake. The Cartel has begun its massacres. When Ofeyi first sees the crane with its rope suspended over the lake, he recalls a similar scene in Scotland and remembers his reaction to the unfinished bridge there.

It seemed to him then that all unfinished things were sublime—a Western romantic notion to which he had clung until this day at Shage Dam. Now he reevaluates that experience, according to the myth of his own culture: "It all remained unfinished, and not sublime." Ofeyi as the Ogun personality cannot accept the chaos of the abyss as the end of the creative effort. The goal must be to restore order, not aesthetically admire the incomprehensible.

When Ofeyi arrives at the bridge that will carry him into Cross-river, he, like Egbo in *The Interpreters*, bathes himself in the purifying waters. Unlike Egbo, however, he then takes the final plunge into the abyss. He enters Cross-river in search of Iriyise. As he experiences at first hand the horrors of war, he moves deeper and deeper into enemy territory and ends in Temoko Prison. He is there not because he is forced to be but because he wills to be. In the final symbolic act of the abyss, he is knocked unconscious, loses his "individuation," and then wills himself back to life. This unrealistic mythical event accompanies his simultaneous rescue of Iriyise from the prison. Their return to Aiyéró with Ahime and Demakin (the warrior aspect of Ogun) means a temporary defeat for society but a victory for Ofeyi, whose will has overcome the recurring temptation of passivity.

A common complaint against Soyinka, in spite of the high acclaim he receives for his artistry and his patriotism, is his failure to speak realistically to the issues confronting African societies. Not only does his complex, allusive style encourage elitism, but also his characters are intellectuals whose problems and solutions have little direct relationship to the larger society. Whereas Western audiences, especially critics, might be attracted to such a highly individualistic aesthetic, African readers and critics might wish for a voice that is closer to their pitch, that seems to echo their complaints. Certainly, many would wish fervently that one who is perhaps the most talented literary figure on the continent could use his gift to effect real and visible change. Nevertheless, three things must be said about Soyinka as an African spokesman. First, his novels have as their underlying theme the freedom of the individual and the use of that freedom in the interests of society. Second, he insists on African roots and traditional African concepts as rationales and sanctions for human behavior. Finally, Soyinka does not indulge in experimentation for its own sake, nor does he employ fiction merely as a medium for presenting the tensions of contemporary conflict; rather, by incorporating ritual and myth in his novels, he seeks to suggest the very communal sense that must ultimately hold the society together.

Other major works

PLAYS: *The Swamp Dwellers*, 1958; *The Lion and the Jewel*, 1959; *The Invention*, 1959; *The Trials of Brother Jero*, 1960; *A Dance of the Forests*, 1960; *Camwood on the Leaves*, 1960 (radio play); *The Strong Breed*, 1963; *Three Plays*, 1963; *Five Plays*, 1964; *Kongi's Harvest*, 1964; *The Road*, 1965;

Madmen and Specialists, 1970, revised 1971; *Jero's Metamorphosis*, 1973; *The Bacchae*, 1973 (adaptation of Euripides' play); *Collected Plays*, 1973, 1974 (two volumes); *Death and the King's Horseman*, 1975; *Opera Wonyosi*, 1977 (adaptation of Bertolt Brecht's play *The Threepenny Opera*).

POETRY: *Idanre and Other Poems*, 1967; *Poems from Prison*, 1969; *A Shuttle in the Crypt*, 1972; *Ogun Abibiman*, 1976.

NONFICTION: *The Man Died*, 1972 (autobiography); *Myth, Literature, and the African World*, 1976; *Aké: The Years of Childhood*, 1981 (autobiography).

TRANSLATION; *Forest of a Thousand Daemons: A Hunter's Saga*, 1968 (of D. O. Fagunwa's novel *Ogboju Ode Ninu Igbo Irunmale*).

Bibliography

Gibbs, James, ed. *Critical Perspectives on Wole Soyinka*, 1981.

Jones, Eldred Durosimi. *Wole Soyinka*, 1971, 1983.

Laurence, Margaret. *Long Drums and Cannons: Nigerian Dramatists and Novelists*, 1969.

Moore, Gerald. *Seven African Writers*, 1962.

───────────. *Twelve African Writers*, 1980.

Nkosi, Lewis. *Tasks and Masks: Themes and Styles of African Literature*, 1981.

Palmer, Eustace. *The Growth of the African Novel*, 1980.

Thomas Banks

RICHARD G. STERN

Born: New York, New York; February 25, 1928

Principal long fiction

Golk, 1960; *Europe: Or, Up and Down with Schreiber and Baggish*, 1961; *In Any Case*, 1962 (reissued as *The Chaleur Network*, 1981); *Stitch*, 1965; *Other Men's Daughters*, 1973; *Natural Shocks*, 1978; *A Father's Words*, 1986.

Other literary forms

In addition to his novels, Richard Stern has published three well-received collections of short fiction: *Teeth, Dying and Other Matters* (1964), *1968: A Short Novel, an Urban Idyll, Five Stories, and Two Trade Notes* (1970), and *Packages* (1980). He has published three miscellanies, comprising essays, reviews, reflections, journal excerpts, interviews, and even a bit of poetry: *The Books in Fred Hampton's Apartment* (1973), *The Invention of the Real* (1981), and *The Position of the Body* (1986). His three plays—*The Gamesman's Island* (1964), *Dossier: Earth. Twenty-four Blackouts from the Middle Electric Age* (1966), and *Reparations* (1958)—have not found a large audience. Stern has also edited two anthologies, *American Poetry of the Fifties* (1967) and *Honey and Wax: The Powers and Pleasures of Narrative* (1966), further testimony to his wide range of abilities and interests.

Achievements

Stern's fiction has been compared to that of Saul Bellow by a number of critics. There are a number of similarities between the two writers, but the differences are, perhaps, more important. Stern does use literary and historical allusions and analogies in the manner of Bellow, but he is not a novelist of ideas as Bellow decidedly is. Stern, in contrast to Bellow, continues to exploit the resources of the traditional novel. His interest is more in character and theme than in the dialectic of ideas. This traditional stance may have limited Stern's audience and his recognition as a writer. He has, however, received some prestigious awards. He received the Longwood Foundation Award in 1960, the Fiction Award of the National Institute of Arts and Letters in 1968, the Carl Sandburg Award for Fiction in 1979, the Award of Merit for the Novel in 1985, and he has been both a Rockefeller and a Guggenheim Fellow. The major complaint about Stern's novels is that they are too consciously allusive or mythical; they lack the confessional note and the excess of feeling so characteristic of contemporary fiction. Marcus Klein is helpful, however, in revealing what Stern's fiction does contain:

> In a time when serious American fiction has tended toward extreme personal assertion and extravagance of manner, Richard G. Stern has been composing a body of work which is notable for its detailed craftsmanship, its intricacy, and its reticencies.

Biography

Richard Gustave Stern was born in New York City on February 25, 1928. He was graduated Phi Beta Kappa from the University of North Carolina, Chapel Hill, in 1947, receiving an M.A. from Harvard University in 1949 and a Ph.D. from the University of Iowa in 1954. He has been a member of the faculty at the University of Chicago since 1955 and has been a visiting lecturer at such institutions as the University of Venice, Harvard University, and the University of Nice. He lives in Chicago, Illinois.

Analysis

In an interview, Robert L. Raeder noted that Richard Stern's "books and stories seemed to lack a center, a common denominator." Stern replied that he adheres to a theory of art in which the artist "detaches" himself from his creations and rejects the Romantic approach, wherein the author includes his own life, opinions, and feelings. Stern immerses himself not only in the personalities of the characters he invents but also in their occupations and milieus. Accordingly, Stern's novels explore the mind and world of a professor of biology, a famous sculptor, a journalist, and a television producer. There is no trace of the author in these diverse creations; nor is there any trace of autobiography in characters who display a very limited range of perception, such as Hondorp in *Golk* or Edward Gunther in *Stitch*.

Despite this diversity, however, there are a few constants in Stern's fiction. One of these is the city. His characters are constantly observing, describing, and identifying their fates with the great cities they inhabit, whether it be the New York of *Golk*, the Venice of *Stitch*, or the Cambridge of *Other Men's Daughters*. Another recurring feature of Stern's novels is their lack of conclusive resolution: What happens to the main characters is a sort of ironic modulation, a subtle change of perception rather than a marked change in character or fortune. Marcus Klein has described the movement of a typical Stern novel as one in which a private man becomes involved in the public world and in the process becomes involved in "contingencies" with which he must deal. "His modest success is that he has become potentially moral."

Stern's first novel, *Golk*, is the tale of a private and reclusive man, Hondorp, who is thrust into the public world by a chance encounter with Golk and his film crew in a bookstore. Up to this point, Hondorp has spent his time wandering around New York City and watching television at home with his father. Suddenly, he is on television and a public figure; he accepts a job with Golk's television crew and joins them in their "Golks," which are the tricks played on unsuspecting people who are filmed in absurd situations. The television program based on these secret glimpses of ordinary people becomes very successful, and the show receives a network contract. Yet Golk, the producer and planner of the show, has larger ambitions: He starts to expose senators, union officials, and bureaucrats. At this point, Golk's empire begins to crumble under the attacks by the politicians and network officials. The climactic moment comes when Hondorp and his girlfriend, Elaine, betray Golk and take over the program. They justify the betrayal with the highest of motives: It is a continuation "of Golk's work." Yet their victory—and their marriage—is short-lived; without the eccentric vision of Golk, the show flounders and is canceled. At the end of the book, everyone returns to his earlier state; Golk is now merely one of the crowd, as he "fits" everywhere; Elaine has gone back to her brutal husband; and Hondorp becomes once more the empty person he was at the beginning, with "all trace of his ambition, all desire for change gone absolutely and forever."

Most critics of the novel have emphasized Stern's satire on the invasion of privacy and the baleful influence of television. Stern, however, suggests that this reading ignores the primary thrust of the novel. According to Stern, *Golk* "deals in large part with genius and its epigones and the nature of contemporary exploitation in its great theater, post-war New York." Golk, then, is, for all of his eccentricities, an authentic original; he pushes his created form to its limits, and, in doing so, encounters the wrath of the establishment. Golk scares them, but his second-rate imitator, Hondorp, takes no risks and eventually fails to excite the audience. Even though Golk has lost his position, he remains a presence; he "fits," while Hondorp does not belong anywhere.

Stern's next important novel, *In Any Case*, also deals with betrayal. The protagonist, Samuel Curry, discovers in a book by a French priest an accusation that his son, Bobbie, has betrayed the Chaleur Network, a group of French, English, and Americans working against the Nazis in the early 1940's. Curry is an unlikely hero; he is comfortable and established in France, and the thought of involving himself in the murk of the recent war is repugnant to him. He first seeks out Bobbie's accuser, Father Trentemille, and confronts him, but he receives no satisfaction: Trentemille simply repeats the charges. He then tries two survivors of the "Network," one of whom defends Bobbie, while the other repeats the accusation. He has better luck with Bobbie's girlfriend in the Network, Jacqueline, who asserts her belief in Bobbie's innocence, although she can offer no proof. He has even better luck with German sources and discovers that the real traitor is an agent whose code name is Robert. Robert is described as a professional agent, one who "doesn't even have sides. He's a sphere." When Samuel Curry confronts Robert, he finds that the matter is more complicated than he had thought. He believes that Robert is a "decent" man and goes into business with him. The climax of the novel comes when Curry decides that he must expose Robert and ask Father Trentemille for a retraction. His motives for this action, however, are complex. He believes that he is punishing Robert for his own "delinquency" in rehabilitating Bobbie's name and because Robert has become a rival for Jacqueline's affections. The result of this series of betrayals is surprisingly tranquil. Robert is exposed, but he is not punished. Samuel Curry and Jacqueline marry and are living on the Riviera and expecting the birth of a child in a few months. Not only is Bobbie's name cleared but also his father and the girl he loved have united to repair the loss of his death—a very satisfying ending.

Stern has spoken of how he drew upon and altered the factual background for *In Any Case*. His source was a factual account of the work of the underground in France. Stern makes it into a moral tale in which "the discoverer finds in himself a treasonous impulse which is related to the official traitor's." This impulse begins when Curry sees the divergence between motive and result, of intention and action. "Action would be too easy a way into the current, too much a short cut to judgment." Curry's own intentions and actions during the war and in his relationship with his son hinder any judgment he might make or any action he might take. Stern's comment on his original title for the novel makes his intention clear. "The idea was that the hero always eschewed an active role because 'in any case' there was so much to be said for either side that to take sides was to simplify the issue. To seek relief in action." Curry seeks this sort of "relief" at the end of the novel when he can no longer control the complexities he discovers.

In *Stitch*, Stern returns to the theme of "genius and its epigones." The protagonist, Edward Gunther, is an American who has left his advertising job to find himself and culture in Europe. He has, however, no sensitivity to or perception of art; he spends his time, instead, in eating, chasing women, and brooding. His wife and children are left behind in a hotel in Venice while he searches for the European experience. His opposite, the genius, is Thaddeus Stitch, an American sculptor who has lived in Italy for many years and is recovering from a prison sentence for supporting Fascism; he is obviously modeled on Ezra Pound. Stitch is now quite old and unable to create great art, but his monuments surround him on his island. Edward and Stitch are brought together by their common interest in Nina, a young American poet. Nina is the opposite of Edward; Nina is a poet, not a cultural hanger-on like Edward, and her epic poem has some of the connections with the past that Stitch's work does. Edward is measured and found wanting by these comparisons. As Stitch remembers creating or re-creating monuments of unaging intellect, and as Nina creates, Edward is literally swelling up with the weight he has gained and the assertions of his ego. His only encounter with Stitch ends with a curt dismissal from the master, and his only encounter with Stitch's art produces only pseudoinsights; he describes the island as "beautiful wreckage." Edward's personal life is also a disaster: His wife finds out about his adulteries and throws him out of the house. He finds cultural salvation in the pompous essays he writes and in the possibility of a place with a foundation. The novel comes to an end with Edward's return to the United States. He is teaching at a secondary school in Santa Barbara while waiting for a foundation position. He does hear news of those he left behind in Europe—news which unsettles him. Nina has married and had her epic poem published; Stitch remains in Venice and was the one who introduced Nina to her husband; Edward's wife has divorced him and has found a new partner. Edward is watching the funeral services for President John F. Kennedy as his dreams of finding himself and Europe fade into nothingness.

In *Stitch*, Stern takes the theme of genius and its epigones much further than he did in *Golk*. The genius of this novel is much more credible; some of the best parts of the book are the descriptions of Stitch's art. The epigone is also more credible: Edward is not merely a nullity who is suddenly placed in a position of power but also a chilling example of the cultural middleman who would not recognize an authentic work of art if he tripped over one. The debate between Edward and Nina over Stitch's art, and art in general, defines the differences between the genius and the epigone. Nina sees the problem in life and in art. "Attempts to be what we aren't. Overprizing our singularity. Egoism. Imperceptivity in situations solved long ago. Failure to adapt. The bloodline runs from the world to art's expression of it." Yet Edward never can escape his egoism, and he remains a bundle of unfulfilled and inexpressible longings.

Other Men's Daughters traces the changes in a relationship and a family, a theme in nearly all of Stern's fiction, especially the later works. The protagonist is a very attractive and settled man, Dr. Merriwether. He is a professor at Harvard Medical School, and he lives in Cambridge in a house passed down to him from his ancestors. He is jolted out of this settled life when a young girl, Cynthia Ryder, comes to him one day for a prescription for the Pill. They meet a few times and eventually become lovers. Dr. Merriwether—Stern emphasizes his title and position rather than his personal identity—resists for a while, but they become deeply involved. When Cynthia returns to Swarthmore, they correspond and keep the relationship alive. They manage to meet when Merriwether delivers a paper in New York and when Cynthia can come to Cambridge, but Merriwether manages simultaneously to keep his domestic life intact. This balance is upset, however, when Cynthia accompanies Merriwether to Italy, where he is reading a paper. Merriwether adds a few "speculations" to his formal paper and is then attacked by an American scientist who tells him to "go back to your child whore and let the rest of us do serious work." The public exposure continues when *Newsweek* prints an item linking Merriwether and Cynthia; this brings Cynthia's father on the scene to confront the couple. The confrontation between Mr. Ryder and Merriwether is reminiscent of *In Any Case*; Mr. Ryder does not despise Merriwether but is, instead, drawn to the seriousness and character he sees in him. He does, however, require Cynthia to undergo psychiatric therapy and for the lovers not to meet for a period. The reaction of Merriwether's wife, Sarah, from whom he has long been emotionally estranged, is angry and bitter. Egged on by her lawyer, she starts acrimonious divorce proceedings, and Merriwether loses all of his comfort and the routines he has established over the years. There are some touching moments, such as the Merriwethers' last Christmas together and the parents' breaking the news of their divorce to the younger children; the mood moves away from bitterness once the painful process has been completed. The last chapter of the novel reunites Merriwether and Cynthia in Colorado. The new environment helps Merriwether to overcome the earlier dislocations, and he has some tender moments with his two youngest children. The last note is a very positive one. "The depth of love after loss. The way of human beings. . . . Linkage. Transmission. Evolving."

Other Men's Daughters emphasizes character and setting more than theme. Stern's portrayal of Robert Merriwether—he acquires a first name when he immerses himself in the private world of relationships—and his world is very full. Even Merriwether's scientific speciality, thirst, is exactly appropriate. Furthermore, Stern also renders Sarah's point of view with an impressive sympathy and fidelity. She reveals that the apparently perfect home and family is a façade that hides long-held feelings of resentment and hatred. In the late twentieth century, divorce may be what marriage was to Jane Austen in the nineteenth century, the essential social transaction to be represented in the novel.

Natural Shocks begins where *Other Men's Daughters* ends; the protagonist, Frederick Wursup, is a new journalist who has been divorced for three years. He now lives across from his children and former wife, and he spends much time peeping into his wife's apartment to see what is happening. This intrusion on privacy is directly related to Wursup's occupation as a journalist, and there are many examples in the book of Wursup's destructive private revelations. He recalls an interview with a famous Hollywood director for *Life* magazine and feels "disgusted" at his unwarranted invasion of the man's privacy. His attempt to help a friend who is having political problems with a forthcoming magazine article revealing that the friend's father is on welfare only makes matters worse. A mutual friend, Knoblauch, sees a central problem in such writing: "The intimacies would be converted into publicity, benevolently but beyond recall. All but the hardest or deepest people would find that unbearable." After establishing the theme of the public revelation of private events and feelings, the novel shifts to deal with the most essential "natural shock," death. Wursup is looking for a topic on which to write, and his editor suggests that he look into the newly popular subject of death. When Wursup visits the hospital to talk to some dying patients, however, he becomes involved in the life of one of them, Cicia Buell. Because of his involvement, or the irreducible nature of death, Wursup finds it difficult to translate the interview with Cicia into his usual brand of journalism. Other shocks follow: His father and a friend commit suicide because of age or anxiety; the reason is never made clear. Wursup's wife remarries, which dislocates his sense of order. He tries to retreat to a Maine island to find some rest and peace; his idyll is interrupted, however, by the news that Cicia is dying. By the time he arrives at the hospital, she is dead, and the novel ends on a note of darkness unrelieved by any saving insight.

The themes are clear in *Natural Shocks*; death and privacy are interwoven throughout the novel. What is more difficult is coming to terms with the main character, Fred Wursup. He is an engaging and witty character, but his prying into people's lives for material for his journalism is disturbing. It is no accident that the book begins and ends with Wursup spying on his former wife's apartment. Wursup does have an epiphany: "Wursup himself had surrendered Cicia upstairs. She was almost as far away as Poppa and Mona. He'd toss off that article for Mike Schilp now. It was just another verbal turn." The people whose lives he has touched have become a product to be marketed. His recognition is, perhaps, what distinguishes him from other revealers of the private life.

A Father's Words is another investigation of domestic life, although the conflict is now not between husband and wife but between parent and children. The father, Cy Riemer, is amicably divorced from his first wife; his four children are in their twenties and, with one exception, settled. Jack is the oldest child and the recipient of most of his father's words; he is a habitual liar and self-deceiver whose unstructured life is a constant source of dismay and disruption to his father. Cy is always encouraging his son to become respectable. When Jack is working in a "bucket shop" selling books by phone, his father suggests that he get a job in a publishing company. Yet Jack resists the advice and continues on his disorderly way. He only impinges on his father's life when he suggests that Cy accept personal advertisements for his scientific newsletter. Cy is in financial difficulty and lets Jack handle it, although he feels soiled by the ads. Jack marries Maria Robusto, the daughter of a pornographic film king, and starts working for a commodities broker, so his father is temporarily relieved. Cy has trouble, however, with his other children. The next oldest, Jenny, has written a Ph.D. thesis on the "Wobbling" family in literature. The youngest son, Ben, has published a book called *The Need to Hurt*, which claims that human personality is formed at the fetal stage. Both works are attacks on Cy's fatherhood and his concept of family. The conflict with Jack comes to a head when Cy confronts Jack in a run-down tenement in New York. Again, Cy's words do not help, and Jack seems to give up on their relationship and on himself. "Face it, Dad. I'm finished. I'm never going to be what you want me to be." There are, however, two important reversals at the end of the novel. First, only a few years later, Jack becomes successful; he is the creator of a television situation comedy which features an addled father who creates problems which the wise son has to solve. It is another attack upon Cy's fatherhood and a curious metamorphosis of their relationship. The second reversal is that Cy has, once more and against all odds and sense, become a father. He resists at first and asks his then girlfriend, Emma, to get an abortion, but at the end he leaves Jack and looks forward to "coming home to a new family."

Riemer seems, at first glance, to be an ideal parent. He encourages, in-structs, and supports all of his children. Yet the words he directs toward his children to accomplish these tasks are resented by his children. Jenny accuses him of "the destructiveness that's there with the generosity and love." She believes that her father does not want anyone to "rival" him and so he cuts down each of the children. Furthermore, the children's success is based on the defeat of the father in Jack's television show, Jenny's thesis, or Ben's book. The theme, then, is the oppressive burden of a father's love, inevitably felt no matter how the father treats the child; each child in the novel must win his independence by supplanting the father in some way. It must be said that this conflict and its resolutions are given a witty rather than oppressive treatment by Stern. In addition, Cy does not, finally, bend under the weight of this conflict but accepts and looks forward to it.

Richard Stern has created a body of work that is equal to that of any of his contemporaries. He was stereotyped early in his career as a follower of Saul Bellow and as a Jewish novelist. Those labels never did fit Stern, and they have become even less accurate as his work has developed. He has moved from such strongly thematic novels as *Golk* and *In Any Case* to novels that emphasize character and plot. Stern's ability to create not only credible char-acters but also their environment is most impressive. His novels are, as one critic has said, "in the great tradition of moral realism."

Other major works

SHORT FICTION: *Teeth, Dying and Other Matters*, 1964; *1968, A Short Novel, an Urban Idyll, Five Stories, and Two Trade Notes*, 1970; *Packages*, 1980.

PLAYS: *Reparations*, 1958; *The Gamesman's Island*, 1964; *Dossier: Earth. Twenty-four Blackouts from the Middle Electric Age*, 1966.

ANTHOLOGIES: *Honey and Wax: The Powers and Pleasures of Narrative*, 1966; *American Poetry of the Fifties*, 1967.

MISCELLANEOUS: *The Books in Fred Hampton's Apartment*, 1973; *The Invention of the Real*, 1981; *The Position of the Body*, 1986.

Bibliography
Bergonzi, Bernard. "Herzog in Venice," in *The New York Review of Books*. V (December 9, 1965), p. 26.
Flower, Dean. "The Way We Live Now," in *The Hudson Review*. XXXI (Summer, 1978), pp. 343-355.
Kenner, Hugh. "Stitch: The Master's Voice," in *Chicago Review*. XVIII (Summer, 1966), pp. 177-180.

Raeder, Robert L. "An Interview with Richard Stern," in *Chicago Review*. XVIII (Summer, 1966), pp. 170-175.

James Sullivan

PAUL WEST

Born: Eckington, England; February 23, 1930

Principal long fiction

A Quality of Mercy, 1961; *Tenement of Clay*, 1965; *Alley Jaggers*, 1966; *I'm Expecting to Live Quite Soon*, 1970; *Caliban's Filibuster*, 1971; *Bela Lugosi's White Christmas*, 1972; *Colonel Mint*, 1972; *Gala*, 1976; *The Very Rich Hours of Count von Stauffenberg*, 1980; *Rat Man of Paris*, 1986.

Other literary forms

Paul West is a remarkably prolific writer whose literary interests also include poetry, criticism, and other nonfiction. In addition to his books of verse, *The Spellbound Horses* (1960) and *The Snow Leopard* (1964), West has published three memoirs: *I, Said the Sparrow* (1963), which recounts his childhood in Derbyshire; *Words for a Deaf Daughter* (1969), one of West's most popular works, which poignantly relates the experiences of his deaf daughter, Mandy; and *Out of My Depths: A Swimmer in the Universe* (1983), which describes the author's determination to learn to swim at middle age. Besides his numerous essays and book reviews in countless periodicals, journals, and newspapers, West has published *The Growth of the Novel* (1959), *Byron and the Spoiler's Art* (1960), *The Modern Novel* (1963), *Robert Penn Warren* (1964), *The Wine of Absurdity: Essays in Literature and Consolation* (1966), and *Sheer Fiction* (1987).

Achievements

When West arrived on the literary scene as a novelist, he was regarded as an author who possessed a compelling voice but also as one who wrote grotesque and verbally complex fictions. The unevenness of critical reaction cannot overshadow, however, the regard with which serious readers have approached his work, and a list of his fellowships and awards clearly indicates a writer of significant stature: He is the recipient of a Guggenheim Fellowship (1962), a *Paris Review* Aga Kahn Prize for Fiction (1974), the National Endowment for the Humanities Summer Stipend for science studies (1975), the National Endowment for the Arts Fellowship in Creative Writing (1980), the Hazlett Memorial Award for Excellence in the Arts (1981), the American Academy and Institute of Arts and Letters Award in Literature (1985), and a National Endowment for the Arts Fellowship in Fiction (1985). Besides teaching at Pennsylvania State University since 1962, West has been a visiting professor and writer-in-residence at numerous American universities. As his fiction has developed, West has shown himself to be a highly imaginative, experimental, and linguistically sophisticated writer. Critics usually commend him for his original style and note the striking diversity of his oeuvre.

Biography

Paul Noden West was born in Eckington, Derbyshire, on February 23, 1930, one of two children, into a working-class family. After attending local elementary and grammar schools, West went to Birmingham University, then to Lincoln College, Oxford, and in 1952 to Columbia University on a fellowship. Although profoundly attracted to New York life, West was forced to return to England to fulfill his military service in the Royal Air Force and there began his writing career. Once he concluded his service, West taught English literature at the Memorial University of Newfoundland, wrote a volume of poems, and did considerable work for the Canadian Broadcasting Corporation. In 1962 he was awarded a Guggenheim Fellowship and returned to the United States, where he took up permanent residence. He has been a member of the English and comparative literature faculties at Pennsylvania State University since 1962, dividing his time each year between teaching and writing in New York. His preference for the United States he has voiced many times, and he has, in fact, become an American citizen.

Analysis

Paul West has long insisted that what is most important to him as a writer is the free play of the imagination. What the imagination invents, he contends, becomes something independent and actual. West himself states the case most clearly when noting that "elasticity, diversity, openness, these are the things that matter to me most." Thus his fictions often revolve, both thematically and structurally, around the interplay between the individual and his or her imagination and an absurd, threatening universe. Often these fictions rely heavily upon dreams of one sort or another, with characters living in their dreams or living out their dreams or becoming confused about where dreams leave off and the world begins.

Consequently, West's fictions often abound with a sense of precariousness as characters who are constrained in one form or another struggle to free themselves and find their places in the world. Sanity frequently becomes the central issue in these lives, with protagonists taking on the forces of conventionality in their private wars with the drab and mundane. Typical West heroes are outsiders, often marginal or largely inconsequential figures, who will not or cannot conform to the forces about them and who, in striking out on their own, pay steep prices for their individuality.

A Quality of Mercy, West's first novel and a work which he largely disowns, deals with a collection of embittered and failed lives overseen by Camden Smeaton, the novel's central consciousness. The novel is otherwise unmemorable except insofar as it anticipates concerns West more successfully developed in later novels: alienation, immersion in dream and illusion, the idea of an irrational universe, and the use of stylistic fragmentation.

On the other hand, *Tenement of Clay*, West's second novel, stands as a far more accomplished work, controlled, stylistically inventive, morally probing. Here West introduces the reader to the voices of two narrators, each of whom is compelling and unique. The work is divided into three chapters, the two shortest forming a frame offered by Pee Wee Lazarus, a dwarf wrestler whose direct idiom immediately assaults the reader and demands his attention. His desire is to "involve" the reader in his tale, a story that revolves around Papa Nick, narrator of the middle section, who along with Lazarus meets a taciturn giant he names Lacland. Lacland appears to have no home or clear destination, so Nick takes him back to his rooms, where Nick presides over a private flophouse for local bums. Kept in the darkened basement, Lacland soon develops, under Lazarus' perverse tutelage, a sexual appetite and his own abusive language. After a series of horrible misadventures, Lacland reverts to his despondency and silence and eventually becomes Nick's legal ward.

All these events, extreme and dramatic as they may appear, actually operate as a backdrop to Nick's personal turmoil. For years he has carried on a fitful relationship with Venetia, a former film actress, who exhorts him to abandon his altruism toward the derelicts and to run off with her to a life of leisure. When Nick physically collapses from the burden of Lacland and Lazarus' escapades, Venetia nurses him back to health, leaves him when he returns to his bums, and dies in a car crash in Florida.

The novel's soul comes in the form of Nick's constant ruminations, which offer a way of coping with and sometimes solving the dilemmas of his existence. Gradually the line between straight narration and Nick's hallucinations begins to dissolve; the two become one, and the reader learns something fundamental about this world: Dream and reality invade each other; there is no escaping one for the other.

The novel is furthermore important for the moral questions it raises. Perhaps the most telling of these involves one's responsibilities to other human beings; in particular terms, is Nick responsible for the lives he admits into his home? As Lacland and Lazarus demonstrate, Nick has assumed the role of a Dr. Frankenstein and created his own monsters, whom he has unwittingly unleashed upon the world. Is the answer to this dilemma incarceration? Lacland's temporary internment in the basement suggests that it is not.

For Nick, these are the questions that finally come with life itself, and his failure to arrive at any fixed solution suggests a form of authorial honesty about the complexity of modern existence. In this context, the epigraph from Samuel Beckett makes sense: "If there were only darkness, all would be clear. It is because there is not only darkness but also light that our situation becomes inexplicable."

The novel's title comes from a passage in John Dryden's *Absalom and Achitophel* (1681-1682), and certainly the images of tenements abound in the work: All the buildings in this metropolis Lazarus calls New Babylon, especially Nick's flophouse, the grave into which Venetia is lowered, and the human body itself, which contains and in many cases entraps the spirit. In their concerns with their corporeal selves, most of these characters miss the important questions Nick poses throughout. Life, then, amounts to inhabiting one vast tenement, and the point is never escape, but how one chooses to live that life.

With his next novel, *Alley Jaggers*, West moved even further into depicting a consciousness at odds with the rest of the world. Alley is as compelling a narrator as Lazarus or Nick, and like them he speaks in a language that is distinct and unique, an idiom that oddly combines Irish brogue, Midlands accent, and personal argot.

Alley is a profoundly frustrated little man who realizes that his job and marriage are unfulfilling but who has no idea how to remedy his situation. He spends his most satisfying moments dreaming of horses and the elaborate names owners concoct for them and creating airplanes in his attic retreat. Alley wants desperately to make an impression of some kind, and one of his creations, an androgynous, semihuman form emitting a silent scream, both intrigues his fellow workers and stands as an effigy of his own condition.

Eventually his boredom and frustration explode into violence when he accidentally kills a young woman during an unsuccessful sexual tryst. In fear and confusion, he wraps her body in plaster and makes a companion for his own statue. When the police inevitably discover the body, Alley has finally and inadvertently stumbled into prominence: In the police he finds his first willing audience in years.

West's purpose here is far more sophisticated than the old cliché of the criminal as artist or as misunderstood noble creature. Instead, Alley represents the alienated individual, the small person cut off from any meaningful existence who struggles in hopeless confusion to make his life somehow mean something. Unfortunately, Alley is locked in the prison of himself, both convict and jailer at once, and remains in fundamental confusion about what to do. Nevertheless, his most vital moments are spent in his imagination, which is infinitely more extravagant and vital than his quotidian existence.

The second novel in the Jaggers trilogy, *I'm Expecting to Live Quite Soon*, represents an entirely different turn in West's career. Here he not only shifts his attention from Alley to his much maligned wife, Dot, but also creates a more controlled, straightforward type of narrative. The real daring in this work comes in West's attempt to enter the consciousness of a woman, to take the same world of the first novel and shift the perspective to see through the eyes of another member of the family.

Where Alley was frustrated and irresponsible to anyone outside himself, Dot lives a life of devotion and caring: attending to Alley's irascible mother, ministering to her dying father in a nursing home, and visiting Alley in the mental hospital. Like Alley, she needs a release from boredom and conventionality, which eventually she achieves through immersion in her sensual self. The measure of her change can be seen in her eventual decision to throw over her old life and run away to Birmingham with Jimsmith Williams, a black bus-driver.

Bela Lugosi's White Christmas, the final volume in the trilogy, finds Alley (now referred to as AJ) in analysis with Dr. Withington (With) in a state institution. Who is counseling whom becomes vague as With is drawn increasingly into AJ's fractured mind, and the two eventually reverse roles, thus effecting AJ's temporary freedom and With's incarceration.

More than any of the previous novels, this one dramatically stakes its claim to stylistic and linguistic experimentation. Attempting to enter AJ's mind as fully as possible, West fashions one of his densest, most verbally complex fictions. While the reader is often at a loss to understand the exact meaning of many passages, what one does comprehend is AJ's indefatigable desire to experience as much as he can as quickly as he can. The result is criminal melee with AJ commandeering a bulldozer and digging up graves in search of his dead father, threatening customers in a bar, sodomizing and murdering a cow, covering himself with the animal's blood and sawdust, and starting a fire in a factory near his mother's home.

AJ's immersion in his own mind becomes so complete that, like a Beckett character, he reaches a state of almost total silence by the end of the novel. Once again, West examines the line between madness and sanity, originality and convention, but like all of his fictions, the work is no polemic; AJ is neither saint nor hopelessly depraved misanthrope but a tortured human being who desperately wants "a bit of individuality." The work is also significant for the fact that West actually intrudes on the fiction in spots, first in a long footnote in which he explains the eccentricities of his characters' names and ends by noting that "in this text, optical illusion is empirically sound," and later in another footnote announcing his own presence throughout the narrative. The point in both cases is to assert artifice as a fictional construct: Fictions are both stories about people and about fiction itself.

West deals with some of these same concerns in *Caliban's Filibuster*, the novel that was published immediately before *Bela Lugosi's White Christmas*. This work represents West at his most experimentally extreme as he takes his deepest plunge into an individual's consciousness. Cal, the narrator, is yet another of West's profoundly frustrated protagonists, in this case a failed novelist-cum-screenwriter who chafes at bastardizing his talent for decidedly mercenary ends. As he travels over the Pacific Ocean with his companions Murray McAndrew, a ham actor, and Sammy Zeuss, a crass film producer and Cal's employer, voices representing various of Cal's divided selves carry on endless debates about his artistic aspirations. Thus the reader is not only taken fully into the character's mind but also given access to the dimensions of his troubled psyche.

To appease these voices and satisfy himself, Cal concocts three separate yet interdependent scenarios in which he and his companions play significant roles. In creating these tales, Cal attempts to convince himself of his abused talent and also to distance himself from his experience, like a viewer before a screen in a theater watching versions of his own life. Like Caliban, his Shakespearean namesake in *The Tempest*, Cal seethes with revenge, cursing those who control him. On his behalf, however, readers must regard his filibuster as an attempt to retain his individuality, which he sees as being eroded by the sterile conventions of his profession.

One way to view the novel is as West's paean to language itself, for it abounds in extravagant verbal complexities: anagrams, anonyms, puns, malapropisms, acronyms, rhymes, and alphabet games. Language operates not only as Cal's professional tool but also as his saving grace; it literally keeps him sane, affording him the diversity of experience that the world denies. Like so many of West's heroes, Cal feels himself trapped, contained by forces which inexorably press against and threaten to destroy him. Language becomes his one potent defense.

In *Colonel Mint*, West operated from a seemingly straightforward, but by no means uncomplicated, premise: An astronaut in space claims that he has seen an angel. Whether he has or not is beside the point; instead, the fact that he *thinks* he has and that others want to disabuse him of this belief becomes the subject of this alternately humorous but morally serious work. For his comment Mint is shunted off to the hinterlands of Washington State and is forced to undergo endless hours of interrogation. If he recants he can go free; otherwise, he must indefinitely remain a prisoner of the space program.

The more Mint refuses to cooperate, the more clever and depraved the methods used against him become. After threats, physical beatings, and sexual sadism fail to make Mint waver, his tormentor, General Lew R., begins, like Dr. With in *Bela Lugosi's White Christmas*, gradually to assume Mint's point of view. He wonders what it would be like to see an angel, what exactly an angel is, and finally he accepts, though he cannot empirically confirm, that Mint has seen an angel.

When the two men escape from the interrogation compound for the wilds of the surrounding woods, it appears they have defeated the forces of conformity and conventional thinking. As is the case in so many of West's fictions, however, those forces track the characters down and exact payment: Lew R. is shot and Mint is frozen. Thus, in this novel, to assert one's individuality becomes tantamount to political treason, and the response of the state is swift, final, and utterly unforgiving.

Stylistically the novel is far more straightforward than *Caliban's Filibuster*, but in at least one important respect it recalls a feature of *Bela Lugosi's White Christmas*. The tone of the novel, for all of its physical and psychological horror, is remarkably level, often nonchalant and conversational. Here the narrator, not necessarily the author, addresses the audience directly a number of times. For example, early in the work, when the reader begins to doubt the plausibility of Mint's abduction, the narrator anticipates one's objections by remarking, "You might ask, now, where is the humanity in all this; where sweet reason went. . . ." The effect here and later in the work, when the intrusions continue, is one of complicity; the audience cannot remain at the safe distance of voyeur but must participate, psychologically and emotionally, in the events that transpire. The forces of conformity involve everyone, and the audience becomes uncomfortably aware of this throughout the narrative.

In *Gala*, West extends the range of his experimentation but also returns to some familiar territory as he develops fictionally the situation described in *Words for a Deaf Daughter*. Here, novelist and amateur astronomer Wight Deulius and his deaf child Michaela construct a model of the Milky Way in their basement. The reader takes a stellar journey through the universe, moving increasingly toward what appear to be the limits of the imagination.

What is especially intriguing about this work is the form West's experimentation takes. Recalling the practice of earlier novels, but especially *Caliban's Filibuster*, West fashions a unique structure for the fiction. Where in the latter work he relies upon the International Date Line and the color spectrum (different sections of the novel are devoted primarily to different colors), in *Gala* elements of physics and the genetic code symbols offer the pattern for the story. West explains this practice when remarking, "I am a compulsive exotic and structural opportunist. I have no idea what structures I will choose next—although I do feel that they will probably be from nature rather than from society."

In his ninth novel, *The Very Rich Hours of Count von Stauffenberg*, West once again shifted focus and style to re-create the details of one of Adolf Hitler's would-be assassins. The novel represents the best in historical fiction, a seemingly effortless blending of fact, elaboration, and pure fantasy, with the result that history becomes for the reader felt experience rather than a catalog of dry, distant details. As West points out in a preface, Stauffenberg is important not only for his public persona but also as someone whose military experience recapitulates, to greater or lesser degrees, that of West's father and all those who lived through World War II. Thus the reader comes to understand an important feature of this writer's fiction, which he expresses as follows: "Whatever I'm writing evinces the interplay between it and my life at the moment of writing, and the result is prose which, as well as being narrative and argumentative and somewhat pyrotechnical, is also symptomatic."

While the narrative, on the surface, seems markedly different from the novels which immediately precede it, one can also see characteristic West concerns emerging. For example, most of the novel places the audience squarely in Stauffenberg's mind as he copes with his war wounds, struggles to express the abiding love he feels for his wife and family, ponders the respon-sibilities that come with his social and military class, and rages increasingly at the psychopathic perversity of Hitler, the displaced paperhanger. West man-ages to avoid the obvious trap of the revisionist historian who might be tempted to make Stauffenberg into a martyr or saint. Instead, he emerges as a deeply committed, idealistic man but also one whose psyche is profoundly bruised and disturbed by the events of which he finds himself a part.

The structure of this novel is also just as experimental as that of earlier novels. West had been reading a number of medieval books of hours, lay bre-viaries that offer devotional prayers alongside richly illuminated paintings. Stauffenberg's rich hours are the last thirty-six of his life; the novel, however, does not stop with his execution. West imaginatively allows the count to speak to the audience from the grave, becoming, then, the most authoritative and omniscient of narrators describing those turbulent last months of the Third Reich.

Rat Man of Paris, his most popular novel, found West exploring yet again the effects of the Third Reich on the life of yet another alienated, marginal figure, in this case a boulevardier of modern Paris who spends his time accosting passersby with a rat he conceals in his overcoat. Étienne Poulsifer, the rat man, has survived the Nazi occupation and destruction of his child-hood village, and carries about with him the emotional and psychological baggage of his horrifying past, as well as the rats which serve as metaphor for that growing legacy.

When he learns of Klaus Barbie's extradition to France, Poulsifer confuses him with the Nazi commander responsible for his parents' death and goes on a personal campaign to become the conscience of an entire nation. Watching all this is Sharli Bandol, Rat Man's lover, who desperately tries to bring some order and love into the chaos of his condition. The birth of a son appears to temper Poulsifer's extremism, but to the end he retains his eccentricity and thus his individuality.

Like *The Very Rich Hours of Count von Stauffenberg*, *Rat Man of Paris* carefully examines the interplay between personal and public trauma, and as West puts it, "Everybody who's born gets the ontological shock, and some people get the historical shock as well, and he has both. Because he has the historical shock, he has the ontological shock even worse, and this has blighted his life." Thus the rat man stands as a contemporary Everyman, radically imperfect, overwhelmed by the world in which he finds himself, but tenaciously determined to make something of his existence.

Also like other of West's protagonists, Poulsifer demonstrates the vitality of the creative imagination. Were it not for his wild musings, the delight he takes in yoking utterly disparate things together in his mind, he would be consumed by history and dreary conventionality. In many ways he is the last free man, an essential primitive who refuses the definitions and restrictions of others for a life created on his own terms.

Throughout his career, West has drawn criticism for his own stylistic ec-centricities and rich verbal texturings, and the usual complaint holds that he is self-indulgent and willfully obscure. While indeed his fiction makes consid-erable demands of his audience, he is anything but deliberately perverse or obscure. In fact, West consistently attempts to reach and communicate with his audience, to involve them, in each of his rich fictional stories. His note at the beginning of *Tenement of Clay*, the interview appended to *Caliban's Fili-buster*, the footnotes in *Bela Lugosi's White Christmas*, the moments of direct address in *Colonel Mint*, the announcement in the middle of *Gala* of the nov-el's particular structure, and the preface to *The Very Rich Hours of Count von Stauffenberg*—all demonstrate that West is fully aware of his audience and always desirous of its sympathetic participation in the fictional experi-ence. West is committed to the proposition that writing matters, and that good writing must present its own unique experience. As he says in his essay "In Defense of Purple Prose," "The ideal is to create a complex verbal world that has as much presence, as much apparent physical bulk, as the world around it. . . . This is an illusion, to be sure, but art *is* illusion, and what's needed is an art that temporarily blots out the real."

Other major works

POETRY: *The Spellbound Horses*, 1960; *The Snow Leopard*, 1964.

NONFICTION: *The Growth of the Novel*, 1959; *Byron and the Spoiler's Art*, 1960; *Byron: Twentieth-Century Views*, 1963 (editor); *I, Said the Sparrow*, 1963; *The Modern Novel*, 1963; *Robert Penn Warren*, 1964; *The Wine of Absurdity: Essays in Literature and Consolation*, 1966; *Words for a Deaf Daughter*, 1969; *Out of My Depths: A Swimmer in the Universe*, 1983; *Sheer Fiction*, 1987.

Bibliography

McLaughlin, Brian. "Paul West," in *British Novelists Since 1960*, 1983. Edited by Jay L. Halio.

West, Paul. "In Defense of Purple Prose," in *The New York Times*. Decem-ber 15, 1985.

——————. "The Writer's Situation II," in *New American Review 10*, 1970.

David W. Madden

JOHN EDGAR WIDEMAN

Born: Washington, D.C.; June 14, 1941

Principal long fiction

A Glance Away, 1967; *Hurry Home*, 1970; *The Lynchers*, 1973; *Hiding Place*, 1981; *Sent for You Yesterday*, 1983; *The Homewood Trilogy*, 1985 (includes *Damballah*, *Hiding Place*, and *Sent for You Yesterday*).

Other literary forms

An intensely lyrical novelist, John Edgar Wideman has also published numerous short stories based upon family members, friends, and neighbors from his childhood community of Homewood, a long-standing all-black subdivision of Pittsburgh, Pennsylvania. Twelve of these pieces are presented as letters in his critically acclaimed collection *Damballah* (1981), which has also been published with two of his novels as *The Homewood Trilogy*. Wideman's autobiographical *Brothers and Keepers* (1984) blends facts with fictionalized characters and incidents as the author scrutinizes his own relationship to his brother Robert Wideman, imprisoned for life in Pennsylvania's Western State Penitentiary. Uncollected poetry, reviews, and essays on black American literature by Wideman abound in the foremost scholarly journals and literary digests.

Achievements

When he emerged upon the literary scene in the late 1960's, Wideman stood out from his peers as a black American writer who did not address exclusively themes of racial conflict and militant nationalism. He concentrated instead on individual psychological struggles that transcend color lines. His earliest novels having been enthusiastically received, he was lauded as a successor to William Faulkner. Nevertheless, it can be argued that he really did not tap the depths of his talent until, influenced in part by slave narratives and African folklore, he initiated his Homewood series. Expressing the black American experience epitomized by Homewood's extensive French family and their fictive kin, *Sent for You Yesterday* received the 1984 Faulkner Award for Fiction from PEN, the International Association of Poets, Playwrights, Editors, Essayists, and Novelists. In spite of favorable reviews of his fiction, many people have accused Wideman of indulging in an unconventional style at the expense of theme. More often than not, though, his experimentation extends meaning by illustrating the impact of the past in addition to the inextricable bonds among generations. In fact, his autobiographical *Brothers and Keepers*, which displays some of his innovative techniques, earned a National Book Critics Circle Award nomination. Hailed as "the most authentic black blues voice since Billie Holliday," Wideman certainly merits consideration as one of the best American writers of his generation.

Biography

Born in Washington, D.C., on June 14, 1941, John Edgar Wideman initially aspired to be a professional basketball player. Consequently, he served as both a Benjamin Franklin Scholar at the University of Pennsylvania and captain of the school's championship basketball team. A member of Phi Beta Kappa, he was graduated from the University of Pennsylvania in 1963 with a B.A. in English. Promptly selected as only the second black Rhodes Scholar in history, he received his B.Ph. degree from Oxford University in 1966, specializing as a Thouron Fellow in the eighteenth century novel. He then spent one year as a Kent Fellow at the University of Iowa Writers' Workshop, subsequently returning to lecture at his alma mater, Pennsylvania. A professor of English at the University of Wyoming, he speaks frequently at other American colleges and universities and has also acted as a consultant to various educational boards and government agencies. He lives in Laramie, Wyoming.

Analysis

The recurring thematic emphasis in John Edgar Wideman's novels is placed upon history, both collective and personal. From homosexual college professors to ghetto junkies, Wideman's characters are often uncomfortable with their places in history and unsure that they even understand those few traditions that they do observe. Therefore, they shuttle between the imaginary and the real in order to rediscover the past, revive it, or at least preserve whatever parts they do recall. Despite Wideman's literary beginnings in the racially turbulent 1960's, when blacks in America articulated their estrangement from Africa, his white as well as black characters crave the rootedness that distinguishes those who have come to terms with their backgrounds. Shifting from the anonymous Northern cities of his first three novels to the clearly delineated Homewood of *Hiding Place* and *Sent for You Yesterday*, Wideman nevertheless consistently indicates that ignorance of heritage results in isolation and psychological turmoil.

Wideman forgoes strictly chronological plot development, adopting instead an intricate experimental style consisting of stream-of-consciousness narrative, long interior monologues, dream sequences, surrealistic descriptions, and abrupt shifts in time, diction, and points of view. Beginning each novel almost exclusively *in medias res*, he employs a technique influenced by the works of T. S. Eliot, James Joyce, and Jean Toomer, yet indisputably original. In *The Lynchers*, for example, he illustrates the traditionally victimized status of black Americans with a preface that cites more than one hundred documented lynchings. Reeling between their own ravaged communities and impenetrable white ones, the black protagonists of his first two novels, *A Glance Away* and *Hurry Home*, occupy a jumbled landscape where blues clubs coexist with biblical icons. Similarly, in *Hiding Place* and *Sent for You Yesterday*, Wideman retells the stories of his ancestors until a shack or a cape acquires the same expressive quality as a cross. As the author himself explains, "You can call it experimentation, or you can call it ringing the changes. . . . I value spontaneity, flexibility, a unique response to a given situation. . . . Getting too close to the edge but then recovering like the heroes of the Saturday matinee serials. That's excitement."

Dedicated to "Homes," Wideman's first novel, *A Glance Away*, creates thematic excitement with its treatment of two drifting men coming to terms with their pasts. After a year spent at a rehabilitation center for drug addicts, Eddie Lawson, a disillusioned young black man, returns to his listless, decaying urban neighborhood. Rather than celebrating, however, he spends his gloomy homecoming confronting the goblins that drove him to the brink in the first place: his mother Martha Lawson's idealization of his dead older brother, his girlfriend Alice Smalls's rejection of him for sleeping with a white woman, and his own self-disgust over abandoning a secure postal job for menial, marginal employment. Dejected and defeated by nightfall, he drags himself to grimy Harry's Place in order to cloak his memories in a narcotic haze. There, he is reconciled by his albino friend Brother Smalls with another outcast named Robert Thurley, a white college professor struggling with his own record of divorce, alcoholism, and homosexuality. Though discrepancies between wealth and power divide the two homeless men, each manages to urge the other to maintain his faith in people despite his guilt-ridden history.

A Glance Away generated much favorable critical response in particular for Wideman's depiction of the alienated Thurley. In trying to disavow his personal past, this connoisseur of food and art embraces a surfeit of creeds and cultures. "In religion an aesthetic Catholic, in politics a passive Communist, in sex a resigned anarchist," he surrounds himself with treasures from both East and West and indulges in a smorgasbord of the globe's delicacies. Yet as a real measure of the displacement that these extravagances so futilely conceal, he quotes lines from T. S. Eliot's "The Love Song of J. Alfred Prufrock," in which a similarly solitary speaker searches for intimacy in a world bereft of its cultural moorings.

Emphasizing his protagonists' self-absorption and the estrangement of their family members and friends, Wideman abandons strictly chronological plot development in favor of lengthy interior monologues. Conversations tend to be short, more likely than not they are interrupted by unspoken flashbacks and asides. Using speech to measure isolation, the author portrays both Eddie and Thurley as incapable of communicating adequately. Eddie, for example, becomes tongue-tied around a group of Southern travelers, shuddering in his bus seat instead of warning them as he wishes of the reality of the Northern mecca that they seek. Similarly, despite the empowering qualities of a gulp of Southern Comfort, Thurley delivers a lecture on Sophocles' *Oedipus Tyrannus* (c. 429 B.C.) fraught with "futility and detachment, . . . introspection and blindness." In one brilliant play on this speechlessness, both men suddenly converse as if they were actors on a stage. This abrupt emphasis on what is spoken—to the exclusion of private thoughts—stresses each man's imprisonment within himself. Flowing from a weaker artist's pen, *A Glance Away* would have become a mere exercise in allusive technique and stream-of-consciousness style. On the contrary, it reads with the effortless ease of a masterfully crafted lyrical poem. Key to its success is Wideman's careful alliance of form and content, not to mention his insightful treatment of a rootlessness that transcends the barriers of race.

The same compact length as the novel which precedes it, *Hurry Home* similarly focuses upon the theme of rootlessness. Its ambitious protagonist, the honors graduate Cecil Otis Braithwaite, is in many ways an upscale Eddie Lawson with a wife and an advanced degree. After slaving through law school, supporting himself with a meager scholarship and his earnings as a janitor, Cecil has lost his aspirations and his love for his girlfriend, Esther Brown. In search of something more, he escapes from his wedding bed to Europe, where he roams indiscriminately for three years among its brothels as well as its art galleries. In the tradition of Robert Thurley of *A Glance Away*, two white men as displaced as Cecil attempt to guide him: Charles Webb, belatedly in search of an illegitimate son, and Albert, a mercenary in Webb's employ who has also abandoned a wife. Too lost to save themselves, however, this pair can offer no enduring words of solace to Cecil.

Hurry Home is more sophisticated than *A Glance Away* in its treatment of the isolation theme. It suggests, for example, that the upwardly mobile Cecil is not merely disturbed by his personal past; he is estranged as well from his African and European cultures of origin. On the other hand, nowhere does *Hurry Home* convey the hope that pervades its predecessor. Cecil travels more extensively than does Eddie to reclaim his past, yet he gains no key to it to speak of. Confronting his European heritage merely confirms his status as "a stranger in all . . . tongues." He flees to the African continent by boat, "satisfied to be forever possessed," only to be forever rebuffed from a past that "melts like a wax casing as I am nearer. . . the flame." When he returns at last to his Washington, D.C., tenement, the fruitlessness of his journey is underscored. There, he finds all the same as when he first entered following his miserable nuptials. Symbolically limning his rootlessness, he switches vocations, abandoning the tradition-steeped protocol of the bar for the faddish repertoire of a hairdresser. Thus, "hurry home," the catchphrase for his odyssey, is an ironic one. Cecil really can claim no place where a heritage nur tures and sustains him, no history that he can truly call his own.

Hurry Home displays a masterful style commensurate with that of the later Homewood novels. In addition to a more controlled stream-of-consciousness technique, recurring Christian symbols, icons of Renaissance art, and fragments from Moorish legend powerfully indicate Cecil's fractured lineage. This second novel being a more refined paradigm than the first, Wideman seemed next inclined to break new ground, to address intently the racial polarization that had unsettled American society by the early 1970's, producing that period's most influential published works.

Distinguished from the previous two novels by its bawdy humor and portrayal of a professional black woman, *The Lynchers* is set in the generic northeastern slum, pockmarked by the self-inflicted wounds of the 1960's, that has become a Wideman trademark. Central to the action are four frustrated black men: Willie "Littleman" Hall, an unemployed dwarf; Leonard Saunders, a ruthless hustler turned repressed postal clerk; Thomas Wilkerson, a plodding fifth-grade schoolteacher; and Graham Rice, an introspective janitor with a persecution complex. Disenchanted with the superficial changes that the Civil Rights movement has wrought—the "job here or a public office there, . . . one or two black faces floating to the top"—these four conclude that violence is the only means to effect a lasting alteration of the white power structure. With Littleman as the ringleader and mastermind, they plan to flex the latent power of the black community and turn the tables on their oppressors by kidnaping and lynching a white policeman.

The plot falls apart, however, once Littleman is badly beaten by the authorities for delivering a militant speech at Woodrow Wilson Junior High School. Suspicion, distrust, and doubt override the remaining conspirators so that they foil themselves instead of their "white butcher pig" enemy. Thus, in a perverse way the weapons of the executioner do revert to black hands. Lynching becomes a symbol of frustration turned inward, of despairing hearts made so taut in their efforts to beat more freely that they burst.

Unlike *A Glance Away* and *Hurry Home*, *The Lynchers* is a total immersion into blackness. Perhaps the critics wanted another black-white character dichotomy, for their assessments of this novel were at best mixed. Nevertheless, Wideman again displays strong gifts of characterization without diminishing the theme's universal appeal. A continuation of his pet preoccupation, rootlessness, *The Lynchers* showcases men who feel acutely that they belong nowhere. Wilkerson, for example, is the Cecil type, the black professional who is alienated from his working-class roots, condescended to by whites possessing similar educational backgrounds and unwelcome in the clubs and restaurants that they patronize. Saunders, like Eddic, is a marginally good citizen, at once attracted to and repelled by "the life" of conning and thieving. In an intricate new twist to this scenario, Wideman depicts the older generation as a group as anchorless as the young. For example, Wilkerson's father, a drunk and a philanderer, stabs a longtime friend to death.

In its familiar inner-city setting and cast of alienated men (a passing reference is even made to Cecil Braithwaite as Littleman's lawyer), *The Lynchers* recalls Wideman's preceding works. In its use of a symbol generated exclusively from the black experience, it acts as a transition between these two novels and Wideman's fourth and fifth endeavors. No longer primarily gleaning symbols from Christianity and the European classics, here Wideman unifies his montage of dialogues with "the hawk," a symbol indigenous to the men's own harsh environment. This frigid, anthropomorphic wind that lashes the streets indicates the blacks' powerlessness and the hollow bravado of their ill-fated intrigue. They cannot even abduct the police officer without using one of their own people, his black girlfriend, Sissie, as a pawn.

After an eight-year interval during which he researched black American literature and culture, Wideman applied folk sources more fully than ever before in *Hiding Place*, one of the three works of fiction which make up *The Homewood Trilogy*. Challenged to enlarge his black readership without limiting the universal relevance of his themes, he chose to emphasize one black family based largely on his own Homewood clan. In this novel's swift, uncomplicated plot, Tommy Lawson, a tough, wisecracking youth from the black neighborhood of Homewood, is running from the police for his involvement in a robbery and killing. He seeks refuge among the weedy plots and garbage piles of desolate Bruston Hill, a once-fertile area to which his ancestor Sybela Owens fled from the South and slavery with Charlie Bell, her white owner's recalcitrant son. In the lone residence at the crest of the Hill, a rotting wooden shack sardonically known as "that doghouse," the reclusive "Mother" Bess Owens reluctantly offers her sister's great-grandson a temporary haven. After Tommy regains the courage to elude the authorities eager to convict him for a murder that he did not commit, Bess reaffirms her ties to her kin and ends her self-imposed isolation. Not knowing whether Tommy is dead, has escaped, or has been captured, she burns her shack and prepares to reenter Homewood to retell Tommy's tragic story so that another like it might never happen again.

Though Bess does not leave her longtime home until the novel's final chapter, *Hiding Place* is as much the story of her isolation from family as it is one of Tommy's. Just as Tommy has shirked his responsibilities as a husband, father, and son, Bess has turned her back upon the younger generations of kin whose ways are alien to her. Widowed and childless, she has retreated into an archaic life-style, shunning the twentieth century amenities of electricity and phones, in order to avoid intimacy with others. Physically rooting herself among Bruston Hill's ruins, she has been running from the present in her mind by focusing her thoughts on the past, especially the deaths of loved ones that have occurred. Only when she becomes involved in Tommy's affairs does she rekindle her active commitment to the family.

In *Hiding Place*, Wideman's style dramatically differs from those of the canonized white writers who were his early models. With a method many reviewers have compared to jazz, his characters unfold the histories of five generations of Lawsons and Frenches. Bess herself repeats certain key events in the family history several times; one of her favorites is the one in which Mary Hollinger revives her cousin Freeda French's stillborn baby by plunging it into the snow. Yet like a jazz improvisation, where instruments alternately play solo and play together, she retells the tale each time in a different way, varying her approach to it with different bits of superstition, mysticism, and folklore. Even Wideman's Clement, an inarticulate orphan similar to Benjy Compson in William Faulkner's *The Sound and the Fury* (1929), bears the unique stamp of the black American experience. As the author himself avows, Clement's assimilation into Homewood reflects the nature of the black community as a tolerant extended family.

Its legacy of songs, tales, and superstitions notwithstanding, the Homewood that finally draws Bess back is a model of urban blight, a "bombed out" no-man's-land of "pieces of buildings standing here and there and fire scars and places ripped and kicked down and cars stripped and dead at the curb." This dying landscape, and in a similar way Bess's ramshackle Bruston Hill homestead, proclaims the present descendants' dissociation from their ancestors and one another. In *Sent for You Yesterday*, the final installment of *The Homewood Trilogy* and the 1984 PEN Faulkner Award winner for outstanding fiction, this undercurrent becomes the novel's predominant theme. Carl French and his lover Lucy Tate relate the stories of a Homewood gone by to the latest generation of listeners, as if the recovery of the past is integral for the entire community's survival and solidarity.

Sent for You Yesterday cannot be divided easily into main story and subplots. All the episodes in it are major in scope and significance. The most memorable ones include the saga of the piano player Albert Wilkes, who slept with a white woman and murdered a white policeman; the tragedy of Samantha, whose college education could not shield her from grief and madness; and the bittersweet adventures of the resilient Brother Tate, an albino and best friend of Carl who communicates only with gestures and scat sounds. Retold by Carl's nephew Doot, a former Homewood resident modeled largely after Wideman himself, each tale conveys a lesson to a younger generation. More than mere exempla, however, the stories emphasize the cyclic nature of the human condition: Each generation rises to further, alter, and often reenact the accomplishments of its predecessors. Thus, Uncle Carl's street in Homewood becomes to Doot "a narrow, cobbled alley *teeming* with life. Like a wooden-walled ship in the middle of the city, like the ark on which Noah packed two of everything and prayed for land." This determination to survive that the ark imagery calls to mind impels Carl and Lucy to share Homewood's history. By remembering past lives, by preserving traditions, they ensure their own enduring places in the memories of their heirs.

From *A Glance Away* to *Sent for You Yesterday*, a span of more than fifteen years, Wideman narrows the geographical mobility of his significant characters and enlarges his focus upon the black American community. Yet he never abandons his central concern for home, heritage, and ancestry, a concern expressed most powerfully through the denizens of Homewood. In retrospect, every one of his novels contains pieces of Homewood, although the connections are not always named (as in the urban setting of *A Glance Away*) or otherwise made immediately apparent. Linked by theme and content, all five underscore the author's own credo: "Past lives live in us, through us. Each of us harbors the spirits of people who walked the earth before we did, and those spirits depend on us for continuing existence, just as we depend on their presence to live our lives to the fullest." It is Wideman's depiction of these spirits, both dead and alive, that has earned for him much-deserved recognition as a pathbreaking literary artist.

Other major works
SHORT FICTION: *Damballah*, 1981.
NONFICTION: *Brothers and Keepers*, 1984.

Bibliography

Coleman, James W. "Going Back Home: The Literary Development of John Edgar Wideman," in *CLA Journal*. XXVII (March, 1985), pp. 326-343.
Frazier, Kermit. "The Novels of John Wideman: An Analysis," in *Black World*. XXIV (June, 1975), pp. 18-38.
O'Brien, John. *Interviews with Black Writers*, 1973.
Samuels, Wilfred D. "Going Home: A Conversation with John Edgar Wideman," in *Callaloo*. VI (February, 1983), pp. 40-59.

Barbara A. McCaskill

A. N. WILSON

Born: Stone, Great Britain; October 27, 1950

Principal long fiction

The Sweets of Pimlico, 1977; *Unguarded Hours*, 1978; *Kindly Light*, 1979; *The Healing Art*, 1980; *Who Was Oswald Fish?*, 1981; *Wise Virgin*, 1982; *Scandal*, 1983; *Gentlemen in England*, 1985; *Love Unknown*, 1986.

Other literary forms

Despite the regularity with which A. N. Wilson produces novels, he has never been limited to that form alone. He is one of the best-known journalists in Great Britain, with particularly close connections to *The Spectator*, the prestigious weekly journal of conservative social and political opinion. He has served as the literary editor of that periodical, but his own writing has not been confined to reviewing books, and he is often a commentator on social and political subjects. Wilson has a special interest in religion, and aside from his occasional essays on that subject, he has published a study of the layman's dilemma in matters of Christian belief, *How Can We Know?* (1985). He teaches at Oxford University and has, since 1980, written a monograph on Sir Walter Scott and biographies of John Milton and Hilaire Belloc.

Achievements

The Sweets of Pimlico gained for Wilson the John Llewelyn Rhys Memorial Prize in 1978, and *The Healing Art* won three prizes, including the Somerset Maugham Award for 1980 and the Arts Council National Book Award for 1981. *Wise Virgin* brought him the W. H. Smith Annual Literary Award in 1983, and his study of Scott, *The Laird of Abbotsford: A View of Sir Walter Scott* (1980), won the Rhys prize for him once again.

There are several formidable writers in Wilson's generation, but it is possible to distinguish Wilson as the best of the new satirists and, as such, one of the most perceptive commentators on Great Britain in the last quarter of the twentieth century. Given his talent, and his capacity to comment attractively (if sometimes improperly) on the excesses of his society, it is not surprising that he has become something of a public personality, the literary figure most often identified with the "Young Fogeys," that amorphous group of literary, social, and political figures who espouse the principles of landowning Toryism and look with nostalgia back to the old Empire and to the days when High Anglicanism was a spiritual power in the land. Part of their conservatism is sheer mischief-making, part of it a matter of temperament and class, but in Wilson's case, it is a love for the aesthetic detail of what he sees as a richer and more caring society (which does not stop him from making wicked fun of it).

Biography

Andrew Norman Wilson, born in Stone, Staffordshire, England, in 1950, was educated at Rugby, one of the great English public schools, and at New College, Oxford. He won the Chancellor's Essay Prize in 1971 and the Ellerton Theological Prize in 1975. He has been a lecturer in English at New College, and at St. Hugh's College, Oxford. Aside from his work in *The Spectator*, he has published in *The Times Literary Supplement* and *The Sunday Telegraph*. Wilson is a Fellow of the Royal Society of Literature. He is married and has two daughters.

Analysis

A. N. Wilson's novels are part of the tradition of sophisticated wittiness, sometimes comic, sometimes satiric, which explores the English caste system (with particular emphasis upon the middle and upper-middle classes), long a subject for English letters, particularly in the 1930's. The promise that World War II would not only stop international tyranny but also destroy the British social hierarchy has not, in fact, come true. Great Britain may have fallen on hard times economically, and may be of less importance politically, but the class structure, though shaken, still prevails.

Evelyn Waugh was the foremost social satirist prior to the war and until his death in 1966, commenting on the dottier aspects of life among the wellborn, the titled, the talented, and the downright vulgar climbers and thrusters, determined to ascend the greasy pole of social, political, and economic success. Wilson's first novel, *The Sweets of Pimlico*, might well have been written by a young Waugh. Thinly plotted, but written with astringent grace and wide-ranging peripheral insights into the fastidious improprieties of the privileged, it tells of the queer love life of Evelyn Tradescant (whose surname alone is appropriately bizarre, but whose credentials are established by the fact that her father is a retired diplomat, Sir Derek Tradescant, of some minor political reputation).

By chance, Evelyn tumbles (literally) into an association with a much older man, Theo Gormann, wealthy, pleased by the attentions of a young woman, and mysteriously ambiguous about his past, which seems to have involved close association with the Nazis before the war. While Theo urges his peculiar attentions on Evelyn, so does his closest friend, John "Pimlico" Price, and Evelyn learns that everybody seems to know one another in varyingly confusing ways. Her father and mother remember the Gormann of Fascist persuasion, and her brother, Jeremy, is also known to Theo through his connection with Pimlico, who proves to be an occasional male lover of Jeremy, who in his last year at Oxford is doing little work but considerable loving, including a sudden excursion into incest with Evelyn. Wilson is teasingly and sometimes feelingly successful in exploring the sexual brink upon which Evelyn and Theo hover in their relationship and which convinces Theo to give part of his estate to Evelyn. Pimlico, the present heir, knows that someone is being considered as a joint recipient of the estate, but he never suspects Evelyn, and Theo dies before the will is changed. All is well, however, since Evelyn and Pimlico decide to marry. It is farce of high order in which coincidence, arbitrary behavior, and sophisticated silliness are mixed with moments of genuine tenderness (but not so tender as to overcome the sly mockery of money and influence in the smart set of south London).

In his next two novels, *Unguarded Hours* and *Kindly Light*, Wilson eschews the underplayed wit of *The Sweets of Pimlico* for comic excess, reminiscent of P. G. Wodehouse in its extravagant playfulness. These theological comedies are strongly cinematic in their incident and character and they display, if ridiculously, Wilson's strong interest in, and deep knowledge of, English Anglicanism and its constant flirtation with Roman Catholicism as well as his affectionate enthusiasm for the detail, the knickknackery of religious ceremony and trapping. The two novels ought to be read in the proper chronological order, since the hero escapes at the end of *Unguarded Hours* in a balloon and begins in the next one, having floated some distance away, once again trying to make his way into the clerical life.

The Healing Art, Wilson's most admired work, reveals how wide his range can be, not only tonally but also thematically. The novel is a "black comedy" in the sense that acts which normally offend are portrayed in such a way that readers enjoy the improprieties without worrying about the moral consequences. Two women, one a university don, one a working-class housewife, meet while having surgery for breast cancer and comfort each other, despite the fact that they otherwise have nothing in common. Their doctor, overworked but peremptory, unfeeling, and vain, may have misread the women's X rays and deems one of them cured and the other in need of chemotherapy. The gifted, handsome, successful younger woman, informed of her possibly fatal condition, refuses treatment, energetically determined to live out her life quickly and to explore her personal relations with some fervor. In the process, she learns much about herself and her male friends and becomes involved in a love affair with the cast-off, occasional mistress of the man whom she presumed was, in fact, her lover (even if such love had not, to the moment, been consummated).

Wilson juxtaposes the range of experience open to a woman of the upper-middle class, searching for some meaning for the last days of her life, surrounded by the many pleasures and alternatives of her world, to the life of a working-class woman, supposedly healthy, but obviously wasting away and ignored by family and by the medical profession as something of a nuisance. The cruelty of it all is subtly explored by Wilson, and the final ironies for both women are unnervingly sad and comic. Wilson proves with this novel that he is serious, and sensitive, particularly in dealing with the emotional lives of the two women.

In *Who Was Oswald Fish?*, which might be called a contemporary black fairy tale, coincidence simply struts through the novel. The mysterious Oswald Fish, a turn-of-the-century architect and designer whose one church, a Gothic ruin in the working-class district of Birmingham, is to be the center of life and death for the parties drawn together to decide its fate, proves to be related to everyone who matters (and some who do not). In the retrieval of Fish's reputation from the neglect and indifference of twentieth century tastelessness and vulgarity, one suicide, one manslaughter, and two accidental deaths occur, the latter two in the rubble of his lovely old church. No one means any harm (although there are two children in this novel who could put the St. Trinian's gang to flight). Fanny Williams, former pop star and model, and survivor of the English rock revolution of the early 1960's, is, in the late 1970's, famous again, as the owner of a chain of trash-and-trend novelty shops dealing in Victorian nostalgia, and she is determined to protect the ruined church from demolition at the hands of soulless civic planners. Sexy, generous, and often charmingly silly, her life is an extravagant mess, a whirlpool of sensual, slapstick nonsense in which some survive and some, quite as arbitrarily, drown. Behind the farcical escapades lies Wilson's deep affection for the rich clutter of Victoriana juxtaposed to the new efficiency.

After the comic excesses of *Who Was Oswald Fish?*, Wilson pulled back into the narrower range of his early work in *Wise Virgin*. There has always been a sense that not only Waugh but also Iris Murdoch influenced him (*The Sweets of Pimlico* had been dedicated to her and to her husband, the literary critic John Bayley), particularly in the way in which she uses love as an unguided flying object, which can strike any character in the heart at any moment. Love tends to strike arbitrarily in Wilson's fiction, for he, like Murdoch, enjoys tracing the madness of fools in love. Also reminiscent of Murdoch, Wilson works interesting technical detail into his novels, often, as has been stated, of the religious world, but in *Who Was Oswald Fish?*, his interest in Victorian architecture and objets d'art predominates and adds amusingly to the texture of the novel. In *Wise Virgin*, Wilson utilizes his own special knowledge as a literary scholar, since his protagonist, Giles Fox, is a medievalist, working on a definitive edition of an obscure text, *A Treatise of Heavenly Love*, on the relation of virginity and the holy life. Fox, irascible, snobbish, and sometimes vicious, has two virgins on his hands, his daughter, whom he has sought to educate without benefit of twentieth century influence, and his assistant, Miss Agar, who is determined to marry him.

Wilson has been accused of gratuitous cruelty in the way in which he allows his characters to comment upon the gracelessness of contemporary British society, and it is true that Fox is a master of the unfair comment and is insensitive to the possibility that some kinds of stupidities, particularly in the less privileged classes, are only innocent gaucheries. Certainly Fox is Wilson's least attractive protagonist, but he is also a man who has suffered much, having lost one wife in childbirth and another in a motor accident, and having himself, in midcareer, gone blind. He is something of a twentieth century Job (although more deserving of punishment), and the tone and plot of the novel suggest black comedy bordering on tragedy. On the lighter side, Wilson satirizes Fox's sister and brother-in-law, who, suffering from that peculiar kind of arrested development which strikes some people as cute, indulge interminably in the baby talk of the schoolboys whom the husband teaches in a public school, clearly based upon Wilson's own school, Rugby.

Gentlemen in England takes place in the late Victorian period of which Wilson is so fond. With this work, Wilson has written a trick novel, partly in the tradition of Thomas Keneally and E. L. Doctorow, in which actual historical events and characters intrude on, and affect, the action. Wilson, however, refuses to use obvious historical allusions carefully chosen to satisfy the vanities of intelligent, well-informed readers. Much of the historical structure requires a deep knowledge of Victorian England. For example, although the novel definitely takes place in 1880, the exact date is never stated but must be gathered from certain facts mentioned by the characters. Allusions to George Eliot and Henry James might be easy to pick up, but those to public figures of the time, such as Charles Bradlaugh, E. B. Pusey, and Sir Charles Wentworth Dilke, require a formidable cultural memory.

The story centers on a father who has lost his Christian faith in the face of Darwinism; a son who is flirting with the late stages of the Oxford movement in religion, with the more theatrical experiments of High Anglicanism, and with the revival of the Roman Catholic Benedictine movement; and a daughter pursued by a disciple of Alma-Tadema, the popular painter of the time. Wilson recounts their family drama in a Victorian style, most reminiscent of the works of Anthony Trollope—slightly arch, witty, but restrainedly so, and inclined to overripe ironies. Like Victorian furniture and design, it is rich and heavy to the point of ponderousness.

Inside this lovingly detailed, historically accurate structure, Wilson plays out pure farce: A mother, still beautiful in early middle age, falls in love with a young painter, who falls in love with the daughter, who is half in love with her mother's old lover, who is half in love with both of them, and who is Wilson's way into the real world of London life. Called, with obvious intent, Chatterway, the former lover is intimately associated with the major figures of London life in that particularly lively year, 1880. *Gentlemen in England* is, in many ways, a work which illustrates Wilson's manipulative curiosity about the ways in which novels can be pushed and pulled about. Kingsley Amis has similar ideas, and his *Riverside Villa's Murder* (1973) anticipated Wilson in its careful re-creation of a 1930's-style English murder mystery in which content, structure, and language were scrupulous imitations of the real thing.

This awareness of the novel as a form which could be used in many ways allows Wilson many humorous moments. In *Who Was Oswald Fish?*, he introduces, in a minor role, Jeremy Tradescant, who was the sexually confused brother of Evelyn, the heroine of *The Sweets of Pimlico*. He goes even further in making a comment on the fate of Evelyn's marriage to Pimlico Price, incomprehensible to all but those who have read the earlier novel. Wilson introduces into *Gentlemen in England* a genuinely thoughtful discussion of the problem of Christian faith, which is tonally at odds with the clutter of Victorian sexual high jinks. He has, in short, no sense of decorum, not because he does not know, but because he knows so well. Sometimes, as in *Scandal* and *Love Unknown*, he seems to have returned to social satire; the latter novel is puzzling until one recognizes that it is based upon the most pathetic kind of popular romance. Wilson is off again, manipulating the genre, enriching junk literature by imposing first-class literary technique on banality and turning it into something it hardly deserves.

Even though Kingsley Amis still holds sway as the linchpin satirist (though less committed to the class theme), A. N. Wilson may succeed him. His range of interests, however, suggests considerable suppleness, and he may yet produce a novel of genuinely tender feeling. He may also simply continue to reinforce his reputation as the cruelest, and sometimes the most amusing, of the new British novelists of the last quarter of the twentieth century.

Other major works

NONFICTION: *The Laird of Abbotsford: A View of Sir Walter Scott*, 1980; *The Life of John Milton*, 1983; *Hilaire Belloc*, 1984; *How Can We Know?*, 1985.

Bibliography

Furbank, P. N. *Unholy Pleasure: Or, The Idea of Social Class*, 1985.
Lowry, Suzanne. *The Young Fogey Handbook*, 1985.
Mason, Philip. *The English Gentleman: The Rise and Fall of an Ideal*, 1982.
Raven, Simon. *The English Gentleman*, 1961.

Charles H. Pullen

LARRY WOIWODE

Born: Carrington, North Dakota; October 30, 1941

Principal long fiction
What I'm Going to Do, I Think, 1969; *Beyond the Bedroom Wall: A Family Album*, 1975; *Poppa John*, 1981.

Other literary forms
Larry Woiwode is known primarily for his longer fiction, but he has frequently published short stories in such prominent literary periodicals as *The Atlantic* and *The New Yorker*; several of his stories have been chosen for anthologies of the year's best. He has also published a well-received book of poetry, *Even Tide* (1977).

Achievements
Woiwode's first novel, *What I'm Going to Do, I Think*, won for him the prestigious William Faulkner Foundation Award for the "most notable first novel" of 1969 and brought him immediate critical attention. It reached the best-seller list and has been translated into several foreign languages. His second novel, *Beyond the Bedroom Wall*, actually begun before *What I'm Going to Do, I Think*, was nominated for both the National Book Award and the National Book Critics Circle Award. It became an even bigger commercial and critical success than his first novel. Woiwode's third novel, *Poppa John*, however, was much less successful commercially and critically. The novel's premise and protagonist indeed represented a departure from the regional narrative Woiwode had successfully employed in his previous fiction, but subsequent criticism may yet redeem it from its detractors.

Poppa John notwithstanding, critics are quick to credit Woiwode's idiosyncratic, family-centered narratives with helping indirectly to rehabilitate the family chronicle, a genre long considered out of fashion. Woiwode's stories are populated with prodigal sons and daughters who, no matter where they tread, fulfill their destiny in rediscovering their roots and the family relationships which nurtured them early in their lives. Woiwode unabashedly admires the traditional nuclear family, and his fiction underscores the value of finding one's way by retracing one's steps. His narrative strength is thus seen in the fact that, even among readers accustomed to despondent, "lost" protagonists preoccupied with discovering the mysteries of life in the squalor of the city or some illicit relationship, Woiwode can make such old-fashioned premises seem startlingly fresh and appealing.

Biography
Larry Alfred Woiwode (pronounced "why-wood-ee") was born in Carring-

ton, North Dakota, October 30, 1941, and spent his early years in nearby Sykeston, a predominantly German settlement amid the rugged, often forbidding north-midwestern terrain. No doubt the beauty as well as the stark loneliness of this landscape heightened the author's appreciation for the effect of nature upon individual character. At the age of ten, he moved with his family to Manito, Illinois, another evocatively Midwestern environment capable of nurturing the descriptive powers of a budding fiction writer.

He attended the University of Illinois for five years but failed to complete a bachelor's degree, leaving the university in 1964 with an associate of arts in rhetoric. He met his future wife, Carol Ann Patterson, during this period and married her on May 21, 1965. After leaving Illinois, Woiwode moved to New York City and supported his family with free-lance writing, publishing in *The New Yorker* and other prestigious periodicals while working on two novels.

He has been a writer-in-residence at the University of Wisconsin, Madison, and has had extended teaching posts at Wheaton College (Illinois) and at the State University of New York at Binghamton, where he has served as a faculty member intermittently since 1983. In 1977, he was awarded the Doctor of Letters degree from North Dakota State University.

Analysis

As a novelist, Larry Woiwode stands apart from most of his contemporaries in refusing to drown his characters in the angst-ridden excesses that have become so conventional in the modern American novel. His characters are not helpless victims of their times but participants in them; they are accountable not so much for what has happened to them but for what they do in response to their circumstances. Their conflicts, from Chris Van Eenanam's enigmatic search for manhood in *What I'm Going to Do, I Think* to Poppa John's drive to recover his self-identity, are not merely contrived psychological dramas played out inside their own consciousness, but compelling confrontations with the very concrete world of everyday life. This is a world which registers as authentic to the reader precisely because of Woiwode's gift for realism.

Woiwode's characters eventually recognize that the answer to their dilemmas is only partly in themselves. In the reestablishment of personal trust in friendships and the nostalgia of forgotten familial relationships, they recover a sense of balance and worth in themselves. However obliquely, each major Woiwode character finds himself in a quest for a transcendent moral order, a renewed trust in God and man that would give him a reference point for his life. This quest animates their rejection of narcissism and a search for a love and security that only marital and familial relationships can foster.

Woiwode's willingness to affirm that these relationships are central to self-fulfillment and to the stability of American culture makes him unique among a generation of writers whose thematic concerns tend to focus on their characters' dehumanization in society and alienation from family life and marital fidelity. Woiwode thus belongs in the company of self-consciously moralistic writers such as Walker Percy and Saul Bellow, who are more interested in the ways human beings survive and thrive in a fallen world than in the ways they capitulate to it.

Nevertheless, when compared with other writers of his caliber, Woiwode has not been a particularly prolific author. In the two decades since he ended an abortive college career to pursue free-lance writing, he has produced only four major works: one long, rather complex family chronicle, one medium-length novel, one short novel, and a book of poems. Yet two of his three novels were critically acclaimed, national best-sellers, and are among the best American novels written since 1960. Despite the negative response to *Poppa John*, Woiwode's reputation as an important American writer in the second half of the twentieth century seems secure.

Woiwode's first novel, *What I'm Going to Do, I Think*, is an absorbing character study of two newlyweds, each of whom is originally drawn to the other as opposites proverbially attract. Chris Van Eenanam, the protagonist, is a listless mathematics graduate student, an unhappy agnostic unsure of his calling in life. The novel's title accentuates his self-doubt and indecision, echoing something Chris's father once said in observing his accident-prone son, "What I'm going to do, I think, is get a new kid." Ellen Strohe, his pregnant bride, is a tortured young woman, dominated by the overbearing grandparents who reared her after her parents' accidental death. Neither she nor Chris can abide their interference and meddling.

Despite the fact that little action takes place "live" before the reader, the psychological realism in Woiwode's use of compacted action and flashbacks and the patterned repetition of certain incidents carry the reader along as effortlessly as might a conventionally chronological narrative. The reader learns "what happens" primarily as events filter through the conversations and consciousness of Chris and Ellen Van Eenanam during their extended honeymoon at her grandparents' cabin near the northwestern shore of Lake Michigan.

In this retreat from the decisions Chris elects not to face, the couple, now intimate, now isolated, confront a grim modern world, which has lost its faith in a supreme being fully in control of his created universe. This loss is exemplified most dramatically in the lives of Chris and Ellen as they try to sort out the meaning of affection and fidelity in their new relationship as husband and wife and as potential parents. Ellen's pregnancy is at first a sign of a beneficent nature's approval of their union, but later, as each has a premonition of their unborn child's death, it becomes a symbol of an ambivalent world's indifference to their marriage and its apparent fruitlessness.

In the absence of a compensatory faith even in mankind itself, a secondary faith arguably derived from faith in God, Chris and Ellen come to realize that they have lost their ability to navigate a hostile world with lasting, meaningful relationships. Neither mathematics nor nature can fill the vacuum left by an impotent faith whose incessant call is to fidelity and perseverance without passion or understanding. In a suspenseful epilogue which closes the novel with an explanation of what has happened to them in the seven years following their marriage, Chris and Ellen return to their honeymoon cabin. Chris retrieves the rifle he has not touched in many years, and, as the action builds toward what will apparently be his suicide, he repeats to himself the beginning of a letter (suicide note?) that he could not complete: *"Dear El, my wife. You're the only person I've ever been able to talk to and this is something I can't say. . . ."*

As he makes his way to the lake, he fires a round of ammunition into a plastic bleach container half-buried in the sand. In the novel's enigmatic final lines, Chris fires "the last round from his waist, sending the bullet out over the open lake." This curious ending seems intended by Woiwode to announce Chris's end of indecision—a recognition that his life can have transcendent meaning only in embracing fully his marriage commitment to Ellen.

The expansiveness and comic vitality of Woiwode's second novel, *Beyond the Bedroom Wall*, offer a marked contrast to *What I'm Going to Do, I Think*. In *Beyond the Bedroom Wall*, Woiwode parades sixty-three characters before the reader by the beginning of chapter 3. True to its subtitle, "A Family Album," *Beyond the Bedroom Wall* is a sprawling, gangly work of loosely connected snapshots of the Neumiller family. An engaging homage to the seemingly evaporating family unit at the end of the twentieth century, the novel's "plot" is nearly impossible to paraphrase, consisting as it does of some narrative, some diary entries, and even its protagonist Martin Neumiller's job application for a teaching position. Since Woiwode published nearly a third of the forty-four chapters of *Beyond the Bedroom Wall* as self-contained short stories in *The New Yorker*, it is no surprise that the book reads as a discontinuous montage of events, images, and personalities.

The novel opens in part 1 with the funeral of Charles Neumiller, a German immigrant farmer who had brought his family to America before the war, and it continues, to part 5, closing with stories of the third generation of Neumillers in 1970, bringing the Neumiller family full circle from birth to life to death. Yet it is Martin Neumiller, Charles's son, a god-fearing, devoutly Catholic man and proud son of North Dakota, whose adventures and misadventures give the novel any unity it possesses. "My life is like a book," he says at one point. "There is one chapter, there is one story after another." The eccentric folks he encounters in and out of his extended family form a burlesque troupe of characters who boisterously sample both the joys and the sorrows of life on Earth. In the Neumiller "family album," Woiwode lends concreteness to his notion that reality is a fragile construction, one that sometimes cannot bear scrutiny "beyond the bedroom wall," that is, beyond the dreamy world of sleep, of its visions of what might be. Woiwode intimates that whatever hope there may be for fulfilling one's dreams, it is anchored in "walking by faith, and not by sight," by trusting in and actively nurturing family intimacy.

The rather sentimental, "old-fashioned" quality Woiwode achieves in this family chronicle, his evocation of once-embraced, now-lamented values, prompted critic and novelist John Gardner to place Woiwode in the company of literature's greatest epic novelists: "When self-doubt, alienation, and fashionable pessimism become a bore and, what's worse, a patent delusion, how does one get back to the big emotions, the large and fairly confident life affirmations of an Arnold Bennett, a Dickens, a Dostoevsky? *Beyond the Bedroom Wall* is a brilliant solution."

Woiwode's eye for the rich details of daily life enables him to move through vast stretches of time and space in executing the episodic structure in this novel. His appreciation for the cadences of Midwestern speech and his understanding of the distinctiveness of prairie life and landscape and its impact on the worldviews of its inhabitants recalls other regional writers such as Rudy Wiebe and Garrison Keillor at their best.

Poppa John is shockingly short when compared with the massive *Beyond the Bedroom Wall*, and is more a novella than a novel. The book takes its title from the character Ned Daley played for many years on a popular television soap opera. His immense popularity beginning to overshadow the show itself, he is abruptly written out of the show in a dramatic "death." Ned thus finds himself suddenly unable to recover a sense of purpose, so long has he lived within the disguise of Poppa John, the fiery father figure, who often quoted Scripture to his television family. Now close to seventy, outspoken and Falstaffian in appearance and behavior, he seeks his deeply lost identity. Ned to his wife, but Poppa John to everyone else, he is lost in the malevolent nostalgia of growing old without self, or self-respect.

The novel opens two days before Christmas, a few months after Poppa John's television "death." Facing the Christmas season with wife, Celia, broke, broken, and without prospects for the future, the couple wander New York City, squandering their savings on gifts they had always wanted to buy for each other. Forced to "be himself," he finds he has leaned too heavily on the preacherlike Poppa John character, and his life begins to unravel. He is finally forced to face his own inconsistencies, his doubts, and even his sins, as Ned, an "elderly boy," is incapable of trusting in a life beyond the present. Speeding to a climax in its closing pages, the novel depicts Poppa John "coming to himself" on Christmas Day, realizing that he, after all these years, does believe in God, and therefore can come to believe in himself.

Poppa John perhaps deserved a better critical reception than it received; as a more than interesting attempt to portray an elderly actor's disintegrating life, it contains some of Woiwode's most lyrical scenes. In the end, however, it remains an unsatisfying chronicle—in part because the complexity apparent in Poppa John's character is never fully realized, presented as it is in a very compressed time frame. While Poppa John emerges as a potentially authentic character in the early parts of the novella, Woiwode gives the reader little insight into the motivations which would prompt his sudden conversion experience at the climax of the story.

To understand Woiwode's craft and achievement, one must finally recognize the essentially religious character of his narratives and their thematic structure. While believing that the most important human questions are, in fact, religious ones, Woiwode rejects the notion that there can be legitimate, compelling "novels of ideas"; for him, such fiction connotes mere propagandizing. Woiwode handles such questions not by placing philosophical soliloquies in the mouths of sophisticated, worldly protagonists, but by creating authentically ordinary characters, and settling them comfortably into the concrete and utterly mundane world of daily life.

In achieving this effective depiction of what might be called heightened normality, Woiwode's prose is consistently active, alive, and unassuming, approaching at times the crisp clarity of Ernest Hemingway but touched with a finely tuned lyricism. While Woiwode has sometimes been criticized for lapsing too easily into didacticism or marring an otherwise evocative scene with excessive detail, his keen eye for the extraordinary ordinariness of life makes his narrative vision compelling and believable.

Woiwode thus stands out as a moderating influence among contemporary novelists, an advocate for restoring a moral, even religious voice to modern letters. Whatever his eventual output, Woiwode promises to remain one of North America's most eloquent and gifted writers of fiction.

Other major work
POETRY: *Even Tide*, 1977.

Bibliography
Connaughton, Michael E. "Larry Woiwode," in *American Novelists Since World War II*, 1980 (second series). Edited by James E. Kibler, Jr.
Gardner, John. Review of *Beyond the Bedroom Wall* in *The New York Times Book Review*. CXXV (September 28, 1975), pp. 1-2.
"An Interview with Larry Woiwode," in *Christianity and Literature*. XXIX (1979), pp. 11-18.

Bruce L. Edwards, Jr.

UPDATES

UPDATES

Amis, Kingsley
BORN: London, England; April 16, 1922
LONG FICTION
Stanley and the Women, 1985
The Old Devils, 1986
ACHIEVEMENTS
Booker Prize

Atwood, Margaret
BORN: Ottawa, Canada; November 18, 1939
LONG FICTION
The Handmaid's Tale, 1986

Auchincloss, Louis
BORN: New York, New York; September 17, 1917
LONG FICTION
Exit Lady Masham, 1983
The Book Class, 1984
Honorable Men, 1985
Diary of a Yuppie, 1986

Ballard, J. G.
BORN: Shanghai, China; November 15, 1930
LONG FICTION
Empire of the Sun, 1984

Barthelme, Donald
BORN: Philadelphia, Pennsylvania; April 7, 1931
LONG FICTION
Paradise, 1986

Beattie, Ann
BORN: Washington, D.C.; September 8, 1947
LONG FICTION
Jacklighting, 1981
Love Always, 1985

Beauvoir, Simone de
BORN: Paris, France; January 9, 1908
DIED: Paris, France; April 14, 1986

Beckett, Samuel
BORN: Foxrock, near Dublin, Ireland; April 13, 1906
LONG FICTION
Worstward Ho, 1983

Berger, Thomas
BORN: Cincinnati, Ohio; July 20, 1924
LONG FICTION
The Feud, 1983
Nowhere, 1985

Bernhard, Thomas
BORN: Heerlen, Netherlands; February 10, 1931
LONG FICTION
Beton, 1982 (*Concrete*, 1984)
Der Untergeher, 1983
Holzfallen: Ein Erregung, 1984

Böll, Heinrich
BORN: Cologne, Germany; December 21, 1917
DIED: Merten, West Germany; July 16, 1985
LONG FICTION
Das Vermächtnis, 1982 (*A Soldier's Legacy*, 1985)

Braine, John
BORN: Bradford, England; April 13, 1922
DIED: London, England; October 28, 1986
LONG FICTION
The Two of Us, 1984
These Golden Days, 1985

Brautigan, Richard
BORN: Tacoma, Washington; January 30, 1935
DIED: Bolinas, California; September, 1984

Burgess, Anthony
BORN: Manchester, England; February 25, 1917

LONG FICTION
Enderby's Dark Lady: Or, No End to Enderby, 1984
The Kingdom of the Wicked, 1985
The Piano Player, 1986

Burroughs, William
BORN: St. Louis, Missouri; February 5, 1914
LONG FICTION
The Place of Dead Roads, 1983
The Burroughs File, 1984
Queer, 1985

Caldwell, Erskine
BORN: White Oak, Georgia; December 17, 1903
DIED: Paradise Valley, Arizona; April 11, 1987

Callaghan, Morley
BORN: Toronto, Canada; September 22, 1903
LONG FICTION
A Time for Judas, 1983
Our Lady of the Snows, 1985

Calvino, Italo
BORN: Santiago de las Vegas, Cuba; October 15, 1923
DIED: Siena, Italy; September 19, 1985
LONG FICTION
Palomar, 1983 (*Mr. Palomar*, 1985)

Canetti, Elias
BORN: Rustschuk, Bulgaria; July 25, 1905
ACHIEVEMENTS
Nobel Prize for Literature, 1981

Capote, Truman
BORN: New Orleans, Louisiana; September 30, 1924
DIED: Los Angeles, California; August 25, 1984

LONG FICTION
Answered Prayers: The Unfinished Novel, 1986

Cassill, R. V.
BORN: Cedar Falls, Iowa; May 17, 1919
LONG FICTION
After Goliath, 1985

Coover, Robert
BORN: Charles City, Iowa; February 4, 1932
LONG FICTION
Spanking the Maid, 1981
Gerald's Party, 1986

Cortázar, Julio
BORN: Brussels, Belgium; August 26, 1914
DIED: Paris, France; February 12, 1984
LONG FICTION
Un tal Lucas, 1979 (*A Certain Lucas*, 1984)

Davies, Robertson
BORN: Thamesville, Canada; August 28, 1913
LONG FICTION
The Deptford Trilogy, 1983 (includes *Fifth Business*, *The Manticore*, and *World of Wonders*)
What's Bred in the Bone, 1985

Delany, Samuel R.
BORN: New York, New York; April 1, 1942
LONG FICTION
Stars in My Pockets Like Grains of Sand, 1984

Desai, Anita
BORN: Mussoorie, India; June 24, 1937
LONG FICTION
The Village by the Sea: An Indian Family Story, 1982
In Custody, 1984

DeVries, Peter
BORN: Chicago, Illinois; February 27, 1910
LONG FICTION
Sauce for the Goose, 1981
Slouching Toward Kalamazoo, 1983
Prick of Noon, 1985
Peckham's Marbles, 1986

Didion, Joan
BORN: Sacramento, California; December 5, 1934
LONG FICTION
Democracy, 1984

Doctorow, E. L.
BORN: New York, New York; January 6, 1931
LONG FICTION
World's Fair, 1985

Donleavy, J. P.
BORN: Brooklyn, New York; April 23, 1926
LONG FICTION
Leila: Further in the Destinies of Darcy Dancer, Gentleman, 1983
De Alfonce Tennis: The Superlative Game of Eccentric Champions: Its History, Accoutrements, Rules, Conduct, and Regimen, 1985

Duras, Marguerite
BORN: Giandinh, Indochina; April 4, 1914
LONG FICTION
La Maladie de la mort, 1982 (*The Malady of Death*, 1986)
L'Amant, 1984 (*The Lover*, 1985)
La Douleur, 1985 (*The War: A Memoir*, 1986)

Durrell, Lawrence
BORN: Julundur, India; February 27, 1912
LONG FICTION
Sebastian: Or, Ruling Passions, 1983
Quinx: Or, The Ripper's Tale, 1985

Elkin, Stanley
BORN: New York, New York; May 11, 1930
LONG FICTION
Stanley Elkin's the Magic Kingdom, 1985

Ellison, Ralph
BORN: Oklahoma City, Oklahoma; March 1, 1914
LONG FICTION
Going to the Territory, 1986

Fowles, John
BORN: Leigh-on-Sea, England; March 31, 1926
LONG FICTION
A Short History of Lyme Regis, 1982
A Maggot, 1985

Frisch, Max
BORN: Zurich, Switzerland; May 15, 1911
LONG FICTION
Der mensch erscheint im Holozän, 1979 (*Man in the Holocene*, 1980)
Blaubart, 1982 (*Bluebeard*, 1984)

Fuentes, Carlos
BORN: Panama City, Panama; November 11, 1928
LONG FICTION
El gringo viejo, 1985 (*The Old Gringo*, 1985)

Gaddis, William
BORN: New York, New York; December 22, 1922
LONG FICTION
Carpenter's Gothic, 1985

Gaines, Ernest J.
BORN: Oscar, Louisiana; February 15, 1933
LONG FICTION
A Gathering of Old Men, 1983

García Márquez, Gabriel
BORN: Aracataca, Colombia; March 6, 1928

LONG FICTION

Relato de un náufrago: Que estuvo diez días a la deriva en una balsa sin comer ni beber, que fue proclamado héroe de la patria, besado por las reinas de la belleza y hecho rico por la publicidad, y luego aborrecido por el gobierno y olvidado para siempre, 1978 (*The Story of a Shipwrecked Soldier: Who Drifted on a Liferaft for Ten Days Without Food or Water, Was Proclaimed a National Hero, Kissed by Beauty Queens, Made Rich Through Publicity, and Then Spurned by the Government for All Time*, 1986)

ACHIEVEMENTS

Nobel Prize for Literature, 1982

Garrett, George

BORN: Orlando, Florida; June 11, 1929

LONG FICTION

The Succession: A Novel of Elizabeth and James, 1983

James Jones, 1984

An Evening Performance, 1985

Poison Pen: Or, Live Now and Pay Later, 1986

Genet, Jean

BORN: Paris, France; December 19, 1910

DIED: Paris, France; April 15, 1986

Golding, William

BORN: Cornwall, England; September 19, 1911

LONG FICTION

The Paper Men, 1984

ACHIEVEMENTS

Nobel Prize for Literature, 1983

Graves, Robert

BORN: Wimbledon, England; July 26, 1895

DIED: Deya, Majorca, Spain; December 7, 1985

LONG FICTION

An Ancient Castle, 1980

Greene, Graham

BORN: Berkhamsted, England; October 2, 1904

LONG FICTION

The Tenth Man, 1985

Handke, Peter

BORN: Griffen, Austria; December 6, 1942

LONG FICTION

Across, 1986

Harris, Mark

BORN: Mount Vernon, New York; November 19, 1922

LONG FICTION

The Doctor Who Technical Manual, 1983

Lying in Bed, 1984

Harrison, Jim

BORN: Grayling, Michigan; December 11, 1937

LONG FICTION

Sundog: The Story of an American Foreman, Robert Corvulstrang, as Told to Jim Harrison, 1984

Hawkes, John

BORN: Stamford, Connecticut; August 17, 1925

LONG FICTION

Adventures in the Alaskan Skin Trade, 1985

Heller, Joseph

BORN: Brooklyn, New York; May 1, 1923

LONG FICTION

God Knows, 1984

Hemingway, Ernest

BORN: Oak Park, Illinois; July 21, 1899

DIED: Ketchum, Idaho; July 2, 1961

LONG FICTION

The Garden of Eden, 1986

Hersey, John

BORN: Tientsin, China; June 17, 1914

LONG FICTION
The Call, 1985

Irving, John
BORN: Exeter, New Hampshire;
March 2, 1942
LONG FICTION
The Cider House Rules, 1985

Kemal, Yashar
BORN: Adana, Turkey; 1922
LONG FICTION
Deniz küstü, 1979 (*The Sea-crossed
Fisherman*, 1985)

Laurence, Margaret
BORN: Manitoba, Canada; July 18, 1926
DIED: Lakefield, Ontario, Canada;
January 6, 1987

Le Carré, John
BORN: Poole, England; October 19, 1931
LONG FICTION
A Perfect Spy, 1986

Le Guin, Ursula K.
BORN: Berkeley, California; October 21,
1929
LONG FICTION
The Adventure of Cobbler's Rune, 1982
The Eye of the Heron, 1983
In the Red Zone, 1983
*Solomon Leviathan's Nine Hundred
Thirty-first Trip Around the World*,
1983
Always Coming Home, 1985

Lessing, Doris
BORN: Kermanshah, Persia; October 22,
1919
LONG FICTION
The Diary of a Good Neighbour, 1983 (as
Jane Somers)
*Document Relating to the Sentimental
Agents in the Volyen Empire*, 1983
The Diaries of Jane Somers, 1984

If the Old Could—, 1984 (as Jane
Somers)
The Good Terrorist, 1985

McMurtry, Larry
BORN: Wichita Falls, Texas; June 3, 1936
LONG FICTION
The Desert Rose, 1983
The Lonesome Dove, 1985

Madden, David
BORN: Knoxville, Tennessee; July 25,
1933
LONG FICTION
Cain's Craft, 1985

Mailer, Norman
BORN: Long Branch, New Jersey;
January 31, 1923
LONG FICTION
Ancient Evenings, 1983
Tough Guys Don't Dance, 1984

Malamud, Bernard
BORN: Brooklyn, New York; April 26,
1914
DIED: New York, New York; March 18,
1986
LONG FICTION
God's Grace, 1982

Moore, Brian
BORN: Belfast, Northern Ireland;
August 25, 1921
LONG FICTION
Cold Heaven, 1983
The Black Robe, 1985

Murdoch, Iris
BORN: Dublin, Ireland; July 15, 1919
LONG FICTION
The Philosopher's Pupil, 1983
The Good Apprentice, 1986

Narayan, R. K.
BORN: Madras, India; October 10, 1906

LONG FICTION
A Tiger for Malgudi, 1983

Ngugi, James
BORN: Limuru, Kenya; January 5, 1938
LONG FICTION
Caitaani Mũtharaba-Inĩ, 1980 (*Devil on the Cross*, 1982)

Oates, Joyce Carol
BORN: Lockport, New York; June 16, 1938
LONG FICTION
Luxury of Sin, 1984
Mysteries of Winterthurn, 1984
Solstice, 1985
Wild Nights, 1985
Marya: A Life, 1986

Percy, Walker
BORN: Birmingham, Alabama; May 28, 1916
LONG FICTION
Lost in the Cosmos: The Last Self-Help Book, 1983

Powell, Anthony
BORN: London, England; December 21, 1905
LONG FICTION
O, How the Wheel Becomes It, 1983
The Fisher King, 1986

Price, Reynolds
BORN: Macon, North Carolina; February 1, 1933
LONG FICTION
Kate Vaiden, 1986

Priestley, J. B.
BORN: Bradford, England; September 13, 1894
DIED: Stratford-on-Avon, England; August 14, 1984

Pritchett, V. S.
BORN: Ipswich, England; December 16, 1900

LONG FICTION
The Turn of the Years, 1982

Purdy, James
BORN: Fremont, Ohio; July 14, 1923
LONG FICTION
On Glory's Course, 1984
In the Hollow of His Hand, 1986

Pym, Barbara
BORN: Oswestry, England; June 2, 1913
DIED: Oxford, England; January 11, 1980
LONG FICTION
Crampton Hodnet, 1985
An Academic Question, 1986

Renault, Mary
BORN: London, England; September 4, 1905
DIED: Capetown, South Africa; December 13, 1983
LONG FICTION
The Alexander Trilogy, 1984 (includes *Fire from Heaven*, *Persian Boy*, and *Funeral Games*)

Robbe-Grillet, Alain
BORN: Brest, France; August 18, 1922
LONG FICTION
Souvenirs du triangle d'or, 1978 (*Recollections of the Golden Triangle*, 1984)

Roth, Philip
BORN: Newark, New Jersey; March 19, 1933
LONG FICTION
The Anatomy Lesson, 1983
The Prague Orgy, 1985
The Counterlife, 1987

Sarton, May
BORN: Wondelgem, Belgium; May 3, 1912
LONG FICTION
The Magnificent Spinster, 1985

Sillitoe, Alan
BORN: Nottingham, England; March 4, 1928
LONG FICTION
Down from the Hill, 1984
The Lost Flying Boat, 1984
Life Goes On, 1985

Simenon, Georges
BORN: Liège, Belgium; February 13, 1903
LONG FICTION
La Marie du port, 1938 (*Chit of a Girl*, 1949)
Le Rescapés du Télémaque, 1938 (*The Survivors*, 1949)
Cour d'assises, 1941 (*Justice*, 1949)
Il pleut bergère, 1941 (*Black Rain*, 1947)
Les Caves du Majestic, 1942 (*Maigret and the Hotel Majestic*, 1977)
Cécile est morte, 1942 (*Maigret and the Spinster*, 1977)
Le Petit Docteur, 1943 (*The Little Doctor*, 1978)
Les Noces de Poitier, 1946 (*The Couple from Poitier*, 1985)
Les Mémoires de Maigret, 1950 (*Maigret's Memoirs*, 1963)
Maigret, Lognon et les gangsters, 1952 (*Maigret and the Killers*, 1954)
Marie qui louche, 1952 (*The Girl with a Squint*, 1978)
Le Revolver de Maigret, 1952 (*Maigret's Revolver*, 1956)
Maigret et le fantôme, 1964 (*Maigret and the Apparition*, 1976)
La Patience de Maigret, 1965 (English translation, 1966)

Simon, Claude
BORN: Tananarive, Madagascar; October 10, 1913
LONG FICTION
Leçon de choses, 1975 (*The World About Us*, 1983)

La Chevelure de Bérénice, 1983
ACHIEVEMENTS
Nobel Prize for Literature, 1985

Singer, Isaac Bashevis
BORN: Leoncin, Poland; July 14, 1904
LONG FICTION
The Penitent, 1983

Spark, Muriel
BORN: Edinburgh, Scotland; February 1, 1918
LONG FICTION
The Only Problem, 1984

Stuart, Jesse
BORN: W-Hollow, Riverton, Kentucky; August 8, 1907
DIED: W-Hollow, Riverton, Kentucky; February 17, 1984
LONG FICTION
My World, 1975

Sturgeon, Theodore
BORN: Staten Island, New York; February 26, 1918
DIED: Eugene, Oregon; May 8, 1985
LONG FICTION
Alien Cargo, 1984
Godbody, 1986

Theroux, Paul
BORN: Medford, Massachusetts; April 10, 1941
LONG FICTION
Doctor Slaughter, 1984
Half Moon Street, 1984
O-Zone, 1986

Tournier, Michel
BORN: Paris, France; December 19, 1924
LONG FICTION
Gilles et Jeanne, 1983 (*Gilles and Jeanne*, 1987)
La Goutte d'or, 1985

Tyler, Anne
BORN: Minneapolis, Minnesota;
  October 25, 1941
LONG FICTION
The Accidental Tourist, 1985

Updike, John
BORN: Shillington, Pennsylvania;
  March 18, 1932
LONG FICTION
The Witches of Eastwick, 1984
Roger's Version, 1986
ACHIEVEMENTS
Pulitzer Prize in Letters, 1982, for *Rabbit
  Is Rich*

Vargas Llosa, Mario
BORN: Arequipa, Peru; March 28, 1936
LONG FICTION
Historia de Mayta, 1984 (*The Real Life of
  Alejandre Mayta*, 1986)

Vidal, Gore
BORN: West Point, New York; October 3,
  1925
LONG FICTION
Duluth, 1983
Lincoln, 1984

Vonnegut, Kurt, Jr.
BORN: Indianapolis, Indiana;
  November 11, 1922
LONG FICTION
Galapagos, 1985

Wain, John
BORN: Stoke-on-Trent, England;
  March 14, 1925
LONG FICTION
Lizzie's Floating Shop, 1981
Young Shoulders, 1982

Walker, Alice
BORN: Eatonton, Georgia; February 9,
  1944
ACHIEVEMENTS
Pulitzer Prize in Letters, 1983, for *The
  Color Purple*

Waters, Frank
BORN: Colorado Springs, Colorado;
  July 25, 1902
LONG FICTION
The Lizard Woman, 1984
Flight from Fiesta, 1986

Wiesel, Elie
BORN: Sighet, Transylvania;
  September 30, 1928
ACHIEVEMENTS
Nobel Prize for Peace, 1986

Wouk, Herman
BORN: New York, New York; May 27,
  1915
LONG FICTION
Inside, Outside, 1985

Yerby, Frank
BORN: Augusta, Georgia; September 5,
  1916
LONG FICTION
Devilseed, 1984

Yourcenar, Marguerite
BORN: Brussels, Belgium; June 8, 1903
LONG FICTION
Alexis: Ou, Le Traité du vain combat,
  1929 (*Alexis*, 1984)
Comme l'eau qui coule, 1982 (*Two Lives
  and a Dream*, 1986)

CRITICAL SURVEY
OF
LONG FICTION

INDEX

I

INDEX